THE

Distinguished Jurist's Primer

VOLUME II

The Center for Muslim Contribution to Civilization

THE
Distinguished Jurist's Primer

VOLUME II

Bidāyat al-Mujtahid

Ibn Rushd

Translated by Professor Imran Ahsan Khan Nyazee

Reviewed by Professor Mohammad Abdul Rauf

Garnet
PUBLISHING

THE DISTINGUISHED JURIST'S PRIMER
VOLUME II

Published by
Garnet Publishing Limited
8 Southern Court
South Street
Reading
RG1 4QS
UK

ISBN-13: 978-1-85964-139-2
ISBN-10: 1-85964-139-3

First Edition 1996
First Paperback Edition 2000
Reprinted 2003, 2006

British Library Cataloguing-in-Publication Data
A catalogue record for this book is available from the British Library

Printed in Lebanon

CONTENTS OF VOLUME II

(IN BRIEF)

CONTENTS OF VOLUME II

In the Name of God, the Beneficent, the Merciful

FOREWORD

THE interrelationship and interaction of human cultures and civilisations has made the contributions of each the common heritage of men in all ages and all places. Early Muslim scholars were able to communicate with their Western counterparts through contacts made during the Crusades; at Muslim universities and centres of learning in Muslim Spain (al-Andalus, or Andalusia) and Sicily to which many European students went for education; and at the universities and centres of learning in Europe itself (such as Salerno, Padua, Montpellier, Paris, and Oxford), where Islamic works were taught in Latin translations. Among the Muslim scholars well-known in the centres of learning throughout the world were al-Rāzī (Rhazes), Ibn Sīnā (Avicenna), Ibn Rushd (Averroes), al Khwārizmī and Ibn Khaldūn. Muslim scholars such as these and others produced original works in many fields. Many of them possessed encyclopaedic knowledge and distinguished themselves in many disparate fields of knowledge.

In view of this, the Center for Muslim Contribution to Civilization was established in order to acquaint non-Muslims with the contributions Islam has given to human civilisation as a whole. The Great Books of Islamic Civilization Project attempts to cover the first 800 years of Islam, or what may be called Islam's Classical Period. This project aims at making available in English a wide selection of works representative of Islamic civilisation in all its diversity. It is made up of translations of original Arabic works that were produced in the formative centuries of Islam, and is meant to serve the needs of a potentially large readership. Not only the specialist and scholar, but the non-specialist with an interest in Islam and its cultural heritage will be able to benefit from the series. Together, the works should serve as a rich source for the study of the early periods of Islamic thought.

In selecting the books for the series, the Center took into account all major areas of Islamic intellectual pursuit that could be represented. Thus the series includes works not only on better-known subjects such as law, theology, jurisprudence, history and politics, but also on subjects such as literature, medicine, astronomy, optics and geography. The specific criteria, used to select individual books, were these: that a book should give a faithful and comprehensive account of its field; and that it should be an authoritative source. The reader thus has at his disposal virtually a whole library of informative and enlightening works.

Each book in the series has been translated by a qualified scholar and reviewed by another expert. While the style of one translation will naturally differ from another, the translators have endeavoured, to the extent it was possible, to make the works accessible to the common reader. As a rule, the use of footnotes has been kept to a minimum, though a more extensive use of them was necessitated in some cases.

This series is presented in the hope that it will contribute to a greater understanding in the West of the cultural and intellectual heritage of Islam and will therefore provide an important means towards greater understanding of today's world.

May God Help Us!

Muhammad bin Hamad Al-Thani
Chairman of the Board of Trustees

ABOUT THIS SERIES

THIS series of Arabic works, made available in English translation, represents an outstanding selection of important Islamic studies in a variety of fields of knowledge. The works selected for inclusion in this series meet specific criteria. They are recognized by Muslim scholars as being early and important in their fields, as works whose importance is broadly recognized by international scholars, and as having had a genuinely significant impact on the development of human culture.

Readers will therefore see that this series includes a variety of works in the purely Islamic sciences, such as Qurʾān, *ḥadīth*, theology, prophetic traditions (*sunna*), and jurisprudence (*fiqh*). Also represented will be books by Muslim scientists on medicine, astronomy, geography, physics, chemistry, horticulture, and other fields.

The work of translating these texts has been entrusted to a group of professors in the Islamic and Western worlds who are recognized authorities in their fields. It has been deemed appropriate, in order to ensure accuracy and fluency, that two persons, one with Arabic as his mother tongue and another with English as his mother tongue, should participate together in the translation and revision of each text.

This series is distinguished from other similar intercultural projects by its distinctive objectives and methodology. These works will fill a genuine gap in the library of human thought. They will prove extremely useful to all those with an interest in Islamic culture, its interaction with Western thought, and its impact on culture throughout the world. They will, it is hoped, fulfil an important rôle in enhancing world understanding at a time when there is such evident and urgent need for the development of peaceful coexistence.

This series is published by the Center for Muslim Contribution to Civilization, which serves as a research centre under the patronage of H.H. Sheikh Hamad bin Khalifa al-Thani, Amir of Qatar. It is directed by a Board of Trustees chaired by H.E. Sheikh Muhammad bin Hamad al-Thani, the former Minister of Education of Qatar. The Board is comprised of a group of prominent scholars. These include H.E. Dr Abul-Wafa al-Taftazani*, Deputy Rector of Cairo University, and Dr Yusuf al-Qaradhawi, Director of the Sira and Sunna Research Center. At its inception the Center was directed by the late Dr Muhammad Ibrahim Kazim, former Rector of Qatar University, who established its initial objectives.

The Center was until recently directed by Dr Kamal Nagi, the Foreign Cultural Relations Advisor of the Ministry of Education of Qatar. He was assisted by a

* Died 1994, may Allāh have mercy on him.

Board comprising a number of academicians of Qatar University, in addition to a consultative committee chaired by Dr Ezzeddin Ibrahim, former Rector of the University of the United Arab Emirates. A further committee acting on behalf of the Center has been the prominent university professors who act under the chairmanship of Dr Raji Rammuny, Professor of Arabic at the University of Michigan. This committee is charged with making known, in Europe and in America, the books selected for translation, and in selecting and enlisting properly qualified university professors, orientalists and students of Islamic studies to undertake the work of translation and revision, as well as overseeing the publication process.

CENTER FOR MUSLIM CONTRIBUTION TO CIVILIZATION

INTRODUCTION

Bidāyat al-Mujtahid is considered to be a book on *khilāf*, a discipline that records and analyzes the differences among Muslim jurists. It is sometimes treated as a book on comparative Islamic law that records the views of different schools and compares them, which is in fact the same thing as *khilāf*. Yet, this is not its declared purpose. Ibn Rushd states in this book, on various occasions and in different ways, that his purpose in writing this book, over which he spent more than twenty years, is the imparting of skills that make a student of law a competent jurist (*mujtahid*), someone who can independently derive the law from its sources. In an important passage, within the Book of *Ṣarf* (Exchange), he uses a simple analogy to point out the purpose of the book and also what the term jurist has come to mean in his own times and what it should mean.

> As our purpose is to record the issues that are expressly covered by the law or are very close to those expressly covered, we thought it desirable to record in this book seven well-known issues, which are like principles, or models, for the guidance of the (would-be) *mujtahid* in whatever he may encounter of the issues of this book. We have designed the book in such a way that with the help of its methodology he may attain the status of *ijtihād*, if he has acquired what is sufficient for him of *ʿilm al-nahw* (grammar), language, and the methodology of usuūl *al-fiqh*—and out of these it is sufficient to know what is proportionate to the requirements of this book or even less. It is by learning the relevant issues, and being equipped with these tools, that he deserves to be called a jurist (*faqīh*), not by merely learning too many details of *fiqh*, even if he has memorized the maximum that is possible for a human being. We find the (so called) jurists of our times believing that the one who has memorized the most opinions has the greatest legal acumen. Their view is like the view of one who thought that a cobbler is he who possesses a large number of shoes and not one who has the ability to make them. It is obvious that the person who has a large number of shoes will (some day) be visited by one whose feet the shoes do not fit. He will then go back to the cobbler who will make shoes that are suitable for his feet. This is the position of most of the *faqīhs* of these times.[1]

[1] See the third paragraph in the Book of *Ṣarf*.

He adds on another occasion:

> It is, however, a strength of this book that through it a person can attain, as we have said, the status of *ijtihād* as he proceeds, along with a knowledge of the Arabic language and of uṣūl al-fiqh that is sufficient for this purpose. It is for this reason that we thought that the most suitable title for this book would be if we name it: *Bidāyat al-Mujtahid wa Kifāyat al-Muqtaṣid.*[2]

To achieve this purpose, he rises above school bias and treats all the great jurists equally. He analyzes their methodology and is at times critical even of his own school. This makes his book unique in Islamic legal literature, and a powerful tool for legal instruction. Anyone who has the determination to read through and understand this powerful, yet difficult, book will not only understand the nature of Islamic law, but also develop skills that will help him derive the law independently. In short, he will be on his way to becoming a jurist.

The Author

Abū al-Walīd Muḥammad ibn Aḥmad ibn Rushd (d.595/1198),[3] famous in the Medieval West under the name of Averöes, belonged to an important Spanish family. His grandfather (d.520/1126),[4] who had the same name and with reference to whom Ibn Rushd is known as the grandson (*al-ḥafīd*), was a well-known *Mālikī* jurist, a *qāḍī*, and the *imām* of the Great Mosque of Cordova. His father too was a *qāḍī*. Ibn Rushd himself is better known as a philosopher or even as a physician, although he had been a *qāḍī* most of his life. He was born at Cordova in the year 520 of the Hijrah, the same year that his grandfather died In his youth he received an excellent education in *fiqh*, *ḥadīth*, *kalām*, and medicine. Some of the well-known teachers mentioned by

2 See the last paragraph in the Book of *Kitāba*.

3 For a detailed description of the life and works of the Author see the excellent article "Ibn Rushd" in the Encyclopaedia of Islam; see also George F. Hourani, Averroes on the Harmony of Religion and Philosophy (London, 1961) 1–43. For his work as a jurist see R. Brunschvig, "Averroès Juriste", in *Études d'Orientalisme Dédiées a la Mémoire de Lévi-Provençal*, tome i (Paris, 1962) 35–68. Also published in *Études d'Islamologie: Droit Musulman* 2 (1976) 167–200. This article presents a reasonable overview of *Bidāyat al-Mujtahid*

4 He wrote a number of well-known works on Mālikī law. See Abū al-Walīd Muḥammad ibn Aḥmad ibn Rushd (1058/1126), *Fatāwá Ibn Rushd*, 3 vols. (Bayrūt: Dār al-Gharb al-Islāmī, 1987); *Al-Bayān wa-al-Taḥsīl wa-al-Sharḥ wa-al-Tawjīh wa-al-Taʿlīl fī Masāʾil al-Mustakhraja*, 20 vols. (*Bayrūt: Dār al-Gharb al-Islāmī*, 1984–1987); and *al-Muqaddimāt al-Mumahhidāt li-Bayān mā Iqtaḍathū Rusūm al-Mudawwana min al-Aḥkām al-Sharʿīyāt wa-al-Taḥṣīlāt al-Muḥkamāt li-Ummahāt Masāʾilihā al-Mushkilāt*, 3 vols. (Bayrūt: Dār al-Gharb al-Islāmī, 1988); see also *Jāmiʿ min al-Muqaddimāt* (ʿAmmān: Dār al-Furqān, 1985).

his biographers[5] are Muḥammad ibn Rizq, Ibn Bashkuwāl, Abū Jaᶜfar Hārūn al-Tajallī, and Abū Marwān ibn Jurrayūl. These were the days when the Almoravid dynasty founded by Yūsuf ibn Tashfīn was replaced by the Almohad dynasty in North Africa (in 541) and the Andalusian provinces were conquered in the next few years. In 565 Hijrah, Ibn Rushd was a *qāḍī* at Seville. This he mentions himself in one of his works. In 567 he was a *qāḍī* at Cordova. In 578, at Marrākush, he succeeded Ibn T.ufayl as the chief physician to Abū Yaᶜqūb Yūsuf (558–80). Later he became the chief *qāḍī* of Cordova. He continued to enjoy the favour of the authorities even during the reign of Yaᶜqūb al-Manṣūr (580–95). It was towards the end of his reign, when animosity was reflected towards philosophers due to political reasons, that Ibn Rushd was criticised by some jurists. This criticism, however, appears to be based on envy and not on doctrinal grounds. He died at Marrākush on 9 Safar 595, 11th December 1298. His body was taken to Cordova for burial.

Ibn Rushd's works on philosophy are well known. Some of these works are available in Latin translations and not in Arabic. Translations of his works on philosophy are available today in English and other languages.[6] In medicine he wrote the book *al-Kulliyāt fī al-Ṭibb*.[7] He is also said to have been interested in Astronomy. A reflection of this can be seen in the section on the sighting of the moon for Ramaḍān in this book. In the area of law, he mentions having written a book on *uṣūl al-fiqh*,[8] and expresses the desire to write a comprehensive and analytical book on the issues dealt with by Mālikī law. He says:

> We hope, God willing, after being free of this book, to compile a book for Mālik's school that assimilates the principles of his school and the well-known issues that work as principles for further derivation. This is what Ibn al-Qāsim did in *al-Mudawwana*. He reconciled that in which he did not have his opinion with what he possessed of the issues of Mālik in the same category and that resembled principles insofar as people (jurists) adopted them for purposes of practice and *taqlīd* in rendering *aḥkām* and verdicts.[9]

[5] Notable among these are Muḥammad ibn ᶜAbd Allāh ibn Abbār (1199–1260), *al-Takmila li Kitāb al-Ṣila*, 2 vols. (Cairo: Maktab Nashr al-Thaqāfa al-Islāmīya, 1955–56) and ᶜAbd al-Walīd al-Marrākushī (b. 1185), *al-Muᶜjib fī Talkhīs Akhbār al-Maghrib* (1978).

[6] See, e.g., George F. Hourani, *Averroes on the Harmony of Religion and Philosophy* (London, 1961). This is the translation of *Kitāb Faṣl al-Maqāl*. See also Simon Van den Bergh, *Averroes, Tahafut al-Tahafut* (*The Incoherence of the Incoherence*) 2 vols. (London, 1954).

[7] See also Ibn Rushd, *Rasāʾil ibn Rushd al-Tibbīya* (Cairo, 1987).

[8] See the first issue under section 2.2.1.2 in the Book of Prayer.

[9] See the last paragraph in the Book of *Kitāba*. He adds on another occasion: "If Allāh were to grant me a long life, I will compile a book about the cases in the school of Mālik ibn Anas, arranging them in an organized manner, as that is the school followed in this peninsula, the peninsula of Andalus, so that the reader may attain the status of a *mujtahid* within Mālik's school. The enumeration of all the narrations, I think, is a task in which life terminates before it (the task) can come to an end". See section 56.7, the Book of *Qadhf*.

It appears that he never found time for the latter book. His book on *uṣūl al-fiqh* is not available in print, and it is not clear whether it is available in manuscript form either. It took him twenty years to compile *Bidāyat al-Mujtahid*. He says at the end of the Book of *Ḥajj* (which was the last portion he compiled):

> It was finalized on Wednesday, the ninth of Jumādī al-Ūlā, which is in the year five hundred and eighty-four. It is a part of *Kitāb al-Mujtahid*, which I have been compiling for more than twenty years or close to it. All praise is for Allāh, the Lord of the Worlds.[10]

The Significance and Method of *Bidāyat al-Mujtahid*

Is *Bidāyat al-Mujtahid* a manual of law like all other manuals, which record the opinions of jurists within their own school? Is it a book on *khilāf* that gives the different opinions of the jurists and records the reasons for their disagreement? Finally, is it a book of law that can be relied upon for opinions expressed by jurists? It serves all these purposes and is used as such by scholars all over the Muslim world, but it is intended by the Author, as has been explained above, to serve a much higher purpose. The true significance and method of this treatise on the law cannot be appreciated unless the nature of Islamic law itself is understood. A brief explanation, therefore, follows.

An exact parallel for Islamic law does not exist in modern legal systems; however, some aspects of its nature may be understood by looking at English common law. Islamic law is an unwritten law, that is, it does not exist in a codified form. English common law is also an unwritten law and it is based on principles that are contained in ancient decisions. The principles of Islamic law are stated, expressly or impliedly, in the Qurʾān and the *sunna* (decisions and practices) of the Prophet Muḥammad (God's peace and blessings be upon him). The principles of the common law may be modified and amended by the judges while deciding new cases arising before them, but some of the principles of Islamic law are relatively fixed and immutable.

It is difficult for the layman, however learned he may otherwise be, to determine on the basis of the principles of the common law what the ruling is on a case. It requires a judge skilled in the art of legal reasoning to decide a case. Likewise, deriving a ruling based on the principles of Islamic law is no easy matter for a layman, whether he is a scholar of *tafsīr* (interpretation of the

[10] See the last paragraph in the Book of *Ḥajj*.

Qurʾān) or of the science of *ḥadīth* (traditions). It requires a jurist (*mujtahid*), who has acquired special skills through rigorous training, to derive such a ruling. The reason is that though the principles of Islamic law are stated in the texts of the Qurʾān and the *sunna* they are not obvious through a direct reading of these texts. It is not possible to read one verse of the Qurʾān or one tradition and say that this is what it means, therefore, this is the law. In some cases, it may not be clear what the law is, even when it is stated explicitly in the texts. Take the case mentioned in the following verse of the Qurʾān:

> And those who accuse chaste women but bring not four witnesses, scourge them (with) eighty stripes and never (afterward) accept their testimony, and they indeed are the *fāsiqūn* (evil-doers), *except those who afterward repent and make amends*, (For such) lo! Allāh is Forgiving Merciful.[11]

There are three penalties mentioned in this text for a person who falsely accuses an honourable woman of having committed unlawful sexual intercourse: eighty stripes, non-acceptance of testimony in other cases, and the public imputation of *fisq*. The question here relates to the impact of the exception mentioned in the words "except those who afterward repent". If a person were found guilty of this offence and he repents promising not to do it again, would it be possible to waive all three penalties for him and let him go? In other words, does the exception apply to all three penalties, to two, or to just one of them?

It is possible here to assign a number of reasons for choosing one of the penalties and relinquishing the others. If such reasoning, however, is based on human reason and expediency alone it would not be acceptable. As the law derived finally would be declared a *ḥukm* (injunction) of Allāh, it is a matter of grave responsibility, and the person has to be careful in arriving at a final ruling. His own reasoning, however plausible it might be, has little value and is considered mere guesswork. He must, therefore, adduce further evidence from within the Qurʾān and the *sunna* in support of his opinion. When he does so, he has a reliable basis for showing the true intention of the Lawgiver. How can the layman, in this case, be sure about the true intention of the Lawgiver? This is clearly the task for the jurist, who will first declare the principles of interpretation that he is using, so that others who follow similar or different principles may be able to evaluate his opinion. He will then undertake a search for one or more principles of law that operate in this case,[12] and determine how the general principles as a whole interact to yield the final view.

[11] Qurʾān 24 : 4.

[12] It should be obvious that the principles of law are not the same thing as the principles of interpretation.

Take another case where three separate verses apparently indicate three different penalties for the same offence:

> As for those of your women who are guilty of *fāhisha* (lewdness), call to witness four of you against them. And if they testify (to the truth of the allegation) then confine them to the houses until death take them or until Allāh appoint for them a way.[13]
> And as for the two of you who are guilty of it (*fāhisha*), punish them both. And if they repent and improve, let them be. Lo! Allāh is Relenting, Merciful.[14]
> The *zānī* and the *zāniyya*[15] scourge ye each one of them with a hundred stripes. And let not pity for the twain withhold you from obedience to Allāh, if ye believe in Allāh and the Last Day. And let a party of the believers witness their punishment.[16]

Is the term *fāhisha* in the first two verses applied to mean the offence of *zinā* mentioned in the third verse, or does it mean something else? In either case the evidence has to be provided from the Qurʾān and *sunna*, and mere literal meanings of the term will have very little force, as grave penalties are being assigned to these acts. If it is assumed, on the basis of some evidence, that the offence is the same in all three verses, are all three penalties to be awarded? Is this possible? Is that the intention of the Lawgiver? The situation becomes highly complex when the *sunna* introduces two more penalties of exile for the unmarried person and stoning to death for the married. Can some of these laws be said to have superseded the others, that is, can one text in the Qurʾān and *sunna* be said to abrogate another text? If we make the assumption that one text can abrogate another, it amounts to choosing a principle of interpretation. Once we choose such a principle, we have to abide by it and apply it to other cases too where it may be applicable. We cannot turn around in another case and say that one text cannot abrogate the other, as in doing so we would be following our own fancy and not a consistent system. This is the crux of the matter. A *mujtahid* must define and declare all his principles of interpretation before he can attempt to interpret the law. Further, the system of interpretation he devises must be internally consistent, that is, one principle should not attempt to contradict or demolish the effect of another principle, as this would ultimately lead to an inconsistency in the derived law.

[13] Qurʾān 4 : 15.

[14] Qurʾān 4 : 16.

[15] The terms *zānī* and *zāniyya* are applied to mean a male and a female, whether married or unmarried, who indulge in unlawful sexual intercourse. It is incorrect to use the terms adulterer and adultress here, as many translators of the Qurʾān tend to do, insofar as the term adultery applies to unlawful sexual intercourse by married persons. The terms used here apply to all persons, whether married or unmarried.

[16] Qurʾān 24 : 3.

The schools of Islamic law, that is, those within the *Sunnī* schools are not sects; their disagreement is not based on theological issues. They represent groups of jurists who uphold different theories of interpretation of the law. Each school has its own set of principles for interpreting the texts. What is common among the four *Sunnī* schools is that they all agree on four sources of Islamic law. They disagree on other principles of interpretation. This is not to be seen as some kind disunity among the Muslims; it is a characteristic found in all legal systems. Take the case of the English common law again. The English common law as practised in England is different to some extent from that applicable in the United States of America, and these systems may differ somewhat from what is practised in Australia and New Zealand, yet they are all based on the English common law and have grown from it. Further, there may be several theories of interpretation within each system. The differences between the views of legal philosophers like Lon Fuller, H.L.A. Hart, and Ronald Dworkin, as well as many others, does not mean that they are talking about different legal systems, yet they are all proposing a different analysis of the methodology of the judge for the same law. It is the same in Islamic law. Each school is advocating a method of interpretation, which not only indicates the maturity of the law, but a richness and variety that helps accommodate a multiplicity of cultures within its fold.[17]

The schools of law did not appear all at once. In the first century of Islam, the law started growing to meet the needs of an expanding empire. The leaders in the law, to whom the people looked up for guidance, were the Companions of the Prophet (God's peace and blessings be upon him). The Companions, as is obvious, did not adopt a common methodology of interpretation. Some of the learned Companions settled in areas that became centres of learning. Within each centre of learning, a more or less common methodology of interpretation started evolving. This led, by the beginning of the second century, to at least two major organized systems of interpretation. The first system was devised by Imām Mālik, who lived in Medina, and the second by Imām Abū Ḥanīfa in Iraq. Both jurists had predecessors whose practices and methods they followed. These leaders in the law were considered the founders of schools because the comprehensive and internally consistent systems of interpretation followed by their respective schools are said to have been devised by these Imām. In other words, the methodology through which the law had to be developed and derived from its sources was laid down by these jurists. Jurists within these schools derived the law independently, but they did not frame new theories of interpretation. They followed the rules chosen by

[17] The views of some Muslim scholars who see the jurists as having caused disunity among the Muslims is naive at best. Such views arise from a lack of understanding of the nature of this law.

their Imāms. By the end of the second century a new theory of interpretation was proposed by Imām al-Shāfiʿī. This was followed by the theory proposed by Imām Aḥmad ibn Ḥanbal. Another theory proposed by Dāwūd al-Ẓāhirī did not survive in the form of an established school.

Can one theory be said to be better than the other? This cannot be decided by the layman, not because he has no right to do so, but because he does not have the ability to prefer one to the other. The layman is known as the *muqallid*, or one who follows the opinion of another, that is, the layman who follows the opinion of an Imām or the preferred opinion of his school. This he does on the basis of faith that he has in the decisions of one school. It is the same thing as following the opinion of a physician in whom one has developed faith or that of a lawyer whose advice one values. The process is known as *taqlīd* in Islamic law. This process has been criticised by many modern scholars, and is deemed to have been the cause of stagnation and decadence. This criticism in unjustified as *taqlīd* is rampant in every area of human life today as it has been in the past, and the causes of stagnation and decadence lie elsewhere. A distinction needs to be made between the principle of *taqlīd* and the inability of jurists in a certain age to independently derive the law. It also needs to be distinguished from the social pressure that the conservative element may exert on a jurist who is competent to undertake *ijtihād*. Ibn Rushd narrates a story about his grandfather, who was forced to take back his opinion that clashed with the established doctrine of the school. The case relates to the time when the right of retaliation is to be exercised, if there are minors among the heirs of the victim.

> On the basis of this opinion, if the victim has heirs who include majors as well as minors, it is necessary to postpone retaliation till the minors grow up to exercise their option, especially when the minors exclude the adults (in inheritance), like children along with brothers.
> The *Qāḍī* (Ibn Rushd) says: This case came up in Cordoba, during the time of my grandfather (God bless him) and the jurists of his time issued the verdict according to the well-known narration (from Mālik), which requires that they should not wait for the minors (to grow up), but he, may *Allāh* have mercy on him, issued the verdict of waiting on the basis of analogy. His contemporaries declared this as abominable, due to the intensity of their *taqlīd*, so much so that he was compelled to issue a verdict in which he supported this school, and this (decision) can be found with people.[18]

It is also said that Jalāl al-Dīn Suyūṭī claimed the status of a *mujtahid* for himself. He was confronted by the jurists, who challenged him to a debate so that they could ascertain whether he was really a *mujtahid*. He declined on the

[18] See section 56.1.2. under the Book of *Qiṣāṣ*.

grounds that a *mujtahid* cannot engage in such an encounter with a *muqallid*, because the opponent must also be a *mujtahid* and there should be a third *mujtahid* to judge between them. Such jurists he maintained did not exist in his times.[19]

Taqlīd, as distinguished from blind conservatism, is the foundation of all relationships based on trust, like those between a patient and his doctor, a client and his lawyer, and a business and its accountant. It is a legal method for ensuring that judges who are not fully qualified *mujtahid*s may be able to decide cases in the light of precedents laid down by independent jurists. It is similar to the case of a subordinate court following the precedent established by a higher court. On the other hand, a Muslim is at liberty to follow one school and then move to another if he is not satisfied, just as he can visit one doctor and then move to another. The system of *taqlīd* implies that as long as the layman does not get the training for becoming a doctor he cannot practise medicine, for example. In the case of medicine, such a person may be termed a quack and may even be punished today, but in the case of Islamic law he is assuming a much graver responsibility: he is claiming that the opinion he is expressing is the law intended by Allāh.

Does this mean that no new theory of interpretation can be proposed today? Certainly not. The Muslim jurists have never placed this restriction. They have never said that jurists should not exercise *ijtihād*. In fact, they maintain that if a person has the necessary ability, it is binding upon him to follow his own opinion. The only requirement is that whoever desires to interpret the law may either use one of the existing systems of interpretation, without mixing it with another to preserve internal consistency, or he should come up with a new theory of interpretation, in which case it would be binding upon him to use his own system. The only requirement is that he must declare his principles of interpretation so that other jurists should be able to judge his competence. In fact, there have been cases in Islamic legal history where new theories have been proposed, although they have been considered extensions of the existing theories rather than as completely indepedent methods. One such theory was proposed by the famous Imām al-Ghazālī, which was refined from the work of his teacher al-Juwaynī. This is the theory based on the purposes of the law, and it comes very close to the methods used in modern law. The full potential of his theory is yet to be utilized by the Muslims. Imām al-Ghazālī died in 505 Hijrah, and Ibn Rushd was born in the year 520.

Did Ibn Rushd lay a claim to the status of a *mujtahid*? He did not do so openly, but if he is claiming to impart skills to would-be *mujtahids* through his

[19] See the introduction to Jalāl al-Dīn Abū Bakr al-Suyūṭī *al-Ashbāh wa al-Naẓā'ir* (Beirut, 1987) 15–16.

work, he is definitely implying that. His competence, his general tone in this book, and the way he prefers opinions expressed by other jurists bears ample testimony to the fact that he considered himself to be a full *mujtahid.* He even expresses new opinions, on several occasions, after declaring that no one had expressed them before him.

Ibn Rushd does not propose a new theory of interpretation in *Bidāyat al-Mujtahid*, although if his book on *uṣūl al-fiqh* is discovered we may find that this may very well be the case. He is fully aware of the developments before him, including the work of al-Ghazālī on the law. He begins the book with a brief statement on the principles of interpretation. He avoids technicalities and presents the principles in a few pages in a manner that only he is accomplished to do. He tries to find a common ground between the different principles of interpretation that are preferred by the leading schools. A thorough grasp of these details is essential for anyone who wishes to understand his book. The system of literal interpretation that he describes uses the terminology adopted by the majority of the schools as compared to the Ḥanafites. He describes how the law is conveyed to us in the form of reports about words, acts, and approvals. The way in which words are used, for example, and the way in which they relate to the acts of the subject determines what the derived law will be. He determines what is to be given preference when words and acts appear to convey different meanings. He does not consider consensus of opinion (*ijmāʿ*) to be an independent source of law, unless it is based directly on a text from the Qurʾān or the *sunna*.

The most important aspect of his method is the way he treats analogy (*qiyās*) and also general principles (*uṣūl*) arising from the texts. He divides analogy into two types: *qiyās al-ʿilla* and *qiyās al-shabah*. This is not to be confused with the division of analogy into *qiyās al-maʿnā* and *qiyās al-shabah* adopted by al-Shāfiʿī in his book *al-Risāla*. Ibn Rushd's method of *qiyās al-shabah* is a much wider form of extension as compared to the restricted form proposed by al-Shāfiʿī. Whenever the phrases like "held it to be similar to" or "considered it to be similar to" appear in his book, the underlying rule is that of *qiyās al-shabah*. The method of *qiyās al-shabah* is usually applied by Ibn Rushd to explain the extensions to the law made by the Mālikī jurists. This method may have much in common with analogy used in the modern law today.

The way Ibn Rushd can identify general principles related to an issue is simply remarkable. General principles play a greater role in the system of interpretation used by the ḥanafites as well as the Malikīs, as compared to the Shafiʿite system in which the emphasis and preference is always given to the text of a sound tradition. These general principles are not based on the jurist's own reasoning or experience, but are based on the texts of the Qurʾān and *sunna*. What is significant is the way Ibn Rushd brings out these principles and explains their operation. This type of exposition is rare in Islamic legal literature, yet it may be essential for the modern lawyer.

When the details of Ibn Rushd's method are considered as a whole, and are related to each other, they begin to reveal a slightly different picture, and this may be termed a somewhat modified, if not a new theory of interpretation.

The arrangement of chapters, or of books as they are called, in the main book follows that in many other manuals of the law, especially Mālik's *al-Muwaṭṭa*ʾ. This facilitates the tracing of issues in books that lack an index or a detailed table of contents. The only section that Ibn Rushd appears to have left out intentionally is the topic of *waqf*. It is the treatment of the topic in which Ibn Rushd's method differs from the rest. He begins each topic by stating the main proposition and then classifies it into its detailed components assigning them to detailed sub-chapters accordingly. Each sub-chapter is divided into detailed issues. The criterion for selecting these issues is described by Ibn Rushd on numerous occasions. He says that these issues are either expressly stated in the texts or are closely related to those that are. In this sense, they serve as the fundamental principles governing a topic. In other words, he discusses only those issues that need to be understood by the student of law, the would-be jurist, and the rest he can derive on his own.

> The purpose is the recording of the well-known issues over which disputes arose between the jurists of the regions together with the issues expressly stated by the *shar*ʿ. This is so, and we have stated this more than once, because our intention in this book is to establish the issues expressly stated by the texts, agreed upon or disputed, and to mention those issues about which the texts are silent, but in which disagreement of the jurists of the regions has become well-known.[20]

Thus, all the detailed issues that may be found in other manuals are not covered by this book.

A distinct pattern can be seen in the statement and discussion of the detailed issues. Ibn Rushd first states the issue and then the opinions of the jurists. He does not give much importance to the author of the opinion; it is the opinion itself that is important. Thus, the opinion may be expressed by a Companion, an individual jurist, or by the leader of a school of law. He makes it a point, though, not to miss the opinions, if known, of the three well-known jurists: Mālik, Abū Ḥanīfa, and al-Shāfiʿī. If there are a large number of opinions on an issue, he classifies them into different groups and refers to them later as the first group, the second group, and so on. Once the opinions have been described he begins by giving the reasons for the formulation of an opinion. A pattern can be seen here too, and it is not too often that Ibn Rushd deviates

[20] See the last sections of the Book of *Kitāba*.

from this pattern. The first basis for an opinion are the texts of the Qurʾān and the *sunna*, that is, if the opinion is directly based on them. This is followed by a description of the methods of interpretation and preference (*tarjīḥ*) used by a jurist. If the jurist relied on analogy in addition to the texts, the basis for such analogy is described and analysed. The special methods of interpretation used by certain schools or jurists are given separate treatment. Thus, Imām Mālik may have used *maṣlaḥah mursala* or *istiḥsān*, or Abū Ḥanīfa may have used his method of preferring general principles. These are explained in detail by the Author. Commenting upon the use of *maṣlaḥa*, for example, he says:

> The rejection of the permissibility of marriage on account of (with the intention of) the inclusion of an additional heir is an analogy based upon *maṣlaḥa*, which is not permitted according to the majority of the *fuqahāʾ*. Taking interests into account in a genus that is remote from the genus that is desired for the establishment of the *ḥukm* according to (the principle of) *maṣlaḥa* led some jurists to the conclusion that upholding such an opinion amounts to legislating additional law, and the adoption of such an analogy dilutes the principle of submission to the *sharīʿa*, neither adding to it nor detracting from it. Yet reluctance to pay attention to *maṣlaḥa* might cause the people to be pushed, because of a lack of precedents in this genus, toward injustice. Such interests should be brought to the scholars of the *ḥikma* (philosophy) of the law, the learned who will not be accused of judging by it, especially nowadays when the qualified persons think that adoption of the letter of the law (apparent meaning) leads to injustice. The proper methodology of the learned scholar in this should be to examine the evidence in the circumstances of the case. If such evidence indicates that he (the *marīḍ*) intends betterment through the marriage, he should not prohibit the marriage, but if it indicates that he intends harm to his heirs, he should disallow it. This is the case in many things among skills and services where the professional is faced with opposing results in what he is trying to do upon the strength of his skill, for it is not possible to lay down fixed limits for the service. This (situation) is usually faced in the profession of medicine and also in various other professions.

Ibn Rushd always makes an attempt to accommodate traditions as far as possible even when they are conflicting with the general principles. If the general principle can be restricted to the extent of the impact of the tradition, he does not hesitate to do so. On many occasions, the criterion he uses for preferring an opinion is the final impact of the opinion on human affairs, that is, he focuses more on the result of the opinion rather than the opinion or the reasoning itself, as in the case cited above, though he tries to find the best reasoning in this case too. When Ibn Rushd is expressing his own opinion it is preceded by the phrase, "The Qāḍī said". This of course is the work of the scribe and not the Author's own language.

Ibn Rushd's method of presenting an issue and explaining its underlying reasoning is highly systematic; however, it must be mentioned that even in its translated form the book is not intended to be taken lightly. He expects the reader to be on his toes, remembering the rules of interpretation along with the evidences stated for an issue. On some occasions the reasoning is so complex that it can be understood only by sketching it out on paper. This means that if the reader is not careful, he will soon find himself facing a void. For the serious reader, however, this book is one of the most powerful tools of legal instruction. Working through the issues will be highly rewarding for him.

It is likely that one who works through these issues and understands the principles of the causes that generated the disagreement of the jurists in them, will be able to derive what is required in each particular case, I mean, what is the answer for it in the opinion of each one of the *fuqahā*ʾ of the regions, that is, in one particular issue itself, and will know when a jurist has opposed his own principle and when he has not. This is the case when an opinion has been related from him in that issue. If, however, a verdict has not been related from him or it has not reached the investigator of these principles, it is possible for him to come up with the answer in accordance with the principles of that jurist according to whose school he is rendering an opinion, and according to the truth to which his *ijtihād* leads him.[21]

At the end of the book Ibn Rushd makes an important statement in which he attempts to summarize the purpose of the *sharīʿa*. In doing so he allows us a glimpse into his own personality.

The *Qāḍī* (Ibn Rushd), may Allāh be pleased with him, said: It is necessary to know that the *aḥkām* of the *sharīʿa* are divisible into two kinds. One of these kinds is adjudicated by the judges, and the majority of the *aḥkām* we have mentioned fall under this category. The second kind are those not adjudicated by the judges, and most of these are in the recommended (*mandūb*) category. This category of the *aḥkām* are like responding to the Muslim greeting (*salām*), blessing one who sneezes, and the like, which are mentioned by the jurists at the end of their books that are called *Jawāmiʿ*. We have also thought of mentioning the best known of this category, God willing.

It is necessary, before this, to know that the legal *sunan* (practices) pertaining to conduct have as their purpose the virtues of the believer. Some of them refer to respect, to whom it is due, and to the expression of gratitude, to whom that is due. The *ʿibādāt* are included in this category. These are the *sunan* relating to ethical values. Some of the *sunan* relate to the virtue call *ʿiffa* (chastity, abstinence from undignified habits), and are of two kinds: *sunan* laid down about food and beverages, and *sunan* laid down about marital affairs. Some *sunan* refer to the requirement of justice and abstention from tyranny. These are the categories of *sunan* that require the maintenance of a balance in financial dealings, and the maintenance of a balance in personal relations (physical contact). Related to this category are (the *aḥkām* of) *qiṣāṣ*, wars, and punishments, as the maintenance of

[21] See the section in the Book of *Kitāba* referred to above.

justice is the aim of all of these. Among them are *sunan* laid down for individual integrity, and *sunan* laid down for all kinds of wealth and its valuation, through which is intended the attainment of the merit called generosity, and the avoidance of the meanness called *bukhl* (covetousness). *Zakāt* is included in this category from one aspect, and is included in the communal sharing of wealth from another; same is the case with charity (*ṣadaqāt*). There are *sunan* laid down for social life, which is the essential condition for human life, and the preservation of its benefits relating to conduct and knowledge, which are called statehood. It is for this reason that these *sunan* should be upheld by the leaders and the upholders of the *Dīn*. Among the important *sunan* for social life are those related to love and hate, and to cooperation for the maintenance of all these *sunan*, which is called *al-nahy ʿan al-munkar, waʾl-amr biʾl-maʿrūf* (prohibiting the blameworthy and requiring what is good), and which is love and hate, that is religious, which occurs either due to the evasion of these *sunan* or due to the evil intent of the believer in the *sharīʿa*. Most of what the jurists mention in the *Jawāmiʿ*, among their books, is that which deviates from the four categories that are the merit of chastity, the merit of justice, the merit of courage, and the merit of generosity, and all kinds of worship (*ʿibāda*) are like conditions for the fulfilment of these merits.[22]

THE TRANSLATION

This is the first time that an entire manual of Islamic law has been translated into English from the original Arabic. This means that the entire terminology of Islamic law has been rendered into English for the first time. The first manual that was rendered into English from a Persian translation was the *Hedaya*, which was translated in 1772 by Charles Hamilton on the order of Warren Hastings, the Governor-General of Bengal. This was not an exact translation of the original. It was more like a summary of al-Marghinānī's views, as they appeared in the Persian translation, expressed in Hamilton's language. The text in English does not conform with the statements of the Author in Arabic. Nevertheless, it was a commendable effort in those early days. Further, Hamilton's translation was meant to be used by the courts, and did not render into English the portions relating to the *ʿibādāt*. As the law in India was changed gradually, some more sections of the translation were deleted from the later editions. Some manuals, Mālikī and Shafiʿī, were translated into French, especially al-Nawawī's *Minhāj al-Ṭālibīn*, which was then translated into English from the French, but they suffered from various defects.[23]

The reason for the lack of translations of such legal texts is obvious. The type of language used by the jurists in their manuals is often so concise that it

[22] See the end of the Book of Judgments.

[23] See the comments made by Joseph Schacht, *Introduction to Islamic Law* (Oxford, 1964) 261–62.

defies rendition into another language. It is not the usual language that one finds in works relating to history or to literature. Most of the manuals were written to facilitate memorization by those aspiring to be judges. Each sentence carries within it an argument that has to be understood in the context of the issue and the underlying principles, many of which are not stated and their prior knowledge is assumed by the authors. It is for this reason that one finds the translations straying away from the original text and the arguments of the author. The task of translating such texts is further complicated by the lack of exact equivalents for the legal terminology employed by the jurists. Thus, there can be no simple formula for translating these texts, and the safest course appears to be to stay with the literal meaning, trying to preserve the intent of the author, even if this is at the expense of style. This was the method adopted for this translation.

Another feature of Islamic legal literature, as with any other technical subject, is that the authors assume a reasonable knowledge of the entire law, including the law relating to ritual, as well as a fair knowledge of legal theory (*uṣūl al-fiqh*). It is not merely a question of transmitting the text from one language into another. Such a knowledge may on some occasions be required of the reader of the translated text. An effort has been made to provide notes for the reader where the text is unduly complex; however, a full treatment of all difficult points is not possible, as that would turn into a full commentary and the sheer magnitude of the project makes that task difficult, at least for the present. A system of numbering the chapters and issues has been adopted to facilitate easy access. The translation of the Qurʾān by Marmaduke Pickthall has been followed generally; however, it has been necessary, several times, to change this to convey the exact meaning intended within the discussion of issues. Ibn Rushd has quoted about eighteen hundred traditions in this book in support of the arguments of the jurists, and on many occasions he refers to one of the *Saḥīḥ* compilations. It has not been possible to document all these traditions, as that would have expanded the project to at least twice its present size. The interested reader may refer to Aḥmad Ibn al-Ṣiddīq, *al-Hidāya fī Takhrīj Aḥādīth al-Bidāya*, 8 vols. (Beirut, 1407/1987).

There are at least three editions of *Bidāyat al-Mujtahid* in Arabic available in print. The only difference in these editions appears to be on how the publisher has divided them into volumes. The text has not been edited, though different manuscripts appear to have been used for compiling the published text. There are a number of typographical errors, and on one occasion a marginal note from one manuscript appears to have crept into the text. On another occasion some sentences have been copied out of order. Despite these errors the text appears to be in a sound and complete condition, and it can safely be assumed to be a complete copy of the Author's original text. The edition used for this translation was published at Beirut by Dār al-fikr, as two volumes in a single volume. There is no date on the book. The system of transliteration followed for this translation is that adopted by the Library of Congress, with slight modifications.

This translation was undertaken for the Center for Research on the Contribution to Muslim Civilization and was supported by a generous grant. It took over four years to complete.

Imran Ahsan Khan Nyazee
Ann Arbor, Michigan
1994

Dr Muhammad Abdul Rauf
Cairo
1994

PREFACE

Praise be to Allāh with all due praise, and prayers and blessings on His Prophet, Muhammad, his family and Companions.

My purpose in this treatise is to lay down in it for myself, by way of remembrance, the issues (*masāʾil*) of the *aḥkām*[1] that are agreed upon and those that are disputed, along with their evidences,[2] and to indicate those bases of the disputes that resemble general rules and principles, for the jurist may be presented with problems on which the law (*sharʿ*) is silent. The issues are mostly those that are expressly stated in the law, or are closely related to those that are so stated. They are the issues agreed upon by the Muslim jurists since the generation of the Companions (God be pleased with them) till such time that *taqlīd*[3] was rampant, or those over which a difference of opinion among them became widely known. Before recording these issues we will mention for you, as briefly as possible, the different channels through which the *aḥkām* of *sharīʿa* were received, the various categories[4] of such *aḥkām*, and the causes that necessitated controversy.

[1] The word *ḥukm* (pl. *aḥkām*) has been translated in various ways by different writers. Some of these meanings are: *sharīʿa* value, injunction, prescription, rule, and command, among others. None of these words, however, conveys the exact meaning of the term *ḥukm* as used in Islamic law, particularly the meaning implied by the *ḥukm waḍʿī* or the determining *ḥukm*. The term *sharīʿa*-value comes very close to capturing the whole meaning, but the term itself is too general and can be used for other meanings. It is, therefore, preferable to retain the term *ḥukm* and allow its meaning to unfold through the text. The term *ḥukm* is also used to mean "legal effects", particularly in contracts (*ʿuqūd*).

[2] The term *adilla* is the plural of *dalīl*, which literally means "guide", "proof", "evidence" and is used here as something that leads to another thing. Technically, the *dalīl* may be transmitted, that is, it may be a text, or it may be rational, like analogy (*qiyās*). The term "proof" is also used by some to denote *dalīl*. Also note the term *adilla tafṣīliyya* or "detailed proofs".

[3] *Taqlīd* means following the opinion of another without questioning the basis of such opinion or its *dalīl* (evidence). Technically it applies to a judicial method adopted by the jurists that ensured the application of the preferred opinion of a particular school in rendering judicial verdicts and in deciding cases. Perhaps, the author implies here that differences of opinion were encouraged during the time of the Companions but *taqlīd* put a stop to such an exchange of ideas and views.

[4] The categories of the *ahkām* were fully developed by the classical jurists, but the origins can easily be traced back to the texts. The categories were also necessitated by the structure of Islamic law.

We say: The channels through which the *aḥkām* were received from the Prophet (peace be upon him) are three in genus: word, act, and approval. With respect to the *aḥkām* about which the Lawgiver is silent, the majority (*jumhūr*) say that the method of attaining them is analogy (*qiyās*). The Ẓāhirites[5] maintain that analogy in law (*sharʿ*) is illegal and that about which the Lawgiver is silent has no *ḥukm*. Reason, they say, supports this assertion as the incidents (occurring) among individuals are unlimited, while words, acts, and approvals are limited, and it is impossible to juxtapose the finite and the infinite.

The kinds of words through which the *aḥkām* are received, by means of transmitted evidences, are four in number; three are agreed upon while the fourth is disputed. The three that are agreed upon are the general word (*ʿāmm*) when applied to all its categories, the particular word (*khāṣṣ*) applied to its single category, the general word when its application is particular, and the particular word when its intended implication is general. Included in this is the use of the higher order meaning to denote the lower order meaning, and the employment of the lower order meaning to indicate the higher order meaning, as well as the indication of equivalent meanings.[6] The example of the first (of the four types of terms) is found in the words of the Exalted, "Forbidden unto you [for food] are carrion and blood and swine-flesh".[7] The Muslim jurists agreed that the word swine (*khinzīr*) includes all kinds of swine, unless it belongs to the category to which the name is not applied, except by way of equivocality (*ishtirāk*), like the term "swine of the sea (porpoise)".[8] The example of the general word implying the particular is found in the words of Allāh, "Take alms of their wealth, wherewith thou mayst purify them and mayst make them grow".[9] The Muslim jurists agreed

[5] The Ẓāhiriyya adopted a system of interpretation that emphasized the literal and the apparent meanings of the texts.

[6] This may sound confusing. The author is saying that the general word sometimes acts like itself and sometimes like the particular word. The same is true of the particular word; that is, it may act like itself or it may act like the general word. For instance, in the example of the verse of *zakāt* (see below), the term "wealth" is used as a general word without any restriction. The meaning it conveys is that *zakāt* is levied on all kinds of wealth; however, we know from other provisions of the *sharīʿa*, that *zakāt* is levied on certain kinds of wealth The word "wealth" will, therefore, be read to mean certain kinds of wealth and not all kinds without restriction. In other words, the general word in this example is meant to convey a particular meaning. It is obvious that in this case the restricted implication of the word "wealth" is dictated by other provisions of the law. Take the other example of the use of the word "fie". This word has a particular implication, but we know that if merely saying "fie" is prohibited all other aggressive and rude behaviour must also be prohibited. The word "fie" is particular, but it has a general implication.

[7] Qurʾān 5 : 3.

[8] This is the name given to the porpoise, which in turn, according to the dictionary, is a name for a number of gregarious, toothed whales. *Porcus* in Latin is pig, while *piscis* is fish The term used here in Arabic is *khinzīr al-māʾ*.

[9] Qurʾān 9 : 103.

that *zakāt* is not obligatory on all kinds of wealth (*māl*).[10] The example of a particular word having a general intent is evident in the words of the Exalted: "Say not 'fie' unto them nor repulse them, but speak to them a gracious word".[11] This is the case of the indication of a higher order meaning through the lower as the prohibition includes beating, abuse, and whatever is more grievous.

The authority demanding the commission of an act uses either the form of a command or the form of a report implying a command. Similarly, the authority demanding omission of an act employs the form of a proscription (*nahy*), or the form of a report implying proscription. If words occur in these forms, is the demand for the commission of an act to be interpreted as an obligation (*wujūb*) or a recommendation (*nadb*)—as will be discussed under the definition of *wājib* and *mandūb*—or is interpretation to be abstained from till another evidence indicates either one of the two? There is a difference of opinion among the jurists in this, recorded in books on *uṣūl al-fiqh*.[12] Same is the case with the forms of proscription, whether they indicate disapproval (*karāha*) or prohibition (*taḥrīm*), or do not indicate either? In this too there is, recorded, a difference of opinion.

The entities to which the *ḥukm* is related[13] are indicated by it either through a word with a single meaning, and this is known in the discipline of *uṣūl al-fiqh* as *naṣṣ* (explicit)—there being no dispute about the obligation of acting in compliance with it—or through a word having more than one meaning and this is of two types. The word may indicate an equal disposition toward the different meanings and is known in *uṣūl al-fiqh* as *mujmal* (having equal probabilities) and there is no dispute that it does not obligate a *ḥukm*; or it may be inclined toward some of these meanings more than it is toward the others, and is known, with reference to such indicated meanings, as *ẓāhir* (manifest, apparent), and with reference to other (probable) meanings as *muḥtamal* (probable).[14] If such a word is used in an unqualified sense it is to be applied to its apparent meaning unless another evidence indicates its

[10] That is, it is applied to certain kinds of wealth; therefore, it is a case of a particular word applied to the specific.

[11] Qurʾān 17: 23.

[12] The term *uṣūl al-fiqh* has been called Islamic jurisprudence, legal theory, and methodology of Islamic jurisprudence, besides other things. It is best left untranslated. Technically it means "the knowledge of the principles that lead to the discovery or derivation of the *sharʿī aḥkām* from their detailed proofs in the sources of Islamic law".

[13] The *ḥukm* is always related to the act of the subject (*mukallaf*) and not to entities or things. It is the act of the subject related to things that is *ḥalāl* or *ḥarām* and not things in themselves. Thus the relationship of the *ḥukm* to entities is indirect.

[14] The division of words into *naṣṣ*, *mujmal*, *ẓāhir*, and *muḥtamal* is in conformity with the system of the Mutakallimūn. The division is slightly different in the system of the Ḥanafites, with some practical consequences.

application to its other probable meanings. Thus there occurs a difference of opinion among the jurists about the *aḥkām* of the Lawgiver. It, in fact, takes place mostly due to three meanings (reasons): the equivocality (*ishtirāk*) of the word applied to an entity with which the *ḥukm* is associated; the equivocality of the definite article "*al*" accompanying the genus of the entity, whether the whole is implied or a part; and the equivocality of the words used for commands and proscriptions. A fourth way, however, is to understand from the obligation of the *ḥukm* for a thing, the negation of things besides it, and from the negation of a thing the obligation of all things besides it. This is known as the (indirect) indication of the communication (*dalīl al-khiṭāb*).[15] It is a rule that is disputed, like the words of the Prophet (peace be upon him), "In the *sāʾima* out of cattle there is *zakāt*". Some have understood from this that there is no *zakāt* in cattle other than the *sāʾima* (pasturing animals).

Legitimate analogy (*qiyās*) is the assigning of the obligatory *ḥukm* for a thing to another thing, about which the law is silent, due to its resemblance to the thing for which the law has obligated the *ḥukm* or due to a common underlying cause (*ʿilla*)[16] between them. It is for this reason that legal analogy is of two types: *qiyās al-shabah* and *qiyās al-ʿilla*. The difference between legal analogy and the particular word implying a general meaning is that analogy can be undertaken only in the case of a particular word that implies just its single category.[17] The other similar cases are then joined with it, that is, those not covered by the text are joined to the one that is, due to a resemblance between them, not through an implication of the word. This is so because the extension of the *ḥukm* to an unstated yet implied category is not analogy, but an indication (connotation) of the word (*dalālat al-lafẓ*). These two kinds (of extensions of the *ḥukm* to the unstated entity) are very close as in both there is a joining of the explicit and the implicit cases and is often a cause of confusion for the jurists. Examples of analogy are the joining of one who drinks wine with the slanderer (*qādhif*) as regards the fixed punishment (*ḥadd*), and the joining of (the amount of) dower (*ṣadāq*) with the minimum scale (*nisāb*) in the case of the cutting of the hand (of the thief). The joining, on the other hand, of things carrying usury (*ribā*) with food, things measured or eatables, is the case of a particular word implying the general. So ponder over this as it is a source of confusion.

[15] The term *khiṭāb*, literally address or communication, of the Lawgiver is distinguished by some from the text of the *Qurʾān*. The *khiṭāb* is eternal and the text is the evidence or *dalīl* of this *khiṭāb*, that is, it leads to the discovery of the meaning of the *khiṭāb*. The distinction indicates the meaning of the term *dalīl*.

[16] The term *ʿilla* too, like the term *ḥukm*, is sometimes translated as *sharīʿa*-value. See *supra* note 1.

[17] The distinction drawn by the author is crucial for understanding the nature of analogical reasoning (*qiyās*) in Islamic law.

It is possible for the Ẓāhirites to dispute the first genus (i.e. analogy), while they are not obliged to dispute the second (i.e., extension through implied meanings) for it is a case of authoritative transmission and he who rejects this rejects a style of communication (*khiṭāb*) employed by the Arabs.

The report of an act, according to many, is one of the channels through which the *aḥkām* are received. Some have said that reports of the Prophet's deeds (acts) do not yield *aḥkām*, as they do not have linguistic patterns. Those who accept that *aḥkām* can be received through acts differ about the kind of *ḥukm* indicated by them. Some say that they indicate obligation while others say that they indicate recommendation (*nadb*). The preferred opinion of the learned scholars is that if they occur as an explanation (*bayān*), of an obscure (*mujmal*) obligatory act, they indicate an obligation, and if they occur as an explanation of an obscure recommended act then they indicate recommendation. If they do not occur as an explanation for an obscure act, but belong to a recommended category, then they indicate recommendation. If they belong to the genus of permissible (*mubāḥ*) acts then they indicate permissibility. Approval (*iqrār*), on the other hand, indicates permissibility. These, then, are the kinds of channels through which the *aḥkām* are received.

Consensus (*ijmāʿ*) relies on one of these four channels, except that when it takes place on the basis of one of these channels, which is not definitive (*qaṭʿī*) the *ḥukm* is considered definitive due to predominant probability. *Ijmāʿ*, however, is not an independent source in itself unless reliance is placed on one of these (four) channels.[18] Had it been so it would have amounted to the establishment of additional law after (the time of) the Prophet (peace be upon him), as it would not have been based on one of the legally valid principles.

The functional terms denoting the *aḥkām* derived from these literal modes for the subjects (*mukallafūn*) are, as a whole, either a command for a thing or a proscription or a choice between the two. When the command is decisive and an omission (to do the act) invokes punishment the act is called obligatory (*wājib*). If there is reward (*thawāb*) for the act and punishment is absent it is called a recommended act (*mandūb*). Similarly, when the proscription is decisive and the commission of the act invokes punishment, the act is prohibited (*ḥarām*), and if there is an urging to abstain from the act without invoking punishment for commission it is called reprehensible (*makrūh*).[19] Where a choice has been given (between commission and omission) the act is permitted (*mubāḥ*). The kinds of *aḥkām* acquired through these channels are

[18] The evidence on which reliance is placed for purposes of *ijmāʿ* is called the *sanad* of *ijmāʿ*.

[19] The term "disapproved" will sometimes be used to indicate this category.

five: obligatory, recommended, prohibited, reprehensible or disapproved, and permissible.

The causes of conflict of opinion (*ikhtilāf*), by genus, are six.[20] First is the vacillation of the words between these four modes, that is between the general word meant as a particular word, or the particular word implying generality, or a general word implying generality, or a particular word intending a particular meaning, or there is present, or absent, an indirect indication of the communication. The second cause is the equivocality (*ishtirāk*) in words. This occurs sometimes in the individual word like the word "period" (*qurʾ*) that is applied both to purity (*ṭuhr*) and to menstruation (*ḥayḍ*); similarly, the word command (*amr*) whether it is to be given the (initial) meaning of obligation or of recommendation and the word proscription (*nahy*) whether it is to be given the meaning of prohibition or of disapproval. Sometimes it occurs in the compound word as in the words of Allāh: "Save those who afterward repent".[21] It is likely that this refers to the transgressing person (*fāsiq*) only and it is also probable that it refers to both the transgressor and the witness (*shāhid*). Thus, repentance can remove the consequences of transgression and it can also permit the testimony of the slanderer.[22] The third cause lies in the (different probabilities of the) grammatical structure. The fourth is the ability of the word to indicate its literal meaning, and an allegorical or metaphorical sense resulting from an implied omission or addition or from the reversal of the normal order of the sentence by advancing or deferring a word from its legitimate place, or it may be the vacillation of the word between its actual application and the figurative meaning. The fifth cause is the occasional use of the word in its absolute/unqualified (*muṭlaq*) meaning or in a qualified sense, like the unqualified use, on occasions, of the word slave (*raqabah*; literally neck) in manumission and then qualifying it with faith (*īmān*) at other times. The sixth cause is the conflict between two texts, in all kinds of words from which the law derives the *aḥkām*. Moreover, the conflict may exist between reported acts or approvals or between different kinds of analogy themselves, or the conflict may be between one of these four channels with another channel: that is, the conflict of a word with a reported act, approval, or analogy; the

[20] The accepted principle is that there is no conflict in the evidences of *sharīʿa*. The conflict exists in the mind of the jurist that he seeks to resolve through the science of *uṣūl al-fiqh*.

[21] Qurʾān 24: 5. The verse relates to those who falsely accuse chaste women: "And those who accuse honorable women but bring not four witnesses, scourge them (with) eighty stripes and never (afterward) accept their testimony. They indeed are the evildoers. Save those who afterward repent and make amends. (For such) lo! Allāh is Forgiving, Merciful". Qurʾān 24 : 4, 5.

[22] The question here is whether repentance on the part of the slanderer (*qādhif*) will have the effect of waiving the restriction placed through the words, "and never (afterward) accept their testimony", (Qurʾān 24: 4) or it will only do away with the imputation, "they indeed are the evildoers". The exception, "save those who afterward repent", can be interpreted both ways.

conflict of a reported act with approval or analogy; and the conflict of approval with analogy.

The Qāḍī (Ibn Rushd) (God be pleased with him) said: After this brief discussion, we begin with our purpose, seeking the help of Allāh, and to do so we start with the Book of Purification (*Ṭahāra*) as is customary with them (the jurists).

XVIII
THE BOOK OF *NIKĀḤ* (MARRIAGE)

The principles of this book are covered in five chapters:
Chapter 1: Preliminaries of marriage;
Chapter 2: Requirements for the validity of marriage;
Chapter 3: Requirements for an option (*khiyār*) in marriage;
Chapter 4: Marital rights; and
Chapter 5: Marriages prohibited by law.

18.1. Chapter 1: Preliminaries of Marriage

In this chapter there are four issues: the *ḥukm* of marriage; the *ḥukm* of the proposal (*khiṭba*) for marriage; proposal to a woman proposed to already; and glancing at the woman to be proposed to (*makhṭūba*).

18.1.1. Issue 1: The *ḥukm* of marriage

A group of jurists maintained that the *ḥukm* of marriage conveys recommendation. These are the majority (*jumhūr*). The Ẓāhirites said that it is obligatory. The later Mālikites held that for some it is obligatory, for others recommended, and for the rest it is permitted. This depends on the extent to which an individual fears falling into evil.

The reason for their disagreement lies in whether the form (*sīgha*) of the command—in the verse: "[M]arry of the women who seem good to you",[1] and in the tradition, "Marry, for through you I wish to outnumber the nations", and in other traditions like it—implies obligation, recommendation, or permissibility. Those who say it is obligatory for some, recommended for others, and permitted for the rest, have recourse to *maṣlaḥa* (secured interest), which is a kind of analogy called *mursal*.[2] It is a principle for which there is no determined source of reliance; it has been rejected by a number of jurists. The preferred opinion in Mālik's school is based on it.

[1] Qur'ān 4 : 3

[2] The word *mursal*, from *irsāl*, means "to let go". This term is used with reference to *qiyās*, which is analogy within a narrow framework tied down to a particular text. *Maṣlaḥa* is undertaken with reference to the meaning of the texts considered collectively, free from the hold of a particular text.

The form of the proposal for marriage transmitted from the Prophet (God's peace and blessings be upon him) is not obligatory according to the majority. Dāwūd said it is obligatory. The reason for their disagreement lies in whether the act of the Prophet (God's peace and blessings be upon him) related to this implies an obligation or recommendation.

18.1.2. & 18.1.3. Issues 2 & 3: Proposal of marriage (*Khiṭba*) and the *ḥukm* of proposal to a woman proposed to already

The proscription from the Prophet (God's peace and blessings be upon him) about a proposal made while another's proposal is pending is well established. The jurists differed as to whether it indicates rescission of the second proposal? If it does indicate rescission, then under what circumstances? Dāwūd said it is rescinded while al-Shāfiʿī and Abū Ḥanīfa said it is not. Both opinions are narrated from Mālik, and a third is that it is rescinded, before consummation and not after it. Ibn al-Qāsim said that the proscription has meaning when a righteous person proposes during the proposal of another righteous person; however, if the first person is not righteous while the second is, it is permissible.

About the time of the second proposal, the majority are of the opinion that it arises when the matter of the first has been referred to a third party, but not in the early stages of the proposal. This is based on the tradition of Fāṭima bint Qays "when she came to the Prophet (God's peace and blessings be upon him) and mentioned to him that Abū Jahm ibn Hudhayfa and Muʿāwiya had both proposed to her. He said, 'As for Abū Jahm, he is a person who does not lift his stick off women, and Muʿāwiya is destitute having no wealth, but marry Usāma' ".

18.1.4. Issue 4: Glancing (for approval) at the woman to be proposed to

Glancing at a woman prior to proposal was permitted by Mālik up to the face and hands alone, while others permitted it for the whole body except the private parts. Some have prohibited this without qualification. Abū Ḥanīfa permitted glancing at the feet along with the face and the hands. The reason for their disagreement is that the command permits glancing at women in general terms and the proscription also prohibits it in general terms. It is also laid down in qualified terms, that is, glancing at the face and the hands, which was the interpretation of most of the jurists of the words of the Exalted, "[Women] are not to display their adornment save that which is apparent",[3] that they mean the face and the hands. Further, there is the analogy of the permissibility, according to the majority, of uncovering them during *ḥajj*. Those who forbade the use of this principle did so because of the absolute prohibition of looking at women.

[3] Qurʾān 24 : 31

18.2. Chapter 2: Requirements for the Validity of Marriage

This chapter is divided into three elements (*arkān*; sing. *rukn*). The first element is about the identification of the formation of this contract. The second element is about the identification of the subject-matter (*maḥall*) of this contract. The third element is about the identification of the conditions of the contract.

18.2.1. Element 1: Formation of the Contract

The study of this element is undertaken from different aspects: the nature of the permission with which the contract is concluded; the person whose permission is acknowledged for the validity of this contract; whether the contract of marriage is permitted with an option; and whether the contract is obligatory with delay from one of the parties, or whether immediate acceptance is a condition?

18.2.1.1. Aspect 1: Consent in marriage

Permission in marriage is of two types. It takes place for men and deflowered women by means of words and for consulted virgin women through their silence, that is, their consent; rejection, however, is by words. There is no dispute about this, as a whole, except what is narrated from the followers of al-Shāfiʿī that the permission of the virgin is by words, when the person giving her away in marriage (her guardian) is other than the father or the grandfather. The majority inclined towards permission through silence because of what is established from the Prophet (God's peace and blessings be upon him) that "the deflowered woman has a greater right over herself than her guardian (*walī*), but the virgin is to be asked about herself and her silence is her permission".

They agreed that in order to be valid, the marriage contract of a person whose permission is by words has to be concluded by the use of the word "*nikāḥ*" or "*tazwīj*". They differed about its conclusion through the word "gift" or the word "sale" or "sacrifice". Some jurists, like Mālik and Abū Ḥanīfa, permitted this. Al-Shāfiʿī said that it cannot be concluded except by the word "*nikāḥ*" or by the word "*tazwīj*". The reason for their disagreement lies in whether it is a contract in which, along with intention (*niyya*), a particular word is required, or whether the employment of such a word is not necessary for its validity. Those who attach it to the category of contracts that require the consideration of both factors said that the contract is not concluded except by the word "*nikāḥ*" or "*tazwīj*". Those who said that particular words are not a condition in it, keeping in view those contracts in which words are not a condition, permitted marriage by means of any word that renders the legal meaning, that is, if between it and the legal meaning there is a common basis.

18.2.1.2. Aspect 2: The person whose consent is taken into account for the validity of the contract

The person whose acceptance is taken into account for the validity of this contract is identified in the law (*sharᶜ*) in two ways. In the first, the consent of the parties (themselves) to the marriage, the groom and the bride, is taken into account, either with the consent of the guardian, or without his consent, according to the opinion of those who do not stipulate a guardian in the case of consent by a woman who possesses the right herself. In the second, the consent of the guardians alone is taken into account. In both methods there arise issues that are agreed upon and those that are disputed. We shall mention out of these the (issues that furnish) principles and rules.

We say: The jurists agreed about the stipulation of the consent and acceptance of men who had attained puberty, were free, and were in charge of their own affairs. They disagreed whether the master could force his slave to marry, and the executor (*waṣī*) his *bāligh*[4] interdicted protégé. Mālik said that the master could force his slave to marry. The same is the opinion of Abū Ḥanīfa. Al-Shāfiᶜī said that he is not to be forced. The reason for their disagreement is based on whether this (the contract of marriage) is one of the rights of the master. Similarly, they disagreed about the executor forcing his interdicted ward, and this dispute exists within the school (of Mālik). The reason for their disagreement, thus, lies in whether marriage is one of the interests (*maṣlaḥa*) secured for him, or is not an interest but a means for pleasure. On the basis of the opinion that marriage is obligatory there should be no hesitation in this.

On the question of women, whose consent is taken into account in marriage, they agreed that the consent of the deflowered *bāligh* (major) woman is to be taken into account, because of the saying of the Prophet (God's peace and blessings be upon him), "The deflowered woman expresses her own consent", except what is narrated from al-Ḥasan al-Baṣrī. They disagreed about the *bāligh* virgin and the non-*bāligh* deflowered girl (when she does not exhibit bad behaviour). About the *bāligh* virgin, Mālik, al-Shāfiᶜī and Ibn Abī Laylā said that it is only for the father to force her to marry. Abū Ḥanīfa, al-Thawrī, al-Awzaᶜī, Abū Thawr and a group of jurists said that it is necessary to take her consent into consideration. Mālik agreed with them about the virgin spinster in one of his opinions.

[4] The term *bāligh* is used for someone who has attained the age of puberty (*bulūgh*). This is the age of majority in Islamic law, however, the terms "major" and "adult" are being avoided, as they indicate a person who is usually older than the *bāligh*. The age of *bulūgh* depends on the actual physical puberty of the individual concerned, and may start at twelve for a boy and even lower for a girl. In the absence of any physical signs of puberty, the presumption of puberty is linked to different ages determined by the *fuqahā*ʾ.

The reason for their disagreement is based on the conflict of the indirect indication of the communication (*dalīl al-khiṭāb)* with the relevant general meaning in this, which is found in the saying reported from the Prophet (God's peace and blessings be upon him) that "the orphan girl is not to be married without her permission", and his saying, "The orphan girl is to be asked about herself". It is narrated by Abū Dāwūd. The meaning derived from it through the indication of the communication is that one having a father is different from the orphan girl. The saying of the Prophet in the well-known tradition of Ibn ᶜAbbās, "The virgin is to be asked (for permission)", makes the seeking of permission from each virgin obligatory through its generality. The general meaning is stronger than the indirect indication of the text, but Muslim has narrated, in the tradition of Ibn ᶜAbbās, an addition that "the virgin's permission is to be sought by the father". This is decisive on the point of dispute.

Mālik and Abū Ḥanīfa said about the non-*bāligh* deflowered woman that the father can force her to marry, while al-Shāfiᶜī said that he is not to force her. The later Mālikites said that there are three views about her in the school. First, that the father can force her as long as she has not attained puberty after divorce. This is the opinion of Ashhab. Second, that he can force her even though she has attained puberty. This is the opinion of Saḥnūn. Third, that he is not to force her even if she has not attained puberty. This is the opinion of Abū Tammām. What we have narrated from Mālik is what is narrated by the writers of *khilāf*, like Ibn al-Qassār and others.

The reason for their disagreement is based on the conflict of the indirect indication of the text with the general implication. This is witnessed in the saying of the Prophet (God's peace and blessings be upon him) that "the orphan girl is not to be married without her consent",—from which it is understood that permission of one having a father is not to be sought except as agreed upon by the majority (*jumhūr*) in the case of the divorced *bāligh* woman—and in the general implication of his (God's peace and blessings be upon him) saying that "the deflowered woman has a greater right over herself than the guardian", which includes the *bāligh* and the non-*bāligh*. So also his saying that "the widow (*ayyim*) is not to be married till her permission is sought, and is not to be married till she gives her consent", which indicates through its general implication what has been said by al-Shāfiᶜī.

There is another reason for their disagreement upon these two issues. It is the construction of an analogy upon a point of consensus (*ijmāᶜ*). They arrived at the consensus that the father can force a non-*bāligh* virgin and that he cannot force a divorced *bāligh* woman, except for isolated instances of disagreement in all this, as we have indicated.

They disagreed about the underlying cause of forced consent whether it is virginity or minority (*ṣighar*). Those who said it is minority maintained that the *bāligh* virgin is not to be forced, while those who considered it to be virginity said that the *bāligh* virgin is forced, but not the deflowered minor girl. Those who considered both as causes made forced consent obligatory when either was found and said that the *bāligh* virgin is to be forced and so is the non-*bāligh* deflowered woman. The determination of the underlying cause (*taʿlīl*) in the first case is by Abū Ḥanīfa, in the second by al-Shāfiʿī, and in the third by Mālik. The sources, however, lend greater support to the cause determined by Abū Ḥanīfa.

They disagreed about the loss of virginity that does away with compulsion and obligates the expression of consent or rejection. Mālik and Abū Ḥanīfa said that it is loss of virginity that results from a valid marriage, or from a semblance of marriage, or from ownership (*milk*), and that does not result from illegal intercourse (*zinā*) or from rape following abduction (*ghaṣb*). Al-Shāfiʿī said that each kind of loss of virginity does away with compulsion. The reason for their disagreement lies in whether the *ḥukm* is linked to the legal meaning or the literal meaning of the loss of virginity in the saying of the Prophet (God's peace and blessings be upon him) that "the deflowered woman has a greater right over herself than her guardian".

They agreed that the father can compel his minor son to marry and also his minor virgin daughter, and he may not seek her permission, as it has been established that "the Messenger of Allāh (God's peace and blessings be upon him) married ʿĀʾisha (God be pleased with her) when she was a girl of six or seven and consummated the marriage with her when she was nine, through a marriage contracted with Abū Bakr (God be pleased with him)", except for the disagreement narrated from Ibn Shubrama. In this, they disagreed about two issues. First, whether the minor girl can be given away in marriage by someone other than the father. Second, whether the minor boy can be married away by someone other than the father.

About the marriage of the minor girl undertaken by someone other than the father, al-Shāfiʿī said that only the paternal grandfather can give her away in marriage. Mālik said that no one can give her away in marriage except the father, or one to whom the father has delegated this task, unless she is likely to fall into corruption and loss. Abū Ḥanīfa said that the minor can be married away by anyone who enjoys guardianship over her, including the father, relatives, and others, but when she attains puberty she has the option (*khiyār*) (of revocation).

The reason for their disagreement is the conflict of analogy with the general meaning. This is because of the saying of the Prophet (God's peace and blessings be upon him), "Seek permission from the virgin, her silence being her consent", implies a generality in the case of all virgins except one having a father, as her case was qualified by consensus (*ijmāʿ*), besides the disagreement we have mentioned. As it is known about all guardians that they will be cautious and will watch the interest of their wards, it is necessary that they be deemed equivalent to the father. Some included all guardians in this meaning, while some included only the grandfather as he is a father who is an ascendant. This was done by al-Shāfiʿī. Those who restricted the right to the father said that what the father possesses is not proper for anyone else, either because the law has singled him out for this or because the sympathy and kindness exhibited by the father are not found to the same degree in anyone else. This is what Mālik (God be pleased with him) has upheld and what he has upheld is the most outstanding, Allāh knows best, except in the case of necessity.

The Ḥanafites argued for the permissibility of contracting the marriage of minors by persons other than the father on the basis of the words of the Exalted: "And if ye fear that ye will not deal fairly by the orphans, marry of the women, who seem good to you".[5] They said the word "orphan" (*yatīm*) is not applied to anyone except the non-*bāligh* girl. Others have said the name orphan is applied to the *bāligh* girl because of the evidence in his (God's peace and blessings be upon him) saying, "Seek permission from the orphan girl", and the girl whose permission is sought is one who is capable of consent, and she is the *bāligh* girl. Thus, their disagreement has another reason and that is the equivocality (*ishtirāk*) of the word orphan (*yatīm*). Those who have not permitted marriage through someone other than the father, have argued on the basis of his (God's peace and blessings be upon him) saying that "the orphan girl is to be asked about herself". They said that the minor, by agreement, is not one of those who grant permission, therefore, denial of the right of persons other than the father is obligatory. And they may also add that this is the *ḥukm* of the orphan girl who is capable of giving consent. The case of the minor is not (expressly) covered by the *sharīʿa*.

In response to the question whether the guardian, who is not a father, can contract the marriage of a minor boy, Mālik granted permission to the executor (*waṣī*) and Abū Ḥanīfa permitted this to the guardians (*awliyāʾ*), except that he granted the minor the option (*khiyār*) upon attaining puberty, while Mālik did not make this obligatory. Al-Shāfiʿī said that none other than the father can contract his marriage. The reason for their disagreement in this is the construction of the analogy for those other than the father from the case of the father. Thus, those who did not find in the person other than the father the reasons uncovered by *ijtihād* that permitted the father to contract the marriage of one of his minor children, did not permit this, while those who said that such reasons were to be found for others did permit it. Those who made a distinction in this between the minor boy and the minor girl were of the view that a male

[5] Qurʾān 4 : 3

possesses the right to divorce upon attaining puberty, while the female does not. For this reason Abū Ḥanīfa has granted both an option upon attaining puberty.

18.2.1.3. Aspect 3: Is the contract permissible with an option (*khiyār*)?

The third aspect is whether the contract of marriage is permitted with an option (*khiyār*). The majority are of the view that it is not permitted. Abū Thawr said it is. The reason for their disagreement is the vacillation of the contract of marriage between sales (*buyūʿ*) in which an option is not permitted and those sales in which it is. We can say that the principle in sales is that there is no option except when there is a text supporting it, and the burden of proof is upon one who wishes to establish it. We can also say that the principle is the prohibition of option in sales and that its basis is hazard (*gharar*). In marriages there is no hazard because their object is quality and not measure, and because the need for option and examination in marriage is more than that in sales. With respect to delay in acceptance on the part of one of the parties to the contract, Mālik permitted a slight delay, while some prohibited it. Others permitted it in a manner that the guardian contracts a woman's marriage without her consent, but when the information reaches her she permits it. From among those who prohibited it absolutely is al-Shāfiʿī and from those who permitted it absolutely are Abū Ḥanīfa and his disciples, while Mālik distinguished between an extended and a short delay. The reason for disagreement is whether (the existence of) acceptance by both parties simultaneously is a condition for the validity of the contract. A similar disagreement is presented in sales.

18.2.2. **Element 2: The Conditions of the Contract**

In this topic there are three sections:
Section 1: Guardians (*Awliyāʾ*);
Section 2: Witnesses;
Section 3: Dower (*ṣadāq*).

18.2.2.1. *Section 1: The Guardians* (Awliyāʾ)

The study of guardians is undertaken from four aspects. First, the stipulation of guardianship (*wilāya*) for the validity of marriage. Second, the qualifications of a guardian. Third, the kinds of guardians, their priority for guardianship, and related issues. Fourth, the prevention of ward marriages by the guardians and differences arising between a guardian and his ward.

18.2.2.1.1. Aspect 1: Is guardianship a condition for the validity of the contract of marriage?

The jurists disagreed whether guardianship is one of the conditions for the validity of marriage. Mālik, in Ashhab's narration from him, said that there is no marriage without a guardian and that it (guardianship) is a condition of validity. Al-Shāfiʿī held the same opinion. Abū Ḥanīfa, Zufar, al-Shaʿbī and al-Zuhrī said that if a woman contracts her marriage without a guardian, and with someone of equivalent status (*kufʾ*), it is permitted. Dāwūd distinguished between a virgin and a deflowered woman and stipulated the existence of a guardian as a condition in the case of a virgin, but did not stipulate it in the case of a deflowered woman. The fourth opinion is Mālik's, as derived from Ibn al-Qāsim's narration, that its stipulation as a demand is recommended (*sunna*), but not obligatory. This is because it is narrated from him that he used to view inheritance among parties married without a guardian (as valid), and permitted an unchaste woman to appoint a man as her guardian for her marriage, and he held as recommended that a deflowered woman present a guardian who could contract on her behalf. Thus, guardianship for him is one of the complementary demands and not a condition for validity, as against the statement of Mālik's disciples from Baghdad, who consider it a condition of validity and not that of perfection. The reason for their disagreement is the absence of a verse or tradition that is apparent (*ẓāhir*), not to say explicit, about the stipulation of guardianship as a condition of marriage. In fact the verses and traditions that are quoted in practice, by those who stipulate it as a condition, are all subject to interpretation. Similarly, the verses and traditions that are quoted in support of its absence as a condition are also not so clear on the issue. The traditions, besides being unclear in meaning, are disputed as to their authenticity, except the tradition of Ibn ʿAbbās, which negates it, but it lacks persuasive force as the original rule requires freedom from all liability.

We will state the most prominent sources from among those cited for support by both parties and explain the aspects of probability in them. The most prominent sources used from the Qurʾān, by those who lay down guardianship as a condition, are the words of the Exalted: "[When] they reach their term, place not difficulties in the way of their marrying their husbands".[6] They said that this is addressed to the guardians. If they had no right of guardianship how is it that they were prohibited from prevention (of marriage)? About the words of the Exalted: "And do not marry idolaters till they believe",[7] they said that this too is addressed to the guardians. The most prominent tradition used by them is narrated by al-Zuhrī from ʿUrwa from ʿĀʾisha that she said, "The Messenger of Allāh (God's peace and blessings be

[6] Qurʾān 2 : 232
[7] Qurʾān 2 : 221

upon him) said: 'Any woman who marries without the consent of her guardian, her marriage is void, void, void, and if the wedding takes place she is entitled to dower according to her status (*mahr al-mithl*). And if they should disagree, then, the sultan is the guardian of whoever is without a guardian'." It is narrated by al-Tirmidhī who said it is a *ḥasan* tradition.

Among the verses from the Qurʾān and the traditions, used by those who do not lay down guardianship as a condition, are the words of the Exalted: "[T]hen there is no sin for you in aught that they (widowed women) may do with themselves in decency".[8] They maintain that this is proof of the permissibility of her entering into a contract for her marriage on her own. They said that in addition to this, the act (of marrying independently) is attributed to them in several other verses. Thus, the words, "[I]n marrying their husbands"[9] and "until she hath wedded another husband".[10]

In their reliance on traditions, they argued on the basis of a report by Ibn ʿAbbās, the authenticity of which is agreed upon. It is the saying of the Prophet (God's peace and blessings be upon him) that "the deflowered woman has a greater right over herself than her guardian, and the virgin is to be asked about herself, and her silence is her consent". It is on the basis of this tradition that Dāwūd argued about the distinction he made between the deflowered woman and the virgin. These, then, are the best-known evidences put forward by both parties from the transmitted texts.

In the words of the Exalted: "[A]nd [when] they reach their term do not place difficulties in their way of marrying their husbands",[11] there is nothing more than a proscription for the relatives and residuaries that they may not prevent her (the woman) from marrying, and from this proscription for non-prevention it is not understood, either in its metaphorical or actual meaning, that their (the guardian's) consent is stipulated for the validity of the contract. I mean, from any aspect of the apparent or explicit indication of the communication (*khiṭāb*). In fact, the opposite may be understood from it, which is that there is no way the guardians can prevent their wards (from marrying). Similarly, the words of the Exalted: "And do not marry idolaters till they believe",[12] are better understood as a communication for the rulers (*ūlūl amr*) of the Muslims or for all the Muslims collectively rather than a communication for the guardians. On the whole, it vacillates between being a communication for the guardians or for the rulers. Thus, those who have argued on the basis of this verse are under the obligation to explain how the

[8] Qurʾān 2 : 234
[9] Qurʾān 2 : 232
[10] Qurʾān 2 : 230
[11] Qurʾān 2 : 232
[12] Qurʾān 2 : 221

communication is addressed, through its apparent meaning, to the guardians and not to the rulers.

If it is maintained that it has a general implication, and being general it includes both rulers and guardians, it will be said that this communication implies the denial of a right in which the guardians and others are equal, and their being addressed does not grant them exclusive authority for giving consent. If we say that it is a communication addressed to the guardians, making it obligatory that they stipulate their consent for the validity of marriage, it would nevertheless be an unelaborated (*mujmal*) communication and acting according to it would be difficult as there is no indication in it about the kinds of guardians, their qualifications and their grades. The explanation (*bayān*) must not be delayed from the time of its need. Had there been a known law practised on this issue it would have come down through a collective communal transmission or through a transmission close to it as this was a point of general need and it is known that there were those in Medina who had no guardians. In addition, it has not been related from the Prophet (God's peace and blessings be upon him) that he used to administer their marriage contracts or that he appointed someone who performed this function. Further, the purpose of the verse is not to expound the *ḥukm* of *wilāya*, but the (purpose is) to prohibit marriage with the polytheists, men and women. This is evident—Allāh knows best.

ʿĀʾisha's tradition is disputed with respect to the obligation of acting upon it. The preferred course is that a tradition disputed with respect to its soundness does not give rise to the obligation of acting upon it, and even if we concede the soundness of the tradition, there is nothing in it beyond the stipulation of seeking the permission of the guardian by one who has a guardian, I mean, the female ward. If we concede that it is general for all women, it does not contain the prohibition for a woman to contract her own marriage, that is, she cannot herself conclude the contract. In fact, it is evident from it that if the guardian grants her his permission, it is permitted to her to form her own contract without there being the stipulation of including the guardian among the witnesses for the validity of the contract.

The meaning of what is adduced as proof by the other party of the words of the Exalted, "[T]here is no sin for you in that which they do of themselves within the recognized limits",[13] indicates a prohibition of attributing blame to them for acting independently to the exclusion of the guardians, and there is no act through which a woman can go against the wishes of her guardian except the contract of marriage. The apparent meaning of the verse, then,

[13] Qurʾān 2 : 240. Pickthall's translation has been altered slightly. He uses the word "rights" for recognized limits.

Allāh knows best, is that a woman has the right to contract her own marriage and the guardians have a right to revoke it if it is not in conformity with her status. This is the manifest requirement of the law, but none of the jurists has expressed it. Arguing on the basis of a part of a verse and not arguing on the basis of the remaining part exhibits weakness (of method). There is no evidence of exclusivity in the verse in attributing the contract of marriage to them (the women), but the principle is that it is exclusive, unless an evidence to the contrary is adduced to contradict this.

The tradition of Ibn ᶜAbbās is, upon my life, explicit in indicating the distinction between a deflowered woman and a virgin, for if permission from each one of them is to be sought and it is their guardian who supervises the contract, then, in what, I wish I knew, does the widow have a greater right over herself than her guardian? The tradition of al-Zuhrī would be better (understood) if it is considered to be in conformity with this tradition rather than being in conflict with it. It is probable that the difference between the two is only to the extent of one being explicit and the other not being so, and silence is sufficient for the contract.

The proof in the words of the Exalted, "[T]here is no sin for you in that which they do of themselves within their recognized limits",[14] indicating that a woman has a right to form her own contract, is stronger than the implication of the words of the Exalted, "And do not marry idolaters till they believe",[15] which are claimed to convey that the guardian has the right to conclude the contract.

The Ḥanafites deemed the tradition of ᶜĀʾisha as weak for the reason that it is a tradition narrated by a group from Ibn Jurayj from al-Zuhrī, and Ibn 'Ulayya related from Ibn Jurayj that he (Ibn Jurayj) asked al-Zuhrī about it, but he did not know of it. They added: "The evidence confirming this is that al-Zuhrī did not make the stipulation of *wilāya*, nor is *wilāya* upheld in ᶜĀʾisha's opinion."

They also argued on the basis of the tradition of Ibn ᶜAbbās, who said, "There is no marriage without a guardian and two *ᶜadl* witnesses". The completeness of its chain, however, is disputed. In the same manner, they differed about the tradition concerning the marriage of the Prophet (God's peace and blessings be upon him) to Umm Salama and his ordering her (young) son to give her away himself in marriage.

The argument of the parties based on reason is equivocal, as it is possible to say that when discretion (*rushd*) is found in a woman, it is sufficient for purposes of the marriage contract, for it is deemed to be so in the case of financial transactions. It may be said, however, that a woman is inclined toward

[14] Qurʾān 2 : 240
[15] Qurʾān 2 : 221

men more than she is inclined toward wealth, and it is for this reason that the *sharᶜ* has been cautious in interdicting her permanently in this respect; the shame that may result from her casting herself in a place out of her status will most likely affect the guardians. It is, however, sufficient to say here that the guardians do have a right of revocation and inquiry. The issue is ambivalent, as you can see, but the point which forces itself upon the mind is that if the lawgiver had intended the stipulation of guardianship, he would have elaborated the categories of the guardians, their types, and grades. Delay of the elaboration, beyond the time of its need, would be harmful. If delay in the needed explanation is not permitted to him (God's peace and blessings be upon him), especially when the general public need requires that the stipulation of guardianship be transmitted through a general communal transmission or in a manner close to it—and yet it is not transmitted—it makes it necessary to believe in one of two possibilities: that guardianship is not a condition for the validity of marriage, and that the guardians have only the right of inquiry in it, or that if guardianship is a condition, then, the explanation of qualifications, types, and grades of the guardians is not a condition for its validity, and it is for this reason that the opinion of those who nullify the contract by a remote guardian in the presence of an immediate guardian, is to be deemed as weak.

18.2.2.1.2. Aspect 2: Qualifications and disqualifications for guardianship

With respect to qualifications establishing entitlement, and disqualifications leading to denial of guardianship, they agreed that the conditions for guardianship are Islam, *bulūgh*, and being a male; the disqualifications are the opposite of these, that is, disbelief, minority, and being a female.

They disagreed about three cases: that of the slave, the *fāsiq*, and the prodigal (*safīh*). Most of the jurists inclined toward the prevention of the slave's guardianship, but it was permitted by Abū Ḥanīfa. The well-known opinion in the school about discretion (*rushd*)—that is, according to the majority of the disciples of Mālik—is that it is not one of its conditions, I mean, of guardianship, which was also Abū Ḥanīfa's opinion. Al-Shāfiᶜī said that it is a condition, and an opinion similar to al-Shāfiᶜī's was related from Mālik. Al-Shāfiᶜī's opinion was also adopted by Ashhab and Abū Muṣᶜab.

The reason for disagreement is the similarity of this kind of guardianship with guardianship over wealth. Those who said that discretion is necessitated in this kind of guardianship, despite its absence from that over wealth, held that it is not a condition that he possess discretion in the case of wealth, but those who maintained that this was impossible ruled that discretion is a must for guardianship over wealth. Discretion, in fact, is of two kinds, as you can see, I mean, the discretion related to wealth is different from discretion required by the woman in making a choice about proportionality of status.

They differed about ʿ*adāla* (probity) due to the fact that it is based on rational inquiry, I mean, in this kind of guardianship, and, therefore, (the guardian) cannot be trusted, in the absence of ʿ*adāla*, to select someone who is an equal match for her. It is possible to say that the situation (here) in which guardians make a choice for their wards, of someone with equal status, is different from the general meaning of ʿ*adāla*. Here it is the fear of shame in case they make the wrong choice. This ʿ*adāla* exists naturally, while the other kind of ʿ*adāla* is acquired. The deficient capacity of the slave causes disagreement about his guardianship, as it does in the case of his ʿ*adāla*.

18.2.2.1.3. Aspect 3: Kinds of guardianship

The bases for the kinds of guardianship, according to those who uphold it, are three: descent, authority, and superior and subordinate clientage. According to Mālik, the qualification of Islam by itself is sufficient for guardianship over one of a low social status. They differed about the *waṣī* (executor). Mālik said that the *waṣī* can be a guardian, while al-Shāfiʿī prohibited this. The reason for disagreement is their dispute whether the nature of guardianship is such that it makes deputization possible. It is for the very same reason that they disagreed about agency (*wakāla*) in marriage, but the majority upheld it, the exception being Abū Thawr. There is no difference between agency and executorship, except that an executor is an agent after death, while agency is terminated at death.

They disagreed about the priorities in guardianship on the basis of lineage. According to Mālik, guardianship is allocated among residuaries, excluding the son (in the case of the mother), thus, whoever is the closest from among the residuaries has the right to be a guardian. The sons, according to him, even if in the lowest rank of descendants, have a higher priority. They are followed by the fathers, uncles german, consanguine uncles, sons of the brother german, sons of consanguine brothers, and the grandfathers on the father's side, in that order. Al-Mughīra said that the grandfather and his father have a higher priority than the brother and his son, for he (the brother or his son) is not an outsider, then come the uncles graded like the brothers, however low in rank, followed by the client (*mawlā*) and then by the sultan.

The higher-order client, according to him (Mālik), has a right prior to that of the lower-order client. The executor, according to him, has priority over the guardian through lineage, that is, the executor appointed by the father. His disciples differed about the priority of the father's executor over a guardian through lineage. Ibn al-Qāsim, in conformity with Mālik's opinion, said that the executor has a superior right, while Ibn al-Mājishūn and Ibn ʿAbd al-Ḥakam said that the guardian has a higher priority.

Al-Shāfiʿī went against Mālik in the guardianship of sons (over their mothers), and also in the preference of brothers over the grandfather, not permitting it as a rule, saying that there is no guardianship for the son. It is related from Mālik that the father has priority over the son, which is preferable. He said that the grandfather has priority over the brother, which was also the opinion of al-Mughīra. Al-Shāfiʿī, on the other hand, considered the residuaries—the son not being among her residuaries—due to the tradition of ʿUmar: "A woman is not to be married without the consent of her guardian, or one of her relatives having authority, or of the sultan". Mālik did not take this into account, in the case of the son, because of the tradition of Umm Salama "that the Prophet (God's peace and blessings be upon him) ordered her son to give her away in marriage himself", and also because they, that is, Mālik and al-Shāfiʿī, agreed that the son inherits the obligatory guardianship of his mother (in other matters), and guardianship according to them is for the residuaries.

The reason for disagreement about the grandfather is based on their dispute about who is closer in relationship, the grandfather or the brother.

There are three important issues related to the grades of the guardians. First, if a remote guardian gives her away in marriage in the presence of the immediate guardian. Second, if the immediate guardian is absent, is guardianship then transferred to the remote guardian or to the sultan? Third, if the father deserts his virgin daughter, is guardianship passed on?

18.2.2.1.3.1. Issue 1: Contract of the remote guardian in the presence of the immediate guardian

Mālik's opinion differed on this issue. He said once that if the remote guardian gives her away in marriage, in the presence of an immediate guardian, the marriage is annulled. On another occasion he said that it is valid. A third time he said that it is up to the immediate guardian to ratify it or repudiate it. These different opinions, related from him, apply to cases other than that of the father and his virgin daughter and that of the executor and his interdicted ward, as in these cases his opinion is firm that the contract would be repudiated, that is, in case of marriage through someone other than the virgin daughter's father, or by someone other than the executor in the presence of the executor. Al-Shāfiʿī said that no one has the right to conclude the contract in the presence of the father irrespective of the bride being a virgin girl or a deflowered woman.

The reason for disagreement is the dispute whether gradation (of the guardians) is a *ḥukm sharʿī*, that is, established through the law (*sharʿ*) in the case of *wilāya*. If it is such a *ḥukm*, is it the right of the immediate guardian or is it the right of Allāh? Those who did not consider gradation as a *ḥukm* of law said that marriage contracted by the remote guardian in the presence of the immediate guardian is valid. Those who considered it a *ḥukm* of law based upon the right of the immediate guardian said that the contract is effective to the extent that if it is ratified by the immediate guardian it is permissible, otherwise it is revoked. Those who maintained that it is the right of Allāh said that the marriage is not deemed to have taken place. Some of the jurists within the school (Mālik's) rejected this interpretation, that is, the contract being void and not effective.

18.2.2.1.3.2. Issue 2: Transfer of guardianship in the absence of the immediate guardian

Mālik said that if the immediate guardian is absent, guardianship is transferred to the next guardian. Al-Shāfiʿī said that it is transferred to the sultan. The reason for their disagreement is the dispute whether absence is equivalent to death, as they have no disagreement about its transfer in the case of death.

18.2.2.1.3.3. Issue 3: Father absent leaving behind a virgin daughter

There are detailed discussions and disagreements about it within the school (Mālik's). They refer to the remoteness of his (the father's) location, prolonged or short absence, and knowledge or ignorance about his location, as well as the daughter's need for marriage, which may be due to the lack of maintenance, fear of inadequate protection, or due to both factors combined.

The school agreed that if the father is absent, having gone to a remote place, or his location is unknown, or he is a prisoner of war, but the daughter is protected and provided for, not requiring marriage, she is not to be married (by the next guardian). If she desires to be married, then, she is to be married in the case of imprisonment of her father or when his location is not known. They disagreed whether she is to be married when his location is known but he is in a remote place. It is said that she is to be married, which is Mālik's opinion, and it is said that she is not to be married, which is the opinion of ʿAbd al-Malik and Ibn Wahb.

In case of lack of maintenance or adequate protection, she is to be married in the three stated situations, that is, in the absence of her father, having gone to a remote place, his imprisonment, and in the case of his location being unknown. Similarly, when both factors are combined (i.e. lack of adequate protection and the need for maintenance). If she has inadequate protection, she is to be married even if she does not demand it. They did not disagree, as far as I think, that she is not to be married when her father has departed to a nearby place and his location is known, because he can be approached. When examined on the basis of the interests to be secured (*maṣāliḥ*), it can be said that when time is short, and the sultan fears unbecoming conduct from her, he is to give her away in marriage even if the location (of her father) is close.

If we were to say that the right of the remote guardian subsists even in the presence of the immediate guardian, and the woman delegates her affair to both, with both making separate contracts of marriage for her, the possibility is that one of them preceded the other in concluding the contract or both finalized the contracts at the same time. It is also possible that the first contract comes to be known or it may not be known. If the first contract comes to be known, they agreed that she is (to be declared) the wife of the husband through the first contract. This is the case when none of them has consummated the marriage with her.

They disagreed when the second husband consummates the marriage with her. One group of jurists said that she is the wife of the first, while another group said that she is the wife of the second, which is the opinion of Mālik and Ibn al-Qāsim. The first opinion was upheld by al-Shāfiʿī and Ibn ʿAbd al-Ḥakam. If both guardians concluded the marriages at the same time, there is no disagreement about the rescission of the contracts, as far as I know. The reason for disagreement in the consideration of consummation is based upon the conflict of the general meaning with analogy, as it is related that the Prophet (God's peace and blessings be upon him) said, "If a woman is given away in marriage separately by two guardians, she belongs to the first (husband) among them". The general meaning of this tradition requires that she is the wife of the first husband, irrespective of the second having consummated marriage with her. Those who took consummation into account compared it to the consumption of goods in a contract of a coerced sale, which is weak. If, however, the first contract was not known, the majority rule for rescission, while Mālik said that it is to be rescinded when none of them has consummated the marriage. Shurayḥ said that she is to be given a choice, and whosoever she chooses is to be her husband. This is a deviant opinion, although it has also been related from ʿUmar ibn ʿAbd al-ʿAzīz.

18.2.2.1.4. Aspect 4: Removal of guardians

They agreed that the guardian does not have the right to decline his ward's marriage, if she desires marriage to a man of equal status and with a dower in keeping with such status. If he does this, her case will be referred to the sultan who will give her away in marriage, except when the father is her guardian, about which there is disagreement in the school. After agreeing on this, they differed about the meaning of *kafāʾa* that is to be taken into account, and whether *ṣadāq al-mithl* (dower conforming with status) constitutes a part of it. They agreed that a woman has a right to refuse marriage when a *mujbir* (coercing) guardian is forcing her into it and there is no proportionality of status, as in the case of a father forcing his virgin daughter. This is so, with complete agreement of the jurists, when the girl has not attained puberty, and with some disagreement in the cases of a major and a deflowered minor, as has preceded. Similarly, when the executor is forcing his ward, according to those who hold this opinion.

They agreed that a factor to be considered in *kafāʾa* is religion, except what has been related from Muḥammad ibn al-Ḥasan about the elimination of the attribute of religion (in this issue). The school was in agreement that if a father were to get his virgin daughter married to a drunkard or a *fāsiq*, she has the right to refuse compliance. The judge is to take cognizance of this and to annul the marriage. Similarly, when he gets her married to a person possessing wealth that is *ḥarām*, or one who is known to pronounce divorce very often.

They disagreed about lineage whether it constitutes a part of *kafāʾa*, as they did about liberty, financial ease, and freedom from bodily defects. It is well known of Mālik that he permitted marriage between the Arabs and the clients, for which he argued on the basis of the words of the Exalted, "Lo! the noblest of you, in the sight of Allāh, is the best in conduct".[16] Sufyān al-Thāwrī and Aḥmad said that an Arab woman is not to marry a client. Abū Ḥanīfa and his disciples said that a Quraysh woman can marry only a Quraysh, and an Arab woman an Arab.

The reason for their disagreement is their dispute over the meaning of the saying of the Prophet (God's peace and blessings be upon him), "A woman is married for her piety (religion), her beauty, her wealth, and her noble descent, but take hold of piety and you will be satisfied with what you have". Some of the jurists held that only piety is to be taken into account, because of the words of the Prophet, "But you should marry the pious and you will be satisfied with what you have". Others said that noble descent, here, stands for piety, as does wealth. Nothing, however, can be eliminated from these, except when excluded by consensus (*ijmāʿ*), as has been done by declaring that beauty does not constitute an element of *kafāʾa*. All those who revoke marriage on the basis of defects maintain that freedom from bodily defects is a part of *kafāʾa*, because of which beauty is taken into consideration, to some extent.

The jurists within the school did not disagree that marriage contracted by a father for his virgin daughter may be revoked on the basis of poverty, that is, when the groom is poor and unable to maintain her. Wealth, thus, constitutes a part of *kafāʾa*. Abū Ḥanīfa does not maintain this opinion. There was no disagreement in the school about liberty that it is a part of *kafāʾa*, because of the established *sunna* granting the female slave a right to choose, if she is liberated (to maintain a pre-liberty marriage or otherwise). About *mahr al-mithl*, Mālik and al-Shāfiʿī maintain that it is not a part of *kafāʾa*, and the father has the right to give his daughter away in marriage for an amount less than the *mahr al-mithl*,

[16] Qurʾān 49 : 13

I mean, his virgin daughter. If a deflowered woman possessing discretion agrees to the amount (of dower), the guardians do not have a right of interference. Abū Ḥanīfa said that *mahr al-mithl* is an essential ingredient of *kafāʾa*.

The reason for disagreement, with respect to the father, is their dispute whether he has the right to reduce a part of the dower of his virgin daughter. In the case of the deflowered woman, it is because of their disagreement whether guardianship is revoked for her with respect to the amount of her dower, when she possesses discretion, just as it is revoked for all her financial transactions, or whether guardianship is not revoked (for the amount of dower) since it is still required in marriage, and dower is one of its elements. This opinion would have suited those who stipulate guardianship rather than those who do not, but the matter has been turned around.

A well-known issue is related to the *aḥkām* of guardianship, which is whether it is permitted to the guardian to marry his ward himself? Al-Shāfiʿī prohibited this on the analogy of a judge and a witness, that is, he does not render judgment for himself nor does he testify for himself. Mālik permitted it, and I am not aware of his argument in this, except what is related that the Prophet (God's peace and blessings be upon him) "married Umm Salama when she did not have a guardian", as her son was a minor, and also the established report "that the Prophet (God's peace and blessings be upon him) emancipated Ṣafiyya and deemed her emancipation to be her dower".[17] The principle for al-Shāfiʿī about the marriages of the Prophet (God's peace and blessings be upon him) is that these were specific to him in the absence of generalized evidence, and the Prophet enjoys a number of exemptions, but his opinion differed in the case of the head of the state.

18.2.2.2. *Section 2: Attestation by Witnesses* (Shahāda)

Abū Ḥanīfa, al-Shāfiʿī and Mālik agreed that attestation by witnesses is a condition of marriage. They disagreed whether it was a condition of completion required over an extended period as to the time of consummation or a condition of validity required at the time of contract. They agreed that a secret marriage was not valid. They disagreed about the witnesses who attest the marriage contract, but are instructed to keep it secret, whether it amounts to a secret marriage. Mālik said that it is a secret marriage and is to be rescinded, while Abū Ḥanīfa and al-Shāfiʿī said that it is not secret. The reason for disagreement is whether attestation is a *ḥukm sharʿī* or it serves the purpose of eliminating disputes or denial. Those who held it to be a proscribed *ḥukm*

[17] In these the Prophet may be said to have exercised his authority as the sulṭān; however, the same rule will apply to such an assertion, that is, whether the sulṭān can render judgment for himself.

said that it is a condition of validity, but those who considered it as attestation of the contract said that it is a condition of completion.

The source for this is what has been related from Ibn ʿAbbās: "There is no marriage without two *ʿadl* witnesses and a supervising guardian". None of the Companions opposed this, and many jurists considered this to have constituted *ijmāʿ*, which is a weak claim. This tradition has been related as *marfūʿ* and is recorded by al-Dār Quṭnī, who mentioned that among its transmitters are unknown persons.

The contract can be concluded, according to Abū Ḥanīfa, even through the attestation of *fāsiq*s, as the purpose in his view is only its publicity. Al-Shāfiʿī is of the view that attestation includes both meanings, that is, proclamation and acceptance, therefore, he stipulates *ʿadāla* as a condition. For Mālik, however, it does not comprise proclamation when the witnesses have been instructed to maintain silence. The reason for their disagreement is whether the act attested by the witnesses can be designated as secret.

The source for the legality of proclamation is the saying of the Prophet (God's peace and blessings be upon him), "Proclaim this marriage and beat the drums". It is recorded by Abū Dāwūd. ʿUmar is reported to have said, "This is a secret marriage, and had they gone ahead with it I would have awarded *rajm*".

Abū Thawr and a group of jurists said that attestation by witnesses is not a condition for the validity of a marriage, neither a condition of validity nor that of completion. Ḥasan ibn ʿAlī is reported to have done this. It is related about him that he married without witnesses and then proclaimed his marriage.

18.2.2.3. *Section 3: Dower* (Ṣaḍāq)

The study of dower comprises six points. First, its *ḥukm* and elements. Second, fixing it entirely for the wife. Third, about its division into parts. Fourth, *Tafwīḍ* and its *ḥukm*. Fifth, void dowers and their *ḥukm*. Sixth, disputes among the spouses over dower.

18.2.2.3.1. **Case 1: The *ḥukm* and elements**

In this section there are four issues. First is about its *ḥukm*. Second, about its amount. Third, about its species and description. Fourth, about its deferment.

18.2.2.3.1.1. Issue 1: The *ḥukm*

In the discussion of its *ḥukm*, they agreed that it is one of the conditions of validity (of marriage), and an agreement to forgo it is not permitted, because of the words of the Exalted, "And give unto the women, (whom ye marry) free gift of their marriage portions",[18] and His words, "[S]o wed them by permission of their folk, and give unto them their portions in kindness".[19]

18.2.2.3.1.2. Issue 2: The amount

They agreed about its amount that it has no maximum limit, but disagreed about its minimum limit. Al-Shāfiʿī, Aḥmad, Isḥāq, Abū Thawr, and the jurists of Medina, among the *Tābiʿūn*, said that there is no minimum limit for it, and anything that can be a price or value for a thing may be the dower. This was the opinion of Ibn Wahb, from among the disciples of Mālik. A group of jurists upheld the obligation of fixing the minimum amount of dower, but they differed about its extent. Two opinions are well known in this. First is Mālik's opinion and that of his disciples, while the second is that of Abū Ḥanīfa and his disciples. Mālik said that the minimum dower is one-fourth *dīnār* of gold, or three measured *dirhams* of silver, or what is equivalent to three *dirhams*, that is, *dirhams* of measure only, according to the well-known opinion; while it is said that whatever is equivalent to any of them (the amounts in gold or silver). Abū Ḥanīfa said that ten *dirhams* is the minimum; it is said five *dirhams*, and it is said forty *dirhams*.

There are two reasons for disagreement over the amount. First is its vacillation between being a compensation—like other counter-values, in which mutual consent is taken into account for small or large amounts, as is the case in sales—and an act of worship, in which it has to have a fixed time. This is so, as from the point of view that he (the husband) comes to own her benefits perpetually, it (dower) resembles compensation, but from the other aspect of the prohibition of consenting to forgo it by mutual agreement it resembles (an act of) worship.

The second reason is the conflict of this analogy, requiring fixation, with the meaning of the tradition, which does not imply fixation. The analogy requiring fixation is, as we have said, an act of worship, and worship is of a determined duration. The tradition implying non-fixation is one tradition related by Sahl ibn Saʿd al-Sāʿidī, which is agreed upon (by al-Bukhārī and Muslim) for its soundness, and in which it is said "that a woman came up to the Messenger of Allāh (God's peace and blessings be upon him) and said to him, 'O Messenger of Allāh, I have bestowed myself to you as a gift.' She, then, waited there (for an answer) for a long time. A man got up (in the meantime) and said, 'O Messenger of Allāh, marry her to me, if you do not have a need for her.' The Messenger of Allāh (God's peace and blessings be upon him) said (to him), 'Do you have something that you can grant her as dower?' He replied, 'I have

[18] Qurʾān 4 : 4
[19] Qurʾān 4 : 25

nothing but this garment (which covers me).' The Messenger of Allāh (God's peace and blessings be upon him) said, 'If you give her that you will be sitting with nothing to cover you. Search for something.' He said, 'I cannot find anything.' He (God's peace and blessings be upon him) said, 'Find it, even if it be a ring made of iron.' The man searched, but could not find a thing. The Messenger of Allāh (God's peace and blessings be upon him) said, 'Do you possess (memorize) anything from the Qurʾān.' The man said, 'Yes, such and such *sūra* (which he named).' The Messenger of Allāh said, 'I hereby marry you to her with what you have of the Qurʾān'. "

They said that the words of the Prophet, 'Find it, even if it be a ring made of iron', are an evidence that there is no minimum limit for it, and had there been such a limit, he would have mentioned it, as a delay in explanation is not permissible from the time of its need. This evidence is manifest, as you can see, along with the fact that the analogy upheld by those who maintain fixation does not have sound premisses. This is so, as it is constructed upon two premisses. First, that dower is an act of worship. Second, that worship must have a fixed time. In each the contender has an objection, which is that there have been laid down in the *sharʿ* kinds of worship that have no fixed duration, but what is required is the least that can come under the term *ʿibāda*. Moreover, it (dower) does not have any pure (real) resemblance with (acts of) worship.

Those who preferred this analogy maintained that the tradition may have been specific to the man in the case, because of the words of the Prophet, 'I hereby marry her to you with what you have of the Qurʾān'. This is against the principles (of interpretation). Though in some versions of this tradition he told him to 'get up and teach her', what he possessed of the Qurʾān, after which the man got up and taught her. It, thus, turned into a marriage on the basis of wages. Yet, when they (these jurists) sought to find a basis for the measure of the dower, they did not find a resemblance better than the minimum scale for amputation due to theft, on the basis of which they could construct their flimsy analogy for fixation of the amount of dower.

The analogy they employed is that it (the female organ here) is a limb that becomes permissible in return for wealth, therefore, it is necessary that it be determined on the basis of amputation (like theft). The weakness of their analogy is evident from the wrong assumption of the existence of a *mushtarak* term, but amputation is different from intercourse; further, amputation has been allowed, even required, as a punishment, involving infliction of pain, and loss of a limb, while that permission is for pleasure with affection. Furthermore, *qiyās al-shabah*, despite its weakness, is that the factors of resemblance on the basis of which the *aṣl* (original case) and the *farʿ* (case in issue) are being compared are the same not through denotation but in meaning, and the *ḥukm* is based in the original case on resembling features, but all this is missing from this analogy. Further, it is a resemblance that is not even indicated through a common term (denotation). It is a type of analogy that is rejected by recognized jurists. These jurists, however, did not employ this analogy for the fixation of dower, in the face of the implication of the tradition that they used to determine what the amount of the fixation would be. The analogy that they employed in opposition to the tradition is stronger than this analogy.

Non-fixation is evidenced by the tradition recorded by al-Tirmidhī "that a woman was married for a pair of sandals. The Messenger of Allāh (God's peace and blessings be upon him) said to her, 'Are you content, in return for yourself and your wealth, on a pair of sandals?' She said, 'Yes.' He, therefore, declared her marriage permissible." Al-Tirmidhī says that it is a sound and *ḥasan* tradition.

After agreeing about the fixation of dower, on the basis of analogy on the minimum scale for theft, those who upheld it, disagreed in accordance with their disputes over the amounts of the minimum scale in the case of theft. Mālik said that it is one-fourth of a *dīnār* or three *dirhams*, as that is the scale for theft, according to him. Abū Ḥanīfa said that it is ten *dirhams*, as that is the scale according to him. Ibn Shubrama said that it is five *dirhams*, for that is the minimum scale (for theft) in his view.

The Ḥanafites argued, for the fixation of dower at this amount, on the basis of the tradition related by them from Jābir from the Prophet (God's peace and blessings be upon him) that he said, "There is no dower less than ten *dirhams*". Had this been established, it would have eliminated the point of contention, for it would become necessary to construe the tradition of Sahl ibn Saᶜd as limited to its specific content (to its case), but this tradition of Jābir is weak, according to the traditionists. They relate it from Mubashshir ibn ᶜUbayd from al-Ḥajjāj ibn Arṭāᶜa from ᶜAṭāʾ from Jābir, but Mubashshir and al-Ḥajjāj are considered weak narrators, while ᶜAṭāʾ had not met Jābir. It is, therefore, not proper to oppose the tradition of Sahl ibn Saᶜd with this tradition.

18.2.2.3.1.3. Issue 3: The species

With respect to its species, it is anything that may be lawfully owned and can be a compensation. About this they disagreed on two occasions: marriage through hire and consideration of manumission of a slave-woman as her dower. About marriage through hire, there are three views in the school: an opinion permitting it, an opinion prohibiting it, and an opinion considering it abhorrent. The best-known opinion from Mālik is (about) its abhorrence. It is for this reason that he considers it revoked prior to consummation (seclusion).

It was permitted, among his disciples, by Aṣbagh and Saḥnūn, which was also al-Shāfiʿī's opinion. It was prohibited by Ibn al-Qāsim and Abū Ḥanīfa, except in the case of a slave, which was permitted by Abū Ḥanīfa.

The reasons for their disagreement are two. First is their dispute over the question whether the *sharʿ* of those before us is binding upon us, till evidence indicates their remission, or whether the matter is the other way round. Those who said that the earlier laws are binding permitted it (marriage through hire) due to the words of the Exalted, "He said: Lo! I fain would marry thee to one of these two daughters of mine on the condition that thou hirest thyself to me for (the term of) eight pilgrimages".[20] Those who said that they are not binding upon us maintained that marriage through hire is not permitted. The second reason is whether an analogy for marriage can be constructed upon hire. This is so, as *ijāra* has been exempted from the rule prohibiting uncertain sales involving *gharar* (and analogy cannot be based upon an exemption). It is for this reason that al-Aṣamm and Ibn ʿUlayya have opposed it, for the principle of mutual exchange requires a determined tangible thing in lieu of another tangible thing, while *ijāra* involves a tangible thing facing which are movements or actions that are not definable or stable or measured. The *fuqahāʾ* have, therefore, differed about (the time) when the wages of *ijāra* are due from the hirer.

The *fuqahāʾ* of the provinces, except for Dāwūd and Aḥmad, have prohibited that manumission be considered as dower. The reason for disagreement is the clash of a tradition, laid down on this issue, with the general principles, that is, the tradition established from the Prophet (God's peace and blessings be upon him) "that he manumitted Ṣafiyya and deemed her emancipation to be her dower", which bears the likelihood of being specific to his case, because of there being many specific rulings for him in this part of the law. The reason for its divergence from the principles is that manumission is the alienation of ownership, and alienation does not include the permissibility of the thing from another case: when she is emancipated she comes to own herself. How, then, can marriage be binding upon her? It is for this reason that al-Shāfiʿī said that if she is repelled by her marriage to him, she owes him her price; as he was of the view that she has caused him to lose her value, since he has destroyed her (value) by stipulating the condition of utilizing her. All this, however, cannot be attributed to the act of the Prophet (God's peace and blessings be upon him), for had it not been permitted to others besides him he would have explained it. The principle is that his acts are binding upon us, except when there arises evidence indicating their being specific to him.

[20] Qurʾān 28 : 27

For the specification of dower, they agreed about the conclusion of marriage for a determined and specified counter-value, that is, determined as to species and amount by description. They disagreed about dower that is unspecified and undetermined, like one saying, "I have married you for a slave or a servant," without a specification that determines his price or value. Mālik and Abū Ḥanīfa said that this is permitted, while al-Shāfiʿī said that it is not. When a marriage takes place in this way, then, according to Mālik, she is entitled to an average value of what has been named, while Abū Ḥanīfa said that he is forced to pay the value (whatever it is). The reason for their disagreement is whether marriage, in this case, resembles sale with the intent of being based on bargaining, or that it does not acquire this state, and the intent is for something else, that is, affection. Those who considered it to be based upon frugality with similarity to a sale said that just as a sale is not permitted for an unspecified thing, similarly, marriage is not permitted. Those who held that it does not resemble it, as the intention is to be noble, said that it is permitted.

A group of jurists did not permit deferment (of the dower) at all, while some did recommending that he advance part of it, at or before consummation, which is Mālik's opinion. Some of the jurists who permitted deferment did so for a limited period and for an amount in proportion to it, which is also Mālik's opinion. Among them were those who permitted deferring it till separation by death or divorce when it becomes due, which is *al-Awzāʿī*'s opinion. The reason for the disagreement is whether marriage resembles sale in deferment. Those who said that it does, did not permit deferment till death or divorce, but those who said that it does not resemble it permitted such deferment. Those who disallowed deferment considered marriage as an act of worship.

18.2.2.3.2. **Case 2: Entitlement to dower**

The jurists agreed that the entire *ṣadāq* becomes due by consummation or death. The basis for its becoming due in the entire amount, following consummation, are the words of the Exalted, "And if ye wish to exchange one wife for another and ye have given unto one of them a sum of money (however great), take nothing from it".[21] I cannot recall transmitted evidence, at the moment, about its obligation upon death (before consummation), except the occurrence of *ijmāʿ* over it.

They disagreed whether consummation for this purpose implies copulation or it merely means being in seclusion[22] with her, which they call drawing of

[21] Qurʾān 4 : 20

[22] The term "seclusion" is being used here to describe a situation after marriage (*nikāḥ*) in which the

the curtains. Mālik, al-Shāfiʿī and Dāwūd said that only one-half dower becomes due with mere seclusion, unless there is intercourse. Abū Ḥanīfa said that (full) dower becomes due with seclusion itself, unless he was in a state of *iḥrām*, ill, fasting in Ramaḍān, or she was menstruating. Ibn Abī Laylā said that full dower becomes due with seclusion, and added no other stipulation.

The reason for their disagreement is the clash of the verdicts of the Companions in this case with the apparent meaning of the Book. This is so as Allāh, the Exalted and Glorious, has laid down a proscription in the case of a woman whose marriage stands consummated that it is not permitted to take back anything from her dower, as in the words of the Exalted, "How can ye take it (back) after one of you hath gone into the other, and they have taken a strong pledge from you".[23] And He stated in the case of a woman divorced before consummation that she has one-half of the dower, thus, the Exalted says, "If ye divorce them before ye have touched them and ye have appointed unto them a portion, then (pay the) half of that which ye appointed".[24] These are explicit, as you can see, in each of the two situations, that is, before touching and after it, and there is no state in between the two. Thus the apparent obligation created by this is that (full) dower does not become due without touching, and touching here, as is obvious from it, is intercourse. It may be construed, however, that "touching" is used here in its normal denotation, not as a polite hint for intercourse, and, perhaps, this is how the Companions interpreted it. It is for this reason that Mālik has said that an impotent person is obliged to pay her the delayed dower, if he divorces her after spending a long period with her; he, thus, fixed it for him without intercourse having any effect upon the obligation of dower. The ruling recorded from the Companions about this is that whoever closes the door behind him or lets down the curtain is obliged to pay dower and no one opposed them in what they decided.

In this topic, those who stipulated touching differed about a case in which the occurrence of touching is disputed. This occurs, for example, when she claims "touching" and he denies it. The well-known opinion of Mālik is that the acceptable statement is hers. It is, however, said that if it was seclusion with

married couple has the opportunity for sexual intercourse, but it may not actually take place. The term "consummation" is being used to denote actual sexual intercourse. The distinction is important for understanding the opinions of the jurists, some of whom maintain that mere seclusion, without sexual intercourse, gives rise to the entitlement to dower, while others say that sexual intercourse must have taken place for such entitlement. "Seclusion" occurs after the wedding ceremony; however, wedding may not necessarily lead to sexual intercourse or even to "seclusion." The use of the term "wedding" is likely to lead to confusion. It is, therefore, being avoided.

[23] Qurʾān 4 : 21

[24] Qurʾān 2 : 237

residence (after marriage), she is to be considered truthful, but if it was merely a visit she is not. It is also said that if she was a virgin, she is to be examined by women. In this case, therefore, three opinions are arrived at in the school. Al-Shāfiʿī and the Ẓāhirites said that it is his statement that is acceptable, for he is the defendant. Mālik, on the other hand, does not give weight to the obligation of oath being upon the defendant in so far as he is the defendant, but to the stronger *prima facie* case. It is for this reason that he prefers the statement of the plaintiff on many occasions when he has a stronger *prima facie* case. This refers to whether the obligation of oath being on the defendant has an underlying reason; similarly, the discussion about the obligation of testimony upon the plaintiff, which will be coming up under its own heading.

18.2.2.3.3. **Case 3: Division of dower**

They agreed generally, when a man divorced (his wife) prior to consummation, and he had fixed a dower, that she has recourse to him for one-half dower, because of the words of the Exalted "If ye divorce them before ye have touched them and ye have appointed unto them a portion, then (pay the) half of that which ye appointed".[25] The study of division of dower relates to three principles: its basis in marriages; the underlying cause of division in different kinds of divorce, that is, those occurring prior to seclusion; and the changes occurring in it before divorce.

Its basis in marriages, according to Mālik, is the validity of a marriage, that is, divorce should have taken place prior to seclusion in a valid marriage. There are two opinions about an irregular marriage, if separation in it does not amount to rescission, and when the husband divorces before rescission. The cause of division is divorce that is pronounced voluntarily by the husband, not on her volition, like the divorce that takes place before she discovers a defect found in him. In this topic they disagreed about the division having as a cause her pressing demand for dower or for maintenance, when he is in difficult straits; there being no difference between residence when he has a defect and between this and the case of her displeasure because of his defect.

There is no disagreement about rescission, that does not amount to divorce, that it does not give rise to sharing of the dower, when the rescission is based upon (a defective) contract or upon (the species of) dower, and generally upon the absence of the requisites of validity, in which she does not have a choice at all. In rescissions that are the result of external contingencies affecting a valid contract, like apostasy or fosterage, if none of them has a choice in it, or she has it but not he, division is not binding; if, however, he has a choice in it, as

[25] Qurʾān 2 : 237

in apostasy, division becomes obligatory. The ruling to which the opinions of the Ẓāhirites lead is that division is obligatory in each divorce occurring before residence is taken up, whether its cause is attributed to him or to her, but in a rescission, not amounting to a divorce, there is no division.

The reason for disagreement is whether it is a practice (*sunna*) that has an underlying rational cause. Those who said that it has a comprehensible meaning, which is that one-half dower becomes due to her, in compensation for her lost right through the return of her commodity and being forced to return the price—as is done by a purchaser; however, marriage differs from sale in this respect and compensation is awarded to her for this (offended) right—(they) upheld that if the cause of divorce arises from her, nothing should be given to her, for she has eliminated any coercion that would have been caused to her by him for returning the price and taking back the commodity. Those who maintained that it is a *sunna* not based on a rational reason, and followed the apparent meaning, said that division (into one-half) is binding in each divorce, whether caused by him or by her.

The changes made in the dower, before divorce, may be either from her or from Allāh. Those that are from Allāh may take one or more of four forms: loss of the whole, reduction, increase, or reduction and increase combined. Those emanating from her may be in the form of disposal by her through consumption as sale, manumission, or donation, or in the form of a disposal for her own benefit or for the preparation of a dowry with it for her groom. According to Mālik, both of them share in the case of loss, or increase or reduction. According to al-Shāfiʿī he has recourse to her for half in the case of reduction and loss but he does not claim half from her in the case of increase. The reason for their disagreement is whether the woman comes to own the dower firmly prior to seclusion or death (of her husband). Those who said that she does not own it through an indisputable ownership maintain that she is a co-owner in it, as long as she does not transgress, and shares in the benefits with him. Those who said that she owns it through an indisputable ownership, and that division is an obligatory right, force her to return all that has been lost in her possession. Further, after the establishment of ownership they have recourse to her for all that passed on to her.

They did not disagree that if she disposes of the revenue, she is liable for one-half, but they disagreed if she purchases with it things necessary for the dowry, as is customary, whether recourse to her is for one-half of what she purchased or for one-half dower, which is the price. Mālik said that he has recourse to her for one-half of what she purchased, while Abū Ḥanīfa and al-Shāfiʿī said that he has recourse to her for one-half of the price, which is the dower.

Under this topic they differed about a well-known case that relates to transmitted (texts), whether the father has the right to forgo one-half dower of his virgin daughter, or the master of his female slave, that is, if she is divorced prior to seclusion? Mālik said that he has the right, while Abū Ḥanīfa and al-Shāfiʿī said that he does not. The reason for their disagreement is the equivocality in the words of the Exalted, "Unless they (the women) agree to forgo it, or he agreeth to forgo it in whose hand is the marriage tie".[26] The word "forgo" (*yaʿfū*), it is said, may mean, in the usage of the Arabs, "to forgo" or "to gift." Also, the pronoun in the words of the Exalted, "in whose hands is the marriage tie", may refer to the guardian or the bridegroom. Those who maintained that it is the bridegroom, deemed the meaning to be "gift", while those who said that it is the guardian, considered it to mean "forgo". Some of the jurists adopted a deviant view saying that each guardian has the right to forgo one-half of the dower that is obligatory for the woman. It appears that both constructions of the meaning of the verse are equal. However, those who considered the subject to be the bridegroom did not assign an additional *ḥukm* to the verse, that is, an additional law, for its permissibility is known through the logical necessity of the law. Those who rendered it as the guardian, either the father or someone else, assigned an additional law. It is necessary for them to come up with evidence indicating that the verse applies primarily to the guardian rather than the bridegroom, which is a difficult feat.

The majority maintain that a minor and an interdicted girl do not have the right to forgo one-half of the dower to which they are entitled. Some jurists maintained a deviant opinion saying that it is permitted pursuing the general meaning of the words of the Exalted, "Unless they (the women) agree to forgo it".[27] In this topic they differed when a woman gifts her dower to her husband and is then divorced prior to seclusion. Mālik said that he cannot have recourse to her for any part of it, while al-Shāfiʿī said that he can claim one-half from her. The reason for their disagreement is whether the half to which the husband is entitled through divorce is linked to the actual dower itself or it can be a liability for the woman? Those who said that it is linked to the actual dower, maintained that he cannot have recourse to her for any part of it, for he had taken possession of the entire dower. Those who said that it has become the woman's liability maintained that he has recourse to her if she had gifted it to him, as if she had made a gift to him of some other wealth of hers. Abū Ḥanīfa made a distinction in this issue on the basis of taking possession and not taking possession: if she had taken possession of it, he has recourse for one-half, but if she had not taken possession when she made the gift, he cannot have anything. It was as if he maintained that the right is associated

[26] Qurʾān 2 : 237
[27] Qurʾān 2 : 237

with the thing as long as possession has not been taken, thus, when she takes possession, it becomes a liability.

18.2.2.3.4. **Case 4: *Tafwīḍ***

They agreed that marriage (contracted) through *tafwīḍ* is permitted, which is the conclusion of the contract of marriage without *ṣadāq* (dower), because of the words of the Exalted, "It is no sin for you if ye divorce women while yet ye have not touched them, nor appointed to them a portion".[28] The jurists disagreed about this on two points. First, when the wife demands the fixation of dower, with no agreement about the amount. Second, when the husband dies without fixing it. Does she get the dower in either case?

18.2.2.3.4.1. Issue 1: When the woman demands fixation of dower

A group of jurists said that an amount equivalent to her status is to be awarded to her, and the husband has no option in this. If he divorces her after the verdict, some of these jurists said that she is entitled to one-half dower, while some of them said that she is not entitled to anything, as fixation did not take place in the contract itself, which is the opinion of Abū Ḥanīfa and his disciples. Mālik and his disciples said that the husband has three choices: he may divorce her without fixation, he may fix the amount demanded by the woman, or he may fix *ṣadāq al-mithl*, which becomes binding upon her.

The reason for their disagreement—that is, among those who determine *mahr al-mithl* for her without granting an option to the husband when he divorces her after her demand for fixation and those who do not determine such dower—is over the meaning of the words of the Exalted, "It is no sin for you if ye divorce women while yet ye have not touched them, nor appointed unto them a portion",[29] whether they are to be construed generally as conveying the dropping of *ṣadāq*, irrespective of the cause of divorce arising from their dispute over *ṣadāq*. Further, whether the absolution from responsibility (from sin) is to be construed as the dropping of dower under all circumstances. This is subject to interpretation, though the obvious meaning implies dropping it under all circumstances due to the words of the Exalted, "Provide for them, the rich according to his means, and the straitened according to his means, a fair provision".[30] There is no dispute, as far as I know, that if he divorces her, right in the beginning (without the discussion of dower), there is no liability upon him. It was logical for the person, who fixed

[28] Qurʾān 2 : 236
[29] Qurʾān 2 : 236
[30] Qurʾān 2 : 236

mutᶜa for her along with half of *mahr* in case he divorces her before seclusion after a marriage not based upon *tafwīḍ*, and fixed *mahr al-mithl* for her in *tafwīḍ*, to fix, along with *mutᶜa*, a part of *mahr al-mithl*, as (the meaning of) the verse does not indicate the dropping of dower in a *tafwīḍ* marriage, it only permits divorce prior to the fixation of dower. If the *tafwīḍ* marriage gives rise to the liability of *mahr al-mithl*, when demanded, it is necessary that it be paid in part if divorce is pronounced, just as it is rendered in part when fixed. It is for this reason that Mālik held that *mahr al-mithl* does not become binding along with the option granted to the husband.

18.2.2.3.4.2. Issue 2: When the husband dies before fixing *ṣadāq* and prior to consummation of marriage

Mālik, his disciples, and al-Awzāᶜī said that she is not entitled to *ṣadāq*, but only to *mutᶜa* and to inheritance. Abū Ḥanīfa said that she is entitled to *ṣadāq al-mithl* and to inheritance, which was also the opinion of Aḥmad and Dāwūd. Both opinions are related from al-Shāfiᶜī, except the opinion supported by his disciples is the one similar to Mālik's.

The reason for their disagreement is the conflict of *qiyās* with a tradition. The tradition is related from Ibn Masᶜūd who, upon being asked about this issue, said: " 'I base the verdict on my own opinion, if it happens to be correct it is from Allāh, but if incorrect it is from me. I hold for her *ṣadāq* equivalent to that paid to women of her status, neither less nor more, and she has to undergo the waiting period and is entitled to inheritance.' Maᶜqal ibn Yasār al-Ashjaᶜī, then, got up and said: 'I bear witness that you have decided in accordance with the judgment of the Messenger of Allāh (God's peace and blessings be upon him) in the case of Barwaᶜ bint Wāshiq.' " It is recorded by Abū Dāwūd, al-Nasāᶜī, and al-Tirmidhī, who declared it to be *ṣaḥīḥ*. The analogy opposing this is that *ṣadāq* is a compensation, and as he has not taken delivery of the counter-value he should not be liable to compensation, on the analogy of sale. Al-Muzanī has related from al-Shāfiᶜī on this issue that if the tradition of Barwaᶜ is proved authentic, there is no force in any one's opinion with the existence of a *sunna*. (Ibn Rushd:) What he has said is correct, Allāh knows best.

18.2.2.3.5. **Case 5: *Fāsid* dowers**

Dower is void either in itself or because of an attribute traceable to *gharar* or to an impediment. The dower that is void in itself may be in the form of wine *(khamr)*, swine *(khinzīr)*, or a thing that cannot be lawfully owned. The dower that is void because of *gharar* or an impediment derives its principles from sales. There are five well-known issues in this.

18.2.2.3.5.1. Issue 1

If dower consists of *khamr*, *khinzīr*, fruit that has not yet begun to ripen, or a stray camel, Abū Ḥanīfa is of the opinion that the contract is valid if it contains a provision for *mahr al-mithl.* From Mālik there are two narrations about it. First, the invalidity of the contract and its rescission before seclusion and after it, which is also Abū ʿUbayd's opinion. Second, that if the marriage is consummated, the contract is effective and she has (the right to) *mahr al-mithl.*

The reason for their disagreement is whether the *ḥukm* of marriage is the same as the *ḥukm* of sale? Those who held that its *ḥukm* is the same as sale said that marriage becomes void with the *fasād* of dower, just as a sale becomes void with the *fasād* of the price. Those who maintained that the validity of dower is not a condition for the validity of marriage, upon the evidence that fixation of dower is not a condition for the validity of the contract, said that marriage is effective and becomes valid with the *mahr al-mithl.* The distinction based upon the occurrence of seclusion and its absence is weak. Mālik's principles lead to the fact that a distinction be made between dower that is prohibited in itself and that which is prohibited due to an (external) attribute, upon the analogy of sale. I do not remember, at this moment, a recorded statement about it.

18.2.2.3.5.2. Issue 2

They disagreed when a sale is associated with dower, like her giving him a slave in return for a thousand dirhams that he gives her for dower along with the price of the slave and does not distinguish the price from the dower. Mālik and Ibn al-Qāsim prohibited such mixing, and it was also the opinion of Abū Thawr. Ashhab permitted it, which was also Abū Ḥanīfa's opinion. ʿAbd Allāh made a distinction in this saying that if one-fourth *dīnār* or more clearly remains after accounting for the sale, it is permitted. Al-Shāfiʿī's opinion differed in this, for he said once that it is permitted, while he said on another occasion that there is *mahr al-mithl* in it.

The reason for their disagreement is whether marriage has a resemblance with sale for this purpose. Those who held it similar to sale disallowed it, while those who permitted a degree of uncertainty in marriage, of a kind that is not permitted in sale, said that it is allowed.

18.2.2.3.5.3. Issue 3

They differed, into three opinions, about the person who gives a woman away in marriage stipulating for the husband a dower in the shape of a gift that is presented to the (girl's) father. Abū Ḥanīfa and his disciples said that the condition is binding and the marriage is valid. Al-Shāfiʿī said that the dower is void and she is entitled to *ṣadāq al-mithl.* Mālik said that if the condition is stipulated at the time of the contract it (the gift) is for his daughter, but if it is stipulated after the contract it is for him.

The reason for their disagreement is the similarity of marriage to sale. Those who compared him (the father) to an agent contracting a sale, while a gift is stipulated for him said that *nikāḥ* is not permitted, just like the sale is not allowed. Those who considered *nikāḥ* to be different from sale said that it is permitted. In the distinction drawn by Mālik, he held him to be subject to blame when the condition is included in the contract of marriage, for what he has stipulated for himself amounts to a reduction in the value of the dower, but he does not subject him to blame when it occurs after the conclusion of the contract with agreement over the dower. Mālik's opinion is the same as that of ᶜUmar ibn ᶜAbd al-ᶜAzīz, al-Thawrī, and Abū ᶜUbayd. Abū Dāwūd, al-Nasāʾī, and ᶜAbd al-Razzāq have recorded from ᶜAmr ibn Shuᶜayb from his father from his grandfather that he said, "The Messenger of Allāh (God's peace and blessings be upon him) said, 'When a woman is married for a gift prior to the conclusion of the contract of marriage, the gift belongs to her, but what takes place after the contract of marriage, it belongs to whom it has been given. The best favour extended to a man is that which is given out of respect for his daughter or his sister.' " ᶜAmr ibn Shuᶜayb's tradition is disputed in so far as he distorted it, but Mālik's opinion is categorically stated. Abū ᶜUmar ibn ʾAbd al-Barr said that when a tradition is reported by trustworthy persons it is to be acted upon.

18.2.2.3.5.4. Issue 4

They disagreed about dower that involves the right of a third party or is found to be defective. The majority said that the marriage is confirmed. They disagreed, however, whether she has recourse to him for its value, a substitute, or for *mahr al-mithl*. Al-Shāfiᶜī's opinion differed in this; he held it once to be the value, and at another time as *mahr al-mithl*. Similarly, the school (Mālik's) differed about it. It is said that she has recourse for the value, and it is also said that she has recourse for *mahr al-mithl*. Abū al-Ḥasan al-Lakhmī said that if it is held to be the lesser of the two, the value or *mahr al-mithl*, it would be the correct standpoint. Saḥnūn deviated from this saying that the contract is void. The basis for disagreement is whether the contract of marriage resembles the contract of sale. Those who held it to be similar said that it is rescinded, while those who did not hold it to be similar said that it is not.

18.2.2.3.5.5. Issue 5

They disagreed about the person who marries a woman agreeing that if he (the bridegroom) has no wife the dower is one thousand (units), but if he has a wife already the dower is two thousand. The majority upheld its validity. They disagreed about the obligation arising in this. One group of jurists said that the condition is valid and she is entitled to dower in accordance with the condition. Another group of jurists said that she is entitled to *mahr al-mithl*, which is the opinion of al-Shāfiʿī and was also upheld by Abū Thawr, but he said that if he divorces her before seclusion she is only entitled to mutʿa. Abū Ḥanīfa said that if he has a wife already she (the new wife) is entitled to one thousand (units), but if he does not have a wife she is entitled to *mahr al-mithl* as long as it is not more than two thousand (units) nor less than one thousand. From these an opinion can be derived that the contract is revoked because of *gharar*, but I do not remember at the moment a recorded statement about this verdict in the (writings of the) school.

These are their well-known opinions upon the subject, though the cases under it are many. They disagreed about the attributes on the basis of which *mahr al-mithl* is determined, when it is awarded in such cases. Mālik said that her beauty, status, and wealth are to be taken into account, while al-Shāfiʿī said that it is to be determined in the light of the dower of women, from among her residuaries. Abū Ḥanīfa said that all the women related to her are to be taken into account, whether her residuaries, or others. The basis for the disagreement is whether similarity pertains to status only or to status, wealth, and beauty, because of the words of the Prophet (God's peace and blessings be upon him) "A woman is married for her faith, beauty, and descent".

18.2.2.3.6. **Case 6: Disagreement among spouses over dower**

Their disagreement may either be about possession, amount, category, or time, that is, the time of obligation. If they differ about the amount, with the woman saying, for example, that it was two hundred and the husband saying that it was one hundred, the jurists disagree extensively about this case. Mālik said that if the disagreement arises prior to seclusion and both the bride and the bridegroom make credible claims, then, both are to be asked to take oaths and to revoke the contract. If one of them takes the oath, while the other refuses, the statement of the one taking the oath will be accepted. If both of them refuse, it will be considered as if both had taken the oath. The statement appearing more likely will be accepted. If the dispute arises after seclusion, the acceptable statement will be the husband's, but a group of jurists said that the acceptable statement will be the husband's along with his oath. This was the opinion of Abū Thawr, Ibn Abī Laylā, Ibn Shubrama and a group of jurists. Another group of jurists said that the acceptable statement will be that of the wife to the extent of the *mahr al-mithl,* and that of the husband to the extent of the excess over the *mahr al-mithl.* A third group of jurists makes them take oaths in case of dispute and makes them revert to *mahr al-mithl* without rescinding the contract, unlike Mālik's opinion. This is the opinion of al-Shāfiʿī, al-Thawrī and a group. It is also said that she is made to have recourse to *mahr al-mithl* without taking an oath, as long as the *ṣadāq al-mithl* is not more than what she is claiming or less than what he is asserting.

Their disagreement is based upon their differing understanding of the words of the Prophet (God's peace and blessings be upon him), "(The burden of) testimony is upon the plaintiff, while the one who denies is to take the oath," whether it has an underlying rational reason. Those who maintained that it has an underlying reason said that the one who has a stronger *prima facie* claim is to take the oath, always, but if their claims are equal (in strength) they are both to take the oath and the contract is rescinded. Those who maintained that it does not have an underlying cause said that the husband is to take the oath as the right is claimed by her, and she is claiming an amount in excess of his statement; he is, therefore, the defendant. It is, however, said that they are both to take the oath, always, as each one of them is a defendant, but this is held by those who do not take into account the probabilities. There is disagreement about this in the school. Those who maintained that the acceptable statement is hers to the extent of *mahr al-mithl*, or his when in excess of the *mahr al-mithl*, were of the view that they can never be considered equal contestants in a claim, and one of them has to have a *prima facie* stronger case. This is so as her claim may either be for a sum equivalent to the *ṣadāq al-mithl* or less than it, in which case it is her statement that is accepted, or it may be more than that, in which case the acceptable statement is his.

The reason for the disagreement between Mālik and al-Shāfiʿī, about rescission after oath-taking and reverting to *mahr al-mithl*, is whether *nikāḥ* is similar to sale. The jurists who said that it resembles it ruled for rescission, while those who said that it does not resemble it, as dower is not a condition for the validity of the contract, ruled for *ṣadāq al-mithl* after oath-taking. The claim of jurists, from among the disciples of Mālik, who thought that it is not permitted to them after oath-taking to arrive at an agreement over an amount, or not permitted to one of them to revert to the claim of the other person with consent, is totally weak. Those who held this opinion compared it to (the procedure) of *liʿān*, which is a weak comparison, along with the fact that the similar *ḥukm* in *liʿān* is disputed.

In their disagreement about taking possession, with the bride saying that she did not take possession and the bridegroom saying that she did, the majority of the jurists maintain that the acceptable statement is that of the woman. These jurists are al-Shāfiʿī, al-Thawrī, Aḥmad and Abū Thawr. Mālik said that the acceptable statement is hers before seclusion and his after seclusion. Some of his disciples said that Mālik made this statement as the custom in Medina was that the husband would not go into seclusion with her till he had paid the dower, but if there is a land that does not have this custom it is her statement that will be accepted always. The opinion that it is her statement that should always be accepted is better, for she is the defendant, but Mālik took into account the strength of his claim after he had consummated the marriage with her. Mālik's disciples differed, when a long time had passed after the wedding, as to which is better: to accept his statement with his oath or without it.

When they differed about the species of the dower, for example, he says, "I married you with this slave as dower", while she says, "I married you with this dress as dower", then, the well-known opinion in the school is that they are both to take oaths and mutually to rescind the contract, when the dispute arises before they take up common residence, but if it is after that then the contract is confirmed and she is entitled to *ṣadāq al-mithl*, as long as it is not more than what she claims or less than what is conceded by the husband. Ibn al-Qaṣṣār said that they take oaths prior to seclusion, and the acceptable statement is that of the husband after seclusion. Aṣbagh said that the acceptable statement is the husband's, if it is credible, irrespective of the similarity of their statements. If the husband's statement does not appear credible, but her statement does, then it is her statement that is accepted. If her statement is also not likely to be true they are both to take the oath and she is entitled to *ṣadāq al-mithl*. Al-Shāfiʿī's opinion on this issue is like his opinion when they dispute over its amounts, that is, they take oaths and revert to *mahr al-mithl*. The reason for the opinions of the *fuqahāʾ* about rescission in sales you will come to know in the Book of Sales, God willing.

Their disagreement about the time is to be conceived through the example of the debt that conforms with Mālik's basic principle in a well-known opinion that the acceptable statement about the period of payment is that of the debtor on the analogy of sale, over which there is dispute. It may also be conceived through the question: when is it due, prior to seclusion or after it? Those who compared *nikāḥ* to sales said that it does not become due, except after seclusion on the analogy of sale, as the price does not become due from the buyer except after the possession of the commodity. Those who held that (payment) dower is an act of worship in which making the act lawful is stipulated said that it is due prior to seclusion. It is for this reason that Mālik recommended that the bridegroom should present part of the *ṣadāq* before seclusion.

18.2.3. **Element 3: The Identification of the Subject-Matter of the Contract**

A woman becomes permissible (to a man) in two ways: by marriage, or by *milk yamīn* (concubinage). The legal impediments to this are first divided, generally, into two kinds: perpetual impediments and temporary impediments. The perpetual impediments are divided into those agreed upon and those disputed. Impediments agreed upon are three: descent, relationship by marriage, and fosterage. Those disputed are *zinā* and *liʿān*. Temporary impediments are divided into nine types: (1) impediment of number; (2) impediment of combination; (3) impediment of bondage; (4) impediment of disbelief; (5) impediment of *iḥrām*; (6) impediment of illness; (7) impediment of the waiting period (*ʿidda*), with the accompanying disagreement about its perpetuity; (8) impediment of pronouncing divorce thrice for the person divorcing; and (9) impediment of an existing marriage. Legal impediments, on the whole, are thus fourteen, therefore, in this part there are fourteen[31] sections.

18.2.3.1. *Section 1: The Impediment of Lineage*

They agreed that women prohibited because of descent are the seven categories in the Qurʾān: mothers, daughters, sisters, paternal aunts, maternal aunts, brother's daughters, and sister's daughters. They agreed that "mother" here is the term for each female related to you as a cause of your birth from the mother's side or the father's side. "Daughter" is the term for each female in whose birth you are the cause through a son or a daughter or directly. "Sister" is the name of each female who shares one parent with you or both, that is, a father or a mother or both of them. "Paternal aunt" is the name of each female who is a sister to your father or to any male who is a cause in your birth. "Maternal aunt" is the term for each female who is a sister to your mother or to the female who is a cause in your birth. "Brother's daughter" is a term for each female in whose birth your brother is a cause from her mother's side or her father's side or directly. "Sister's daughter" is the term for each female in whose birth your sister is a cause directly or from her mother's side or father's side.

I do not know of any disagreement about these seven prohibited categories. The source for these prohibitions are the words of the Exalted, "Forbidden unto you are your mothers, and your daughters, and your sisters, and your father's sisters, and your mother's sisters, and your brother's daughters and your sister's daughters, and your foster-mothers, and your foster-sisters, and your mothers-in-law, and your stepdaughters who are under your protection (born) of your women unto whom ye have gone in—but if ye have not gone in unto them, then it is no sin for you (to marry their daughters)—and the wives of your sons who (spring) from your loins. And (it is forbidden unto you) that ye should have two sisters together, except what hath already happened (of

[31] The sections discussed by the author are actually twelve. Two are deferred to later discussions.

that nature) in the past. Lo! Allāh is ever Forgiving, Merciful".[32] They agreed that descent, which prohibits intercourse through marriage, prohibits intercourse through *milk yamīn*.

18.2.3.2. *Section 2: Impediment of relationship through marriage*

Women prohibited through a relationship of marriage are four. First are the wives of fathers. The source for this are the words of the Exalted, "And marry not those women whom your fathers married, except what hath already happened (of that nature) in the past. Lo! it was ever lewdness and abomination, and an evil way".[33] Second are daughters of sons. The source for this are the words of the Exalted, "[A]nd the wives of your sons who (spring) from your loins".[34] Third are mothers of wives. The source for this are the words of the Exalted, "[A]nd your mothers-in-law".[35] Fourth are the daughters of wives. The source for this are the words of the Exalted, "[A]nd your stepdaughters who are under your protection (born) of your women unto whom ye have gone in—but if ye have not gone in unto them, then it is no sin for you (to marry their daughters)".[36]

Out of these four categories, the Muslim jurists agreed upon the prohibition of two by virtue of the contract itself, namely, the prohibition of the wives of fathers and sons, and upon a third category because of consummation, namely, the wife's daughter. They disagreed in the latter case on two points. First, whether it is a condition that she be in the protection of the husband. Second, whether she becomes prohibited by mere fondling of the mother or through intercourse. They disputed about the wife's mother, whether she becomes prohibited through intercourse with the daughter or through the contract (with her) alone. They also disagreed in this subject on a fourth issue, whether *zinā* gives rise to the same prohibition as is imposed through a valid or irregular *nikāḥ*. There are, then, four issues.

18.2.3.2.1. Issue 1

The issue is whether it is a condition that the wife's daughter be in the care of the husband. The majority maintain that this is not a condition for prohibition. Dāwūd said that it is. The reason for disagreement is whether the words of the Exalted, "[W]ho are under your protection", is a description that is effective in

[32] Qurʾān 4 : 23
[33] Qurʾān 4 : 22
[34] Qurʾān 4 : 23
[35] Qurʾān 4 : 23
[36] Qurʾān 4 : 23

the prohibition, or that it is not effective and has been stated to indicate the usual relationship? Those who maintained that it indicates the common relationship and is not a condition in the case of stepdaughters, for there is no difference in this between those who are under protection and those who are not, said that the prohibition is absolute for all stepdaughters. Those who considered it to be a non-rational condition said that they are not prohibited unless they are under his protection.

18.2.3.2.2. Issue 2

Is the (step-)daughter prohibited by mere (physical) contact with the mother or by intercourse? They agreed that she becomes prohibited by intercourse. They disagreed about what is less than intercourse, like fondling or looking at the sexual organs with or without lust, whether it prohibits (the daughter). Mālik, al-Thawrī, Abū Ḥanīfa, al-Awzāʿī and al-Layth ibn Saʿd said that touching the mother with lust prohibits the daughter, which is one of the opinions of al-Shāfiʿī. Dāwūd and al-Muzanī said that only intercourse can prohibit her, which is an opinion of al-Shāfiʿī that is preferred by him. Looking (at the mother with lust) is like touching for Mālik, whatever the limb at which the gaze is focused with lust, but differing opinions have been narrated from him about it. Abū Ḥanīfa restricted his opinion to looking at the sex organs, while al-Thāwrī construed "looking" to be the same as touching without stipulating lust with it. Ibn Abī Laylā opposed them in this, as did al-Shāfiʿī in one of his opinions, and did not assign any consequence to looking, but he did so to touching. The basis for the disagreement is whether the meaning of the stipulation of seclusion in the words of the Exalted, "[U]nto whom ye have gone in", is intercourse, or pleasure through what is less than intercourse? If it is pleasure, then, is looking included in it?

18.2.3.2.3. Issue 3

The majority of the jurists of the provinces said about the (wife's) mother that she is prohibited by virtue of the contract with the daughter, irrespective of the consummation of his marriage with her. A group of the jurists held that the mother does not become prohibited except through a consummated marriage with the daughter, as is the case with the (wife's) daughter, that is, she does not become prohibited except by consummating marriage with the mother. This is related from ʿAlī and Ibn ʿAbbās, may Allāh be pleased with them both, through channels that are weak.

The basis for disagreement is whether the condition (the pronoun) in the words of the Exalted, "[U]nto whom ye have gone in", refers to the last-mentioned category, who are the stepdaughters, or to the stepdaughters and mothers who are mentioned before the stepdaughters in the words of the Exalted, "And your mothers-in-law, and your stepdaughters who are under your protection (born) of your women unto whom ye have gone in".[37] It is possible that the words "unto whom ye have gone in" refer to both mothers and daughters, and it is also possible that they refer to the last mentioned, that is, the daughters. The proof of the majority is what is related by al-Muthanna ibn al-Sabāḥ from ᶜAmr ibn Shuᶜayb from his father from his grandfather that the Prophet (God's peace and blessings be upon him) said, "When a man marries a woman, and has intercourse with her or he does not, her mother cannot be permissible for him".

18.2.3.2.4. Issue 4

They disagreed about unlawful intercourse whether it gives rise to the same prohibition in such cases as that of marriage through a valid contract or one made in *shubha*, that is, one in which the *ḥadd* penalty is waived. Al-Shāfiᶜī said that unlawful intercourse with a woman does not prohibit marriage with her mother or her daughter or her marriage with the offender's father or son. Abū Ḥanīfa, al-Thawrī, and al-Awzāᶜī said that unlawful intercourse prohibits what is prohibited by marriage. From Mālik an opinion similar to al-Shāfiᶜī's is recorded in *al-Muwaṭṭa*ᵓ that it does not prohibit, and Ibn al-Qāsim has related from him an opinion identical to that of Abū Ḥanīfa's that it does. Saḥnūn said that the disciples of Mālik opposed him (Ibn al-Qāsim) in this, and follow what is in *al-Muwaṭṭā*ᵓ. It is related from al-Layth that intercourse through *shubha* does not prohibit such marriages, but it is deviant.

The reason for the disagreement lies in the equivocality in the meaning of the term "*nikāḥ*", that is, in its conveying both legal and literal meanings. Those who assigned the literal meaning to it in the words of the Exalted, "And marry not those women whom your fathers married", said that unlawful intercourse prohibits such marriages, but those who assigned it the legal meaning said that it does not. Those who determined the underlying cause for the *ḥukm* to be the prohibition that operates between a mother and her daughter and between a father and his son said that unlawful intercourse also prohibits (such marriages), but those who derived the underlying cause from descent said that it does not, because of the consensus of the majority that descent is not linked with unlawful intercourse. They agreed about what is related by Ibn al-Mundhir that intercourse in concubinage prohibits what is prohibited by intercourse in a marriage. They disagreed about the effect of physical contact in concubinage, just as they disagreed about it in marriage.

[37] Qurᵓān 4 : 23

18.2.3.3. *Section 3: The Impediment of Fosterage (Suckling; Wet-nursing)*

They agreed that fosterage, as a whole, prohibits what is prohibited because of the impediment of descent, that is, the foster-mother acquires the status of the mother, and becomes prohibited herself for the foster-child along with all those who are prohibited to the son because of the true mother. They disagreed about this in many issues out of which the primary ones are nine. First, the quantity of milk that leads to prohibition. Second, the number of years of fosterage. Third, the state of the foster-child at that time, according to those who stipulate for the prohibitive suckling a particular time. Fourth, is the child's contact with the breasts and swallowing taken into account? Fifth, is mixing of the milk (with something else) taken into consideration? Sixth, is the reaching of the milk into the gullet considered? Seventh, does the owner of the milk, that is, the husband of the foster-mother, acquire the status of a father, the case being called *laban al-faḥl.* Eighth, is the testimony about suckling. Ninth, the qualification of the foster-mother.

18.2.3.3.1. Issue 1

About the prohibiting quantity of milk, a group of jurists upheld the negation of a limitation, which is the opinion of Mālik and his disciples, is related from Ali and Ibn Masᶜūd, and is also the opinion of Ibn ᶜUmar and Ibn ᶜAbbās. According to them any quantity is sufficient for prohibition. It was also the opinion of Abū Ḥanīfa and his disciples, as well as that al-Thawrī, and al-Awzāᶜī. Another group of jurists upheld a limitation upon the quantity of milk that prohibits. These jurists are divided into three groups. One group said one or two sucklings do not prohibit, but three or more do. This was upheld by Abū ᶜUbayd and Abū Thawr. The second group said that five sucklings lead to prohibition, which was al-Shāfiᶜī's opinion. The third group said that ten sucklings are prohibitive.

The reason for their disagreement over this issue is the conflict of the general meaning of the Book with the traditions which imply limitation, and also the conflict of some traditions with the others. The general meaning in the Book is found in the words of the Exalted, "[A]nd your (mothers who have suckled you) foster-mothers, and your foster-sisters, and your mothers-in-law..."[38] This indicates whatever the term fosterage is applied to. The conflicting traditions are essentially two. First is the tradition of ᶜĀʾisha, including the other traditions which convey the same meaning, that the Prophet (God's peace and blessings be upon him) said, "One or two sucks or one or two feedings do not lead to prohibition". It is recorded by Muslim once through ᶜĀʾisha, another time

[38] Qurʾān 4 : 23

through Umm al-Faḍl, and through a third channel, and in it is said, "The Messenger of Allāh (God's peace and blessings be upon him) said, 'One or two sucks do not lead to prohibition.' ". The second tradition is of Sahla about Sālim that the Prophet (God's peace and blessings be upon him) said to her, "Give him five feedings (sucklings)". There is a report from ʿĀʾisha conveying the same meaning, in which she said: "There were ten sucklings relating to what was revealed in the Qurʾān, but were later abrogated by five. The Messenger of Allāh (God's peace and blessings be upon him) died and these are what is read in the Qurʾān (as a commentary)". Those who refer the apparent interpretation of the Qurʾān to these traditions say that one or two sucks lead to prohibition, but those who considered the traditions as an elaboration of the Qurʾān, and reconciled them with the Qurʾān, and interpreted the indirect indication of the text through the words of the Prophet, in the tradition of Sālim, "A suck or two do not lead to prohibition", said that three or more feedings lead to prohibition. This is so as the indirect indication of the text in the words of the Prophet (God's peace and blessings be upon him), "One or two sucks do not lead to prohibition", requires that what is beyond three leads to prohibition, while the indication of the text in his words, "Give him five feedings", means that what is less than this does not lead to prohibition. There is a possibility of preferring either of these indications.

18.2.3.3.2. Issue 2

They agreed that suckling in the first two years (of the age of the child) leads to prohibition, and they differed about the nursing of an older child. Mālik, Abū Ḥanīfa, al-Shāfiʿī, and most of the other jurists said that nursing an older child does not lead to prohibition. Dāwūd and the Ẓāhirites held that it does, which is ʿĀʾisha's opinion. The opinion of the majority is also the opinion of Ibn Masʿūd, Ibn ʿUmar, Abū Hurayra, Ibn ʿAbbās, and all the other wives (besides ʿĀʾisha) of the Prophet (God's peace and blessings be upon him).

The reason for their disagreement is the conflict of the relevant traditions. Two traditions have been related in this. First is the tradition of Sālim that has preceded, while the second is ʿĀʾisha's tradition recorded by al-Bukhārī, where she said, "The Messenger of Allāh (God's peace and blessings be upon him) came into the house and there was a man with me. He felt perturbed and I could see anger upon his face. I said, 'O Messenger of Allāh he is my foster-brother'. He said, 'See who your foster-brothers are, for fosterage relates to hunger'. " Those who prefer this tradition said that the milk, which does not constitute sustenance for the infant, does not lead to prohibition. Further, Sālim's tradition is laid down in a specific issue, and all the other wives of the Prophet (God's peace and blessings be upon him) maintained that it was a case of exemption for Sālim. Those who preferred Sālim's tradition and reasoned about ʿĀʾisha's tradition that she (herself) did not act upon it maintained that nursing an older child does lead to prohibition.

18.2.3.3.3. Issue 3

They disagreed when the infant becomes independent of food (suckling) before a period of two years, has weaned, and then a woman suckles him. Mālik said that this suckling does not prohibit (marriage), while Abū Ḥanīfa and al-Shāfiʿī said that it leads to prohibition. The reason for disagreement is their difference in construing the words of the Prophet (God's peace and blessings be upon him), "Fosterage is related to hunger", which could imply that he intended the years of hunger whatever the state of the infant, and these would be the years of fosterage, but it is also possible that he meant when the child has not weaned, and once he has weaned within two years it no longer remains suckling due to hunger. The disagreement, therefore, refers to the fact whether in fosterage, the cause of which is hunger and the need for milk, the natural physical need of infants for milk is considered, which is a need based on the age of suckling, or the actual need of the infant himself, which is removed with weaning but is present by nature, is to be taken into account.

Those who upheld the effectiveness of suckling in the period of fosterage, irrespective of their stipulation of weaning, differed about this duration. Some held it to be a period of two years only, which is Zufar's opinion, while Mālik resorted to *istiḥsān* for purposes of prohibition and included a short duration beyond two years; in one opinion from him it is a month, and in another it is three months. Abū Ḥanīfa held it to be two years and six months. The reason for their disagreement is based on the presumed conflict between the verse of suckling and ʿĀʾisha's tradition that has preceded. This is so as in the words of the Exalted, "Mothers shall suckle their children for two whole years; (that is) for those who wish to complete the suckling", imply that whatever is beyond these two years is not suckling based upon hunger for milk, while the words of the Prophet (God's peace and blessings be upon him), "Fosterage is related to hunger" imply by their generality that as long as the food of the infant is milk, suckling will lead to prohibition.

18.2.3.3.4. Issue 4

Does the feeding (of extracted milk) by pouring it or administering it lead to prohibition, that is, the passing of milk through the gullet by means other than suckling? Mālik said that feeding of extracted milk without direct suckling, by pouring it or administering it, leads to prohibition. ʿAṭāʾ and Dāwūd said that it does not. The reason for their disagreement is whether the consideration is for the consumption of the milk, howsoever it reaches the mouth, or is it for (consumption in) the usual way? Those who were of the view that it should be fed in the usual way, which is designated by the term 'suckling,' said that other methods of feeding do not lead to prohibition, while those who took into account the reaching of milk into the child's stomach, whatever the channel, said that it does.

18.2.3.3.5. Issue 5

They also disagreed about the question whether it is a condition for prohibiting milk that it should not be mixed with something else. Ibn al-Qāsim said that if the milk is mixed with water or with something else and is then fed to the infant there is no prohibition. This was also the opinion of Abū Ḥanīfa and his disciples. Al-Shāfiʿī, Ibn Ḥabīb, Muṭarrif, and Ibn al-Mājishūn from among the disciples of Mālik said that prohibition is caused by it in case the milk is not mixed and its essence is not lost. The reason for their disagreement is whether the *ḥukm* of prohibition for milk subsists when it is mixed with something else or it does not, as is the case with filth when it is mixed with a permissible pure thing. The principle to be considered is that prohibition is found as long as application of the term "milk" to the mixture remains valid, as is the case of water when something clean is mixed with it.

18.2.3.3.6. Issue 6

Is the passage of milk through the gullet essential (for prohibition)? It appears that this is the cause for disagreement in the cases of snuffing and enema with milk, and the disagreement is apparently based on their doubt as to whether milk passed on through these organs reaches the stomach.

18.2.3.3.7. Issue 7

Does the man who has authority over the milk, that is, the woman's husband, become the foster-father of the child, so that prohibition is applied to them: to this foster-father, and to their ascendants and offspring? This is what they term as *laban al-faḥl*. The jurists disagreed about this. Mālik, Abū Ḥanīfa, al-Shāfiʿī, Aḥmad, al-Awzāʿī and al-Thawrī said that *laban al-faḥl* leads to prohibition. Another group of jurists said that it does not. The former opinion was held by ʿAlī and Ibn ʿAbbās, while the latter was maintained by ʿĀʾisha, Ibn al-Zubayr and Ibn ʿUmar.

The reason for their disagreement is the conflict of the apparent meaning of the Book, that is, the verse of suckling, with the well-known tradition related by ʿĀʾisha. The tradition of ʿĀʾisha is the one in which "she said, ʿAflaḥ, the brother of Abū al-Quʿays, sought permission to enter after the coming down of the *ḥijāb* obligation, so I refused to let him in. I asked the Messenger of Allāh (God's peace and blessings be upon him), who said, 'He is your uncle, so grant him permission'. I said, 'O Messenger of Allāh, it is the woman who suckled me, not the man'. He said, 'He is your uncle and can enter in your presence'."

It is recorded by al-Bukhārī, Muslim and Mālik. Those who maintained that the content of the tradition is an addition over the provision of the Book, that is, the words of the Exalted, "And your foster-mothers, and your foster-sisters", and also upon the words of the Prophet (God's peace and blessings be upon him), "Fosterage prohibits what is prohibited by birth", said that *laban al-faḥl* leads to prohibition. Those who held that the verse of suckling and the words, "Fosterage prohibits what is prohibited by birth", were laid down to strengthen the *ḥukm* of suckling, as delaying the explanation beyond the time of its need is not permitted, said that if the requirements of this tradition are acted upon it becomes necessary to consider it as abrogating the principles, as an addition that alters the *ḥukm* abrogates it. Further, prohibition caused by *laban al-faḥl* was not ʿĀʾisha's opinion, and she is the narrator of the tradition. It becomes difficult to reject the declared principles that seek to strengthen and explain (the *ḥukm*) at the time of need, on the basis of rare traditions, especially those that are for a specific case. It was for this reason that ʿUmar (God be pleased with him) said about the tradition of Faṭima bint Qays: "We cannot relinquish the Book of Allāh for a woman's fables".

18.2.3.3.8. Issue 8

A group of jurists said about the testimony regarding suckling that nothing but the testimony of two women is acceptable in this. Another group said that the testimony of at least four is required, which was the opinion of al-Shāfiʿī and ʿAṭāʾ. A third group of jurists said that the testimony of a single woman is acceptable. Some among those who said that the testimony of at least two women is acceptable stipulated the spread of the news about suckling prior to the acceptance of their testimony. This is the opinion of Mālik and Ibn al-Qāsim. There were others who did not stipulate this, which is the opinion of Muṭarrif and Ibn al-Mājishūn. Among those who allowed the testimony of a single woman are some who did not stipulate spread of her claim prior to testimony, which is Abū Ḥanīfa's opinion, and there are some who did stipulate this, which is one report from Mālik, from whom it is also related that the testimony of less than two women is not acceptable.

The reason for their disagreement, over four and two women, is their dispute about the testimony of women whether two women are equivalent to one man, in cases where the testimony of a man is not acceptable, or that two women are sufficient. This issue will be coming up in the Book of *Shahādāt*, God willing. Their disagreement about the acceptance of the testimony of a single woman arises because of its conflict with the traditions relevant to the issue and with principles that are agreed upon, that is, the testimony of less than two males is not acceptable, and that the position of women in this is either weaker than that of men or is equivalent to it. Further, there is consensus on the point that judgment cannot be rendered upon the testimony of a single woman. The command that is laid down on this issue is found in the tradition of ʿUqba ibn al-Ḥārith, who said, " 'O Messenger of Allāh, I married a girl and a woman turned up saying: I suckled both of you.' The Messenger of Allāh (God's peace and blessings be upon him) said, 'How can this be apparent after what had been said? Turn her away'. " Some of the jurists interpreted this tradition as conveying a recommendation, after reconciling it with the principles, and that is more likely; it is one of the narrations from Mālik.

18.2.3.3.9. Issue 9

They agreed about the condition of the wet-nurse that the milk of any woman, *bāligh* or non-*bāligh*, even beyond the age of menopause, married or single, pregnant or not, leads to prohibition. Some of them gave an absurd opinion imposing prohibition because of male-milk. This is non-existent let alone that there be a legal *ḥukm* for it. If it is found, it is not milk except by the equivocality of the name. Under this subject, they differed about the milk of a corpse. The reason for the disagreement is whether it is included in the general meaning. There is no milk from a corpse, and if found it is only designated as such through the equivocality of the term. It is possible that an issue be hypothetical, thus, it has no existence, except as a conjecture.

18.2.3.4. *Section 4: The Impediment of Unlawful Intercourse (*Zinā*)*

They disagreed about the marriage of a *zāniya*.[39] The majority permitted this, while a group of jurists disallowed it. The reason for their disagreement is their dispute about the meaning of the words of the Exalted, "[A]nd the adulteress none shall marry save an adulterer or an idolater. All this is forbidden unto believers", whether it implies blame or prohibition, and whether the reference in the words, "All this is forbidden unto believers"[40], is to *zinā* or to marriage? The majority decided to construe the verse to mean blame and not prohibition because of what is laid down in the tradition "that a man said to the Prophet (God's peace and blessings be upon him) about his (the man's) wife that she does not turn away the hand of anyone who touches her. The Prophet (God's peace and blessings be upon him) said, 'Divorce her'.

[39] A woman who has indulged in unlawful sexual intercourse, by way of fornication or adultery.

[40] Qurʾān 24 : 3. The use of the term "adulteress" in Pickthall's translation is not correct, in so far as it does not indicate every woman who has committed unlawful sexul intercourse. The term "adulteress" is applicable to a married woman alone, while the word *zāniya* has a wider meaning, and includes married as well as unmarried women. The phrase "unlawful sexual intercourse" has, therefore, been used to convey the meaning of the term *zinā*.

The man replied, 'I love her'. The Prophet said, 'Then hold on to her'. " A group of jurists also said that unlawful intercourse annuls marriage on the basis of this principle, which was the opinion of al-Ḥasan. We shall discuss in the Book of *liʿān* (Imprecation) the marriage of a woman, accused in *liʿān*, to her husband who accused her.

18.2.3.5. *Section 5: The Impediment of Number (of Marriages)*

The Muslim jurists agreed about the permissibility of (a man) marrying four women at the same time. This is for freemen. They disagreed on two points: in the case of slaves and about a number beyond four.

Mālik said about the slave, in his well-known opinion, that it is permitted to him to marry four (wives); this was also the opinion of the Ẓāhirites. Abū Ḥanīfa and al-Shāfiʿī said that it is permitted to him to have two wives only (at one time). The reason for their disagreement is whether bondage is effective in discarding this number, just as it is effective in remitting one-half of the *ḥadd* that is obligatory for the freeman for fornication; similarly, in divorce, according to those who uphold it. This is so as the Muslim jurists agreed about reducing his *ḥadd* to one-half in *zinā*, that is, his *ḥadd* is one-half that of the *ḥadd* of the freeman, but they disagreed about other things.

About marrying more than four, the majority maintain that a fifth wife is not permitted, because of the words of the Exalted, "[M]arry of the women who seem good to you, two or three or four"[41] and also because of a tradition related from the Prophet (God's peace and blessings be upon him) that he said to Ghaylān when he converted to Islam and had ten wives, "Hold on to four and let go the rest". A sect says that nine are permitted. It appears that those who permitted nine held that opinion on the basis of addition of numbers occurring in the preceding verse, that is, addition of the numbers in the words of the Exalted, "two and three and four".

18.2.3.6. *Section 6: The Impediment of Combination*

They agreed that two sisters are not be combined (married together) through marriage contracts, because of the words of the Exalted, "And (it is forbidden unto you) that ye should have two sisters together, except what hath already happened (of that nature) in the past". They disagreed about combining them through the ownership of the right hand. The *fuqahāʾ* (in general) prohibit it, but one group held that it is permissible.

[41] Qurʾān 4 : 3

The reason for their disagreement is the conflict of the general meaning in the words of the Exalted, "[T]hat ye should have two sisters together", with the generality of the exemption at the end of the verse, "[S]ave those (captives) whom your right hands possess".[42] It is likely that this exemption extends backwards to the last-mentioned category, and it is also possible that it extends to all that is included in the verse as to prohibition, except cases over which there is consensus that it does not affect them; in this way *milk al-yamīn* is excluded from the words of the Exalted, "[T]hat ye should have two sisters together". It is likely that the exemption relates to the last-mentioned category whereby the words of the Exalted, "[T]hat ye should have two sisters together", retain their generality, especially when we assign it the underlying cause of sisterhood or another cause found within it. Those who upheld its prohibition in *milk al-yamīn* differed in the case where one of them was (associated) through marriage while the other through *milk al-yamīn*. Mālik and Abū Ḥanīfa prohibited it, but it was permitted by al-Shāfiʿī.

Similarly, they agreed, as far as I know, about the prohibition of combining a woman with her paternal aunt, and a woman with her maternal aunt, as this has been established from the Prophet (God's peace and blessings be upon him) in the *mutawātir* tradition of Abū Hurayra in which the Prophet is reported to have said, "A woman is not to be married together with her paternal aunt nor with her maternal aunt". They agreed that a paternal aunt is every female who is a sister of a male who is the cause of one's birth, either directly or through another male, and that a maternal aunt is each female who is a sister of every female who is the cause of one's birth, either directly or through another female; these are free-women from the mother's side. They disagreed whether it is a case of a particular meaning whose implication is also particular or it is from the category of a particular word whose implication is general. Those who said that it is from the category of a particular word with a general implication, disagreed what kind of generality is intended by it. A group of jurists, and they are the majority of the jurists of the regions, said that it is a particular word with a particular implication, and the prohibition does not extend beyond the case delineated. Another group of jurists said that it is a particular word with a general implication, which includes any two women between whom there is a prohibiting or non-prohibiting relationship. Thus, according to them, it is not permitted to marry together two daughters of paternal uncles or an aunt, nor two daughters of maternal uncles or an aunt, nor a woman and a daughter of her paternal uncle or aunt, nor a woman and the daughter of her maternal aunt.

[42] Qurʾān 4 : 24

One group of jurists said that it is prohibited to marry together any two women between whom there is a prohibiting relationship, that is, when one of them is a man and the other a woman, they could not have been legally permitted to marry. That is, if one of these two women had been a man. There are among them those who stipulate this from both sides, that is, if each one of them is considered a man and the other a woman, in turn, and it turns out that they are not legally permitted to marry.[43] These would be the cases where marrying them together is not permitted. If, however, one side is considered a male and marriage is prohibited, but it is not prohibited when assumed from the other side, then, marrying together is permitted, as in the case of marriage with a man's (former) wife and his daughter from another woman. Here, if we consider the daughter a male, it would not be permitted to her to marry the woman, for she is the wife of her father, but if we consider the woman as a male, she would be permitted to marry the daughter of her husband, for she is the daughter of a stranger. These rules were preferred by the disciples of Mālik. The other jurists disallow simultaneous marriage with a man's wife and his daughter from another woman.

18.2.3.7 *Section 7: The Impediment of Slavery*

They agreed that it is permissible for the slave to marry a female slave, and for a free-woman to marry a male slave, if she agrees to this and so do her guardians. They disagreed about the marriage of a freeman to a female slave. Some jurists said that it is permitted without qualification, which is the well-known opinion of Ibn al-Qāsim. Others said that it is not permitted, except on two conditions: lack of resources (dower of a free-woman), and the fear of falling into evil. This is the well-known opinion of Mālik, and also of Abū Ḥanīfa and al-Shāfiʿī.

The reason for their disagreement is the conflict between the indirect indication of the text in the words of the Exalted, "And whoso is not able to afford to marry chaste (or free), believing women, let them marry from the believing maids whom your right hands possess",[44] and the generality of His words, "And marry such of you as are solitary and the pious of your slaves and maidservants".[45] This is so as the meaning of the indirect indication of the text in the words of the Exalted, "And whoso is not able to afford to marry free, believing women, let them marry from the believing maids whom your right hands possess", requires that marriage with a female slave is not permitted except with two conditions. First, is the absence of means to marry a free-

[43] That is, if one of these two women had been a man.
[44] Qurʾān 24 : 32
[45] Qurʾān 24 : 32

woman, while the second is the fear of falling into sin. The words of the Exalted, "And marry such of you as are solitary and the pious of your slaves and maidservants",[46] require, through their generality, the permissibility of their marriage with a freeman or slave, whether the freeman is a bachelor, and whether he is in fear of falling into sin. Yet, the indirect indication of the command in the text here has greater strength than the generality, Allāh knows best, as in this general implication the qualifications of the prospective husbands for the slave-girls are not stipulated. The aim in this verse is to issue the command for marrying them and to forbid their coercion, which is also construed by the majority to be a recommendation, though the man will cause his offspring from this marriage to go into bondage.

In this topic, they differed about two widely known cases, that is, those who did not permit marriage (with a female slave) except on two prescribed conditions. The first is that if the man is already married to a free-woman, does it amount to a possession of means? Abū Ḥanīfa said that it amounts to a possession of means, while others said that it does not. From Mālik both opinions are related. The second issue is whether the person, in whom both these conditions are found, can marry more than one slave-woman, three, four, or two.

Those who maintained that a man married to a free-woman cannot fear falling into sin, as he is not a bachelor, said that such a man is not permitted to marry a slave-woman (because children from a slave go into bondage). Those who said that the fear of falling into sin can always exist, whether the man is single or married, for the first wife may not be sufficient to protect him from sin, and he is not able to marry another free-woman so as to avoid sin, said that he may marry a slave-woman. His position with respect to this free-woman is the same as his condition prior to marriage with her, especially when he fears falling into sin with the slave-woman whom he wishes to marry. This is exactly the cause in their disagreement over the issue whether he could marry a second female slave on top of the first. Those who limit the fear of falling into sin to a bachelor, for such a fear is greater for bachelors, said that he cannot marry more than one slave-woman. Those who do not impose such a limitation said that he may marry more than one slave-woman; similarly, they say that he may marry her with an existing marriage with a free-woman.

The generalization of the fear of falling into sin without qualification is subject to examination. If we say that a man married to a free-woman follows the opinion that he has the right to marry a slave-woman without the permission of the free-woman, does she have an option to stay with him or to annul the marriage? Mālik's opinion differed on this. They also disagreed

[46] Qurʾān 24 : 32

when he acquires the means to marry a free-woman after marrying the slave-woman, is he to be separated from the slave-woman? They did not disagree, that is, the disciples of Mālik, that when the fear of falling into sin has left him he is not to be separated from the slave-woman. They agreed under this topic that it is not permitted to a woman to marry her own slave; if she comes to own her husband, the marriage is rescinded.

18.2.3.8. *Section 8: The Impediment of Disbelief (*Kufr*)*

They agreed that it is not permitted to a Muslim to marry an idolatress due to the words of the Exalted, "And hold not to the ties of disbelieving women". They disagreed about marrying slave idolatresses. They agreed that he may marry a free *kitābiyya*, except what is related about it from Ibn ʿUmar. They disagreed about marrying a slave *kitābiyya*, but they were in agreement about her permissibility through *milk al-yamīn.*

The reason for their disagreement about marrying enslaved idolatresses is the conflict of the general meaning of the words of the Exalted, "And hold not to the ties of disbelieving women", and of the words of the Exalted, "Wed not idolatresses till they believe",[47] with the words of the Exalted, "And all married women (are forbidden unto you) save those (captives) whom your right hands possess",[48] that is, the female prisoners of war, with the apparent meaning implying generality, without distinction of a *kitābiyya* or idolatress. The majority of the jurists prohibit this, while Ṭāwūs and Mujāḥid upheld its permissibility. Their argument is supported by what is related about the marriages of the prisoners in the battle of Awṭās when they sought the Prophet's permission for *ʿazl* (ejaculating outside) and he permitted them to do so.

The majority upheld the permissibility of marriage with the *kitābiyāt* who are free through a contract, as the principle is to construe (by exemption) the particular from the general. The words of the Exalted, "[A]nd the virtuous women (out) of those who received the Scripture", is particular, while His words, "Wed not idolatresses till they believe",[49] is general; the majority, thus, exempted the particular from the general. Those who inclined toward its prohibition, which is the opinion of some of the *fuqahāʾ*, considered the general meaning to have abrogated the particular.

They disagreed about the permissibility of a slave *kitābiyya* through marriage, because of the conflict of the generality in this case with analogy.

[47] Qurʾān 2 : 221
[48] Qurʾān 4 : 24
[49] Qurʾān 2 : 221

This is so as analogy in her case upon a free-woman requires the permissibility of her marriage, while the remaining general meaning, after the free-woman has been exempted from the prohibition, opposes it, as it necessitates her prohibition, according to the opinion of those who maintained that an exemption made from a general meaning leaves the remaining categories within the generality. Those who restricted the remaining generality with analogy, and those who did not view the restricted general meaning as applicable generally, said that the marriage of a slave *kitābiyya* is permissible. Those who preferred the remaining generality, not restricting it with analogy, said that the marriage of a slave *kitābiyya* is not allowed.

There exists another reason for their disagreement, which is the conflict of the (indirect) indication of the text with analogy. This is so as the words of the Exalted, "let them marry from the believing maids whom your right hands possess",[50] implies through the (indirect) indication of the text that the marriage of a non-believing slave is not permitted, while analogy upon the free-woman implies that it is.[51] They agreed on the permissibility of the *kitābiyya* on the basis of the Qurʾānic words, "except those whom your right hands possess", and also on the basis of their consensus over the fact that enslavement makes the unmarried enslaved woman permissible.

They disagreed about a married woman whether imprisonment (in war) demolishes her marriage, and if it is demolished then at what time? A group said that the marriage of couple imprisoned together is not annulled, but the imprisonment of one prior to the other annuls their marriage. This was Abū Ḥanīfa's opinion. Another group of jurists said that imprisonment annuls the marriage whether they are imprisoned together or one before the other, which was al-Shāfiʿī's opinion. There are two opinions from Mālik. First, that imprisonment does not annul marriage at all. Second, that it annuls it absolutely, as in al-Shāfiʿī's opinion.

The reason for their disagreement about annulment is the vacillation of the captives who have escaped slaying in being considered as the women of the *dhimmīs* having a pact (in which case they could not be treated as concubines) and in considering them as disbelieving women who have no husbands or who have been hired by the disbelievers. In the distinction drawn by Abū Ḥanīfa between couples taken captive together and those taken separately, one before the other, the effective factor according to him in their permissibility is the difference of *dār* (legal jurisdiction) not slavery. The factor effective in

[50] Qurʾān 4 : 25

[51] There are two lines after this, which according to the note given by the editor of the original are found in some manuscripts. The text in these lines appears to be a gloss, which was somehow incorporated into the text at some stage. As these lines have no relevance to the discussion they have been omitted.

permissibility according to others besides him is slavery. What is to be investigated here is whether slavery governs cases of single female captives, or it applies generally to single as well as married captives. It appears that being married in this case should not receive protection, as the effective factor in enslavement is disbelief, which is the cause of permissibility. Her comparison with a *dhimmiyya* is far-fetched, as the *dhimmī* has agreed to pay *jizya* so that he may retain even his religion, let alone his marriage.

18.2.3.9. *Section 9: The Impediment of (the Ritual State of)* Iḥrām

They disagreed about the marriage of the *muḥrim* (person in the ritual state of *iḥrām*). Mālik, al-Shāfiᶜī, al-Layth, al-Awzāᶜī and Aḥmad said that a muḥrim does not marry and cannot be married. If he should go through a marriage contract, the marriage is void. This was the opinion of ᶜUmar ibn al-Khaṭṭāb, ᶜAli, Ibn ᶜUmar and Zayd ibn Thābit. Abū Ḥanīfa said that there is no harm in this.

The reason for their disagreement is the conflict of transmitted traditions on this subject. Among these is the tradition of Ibn ᶜAbbās "that the Messenger of Allāh (God's peace and blessings be upon him) married Maymūna when he was a muḥrim". It is a tradition with an established transmission and is recorded by the compilers of the *Ṣaḥiḥs*. This, however, is opposed by many traditions. First, from Maymūna "that the Messenger of Allāh (God's peace and blessings be upon him) married her when he had relinquished the state of *iḥrām*". Abū ᶜUmar said that it is related from several channels, from Abū Rāfiᶜ, from Sulaymān ibn Yasār who was her client, and from Yazīd ibn al-Asamm. Mālik also related it through the tradition of ᶜUthmān ibn ᶜAffān, who said along with this, that "The Messenger of Allāh (God's peace and blessings be upon him) said, 'A *muḥrim* is neither to marry nor to be married, nor to be proposed to.' " Those who preferred this tradition over the tradition of Ibn ᶜAbbās said that a *muḥrim* is not to marry nor is to be married. Those who preferred the tradition of Ibn ᶜAbbās or reconciled it with the tradition of ᶜUthmān ibn ᶜAffān, by construing the prohibition to indicate disapproval, said that he may marry and may be given away in marriage. This refers to a conflict between practice and word, and the right method is either reconciliation or giving predominance to the word.

18.2.3.10. *Section 10: The Impediment of Illness*

They disagreed about the marriage of the *mariḍ* (sick person). Abū Ḥanīfa and al-Shāfiᶜī said that it is permitted. Mālik in a well-known opinion of his said that it is not permitted. It may be derived from his opinion that he rules for separation between them even if the *mariḍ* recovers, and it may also be derived from his opinion that he does not uphold separation between them, but separation is recommended not obligatory. The reason for their disagreement is the vacillation of marriage between sale and a gift, because the gift of a *mariḍ* is not permitted except to the extent of a third (of his estate), but his sale is permitted. There is another reason for their disagreement, which is the fear that he (the *mariḍ*) may be accused of intending to harm the heirs by introducing an additional heir?

The analogy of marriage upon a gift is incorrect, for they agreed that a gift is valid if it can be accommodated within a third, but they did not associate marriage, here, with a third. The rejection of the permissibility of marriage on account of the inclusion of an additional heir is an analogy based upon *maṣlaḥa*, which is not permitted according to the majority of the *fuqahāʾ*. Taking interests into account in a genus that is remote from the genus that is desired for the establishment of the *ḥukm* according to (the principle of) *maṣlaḥa* led some jurists to the conclusion that upholding such an opinion amounts to legislating additional law, and the adoption of such an analogy dilutes the principle of submission to the *sharīʿa*, neither adding to it nor detracting from it. Yet, reluctance to pay attention to *maṣlaḥa* might cause the people to be pushed, because of a lack of precedents in this genus, toward injustice. Such interests should be brought to the scholars of the *ḥikma* (philosophy) of the law, the learned who will not be accused of judging by it, especially nowadays when the qualified persons think that adoption of the letter of the law (apparent meaning) leads to injustice. The proper methodology of the learned scholar in this should be to examine the evidence in the circumstances of the case. If such evidence indicates that he (the *mariḍ*) intends betterment through the marriage, he should not prohibit the marriage, but if it indicates that he intends harm to his heirs, he should disallow it. This is the case in many things among skills and services where the professional is faced with opposing results in what he is trying to do upon the strength of his skill, for it is not possible to lay down fixed limits for the service. This (situation) is usually faced in the profession of medicine and also in various other professions.

18.2.3.11. *Section 11: The Impediment of* ʿIdda *(Waiting Period)*

They agreed that marriage is not permitted during the (woman's) waiting period, whether it is the waiting period of menstruation, of pregnancy, or of months. They disagreed about the person who marries a woman during her waiting period and consummates it. Mālik, al-Awzāʾī, and al-Layth said that they are to be separated and she is not to be permissible for him, ever. Abū Ḥanīfa, al-Shāfiʿī, and al-Thāwrī said that they are to be separated and when her *ʿidda* is over there is no harm in his marrying her a second time.

The reason for their disagreement is whether the opinion of a Companion has binding force. This is so as Mālik related from Ibn Shihāb from Saʿīd ibn al-Musayyib and Sulaymān ibn Yasār that ʿUmar ibn al-Khaṭṭāb ruled for a separation between Ṭalīḥa from the tribe of Asad and Rāshid al-Thaqafī when he married her during her *idda* from another husband, saying, "If a woman marries during her *idda*, and if the husband whom she marries has not consummated the marriage with her, they are to be separated, and she will then complete the remaining *idda* from the first, after which the second husband may be one of those who can propose. If he consummates the marriage with her, they are to be separated, after which she will complete her *idda* from the first and then the second, but then they can never come together in marriage, ever". Saʿīd said that she is entitled to dower in view of his irregular marriage to her. Perhaps, those who ruled for perpetual prohibition supported this analogy with *qiyās al-shabah* that was weak and disputed with respect to its basis, which is that this invalid marriage, during the *ʿidda*, may cause confusion in lineage and thus (his position) is similar to the accuser in *liʿān*.

It is related that ʿAli and Ibn Masʿūd opposed ʿUmar's ruling on this case. The principle is that she is not to be forbidden to him unless evidence to that effect can be adduced from the Book, *sunna*, or the consensus of the community (of jurists). Some of the narrations state that when ʿAli heard that ʿUmar had ruled for her prohibition, and for the dower being the liability of the treasury, he denied it, upon which ʿUmar retracted from it placing the liability for dower on the husband and not declaring her to be prohibited for him. This is related by al-Thāwrī from Ashʿath from al-Shaʿbī from Masrūq. (The opinion of) those who declared her to be prohibited for him merely on the basis of the contract is weak.

They agreed unanimously that intercourse is not to be had with a pregnant enslaved prisoner, unless she delivers, because of the *mutawātir* reports from the Messenger of Allāh (God's peace and blessings be upon him) to this effect. They disagreed, when the master has had intercourse with her, whether the child is to be manumitted on his account. The majority maintain that the child is not to be manumitted. The reason for the disagreement is whether his sperm has any effect in its growth. If we maintain that it has been effective, the child is his to some extent, but if we say that it does not have any effect this would not be the case. It is related from the Prophet (God's peace and blessings be upon him) that he said, "How can he enslave it, when he has fed it with respect to sight and hearing".

The examination of the impediment of pronouncing divorce thrice will be taken up in the Book of Divorce.

18.2.3.12. *Section 12: The Impediment of Marriage*

They disagreed, regarding the impediment of marriage, that marriage among Muslims amounts to a prohibition, as it does among the *dhimmīs*. They disagreed about an enslaved female prisoner of war as has preceded. They also disagreed over whether the sale of a slave-girl amounts to a divorce. The majority maintain that it does not amount to a divorce, while a group said that it does, which is related from Ibn ᶜAbbās, Jābir, Ibn Masᶜūd, and Abū ibn Kaᶜb.

The reason for their disagreement is the conflict of the tradition of Barīra with the generality of the words of the Exalted, "And all married women (are forbidden unto you) save those (captives) whom your right hands possess[52]," which includes captives as well as others besides them. The granting of a choice to Barīra implies that her sale was not a divorce, for had it been a divorce the Messenger of Allāh (God's peace and blessings be upon him) would not have granted her a choice in the matter after manumission, and her purchase itself by ᶜĀʾisha would have amounted to a divorce.

The evidence for the majority of the jurists is what is recorded by Ibn Abī Shayba from Abū Saᶜīd al-Khudrī "that the Messenger of Allāh sent out, on the day of Hunayn, a troop that came upon an Arab camp on the day of Awṭās. They defeated them and slew them, and found women who had husbands. Some Companions hesitated to touch them fearing it was not permissible because of their existing marriages. Thus, Allāh sent down the verse, 'And all married women (are forbidden unto you) save those (captives) whom your right hands possess'."[53] This issue is better suited to the Book of Divorce.

These are all the things that influence the validity of the marriage contract. They refer, as we have said to three categories: the qualifications of the party to the contract and the description of the subject-matter of the contract, the description of the contract, and the description of the conditions of the contract. About marriages that were concluded prior to Islam and then became subject to Islam, they agreed that if both converted to Islam simultaneously, that is, the husband and the wife, and the parties to the marriage were mutually

[52] Qurʾān 4 : 24
[53] Qurʾān 4 : 24

permissible in Islam, then, Islam confirmed such a marriage. They disagreed on two points. First, when marriage was polygamous with more than four (wives) or with those who cannot be married together in Islam. Second, when one of them converted to Islam before the other.

18.2.3.12.1. Issue 1

When a disbeliever converted to Islam and had more than four women or he converted and had two sisters (as wives), Mālik said that he is to choose four from among them and one from the sisters, whomsoever he likes. This was also upheld by al-Shāfiʿī, Aḥmad, and Dāwūd. Abū Ḥanīfa, al-Thawrī and Ibn Abī Laylā said that he is to hold on to those who were first in the order of the contracts. If he has married them (all) through a single contract a separation is ordered between them and him. Ibn al-Mājishūn, one of the disciples of Mālik, said that if he converts to Islam and is married to two sisters, both are to be separated (from him) and he concludes a new contract with the one he likes. No one else among Mālik's disciples held this opinion.

The reason for their disagreement is the conflict of analogy with traditions, as there are two traditions that are related to this issue. First is the *mursal* by Mālik "that Ghaylān ibn Salāma al-Thaqafī converted to Islam and he had ten wives, who converted to Islam with him. The Messenger of Allāh (God's peace and blessings be upon him) ordered him to select four out of them". The second tradition is that of Qays ibn al-Ḥārith that he converted to Islam having two wives as sisters. The Messenger of Allāh (God's peace and blessings be upon him) said to him, "Choose whomsoever you like". The analogy opposing these traditions is the similarity of the contracts of later wives concluded before Islam with the forbidden contracts after Islam, that is, just as the contracts with them were void in Islam it should be the same for the contracts prior to Islam. This is weak.

18.2.3.12.2. Issue 2

When one of them converts to Islam before the other, which is the second issue, they disagreed about it. Mālik, Abū Ḥanīfa, and al-Shāfiʿī said that if he accepts Islam[54] before her and she is a *kitābiyya*, her contract is confirmed, but if the woman accepts Islam before him, he has a right to her if he accepts Islam during her *ʿidda* (waiting period), because of the tradition of Ṣafwān ibn ʿUmayya about this "that his spouse ʿĀtika daughter of al-Walīd ibn al-Mughīra converted to Islam before he did, then he also accepted Islam and the Messenger of Allāh (God's peace and blessings be upon him) ratified his original contract of marriage". They said that between the conversion of Ṣafwān and his wife there was a duration of approximately one month. Ibn Shihāb said that word has not

[54] The text in the original was not clear at this point. The problem was resolved by switching this sentence with the one following it.

reached us that a woman migrated to the Messenger of Allāh (God's peace and blessings be upon him) and her husband was a disbeliever residing in the *dār al-kufr*, except that her migration caused a separation between her and her husband, unless her husband came over too as a migrant prior to the termination of her *ʿidda*.

If the husband converted to Islam prior to the conversion of the wife, they differed about this. Mālik said that if the husband converted to Islam earlier and the wife is offered conversion, but she refuses, a separation is to be effected between them. Al-Shāfiʿī said that whether the husband converts to Islam before the wife or the wife before the husband, if the conversion to Islam of the later is within the period of the *ʿidda* the marriage is confirmed.

The reason for their disagreement is the conflict of a general meaning with traditions and analogy. The general meaning is found in the words of the Exalted, "And hold not to the ties of disbelieving women,"[55] which implies immediate separation. The tradition opposing the implication of this general meaning is that related about Abū Sufyān ibn Ḥarb, who converted prior to Hind bint ʿUtba, his wife. His conversion took place at Marr al-Ẓahrān (during the conquest of Mecca). He then returned to Mecca where Hind was still a disbeliever. She took hold of his beard and said, "Slay the misguided old man". Within a few days she accepted Islam, and they were confirmed upon their marriage. In the analogy opposing the tradition, it is obvious that there is no difference whether she converts to Islam before him or he converts before her. If the *ʿidda* is to be considered in her accepting Islam prior to him, it should be acknowledged in his prior conversion too.

18.3. **Chapter 3: The Requisites of an Option in Marriage**

The causes for an option are four: defects; inability to pay the dower, maintenance, and clothing; absence, that is, absence of the husband; and manumission of a married slave-woman. Thus, there are four sections in this chapter.

18.3.1. *Section 1: The Option of Defects*

The jurists disagreed about the causes of the option of defects for each one of the spouses. This they did on two points. First, is it revoked because of defects? If we say that it is to be revoked, then, by whom is it revoked, and what is its *ḥukm*.

About the first point, Mālik, al-Shāfiʿī and their disciples said that defects give rise to the option of revocation or of retaining the marriage. The Ẓahirites said that

[55] Qurʾān 60:10

they do not give rise to the option of revocation or of retaining the marriage, which was the opinion of ʿUmar ibn ʿAbd al-ʿAzīz. The reason for their disagreement is based on two factors. First, (upon the question) whether the opinion of a Companion is binding as a source (of law). Second, on the analogy for marriage, in this case, upon sale. The opinion of a Companion laid down in this is what has been related from ʿUmar ibn al-Khaṭṭāb that he said, "When a man marries a woman and she is suffering from insanity, leprosy, or a skin disease"—in some narrations is added the word *qarn* (see the meaning of *ratq* a few lines below)—"she is entitled to full dower, and it is a debt to be claimed by the husband from her guardian". Regarding analogy upon sale, those who upheld defects to be a cause for an option in marriage, said that marriage in this case resembles sale. Their opponents asserted that it does not resemble sale, because of the unanimity of the Muslims on the point that it is not every defect that can lead to the revocation of marriage, while sale can always be revoked because of defects.

In the second point about revocation due to defects, they disagreed about the defects that can entail revocation, and those that did not, and also about the *ḥukm* of revocation. Mālik and al-Shāfiʿī agreed that revocation is on the basis of four defects: insanity, leprosy, *baraṣ* (skin disease like leprosy), and disease of the sex organ that prevents intercourse—*qarn* or *ratq* (birth defect in which the vulva is blocked, or the sides of the vulva are joined together) in a woman, and impotence or castration in a man. Mālik's disciples differed about four defects: black colour, baldness, excessive vaginal odour, and foul breath. It is said that marriage can be revoked because of them, and it is said that it cannot. Abū Ḥanīfa, his disciples, and al-Thāwrī said that a woman cannot be rejected in a marriage except for two defects: *qarn* and *ratq*.

In relation to the *aḥkām* of revocation, those who upheld revocation (due to defects) agreed that if the husband came to know about the defects prior to seclusion, he pronounces divorce and there is nothing due from him. They disagreed when he comes to know about them after seclusion and "touching". Mālik said that if her guardian who gave her away in marriage, about whom it can be said because of his closeness to her as in the case of a father or brother that he was aware of the defects, then, he is a deceiver and the husband has recourse to him for the dower, but he has no claim against the woman for anything. If the guardian is a distant relative, the husband has recourse to the woman for the entire dower, except for one-fourth *dīnār*. Al-Shāfiʿī said that if he consummates marriage with her, he is obliged for the dower and he cannot have recourse to the woman for it, or to the guardian.

The reason for their disagreement is the similarity of marriage with sale and its similarity with void marriages in which consummation has occurred. They agreed about the obligation of paying dower in void contracts on the basis of the words of the Prophet (God's peace and blessings be upon him), "When a woman enters into a marriage without the permission of her guardian, her marriage is void, and she has dower as compensation for her". The point of disagreement turns on the vacillation of this rescission between the *ḥukm* of revocation due to defects in sale, and the rescinded marriages, that is, after consummation.

Those who upheld the rescission of the marriage of an impotent person, agreed that it is not rescinded until they are left alone with each other without any hindrance for a year. The disciples of Mālik disagreed about the underlying reason due to which revocation has been confined to these four defects. It is said that it is so because it is a non-rational law. It is said that because they are hidden defects. The implication about the remaining defects is that they are not concealed. It is also said that (the underlying reason is that) they may be passed on to the children. On the basis of this reasoning they repudiate because of blackness of colour and baldness, while on the basis of the former they revoke (marriage) because of every defect if it is known that it was concealed from the husband.

18.3.2. *Section 2: Option on Inability to Pay Dower and Maintenance*

They disagreed about inability to pay dower. Al-Shāfiʿī used to say that the wife is to be given a choice if the husband has not consummated the marriage with her. This was also Mālik's opinion, but his disciples differed about the extent of delay permitted to him. It is said that there is no limit on this for him, while it is said it is a year, and it is also said that it is two years. Abū Ḥanīfa said that he is a debtor like all other debtors and there is to be no separation between them, but he is to be taken to task for maintenance; and she has the right to refuse access to herself till he pays her the dower.

The reason for their disagreement is the predominance of the similarity of marriage with sale, or the predominance of the harm to be caused to the woman, because of the absence of intercourse just as in in the cases of *al-īlāʾ* and impotence.

About the inability to pay maintenance, Mālik, al-Shāfiʿī, Aḥmad, Abū Thawr and Abū ʿUbayd said that they are to be separated, which is also related from Abū Hurayra and Saʿīd ibn al-Musayyib. Abū Ḥanīfa and al-Thāwrī said that they are not to be separated, which was also the opinion of the Ẓāhirites.

The reason for their disagreement is the similarity between harm resulting from this with harm resulting from impotency, as the majority uphold the pronouncement of divorce in the case of the impotent person, and Ibn al-Mundhir has gone so far as to say that there is consensus (*ijmāʿ*) over it. Perhaps they maintained that maintenance is a counter-value for (sexual) utilization, on the evidence that there is no maintenance for the recalcitrant woman according to the majority. If maintenance is not available, utilization lapses and the option becomes obligatory. Those who do not acknowledge analogy (as a principle) said that if the bond has been established through consensus, it cannot be severed except by another consensus or by an evidence from the Book of Allāh or the *sunna* of the Prophet. The reason for their disagreement, then, is the conflict of analogy with *istiṣḥāb al-ḥāl*.[56]

18.3.3. *Section 3: Option upon Absence*

They disagreed over the missing person about whose life or death nothing is known in the land of Islam. Mālik said that his wife is to be given a period of four years from the day her case is brought before the judge. If search for information about his life and death terminates and (his whereabouts) become unknown, the judge will determine a period for her; upon the termination of the period she will begin to observe the waiting period of four months and ten days, after which she will be free. About his wealth, he said that it is not to be distributed among his heirs till such a time has passed after which he is not likely to survive. It is said that this is seventy years, or eighty, or ninety, and it is said a hundred years, if he disappeared before reaching this age. This opinion is related from ᶜUmar ibn al-Khaṭṭāb, and is also related from ᶜUthmān. It was upheld by al-Layth. Al-Shāfiᶜī, Abū Ḥanīfa and al-Thāwrī said that the wife of a missing person is not to be released (from the marriage contract) till his death is verified; their opinion is related from ᶜAlī and Ibn Masᶜūd.

The reason for their disagreement is the conflict of *istiṣḥāb al-ḥāl* with analogy, as *istiṣḥāb al-ḥāl* requires that the bond should not be severed except through death or divorce, unless evidence indicates the contrary. The analogy here is the similarity of harm caused to her because of absence with the harm in *al-īlāʾ* and impotence; she thus has an option, as she has in these two cases.

Missing persons according to the authorities in Mālik's school are of four types: persons missing within the Islamic lands, and there was a disagreement over this category; persons missing in enemy lands; persons missing in Muslim wars, I mean, those that are among the Muslims; and persons missing in the wars with the disbelievers. There is a substantial disagreement reported from Mālik and his disciples about three of these types.

[56] This principle requires the maintenance of the *status quo* in accordance with the previous rule applicable to the case, if any, unless valid evidence from the Qurʾān, *sunna* or consensus can be adduced to change the ruling. This principle arises from another principle, which maintains: "The original rule for all things is permissibility, unless evidence can be adduced to the contrary".

The *ḥukm* of a person missing in enemy lands, according to them, is the *ḥukm* of the captive. His wife cannot marry again and his wealth is not to be divided till his death is confirmed, except that Ashhab ruled in his case by the *ḥukm* of a person missing in Muslim lands. Regarding a person missing in wars among the Muslims, he (Mālik) said that his *ḥukm* is that of the slain person, without there being any delay, and it is said that he is to be awaited in accordance with the distance of the place where the battle took place; the maximum period in this case is a year. There are four opinions in the school about the person missing in the wars with the disbelievers: (1) That his *ḥukm* is that of a captive; (2) That his *ḥukm* is that of the slain person after a waiting period of a year, except that if he was in a place where his fate cannot remain concealed, he is to be assigned the *ḥukm* of the person missing in Muslim wars and insurrections; (3) That his *ḥukm* is that of a person missing in Muslim lands; and (4) That his *ḥukm* is that of a person slain with respect to his wife, and that of a person missing in Muslim lands with respect to his wealth, that is, for life (expectancy), after which it (his wealth) is to be inherited.

All these opinions have been structured upon the proposal of the best interest secured by the *sharᶜ*, which is known as *al-qiyās al-mursal*, and about which there is a disagreement among the *fuqahāᵓ*, that is, among those who uphold analogy.

18.3.4. *Section 4: Option upon Manumission*

They agreed that if the slave-woman is manumitted when she is married to a slave, she has an option, but they disagreed whether she has an option when she is married to a freeman. Mālik, al-Shāfiᶜī, the jurists of Medina, al-Awzāᶜī, Aḥmad and al-Layth said that she has no option. Abū Ḥanīfa and al-Thāwrī said that she has an option whether the husband is a freeman or a slave.

The reason for their disagreement is the conflict of the transmitted texts in the traditions of Barīra with the likelihood of the underlying cause giving rise to the option, being (her master's right of) coercion, which is there absolutely in her marriage as a slave, or (with the likelihood that there) is coercion in her marriage to a slave. Those who maintained that the underlying cause, without qualification, is coercion in marriage said that she is given an option whether she is married to a freeman or slave. Those who limit coercion to her marriage with a slave said that she has an option only when married to a slave. About the conflict with transmission, it is related from Ibn ᶜAbbās that Barīra's husband was a black slave, but it is related from ᶜĀᵓisha that her husband was a freeman. Both narrations are established according to the traditionists.

They also differed about the time when the option is granted to her. Mālik and al-Shāfiᶜī said that she has an option as long as he does not have intercourse with her (after manumission). Abū Ḥanīfa said that she has the option during the session (of manumission). Al-Awzāʿī held that her option lapses with intercourse as long as she knows that her option will lapse with intercourse.

18.4. **Chapter 4: Marital Rights**

They agreed that among the wife's rights over her husband are maintenance and clothing, because of the words of the Exalted, "The duty of feeding and clothing nursing mothers in a seemly manner is upon the father of the child, and no one should be charged beyond his capacity",[57] and the words of the Prophet (God's peace and blessings be upon him), "They have a right over you for food and clothing in a reasonable manner", and his directive to Hind, "Take what is reasonably sufficient for you and your child".

They agreed about the obligation of maintenance, but they differed on four points: the time of the obligation, amount, for whom is it obligatory, and upon whom. With respect to the time of its obligation, Mālik said that maintenance is not obligatory upon the husband unless he has consummated the marriage with her, or he has been asked to consummate the marriage when she is legally capable for intercourse and he has attained puberty. Abū Ḥanīfa and al-Shāfiʿī said that maintenance is obligatory on one who has not attained majority if she has attained it, but when he has attained majority and she is a minor, there are two views about it from al-Shāfiʿī. One is the same as Mālik's, while the other holds that she is entitled to maintenance without qualification.

The reason for their disagreement is whether maintenance is a counter-value for (sexual) utilization, or is compensation for the fact that she is confined because of her husband, as in the case of one absent or sick.

Mālik said about the amount of maintenance that it is not determined by the law and refers to the requirements of the status of the husband and the status of the wife, and that this varies in accordance with a change in location, time and status. This was upheld by Abū Ḥanīfa. Al-Shāfiʿī maintained that it is determined, and for the person in financial ease it is two *mudd*s (a dry measure), for one with average circumstances it is one and one-half *mudd*, and for a person in difficult straits it is one *mudd*. The reason for their disagreement is the vacillation of the interpretation of maintenance for this subject between feeding in expiation and that in clothing. This is so, as they agreed that there is no limit for clothing, while for feeding there is.

They disagreed under this topic whether the maintenance of the wife's servant is upon the husband, and if it is obligatory (upon him) how much is it?

[57] Qurʾān 2 : 233

The majority agreed that the maintenance of the wife's servant is the liability of the husband if she is of a status that needs a servant, while it is also said that the wife has to take care of the household herself. Those who held the maintenance of the wife's servant to be the liability of the husband differed about the number of servants. One group said that he should provide maintenance for one servant, but it is said that he provides for two servants if the wife is accustomed to two servants, which was upheld by Mālik and Abū Thawr. I do not know of a legal source for the obligation of maintenance of a servant except its similarity with the provision of service with residence. They agreed that residence is to be provided by the husband, because of a text laid down for its obligation in the case of a wife whose divorce is retractable.

They agreed regarding the wife for whom maintenance is necessary that it is obligatory for the free-woman, who is not recalcitrant. They disagreed about the recalcitrant woman and about the slave-woman. About the recalcitrant woman, the majority agreed that maintenance is not due to her, but a group of jurists deviated from this and said that it is due. The reason for their disagreement is the conflict of the generality with the implication of the text, as the generality of the words of the Prophet (God's peace and blessings be upon him), "They have a right over you for food and clothing in a reasonable manner", equally include the recalcitrant woman and others besides her, while the implication is that maintenance is in lieu of (sexual) utilization, which conveys that there is no maintenance for the recalcitrant.

The disciples of Mālik disputed extensively the case of the slave-woman. It is said that she is entitled to maintenance like the free woman, which is the well-known opinion, while it is said that there is no maintenance for her. It is also said that if she visits him she has maintenance, but if he visits her there is no maintenance. Further, it is maintained that she is entitled to maintenance at the time she visits him. If the husband is a freeman, they said, she has maintenance, but if he is a slave there is no maintenance for her. The reason for their disagreement is the conflict of the general meaning with analogy, as the general meaning requires the obligation of maintenance for her, while analogy dictates that her maintenance is only upon the master whom she serves, or is to be shared by them as each one of them makes use of her in different ways. It is for this reason that one group held that she is entitled to maintenance when she visits him. Ibn Ḥabīb said that the married slave-woman's master is to be ordered to allow her to visit her husband once every four days.

In response to the question, who is obliged to pay maintenance, they agreed that it is obligatory upon a husband who is present and is a freeman. They disagreed about one absent or one who is a slave. Ibn al-Mundhir said about the slave that all those jurists whose rulings he had studied agreed that the slave is obliged to pay his wife's maintenance, while Ibn al-Muṣʿab said that there is no obligation for maintenance upon him. The reason for their disagreement is the conflict of the general principle with the fact that the slave is interdicted with respect to his wealth. The majority uphold the obligation of maintenance upon the person who is absent, but Abū Ḥanīfa said that it does not become obligatory except by the decree of the sultan.

They disagreed about the person whose statement would be acceptable in case of dispute about maintenance. This will be coming up, God willing, in the Book of *Aḥkām* (Judgments).

They agreed that among the wife's (basic) marital rights (in case of a polygamous marriage) is justice between the wives in sharing (of the husband's favours), because of the established practice of the Prophet (God's peace and blessings be upon him) who distributed his favours fairly between his wives, and also because of his words, "When a person has two wives and he feels inclined toward one of them, he will appear on the day of judgment with one of his sides inclined". It is also established that the Prophet (God's peace and blessings be upon him), when he wished to go on a journey, used to draw lots between them.

They disagreed about the period of stay of the husband with a (newlywed) wife, who may or may not be a virgin, whether in the case of a polygamous household this period should be taken into account in the process of conjugal sharing. Mālik, al-Shāfiʿī, and their disciples said that he (the husband) stays with a newlywed virgin for seven days and with a newlywed non-virgin for three days, and that this nuptial period is not to be counted in the distribution of conjugal rights among the wives. Abū Ḥanīfa said that stay with newlyweds is equal, whether virgin or non-virgin, and that in a polygamous marriage the initial nuptial period must be taken into account. The reason for their disagreement is the conflict of the tradition of Anas with the tradition of Umm Salama. The tradition related by Anas is "that the Prophet (God's peace and blessings be upon him) when he married a virgin, he stayed with her for seven days, but when he married a non-virgin he stayed with her for three days". The tradition of Umm Salama says "that the Prophet (God's peace and blessings be upon him) married her and the next morning said to her, "You are not to suffer discrimination among your family. If you like I will stay seven days with you, and seven with (each of) them, but if you like I will stay three days with you and take turns (among them accordingly)". She said, "Stay three days". Umm Salama's tradition is Madanī, is agreed upon, and is recorded by Mālik, al-Bukhārī and Muslim. The tradition of Anas is Baṣrī and is recorded by Abū Dāwūd. The jurists of Medina adopted the tradition recorded by the scholars of Baṣra, while the jurists of Kūfa adopted the tradition recorded by the scholars of Medina. Mālik's disciples disagreed whether his stay with a virgin for seven days and with a non-virgin for three is obligatory or recommended. Ibn al-Qāsim said that it is obligatory, while Ibn ʿAbd al-Ḥakam said that it is recommended. The reason for the disagreement is the interpretation of the Prophet's case to indicate recommendation or obligation.

The rights of the husband over the wife with respect to nursing and taking care of the house are structured upon the disagreement of the jurists over this issue. This is so as one group of jurists made nursing absolutely obligatory for her, while another group did not make it obligatory at all. One group of jurists made it obligatory for a woman of lower status and not for one with a higher status, unless the infant will not feed except at her breast, which is Mālik's well-known opinion. The reason for their disagreement is the difference as to whether the verse of suckling conveys the *ḥukm* of suckling, that is, its obligation, or that it merely contains the command of suckling (but not as an obligation). Those who held that it contains only the command said that it is not obligatory upon her as there is no evidence for its interpretation as obligation. Those who held that it implies the command of suckling as well as its obligation, because it is a report meant to be a command said that suckling is obligatory upon her. Those who made a distinction between a woman of lower status and one of a higher status based it upon custom and practice. There is no obligation of suckling upon the divorced woman, unless the infant will not feed at another woman's breast, in which case suckling is binding upon her and the child's father is liable for the wages of suckling. This is a point of consensus, because of the words of the Exalted, "Then, if they give suck for you, give them their due payment and consult together in kindness".[58]

The majority maintain that custody (*ḥaḍāna*) belongs to the mother if she is divorced by the husband and the child is still in a tender age, because of the words of the Prophet (God's peace and blessings be upon him), "He who causes a separation between a mother and her child, Allāh will cause a separation between him and his loved ones on the day of judgment", and in so far as enslaved and captive women cannot be separated from their child, the case of the free-woman becomes stronger. They disagreed when the child has reached the age of discrimination. One group, and among them is al-Shāfiʿī, said that he is to be given an option (to remain with his mother or to go to the father). They argued on the basis of a tradition that is relevant to this, while the others held on to the general principle, as this tradition was not proved authentic according to them. The majority maintain[59] that her marriage to someone other than the (child's) father terminates custody, because of the report that the Messenger of Allāh (God's peace and blessings be upon him)

[58] Qurʾān 65 : 6

[59] According to the editor of the original, the text following this and up to the end of the paragraph is not found in some manuscripts.

said, "You have a prior right to him as long as you do not marry". Those for whom this tradition was not authentic pursued the general principle. There is no basis for it, that can be relied upon, about the transfer of custody from the mother to someone other than the father.

18.5. **Chapter 5: Marriages Prohibited by Law, Void Marriages, and their *Ḥukm***

The marriages about which an express proscription has been laid down are four: *nikāḥ al-shighār*, *nikāḥ al-mutʿa*, proposal during another's proposal, and *nikāḥ al-muḥallil.* They agreed about *nikāḥ al-shighār* that it takes the form of a man giving his female ward in marriage to another on the condition that he will give his ward in marriage to the first, without there being any dower except the body of one woman in exchange for that of the other. They agreed that it is a marriage that is not permitted, because of an established proscription from the Prophet. They disagreed when it did take place, whether it would entail *mahr al-mithl.* Mālik said that it is not valid and is annulled for ever, before consummation and after it. This was also al-Shāfiʿī's opinion, except he added that if a dower is announced for one of them or for both simultaneously, then, the marriage is established on the basis of *mahr al-mithl*, and the dower announced is void. Abū Ḥanīfa said that *nikāḥ al-shighār* is valid on the fixation of *mahr al-mithl.* This was also the opinion of al-Layth, Aḥmad, Isḥāq, Abū Thawr and al-Ṭabarī.

The reason for their disagreement is whether the proscription assigned to it has the absence of a consideration (counter-value) as an underlying reason, or that it has no underlying reason. If we concede that it has no underlying (rational) reason, then rescission is binding without exemptions. If we say that the underlying reason is the absence of dower, it will become valid by fixation of dower as *mahr al-mithl*, like the contracts of marriage in return for wine or swine. They agreed unanimously that a contract of marriage for wine and swine is not rescinded if utilized with consummation, but there will be *mahr al-mithl* in it. It was as if Mālik (God be pleased with him) held the view that though dower was not a condition for the validity of the contract, the invalidity of the contract here, because of the invalidity of the dower, is peculiar for the assignment of the proscription to it, or he was of the view that the proscription is linked to the very formation of the contract, and a proscription (as a rule) indicates the invalidity of the thing proscribed.

In the marriage of *mutʿa*, though the reports from the Messenger of Allāh (God's peace and blessings be upon him) about its prohibition have reached the level of *tawātur*, they have differed about the time of the occurrence of the prohibition. In some narrations it is stated that he prohibited it on the day of Khaybar, in some it is the day of the conquest of Mecca, in some the day of Tabūk, in some the day of the Farewell Pilgrimage, in some it is during the *umrat al-qaḍāʾ*, and in some it is the day of Awṭās. Most of the Companions and all the jurists upheld its prohibition. Its permission by Ibn ʿAbbās became well known, and he was followed in his opinion by his disciples in Mecca and in Yemen. They related that Ibn ʿAbbās used to argue for it on the basis of the words of the Exalted, "And those of whom ye seek content (by marrying them), give unto them their portions as a duty. And there is no sin for you in what ye do by mutual agreement after the duty (hath been done). Lo! Allāh is ever Knower, Wise".[60] In one variant reading from him there is an addition of the words "till a stipulated period". It is related from him that he said, "*Mutʿa* is nothing but a mercy from Allāh, the Mighty, Glorious, through which he had mercy upon the *umma* of Muḥammad (God's peace and blessings be upon him). If ʿUmar had not prohibited it, no one would have had the urge to commit *zinā*, except the doomed". All this that is related from Ibn ʿAbbās is related by Ibn Jurayj and ʿAmr ibn Dīnār. From ʿAṭāʾ is the report that he said, "I heard Jābir ibn ʿAbd Allāh saying, 'We contracted *mutʾa* in the period of the Messenger of Allāh (God's peace and blessings be upon him), in that of Abū Bakr, and in the first half of the period of the caliphate of ʿUmar,' " but ʿUmar forbade the people from undertaking it.

Regarding the disagreement about a marriage in which a proposal was made during the proposal of another, it has preceded that there are three opinions on it. One opinion requiring rescission, another not imposing rescission, and the third making a distinction on the basis of the degree of maturity of the first proposal, which is Mālik's opinion.

Nikāḥ al-muḥallil, that is, a marriage through which the permissibility (for remarriage) of a woman divorced by three pronouncements (to her divorcing ex-husband) is sought, Mālik said that it is a marriage that is rescinded, while Abū Ḥanīfa and al-Shāfiʿī said that it is a valid marriage. The reason for their disagreement is their dispute about the meaning of the words of the Prophet, "The curse of Allāh is upon the *muḥallil*". Those who understood the word 'curse' to mean sin alone said that the contract is valid, but those who understood sin to imply the invalidity of the contract, comparing it to the proscription that implies the nullity of the thing proscribed, said that the marriage is void. These are the marriages that are declared void because of a proscription.

Marriages declared void by implication of the law are invalidated either by

[60] Qurʾān 4 : 24

dropping a condition of validity of marriage, or by the alteration of a *ḥukm* that has been made obligatory by commands from Allāh Almighty, or by making an addition that leads to the nullification of one of the conditions of validity of marriage. Other additions besides these do not invalidate marriage, by agreement of the jurists, rather the jurists disagreed about the binding effect of conditions imposed in this way, for example, when a condition is stipulated for the husband that he will not marry another wife during her marriage, or will not take a slave-girl as a concubine, or move her from her place of domicile. Mālik said that if such conditions are imposed they are not binding upon him, unless they incorporate an oath to manumit or divorce, for these are binding upon him, except when they consist of a condition to manumit or divorce one for whom the oath is taken, in which case the former condition would not be binding either. The same view was expressed by al-Shāfiʿī and Abū Ḥanīfa. Al-Awzāʿī and Ibn Shubrama said that she is entitled to (enforce) her condition and compliance is binding upon him. Ibn Shihāb said that some of the jurists he came across used to issue such a ruling. The opinion of the majority is related from ʿAlī, while the opinion of al-Awzāʿī is related from ʿUmar.

The reason for their disagreement is the conflict of a general with a particular meaning. The general meaning is conveyed in the tradition of ʿĀʾisha (God be pleased with her) "that the Prophet (God's peace and blessings be upon him) addressing the people said, 'Any condition that is not in the Book of Allāh is void, even if it were a hundred conditions.' " The particular meaning is conveyed in the tradition of ʿUqba ibn ʿĀmir from the Prophet (God's peace and blessings be upon him) that he said, "The condition having the highest priority for performance is the one with which you have made intercourse lawful". Both traditions are ahih and have been recorded by al-Bukhārī and Muslim, except that the well known view from the *uṣūliyūn* is for decision on the basis of the particular meaning, which is the binding nature of conditions and is the apparent meaning of what is found in *al-ʿUtbiya*, though the well-known opinion is against it. The school differed extensively about the conditions restricted with respect to the determination of dower, that is, whether they are binding or not, but this book of ours has not been structured for detailed cases.

Under the *ḥukm* of void marriages, when they occur, are some that are agreed upon with respect to rescission, prior to consummation and after it. These are those declared void because of dropping a condition whose existence is obligatory for the validity of the marriage, like marrying a woman who is prohibited for the man. Another category of these *fāsid* marriages is disputed because of the disagreement about the weakness and strength of the underlying reason of invalidity and why it reverts to a disregard of the conditions of validity. In this category, in many of these cases, Mālik issues the ruling of rescission prior to consummation, and of confirmation after consummation.

The principle, according to him, in these is that there is no rescission, but he is being cautious, as in the case of many sales where he considers the subject-matter to be consumed because of the fluctuation of the rates and other factors. It appears that such marriages, in his view, are abominable, otherwise there would be no reason for a distinction between consummation and its absence. The consternation within the school over these matters is extensive. It is as if this refers, according to Mālik, to the strength of the rescinding evidence and its weakness. When the evidence appears strong to him, he rescinds the marriage both before and after consummation, but when it is weak, he rescinds it before consummation and not after it, irrespective of the agreement over the rescinding evidence. In relation to this, the school differed about the right of inheritance resulting from void marriages, when death occurs prior to rescission; similarly, as to the occurrence of a divorce. On one occasion both agreement and disagreement are found, while on another occasion rescission and also its absence have been acknowledged after consummation.

We deem it appropriate to terminate our discussion of the subject here, for what we have recorded about it is sufficient for our desired purpose.

XIX
THE BOOK OF *ṬALĀQ* (DIVORCE)

The discussion on this subject is divided into four parts:
Part 1: The kinds of divorce;
Part 2: The elements of divorce;
Part 3: Revocation; and
Part 4: The *aḥkām* of divorcees.

19.1. **Part 1: The Kinds of Divorce**

In this part there are five chapters. The first chapter is about the identification of *bāʾin* (irrevocable) and *rajʿī* (revocable) divorces. The second chapter is about the distinction between *ṭalaq al-sunna* and *ṭalāq al-bidʿa*. The third chapter relates to *khulʿ* (redemption). The fourth chapter is about the distinction between divorce and rescission. The fifth chapter is about *takhyīr* and *tamlīk*.

19.1.1. **Chapter 1: The Identification of *Bāʾin* and *Rajʿī* Divorces**

The jurists agreed that divorce is of two types: *bāʾin* (irrevocable) and *rajʿī* (revocable). In the *rajʿī* divorce the husband possesses the right over her (the wife's) return, without there being a choice for her in the matter. The condition for doing this is that he should have consummated the marriage with her. They agreed about this because of the words of the Exalted, "O Prophet! When ye (men wish to) divorce women, divorce them when they can begin their waiting period, and reckon the period, and keep your duty to Allāh, your Lord. Expel them not from their houses nor let them go forth unless they commit open immorality. Such are the limits (imposed by) Allāh; and whoso transgresseth Allāh's limits, he verily wrongeth his soul. Thou knowest not: it may be that Allāh will afterward bring some new thing to pass",[61] and also because of the established tradition related by Ibn ʿUmar that the Prophet (God's peace and

[61] Qurʾān 65 :1. Divorce should not take place during the time of the wife's blood discharge, or during a clear period in which copulation has occurred. If it does, such a period cannot be counted as part of the waiting period, and it will prolong the period for which a woman has to wait before she can remarry.

blessings be upon him) ordered him to take her back, when he had divorced his wife during her menstruation. There is no dispute about this.

They agreed that the characteristic of the *bāʾin* divorce of being irrevocable is found in a divorce due to the absence of consummation, or due to the number of pronouncements of divorce, or due to the existence of a counter-value for *khulʿ*, despite the disagreement whether *khulʿ* is a divorce or rescission, as will be coming up later. They agreed that the number giving rise to an irrevocable divorce in a repudiation by a freeman is three, when made separately, because of the words of the Exalted, "Divorce must be pronounced twice, and then (a woman) must be retained in honour or released in kindness".[62] They disagreed when it occurs three times through words, but not (thrice) in (three separate) acts. Similarly, the majority agreed that slavery is effective in the reduction of the number, and the number that makes non-revocation obligatory (for those) in bondage is two. They disagreed whether this was to be acknowledged for the bondage of the husband or that of the wife, or for the bondage of either one of them. In this chapter, then, there are three issues.

19.1.1.1. Issue 1

The majority of the provincial jurists maintained that a triple divorce pronounced once has the effect of the third repudiation. The Ẓāhirites and another group maintained that it takes the *ḥukm* of a single pronouncement and the stated number has no effect. The proof for these jurists is the apparent meaning of the words of the Exalted, "Divorce may be pronounced twice (and retracted)... And if he hath divorced her (the third time), then she is not lawful unto him thereafter until she hath wedded another husband",[63] maintaining that one divorced thrice through words is actually divorced once not thrice. They also argued on the basis of what has been recorded by al-Bukhārī and Muslim from Ibn ʿAbbās, who said, "Divorce in the period of the Messenger of Allāh (God's peace and blessings be upon him), Abū Bakr and in (the first) two years of the *khilāfa* of ʿUmar, if pronounced thrice (at once) was counted as one, but ʿUmar gave it effect against them". They also argued on the basis of what is related by Ibn Isḥāq from ʿIkrima from Ibn ʿAbbās, who said, "Rukāna divorced his wife thrice in a single session, and was greatly saddened in his longing for her. The Messenger of Allāh asked him, 'How did you divorce her?' He said, 'I divorced her thrice in a single session.' He (the Prophet) said, 'That is a single divorce, bring her back by revocation' ".

Those who lent support to the majority opinion argued that the tradition of Ibn ʿAbbās that has occurred in the *Saḥīḥayn*[64] has been related from him by

[62] Qurʾān 2 : 229
[63] Qurʾān 2 : 229, 230
[64] The compilations by al-Bukhārī and Muslim.

one of his disciples, Ṭāwūs, while the great majority of his disciples have related from him the binding nature of a divorce pronounced thrice—among them are Saᶜīd ibn Jubayr, Mujāhid, ᶜAṭāʾ, ᶜAmr ibn Dīnār, and several others—and that the tradition of Ibn Isḥāq is imaginary, for Rukāna, in fact, did not divorce his wife thrice.

The reason for the disagreement is whether the *ḥukm* of irrevocability that the *sharᶜ* has assigned to the third pronouncement comes into effect by the subject imposing it upon himself by means of a single pronouncement or whether this is not the case, and that nothing in it is binding unless it is made so by the *sharᶜ*. Thus, those who compared divorce to acts for the proper performance of which the observance of conditions imposed by law is stipulated, as in marriage and sales, said that (self-imposition) is not binding. Those who compared it to consecrations and oaths, in which whatever the subject vows to do becomes binding upon him whatever its nature, made divorce binding in whatever way the subject (*mukallaf*) has deemed it to be binding upon himself. It was as if the majority imposed the strict *ḥukm* about divorce for plugging the means (of exploitation through threat of frequent use), but this view would nullify a lawful exemption whose aim is compassion, I mean, in the words of the Exalted, "[I]t may be that Allāh will afterward bring some new thing to pass".[65]

19.1.1.2. Issue 2

In their disagreement about taking into account bondage for a reduction in the number (of pronouncements) for an irrevocable divorce, there were those who said that only the bondage of males (the husband's) is taken into account. Thus, if the husband is a slave, his irrevocable divorce will take effect on the second pronouncement, irrespective of his wife being a free woman or a slave. This was upheld by Mālik and Al-Shāfiᶜī, and by ᶜUthmān ibn ᶜAffān, Zayd ibn Thābit, and Ibn ᶜAbbās from among the Companions, though there are different narrations from Ibn ᶜAbbās in this, but this is the better-known opinion. Among the jurists were those who said that the bondage taken into account pertains to women. Thus, if the wife is a slave the irrevocable divorce comes into effect on the second pronouncement, irrespective of the husband being a slave or a freeman. Those among the Companions who maintained this opinion are ᶜAlī and Ibn Masᶜūd, and from the jurists of the provinces Abū Ḥanīfa and others. Within the issue is an opinion that deviates from these two opinions: that divorce is to be effective because of the bondage of either one of them. This was upheld by ᶜUthmān al-Battī and other jurists, and it is related from Ibn ᶜUmar.

[65] Qurʾān 65 : 1

The reason for this disagreement is whether bondage, which is effective in this, is that of the female or the male spouse. Those who maintained that effectiveness in this flows from the will of the person who possesses the right of divorce said that the status of the husband is taken into account, while those who maintained that effectiveness depends on the status of the party who faces divorce said that it is a *ḥukm* related to the woman being divorced, for which they held it similar to the (reduced) waiting period. They agreed (as we know) that the (duration of the) waiting period of women is dependent upon their status, that is, its reduction is dependent upon their bondage. The first party argued on the basis of the tradition related from the Prophet (God's peace and blessings be upon him) through Ibn ʿAbbās, in which he said, "Divorce depends on men and the waiting period (*ʿidda*) upon women". This tradition, however, has not been recorded in the ṣaḥīḥ compilations. Those who took into account the bondage of either one of the spouses considered it without qualification to be slavery of either party irrespective of the gender of the slave.

19.1.1.3. Issue 3

About considering slavery as a factor in the reduction of the number of pronouncements of divorce, a group of jurists have related that it is based upon consensus (*ʿijmā*). Abū Muḥammad ibn Ḥazm and a group of Ẓāhirite jurists, however, oppose it, maintaining that freeman and slave are equal in this.

The reason for their disagreement is the conflict of the apparent meaning with the result of the analogy. The majority adopted this position for the reduction of the number of divorces of the slave, male and female, on the analogy of mitigation of their *ḥudud*, coming to a consensus that bondage is effective in the mitigation of the *ḥadd*. The principle for the Ẓāhirites is that the *ḥukm* of the slave in all religious duties is the same as the *ḥukm* of the freeman, unless excluded by an evidence, and "evidence" in their opinion has to be the literal or apparent meaning of the Qurʾān or *sunna*, and because there is no transmitted evidence in this case, it follows that the slave remains covered by the principle.

It appears that the analogy of divorce upon *ḥadd* is off the mark, as the goal of reduction of *ḥadd* is an exemption for the slave in view of his deficient legal capacity, and an abomination committed by him is not considered as contemptible as that of a freeman. The reduction in the number of pronouncements amounts to an exacerbation (as against an exemption), for the imposition of a prohibition against a human through two pronouncements has greater severity than its imposition by three, it being likely that the action is regretted. The *sharīʿa* has adopted a middle course in this: if revocation could be practised persistently against the wife it would become a source of distress and misery for the woman, and if a single pronouncement should lead to an irrevocable separation it would be a cause of hardship and remorse for the husband, which would be intolerable for him. Allāh has reconciled, by means of this *sharīʿa*, the mutual interests of the parties. It is for this reason that we adopt the view that those who make three divorces binding through a single declaration, Allāh knows best, negate the wisdom behind this legal principle.

19.1.2. Chapter 2: The Distinction between *Sunna* and *Bidʿa* Forms of Divorce

The jurists agreed that the person divorcing his wife, with whom he has consummated the marriage, through *ṭalāq al-sunna* is one who divorces her through a single pronouncement during a period of her purity (from menstruation) in which he has not had intercourse with her. The person divorcing in a period of menstruation or in a period of purity during which he has had intercourse with her is not abiding by the *sunna* form (of divorce). They agreed unanimously about this, because of the established tradition of Ibn ʿUmar "that he divorced his wife during her menstruation in the lifetime of the Messenger of Allāh (God's peace and blessings be upon him). He (the Prophet) sent him a message saying, 'Command him to restore her status until such time she is in the period of purity, and thereafter menstruates and then reaches the next period of purity. If then you like hold on to her or if you like divorce her before you have had intercourse with her. This is the (beginning of the) time-frame (*ʿidda*) in which Allāh has permitted you to divorce women' ".

They disagreed in this topic about three points. The first point is whether it is a condition that he should not follow up with another pronouncement of divorce during the *ʿidda*. Second, whether one divorcing thrice, that is, by using the word "three" (in a single session) is divorcing according to *sunna*. Third is the *ḥukm* of the person who divorces during menstruation.

19.1.2.1. Point 1

Mālik and Abū Ḥanīfa, and those who followed them, differed on this. Mālik said that it is a condition for this form that he should not follow up with another pronouncement of repudiation during the (entire) period of waiting. Abū Ḥanīfa said that if he makes a single repudiation during each period of purity, he is acting according to the *sunna* (form). The reason for the disagreement is whether it is a condition for this form of divorce that it should be made in a state of marriage after revocation. Those who maintained that it is a condition said that he should not follow up with another pronouncement (during the *ʿidda*). Those who said that it is not a condition allowed the issuance of a second pronouncement. There is no disagreement among them that the second pronouncement (if made during ʿ*idda*) does take effect.

19.1.2.2. Point 2

Mālik maintained that the person repudiating thrice through a single pronouncement is not repudiating according to *sunna*. Al-Shāfiʿī held that he is repudiating according to *sunna*. The reason for the disagreement is the conflict of the acknowledgement by the Prophet (God's peace and blessings be upon him) of a person repudiating, before him, thrice through a single pronouncement, with the meaning of the Book about the *ḥukm* of the third repudiation. The tradition relied upon by al-Shāfiʿī establishes that al-ʿAjlānī divorced his wife thrice in the presence of the Messenger of Allāh (God's peace and blessings be upon him) on the conclusion of imprecation (*liʿān*). He said that had it been an innovation (*bidʿa*) why would the Messenger of Allāh (God's peace and blessings be upon him) have confirmed it (tacitly). When Mālik saw that the person repudiating thrice is negating the exemption that Allāh has granted in terms of number, he said that it is not according to *sunna*. His disciples raised an objection about the tradition that, according to him, a separation has been caused between the imprecators through the imprecation itself, and the subsequent repudiation is in vain; it cannot be described either as *sunna* or as *bidʿa*. Mālik's opinion here is more convincing than that of al-Shāfiʿī, Allāh knows best.

19.1.2.3. Point 3

The jurists disagreed on a number of points about the case of the person who repudiates during the menstrual period. The majority held that his repudiation takes effect, while another group said that it is not to be implemented or reckoned. Those who maintained that it is implemented said that he is to be asked to take her back, but then they became divided into two groups. One of these groups held the view that this is obligatory and he is to be forced to do so. It was upheld by Mālik and his disciples. The other group said that it is recommended to him to do so, but he is not to be forced. This was upheld by al-Shāfiʿī, Abū Ḥanīfa, al-Thawrī and Aḥmad.

Those who made retraction obligatory differed about the time-period in which such compulsion is to take place. Mālik and most of his disciples, Ibn al-Qāsim and others, said that he is to be forced as long as her period of waiting is not over. Ashhab maintained that he is to be forced only up to the time of the first menstruation. Those who held that he is to be ordered to take her back differed about the time when he may do so, if he wishes to divorce her after he has taken her back. One group stipulated, as a condition for the restoration of her status, that he has to retain her till she enters the period of purity after the menstruation, menstruates thereafter and enters a period of purity another time. It is then that he may divorce her, if he likes, or retain her. This was the opinion of Mālik, al-Shāfiʿī, and a group of other jurists. Another group said that he takes her back, and when she becomes pure after the first period of menstruation in which he divorced her, he may hold on to her if he likes or divorce her. This was Abū Ḥanīfa's opinion and that of the Kūfīs.

All those who stipulated for *ṭalāq al-sunna* that he divorce her in a period of purity during which he has not cohabited with her, did not require him to take her back if he had divorced her in a period of purity in which he had cohabited with her. In summary, there are four issues. First, whether this divorce is valid. Second, if it is so, is he to be forced to take her back or is merely required to do so? Third, when does the divorce come into effect after such compulsion or recommendation? Fourth, when is he to be compelled?

19.1.2.4. Issue 1

The majority held that if the divorce occurs during the period of menstruation, it is to be deemed a legitimate divorce, because of the words of the Prophet (God's peace and blessings be upon him) in the tradition of Ibn ʿUmar, "Order him to take her back". They maintained that *rajʿa* (return) does not take place, except after divorce. It is related from al-Shāfiʿī from Muslim ibn Khālid from Ibn Jurayj that they sent someone to inquire from Nāfiʿ whether he had taken the (report about the) repudiation of Ibn ʿUmar, which took place during the period of the Prophet (God's peace and blessings be upon him), into account. He replied in the affirmative. It is also reported that Ibn ʿUmar used to issue verdicts in accordance with it.

Those who did not consider such a divorce to have taken legal effect, relied upon the general implication of the words of the Prophet (God's peace and blessings be upon him), "Every act and deed not based upon our practice is rejected". They said that its rejection by the Messenger of Allāh (God's peace and blessings be upon him) implies its non-implementation and invalidity.

The reason, however, for the disagreement here is whether the conditions stipulated by the *sharʿ* for *ṭalāq al-sunna* are conditions of validity and implementation or those of completion and perfection. Those who maintained that they are conditions of implementation said that the divorce does not take legal effect when it does not conform with this description. Those who held that they are conditions of completion and perfection said that it does take effect, but it is recommended that it take its full, perfect form. Therefore, those who upheld the occurrence of divorce, and then compelled him to retract, have contradicted themselves. Ponder over this.

19.1.2.5. Issue 2

The issue is whether he is to be compelled to take her back. Those who went by the accepted opinion, which is the obligation of what has been determined by the majority, said that he is to be compelled. Those who acknowledged the reason that we have stated, as to the validity of divorce, said that the requirement is for a recommendation.

19.1.2.6. Issue 3

The issue is when does the divorce take legal effect after he is compelled? Those who said that he is to hold on to her till she enters the period of purity, menstruates, and then enters purity, decided this because it is stated in the tradition of Ibn ᶜUmar quoted above. They said that the reason for this is that the act of taking her back should become valid by his cohabiting with her in the period of purity that follows menstruation. If he divorces her in the period immediately following menstruation, it would not lead to a waiting period from a second repudiation, and he would be like one who has repudiated prior to consummation.

They said, generally, that a condition of *rajᶜa* is the existence of a time-period in which cohabitation is proper. On the basis of this reasoning, the condition for *ṭalāq al-sunna* is that he should divorce her in a period of purity when he has not divorced her (already) in a period of menstruation that precedes it. This is one of the conditions stipulated by Mālik for *ṭalāq al-sunna* as recorded by ᶜAbd al-Wahhāb. Those who did not stipulate this decided according to what is related by Yūnus ibn Jubayr, Saᶜīd ibn Jubayr, Ibn Sīrīn and those who followed them, from Ibn ᶜUmar. In this version he said that he is to take her back, and when she is pure, he may divorce her if he likes. The reasoning in this is that he was ordered to take her back as a penalty, as he had divorced in a period of time in which divorce is considered reprehensible. When this time-period is over, the divorce will take effect without disapproval. The reason for their disagreement is the conflict of traditions laid down on this issue, and also the conflict of the meaning of the underlying causes.

19.1.2.7. Issue 4

When is he compelled (to take her back)? Mālik held that he is to be compelled to take her back throughout the waiting period, as it is a period in which he has a right to take her back. As for Ashhab, he decided this on the basis of the apparent meaning of the tradition, for it says, "Order him to take her back till she is pure", and this indicates that she is to be accepted back in that period of menstruation. In addition, he said that he was ordered to take her back so that the waiting period is not prolonged for her, because when a divorce occurs in the period of menstruation it (the period of menstruation) is not taken into account, by consensus (*ijmāʿ*). If we uphold that he can take her back in a period other than menstruation it would be a longer waiting period for her. On the basis of this reasoning, it is necessary that the occurrence of a divorce be permitted in the period of purity that immediately follows menstruation. The reason for disagreement is the dispute over the underlying cause of the decreed rejection.

19.1.3. **Chapter 3: *Khulʿ* (Redemption)**

The terms *khulʿ*, *fidya*, *ṣulḥ* and *mubāraʾa* all refer to the same meaning, which is "(a transaction in which) compensation is paid by the wife for obtaining her divorce". The term *khulʿ*, however, in the opinion of the jurists is confined to her paying him all that he spent on her, the term *ṣulḥ* to paying a part of it, *fidya* to paying more than it, and *mubāraʾa* to her writing off a claim that she had against him. The discussion of the principles of this mode of separation is split into four sections. First, the permissibility of its occurrence (legal effectiveness). Second, the conditions for its proper occurrence, that is, its valid occurrence. Third, about its nature, whether it is divorce or rescission. Fourth, about the *aḥkām* related to it.

19.1.3.1. *Section 1: Its Permissibility*

Most of the *fuqahāʾ* uphold its permissibility. Its sources are to be found in the Book and *sunna*. In the Book it is the words of the Exalted, "[I]t is no sin for any of them if the woman ransom herself".[66] The *sunna* is the tradition of Ibn ʿAbbās "that the wife of Thābit ibn Qays came up to the Prophet (God's peace and blessings be upon him) and said, 'O Messenger of Allāh, I do not find anything wrong with him from the religious and moral points of view, but I detest disbelief after entering the fold of Islam.' The Messenger of Allāh (God's peace and blessings be upon him) said, 'Will you return to him his orchard (that he had given to you)'. She said, 'Yes'. The Messenger of Allāh said to (Thābit), 'Accept the orchard and divorce her through a single repudiation' ". It is recorded, in these words, by al-Bukhārī, Abū Dāwūd, al-Nasāʾī, and is a tradition agreed upon for its soundness.

Abū Bakr ibn ʿAbd Allāh al-Mazīnī deviated from the majority opinion and said that it is not permitted to the husband to take anything from his wife. He argued for this on the basis of his understanding that the words of the Exalted, "[I]t is no sin for any of them if the woman ransom herself ",[67] have been

[66] Qurʾān 2 : 229
[67] Qurʾān 2 : 229

abrogated by the words of the Exalted, "And if ye wish to exchange one wife for another and ye have given unto one of them a sum of money (however great), take nothing from it. Would ye take it by way of calumny and open wrong?"[68] The majority, however, maintain that this prohibition applies when it is taken without her consent, but it is permitted with her consent. The reason for disagreement here is whether this meaning of prohibition is to be assigned its general or particular implication.

19.1.3.2. *Section 2: The Conditions for its Permissibility*

Some of the conditions of its permissibility are related to the amount permissible in this transaction, some to the quality of the thing whereby it is permissible, some to the state (of the party) in which it is permitted, and some to the qualifications of the women in whose case it is permitted, or to the qualifications of their guardians when they do not have a say in it themselves. In this section, therefore, there are four issues.

19.1.3.2.1. Issue 1

About the amount with which it is permitted to her to secure redemption, Mālik, al-Shāfiʿī and a group of jurists said that it is permitted to a woman to secure redemption with more than what has come to her from the husband, by way of dower, when she is the cause of discord, or with an equivalent amount, or less. Other jurists held that he [the husband] does not have a right to take more than what he has given her (as dower), according to the apparent meaning of Thābit's tradition. So those who compared this compensation to that in all other transactions held that the amount is dependent upon mutual consent, but those who went by the literal meaning of the tradition did not permit excess, and it was as if they considered it to be the acquisition of wealth without lawful justification.

19.1.3.2.2. Issue 2

Both al-Shāfiʿī and Abū Ḥanīfa stipulate about the description of compensation that it should be determined through description and be known to exist. Mālik permits it even when it is uncertain as to existence, amount, and availability, like a runaway slave, lost camel, and fruit that has not yet begun to ripen, or a slave whose description is not provided. The permissibility of *gharar* is related from Abū Ḥanīfa, but he prohibited it in the case of non-availability.

The reason for disagreement is the vacillation of compensation here between being a compensation in sales and that in things donated or bequeathed. Those who held it similar to compensation in sales stipulated for it what they

[68] Qurʾān 4 : 20

stipulate for sales and for the consideration in sales, but those who held it similar to donated things did not stipulate such conditions.

They disagreed when *khulʿ* takes place on the basis of things that are not permissible, like *khamr*, and *khinzīr*, whether a compensation (in lieu) is obligatory for her, although they had agreed that divorce would occur (in any case). Mālik said that she does not have a right to any compensation, which was also Abū Ḥanīfa's opinion, but al-Shāfiʿī said that she has a right to claim an amount equivalent to *mahr al-mithl.*

19.1.3.2.3. Issue 3

Regarding the conditions in which redemption is permissible, the majority held that it is permitted with the mutual consent of the parties, unless consent to pay him is obtained by fear of injury to her. The basis for this are the words of the Exalted, "O ye who believe! It is not lawful for you forcibly to inherit the women (of your deceased kinsmen), nor (that) ye should constrain them that ye may take away a part of that which ye have given them, unless they be guilty of flagrant lewdness",[69] and His words, "And if ye fear that they may not be able to keep the limits of Allāh, in that case it is no sin for either of them if the woman ransom herself. These are the limits (imposed by) Allāh".[70]

Abū Qalāba and al-Ḥasan al-Baṣrī deviated from this (opinion), with both maintaining that it is not permitted to a man to contract redemption with his wife, unless he has seen her committing fornication. They interpreted the term lewdness (*fāḥisha*) in the verse as fornication. Dāwūd said that it is not permitted, except in the case of fear that they will not be able to maintain the limits imposed by Allāh, according to the apparent meaning of the verse. Al-Nuʿmān deviated too, saying that redemption is permitted even with a threatened injury. Yet, the juristic reasoning is that *fidāʾ* (ransom) grants to a woman something equivalent to what is possessed by the man; namely, (the right to) divorce. A man possesses repudiation when he pressurizes a woman, while a woman possesses *khulʿ* when she wants to pressurize a man (her husband).

Five opinions are, thus, derived for *khulʿ*. First, that it is not permitted at all. Second, it is permitted in all circumstances, that is, even under duress. Third, it is not permitted unless fornication is witnessed. Fourth, it is permitted when there is fear that the limits imposed by Allāh will not be maintained. Fifth, that it is permitted in all circumstances, except under duress, which is the most widely accepted (*mashhūr*) opinion.

[69] Qurʾān 4 : 19
[70] Qurʾān 2 : 229

19.1.3.2.4. Issue 4

With respect to the person to whom *khulᶜ* is permitted, there is no dispute that a woman possessing discretion (a *rashīda*) has a right to transact redemption herself, while a slave-woman does not enter into a transaction of *khulᶜ* without the consent of her master; similarly, a prodigal woman seeks the consent of her guardian, according to those who uphold interdiction. Mālik said that a father transacts redemption on account of his minor daughter, just as he gives her away in marriage. Similarly in the case of his minor son, for according to him, it is he who repudiates on his account. There is a disagreement about the minor son. Al-Shāfiᶜī and Abū Ḥanīfa said that this is not permitted, as he (the father) does not divorce on his behalf, Allāh knows best.

The *khulᶜ* of a sick woman is permitted according to Mālik, if it involves an amount equivalent to his inheritance from her. Ibn Nāfiᶜ has related from Mālik that her *khulᶜ* is permitted to the extent of a complete third (of her wealth). Al-Shāfiᶜī said that if she transacts redemption to the extent of her *mahr al-mithl* it is permitted, but will be deducted from the liquid cash (*rāʾs al-māl*), but if it exceeds this it will be from a third of the estate. About the *muhmala* (that is, one without a guardian), who has no executor or father, Ibn al-Qāsim said that her *khulᶜ* is permitted if it conforms with an amount of *khulᶜ* deemed reasonable for her status. The majority maintain that *khulᶜ* transacted by a woman possessing all rights over herself is valid. Al-Ḥasan and Ibn Sīrīn deviated saying that *khulᶜ* is not permitted except by the permission of the sultan (that is, through a court).

19.1.3.3. *Section 3: The Legal Category of Redemption*

The majority of the jurists agreed that *khulᶜ* amounts to a divorce (repudiation), which was Mālik's opinion. Abū Ḥanīfa deemed divorce and rescission equivalent. Al-Shāfiᶜī said that it is rescission, which was also upheld by Aḥmad, Dāwūd and by Ibn ᶜAbbās from among the Companions. It is related from al-Shāfiᶜī that it is an indirect declaration of intent; if he intends thereby a divorce it amounts to a divorce, otherwise it is a rescission. It is, however, related from him in a later opinion that it amounts to divorce. The reason for making the distinction is whether the number of repudiations in it is taken into account.

The majority of those who consider it to be a divorce deem it irrevocable, for had the husband possessed the right to take her back in the waiting period, the provision of ransom would have been futile. Abū Thawr said that as long as it is not transacted with the use of the word "divorce", the husband has no right to claim her back, but if it has been transacted by the use of the word "divorce" he has this right.

Those who considered it to be a divorce argued that rescission usually arises from causes of separation that do not depend upon the husband's discretion, but this relates to his discretion and is, therefore, not a rescission. Those who did not consider it to be divorce argued that Allāh, the Glorious and Exalted, has laid down in His Book that "Divorce must be pronounced twice, and then (a woman) must be retained in honor or released in kindness".[71] He then mentioned ransom, and said, "And if he hath divorced her (a third time), then she is not lawful unto him thereafter until she hath wedded another husband".[72] Thus, if redemption had been divorce, the (last mentioned) divorce, which makes his wife unlawful for him, except after marrying another husband, would have amounted to a fourth divorce. According to these jurists, rescission takes place with consent, on the analogy of rescission in sales, that is, *iqāla*. In the opinion of their opponents the verse includes the *ḥukm* of ransom, as a factor that is linked to all kinds of divorces, not that it is something other than divorce.

The reason for disagreement is whether the association of compensation with this kind of separation removes it from the category of separation caused by divorce to a category of separation caused by rescission.

19.1.3.4. *Section 4: The* Aḥkām *Associated with Redemption*

A large number of cases are linked with redemption, but we shall mention out of these the most prominent. Among these is the issue whether repudiation is to be pronounced for the woman who has transacted *khulʿ*? Mālik said that redemption is not to be followed up with repudiation, unless it is a statement immediately following the agreement (of *khulʿ*). Al-Shāfiʿī held that it is not to be made even if immediate. Abū Ḥanīfa said that the pronouncement is to be made, and he did not distinguish between immediate or delayed statements.

The reason for disagreement is that the waiting period, according to the first opinion, forms part of the *aḥkām* of divorce, while it is a part of the *aḥkām* of marriage, in Abū Ḥanīfa's opinion, because of which it is not permitted to marry the divorced woman's sister (during the waiting period). Those who considered it as one of the *aḥkām* of marriage ruled for the pronouncement of divorce, while those who did not consider it a *ḥukm* of marriage did not require pronouncement.

One of the issues relates to the consensus of the jurists that the husband does not have the right to take back the woman granted redemption during her waiting period, except what is related from Saʿīd ibn al-Musayyib and Ibn Shihāb, who said that if he returns what he has taken from her, it is testimony of his taking her back. The distinction lies in what we related from Abū Thawr about using the words of repudiation. Another issue is the agreement of the

[71] Qurʾān 2 : 229
[72] Qurʾān 2 : 230

majority that he has a right to marry her during her waiting period with her consent, but a group of the later jurists said that neither he nor anyone else can marry her during the waiting period. The reason for disagreement is whether the prohibition of marrying during the waiting period is a kind of ritual non-rational obedience or whether it has an underlying (rational) cause. They disagreed about the waiting period of a woman granted *khulʿ*, and this will be coming up shortly.

They disagree when the husband and wife have a dispute about the amount of compensation upon which *khulʿ* has been transacted. Mālik said that his statement is to be accepted, if there is no supporting testimony. Al-Shāfiʿī said that they take oaths and then she is obliged to pay mahral-mithl. Al-Shāfiʿī held their dispute to be similar to that of the parties to a sale, while Mālik said that she is the defendant and he is the plaintiff.

The issues in this chapter are many, but further details do not suit our purpose.

19.1.4. **Chapter 4: The Distinction between Divorce and Rescission**

The views of Mālik (God bless him) differed, into two opinions, about the distinction between rescission that is not taken into account in the three repudiations and divorce that is taken into account in the three repudiations. First, if the marriage is disputed in law, and it is well known that in Mālik's opinion it would not be permissible, the separation taking place in it amounts to a divorce. In the cases, for example, of a woman contracting her marriage herself or of marriage within the prohibited degree, the separation, according to this (first) narration, amounts to a divorce and not a rescission. In the second opinion the consideration is of the cause giving rise to separation. If the cause does not refer to the willingness of the spouses, that is, even if they desire to maintain the marriage it cannot be valid, then, it is a case of rescission, for example, marriage prohibited due to fosterage, or a marriage during an *ʿidda*. When it is possible for the spouses to maintain the marriage, like the case of rejection due to defects, it amounts to a divorce.

19.1.5. **Chapter 5: *Takhyīr* and *Tamlīk***

Procedures that are counted among the categories of divorce, and which are considered to have specific *aḥkām*, are *takhyīr* (granting a choice) and *tamlīk* (granting possession of the right). According to Mālik there is a difference between *tamlīk* and *takhyīr* (in this context). *Tamlīk*, in his view, is the granting of a right to a woman to pronounce (her own) divorce. This may be interpreted as one repudiation or more, thus, the man is entitled to deny her the right to more than one repudiation. *Khiyār* is different from this, as far as it implies the execution of divorce leading to the termination of the nuptial tie, unless it is a restricted form of *takhyīr*, like his saying to her: "choose for yourself, a single repudiation, or two repudiations". In the case of unrestricted choice, according to Mālik, she only has the choice to choose her husband or opt for irrevocable separation from him through the pronouncement of three repudiations, but she is not entitled to choose a single repudiation.

The right under *tamlīk*, according to him (Mālik) in one narration, is not annulled even if it is not exercised by the authorized woman for a long period of time, or till they part from the session. According to a second narration from him, the right under *tamlīk* stays with her till she revokes it or exercises it through repudiation. The difference, in Mālik's view, between *tamlīk* and granting of a power of attorney (*tawkīl*) to her to exercise repudiation is that in an agency he can revoke the power of attorney before she exercises such power, but in *tamlīk* he does not have that right. Al-Shāfiʿī said that statements like, "choose yourself" or "your affair is in your hands" mean the same thing, but this does not amount to granting the right of repudiation, unless he intends it to be so, and whatever he intends takes effect: if he intends it to be a single repudiation it is so and if he intends three repudiations, then, that will be the case. He is entitled, according to al-Shāfiʿī, to deny her the right of repudiation itself, or restrict her with respect to the number (of repudiations) in both *takhyīr* and *tamlīk*.

According to him (al-Shāfiʿī), if she divorces herself it amounts to a revocable divorce, which is also the case according to Mālik in *tamlīk*. Abū Ḥanīfa and his disciples said that granting a choice does not amount to divorce, but if she divorces herself even through a single repudiation in *tamlīk*, it amounts to an irrevocable divorce. Al-Thawrī said that *khiyār* and *tamlīk* are the same thing and there is no difference between them.

It is said that the acceptable statement is hers about the number of repudiations in *tamlīk* and the husband cannot rebut her statement. This opinion is related from ʿAlī and Ibn al-Musayyib, and it was also adopted by al-Zuhrī and ʿAṭāʾ. It is said that the woman, in the case of *tamlīk* is not entitled to divorce herself, except through a single repudiation. This is related from Ibn ʿAbbās and ʿUmar, may Allāh be pleased with them both. It is reported that a man came to Ibn Masʿūd and said, "There was between me and my wife, the kind of relationship that exists between people (normally). She said (to me), 'Had the power that you possess over me, been in my hands, you would have known how I would treat you.' I said to her, 'In that case, the authority that I possess over you is now in your hands.' She said, 'Then you are divorced thrice' ". Ibn Masʿūd replied, "I consider this to be a single repudiation, and you have a right over her as long as she is in her *ʿidda*; I will, however, consult the *Amīr al-Muʾminīn*, ʿUmar". He then met ʿUmar and related the case to him. ʿUmar said, "Allāh has given men what He did. If they desire to place in the hands of women, what Allāh has placed in their authority, then, dust is in their jaws. How did you decide it?" He said, "I held it to be a single repudiation, and that he still has a right over her". ʿUmar said, "I hold it to be the same, and if you had decided it differently I would have considered you to be wrong".

It is said that *tamlīk* has no legal force, as it is not permitted that the authority placed in the hands of a man be passed on to the authority of a woman by the act of the assigner. Similarly in the case of *takhyīr*, which is the opinion of Abū Muḥammad ibn Ḥazm. Mālik's opinion about the woman authorized under *tamlīk* is that she has a choice between divorce and holding fast to the nuptial tie as long as she is in the session (of assignment), which is also the opinion of al-Shāfiʿī, Abū Ḥanīfa, al-Awzāʿī, and a group of other jurists of the provinces. According to al-Shāfiʿī, *tamlīk* is like agency *wakāla*, when he intends divorce, and he has the right to retract it whenever he likes, as long as divorce has not come into effect.

The majority decided in favour of *tamlīk* and *takhyīr* and deemed it to be a provision for women, because of what is established about the *takhyīr* of the Messenger of Allāh (God's peace and blessings be upon him) in the case of his wives. ʿĀʾisha said that the Messenger of Allāh (God's peace and blessings be upon him) granted us a choice, and we chose him so it did not amount to a divorce". The Ẓāhirites, however, maintain that the meaning of this would be that if they had opted for themselves, the Messenger of Allāh (God's peace and blessings be upon him) would have divorced them, not that they could divorce themselves by the very option of divorce.

The majority also maintained the validity of *takhyīr* and *tamlīk*, and permitted the granting of these rights to women as the implication of customary usage is that one who transfers the ownership of a right to another, to the effect that he may exercise it or he may not, has granted that person a choice. Mālik, however, is of the opinion that his saying, "choose me or choose yourself", would amount, in legal usage, to a choice for irrevocable repudiation within the meaning of the Messenger of Allāh's option for his wives, and the meaning implied by this option is of irrevocability.

Mālik was of the view, in the case of *tamlīk*, that the husband's statement, to the extent that he did not intend divorce thereby, is not to be accepted (in case of dispute) when he makes such a claim, for it is an authorization clear in its meaning about placing of the right of divorce in her hands. Al-Shāfiʿī, because the words used are not explicit for him, attached weight to intention.

So the basis for the dispute is whether weight should be attached to the apparent meaning of the text or to intention. He did the same in *takhyīr*.

They agreed that he has the right to deny her the (maximum) number (of repudiations), that is, through the implication of the word *tamlīk*, as it does not carry an additional meaning beyond the literal. Mālik and al-Shāfiʿī held that if she divorced herself through his assignment of authority to her, with a single repudiation, it would be a revocable divorce, as divorce in legal usage is *ṭalāq al-sunna*. Abū Ḥanīfa held that it is irrevocable, for if it is revocable it is of no use in view of what she expects from it and also in view of what he intends thereby.

Those who maintained that she has the right to divorce herself thrice through *tamlīk*, and that the husband does not have the right to deny her this, because the meaning of *tamlīk*, according to them, considers all the authority possessed by the man to have passed on to the woman, said that she has a choice in the number of repudiations she pronounces. Those who deemed *tamlīk* to be a single repudiation or a choice (restricted to it), held that it is the minimum (number) to which the term can be applied, as a precaution for the sake of men, because the underlying reason for granting the authority of divorce to men is the weaker rationality of women, their being normally overpowered by emotions, and their inclination to disturb normal life.

The majority of the jurists maintained that if the woman chooses her husband, it (her choice) cannot revert to divorce, because of ʿĀʾisha's preceding tradition. It is, however, related from al-Ḥasan al-Baṣrī that if she chooses her husband it amounts to a single repudiation, but if she chooses herself it amounts to a triple repudiation.

In summation of the issue, we find that there is disagreement on three points. First, that divorce does not result from either category (*tamlīk* or *takhyīr*). Second, that both categories cause separation (divorce) between the two (husband and wife). Third, that there is a distinction between *takhyīr* and *tamlīk* with respect to the right acquired by the woman, that is, through *takhyīr* she possesses the right to an irrevocable divorce, and through *tamlīk* what is less than that. When we concede that it is an irrevocable divorce, it is said that she possesses a single repudiation, and it is said that she possesses a triple repudiation; when it is conceded that she possesses a single repudiation, it is said that it leads to a revocable divorce, and it is said to an irrevocable divorce.

The words that a woman pronounces in *takhyīr* and *tamlīk* refer to the *ḥukm* of words with which divorce is pronounced in so far as they are explicit, indirect, or equivocal. The details will come up in the discussion of words used for divorce.

19.2. **Part 2: Words Used for Divorce**

In this part there are three chapters. The first chapter is about the words of divorce and their conditions. The second chapter is about the details of the person whose divorce is valid. The third chapter is about the details of women against whom a divorce is effective and those against whom it is not.

19.2.1. **Chapter 1: Words Used for Divorce and their Conditions**

There are two sections in this chapter. First, the kinds of words used for an unrestricted divorce. Second, the kind of words used for a contingent divorce.

19.2.1.1. *Section 1: Words Used for an Unrestricted Divorce*

The Muslim jurists agreed that divorce becomes effective when it is accompanied by an intention and the use of unambiguous words. They disagreed whether it can become effective with intention accompanied by words that are not manifest, or with intention without words, or with words without an intention. Those who stipulated the existence of an intention in it as well as unequivocal words did so observing the letter of the law, similarly those who substituted the words with apparent meanings in place of manifest meanings. Those who held it similar to a declaration of a vow, or to a an oath, deemed the divorce effective with intention alone, while those who held suspicion to be operative in this case deemed it effective through words only.

The majority agreed that the words of an unrestricted divorce are of two types: manifest, and indirect. They disagreed about the distinction between manifest and indirect words, about their effect, and about the duties arising from such use. We have, however, aimed at the discussion of the widely known issues, and of those that resemble general principles.

Mālik and his disciples said that the manifest term is the word *ṭalāq* alone, and whatever is besides this is indirect. The latter, according to Mālik, is of two types: obvious and equivocal; which is also Abū Ḥanīfa's opinion. Al-Shāfiʿī said that the manifest words for divorce are three: divorce, separation, and release; and they are mentioned in the Qurʾān. Some of the Ẓāhirite jurists (also) said that divorce cannot occur, except by the use of these three words. This, then, is their dispute about words that are manifest in conveying the meaning of divorce and those that are not.

They agreed that the word *ṭalāq* (divorce) is manifest in meaning, as the implication for this meaning has been assigned to it by the *sharʿ*, and it, therefore, forms a foundation for this issue. The terms *firāq* and *sarāḥ*, on the other hand, vacillate between being words employed by the *sharʿ*, that is, they indicate the meaning of divorce through legal usage, and between being words retaining their literal meaning. If they are used in this meaning, that is, in the sense of divorce they are metaphorical as that is the meaning of being indirect, which means a word that is metaphorical in its application.

Those who held that divorce is not effective, except by the use of these three words, did so as the *sharᶜ* employed only these three words and their use is a kind of a predetermined ritual in which the use of words is a condition (and is not subject to rationalization). Thus, it is obligatory that such use be confined to the words laid down by the *sharᶜ*. In their disagreement about the *aḥkām* of manifest words for divorce, there are two widely known issues. Mālik, al-Shāfiᶜī, and Abū Ḥanīfa agreed about the first issue, but they disagreed about the second.

19.2.1.1.1. Issue 1

Mālik, al-Shāfiᶜī, and Abū Ḥanīfa said that if the repudiator uses the word *talāq*, saying to his wife, "You are divorced", he is not allowed to say that he did not intend divorce thereby. Similar is the case in the use of the words *firāq* and *sarāḥ*, according to al-Shāfiᶜī. The Mālikites, however, made an exemption saying that if there is circumstantial evidence related to the situation or to the woman indicating the truth of his claim (that he did not intend divorce), for example, when she asks him to release her from her shackles, and he says to her: "you are free" (the context showing that it is freedom from a physical tie).

The juristic reasoning underlying the issue, according to al-Shāfiᶜī and Abū Ḥanīfa, is that divorce is not dependent upon intention, but according to Mālik, in the well-known narration from him, it is dependent upon intention. In this case he did not assign intention because of doubtful circumstances. His verdict related to doubt is based upon the principle of prevention of the means (*sadd al-dharīᶜa*), in which he was opposed by al-Shāfiᶜī and Abū Ḥanīfa. Thus, it is obligatory upon those who do stipulate intention and do not issue a verdict in case of doubt that they should accept the claim of the repudiator.

19.2.1.1.2. Issue 2

This issue relates to their disagreement about the person who says to his wife, "you are divorced", and claims that he intended thereby more than one divorce, either two or three. Mālik said that it will be what he intended and that is what is binding upon him. This was also al-Shāfiᶜī's opinion, unless the man adds the words: "*ṭalqa wāḥida*" (a single divorce). The latter opinion is preferred by his disciples. Abū Ḥanīfa said that the use of the word *ṭalāq* does not convey more than one repudiation as words applied to single categories do not imply (multiple) numbers, either in their indirect or their manifest application.

The reason for their disagreement is whether divorce becomes effective with intention without the use of words, or with intention accompanied by equivocal words. Those who upheld (the effectiveness) of intention deemed it to be three (repudiations) if he pretends that he meant three; similarly, those who upheld (the effectiveness of) intention accompanied by equivocal words, and maintained that the word *ṭalāq* implies (more than one) number. Those who held that it does not denote numbers, and that the stipulation of the use of words in divorce is a must, said that multiple numbers are not implied even if the repudiator intended them to be so.

This issue over which they disagreed is one that relates to the conditions for the words of divorce, that is, the stipulation of intention along with words, or the stipulation of each of them separately. The well-known opinion from Mālik is that divorce does not become effective except by words used with intention. This was also Abū Ḥanīfa's opinion, however, it is related from him that it becomes effective with words without intention. In al-Shāfiʿī's view manifest words of divorce are not dependent upon intention.

Those who held intention to be sufficient argued on the basis of the words of the Prophet (God's peace and blessings be upon him), "Acts are dependent on intentions". Those who did not take intention into account along with words argued on the basis of the words of the Prophet, "Liability of my *umma* has been removed for mistake, forgetfulness, and inner resolve", as intention is less than inner resolve. They said that the stipulation of intention in the former tradition does not make it conclusive that intention alone is sufficient.

Mālik's school disagreed whether the pronouncement of the words of divorce imply an irrevocable divorce for a woman with whom marriage has been consummated, when that is the intention of the repudiator and there is no compensation in the case. It was said that it is counted as irrevocable if intended, and it was said that it is not. This is an issue related to the *aḥkām* of manifest words in divorce.

Some of the words of divorce that are not manifest are obviously indirect, according to Mālik, while others are probably so. Mālik's view is that if the repudiator, after use of obviously indirect expressions, claims that he did not intend divorce, his statement is not to be accepted, unless there is circumstantial evidence to indicate this, as is his opinion about the use of manifest words. Similarly, it is not acceptable in so far as he claims to have repudiated less than thrice in the case of obviously indirect expressions. This is the case of the woman with whom marriage has been consummated, though he maintained this in the case of *khulʿ* also. In the case of the woman whose marriage is not consummated, his statement is accepted in a claim for being less than thrice, when indirect expressions have been used, as the divorce of such a woman is irrevocable. The examples of such words are: you have a free rein, you are otherwise, and you are released and absolved.

Al-Shāfiʿī's opinion about indirect expressions is based upon what the repudiator intends, if he had intended divorce it would amount to a divorce, if he had intended three pronouncements it is so, and if one it is taken to be one; he is to be considered truthful in what he claims. Abū Ḥanīfa's opinion in this case is the same as al-Shāfiʿī's, except that on the basis of his principles, when the repudiator intended one or two pronouncements these will be considered as a single irrevocable repudiation, and if there is circumstantial evidence indicating divorce and the repudiator claims that he did not intend it, his statement is not accepted, that is, unless she was in the process of discussing divorce (with him). Abū Ḥanīfa permits divorce with all indirect expressions when supported by the context, except four: you have a free rein, start your waiting period, you are absolved, and veil your face. These expressions, according to him, are ambivalent and not manifest. In ambivalent expressions of divorce, Mālik takes intention into account, as is the case with al-Shāfiʿī for indirect expressions. The majority of the jurists opposed him in this saying that such words have no legal value, even if the repudiator intended divorce.

Three opinions are, thus, arrived at in obviously indirect expressions. The first opinion is that the repudiator's claim is to be confirmed without qualification. This is al-Shāfiʿī's view. The second opinion is that the repudiator's claim is not to be confirmed at all unless there is supporting circumstantial evidence. This is Mālik's view. The third opinion is that his claim is confirmed, unless he was in the process of negotiating divorce. This is Abū Ḥanīfa's opinion.

Within the school, there is disagreement about issues that vacillate between being manifest or equivocal, and there is a disparity in their force or weakness in indicating irrevocability. Dispute, therefore, arose about these issues and it is based upon the following principles. Mālik decided that the statement of the repudiator, in the case of obviously indirect expressions, is not to be accepted in so far as he claims that he did not intend divorce, as both literal and legal usage bear testimony to the fact that these are the words generally employed by people, and they imply divorce, except when there is circumstantial evidence indicating the contrary. He decided that his statement is not to be accepted when he claims that he did not intend three pronouncements, because the manifest meaning in these expressions is that of irrevocability, and an irrevocable divorce, according to him, does not take place unless it is by way of *khulʿ* or is pronounced thrice, so in the absence of compensation, which means it is not a case of *khulʿ*, it is still counted as thrice. This is the case where marriage stands consummated with the woman. It is to be derived from the opinions in the school that an irrevocable divorce takes place without there being compensation (as in *khulʿ*) or multiple pronouncements; the claim of the repudiator in a single pronouncement is to be accepted and will be deemed irrevocable.

Al-Shāfiʿī's argument is that when consensus has occurred that his statement is to be accepted for a claim of less than three repudiations, when manifest expressions of divorce have been used, it is more appropriate that his claim be accepted in the case of his indirect expression, as the indicative force of the manifest expression is greater than that of an indirect expression. It appears that the Mālikites say that a manifest expression, even though it is manifest for purposes of divorce, it is not so for the number of pronouncements. Al-Shāfiʿī's proof in this is the tradition of Rukāna that has preceded, which is ʿUmar's opinion in a case of "you have a free rein". Al-Shāfiʿī came to the decision that a divorce pronounced through manifest expressions, when the intention is for less than three repudiations, is revocable on the basis of the preceding tradition of Rukāna. Abū Ḥanīfa decided that it is irrevocable as the purpose in it is the severance of the bond; he did not consider it to be three repudiations as that has a meaning beyond irrevocability for him.

The reason for disagreement is whether literal usage is to have precedence over intention, or intention is to have precedence over literal usage. If we give precedence to literal usage, does it imply irrevocability alone or multiple repudiations also? Those who gave precedence to intention did not give a ruling according to literal usage, while those who gave precedence to the obvious literal usage did not have recourse to intention. One of the things in this topic, that is, among the category of issues included in this topic, about which the jurists of the first generation and those of the provinces disagreed, was the use of the term "prohibition"—I mean, when a person says to his wife, "you are prohibited for me". Mālik said that for a woman whose marriage stands consummated it is to be construed as decisive, that is, as three repudiations, and for the one whose marriage is not consummated, it is to be referred to the intention (of the repudiator). This is an analogy based upon his preceding view about obviously indirect expressions. It is also the opinion of Ibn Abī Laylā, Zayd ibn Thābit and ʿAlī, from among the Companions, and has been upheld by his disciples, except for Ibn al-Mājishūn, who said that intention is not to be considered for a woman whose marriage has not consummated and is to be taken as three repudiations. This is one of the views on the issue.

The second opinion is that if he (the repudiator) intended by it three repudiations, it is to be taken as three, and if he intended it as a single repudiation, it is treated as one repudiation, but irrevocable; if he intended it to be an oath, it is considered as such and for which there is expiation (*kaffāra*), but if he did not intend anything thereby, neither divorce nor oath, it has no value and is a lie. This was also al-Thawrī's opinion. The third opinion also relates it to intention. If he intended a single repudiation it is taken as one, if three repudiations they are considered as three, but if he did not intend anything thereby it is taken as an oath for which he offers expiation. This was al-Awzāʿī's opinion. The fourth opinion is that intention is to be relied upon for two things: the intention to divorce and the number of repudiations. It will be as he has intended. If he intended one repudiation, it will treated as one revocable repudiation, but if he intended her prohibition without divorce he has to pay expiation for breaking an oath. This is al-Shāfiʿī's opinion. The fifth opinion also considers it to be an intention of two things: divorce and number of repudiations. If he intended one repudiation, it is considered as such, but as irrevocable. If he did not intend divorce, it is considered as an oath and he is financially liable, and if he intended it to be a lie, it has no legal value. This was Abū Ḥanīfa's opinion and that of his disciples. The sixth opinion is that it is an oath and he is liable for the usual expiation fixed for an oath, but some of those jurists who upheld this opinion said that there is enhanced expiation for the oath. This is the opinion of ʿUmar, Ibn Masʿūd, Ibn ʿAbbās and a group of the *Tābiʿūn*. Ibn ʿAbbās, when he was asked about it, said, "In the Messenger of Allāh (God's peace and blessings be upon him), you have an excellent example". It is recorded by al-Bukhārī and Muslim. He supported this with the words of the Exalted, "O Prophet! Why bannest thou that which Allāh hath made lawful for thee, seeking to please thy wives? And Allāh is Forgiving, Merciful".[73] The seventh opinion is that prohibiting a woman is just like the prohibition of water (in imposing prohibition of what Allāh has made permissible), there is no expiation in it nor is there any divorce, because of the words of the Exalted, "O ye who believe! forbid not the good things which Allāh hath made lawful unto you, and transgress not. Lo! Allāh loveth not transgressors".[74] This is the opinion of Masrūq, al-Ajdaʿ, Abū Salama ibn ʿAbd al-Raḥmān, al-Shaʿbī and others. Some of those who did not enhance it imposed in it the liability of *ẓihār*, while others imposed the (the liability of) freeing of a slave. The reason for disagreement is whether it is an oath or an indirect expression, or whether it is not an oath nor an indirect expression.

These are the principles over which disagreement has occurred concerning the words of divorce.

19.2.1.2. *Section 2: Words Used for a Contingent Divorce*

A contingent divorce is of two types: contingent upon a conditional statement and contingent upon an exemption. Contingency based upon a conditional statement may depend either upon the will of the person exercising a choice, or it may be depend on the occurrence of a future happening, or upon the

[73] Qurʾān 66 : 1

[74] Qurʾān 5 : 87

coming into existence of a non-existent thing in the way it is claimed by the person making the divorce contingent and which cannot be known except after its emergence into the world of the senses or by coming into actual existence, or it may depend upon the occurrence of a thing about the possibility of which there can be no prediction.

When divorce is made contingent upon volition, it may either be contingent upon the will of Allāh or upon the will of a mortal. If it is made contingent upon the will of Allāh, either in the form of a condition, like saying "You are divorced if Allāh so wills", or by way of an exemption, like saying, "You are divorced, unless Allāh wills the contrary", then Mālik said that the exemption has no effect upon the repudiation, which comes into effect necessarily. Abū Ḥanīfa and al-Shāfiʿī said that if the repudiator makes an exemption dependent upon the will of Allāh, the divorce will not take effect.

The reason for the disagreement is whether an exemption relates to acts, which occur in the present, in the same way as it relates to acts occurring in the future. This is so as divorce is an act occurring in the present time. Those who maintained that it does not relate to present acts said that an exemption has no effect upon the repudiation nor does the stipulation of volition. Those who maintained that it (the exemption) does relate to present acts said that it has an effect upon the occurrence of the repudiation.

If the repudiator makes divorce dependent upon the will of a person who can be lawfully authorized, and information to the effect reaches her (the wife), then there is no dispute in Mālik's school that the divorce will be dependent upon the will of the person authorized. There is disagreement in the school about linking divorce to the will of a person who is not capable of exercising such will. It is said that divorce will be binding upon him (the husband) and it is said that it will not be binding. The minor and the insane are included in the meaning of such authorization. Those who compared such a divorce to a divorce pronounced in jest, when a divorce pronounced in jest is binding in their view, said that this divorce is legally effective. Those who took into account the existence of the condition said that such a divorce does not take effect as the condition is missing in this case.

When divorce is made contingent upon future acts, such acts are found to be of three types. First, the acts that may or may not happen, like entering a house or the appearance of Zayd. In such a case the coming into effect of the divorce is dependent, without doubt, upon the fulfilment of the condition. In acts that are bound to occur like the rising of the sun in the morning, divorce takes immediate effect in Mālik's view, while it takes effect according to Abū Ḥanīfa and al-Shāfiʿī when the condition is fulfilled. Those who compared it to a condition, the occurrence of which is possible, said that it will not take effect unless the condition comes to pass, while those who compared it to intercourse occurring through a contract of *mutᶜa* during a stipulated period, when it is permitted for that period, said that the divorce comes into effect (immediately). The third type, which are the most common in practice, are those (acts) dependent upon the fulfilment of the condition. In such cases divorce may not take effect, as in the case of delivery of the child or the passing of the menstrual period or that of purity. There are two narrations from Mālik on this. In the first he maintains the occurrence of divorce immediately and in the second upon the fulfillment of the condition imposed by him, which is a view conforming with the views of Abū Ḥanīfa and al-Shāfiᶜī. The view upholding immediate divorce in this case is weak as it is held similar, according to him, to the case in which the condition must come to pass; the disagreement about this (in the school) is intense.

In the suspension of divorce upon a condition the occurrence of which is uncertain, if there is no way of knowing of such occurrence, like his saying that "if Allāh creates today a whale of such and such a description in the Red Sea you are divorced", then there is no dispute in the school, that I know of, that divorce does take place in such a case, but when he links it to a happening the existence of which is likely to be known, like his saying that "if you give birth to a female you are divorced", the divorce is dependent upon the coming into existence of the condition. If he vows to divorce her if she gives birth to a female, then the divorce comes into effect immediately, according to him (Mālik), even though she does give birth to a female (later); this is considered to be a deterrent, though analogy would require that divorce be dependent upon the happening of an event or upon its opposite.

One of Mālik's opinions is that if he (the husband) makes the pronouncement of divorce binding upon himself if he should commit a certain act, he is not liable until he commits the act. But, if he makes a vow to give up the commission of a certain act, then he is liable for breaking a vow till he complies (with it) and is to refrain from intercourse with his wife. If he refuses to act till a time-period that exceeds the period of *al-īlāʾ*, the rules of the period of *al-īlāʾ*, are to be imposed on him, but the divorce does not take effect unless the act is given up, if it is one that can be given up. Some jurists hold the view that he does not violate the vow till the act has come to pass. If it is something that does not come to pass, he remains in that state until his death.

In this topic is their disagreement about the partially divorced woman, and about partial divorce or of a serial divorce. With respect to the question of the partially divorced woman, Mālik said that if he were to say that your hands, feet, or hair are divorced, she stands divorced for him. Abū Ḥanīfa said that she is not divorced, except when a part of the body is mentioned that is used to imply the whole body, like the head, heart, or genitals. According to him, she is divorced when it is a mathematical portion, like a third or a fourth. Dāwūd said that she cannot be divorced by such pronouncements. Similarly, if he were to say, "I have pronounced for you half a divorce", then, according to Mālik she stands divorced, as this cannot be split up in his view, while according to the contender when it is split up it does not take legal effect. If he were to say, "you are divorced, you are divorced, you are divorced", in successive statements, they amount to three divorces according to Mālik. Abū Ḥanīfa and al-Shāfiʿī said that only one has taken place. Those who held the repetition of words to be the same as pronouncing the numbers, that is, like saying "you are divorced thrice", said that divorce has taken place thrice, while those who held that she is irrevocably divorced through a single pronouncement said that the second and third do not take effect. There is no disagreement among the Muslim jurists about successive divorces in *ṭalāq rajʿī*.

Divorce contingent upon an exemption is to be conceived with relation to number only. If he has made several repudiations, it cannot go beyond three cases. He may make an exemption for the same number, like saying, "you are divorced thrice except thrice, or twice except twice", or he may exempt a lesser number. If he exempts a lesser number, he may exempt it from a larger number or he may exempt the larger number from the smaller number. When he exempts the smaller from the larger number there is no dispute, that I know of, that the exemption is valid and the exempted number of pronouncements are cancelled. When he exempts the larger number from the smaller, there are two opinions on it. First, that the exemption is not valid, and this is based on the view of those who prohibit the exemption of a larger from the smaller number. The second is that the exemption is valid, which is Mālik's opinion.

When he is exempting the same number, like saying "you are divorced thrice, except thrice", Mālik holds that the divorce comes into effect as he has created a suspicion that it is a retraction on his part, but when he is not creating a suspicion and his intention is to indicate the impossibility of divorce, divorce is not effective against him, like saying "you are divorced, but not divorced", at the same time, for the occurrence of a thing and its opposite at the same time is impossible.

Abū Muḥammad ibn Ḥazm deviated (from these views) and said that divorce does not come into effect (when associated) with events that have not yet come to pass or with an act that has not yet occurred, as divorce is not effective except at the time it is pronounced by the repudiator. There is no evidence in the Book, *sunna*, or *ijmāʿ* that divorce will come into effect at a time other than that at which it is pronounced by the repudiator, for he has imposed on himself its coming into effect at that particular time. If we uphold such imposition it is binding to await that time and then pronounce it. This is analogy drawn from his opinions and arguments by me, though I do not remember at the moment his supporting evidence for it.

19.2.2. **Chapter 2: The Repudiator whose Pronouncement is Valid**

They agreed that the repudiator has to be the husband who is sane, major (*bāligh*), a freeman, and not under duress. They disagreed about the repudiation of one intoxicated, coerced, or ill, and about the person about to reach puberty.

They agreed that the repudiation of the *marīḍ* (the sick person) is valid if he recovers, but they disagreed whether she will inherit from him if he dies. The repudiation of the person under coercion does not come into effect according to Mālik, al-Shāfiʿī, Aḥmad, Dāwūd and a group of jurists, and it was the opinion of ʿAbd Allāh ibn ʿUmar, Ibn al-Zubayr, ʿUmar ibn al-Khaṭṭāb, ʿAlī ibn Abī Ṭālib and Ibn ʿAbbās. The disciples of al-Shāfiʿī made a distinction based on whether he intended to divorce. In the case of his intention to divorce there are two opinions of which the better view is that it is binding. When he did not intend divorce there are (again) two opinions of which the better view is that it is not binding. Abū Ḥanīfa and his disciples said that it comes into effect as does his manumission, though not his sale, and thus they made distinctions between sale, divorce, and manumission.

The reason for disagreement is whether the person under coercion possesses a will, for there is no coercion in the pronouncement and the words have been uttered of his own volition. The person coerced does not, in fact, possess a will for the performance of anything. Both parties argue on the basis of the words of the Prophet (God's peace and blessings be upon him), "Liability is removed from my *umma* for mistake, forgetfulness, and for what they have been coerced to do". It is obvious, however, that the person coerced into repudiating, though he pronounces the words of his own volition, is one whom the law designates as the coerced, because of the words of the Exalted, "[S]ave him who is forced thereto and whose heart is still content with Faith".[75] Abū Ḥanīfa, however, made a distinction between sale and divorce, as divorce is a solemn matter, and that is why seriousness and jest about it have been deemed similar.

The widely known opinion of Mālik about the repudiation of the minor is that it does not take effect till he attains majority. According to the *Mukhtaṣar mā laysa fīʾl Mukhtaṣar* it is binding upon him if he has approached (the age of) ejaculation. This was also Aḥmad ibn Ḥanbal's opinion, who held it to be the time when the boy could keep the fasts of Ramaḍān. ʿAṭāʾ said that when he reaches the age of twelve his repudiation is valid, which is also related from ʿUmar ibn al-Khaṭṭāb (God be pleased with him).

[75] Qurʾān 16 : 106

About the divorce of the intoxicated person, the majority of the jurists maintain that it comes into effect. One group of jurists, and among them are al-Muzanī and the disciples of Abū Ḥanīfa, said that it is not effective. The reason for their disagreement is whether his *ḥukm* is the *ḥukm* of the insane person or that there is a difference between them. Those who maintained that he and the insane person are similar, for both have lost their senses, and the condition of liability is *ᶜaql* (sanity), said that it does not come into effect. Those who maintained that there is a distinction between them because the intoxicated person has muddled his senses by his own volition, the case of the insane being different, said that it is not effective. This is the case of enhanced liability for him.

The jurists disagreed about the *aḥkām* applicable to the intoxicated person as a whole. Mālik said that he is liable for divorce, manumission, and retaliation for injuries and homicide, but his marriage and sale are not valid. Abū Ḥanīfa held him liable for all things. Al-Layth was of the opinion that there is no liability for all that has resulted from the speech of the intoxicated person and, therefore, he is not liable for divorce, manumission, marriage, sale or the *ḥadd* for *qadhf*, but he is liable for all physical acts, thus, he is to be awarded the *ḥadd* for drinking, homicide, unlawful intercourse, and theft. It is established from ᶜUthmān ibn ᶜAffān (God be pleased with him) that he did not uphold divorce pronounced under the effect of intoxication. Some of the jurists believed that no one from among the Companions opposed ᶜUthmān in this. The opinion that "each repudiation is valid, except that of the idiot", does not make the divorce of the intoxicated person binding as he is an idiot of a kind. This was upheld by Dāwūd, Abū Thawr, Isḥāq and a group of the *Tābiᶜūn*, that is, his divorce is not effective. Both opinions are related from al-Shāfiᶜī and most of his disciples have selected the opinion conforming with that of the majority, while al-Muzanī elected the opinion that his divorce is not effective.

About the *mārid*, who pronounces an irrevocable divorce and then dies from his illness, Mālik and a group of jurists said that his wife inherits from him, while al-Shāfiᶜī and a group do not allow her to inherit. Those who permitted her inheritance are divided into three groups. One group said that she is entitled to inherit as long as she is in her waiting period.[76] Those who maintained this are Abū Ḥanīfa, his disciples, and al-Thawrī. The second group said that she is entitled to inherit as long as she has not married (again). Those who upheld this are Aḥmad and Ibn Abī Laylā. The third group said

[76] This may appear meaningless, however, it is another way of saying that though the divorce of the *marīḍ* is effective, the woman is technically his wife as long as the waiting period lasts, and is, therefore, entitled to inheritance. We may also note here that this opinion is attributed to the Ḥanafites and in their law a divorce pronounced in any circumstances is valid, even one pronounced under coercion. It is possible that they make a minor exemption in this case.

that she inherits whether she is still in the waiting period, and whether she has married. This is the opinion of Mālik and al-Layth.

The reason for disagreement is based upon their dispute over following the principle of preempting the means (*sadd al-dharīʿa*). This is so as the *marīḍ* may have divorced his wife in his illness out of covetousness to cut her off from her share of the inheritance. Those who upheld the principle of *sadd al-dharīʿa*, therefore, held her inheritance to be obligatory, but those who did not uphold it, and took into account the binding nature of the divorce, denied her inheritance. The latter group maintained that if the divorce has come into effect, it must be enforced with all its *aḥkām*. They added that he would not be inheriting from her if she died (before him). On the other hand, if the divorce is not effective, the conjugal relationship is maintained with all its *aḥkām*. This group (inconsistently) holds that the repudiator does not inherit from her if she should die (before him), but if divorce is not effective, then, marriage should survive together with all its *aḥkām*.

The contender must answer this in one of two ways, as he is constrained to do. First, it is inconceivable to claim that there is a kind of divorce in the law, which has some of the *aḥkām* of marriage as well as some *aḥkām* of divorce. A more difficult reply than that would be to postpone the *ḥukm* of repudiation till the repudiator recovers, holding divorce to be effective in such a case, or to postpone it till he dies, in which case the divorce is held to be ineffective, as in this situation it would be a divorce that is suspended till it can be determined whether it is valid. Such claims would be difficult to justify in the *sharʿ*. Yet, those who upheld it identified a decision rendered by ʿUthmān and ʿUmar, so much so that the Mālikites believed it to be the consensus of the Companions, but their claim is not justified, as opposition to this opinion from Ibn al-Zubayr is widely known.

Those who maintained that she inherits (if the repudiator dies) during the waiting period do so because the waiting period is subject to some of the *aḥkām* of marriage, and it was as if they held her to be similar to a woman whose divorce has been retracted. This opinion is related from ʿUmar and from ʿĀʾisha. Those who stipulated for her inheritance that she should not have married, took into account for this view the consensus of the Muslim jurists that one woman cannot inherit from two husbands; and also because their reasoning incorporates suspicion (about the husband's intentions).

They disagreed when she asked for divorce herself or the husband had delegated her the right through which she divorced herself. Abū Ḥanīfa said that she does not inherit in both cases, while al-Awzāʿī made a distinction between *tamlīk* and divorce (by the husband), saying that she does not inherit in the case of authorization (*tamlīk*), but she does in repudiation.

Mālik did not make a distinction in these cases, and said that if she dies, he does not inherit from her, but if he dies she inherits from him. This is very much opposed to the general principles.

19.2.3. **Chapter 3: Women Affected by Divorce**

They agreed about the women against whom divorce becomes effective that these are the women who are in the protection of their husbands, and those whose waiting periods have not terminated in a revocable divorce. They agreed that it has no effect against women who are strangers, that is, a conditional divorce. About the divorce of strange women upon the condition of marriage, like saying that "if I marry so and so, she is divorced", the jurists have three opinions. First, that divorce does not affect strange women, whether it is made general for all or is specific. This is the opinion of al-Shāfiᶜī, Aḥmad, Dāwūd and a group of jurists. Second, that it is effective upon the condition of marriage whether made general for all women or specific. This is Abū Ḥanīfa's opinion and that of a group of jurists. Third, that if he has made it general for all women, it is not binding upon him, but it is binding when he makes it specific, which is Mālik's opinion and also of a group of jurists. For example, if he says that "any woman I marry from such and such a tribe or from such and such a land is divorced", and also when he stipulates a time, then, these women stand divorced, if married, according to Mālik.

The reason for disagreement is whether ownership of marital rights prior to the time of divorce is a condition for divorce to be effective. Those who maintained that it is a condition said that divorce does not affect women strangers, while those who said that the only condition is the existence of ownership (not prior) said that it can be effective against strangers.

The distinction between making it general (for all women) or specific is based on the exercise of *istiḥsān* grounded upon the doctrine of *maṣlaḥa*. If divorce of all strange women is made effective we would be imposing upon him a general rule through which he will not find a means to permissible marriage; it would cause inconvenience and hardship for him, and would amount to a vow to commit a sin. When he makes it specific, the case is different if we make divorce binding against him.

Al-Shāfiᶜī argued on the basis of the tradition of ᶜAmr ibn Shuᶜayb from his father from his grandfather, who said, "The Prophet (God's peace and blessings be upon him) said 'There is no divorce, except after marriage' ". Another version states, "There is no divorce without ownership, nor manumission without ownership". The tradition has been related from ᶜAlī, Muᶜādh, Jābir ibn ᶜAbd Allāh, Ibn ᶜAbbās and ᶜĀʾisha. But an opinion similar to that of Abū Ḥanīfa is related from ᶜUmar and Ibn Masᶜūd, though some have considered the narration from ʿUmar (God be pleased with him) to be weak.

19.3. Part 3: Retraction after Divorce

As divorce is of two types, irrevocable and revocable, and the *aḥkām* of retraction after an irrevocable divorce are different from those of retraction after a revocable divorce, it is necessary that under this category there be two chapters: the first chapter is about the *aḥkām* of retraction after a revocable divorce and the second about the *aḥkām* of retraction after an irrevocable divorce.

19.3.1. Chapter 1: Retraction after a Revocable Divorce

The Muslim jurists agreed that the husband possesses the right to have recourse to his wife after a *ṭalāq rajʿī* as long as she is in her waiting period, even without her consent, on the basis of the words of the Exalted, "And their husbands would have a greater right to take them back in that case if they desire a reconciliation".[77] It is a condition for this kind of divorce that the wife must have been wed to the husband, that is, their marriage must have been consummated before divorce.

They agreed that recourse (*rujūʿ*) is by words and by witnessing. They disagreed whether witnessing was a condition for this. Similarly, they disagreed whether recourse is valid through intercourse. As to witnessing, Mālik held that it is recommended, while al-Shāfiʿī said that it is obligatory. The reason for disagreement is the conflict of analogy with the apparent meaning of the text. The apparent meaning is found in the words of the Exalted, "Then, when they have reached their term, take them back in kindness or part from them in kindness, and call to witness two just men from among you, and keep your testimony upright for Allāh",[78] which imply an obligation. A comparison of this right with all other rights that a human being possesses indicates that there be no obligatory witnesses. The reconciliation between analogy and the verse leads to construing the meaning of the verse as a recommendation.

Regarding their disagreement about how recourse is achieved, a group of jurists said that recourse is only by words, which was al-Shāfiʿī's opinion. Another group of jurists said that recourse may be through intercourse. These jurists are divided into two groups. The first group said that recourse is not valid through intercourse, unless he intended it to be so, as an act according to them can only be equivalent to words when accompanied by intention.

[77] Qurʾān 2 : 228
[78] Qurʾān 65 : 2

This is Mālik's opinion. Abū Ḥanīfa permitted recourse through intercourse when he (the husband) meant it to be so, without manifest intention. Al-Shāfiʿī held recourse to be analogous to marriage and said that Allāh has ordered the presence of witnesses, and such witnesses only bear witness to a declaration.

The reason for disagreement between Mālik and Abū Ḥanīfa is that Abū Ḥanīfa considers recourse as making intercourse permissible on the analogy of a woman repudiated through *al-īlāʾ* and *ẓihār*, and also because the ownership has not been alienated, because of which inheritance is permissible among them. According to Mālik intercourse with a woman after a revocable divorce is prohibited, unless there is recourse, and, therefore, he stipulated intention for it. This is their disagreement about the conditions of validity of recourse.

They disagreed about what part of the divorced wife's body can the repudiating husband look at, as long as she is in her waiting period. Mālik said that he cannot be alone with her and he cannot visit her except by her permission, he cannot look at her hair, but there is no harm if they eat together, as long as there is someone else with them. Ibn al-Qāsim has related that he withdrew the permission of eating with her. Abū Ḥanīfa said that there is no harm if the woman adorns herself for her husband, uses perfume, reveals the tips of her fingers, and uses cosmetics for him. This was also the opinion of al-Thawrī, Abū Yūsuf and al-Awzāʿī. All of them said that he is not to go into her (quarters) unannounced either through words or movement, like clearing his throat or the sound of his shoes.

In this topic, they differed about the case of a person who repudiates his wife through a revocable divorce and takes her back, when he is absent. She then comes to know of the repudiation, but not the retraction, and upon the termination of her waiting period she gets married. Mālik held that she belongs to the person who has now contracted marriage with her, irrespective of the consummation of such marriage. This is his opinion in *al-Muwaṭṭaʾ*. It is also the opinion of al-Awzāʿī and al-Layth. Ibn al-Qāsim has related from him (Mālik) that he withdrew his earlier opinion and said that the first husband has a prior right, unless the second husband has consummated the marriage with her. The first opinion was adopted by his disciples in Medina, who said that he did not retract from this opinion and confirmed it in his *al-Muwaṭṭaʾ* till he died as it used to be read out to him, and that it is also an opinion of ʿUmar ibn al-Khaṭṭāb from whom it was related by Mālik in *al-Muwaṭṭaʾ*.

Al-Shāfiʿī and the Kūfīs, Abū Ḥanīfa and the others, said that the first husband has a superior right to her, irrespective of the second husband having consummated the marriage with her. This is also the opinion of Dāwūd and Abū Thawr. It is related from ʿAlī, and is obviously the better opinion. It is related from ʿUmar ibn al-Khaṭṭāb (God be pleased with him) that he said,

"The husband who had recourse to her has an option to take her back as his wife or demand what he had paid her as her dower".

The evidence for Mālik in the first opinion is what has been related by Ibn Wahb from Yūnus from Ibn Shihāb from Saᶜīd ibn al-Musayyib, who said that "There is a precedent about the person who divorces his wife and then takes her back without letting her know about it till such time that she is free to marry, and she does marry a second husband, that he has no right over her and she belongs to the person who has now married her". It is, however, said that this tradition is related from Ibn Shihāb alone. The argument of the other group is that the jurists agreed unanimously that recourse is valid even when the woman is not aware of it. This is based on the evidence of their agreement that the first has a prior right to her before she gets married. If the retraction was valid then the second marriage is void, and the second marriage has no affect in nullifying the retraction, either before consummation or after it. This is better, God willing. It is supported by what is recorded by al-Tirmidhī from Samura ibn Jundub that the Prophet (God's peace and blessings be upon him) said, "When a woman is married to two men, she belongs to the first, and when one sells something to two persons, it belongs to the first".

19.3.2. **Chapter 2: Retraction after an Irrevocable Divorce**

A divorce with less than three repudiations is effective without dispute against a woman with whom marriage has not been consummated, but there is disagreement about the (nature of the divorce of a) woman granted redemption (*khulᶜ*). Can an irrevocable divorce occur without compensation? About this too there is dispute. The *ḥukm* of retraction for this type of divorce is the same as that of a new marriage, that is, regarding the stipulation of dower, guardianship, and consent. The termination of the waiting period, however, is not taken into account by the majority, while a group deviated from this saying that a woman granted redemption is not to be married by her husband either during the waiting period or after it. It was as if these jurists viewed the prohibition of marrying within the waiting period as a religious ritual having a non-rational underlying cause.

All the jurists agreed about the woman divorced irrevocably with a triple repudiation that she is not permitted to her first husband, unless she has intercourse (with a second husband through a lawful marriage), because of the tradition of Rifāᶜa ibn Samawʾal that he divorced his wife Tamīma daughter of Wahb during the period of the Messenger of Allāh (God's peace and blessings be upon him) through a triple repudiation and she married ᶜAbd al-Raḥmān ibn al-Zubayr, who abandoned her and was not able to have intercourse with her and separated from her. After this, the first husband

Rifāʿa wanted to marry her, and mentioned this to the Messenger of Allāh (God's peace and blessings be upon him), who prohibited him from marrying her, saying, "She is not permissible for you, unless she tastes the sweetness of another". Saʿīd ibn al-Musayyib deviated from this and said that it is permitted to her to return to her first husband by merely entering into a contract of marriage (without intercourse), because of the general meaning of the words of the Exalted, "[U]ntil she hath wedded another husband", as the term *marriage* is applied to mean the contract. All of them (those who stipulated intercourse) said that the mere contact of the genitals (penetration) makes her permissible (for the first husband), but al-Ḥasan al-Baṣrī maintained that she does not become permissible without intercourse and accompanying ejaculation, but the majority of the jurists maintain that intercourse, which imposes *ḥadd*, nullifies fasting and *ḥajj*, makes permissible a divorced wife, converts the spouses to *muḥṣans*, and makes dower obligatory is that in which there is simple penetration.

Mālik and Ibn al-Qāsim added that a divorced woman does not become permissible, unless the intercourse is permissible, which results from a valid contract and is not committed during a fast, *ḥajj*, menstruation or *iʿtikāf*. A *dhimmī* woman (in their view) does not become permissible for a Muslim through marriage with a *dhimmī*, nor a woman who has intercourse (through marriage) with a minor. In all this they (Mālik and Ibn al-Qāsim) were opposed by al-Shāfiʿī, Abū Ḥanīfa, al-Thawrī and al-Awzāʿī, who said that intercourse makes her permissible even if it occurs in a void marriage or at a time in which it is not permissible. Similarly, intercourse with an adolescent makes her permissible, as does the intercourse of a *dhimmiyya* with a *dhimmī*, so also the intercourse of an insane person or of a castrated individual, as long as there is some part which penetrates. The disagreement in all this refers to the question whether the term intercourse (*nikāḥ*) includes all kinds of deficient intercourse.

Within this subject they disagreed about marriage with the *muḥallil*, that is, one who marries her upon the condition that he would make her permissible for her first husband. Mālik said that the marriage is void and is rescinded before consummation and after it, and the condition too is void, and cannot make her permissible. In this case, according to him, it is not the intention of the woman that is considered, but the intention of the man. Al-Shāfiʿī and Abū Ḥanīfa said that the marriage is valid and intention is not relevant in it, which was also the opinion of Dāwūd and a group of jurists. They said that he makes her permissible for the husband who has repudiated her thrice. Some of them said that the contract is valid, but the condition (that the *muḥallil* divorce her) is void, that is, he will not make her permissible. It is the opinion of Ibn Abī Laylā, and is related from al-Thawrī.

Mālik and his disciples argued on the basis of what is related from the Prophet (God's peace and blessings be upon him) through a narration of ᶜAlī ibn Abī Ṭālib, Ibn Masᶜūd, Abū Hurayra, and ᶜUqba ibn ᶜĀmir that he (the Prophet) said, "The curse of Allāh is upon the *muḥallil* and upon the person for whom he is making her permissible". This curse is the same as the curse upon the person who indulges in usury or one who drinks wine; it indicates a proscription, and a proscription indicates the invalidity of the thing prohibited (the contract in this case). The term legal marriage is not applied to a marriage that is prohibited. The other party relied on the general meaning of the words of the Exalted, " [U]ntil she hath wedded another husband",[79] saying that this person is contracting a marriage. They added that there is nothing in the proscription of the intention to make permissible, anything that indicates that its absence is a condition for the validity of marriage, just as the proscription of praying in usurped property does not indicate that a condition for the validity of prayer is the ownership of the site or the permission of the owner. They said that if the proscription does not indicate the invalidity of the marriage contract, it is appropriate that it should not indicate the nullification of *taḥlīl*.

Mālik did not take the intention of the woman into account, because if the man did not comply with her intention, her intention would have no significance, as she does not possess the power of divorce.

They disagreed whether marriage to a *muḥallil* negates less than three repudiations. Abū Ḥanīfa said that it does, while Mālik and al-Shāfiᶜī said that it does not, that is, if the wife marries a second husband before the third repudiation, and the first husband decides to take her back, is the *ḥukm* of less than three repudiations the same? Those who maintained that it was something specific, in law, to the third repudiation said that the husband does not negate what is less than three. Others held that if he could negate the third, it is proper that he be able to negate what is less than that. Allāh knows best.

19.4. Part 4: Waiting Period (*ᶜIdda*) and the Gift of Consolation (*Mutᶜa*)

In this part there are two chapters. The first is about the waiting period, while the second is about compensation for a divorced woman (*mutᶜa*).

[79] Qurʾān 4 : 230

19.4.1. **Chapter 1: The Waiting Period (*ᶜIdda*)**

The discussion in this chapter is undertaken in two sections. The first section is about the determination of the waiting period, while the second about the *aḥkām* of the waiting period.[80]

19.4.1.1. *Section 1: The Determination of the Waiting Period*

The discussion of the waiting period for wives is divided into two categories. First, the waiting period for wives and second the identification of the waiting period of those in the *milk al-yamīn* (slave-girls).

19.4.1.1.1. Category 1: The waiting period for wives

A wife may be a free woman or a slave. The marriage of each one of them may have been consummated or it may not have been consummated. There is no waiting period, by consensus, for a divorced wife whose marriage has not been consummated, because of the words of the Exalted, "O ye who believe! If ye wed believing women and divorce them before ye have touched them, then there is no period that ye should reckon. But content them and release them handsomely".[81]

The divorced woman whose marriage stands consummated may or may not be one who menstruates. If she does not menstruate, she may be a minor or beyond the age of menstruation. Those who menstruate may be pregnant or they may be undergoing their usual periods of menstruation. (In the latter case) their menstruation may have ceased (recently) or it may be continuing. Those who menstruate, but their menstruation has ceased, may have conceived, that is, it can be felt from (the changes in) their body, or they may not have conceived. Those who have not conceived may know the reason for the cessation of blood such as suckling or illness, or they may not know the reason.

The waiting period of free women, who menstruate according to their usual cycles, is three periods (*qurūᶜ*), but those among them who are pregnant, their waiting period is up to the time of delivery. The waiting period for those among them who are beyond the age of menstruation is three months. There is no dispute about this as it is explicitly stated in the words of the Exalted, "Women who are divorced shall wait, keeping themselves apart, three (monthly) courses"[82] and His words, "And for such of your women as despair of menstruation, if ye doubt, their period (of waiting) shall be three months,

[80] The text under this section had to be switched with that under the following heading. Apparently it had been mixed up through a scribe's error.

[81] Qurʾān 33 : 49

[82] Qurʾān 2 : 228

along with those who have it not. And for those with child, their period shall be till they bring forth their burden. And whosoever keepeth his duty to Allāh, He maketh his course easy for him".[83]

In these verses, they differed about the meaning of the term "periods"(sing. *qurʾ*). Some jurists said that these are the periods of purity, that is, the periods between two menses. Some said that these are the periods of menstruation itself. Among the jurists of the provinces, those who said that the periods are those of purity, are Mālik, al-Shāfiʿī, most of the jurists of Medina, Abū Thawr and a group of jurists; and among the Companions are Ibn ʿUmar, Zayd ibn Thābit and ʿĀʾisha. Among the jurists of the provinces, who said that the periods are those of menstruation, are Abū Ḥanīfa, al-Thawrī, al-Awzāʿī, Ibn Abī Laylā, along with a group of other jurists; and among the Companions are ʿAlī, ibn al-Khaṭṭab, Ibn Masʿūd and Abū Mūsā al-Ashʿarī. Al-Athram has related from Aḥmad that he said, "The foremost Companions of the Messenger of Allāh (God's peace and blessings be upon him) said, 'The periods are menstruation' ". It is also related from al-Shaʿbī that it is the opinion of eleven or twelve Companions of the Messenger of Allāh (God's peace and blessings be upon him). As for Aḥmad ibn Ḥanbal, the narration from him has differed. It is related from him that he used to say, "The periods are (the days) of purity in the opinion of Zayd ibn Thābit, Ibn ʿUmar and ʿĀʾisha, but now the judgment is reserved, because of the opinion of Ibn Masʿūd and ʿAlī to the effect that it is menstruation".

The difference between the two opinions is (based on the reason) that those who held it to be purity said that once the divorced woman begins her third menses, the husband would have no right to have recourse to her in a retractable divorce and she would be free to marry again, while those who held it to be menstruation prohibited her remarriage until the third period of menstruation had terminated.

The reason for disagreement is the equivocality of the term '*qurʾ*', for it is applied to both purity and menstruation in Arabic usage. Each group desired to show that the meaning of the term in the related verse is obviously what each considers it to be. Those who held that it is the period of purity said that this pattern of plural (*qurūʾ*) is specific to purity, because the term *qurʾ*, which has *aqrāʾ* as its plural and not *qurūʾ*, applies specifically to menstruation. They related this from Ibn al-Anbārī. They also added that *ḥayḍa* (menstruation) is feminine, while *ṭuhr* (purity) is masculine, thus, had the term *qurʾ* denoted menstruation the feminine letter *tāʾ* could not have survived in the numerical word *thalāthata* (three) annexed to the term *qurūʾ*, according to the rule.[84] They also said that etymology indicates it too, for the

[83] Qurʾān 65 : 4

[84] That is, when the numerical Arabic words denoting three, four... ten, are annexed to a masculine term,

phrase "to gather water in the pond", means to collect it; the period of collecting blood is the period of purity. All the above are the strongest arguments that the first party advanced about the adoption of what they believed to be the obvious meaning of the verse.

About the meaning adopted by the second party, they said that the words of the Exalted, "three periods", or "three courses" obviously imply the completion of each of the three periods, for the term "period" cannot be applied to a part of the period, except by way of metaphor. If the periods are designated as the periods of purity, it is possible that the waiting period may result in two periods and a part of a period, for according to them (the first party) she reckons the duration in time in which she was divorced, even if most of it was over. If that is the case, the term "three" cannot be applied to it without violation and the term three is manifest for the completion of each of the periods, which cannot be unless the term "period" is applied to the period of menstruation, because of the consensus that if she is divorced during menses she is not to take that period into her reckoning.

So each party has equally strong arguments regarding the word "period" (*qurʾ*) and that which satisfies the astute jurists is that the verse is unelaborated (and needs explanation) and the explanatory evidence should be sought from a different aspect. The strongest evidence adduced by those who view that the periods mean periods of purity is the preceding tradition of Ibn ʿUmar and also the words of the Prophet (God's peace and blessings be upon him), "Order him to take her back (and wait) till she has her menses then the period of purity then menses and then the period of purity. He may then divorce her if he likes before cohabiting with her. This is the waiting period which Allāh has commanded you to observe when you divorce women". They also added that there is consensus that *ṭalāq al-sunna* takes place only in a period in which the divorcing husband has not cohabited with her and the words of the Prophet, "This is the period in which Allāh has commanded you to divorce women (if you should divorce them)", is a clear evidence that the waiting period is that of purity so that the repudiation falls within the waiting period. It is possible that the words of the Prophet, "This is the *ʿidda*", that is, this is the post-divorce waiting period, imply the commencement of the *ʿidda* so that the period is not split up due to a repudiation during menses.

The strongest argument adduced by the second party is that *ʿidda* has been ordained for (ascertaining) the vacation of the womb and such vacation is decided through menstruation not through purity. It is for this reason that the *ʿidda* of one whose menstrual period has ceased is reckoned in days. It is,

it is followed by the feminine term *tā*. When annexed to a feminine word, the numerical term cannot carry the feminine *tāʾ*. In the Qurʾānic verse here *thalāthata* (three) annexed to *qurūʾ* has the feminine *tāʾ*.

therefore, menstruation that is the basis for the *ʿidda* being reckoned in periods, which makes it necessary that the "periods" be those of menstruation.

Those who maintained that the "periods" are those of purity, argued (in response) that the factor taken into account for the vacation of the womb is the transition from purity to menstruation not the termination of menstruation, therefore, the (length of the) last period of menstruation has no significance. The stipulation is for the completion of the three periods, thus, the actual stipulation is for periods of purity not of menstruation.

Both parties have lengthy arguments and the opinion of the Ḥanafites is better from the aspect of reason, while their arguments based on transmission are equally strong, or almost equal.

Those who maintained that *ʿidda* is based on the periods of "purity" did not disagree that it (*ʿidda*) terminates with her entering the third period of menstruation. Those who maintained that it is based on the periods of menstruation differed. It is said that it terminates with the cessation of bleeding in the third menstruation. This was al-Awzāʿī's opinion. It is also said that it terminates after she takes a bath when the third period of menstruation is over. This was held, from among the Companions, by ʿUmar ibn al-Khaṭṭab, ʿAlī and Ibn Masʿūd and, from among the *fuqahāʾ*, by al-Thawrī and Isḥāq ibn ʿUbayd. It is said that (it extends) till the time of prayer, prior to which she has entered the period of purity, is over. It is maintained that the husband has the right of retraction even if she delays taking a bath for twenty years. This is related from Shurayk. It is also said that it terminates upon her entering the third period of menstruation, which is a deviant opinion.

This, then, is the position of the menstruating woman, who is having her usual periods.

The divorced menstruating woman whose periods have ceased, but she is in the age group where menstruation is likely and there is no suspicion about the cessation of menstruation due to suckling or illness, waits in Mālik's opinion for nine months. If she does not have her menses in this time, she undergoes her *ʿidda* for three (further) months. If she menstruates during these months, she is to reckon on the basis of menstruation and awaits it (the next course). If another nine months pass before she has menstruated a second time, she undergoes an *ʿidda* of three months. If she menstruates before the three months of the second year are over, she is to await the third menstruation. If nine months go by before she has menstruated again, she undergoes *ʿidda* for three months. If she menstruates in these three months, she has fulfilled her *ʿidda* on the basis of menstruation and the waiting period is over. Her husband has a right to take her back as long as she is not free to marry. The narration from Mālik as to when she begins to reckon nine months has differed. It is said that she does so from the day she is divorced, which is his opinion in *al-Muwaṭṭa*ʾ. Ibn al-Qāsim has reported from him that this time is the day when her menstruation ceases.

Abū Ḥanīfa, al-Shāfiʿī and the majority said about the woman whose menstruation has ceased and she has not recently undergone a menopause, that she continues to await menstruation till she enters the age when she would despair of menstruation. It is then that she undergoes the *ʿidda* for three months, unless she menstruates prior to this.

Mālik's opinion has also been related from ʿUmar ibn al-Khaṭṭāb and Ibn ʿAbbās, while the opinion of the majority has been related from Ibn Masʿūd and Zayd. Mālik's argument by way of reasoning is that the purpose of *ʿidda* is to ascertain the vacation of the womb through an overwhelming probability, because even a pregnant woman may sometimes menstruate. If this is the case then the *ʿidda* of pregnancy is sufficient to ascertain the vacation of the womb, in fact, it is definitive in indicating this. She may then undergo the *ʿidda* of one who has despaired of menstruation. If she menstruates before the end of the year, she is subject to the *ḥukm* of women who menstruate. She reckons this to be one period and awaits the second period, or she waits for a year till the three periods are complete.

The majority decided according to the apparent meaning of the words of the Exalted, "And for such of your women as despair of menstruation, if ye doubt, their period (of waiting) shall be three months, along with those who have it not. And for those with child, their period shall be till they bring forth their burden. And whosoever keepeth his duty to Allāh, He maketh his course easy for him".[85] The woman who is likely to menstruate is not among those who have despaired. This opinion invokes difficulty and harm. If it had been said that she is to undergo *ʿidda* for three months, it would have been better, if the meaning of "one who has despaired" is that the woman is not positive about the menopause. The meaning of the words of the Exalted, "if ye doubt", refers to the (doubt about the) *ḥukm* and not to menstruation, as interpreted by Mālik. If (the meaning of) a despairing woman is one who is certain that she is not one of those who menstruate, then, it would appear as if Mālik did not make his opinion conform with his interpretation of the verse, since this (such certainty) comes only at a certain age. It is for this reason that he deemed the words of the Exalted, "if ye doubt", to refer to the *ḥukm* and not menstruation, that is, "if ye are in doubt about their *ḥukm*". He then elaborated that the woman who did not menstruate for nine months, though she was within the age-span for menstruation, should reckon her waiting period by way of months.

His disciples, Ismāʿīl and Ibn Bukayr, held that the reference to doubt (in

85 Qurʾān 65 : 4

the verse) is about menstruation and in the usage of the Arabs, the woman who despairs is one to whom the *ḥukm* of what she has despaired of is not certain. By doing this they brought their opinion to conform with the verse and with Mālik's view. What they did was good, for if the meaning of despair is to be understood to imply certainty, then it is necessary that she should await menstruation and remain in the waiting period till she reaches the age, that is, the age of despair, but if uncertainty is to be understood from it, then, the woman whose menstruation has ceased while she is within the age-group in which menstruation is likely, she undergoes the waiting period on the basis of months. This is an analogy upon the opinion of the Ẓāhirites, for the woman who has despaired is not among those who undergo a waiting period, neither by (menstrual) periods nor by months. The distinction between the two, regarding what is prior to nine months and what is after it, is based upon *istiḥsān*.

Mālik's widely known opinion about the woman whose menstruation has ceased because of suckling or illness, is that she awaits menstruation, whether the period is short or prolonged. It is said that the sick woman's case is the same as one whose menstruation has ceased without a reason.

In Mālik's view, the *ʿidda* of a woman with extended menstruation is a year when a distinction cannot be made between the two kinds of bleeding (the normal blood discharge and bleeding due to sickness). When a distinction can be made between the two kinds of bleeding, there are two opinions from him. First, that her *ʿidda* is for a year. The other opinion is that she is to abide by the distinction and undergo *ʿidda* by periods. Abū Ḥanīfa said that her *ʿidda* is based upon periods, if she can distinguish, but if she cannot then it is three months. Al-Shāfiʿī said that her *ʿidda* is based upon distinction. When the blood is separated from her it will be a deep red in the days of menstruation and yellowish in the days of purity. If the blood discharge continues without distinction, she undergoes a waiting period on the basis of (the length of) her (previous) menstruation when she was in good health. Mālik upheld the waiting period of a year for he deemed her to be similar to a woman who does not menstruate, when she is one of those who should. Al-Shāfiʿī upheld that the woman who can identify her days of menstruation is to be subject to their identification, on the analogy of prayer, because of the words of the Prophet (God's peace and blessings be upon him) to a woman with extended menstruation: "Relinquish prayer in the days of your (previous) periods and when these days are over, resume the performance of prayers, but wash away the blood".

Those who took into account this distinction did so because of the words of the Prophet (God's peace and blessings be upon him) to Fāṭima daughter of Ḥubaysh, "If it is the blood of menstruation, it is dark and can be identified.

If it is so, refrain from prayer, but if it is of the other kind, perform ablutions and pray for it is merely blood". It is recorded by Abū Dāwūd. Those who maintained that her ʿ*idda* is to be reckoned by months when she cannot distinguish between the two kinds of blood, argued that if it is commonly known that she menstruates every month her ʿ*idda* is to be reckoned by months, because Allāh has fixed ʿ*idda* by months upon the cessation of menstruation and its reduction is just like its cessation.

The suspecting woman, I mean, one who can sense from her body that she is pregnant, is to wait for the longest gestation period, but they differed about it. It is said in the school that it extends up to four years, while it is also held to be five years. The Ẓāhirites said that it is for nine months. There is no dispute, however, that the termination of the waiting period of the divorced pregnant women is at the time of delivery, on the basis of the words of the Exalted, "And for those with child their period shall be till they bring forth their burden".[86]

19.4.1.1.2. Category 2: The waiting period for those in bondage

The wives who are not free women are divided into exactly the same categories, that is, with respect to menstruation, despair, extended menstruation and those whose menses have ceased but they have not despaired as yet.

The majority maintain about menstruating (slave) women who are still undergoing their monthly courses that their ʿ*idda* is two periods. Dāwūd and the Ẓāhirites maintained that their ʿ*idda* is also for three menstrual periods like free women. This was also Ibn Sīrīn's opinion.

The Ẓāhirites relied upon the general implication of the words of the Exalted, "Women who are divorced shall wait, keeping themselves apart, three (monthly) courses",[87] saying that these woman are also covered by the term "divorced". The majority relied upon the restriction of this general meaning through *qiyās al-shabah*. They compared (the waiting for a number of) menstruation(s) to a repudiation and the *ḥadd*, both of which are reduced into halves on the basis of bondage. Thus, they reduced the ʿ*idda* of the female slave to two menstruations, not one and one-half, as a single menstruation cannot be divided up into halves.

About the slave-woman who has despaired of menstruation, or one who is a minor, Mālik and most of the jurists of Medina said that her ʿ*idda* is three months. Al-Shāfiʿī, Abū Ḥanīfa, al-Thawrī, Abū Thawr and a group of jurists

[86] Qurʾān 65 : 4
[87] Qurʾān 2 : 228

held that her waiting period is a month and a half, being one-half of the *ʿidda* of the free woman, which is based upon analogy, if we concede the restriction of the general meaning. It appears that Mālik's opinion differed in an irregular way. He adopted the general meaning once, that is, in the case of despairing women, while he adopted analogy in the case of menstruating women, whereas analogy should lead to consistent conclusions. With respect to the slave-woman whose menstrual cycle has ceased without a reason, the opinion is the same as that in the case of the free woman, but there is disagreement in this; so also in the case of the woman with extended menstruation. They agreed in the case of a slave-woman divorced prior to consummation that there is no waiting period for her.

The disagreed about the case of the person who takes back his wife during the waiting period after a revocable divorce and then divorces her before cohabiting with her, whether she is to start a fresh *ʿidda* or continue the earlier one. The majority of the jurists of the provinces said that she is to start a new *ʿidda*. A group of jurists said that she remains in her *ʿidda* following the first divorce, which is one opinion of al-Shāfiʿī. Dāwūd said that she does not have to complete her *ʿidda* nor does she undergo a new one.

As a whole, according to Mālik, each retraction demolishes the *ʿidda*, even if there is no cohabitation, except in the case of *al-īlā*. Al-Shāfiʿī said that if he divorces her after retraction and prior to cohabitation, she remains in her first waiting period. Al-Shāfiʿī's opinion is better.

Similarly, according to Mālik, a person who is unable to provide maintenance, the validity of his retraction rests upon his ability to provide maintenance, if he can provide maintenance his retraction is valid and the waiting period is annulled when it is a case of divorce, but if he cannot provide maintenance, she remains in her first waiting period. If she marries again during her waiting period, then, from Mālik there are two opinions. The first upholds the merging of the two waiting periods, while the other opinion holds the negation of the merger. The basis for the first is the vacation of the womb, as this is achieved by merging the two waiting periods. The basis for the second is that *ʿidda* is a kind of ritual (non-rational *ḥukm*), therefore, it must be renewed with each lawful cohabitation. If the slave-woman is emancipated during the waiting period of divorce, she continues within the waiting period of a slave and does not move to that of a free woman. Abū Ḥanīfa said that she does move to the waiting period of a free woman in a revocable divorce, but not in an irrevocable divorce. Al-Shāfiʿī said that she moves to it in both cases.

The reason for disagreement is whether *ʿidda* falls under the *aḥkām* of marriage or under the *aḥkām* of its dissolution. Those who maintained that it relates to the *aḥkām* of marriage said that her *ʿidda* is not transferred, while those who maintained that it relates to the dissolution of marriage said that it is transferred, as if she was emancipated while she was married and was divorced thereafter. In the case of those who distinguished between revocable and irrevocable divorces the reason is obvious. In a revocable divorce there is a likelihood of continued protection, as it is agreed that she is entitled to inheritance if he dies while she is undergoing the *ᶜidda* of a revocable divorce and then she would move to the *ᶜidda* for a widow.

This is the first section out of the two sections relating to the study of the waiting period.

19.4.1.2. *Section 2: The* Aḥkām *of the Waiting Period*

In the topic of the *aḥkām* relating to waiting periods, they agreed that a woman undergoing a waiting period after a revocable divorce is entitled to maintenance and residence, similarly, the pregnant woman (separated by divorce or death), because of the words of the Exalted, "Lodge them where ye dwell, according to your wealth and harass them not so as to straiten life for them", and His words, "And if they are with child, then spend for them till they bring forth their burden".[88]

They disagreed about providing residence to the woman divorced irrevocably and also about her maintenance when she was not pregnant, into three opinions. First, that she has maintenance and residence, which is the opinion of the Kūfīs. Second, that there is neither residence nor maintenance for her, which is the opinion of Aḥmad, Dāwūd, Abū Thawr, Isḥāq and a group of jurists. Third, that she is entitled to residence, but not maintenance, which is the opinion of Mālik, al-Shāfiᶜī and a group of jurists.

The reason for their disagreement is the conflict of different versions of the tradition of Fāṭima bint Qays and also the conflict of the apparent meaning of the Book with this tradition. Those who did not assign to her residence or maintenance argued on the basis of the tradition of Fāṭima bint Qays, who said, "My husband divorced me thrice during the period of the Messenger of Allāh (God's peace and blessings be upon him). I went up to the Prophet (God's peace and blessings be upon him), but he neither granted me residence nor maintenance". This is recorded by Muslim. In some narrations it is laid down that the Messenger of Allāh (God's peace and blessings be upon him) said, "Residence and maintenance are for one whose husband has a right to take her back". This opinion is related from ᶜAlī, Ibn ᶜAbbās and Jābir ibn ᶜAbd Allāh. Those who made residence obligatory for her to the exclusion of maintenance, argued on the basis of a version of the preceding tradition of Fāṭima related by Mālik in his *al-Muwaṭṭaʾ*, which states, "The Messenger of

[88] Qurʾān 65 : 6

Allāh (God's peace and blessings be upon him) said, 'You are not entitled to claim maintenance from him' ". He ordered her to undergo her waiting period in Umm Maktūm's son's house. This narration does not relinquish her right of residence and, therefore, conforms with the generality of the words of the Exalted, "Lodge them where ye dwell, according to your wealth and harass them not so as to straiten life for them".[89] They said that the underlying cause for the Prophet's command that she stay during her *ʿidda* at Umm Maktūm's son's house was her foul tongue.

Those who made residence as well as maintenance obligatory for her determined the obligation of residence for her from the general meaning of the words of the Exalted, "Lodge them where ye dwell, according to your wealth and harass them not so as to straiten life for them",[90] and they upheld her right for maintenance, as an obligation consequential to residence, since it is the case of a revocable divorce, of pregnancy and of marriage itself. Thus, wherever residence becomes obligatory in the law, maintenance becomes obligatory too. It is related from ʿUmar that he said, "We cannot relinquish our Prophet's Book and his practice for the narration of a woman", intending thereby the words of the Exalted, "Lodge them where ye dwell, according to your wealth and harass them not so as to straiten life for them".[91] Moreover, the Prophet's practice is well known that he always granted maintenance whenever residence became obligatory.

In this issue there are two opinions; namely, that she is entitled to both (residence and maintenance) relying upon the apparent meaning of the Book and the well-known *sunna*. It is also said that this general meaning be restricted by the preceding tradition of Fāṭima. The distinction between residence and maintenance is difficult and the basis for this difficulty is the weakness of the evidence.

It is essential to know that the Muslim jurists agreed that *ʿidda* results from three cases: divorce, death and the option granted to the (married) slave-woman when she is emancipated. They disagreed in the case of rescinded contracts, with the majority upholding its obligation.

19.4.1.2.1. **Case 1: Waiting period following (husband's) death**

As the discussion of the waiting period is related to the *aḥkām* of *ʿidda* following (the husband's) death, we deem it appropriate to discuss it here. We, therefore, say: The Muslim jurists agreed that the waiting period for a free woman, because of (the death of) her husband who is a freeman, is four months and ten days, on the basis of the words of the Exalted, "Such of you

[89] Qurʾān 65 : 6
[90] Qurʾān 65 : 6
[91] Qurʾān 65 : 6

as die and leave behind them wives, they (the wives) shall wait, keeping themselves apart, four months and ten days".[92] They disagreed about the waiting period of the pregnant woman and about the waiting period of the slave-woman, as to what is her *ḥukm* when she did not receive her menses during the four months and ten days. Mālik said that a condition for the completion of her waiting period is that she have one menstrual course during this period, if she does not she is considered to be under the doubt of conception and has to undergo the entire waiting period of a pregnant woman. It is also related from him that she may neither be menstruating nor be under a doubt of conception. This is the case when her usual menstrual cycle exceeds the duration of the *ᶜidda*. This either does not occur or it is rare. This is in case her menstrual course exceeds the period of four or more than four months. The narrations from him differ about a woman who actually finds herself in this situation. It is said that she waits for the next menstrual course, but Ibn al-Qāsim has narrated from him that she is to marry if after the *ᶜidda* of death she does not find herself to be pregnant. This is the opinion of the majority of the jurists of the provinces, Abū Ḥanīfa, al-Shāfiᶜī and al-Thawrī.

19.4.1.2.2. Case 2: Pregnancy and the waiting period following death

The majority and all the jurists of the provinces said that the waiting period of the pregnant woman whose husband has died extends up to the time she delivers her burden, on the basis of the words of the Exalted, "And as for the conceiving women, their term shall be the delivery of their burden",[93] though the verse is related to divorce. They also relied on the tradition of Umm Salama, "that Subayᶜa al-Aslamiyya gave birth one-half month after the death of her husband". This tradition states that "She came to the Messenger of Allāh (God's peace and blessings be upon him) who said to her: 'You are now free so marry whom you like' ".

Mālik has related from Ibn ᶜAbbās that her *ᶜidda* extends to the end of the two periods (the time of delivery and the end of the four months and ten days), intending thereby that it extends to the greater of the two periods (whichever is later), either the (termination of) pregnancy or the termination of *ᶜidda* after death. A similar opinion is related from ᶜAlī ibn Abī Ṭālib (God be pleased with him). Their argument is that this is what is required by the reconciliation between the general meaning of the verses; namely, that relating to pregnant women and the verse relating to those whose husbands have died.

When the person for whom the *ama* was permissible has died, she may either be a wife or owned through the *milk yamīn* (bondage) or an *umm al-walad* (a slave-girl who conceives from her master) or just a slave other than the *umm al-*

[92] Qurʾān 2 : 234

[93] Pickthall's translation has been changed here.

walad. About the wife, the majority said that her ᶜ*idda* is one-half that of the free woman on the analogy of ᶜ*idda* (after divorce). The Ẓāhirites said that her ᶜ*idda* is the same as that of the free woman; the same is the case, according to them, of the waiting period after divorce following the general meaning (of the texts).

About the *umm al-walad*, Mālik, al-Shāfiᶜī, Aḥmad, al-Layth, Abū Thawr and a group of jurists said that her ᶜ*idda* is one menstrual course, which was the opinion of Ibn ᶜUmar. Mālik said that if she is one of those who do not menstruate, she is to wait for three months, during which she is entitled to residence. Abū Ḥanīfa, his disciples and al-Thawrī said that her ᶜ*idda* extends up to three menstrual courses, which is the opinion of ᶜAlī and Ibn Masᶜūd. A group of jurists said that her ᶜ*idda* is one-half the waiting period of the free woman whose husband has died, while another group said that her waiting period is the same as that of the free woman, four months and ten days.

Mālik's argument is that she is not a wife so that she may undergo the ᶜ*idda* following death, nor is she divorced so that she may wait up to three menstrual courses, thus, nothing is left except the confirmation of the vacation of her womb and this takes place through one menstrual course comparing her to the slave-woman whose master has died, about which there is no dispute. Abū Ḥanīfa's argument is that the waiting period became obligatory upon her because she is free, she is not a wife that she may undergo the ᶜ*idda* following death, nor is she an *ama* so that she may undergo the ᶜ*idda* of the *ama*, it is, therefore, necessary that the vacation of her womb be established through the ᶜ*idda* of a free woman.

Those who imposed upon her the (regular) ᶜ*idda* following death argued on the basis of the tradition of ᶜAmr ibn ᶜĀṣ, who said, "Do not confuse for us the practice of our Prophet, the ᶜ*idda* of the *umm al-walad*, when her master has died, is four months and ten days". Aḥmad considered this tradition to be weak and did not follow it. Those who imposed upon her one-half the ᶜ*idda* of a free woman did so comparing her to the slave-woman who is a wife. The reason for disagreement is that she is not expressly mentioned in the texts and her case vacillates between those of the *ama* and the free woman. Those who compared her ᶜ*idda* with that of the slave-woman who is a wife, made a weak comparison and weaker than that is its comparison with the ᶜ*idda* of a divorced free woman, which is Abū Ḥanīfa's opinion.

19.4.2. **Chapter 2: Gift of Consolation Paid to a Divorced Woman (*Mut*ᶜ*a*)**

The majority maintain that a gift of consolation is not obligatory for each woman divorced, while a group of the Ẓāhirites said that it is obligatory for each woman divorced. Another group said that it is recommended, but not obligatory, which was upheld by Mālik. Those who considered it obligatory in the case of some categories of divorced women differed about this. Thus, Abū Ḥanīfa said that it is obligatory in the case of the woman divorced prior to consummation, when no dower was fixed for her. Al-Shāfiʿī said that it is obligatory for each woman divorced, when the separation is initiated by him, except for the case of the woman whose dower was fixed, but she was divorced prior to consummation. This is (also) the opinion of the majority.

Abū Ḥanīfa argued on the basis of the words of the Exalted, "O ye who believe! If ye wed believing women and divorce them before ye have touched them, then there is no period that ye should reckon. But content them and release them handsomely".[94] Thus, *mutʿa* was stipulated in the absence of consummation. Further, Allāh, the Exalted, said, "If ye divorce them before ye have touched them and ye have appointed to them a portion, then (pay the) half of that which ye have appointed".[95] This indicates that there is no compensation for her in the case of fixation (of dower) and divorce prior to consummation and as dower is not obligatory for her it is more appropriate that compensation should not be obligatory. This, upon my life, is conjectural, for when dower was no longer obligatory for her, compensation (*mutʿa*) was substituted for it, but if she or the one who possesses her marriage tie decide to forgo one-half dower, she is entitled to nothing more.

Al-Shāfiʿī construed the commands, laid down about compensation, in the words of the Exalted, "Provide for them, the rich according to his means and the straitened according to his means, a fair provision",[96] in their general meaning for every divorced woman, except one for whom the dower is fixed and is divorced prior to consummation.

The Ẓāhirites interpreted the command in its general meaning, while the majority maintain that there is no compensation (*mutʿa*) for a woman separated through redemption (*khulʿ*), as she is the payer and her case is like that of the woman divorced prior to consummation and after the fixation of dower. The Ẓāhirites maintain that it is the (general) law, she may take and give at the same time.

Mālik interpreted the command for compensation to mean recommendation, because of the words of the Exalted at the end of the verse, "(This is) a bounden duty for those who do good",[97] that is, the generous and the gracious and whatever falls under the category of generosity is not obligatory.

They disagreed whether mourning (*iḥdād*) is obligatory for a divorced woman undergoing ʿ*idda*. Mālik said it is not.

[94] Qurʾān 33 : 49
[95] Qurʾān 2 : 237
[96] Qurʾān 2 : 236
[97] Qurʾān 2 : 236

19.4.3. **Chapter 3: Appointment of Arbitrators**

The jurists agreed about the permissibility of appointing arbitrators in case of discord between the spouses, when their positions are not known, as to which one of the couple is right and who is wrong, because of the words of the Exalted, "And if ye fear a breach between them twain (the man and wife), appoint an arbiter from his folk and an arbiter from her folk. If they desire amendment Allāh will make them of one mind. Lo! Allāh is ever Knower, Aware".[98] They agreed that the arbiters could only be from the families of the spouses, one representing the husband and the other the wife, except when no one in their families is to be found who can negotiate a settlement between them, in which case someone else is to be appointed.

They agreed that if the arbiters were not unanimous their decision would not be implemented and they also agreed that their decision to maintain the marriage tie is to be executed without there being a specific delegation of powers to them by the spouses. They disputed the agreed decision of the arbiters to separate them, whether it would require the consent of the husband. Mālik and his disciples said that their decision about separation and union is valid without specific delegation by the spouses and without their consent. Al-Shāfiʿī, Abū Ḥanīfa and their disciples said that they have no right to separate them, except when the husband delegates such authority to them.

The evidence for Mālik is what he has related from ʿAlī ibn Abī Ṭālib about this, when he said about arbitrators that "they have a right to cause a separation or a union between the spouses". The evidence for al-Shāfiʿī and Abū Ḥanīfa is that as a fundamental principle, the right to divorce does not belong to anyone but the husband or to one whom the husband has delegated such power.

Mālik's disciples disagreed about the case where the arbiters repudiate thrice. Ibn al-Qāsim said that it amounts to a single repudiation, while Ashhab and al-Mughīra said that it is a triple repudiation if they have pronounced it thrice.

The principle, however, is that divorce is a right possessed by the husband, unless evidence to the contrary is adduced. Al-Shāfiʿī and Abū Ḥanīfa argue on the basis of a verdict by ʿAlī, when he said to the arbiters, "Do you know what (authority) you possess? If you decide to maintain their union, you may do so and if you decide to cause a separation between them you may do so". In response to this, the woman said, "I agree to abide by the Book of Allāh and by what is in it for me and against me". The husband said, "I disagree about separation". ʿAlī said, "By Allāh, you will not go till you agree in the same way in which the woman has agreed". This was taken as his consent for

[98] Qurʾān 4 : 35

this. Mālik, on the other hand, compares the arbiters to the sultan and the sultan has the right to divorce because of harm, according to Mālik, when it becomes manifest.

XX
THE BOOK OF *AL-ĪLĀʾ* (VOW OF CONTINENCE)

The basis for this subject are the words of the Exalted, "For those who forswear their wives, there is a period of waiting of four months; then if they change their mind, lo! Allāh is Forgiving, Merciful".[99] *Al-īlāʾ* is the swearing of an oath by a man that he will not have intercourse with his wife, either for a period in excess of four months, or for a period of four months, or for an unlimited period, over which there is (juristic) dispute, as will be discussed in what follows.

The jurists of the provinces differed about *al-īlāʾ* on a number of points. One of these is whether a woman is to be considered as divorced by the person taking the oath after the completion of the period of four months laid down in the text, or whether she is divorced if he abstains from it even after the period of four months—after which he may return to her (*fāʾa*) or divorce her. Another point is whether *al-īlāʾ* comes into effect with any oath, or only through oaths that are considered permissible by the law (*sharʿ*). If he exercises continence without taking the oath, will he be considered to have taken the oath? Is the person swearing considered to be covered by *al-īlāʾ* if he specifies the period of four months, or is the period to be in excess of that? And what if he has not specified a period at all? Is the divorce resulting from *al-īlāʾ* revocable or irrevocable? If he refuses to divorce or to return, is the *qāḍī* to divorce on his behalf? Does *al-īlāʾ* recur if he divorces her and then takes her back without a new vow of continence in the renewed marriage tie? Is it a condition for retraction by the person taking the vow of continence that he have intercourse with her during the waiting period? Does the vow of continence by a slave give rise to the same *ḥukm* as is applicable to a freeman? If he divorces her after the completion of the period of *al-īlāʾ*, is it binding on her to undergo a waiting period?

These are the issues related to *al-īlāʾ* over which disagreement among the *fuqahāʾ* of the provinces is widely known. These issues act as the principles underlying this subject and we shall discuss in each, as is our aim, the disagreement, the major evidence and the reasons for disagreement.

[99] Qurʾān 2 : 226. Pickthall's translation changed for this verse.

20.1. Issue 1

About their disagreement whether divorce comes into effect by the end of the four-month period itself, or divorce does not take effect, in which case the *ḥukm* is suspended till he returns to her or divorces her, Mālik, al-Shāfiʿī, Aḥmad, Abū Thawr, Dāwūd and al-Layth held that the *ḥukm* is suspended till he returns to her or divorces her. This was the opinion of ʿAlī and Ibn ʿUmar, though other opinions have also been related from them, but this is the correct record. Abū Ḥanīfa, his disciples, al-Thawrī and the Kūfīs generally held that divorce comes into effect at the time of the completion of the four-month period, unless he approaches his wife during that period. This was the opinion of Ibn Masʿūd and a group of the *Tābiʿūn*.

The reason for disagreement is whether the words of the Exalted, "Then if they change their mind, lo! Allāh is Forgiving, Merciful",[100] imply that they should change their minds before the completion of four months or after it. Those who understood them to mean before the completion of the period said that divorce comes into effect (upon completion of the period). According to these jurists the term "decide" in the words of the Exalted, "And if they decide upon divorce (let them remember that) Allāh is Hearer, Knower",[101] imply that he has not changed his mind during that period. Those who understood by the stipulation of return as its being effective after the end of the period said that the meaning of the words "if they decide upon divorce" imply "if they pronounce divorce with words" then "Allāh is Hearer, Knower".

The Mālikites have four arguments related to the verse. First, that the period of waiting has been deemed to be the right of the husband and not that of the wife; it, therefore, resembles the period of delay in debts. Second, that Allāh has made divorce dependent upon his (the husband's) act, while according to the others it does not result from his act except by way of infraction, that is, it is not attributed to him according to the opinion of the Ḥanafites except as an infraction and it cannot be interpreted as a metaphorical use from the apparent meaning except with supporting evidence. The third evidence is that the words of the Exalted, "And if they decide upon divorce (let them remember that) Allāh is Hearer, Knower",[102] imply that divorce occurs in a way that it can be heard, through words and not by the completion of the period. Fourth, that the conjunction *fāʾ* (then) in the words of the Exalted, "then if they change their mind, lo! Allāh is Forgiving, Merciful",[103] implies consequential action, which indicates that changing his mind (returning) is after the period. Perhaps, they compared this period to the period in manumission.

[100] Qurʾān 2 : 226
[101] Qurʾān 2 : 227
[102] Qurʾān 2 : 227
[103] Qurʾān 2 : 226

Abū Ḥanīfa relied in this upon the resemblance of this period with the period in a revocable divorce, the period being stipulated so that he may not do something regrettable. On the whole, they compared *al-īlāʾ* with a revocable divorce and compared the period here with *ʿidda*, which is a strong resemblance. This is also related from Ibn ʿAbbās.

20.2. Issue 2

About their disagreement over the oath through which *al-īlāʾ* takes place, Mālik said that it (*al-īlāʾ*) occurs through every kind of oath, while al-Shāfiʿī said that it can only be invoked through oaths permissible under the law, like swearing by Allāh or by one of His attributes. Mālik relied upon the general meaning, that is, the general meaning implied by the words of the Exalted, "Those who forswear their wives must wait four months". Al-Shāfiʿī, on the other hand, compared *al-īlāʾ* with the oath of expiation. The reason is that both kinds of oath lead to a legal *ḥukm*, thus, it becomes obligatory that the oath upon which the *ḥukm* of *al-īlāʾ* was based be the same as the oath upon which the *ḥukm* of expiation was structured.

20.3. Issue 3

With respect to the application of the *ḥukm* of *al-īlāʾ* to the husband who gives up cohabitation with his wife without swearing an oath, the majority maintain that the *ḥukm* of *al-īlāʾ* is not applicable to him without the oath. Mālik makes it applicable if he intends to harm his wife by abstention, even without swearing the oath. The majority relied upon the apparent meaning, while Mālik considered the underlying reason, as the *ḥukm* has been applied to him because of practising continence, whether such an act has been strengthened with a vow or is undertaken without it. The harm is caused in both ways.

20.4. Issue 4

In their dispute about the duration of *al-īlāʾ*, Mālik and those who agreed with his opinion held that the period for *al-īlāʾ* must be in excess of four months, as returning (changing his mind), according to them, takes place after four months. For Abū Ḥanīfa the period of *al-īlāʾ* is only four months, as returning to the wife takes place, according to him, within this period. Al-Ḥasan and Ibn Abī Laylā said that if he swears an oath for any determined period, even when such a period is less than four months, the period assigned for him will be four months from the time when he swore the oath. It is related from Ibn ʿAbbās that the person taking the oath of *al-īlāʾ* is one who swears not to cohabit with his wife, ever.

The reason for their disagreement is the unrestricted implication of the verse. Their disagreement about the time of return, the nature of the oath and its duration arises because the verse assigns general meanings to these terms or it does not provide details. Similarly, their dispute about the description of the person taking the oath and the woman against whom it is sworn and also about the kind of divorce resulting from it, as will be coming up in what follows. The reason for disagreement, thus, is due to the silence about these things, which are the essential elements of *al-īlāʾ*, that is, the identification of the kind of oath, the time of return, the duration, the description of the man taking the oath, the woman who is the object of the oath and the kind of divorce resulting from it.

20.5. Issue 5

According to Mālik and al-Shāfiʿī the divorce resulting from *al-īlāʾ* is revocable, as the principle dictates that any divorce under the law is to be interpreted as being revocable, unless evidence indicates that it is irrevocable. Abū Ḥanīfa and Abū Thawr said that it is irrevocable. The reason being that if it were revocable the harm caused by it would not be removed from her, as he would be able to force her to come back to him. The reason for disagreement is the conflict of the interest to be secured by the law of *al-īlāʾ* with a well-known principle in divorce. Those who preferred the principle said it is revocable, while those who preferred the secured interest said that it is irrevocable.

20.6. Issue 6

Does the *qāḍī* pronounce the divorce when he refuses to return or to divorce her, or is he to be imprisoned till he divorces her. Mālik said that the *qāḍī* is to pronounce the divorce, while the Ẓāhirites said that he is to be confined till he divorces her himself. The reason for disagreement is the clash of an established principle with a secured interest. Those who preserved the declared principle in divorce said that a divorce does not take place except when pronounced by the husband, while those who took into account the inherent harm caused to women said that the sultan is to divorce in view of the general interest to be secured. This is what is known as *qiyās mursal* and its practice is related from Mālik when many other jurists rejected it.

20.7. Issue 7

Does *al-īlāʾ* recur if he divorces her and then takes her back? Mālik said that if he takes her back and does not cohabit with her, *al-īlāʾ* becomes operative against him again. This is the case, according to him, in both revocable and irrevocable divorces. Abū Ḥanīfa said that an irrevocable divorce annuls *al-īlāʾ*, which is also one of al-Shāfiʿī's opinions and is the opinion selected by al-Muzanī. A group of jurists maintain that *al-īlāʾ* does not recur after divorce, except by the repetition of the vow.

The reason for their disagreement is the clash of *maṣlaḥa* with an apparent condition of *al-īlā*ʾ. The reason is that there is no vow of continence under the law unless it occurs within the same marriage tie, not a renewed contract (after an irrevocable divorce). But when we take this into account, the harm that was desired to be removed through *al-īlā*ʾ is found to exist. It is for this reason that Mālik applied the *ḥukm* of *al-īlā*ʾ in the absence of the vow when the meaning of *al-īlā*ʾ was to be found (in the act).

20.8. Issue 8

Is the ʿ*idda* binding upon the wife of the person swearing continence? The majority maintain that ʿ*idda* is binding upon her. Jābir ibn Zayd said that ʿ*idda* is not binding upon her if she has menstruated thrice in the four-month period. A group of jurists adopted his opinion, which is also related from Ibn ʿAbbās. His argument is that ʿ*idda* has been prescribed to verify the vacation of the womb and vacation is established for the woman in such a case. The majority's argument is that she is a divorced woman and it is necessary that she undergo ʿ*idda* like all other divorced women. The reason for disagreement is that ʿ*idda* combines in itself a *maṣlaḥa* as well as non-rational obedience. Those who took into account the secured interest did not prescribe ʿ*idda* for her, while those who gave prominence to obedience (worship) made ʿ*idda* obligatory for her.

20.9. Issue 9

About the vow of continence by the slave, Mālik said that the period for *al-īlā*ʾ of the slave is two months, one-half the period for a freeman on the analogy of *ḥudūd* and divorce in his case. Al-Shāfiʿī and the Ẓāhirites said that the period in his vow is the same as that of the freeman—four months, taking into account the general implication (of the verse). The apparent rule is that the swearing of oaths by the slave and the freeman are the same and *al-īlā*ʾ is an oath; so also on the analogy of the duration of impotence. Abū Ḥanīfa said that the inherent harm caused in *al-īlā*ʾ is to be considered from the view of women not men, as in the case of ʿ*idda*. If the woman is free, the period of *al-īlā*ʾ will be that of a free-woman, even if the husband is a slave, but if she is a slave, the period will be one-half.

The analogy of *al-īlā*ʾ upon *ḥadd* is not good, because the *ḥadd* of the slave is less than the *ḥadd* of the freeman, as an offence on his part is less offensive, while it is more offensive when committed by a freeman. The period of *al-īlā*ʾ, on the other hand, combines in it flexibility for the husband and the removal of harm from the wife. If we stipulate a period narrower than this, it would be confining for the husband and enhanced in its removal of harm from the wife, but the freeman too is entitled to relief and protection from harm.

It follows from this analogy that the period of *al-īlāʾ* can only be reduced when the husband is a slave or the wife is a free woman, but this is an opinion proclaimed by none. A compromise is, therefore, necessary.

Those who maintained the effectiveness of bondage in the reduction of the period of *al-īlāʾ*, disagreed about the elimination of bondage after the vow, whether it would convert into the period prescribed for freemen. Mālik said that it would not be converted from the period of slaves to the period for freemen. Abū Ḥanīfa said it will; according to him, if the slave woman is emancipated after her husband has sworn a vow of continence against her, the period will be converted to the period of free persons.

Ibn al-Qāsim said that there is no operation of the vow of continence against a minor girl at whose age cohabitation is not practised. If, however, an oath is sworn and he persists with it, the four months will be counted from the day she attains puberty. He said this because there is no harm being caused to her as a result of continence. He also said that there is no operation of the vow in the case of a castrated man and also in the case of one who is not capable of intercourse.

20.10. Issue 10

Is it a condition for retraction by the person making a vow of continence that he cohabit with his wife during her *ʿidda*? The majority maintained that this is not one of the conditions. Mālik, however, said that if he does not cohabit with her, without a cause of illness or something similar to it, his retraction (of divorce after *al-īlāʾ*) will not be valid and she will continue with her *ʿidda* and there would be no chance of his taking her back if the *ʿidda* is completed.

The argument of the majority is that after retraction *al-īlāʾ* may be repeated by him during the *ʿidda* or it may not be. If he repeats it, the first one is not taken into account and is renewed from the time of retraction, that is, the period of *al-īlāʾ* is calculated from the time of retraction. If he does not repeat the vow, the first one is not taken into account at all, except according to the opinion of those who maintain that *al-īlāʾ* can take place without an oath. Thus, whatever the case, the four months are counted from the time of the retraction. Mālik said that every retraction from divorce is meant to avoid harm and the validity of this retraction is to be taken into account for the removal of this harm. The principle is the same as that in the case of one in straitened circumstances. If a divorce is pronounced against him and he retracts it, his retraction will only be valid if he has attained financial ease. The reason for disagreement is *qiyās al-shabah*. The basis is that those who compared it to a renewal of the contract of marriage made the renewal of *al-īlāʾ* obligatory in it, while those who held this retraction to be similar to the retraction of a person divorced because of harm and from whom the cause of the harm has not been removed, said that he maintains the original status.

XXI
THE BOOK OF *ẒIHĀR* (INJURIOUS ASSIMILATION)

The sources for (the *aḥkām* of) *ẓihār* are the Book and the *sunna*. In the Book, it is the words of the Exalted, "Those who put away their wives (by saying they are as their mothers) and afterward would go back on that which they have said, (the penalty) in that case (is) the freeing of a slave before they touch one another. Unto this they are exhorted; and Allāh is informed of what ye do".[104] In the *sunna* it is the tradition of Khawla bint Mālik ibn Thaʿlaba, who said, "My husband, Uways ibn al-Ṣāmit, pronounced *ẓihār* against me, so I went up to the Messenger of Allāh (God's peace and blessings be upon him) and complained to him. The Messenger of Allāh argued about the matter with me and said, 'Fear Allāh, for he (your husband) is the son of your uncle'. As soon as I left, Allāh sent down the verse, 'Allāh hath heard the saying of her that disputeth with thee (Muḥammad) concerning her husband and complaineth unto Allāh. And Allāh heareth your colloquy. Lo! Allāh is Hearer, Knower—(followed by the next three verses)' ".[105] He (the Prophet) said, 'He must set free a slave'. She replied, 'He does not have one'. He said, 'He should fast consecutively for two months'. She said, 'O Messenger of Allāh, he is an old man and is not able to fast'. He said, 'Then he must feed sixty needy persons'. She replied, 'He does not have anything that he can give away as charity'. He said, 'I will support him with a load of dates'. She said, 'And I will support him with another'. He said, 'You have done well, go and feed sixty needy ones on his behalf'. It is recorded by Abū Dāwūd. Another (similar) tradition is that of Salama ibn Ṣakhr al-Bayāḍī from the Messenger of Allāh (God's peace and blessings be upon him).

The discussion about the principles of *ẓihār* is dealt with in seven sections: the words of *ẓihār*; the conditions of the obligation of expiation in it; persons in whose case *ẓihār* is effective; what is prohibited for the person pronouncing *ẓihār*; is *ẓihār* renewed by the renewal of marriage; is *al-īlāʾ* applicable to him; and the discussion of the *aḥkām* of the penance of *ẓihār*.

[104] Qur'ān 58 : 3
[105] Qur'ān 58 : 1

21.1. *Section 1: Words Used for* Ẓihār

The jurists agreed that if the man says to his wife, "You are for me like my mother's back", it amounts to *ẓihār*. They disagreed when he mentions another part of the body, or when he mentions the back of women, other than the mother, who are perpetually prohibited for him. Mālik said it is *ẓihār*, while a group of jurists said that it does not amount to *ẓihār*, except by the employment of the words "back" and "mother". Abū Ḥanīfa said that it amounts to *ẓihār* by naming any part of the body, which it is prohibited to look at.

The reason for disagreement is the conflict of the underlying meaning with the literal interpretation. On the one hand, the mother and other prohibited women, as well as the backs of women and their other limbs are similarly prohibited. Yet, according to the law, *ẓihār* only applies when the words "back" and "mother" are used.

If, however, he says that she is like his mother, but does not use the word "back", Abū Ḥanīfa and al-Shāfiʿī say that his intention is to be taken into account, as he may mean to indicate his respect and love for her. Mālik said that this is *ẓihār*. If the person compares his wife to a strange woman who is not prohibited to him perpetually, it is *ẓihār* according to Mālik, but according to Ibn al-Mājishūn it is not. The reason for disagreement is whether the comparison of the wife with a prohibited woman, who is not prohibited perpetually, is the same as comparing her to one prohibited perpetually.

21.2. *Section 2: Conditions for the Obligation of Expiation (*Kaffāra*)*

As a condition of the obligation of expiation, the majority maintain that it does not become obligatory without retraction. Mujāhid and Ṭāwūs deviated from this saying that it becomes obligatory even without retraction. The evidence for the majority are the words of the Exalted, "Those who put away their wives (by saying they are as the backs of their mothers) and afterwards would go back on that which they have said, (the penalty) in that case (is) the freeing of a slave before they touch one another. Unto this they are exhorted; and Allāh is informed of what ye do".[106] This text is explicit about the relationship of expiation with retraction. It is also obvious by way of analogy, as (expiation in) *ẓihār* resembles expiation in an oath; just as expiation becomes binding by going against the oath or by the resolve to go against it, the same is the case in *ẓihār*.

The argument of Mujāhid and Ṭāwūs is that it is an act invoking the extreme type of expiation, it is, therefore, necessary that it should give rise to it on its own and not through any additional reason, the same as the expiation of homicide and the violation of a fast. They also said that it was a form of

[106] Qurʾān 58 : 3. Pickthall's parenthetical phrase changed slightly.

divorce during *jāhiliyya* and it was annulled by means of expiation, which is the meaning of the words of the Exalted, "and afterwards would go back on that which they have said". Going back here, for them, is like going back into the fold of Islam.

Those who uphold the stipulation of retraction in the obligation of expiation, disagreed as to how it is constituted. There are three narrations from Mālik about it. First, that he resolves to keep her and to have intercourse with her. Second, that he resolves to have intercourse with her. This is the correct and widely known narration from his disciples and is also the opinion of Abū Ḥanīfa and Aḥmad. The third is that retraction occurs through intercourse itself (irrespective of resolve) and this is the weakest of the three narrations, according to his disciples. Al-Shāfiʿī said that retraction is the act of retaining her. He said that when considerable time has passed in which he could have divorced her, but did not, he is to be assumed to have gone back (on what he said) and is obliged to make expiation, as his waiting for a period of time in which he could have divorced and did not do so is to be taken as a substitute for his resolve to take her back, or it is an indication of it. Dāwūd and the Ẓāhirites said that retraction is by repeating the words of *ẓihār* a second time.[107] If he does not do so, he has not retracted and is not liable for expiation.

The evidence, for the widely known narration from Mālik, is structured upon two principles. The first is that the concept of *ẓihār* requires that the obligation of expiation should arise from the resolve of the man to go back to what he has prohibited to himself and which is intercourse. If that is the case, it is necessary that going back be through intercourse itself, or through the determination and resolve to revert to it. The second principle is that it is not possible that going back itself should be intercourse, because of the words of the Exalted, "(the penalty) in that case (is) the freeing of a slave before they touch one another".[108] Intercourse is, therefore, prohibited till expiation. They (Mālik's disciples) said that had (the resolve of) retraction itself meant taking her back, then, *ẓihār* would have prohibited taking her back, which would mean that *ẓihār* amounted to divorce.

The solution, on the whole, according to them, in this issue is what is referred to by the *fuqahāʾ* as *sabr wa al-taqsīm* (division and elimination). This takes place by saying that the meaning of going back may either be the repetition of the word, as is held by Dāwūd, or intercourse itself, or taking her back, or the resolve of having intercourse. It cannot be the repetition of the word (*ẓihār*), for this is mere emphasis and emphasis cannot obligate

[107] That is, incorporating the words within the retraction.

[108] Qurʾān 58 : 3

expiation, nor can it be the resolve to take her back for intercourse and the act of taking her back is present in any case. It, therefore, remains that it is the resolve for intercourse and even if he has decided to take her back for purpose of intercourse, he still intends intercourse. It is, therefore, established that retraction means (resolve for) intercourse.

The reliance of the Shāfiʿites in considering the intention to hold on to her as being the intention of intercourse is on the point that holding on to her itself makes intercourse necessary. Thus, they considered the consequence of the thing to be the thing itself and assigned them the same *ḥukm*. This opinion comes close to the second narration (from Mālik). Perhaps, the Shāfiʿites argued that the intention of retaining her is the cause of the obligation of expiation and the obligation is removed with the removal of the intention to retain her. This is the case when he divorces her following *ẓihār*. It is for this reason that Mālik was cautious in the second narration and deemed retraction the resolve to do both things, I mean, intercourse and retaining her.

The opinion that retraction is intercourse itself is weak and opposed to the text. The reliance in this is on the similarity of *ẓihār* with an oath, that is, just as the expiation for the oath becomes obligatory upon breaking it, the same is the case here, which is *qiyās al-shabah* that is opposed by the text.

Dāwūd went by the literal meaning of the words of the Exalted, "and afterwards would go back on that which they have said".[109] These words imply going back upon the word itself. According to Abū Ḥanīfa it is going back to the *jāhiliyya* practice of *ẓihār* after coming into the fold of Islam, in accordance with what has preceded about their practice of *ẓihār* in *jāhiliyya*, while according to Mālik and al-Shāfiʿī it is the underlying meaning of the words "and afterwards would go back on that which they have said".

The reason for disagreement, on the whole, is the conflict of the literal with the underlying meaning. Those who considered the underlying meaning deemed retraction to be the resolve for intercourse, or of retaining her (without divorce). The meaning of the letter *lām* in the words of the Exalted, "*thumma yaʿūdūna li-mā qālū*—and afterwards would go back on that which they have said", was interpreted to mean the same as the preposition *fī* to be read as the letter *fāʾ* (standing for "because of what"). On the other hand, those who considered the literal meaning deemed going back to be the repetition of the word and as going back a second time, which is second with respect to the first that was in *jāhiliyya* (that is, doing the same thing as was done in *jāhiliyya*). For those who interpreted it to be either of these two meanings, it is proper for them to believe that expiation becomes obligatory with the act of *ẓihār* itself, as was understood by Mujāhid, unless an implied word is assumed, which is the intention of keeping her.

109 Qurʾān 58 : 4

Here, then, we have three opinions: that retraction may either be the repetition of the words, or it should be the intention to hold on to her, or it may be the retraction that was in Islam. These two, that is, the first and the third are divided in two ways. First, that an implied word be assumed in the verse, which is the intention of keeping her and thus stipulate this condition in the obligation of expiation. Second, that no implication is assumed and expiation becomes obligatory by the act of *ẓihār* itself.

In this topic they differed about cases. The first arises when he divorces her before forming an intention of keeping her, or when the woman dies (before this), is he obliged to make expiation? The majority of the jurists maintain that there is no expiation for him, unless he divorces (her) after forming an intention to retract or after taking her back through the passage of a long period, as is the view of al-Shāfiʿī. It is related from ʿUthmān al-Battī that he is liable for expiation after divorce, but if she dies before the intention to retract, he is not entitled to inherit from her, except when he makes expiation. This is a deviation opposing the text. Allāh knows best.

21.3. *Section 3: Persons in Whose Case* Ẓihār *is Effective*

They agreed about the effectiveness of *ẓihār* in the case of a wife who is in the protection of the husband, but they differed in the case of *ẓihār* related to a slave-woman and about one not under protection. Similarly, they disagreed about *ẓihār* of a woman against a man.

About *ẓihār* related to a slave-woman, Mālik, al-Thawrī and a group of jurists said that the consequences of *ẓihār* in her case are the same as those in the case of a wife who is a free woman. Same is the case of a *mudabbara*, or that of an *umm al-walad*. Al-Shāfiʿī, Abū Ḥanīfa, Aḥmad and Abū Thawr said that *ẓihār* does not apply to a slave-woman. Al-Awzāʿī said that if he uses the slave-woman as a concubine, then, his *ẓihār* is applicable to her, otherwise it amounts to an oath and there is expiation of an oath in it. ʿAṭāʾ said that his *ẓihār* is effective (in her case), but there is one-half the amount of expiation in it.

The evidence of those who give effect to *ẓihār* in the case of a slave-girl is found in the general application of the words of the Exalted, "Those who put away their women (by saying they are as their mothers)",[110] as slaves are among these women. The argument of those who do not consider *ẓihār* in her case to be effective is based on their agreement that the word *nisāʾ* in the words of the Exalted, "Those who forswear their wives must wait four months",[111] is applied to wives; similarly, the word *nisāʾ* in the verse of *ẓihār*.

[110] Qurʾān 58 : 4. The word "wives" now changed to "women" in Pickthall's translation so that it may conform with the author's discussion.

[111] Qurʾān 2 : 226

The reason for disagreement is the conflict of *qiyās al-shabah* with the general meaning, that is, the comparison of *ẓihār* with *āl-īlā*ʾ and the general meaning of the word *nisā*ʾ, I mean, the general meaning implies the inclusion of the slave-women in *ẓihār* and the comparison with *āl-īlā*ʾ implies their exclusion from *ẓihār*.

Mālik's opinion about the question whether it is a condition of *ẓihār* that the woman be in the protection of the person swearing against her is that it is not a condition and one who identifies a particular woman and proclaims *ẓihār* against her upon the condition of future marriage has made *ẓihār* effective against her. Similarly, when he does not identify a particular woman and says that any woman he may marry is like his mother's back for him. This is contrary to the rule in divorce. Abū Ḥanīfa, al-Thawrī and al-Awzāʿī went by Mālik's opinion. Others said that *ẓihār* does not operate, except in that which is owned by a man. Among those who held this opinion are al-Shāfiʿī, Abū Thawr and Dāwūd. One group made a distinction saying that if he makes a categorical statement he is not liable for *ẓihār*, for example, he says: "Any woman that I will marry is for me like my mother's back". If he qualifies it, it becomes binding against him, like his naming a woman, or naming a village or a tribe. Those expressing this opinion are Ibn Abī Laylā and al-Ḥasan ibn Ḥayy.

The evidence of the first group are the words of the Exalted, "Abide by your agreements", as this is an agreement with the condition of ownership and becomes likely when he comes to own. Further (evidence is) the saying that the believers have to abide by their conditions, which is ʿUmar's view. Al-Shāfiʿī's argument is based on the tradition of ʿAmr ibn Shuʿayb from his father from his grandfather "that the Prophet (God's peace and blessings be upon him) said, 'There is no divorce except in what is owned, no manumission except in what is owned, no sale except in what is owned and no performance of a vow except in what is owned' ". It is recorded by Abū Dāwūd and al-Tirmidhī. Another argument is that *ẓihār* resembles divorce, which is the opinion of Ibn ʿAbbās.

Those who made a distinction between generalization and specification held that categorical statements in *ẓihār* lead to harm and Allāh, the Exalted, has said, "He hath chosen you and hath not laid down for you in religion any hardship".[112]

Within this topic they also disagreed over whether a woman can also proclaim *ẓihār* against a man. There are three opinions of the jurists about it. The best known is that there can be no *ẓihār* initiated by her, which is the opinion of Mālik and al-Shāfiʿī. Second, that she will be liable to expiation for

[112] Qurʾān 22 : 78

an oath. Third, that she is liable for the expiation of *ẓihār*. The reliance of the majority is upon the similarity between *ẓihār* and divorce. Those who made it effective in her case held *ẓihār* to be similar to an oath. Those who made a distinction, did so as they held that the minimum obligation for her in this is the expiation of an oath, which is weak. The reason for disagreement is the conflict of similarities in this concept.

21.4. *Section 4: Prohibitions for the Person Pronouncing* Ẓihār

They agreed that sexual intercourse (with penetration) is prohibited to the person pronouncing *ẓihār*, but they disagreed about what is less than sexual intercourse, like fondling, playing with the sexual organs and looking at the woman with lust. Mālik held that sexual intercourse and all kinds of sexual gratification that is less than intercourse, like playing with the sexual organs, fondling, kissing and looking with lust at parts of the body other than the face, hands and forearms is prohibited. This was also the opinion of Abū Ḥanīfa, though he considered only the looking at genitals as reprehensible. Al-Shāfiʿī said that to the person pronouncing *ẓihār* only the agreed upon intercourse with penetration is prohibited and not the other acts, which was also the opinion of al-Thawrī, Aḥmad and a group of jurists.

Mālik's evidence is in the words of the Exalted, "before they touch one another".[113] The apparent meaning of touching implies physical contact and what is more than that. In addition it (*ẓihār*) is a word by which she becomes prohibited for him and it, therefore, resembles divorce. The evidence for al-Shāfiʿī's opinion is that touching here is a figurative use alluding to sexual intercourse, upon the evidence of their consensus that it is intercourse that is prohibited. If it indicates intercourse, it cannot indicate what is besides that, for it may either indicate sexual intercourse or indicate what is besides it, which is a metaphorical meaning. As they agreed that it indicates intercourse, the metaphorical implication is negated, for a word cannot imply two things at the same time, the actual and the metaphorical.

I would say: For those who hold that the equivocal word has a general implication, it is possible for a word to indicate two meanings at the same time, that is, actual and metaphorical, though it is not normal in the Arab usage. It is for this reason that an opinion based upon it is considered weak. If, however, it is known that the law has used it in this way, it would be permitted. In addition to this *ẓihār* resembles *āl-īlāʿ*, it is, therefore, necessary according to them that it be confined to sexual intercourse.

[113] Qurʾān 58 : 3

21.5. *Section 5: Renewal of* Ẓihār *with the Renewal of Marriage?*

There is disagreement about the recurrence of *ẓihār* after divorce, that is, if he divorces her after *ẓihār* before retracting it and then takes her back, does *ẓihār* come into force again, so that he cannot touch her till he retracts it? Mālik said that if he divorces her less than three times and thereafter takes her back during the waiting period or after it, he is to offer expiation. Al-Shāfiʿī said that if he takes her back during the *ʿidda*, he is liable for expiation, but if he takes her back in a time other than the waiting period he is not liable for expiation. There is another opinion from him identical to Mālik's opinion. Muḥammad ibn al-Ḥasan said that *ẓihār* recurs whether he marries her after three repudiations or after one. This issue resembles the case of the person who takes an oath to divorce, after which he pronounces the divorce and then takes the woman back, is the earlier oath still in force to his detriment?

The reason for disagreement is whether divorce eliminates all the *aḥkām* of the marriage bond and annuls them. Some jurists were of the opinion that the irrevocable divorce, resulting from a triple-repudiation annuls them, but a divorce that is less than that does not. There are also others who believe that no form of divorce annuls those *aḥkām* and I think it is the Ẓāhirites who maintain that all forms of divorce annul such *aḥkām*.

21.6. *Section 6: The Operation of* al-Īlāʾ *in* Ẓihār

Does *al-īlāʾ* become operative in *ẓihār* if he persists in his injurious act? This occurs when he does not retract when he is capable of doing so. There is disagreement in this too. Abū Ḥanīfa and Al-Shāfiʿī said that the two separate *aḥkām* cannot be combined, as the *ḥukm* of *ẓihār* is different from the *ḥukm* of *al-īlāʾ*. It is the same for them whether his act entails an injurious intention. This was also the opinion of al-Awzāʿī, Aḥmad and a group of jurists. Mālik said that *al-īlāʾ* can be imposed upon *ẓihār* on the condition that his intention is to inflict harm. Al-Thawrī said that *al-īlāʾ* is enforced in *ẓihār* in which case she becomes divorced from him irrevocably on the termination of the period of four months, without considering his intention to harm.

There are, thus, three opinions. First, that *al-īlāʾ* can be imposed upon *ẓihār* without qualifications. Second, it cannot be enforced at all. Third, that it can be enforced in case of an intention to harm, but not in its absence. The reason for disagreement is the concern for the underlying reason and consideration of the apparent meaning. Those who went by the apparent meaning said that the two cannot be combined, while those who regarded the underlying reason said that they can be combined when the intention is to inflict harm.

21.7. Section 7: The Aḥkām *of Expiation for* Ẓihār

The study of expiation of *ẓihār* involves a number of things: the number and kinds of expiation and their priority; the conditions of their different kinds, that is, the conditions of validity; and when do single and multiple expiations become obligatory?

They agreed that the kinds of expiation are three: setting free a slave; fasting for two months; and the feeding of sixty needy persons, in this order of priority. First comes the manumission of a slave; if he cannot afford it then fasting (is obligatory) and if he cannot sustain it then the feeding of needy persons. This applies to the freeman. They disagreed about the slave whether he can offer expiation through manumission or feeding, after they had agreed that he begins with fasting, thus, can he do so if he is not able to fast? Abū Thawr and Dāwūd permitted the slave to manumit a slave if he was authorized by his master to do so, but all the other jurists disallowed this. Mālik permitted him feeding when he fed them with the consent of his master, but Abū Ḥanīfa and al-Shāfiʿī did not allow this. The reason for disagreement in this issue arises from their dispute whether the slave can own (property) under the law.

Their disagreement about the validating conditions includes the dispute over the effect of intercourse if it should take place during the fasting of two months, whether he has to start the fast all over again, not counting the days he kept the fasts before the incident. Mālik and Abū Ḥanīfa said that he would have to renew the fasting, but he (Abū Ḥanīfa) did stipulate intentional violation for this. Mālik, on the other hand, did not differentiate between intention and forgetfulness, while al-Shāfiʿī said that he would not renew fasting in any circumstances.

The reason for disagreement is the similarity between the expiation of *ẓihār* with the expiation for an oath and the condition laid down for the expiation of *ẓihār*, that is, it should be performed before cohabitation. Those who considered this condition said that he should renew the fasts, but those who compared it to the expiation for an oath said that he is not to renew fasting, as the expiation for an oath eliminates the effect of violation, by agreement, even after it has occurred. They also disagreed over the issue whether it is a condition that the slave to be set free be a believer. Mālik and al-Shāfiʿī held that it is a condition of validity. Abū Ḥanīfa said that fulfilment can be achieved when the slave is a non-believer, but not if he is an idolater or an apostate.

The argument of the first party is that the purpose of emancipation here is seeking the pleasure of Allāh, it is, therefore, obligatory that the slave be a Muslim; the basis being the emancipation in the case of homicide. It may be argued, however, that this is not a case of analogy, but of interpreting an absolute term as restricted. Restriction of the slave with the qualification of faith occurred in the case of the expiation for homicide, whereas it has been rendered absolute here. It follows that this should also be restricted. Yet, there is a disagreement about restricting an absolute term in this manner and the Ḥanafites do not permit it, as the causes in the two cases are different.

The argument of the Ḥanafites is based upon the apparent general implication and according to them there is no clash between the absolute and the restricted meaning. It is, therefore, necessary that the terms be assigned their existing meanings, in their view.

Their disagreement also includes the issue whether the slave being emancipated should be free of defects. And what are those defects the absence of which is stipulated? The majority maintain that defects adversely affect the validity (or the fulfilment of) manumission. A group of jurists, however, maintained that defects have no such effect. The argument of the majority is based upon its similarity with (ᶜ*Īd*) sacrifices and vows, all of which seek the pleasure of Allāh. The argument of the other party is based upon the unrestricted form of the term in the verse. The reason for disagreement is the conflict of the obvious implication with *qiyās al-shabah*.

Those who maintained that defects are effective in preventing the validity (of expiation) fulfilment, disagreed about the kind of defect that is to be taken into account for the presence or absence of validity. There is no disagreement among them that (total) blindness or the loss of both hands or feet preclude validity, but they differed about lesser defects. Is the lack of one hand permitted? Abū Ḥanīfa permitted it, but Mālik and al-Shāfiᶜī did not. About the loss of one eye, Mālik said that it is not permitted, while ᶜAbd al-Malik said that it is. Expiation (by emancipation) of a slave with slitted ears is not valid in Mālik's view, while the disciples of al-Shāfiᶜī said that it is. There is dispute about the deaf slave in Mālik's school; it is said that it is valid, while it is said that it is not. Emancipation of a dumb slave (for expiation) is not valid in Mālik's opinion, while there are two opinions about him in al-Shāfiᶜī's school. The (emancipation of the) insane slave will not lead to validity. About the castrated slave, Ibn al-Qāsim said that it did not appeal to him, while others said that it is not valid, but al-Shāfiᶜī held that it is. The emancipation of a minor is permitted (for this purpose) according to the majority of the jurists of the provinces, while its insufficiency is related from some of the earlier jurists. Slight limping does not affect validity, according to the school (Mālik's), but obvious lameness does. The reason for disagreement is their dispute over the extent of the defect that is effective in this ritual obligation. It has no basis in the law, except (the analogy upon) sacrificial animals.

In the same way, it is not valid (in expiation) to emancipate a slave who is jointly owned, or one who is partly free, as in the case of *kitāba* and *tadbīr*, because of the words of the Exalted, "the freeing of a slave", for setting free means emancipation *ab initio* and when there are existing contracts of freedom, like *kitāba*, it would amount to completion not emancipation. Similarly, in the case of partnership, as part of a slave is not a (full) slave. Abū Ḥanīfa said that if the *mukātab* has made part of the payment of *kitāba*, it is not permitted, but when he has not paid it is.

They disagreed whether it is valid for him to emancipate a *mudabbara*. Mālik, comparing it to *kitāba*, said that it is not, as it is a contract that he cannot undo. Al-Shāfiʿī said that it is valid. According to Mālik, it is not sufficient to manumit an *umm al-walad*, nor is it sufficient to emancipate a slave with a period of delay. The reason is that the contract of an *umm al-walad* is stronger than the contracts of *kitāba* and *tadbīr*. The evidence is that these can be revoked; the contract of *kitāba* because of the inability to pay the instalments and *tadbīr* when the value exceeds a third of the estate. The contract of emancipation with a period, however, is an agreement in which the period cannot be curtailed.

Mālik and al-Shāfiʿī differed with Abū Ḥanīfa on the sufficiency of a slave who is to be necessarily set free by him, because of descent (for example, when his father has become his slave). Mālik and al-Shāfiʿī said that it is not valid, while Abū Ḥanīfa said that if he resolves to set him free on account of *ẓihār* it is valid. Abū Ḥanīfa compared this to the case of the slave whose emancipation is not obligatory, as in both types of slave it is not obligatory upon him to buy them and to pay their value with the object of emancipation, thus, if he intends expiation thereby it is permitted. The Mālikites and Shāfiʿites held that if he buys someone whose emancipation is obligatory upon him without regard for his intention to emancipate him, it is not valid. Abū Ḥanīfa held the intention to buy to be a substitute for the intention to emancipate, but they said that he must form the intention of emancipation itself. In both cases he is designated an emancipator by choice, but in one he is emancipating through a primary choice, while in the second he is emancipating through a consequence of the choice and it is as if he has emancipated through a secondary choice. The buyer (intending expiation) exercises the primary choice, while in the other case it is the opposite. Mālik and al-Shāfiʿī differed about the person who is emancipating one-half of two slaves. Mālik said that this is not permitted, while al-Shāfiʿī said that it is, for it amounts to one slave. Mālik held on to the apparent meaning of the term.

This is their disagreement about the conditions of emancipated slaves.

In the stipulation of feeding, they disagreed about the amount of food that would be sufficient in the case of each of the sixty needy persons who have been mentioned in the text. There are two narrations in this from Mālik. The widely known report is that it is one *mudd*, measured by the *mudd* of Hishām, which would amount two *mudds* used by the Prophet (God's peace and blessings be upon him), but it is said that it is less, while it is said that it is one and one-third mudd. The second narration is that it is one *mudd* for each needy person in accordance with the *mudd* used by the Prophet and that is also al-Shāfiʿī's opinion. The basis for the first narration is the consideration of hunger generally, that is lunch and dinner, while the basis for the second narration is the comparison of this expiation with that of the expiation in an oath.

This, then, is their disagreement about the conditions of validity of the obligations arising out of this form of expiation.

In their disagreement about its multiplicity and unity (of several), one of the points of disagreement is that if he pronounces *ẓihār* with a single statement with respect to more than one woman, is a single expiation sufficient, or will he have to offer expiation according to the number of women involved? According to Mālik a single expiation will be sufficient, while according to al-Shāfiʿī and Abū Ḥanīfa the number of expiations must conform with the number of women denounced through *ẓihār;* if they are two he has to offer two expiations, if they are three he offers three and if they are more he offers more. Those who considered it similar to divorce made an expiation obligatory for each woman, but those who considered it similar to *al-īlāʾ* considered one expiation to be sufficient. The resemblance with *al-īlāʾ* is stronger.

Another point is that if he pronounces *ẓihār* for his wife in different sessions, is he liable for a single expiation or for the number of times that he has pronounced *ẓihār*? Mālik said that he is liable for a single expiation, except when he pronounces *ẓihār* then retracts from it and then pronounces it again, in which case he is liable for expiation a second time. This was also upheld by al-Awzāʿī, Aḥmad and Isḥāq. Abū Ḥanīfa and al-Shāfiʿī said that there is to be expiation for each *ẓihār*. When this takes place in a single session, there is no dispute in Mālik's school that there is a single expiation for it. Abū Ḥanīfa said that this depends upon his intention, if his purpose was emphasis there is only one expiation, but if he intended the renewal of *ẓihār*, it will be as he intended and he will be liable for expiation according to the number of pronouncements of *ẓihār*. Yaḥyā ibn Saʿīd said that expiation becomes binding according to the number of pronouncements, irrespective of the number of sessions in which this took place.

The reason for this disagreement is that a single *ẓihār*, in actual fact, occurs through a single pronouncement for a single woman and at one time. Two pronouncements, without dispute, would be through two utterances for two women at separate times. Therefore, if the word is repeated with respect to one wife, does it lead to multiple pronouncements of *ẓihār*? Similarly, when a single statement is used, but the women involved are more than one? Thus, the question is equipoised between these two extremes and so those for whom one extreme had greater weight, they gave preference to the *ḥukm* of that extreme, but those for whom the other extreme carried greater weight, they assigned it the relevant *ḥukm*.

Another issue is that if he pronounces *ẓihār* against his wife and then cohabits with her without offering expiation, is he liable to a single expiation? The majority of the jurists of the provinces, Mālik, al-Shāfiᶜī, Abū Ḥanīfa, al-Thawrī, al-Awzāᶜī, Aḥmad, Isḥāq, Abū Thawr, Dāwūd, al-Ṭabarī and Abū ᶜUbayd maintained that there is a single expiation in this case. Their evidence is the tradition of Salama ibn Ṣakhr al-Bayāḍī "that he pronounced *ẓihār* against his wife in the time of the Messenger of Allāh (God's peace and blessings be upon him) and then cohabited with her before offering expiation, he then came up to the Messenger of Allāh (God's peace and blessings be upon him) and mentioned it to him. He ordered him to offer a single expiation". A group of jurists said that he has to offer expiation twice, an expiation for the resolve to commit intercourse and an expiation for actually committing intercourse, for that intercourse was prohibited. This is related from ᶜAmr ibn al-ᶜĀṣ, Qabīṣah ibn Dhuʾayb, Saᶜīd ibn Jubayr and Ibn Shihāb. It is also said that he is not liable for anything, neither for retraction nor for intercourse, as Allāh has stipulated the validity of expiation prior to cohabitation when he cohabits with her, the time for expiation is over and it can only be imposed with a new command and such a *ḥukm* is absent from the issue. This is deviant. Abū Muḥammad ibn Ḥazm said that the person for whom the obligation is feeding, for him cohabitation is not prohibited before such feeding; cohabitation is prohibited only for those whose obligation it is to manumit or to fast.

XXII
THE BOOK OF *LIᶜĀN* (IMPRECATION)

The discussion in this book, after the explanation of the obligation of *liᶜān*, extends over five sections. The first section is about the kinds of complaints giving rise to it and their conditions. The second section is about the description of the imprecators. Third is about the description of *liᶜān*. Fourth is about the refusal of either of them (the spouses) to take the oath. Fifth is about the *aḥkām* necessary for the completion of *liᶜān*.

The source for the legitimacy of *liᶜān* in the Book are the words of the Exalted, "As for those who accuse their wives but have no witnesses except themselves; let the testimony of one of them be four testimonies (swearing) by Allāh that he is of those who speak the truth; and yet a fifth, invoking the curse of Allāh on him of those who lie. And it shall avert the punishment from her if she bear witness before Allāh four times that the thing he saith is indeed false and a fifth (time) that the wrath of Allāh be upon her if he speaketh the truth".[114] The *sunna* is found in what was related by Mālik and other recorders of the *ṣaḥīḥ* traditions about the tradition of ᶜUwaymir al-ᶜAjalānī "when he came up to ᶜĀṣim ibn ᶜAdiyy al-ᶜAjalānī, a man from his tribe and said to him, 'O ᶜĀṣim, what do you think about the man who finds another man with his wife. Should he kill him, so that he may be executed himself? What is he to do? Ask the Messenger of Allāh (God's peace and blessings be upon him) about this, O ᶜĀṣim'. ᶜĀṣim asked the Messenger of Allāh (God's peace and blessings be upon him) about it and when he returned to his people, ᶜUwaymir came up and said, 'O ᶜĀṣim, what did the Messenger of Allāh (God's peace and blessings be upon him) tell you'. He said, 'You have not brought me something good (he said). The Messenger of Allāh looked down upon the issue I asked him about'. He said, 'By Allāh, I will not stop till I have asked him about it'. He set off till he came up to the Messenger of Allāh (God's peace and blessings be upon him) when he was in the midst of people. He said, 'O Messenger of Allāh, what do you think about the man who finds another man with his wife. Should he kill him, so that he may be executed himself? What is he to do?' The Messenger of Allāh (God's peace and blessings be upon him) said, 'The Qurʾān has been revealed about you and your wife, so go and bring

[114] Qurʾān 24 : 6-9

her here' ". Sahl says that "They underwent the *liᶜān* procedure, when I was among the people with the Messenger of Allāh (God's peace and blessings be upon him). When they had completed the procedure, ᶜUwaymir said, 'I would be lying against her, O Messenger of Allāh, if I retain her' ". He then divorced her thrice, before the Messenger of Allāh had ordered him to do so. Mālik related from Ibn Shihāb the report that this has continued (since then) to be the *sunna* for the imprecators. Similarly, by way of a rational evidence, as marriage is the basis for the association of paternity, there was a need for the people to have a method by which they could negate it when they had established corruption in it. This method is *liᶜān*.

Thus, *liᶜān* is a *ḥukm* established by the Book, *sunna*, *qiyās* and *ijmāᶜ*. I do not know of any dispute about this. This, then, is the discussion about the establishment of its *ḥukm*.

22.1. *Section 1: Kinds of Complaints Leading to* Liᶜān *and their Conditions*

The complaints that can give rise to *liᶜān* are of two types: first is the complaint of *zinā* and second, the denial (of paternity) of the foetus. The complaint of *zinā* may be based upon testimony, that is, he (the husband) alleges that he saw her committing *zinā*, or it may be a general complaint. If he denies the (paternity of) the embryo, he may also be denying it absolutely or may allege that he did not approach her after she was free of menstruation. These are four simple cases and all the other complaints are structured upon them. For example, he accuses her and denies the paternity of the foetus, or he may acknowledge the paternity of the foetus and accuse her of *zinā*.

There is no dispute about the validity of *liᶜān* after the accusation of *zinā* (*qadhf*), when he claims that he witnessed it. The Mālikites said that this is possible if he claims that he did not have intercourse with her afterwards. The majority, that is, al-Shāfiᶜī, Abū Ḥanīfa, al-Thawrī, Aḥmad, Dāwūd and others, permit the operation of *liᶜān* by *qadhf* alone. The widely known opinion from Mālik is that *liᶜān* does not arise from the complaint of *qadhf* alone. Ibn al-Qāsim said that it is permitted and it is also another narration from Mālik.

The argument of the majority is based upon the general meaning of the words of the Exalted, "As for those who accuse their wives but have no witnesses except themselves; let the testimony of one of them be four testimonies (swearing) by Allāh that he is of those who speak the truth". *Zinā* here has not been qualified with different characteristics, as was the case in the obligation of the *ḥadd* of *qadhf*. Mālik's argument is based on the apparent meaning of the traditions relevant to this issue. Among these is the tradition of (Sahl ibn) Saᶜd, "What do you think of the man who finds another man with his wife ...", and the tradition of Ibn ᶜAbbās, which says, "He came up to the Messenger of Allāh (God's peace and blessings be upon him) and said,

'By Allāh, O Messenger of Allāh, I saw it with my own eyes and heard it with my own ears'. The Messenger of Allāh disliked what he reported and then the verse, 'As for those who accuse their wives ...', was revealed". Further, the complaint itself is a kind of evidence like testimony.

Within this issue is a case about which Mālik's opinion differed. It is a case where she is found to be pregnant after the complaint of *liᶜān* and there are two opinions about it from Mālik. First, that the association of the foetus with him is discarded. Second, that it (the paternity of the foetus) is associated with him.

They agreed, as far as I know, that a condition for the complaint of *zinā* giving rise to *liᶜān*, where the act has been witnessed, is that the wife still be in his protection. They disagreed about the person who makes a complaint of *zinā* against his wife and then divorces her, whether *liᶜān* can take place between them. Mālik, al-Shāfiᶜī, al-Awzāᶜī and a group of jurists said that *liᶜān* proceedings may be instituted, while Abū Ḥanīfa said that there is to be no *liᶜān* between them, unless he denies the paternity of the child and there is no *ḥadd* in this case. Makḥūl, al-Ḥakam and Qatāda said that he is to be awarded *ḥadd*, but there is no *liᶜān*.

If he denies paternity of the embryo, then, as we have said the case has two aspects. First, he may claim that he had avoided her since her menses and did not have intercourse with her after that. There is no dispute in this case. Mālik's opinion differed about the nature of *istibrāʾ* (assuring the vacation of the womb). He said once that this is through (avoiding her for a duration of) three menstrual periods, but at another time he said it is through one. The well-known opinion of Mālik about absolute denial is that *liᶜān* is not necessary for it; he was opposed in this by al-Shāfiᶜī, Aḥmad and Dāwūd, who said that this does not mean much as a woman may be pregnant, even when blood can be noticed. ᶜAbd al-Wahhāb has related from the disciples of al-Shafiᶜī that an absolute denial of paternity is not permitted without accompanying *qadhf*.

They disagreed in this topic about a sub-issue, which is the time of denying paternity of the embryo. The majority said that he should deny it while she is still pregnant. Mālik further stipulated that if he does not deny while the pregnancy continues, he cannot deny it later through the process of *liᶜān*. Al-Shafiᶜī said that if the husband came to know about the pregnancy and the judge granted him the opportunity to invoke *liᶜān*, but he did not do so, he is not entitled to deny paternity through *liᶜān* after birth. Abū Ḥanīfa said that paternity of the child is not to be denied till birth.

Mālik's argument and the argument of those who held the same opinion, is based upon *mutawātir* traditions, like the traditions of Ibn ᶜAbbās, Ibn Masᶜūd, Anas and Sahl ibn Saʾd "that the Prophet (God's peace and blessings be upon him) when he ordered *liᶜān* proceedings between two imprecators said,

'Whenever she (the woman) comes in such and such condition (i.e. pregnant), I have always seen that he is telling the truth' ". They said that this indicates her being pregnant at the time of *liᶜān*. Abū Ḥanīfa's argument is that the womb may become bloated or subside (for different reasons) and there is no cause for *liᶜān*, except in the case of certainty. One of the arguments of the majority is that the law has made a number of *aḥkām* dependent upon pregnancy, like maintenance, waiting period and prohibition of intercourse; it is, therefore, necessary that the analogy for *liᶜān* be the same. According to Abū Ḥanīfa, he may proceed with *liᶜān* without denying paternity, except at the time of birth or close to it, but he did not fix a time for this. His disciples, Abū Yūsuf and Muḥammad, did fix a time saying that he may deny paternity in the forty nights before (expected) birth.

Those who made *liᶜān* obligatory upon the appearance of pregnancy agreed that he has to deny paternity during the period of tie (of marriage), but they disagreed about the denial of paternity after divorce. Mālik held that he may do this in the entire period during which the child can be associated with the conjugal relationship, which is the maximum period of gestation, according to him and that is four years or five years. Similar is the *ḥukm*, according to him, for the denial of (the paternity of) the child after divorce, if he persists in denying it. An almost similar opinion was expressed by al-Shāfiᶜī. A group of jurists said that he does not have the right to deny the paternity of the embryo, except during the *ᶜidda*. If he denies it in a period other than the *ᶜidda* he is to be awarded *ḥadd* (for *qadhf*) and the child is to be attributed to him. The *ḥukm*, then, according to the majority in which this is possible is the maximum length of the gestation period, despite their accompanying disagreement about it (the length). The Ẓāhirites held that the maximum[115] period of gestation in which the *ḥukm* is obligatory is the usual period and it is equivalent to nine months or close to it.

There is no dispute among them that the *ḥukm* becomes obligatory during the time of protection (of marriage), which is not less than six months after the time of actual consummation, that is, the woman should give birth within six months of the time of consummation or the likelihood of consummation and not the time of the contract. Abū Ḥanīfa deviated from this and said that it is from the time of the contract, even when it is known that intercourse was not possible, so much so that according to him if a man in the remote west is married to a woman in the remote east and she gives birth to a child after six months from the time of the contract, the child will be attributed to him, unless he denies paternity through *liᶜān*. He is being too literal in this issue,

[115] The original text says "minimum", however, the word should be "maximum". This is the well-known opinion of the Ẓāhirites. The author himself says a few lines below that there is no dispute among the jurists that the minimum period is six months, which is based on the interpretation of Qurʾānic texts.

for he relies upon the general meaning of the words of the Prophet, "*al-walad lil-firāsh*",[116] and the woman in this case is associated with him through a conjugal relationship. It was as if he considered this not to be subject to rationalization. This is something that is weak.

Mālik's opinion differed within this issue about a sub-issue. If he claims that she committed *zinā*, but he acknowledges paternity of the embryo, then, there are three narrations from Mālik. First, that he is to be awarded *ḥadd* (for *qadhf*), the child is attributed to him and he cannot invoke *liʿān*. Second, that he is to invoke *liʿān* and deny paternity. Third, that the child is attributed to him, but he is to invoke *liʿān* in order to avoid the *ḥadd* penalty. The reason for the difference is whether he can establish paternity along with a denial of its cause, that is, his claim of *zinā*.

They disagreed in this topic about another issue. If testimony about *zinā* has been rendered, is he to invoke *liʿān* too? Abū Ḥanīfa and Dāwūd said that he does not invoke *liʿān*, as *liʿān* is a substitute for witnesses, because of the words of the Exalted, "As for those who accuse their wives but have no witnesses except themselves ...". Mālik and al-Shafiʿī said that he is to invoke *liʿān* as the witnesses have no affect upon the denial of paternity.

22.2. *Section 2: The Qualifications of the Imprecators*

About the qualifications of the imprecators, a group of jurists said that *liʿān* is permissible between spouses, whether they are free or slave, or when one of them is free and the other a slave, whether they have been subjected to *ḥadd* or are virtuous, or when one of them is such and when they are Muslims or when the husband is a Muslim and the wife a *kitābiyya*. There is no *liʿān* between disbelievers, unless they bring the matter before the Muslim court. Among those who held this opinion are Mālik and al-Shāfiʿī, while Abū Ḥanīfa and his disciples said that *liʿān* is only possible between free, *ʿadl*, Muslims. As a general rule, according to them, *liʿān* is possible between people who qualify as witnesses.

The argument of the first group is based upon the general meaning of the words of the Exalted, "As for those who accuse their wives but have no witnesses except themselves", and the verse did not add any condition to this. The reliance of the Ḥanafites is on the argument that *liʿān* is testimony, so the conditions of testimony are to be stipulated for *liʿān* and Allāh too has called them witnesses, "let the testimony of one of them be four testimonies (swearing) by Allāh that he is of those who speak the truth". They also say

[116] Literally: The child belongs to the bed. The phrase conjugal relationship is being used here, but this only indicates the relationship of marriage and not the relationship with female slaves, which is included in the maxim. The phrase actually means that paternity is attributed to the person who has legal access to the woman for sexual intercourse.

that *liʿān* is only possible between persons who can be liable for *qadhf* that may come to exist between them.

They agreed that the slave is not subjected to *ḥadd* because of his *qadhf*; similarly the disbeliever. They compared a person qualified for *liʿān* to one who may be liable for the *ḥadd* of *qadhf*, as *liʿān* has been ordained for the evasion of *ḥadd* along with the denial of descent. Perhaps, they argued on the basis of what is related by ʿAmr ibn Shuʿayb from his father from his grandfather that the Messenger of Allāh (God's peace and blessings be upon him) said, "There is no *liʿān* between four persons: two slaves and two disbelievers". The majority maintain that it (*liʿān*) is like an oath, even though it has been termed as testimony, as no one testifies for himself and an oath is sometimes referred to as testimony, which is obvious from the words of the Exalted, "When the hypocrites come unto thee (O Muḥammad), they say: We bear witness that thou art indeed Allāh's messenger. And Allāh knoweth that thou art indeed His messenger and Allāh beareth witness that the Hypocrites are speaking falsely",[117] followed by, "They make their oaths a pretext so that they may turn (men) from the way of Allāh".[118]

They agreed about the validity of the *liʿān* of the blind, but disagreed about that of the dumb. Mālik and al-Shafiʿī said that the deaf can invoke *liʿān*, if their gestures are comprehensible. Abū Ḥanīfa said that they cannot invoke *liʿān* as they are not a qualified witnesses. They agreed unanimously that among the conditions are sanity and the attainment of the age of majority (*bulūgh*).

22.3. *Section 3: The Procedure of* Liʿān

The descriptions of *liʿān*, given by the majority, are almost similar and there is not much difference, because of the obvious implications of the verse.

The husband takes an oath swearing four times by Allāh that he saw her committing unlawful intercourse and the child that she carries is not because of him. In the fifth oath he says that may the curse of Allāh be upon him if he is lying. The woman then swears four times rebutting him (to evade the *ḥadd*) and swears the fifth invoking the wrath of Allāh (in case she is lying). All this is agreed upon. Some jurists differed whether it is permitted to substitute wrath for curse, curse for wrath, swearing for testifying and one of the attributes of Allāh for "by Allāh". The majority maintained that none of the substitutions is permitted, but only the words which are mentioned in the text, the basis being the number of testimonies. They agreed that a condition for its validity is that it (*liʿān*) should be invoked under orders from the judge.

[117] Qurʾān 63 : 1

[118] Qurʾān 63 : 2. Pickthall translates it as "They make their faith a pretext so that they may turn (men) from the way of Allāh". The text says "*aymānahum*," "their oaths," not "*īmānahum*," "their faith".

22.4. *Section 4: Refusal to Take the Oath and Retraction*

If the husband refuses to take the oath, the majority maintain that he is to be subjected to *ḥadd*. Abū Ḥanīfa said that he is not to be subjected to *ḥadd*, but is to be confined (imprisoned).

The basis for the majority opinion is the general implication of the words of the Exalted, "And those who accuse honourable women but bring not four witnesses, scourge them (with) eighty stripes and never (afterwards) accept their testimony—They indeed are evil doers". This is general with respect to a stranger as well as a husband and the imprecation of the husband is substituted for the testimony of witnesses. It is, therefore, necessary that when he refuses to swear he should be considered as one who has committed *qadhf* and does not have four witnesses, I mean, that he should be awarded the *ḥadd*. They also relied on the traditions of Ibn ᶜUmar and others about the incident of al-ᶜAjalānī and the words he said to the Prophet (God's peace and blessings be upon him) "If I kill him I would be killed, if I speak out I will be whipped and if I remain silent I will do so with anger".

The other party argued that the verse of *liᶜān* does not include his liability for *ḥadd* when he refuses to swear and the proposal for its obligation is an addition to the text; an addition for them amounts to abrogation and an abrogation is not possible through analogy or through individual narrations. They added that if *ḥadd* is imposed there is no utility in *liᶜān*, nor will it have any effect in its avoidance, as *liᶜān* is an oath that does not waive the *ḥadd* in the case of a stranger, so also in the case of the husband.

The truth, however, is that *liᶜān* is a special oath, which makes it necessary that it have a special *ḥukm*. Further, it is stated in the text about the woman that the oath will avert the torment from her. The question is what is this torment that will be waived because of the oath?

The equivocality that is found in the term torment also led them to differ about the consequences for her if she refused to swear. Al-Shāfiᶜī, Mālik, Aḥmad and the majority said that she is to be subjected to *ḥadd* and her *ḥadd* is stoning to death if he has had intercourse with her and she fulfils the conditions of *iḥṣān*. If he has not had intercourse with her she is to be subjected to stripes. Abū Ḥanīfa said that if she refuses she is liable for confinement till she invokes *liᶜān*. His evidence is the words of the Prophet (God's peace and blessings be upon him), "The shedding of a Muslim's blood does not become permissible, except for three reasons: *zinā* after *iḥṣān*; disbelief after faith; and the taking of a life without cause for retaliation". In addition to this, the spilling of blood because of refusal to swear is an act that is rejected by the principles. If a large number of jurists do not impose a financial liability because of a refusal to swear, it appears appropriate that they should not spill blood because of such refusal. On the whole, the basis in the law for the rule for spilling blood is that it should not be shed except through legally admissible testimony or by confession. It must not be that this rule is restricted by means of an equivocal term. Abū Ḥanīfa in this issue is closer to the truth, God willing. Abū al-Maᶜālī, in his book *al-Burhān*, has acknowledged the strength of Abū Ḥanīfa's reasoning in this issue and he was a Shāfiᶜite.

They agreed that if he declares himself a liar, he is to be subjected to *ḥadd* and the child is to be attributed to him, even if he has denied its paternity. They disagreed whether he has the right to take her back, after their agreement that separation (divorce) becomes obligatory through *liᶜān*, either on its own or by the decree of the judge, which we will discuss later. Mālik, al-Shāfiᶜī, al-Thawrī, Dāwūd, Aḥmad and the majority of the jurists of the provinces said that they cannot be together again, ever, even when he declares himself to be a liar. Abū Ḥanīfa and a group of jurists said that if he declares himself to be a liar and is awarded the *ḥadd*, he may propose to her along with the others. Other jurists said that his wife is to be returned to him.

The argument of the first party is based on the words of the Prophet (God's peace and blessings be upon him), "You have no means of attaining her". The Prophet did not make an exception for this and it was construed as absolute for prohibition. The argument of the second party is that he has called himself a liar, therefore, the *ḥukm* of *liᶜān* stands annulled. Just as the child is associated with him, in the same way his wife is to be returned to him. The reason is that the cause of prohibition is the lack of knowledge about the verification of the veracity of one of them, along with the certainty that one of them is a liar. As soon as this is established, the prohibition stands removed.

22.5. *Section 5:* Aḥkām *Necessary for the Completion of* Liᶜān

The jurists differed about the consequences of *liᶜān* on a number of issues. Among these are whether separation becomes obligatory. If it does, when? Does it become obligatory due to *liᶜān* itself, or through the decree of the judge? If separation does occur, is it divorce or rescission?

The majority held that separation occurs because of *liᶜān*, as has become widely known through the traditions of *liᶜān* that the Messenger of Allāh caused a separation between them. Ibn Shihāb said, as reported from him by Mālik, that this has not ceased to be the *sunna* for the imprecators. Further, because of the words of the Prophet (God's peace and blessings be upon him), "You have no means of attaining her". ᶜUthmān al-Battī and a group of jurists from Baṣra said that *liᶜān* is not followed by separation. They argued that this is a *ḥukm* that is not included in the verse of *liᶜān*, nor is it explicit in the traditions. In the best-known tradition the person divorced her in front of the Prophet and he (the Prophet) did not disapprove it. In addition to this, *liᶜān* has been ordained for waiving the *ḥadd* of *qadhf* and it does not obligate prohibition, as in the case of testimony.

The argument of the majority is that mutual discord, hate and confrontation with similar testimony and a violation of the limits set by Allāh has occurred between them, which makes it necessary that they should never come together again, ever. This is so as marriage is structured upon love and compassion, while these two are devoid of it completely. The least that can be said is that their penalty should be separation. On the whole, the evil that exists between them is of an extreme form.

About the time of separation, Mālik, al-Layth and a group of jurists said that it comes into effect when both are done with imprecation. Al-Shafiʿī said that as the husband finishes his imprecation separation comes into effect. Abū Ḥanīfa said that it does not come into effect, except by the decree of the judge, which was also upheld by al-Thawrī and Aḥmad. Mālik's argument against al-Shafiʿī is based upon the tradition of Ibn ʿUmar, who said that "the Messenger of Allāh ordered separation between imprecators and said, 'Your reckoning is with Allāh, as one of you is a liar. And you (the husband) do not have any means of attaining her' ", and also the report that he did not order separation between them, until the completion of *liʿān* proceedings. Al-Shāfiʿī's argument is that her imprecation causes only the *ḥadd* to be waived from her and it is the man's imprecation that is effective in the denial of descent. It is, therefore, necessary that if the *liʿān* is effective in separation, the man's *liʿān* should be deemed equivalent to a divorce. Their joint argument against Abū Ḥanīfa is that the Prophet (God's peace and blessings be upon him) informed the imprecators about the occurrence of separation between them with their act of imprecation, which indicates that it is *liʿān* that is the cause of separation. Abū Ḥanīfa, on the other hand, is of the view that separation was implemented against them with the decree and the order of the Prophet (God's peace and blessings be upon him), when he said, "You have no means of attaining her". He, therefore, held that his (the judge's) *ḥukm* is a condition for the occurrence of separation, just as his *ḥukm* is essential for the validity of *liʿān*.

The reason for disagreement between those who held that it is because of it (the *ḥukm*) that separation occurs and between those who do not hold it to be so, is that the separation caused by the Prophet (God's peace and blessings be upon him) is not manifest in the well-known tradition as the man took sudden initiative himself and divorced her before he informed him of the separation. The principle is that there is no separation without divorce and that there is no prohibition in the law that can become perpetual, that is, one agreed upon. Those who imposed this principle upon the meaning, because of the likelihood that such meaning negates the obligation of separation, did not hold separation to be obligatory (through *liʿān*). The disagreement between those who stipulate the decree of the judge and those who do not is based upon the vacillation of this *ḥukm* between those *aḥkām* for whose validity the decree of the judge is stipulated and those for which it is not.

The fourth issue, which arises if we say that separation does arise through *liʿān*, relates to the question whether such separation amounts to a rescission or a divorce? Those who uphold separation (through *liʿān*) differed about this. Mālik and al-Shafiʿī said that it is rescission, while Abū Ḥanīfa said that it is an irrevocable divorce. Mālik's argument depends upon the perpetuity of the prohibition and, therefore, the woman comes to resemble those in the prohibited category.

Abū Ḥanīfa, on the other hand, held that it resembled divorce, on the analogy of separation, by a decision of the court, from one who is impotent.

XXIII
THE BOOK OF *IḤDĀD* (MOURNING)

The Muslim jurists, except for al-Ḥasan alone, agreed that mourning is obligatory for free Muslim women during the waiting period following death (of their husbands). They disagreed in the cases of the other wives, and also regarding the kinds of *ʿidda* other than the *ʿidda* following death, and also about what the mourning woman is required to abstain from.

Mālik said that mourning is necessary for the women who are Muslim or from the People of the Book, are minor or major. There is no mourning for a slave-woman whose master has died, irrespective of her being an *umm al-walad*. This opinion was upheld by the jurists of the provinces. Mālik's opinion about the *kitābiyya*, however, was opposed by Ibn Nāfiʿ and Ashhab, who related that too from Mālik. This was also upheld by al-Shāfiʿī, that is, there is no mourning for the *kitābiyya*.

Abū Ḥanīfa said that there is no mourning for a minor or for a *kitābiyya*. A group of jurists said that there is no mourning for a married slave-woman, and this has been related from Abū Ḥanīfa. This, then, is their well-known disagreement about the categories of wives for whom mourning has been prescribed and those for whom it has not been prescribed.

In their disagreement about the categories of *ʿidda* that involve mourning, Mālik said that there is no mourning, except in the waiting period following death. Abū Ḥanīfa and al-Thawrī said that mourning is obligatory in the waiting period of an irrevocable divorce. Al-Shāfiʿī preferred it for a divorced woman, but did not make it obligatory.

The third point relates to what is prohibited to the mourning woman and what is not. She is disallowed, by the *fuqahāʾ* as a whole, all kinds of adornment that is meant to attract men to women, like wearing jewellery or darkening of the eyes, unless this is not meant as an adornment. She is also not allowed to wear colourful clothes, except black, as Mālik did not consider reprehensible her wearing black. All of them made an exemption for using kohl (*kuhl;* antimony sulphide for darkening the eyes) in the case of necessity, though some of them stipulated that it be in a way that does not amount to an adornment, while others did not make such a stipulation, and yet others permitted its use during the night and not during the day. On the whole, the opinions of the jurists in things avoided by the mourning woman are quite similar, and they amount to saying that it is anything that draws the attention of men toward them.

The majority decided in favour of the obligation of mourning generally because of an established *sunna* about it from the Messenger of Allāh. One of the traditions is that of Umm Salama, wife of the Prophet, that "a woman came up to the Messenger of Allāh (God's peace and blessings be upon him) and said, 'O Messenger of Allāh, my daughter's husband has died, and her eyes hurt. May I use kohl for her eyes?' The Messenger of Allāh (God's peace and blessings be upon him) said 'No' two or three times. Each time he said, 'No', and then said, 'It is a period of four months and ten days'. " Abū Muḥammad said that in accordance with this tradition it is, necessary, to construe the obligation of mourning. In the tradition of Umm Ḥabībah—when she called for perfume and applied it on the sides of her face, saying, "By Allāh, I have no need for this, but I heard the Messenger of Allāh saying, 'It is not permitted to a believing woman, who believes in Allāh and the Day of Judgment, to mourn the dead more than three nights, except in the case of the husband, for whom it is four months and ten days' "—there is no evidence, except an exemption in mourning and it denotes permissibility rather than an obligation; similarly, the tradition of Zaynab bint Jahsh.

The Qāḍī (Ibn Rushd) said: In the case where a command is issued after a prohibition, there is dispute among the *Mutakallimīn*, I mean, whether it implies an obligation or permissibility.

The reason for disagreement in making mourning obligatory for a Muslim woman and not a disbeliever is that those who considered mourning to be kind of worship did not make it binding upon the disbeliever, while those who held it to have an underlying rational reason, which is the attraction of men toward her and she being attracted to them, deemed the disbeliever and the Muslim woman to be equal. Those who took into account the attraction of men and not that of women, made a distinction between the minor and the mature woman, as men are not likely to be attracted to minors. The evidence of those who made it obligatory on Muslim women to the exclusion of disbelievers is in the words of the Prophet, "It is not permitted to a believing woman, who believes in Allāh and the Day of Judgment to mourn, except for her husband". They said that the stipulation of faith in mourning indicates that it is a kind of worship.

Those who made a distinction between a slave and a free woman, and also the *kitābiyya*, did so because they thought that the waiting period following death gives rise to two things, by agreement: first is mourning and the second is not to go out (of the house). As the relinquishment of (the prohibition of) going out in the case of the slave-woman became necessary through her employment and the need for her services, the prohibition of adornment also had to be dropped. Their disagreement about the *kitābiyya* relates to her vacillation between a free woman and a slave. With respect to the difference between the slave-woman possessed by the right hand and the *umm al-walad*, the *fuqahā*ʾ decided to forgo mourning in her case, because of the words of the Prophet, "It is not permitted to a believing woman, who believes in Allāh and the Day of Judgment to mourn, except for her husband". The indication of the text reveals that those who are not wives are not obliged to mourn.

Those who made mourning obligatory for the widow, but not a divorced woman, relied upon the literal construction of the case stated (in the text), while those who extend the *ḥukm* to the divorced women did so through reasoning. The reason is that it becomes obvious from the underlying cause of mourning that the purpose is to prevent the attraction of men toward them during the waiting period, nor should they be attracted to them. This is a case of *sadd al-dharīʿa* for the preservation descent, Allāh knows best.

The Book of Divorce is completed, praising Allāh for His favours and thanking Him for His grace. This will be followed by the Book of Sales, God willing.

XXIV
THE BOOK OF *BUYŪ*ᶜ (SALES)

The discussion of sales is covered in five parts:[119]

identification of the kinds of sales;
conditions of the validity of each kind;
causes of vitiation (*fasād*);[120]
the *aḥkām* of valid sales; and
the *aḥkām* of vitiated sales.

We will first describe the kinds of absolute sales and then the conditions of validity and vitiation of each (separate) kind, followed by the *aḥkām* of valid and vitiated sales. As the reasons for vitiation and validity are either general for all kinds of sales, or for most of them, or particular to some—so also the *aḥkām* of validity and vitiation are either general or particular—the technical approach requires that we first mention the common elements of these four categories, that is, the general features of the causes of vitiation, the requisites of validity, the *aḥkām* of validity and the *aḥkām* of vitiation. We will then mention the particular features of these four categories within each kind of sale. This book is, then, divided by necessity into six parts:[121]

[119]The general principles of sales are discussed in five parts. This is followed by a sixth part that deals with individual sales like *ṣarf, salam, bay*ᶜ *al-khiyār* and *bay*ᶜ *al-*ᶜ*ariyya*. Each of these sales, however, is treated as an independent book. This division is explained by the author below. *See infra* note 121 and accompanying text.

[120]The term *fāsid* is sometimes translated as "irregular". Here the term "vitiated" has been preferred. It should be noted that the term *fāsid* does not have the same meaning as "voidable", which is used in English common law. An agreement or contract is voidable at the option of the parties. If the parties choose not to exercise this option, the agreement or contract will take effect. *Fāsid*, on the other hand, is the same as void (*bāṭil*) according to the majority of the Muslim jurists. It has no legal effects. The reason of *fasād* is the stipulation of a condition that has been prohibited by the Lawgiver. The Hanafites maintain that a *fāsid* contract is not void *ab initio* and it can have legal effects. In fact, it will become a valid (*ṣaḥiḥ*) contract if the obnoxious condition is expunged; till such time that this is done, the contract will remain in a state of suspension. The manner in which the term is being used by the author will be determined by the context.

[121] See *supra* note 119

Part 1: Kinds of absolute sales;

Part 2: The general causes of vitiation in absolute sales, that is, in all or most of them, (discussed first) as they are better known than the requisites of validity;

Part 3: The requisites of validity in absolute sales;

Part 4: *aḥkām* of valid sales, that is, the *aḥkām* common to all valid sales or most of them;

Part 5: *aḥkām* common to vitiated sales, that is, when they take effect;

Part 6: Each individual sale with its particular reasons of validity and vitiation and its particular *aḥkām*.

24.1. Part 1: Definition of the Kinds of Absolute Sales

Each transaction between two individuals is an exchange, either of corporeal property[122] for corporeal property, or of corporeal property for a corresponding liability,[123] or of a liability for another liability. Each one of these three is either delayed or immediate. Each one of these again is either immediate for both parties or delayed for both, or is immediate for one party and delayed for the other. The kinds of sales (that emerge) are thus nine in number. Delay from both sides is not permitted by consensus (*ijmāᶜ*) either in corporeal property or in liabilities as it amounts to a proscribed exchange of a debt for a debt.

The names of these sales are derived from the condition of the goods being exchanged and the form of the contract of sale itself. Thus, when two commodities are exchanged, one may serve as a currency[124] and the other as a priced commodity, or both may be currencies. When a currency is exchanged for a currency the sale is called *ṣarf*; when a currency is exchanged for a priced commodity the transaction is sale proper (*bayᶜ*). Similar is the sale of a priced commodity for another priced commodity (barter) upon conditions that will be mentioned later. When corporeal property is exchanged for a liability, the sale is called *salam*. If an option is introduced the transaction is called sale with an option (*bayᶜ al-khiyār*). If it is made with a stated profit (mark-up) it is called *murābaha*; when bids are called it is called *muzāyada* (auction).

[122] The term *ᶜayn* is applied to mean something determined and present as compared to something that is not determined by (weight or measure in a contract like *currencies*, *dirhams* and *dīnārs*, because these are standardized with respect to weight). The term corporeal property has, therefore, been preferred over the terms "thing" and "subject-matter". The term "subject-matter of the contract" is the equivalent of *maḥall al-ᶜaqd* and is a more comprehensive term than "*ᶜayn*". It has been used on occasions for purposes of clarity.

[123] The term "liability" is used here to indicate the Arabic term *dhimma*.

[124] The term currency is being used in place of price (*thaman*) which has been used by the author. In Islamic law when two commodities are exchanged, one of them may be called the "price" while the other is the subject-matter of the sale or *mabīᶜ*. The situation is different though in the contract of *ṣarf* where both counter-values are currencies or commodities having currency value. The use of the term "price" is likely to prove confusing in *ṣarf* and has, therefore, been avoided throughout to maintain consistency.

24.2. Part 2: Definition of the General Causes of Vitiation in Absolute Sales

When the causes due to which legal proscription has been laid down are considered and these are the general causes of vitiation, they are found to be four: first is the prohibition of the commodity itself; second is usury (*ribā*); third is hazard or uncertainty (*gharar*); fourth are stipulated conditions that lead to one of the last two or both simultaneously. These four causes are in fact the causes of vitiation as the proscription is related to them in sales, with respect to their being sales and not due to some external factor. Among those in which the proscription is linked to an external factor are misrepresentation (*ghishsh*), injury (*ḍarar*), sale in a period of time assigned to a more important activity,[125] and sale prohibited in itself. In this part, then, there are several chapters.

24.2.1. Chapter 1: Corporeal Property Prohibited for Sale

These are of two kinds: filth (*najāsa*) and that which is other than filth. The source for the prohibition of the sale of filth is the tradition of Jābir, recorded in the *Ṣaḥīḥayn,* in which he said, "The Messenger of Allāh (God's peace and blessings be upon him) said, 'Allāh and His Messenger have prohibited the sale of wine (*khamr*), carrion (*mayta*), swine (*khinzīr*) and idols (*aṣnām*)'. It was said, 'What about the fat of corpses with which (the crevices of) boats are filled and it is used for illumination?' He replied, 'Allāh has cursed the Jews. Fat (of corpses) was prohibited for them, but they sold it and consumed its value'". He (the Prophet) said about *khamr*, "He, who has prohibited its drinking, has also prohibited its sale".

Filth is of two kinds. First is that about the prohibition of whose sale the Muslims are all agreed. Of these is wine (*khamr*). It is considered filth except for slight disagreement, regarding its being filth. So is carrion with all its sensitive non-disposable ingredients and similarly swine and those parts of it that accommodate organic life (that is, they are prone to decay).[126] There is disagreement, though, about the utilization of its bristles. Ibn al-Qāsim permitted this. The second kind is filth the utilization of which is required by necessity, like excrement and dung utilized in gardens (as manure); there is a disagreement in the school (of Mālik) about its sale. Some have prohibited this absolutely, some have permitted it without qualification, while others distinguish between manure and excrement, that is, they permit sale of manure and prohibit that of excrement. They disagreed about the tusks of elephants

[125] Like the Friday congregation prayer.

[126] The parts of the body of a *ḥarām* animal that "do not accept death", like the bristles of swine, may be utilized according to a Mālikī opinion. The use of the term "organic" is, therefore, not very helpful.

(ivory), because of their disagreement whether they are filth. Those who consider them as teeth assign them the *ḥukm* of carrion, while those who consider them inverted horns assign them the *ḥukm* of horns. There is a controversy in Mālik's school about this too.

Among those things whose sale is prohibited but they are not filth, or their being filth is disputed, are dogs and cats. They disagreed about the sale of a dog. Al-Shāfiʿī said the sale of a dog is not permitted at all. Abū Ḥanīfa said that it is. The disciples of Mālik distinguished between a sheep- or farm-dog that can be lawfully owned and that which cannot. They agreed that a dog which cannot be owned cannot be sold for use, or for ownership. There is controversy about the person who needs it for consumption (as food). Those who permit its consumption, permit its sale, while those who do not permit its consumption, on the narration of Ibn Ḥabīb, do not permit its sale. They also disagreed about the (sale of a) dog that can be lawfully owned and it is said that this is prohibited, or that it is disapproved (*makrūh*).

Al-Shāfiʿī relies (for his view) on two things. First, the established proscription from the Prophet (God's peace and blessings be upon him) about charging a price for a dog; second, a dog according to him is filth in itself like swine and we have mentioned his proof about this in the Book of (Ritual) Purification. The basis according to those who have permitted its sale is that a dog is clean (*ṭāhir*) in essence and its consumption is not prohibited, therefore, its sale is allowed like that of other clean things. The proof of those who consider it clean has also preceded in the Book of Purity. In the Book of Foods can be found the proof of those who consider it permissible for consumption. The basis for those who make a distinction is that neither its consumption nor its utilization is permitted except what has been exempted by the tradition about the sale of sheep, farm, or other similar dogs. Less known traditions have been narrated in which the prohibition of charging a price for dogs generally is accompanied by an exemption for charging a price for dogs that can lawfully be maintained.

The proscription of charging a price for a cat is established, but the majority (*jumhūr*) permit it as it is clean in essence and its benefits too are lawful. The reason for their disagreement about dogs is the conflict of evidence.

Related to this is the disagreement about oil extracted from filth and what resembles it, after their agreement about the prohibition of its consumption. Mālik said that the sale of *najis* oil is not permitted. Al-Shāfiʿī had the same opinion. Abū Ḥanīfa, on the other hand, said that it is permitted if the oil is separated not mixed. Ibn Wahb, one of the disciples of Mālik, held the same opinion. The proof of those who prohibit it is the tradition of Jābir, that has preceded, that he heard the Messenger of Allāh, on the day of the conquest of Mecca, saying that, "Allāh and His Messenger prohibited wine, carrion and swine". The reliance of those who permit its sale is (on the basis) that when a thing has more than one benefit, the prohibition of one of its benefits does not prohibit the rest of its benefits, especially if the need for the disputed benefits is equivalent to that of the prohibited benefits. If from this principle wine (*khamr*), carrion (*mayta*) and swine (*khinzīr*) are excluded leaving the rest of the things prohibited for consumption, but useful in other ways, it follows that they can lawfully be sold for those other benefits, that is, if they consist of benefits other than consumption. If they consist of benefits other than consumption and are sold for such benefits, it is permitted.

It is narrated from ᶜAlī, Ibn ᶜAbbas and Ibn ᶜUmar that they permitted the sale of *najis* oil for illumination. In Mālik's school there is found the permission of illumination with it and also the making of soap from it, although its sale is prohibited. Al-Shāfiᶜī also permitted this along with the prohibition of charging a price for it. All this, however, is somewhat weak. It is said that in the school (of Mālik) there is another narration that prohibits illumination with it (the oil) and this is more in conformity with the basic rule, that is, the prohibition of its sale. They also disagreed in the school (of Mālik) about washing and heating the *najis* oil as being effective in removing the filth from it. There are two opinions (on this). The first stands for its permission while the second calls for its prohibition. They are based on the question whether oil, mixed up with the filth, is filthy in its essence or is it filth of contiguity. Those who consider it external, caused only by contiguity, deem it cleaned when washed and heated while those who consider it filthy do not consider it clean, even on heating and washing.

Among the well-known issues related to this topic is their disagreement about the permissibility of the sale of the milk of a woman when extracted. Mālik and al-Shafiᶜī permit this, but Abū Ḥanīfa does not. The reliance of those who permit its sale is on the argument that it is milk the drinking of which is permitted, thus by analogy upon the milk of all cattle, its sale is permitted. Abū Ḥanīfa is of the opinion that its permission is based on the necessity arising from the need of the child for it, but it is actually prohibited just as the flesh of human beings is prohibited and the principle is that milk follows the *ḥukm* of the flesh. The analogy is that human beings are animals whose flesh is not eaten and, therefore, the sale of their milk is not permitted. The basis of this analogy is the milk of swine and asses. The reason for their disagreement then is the conflict of similar analogies. The cases falling under this rule are many and we mention only the well-known issues so that they may be regarded as principles.

24.2.2. Chapter 2: Usurious Sales

The jurists agreed that usury is found in two things: sales and that which is established as a liability through sale, credit, or other transactions. *Ribā* which is incurred as a liability is of two kinds. First is that about which there is an agreement and this is the *ribā* of the period of *jāhiliyya* (the pre-Islamic age) which is prohibited, as they used to stipulate excess in loans and then delay the period (of repayment). They used to say, "Grant me further delay and I will increase it (the amount)". This is what the Prophet (God's peace and blessings be upon him) meant when he said at the farewell pilgrimage, "Take heed, verily the *ribā* of *jāhiliyya* is annulled and the first (claim) of *ribā* I cancel is that of ᶜAbbās ibn ᶜAbd al-Muṭṭalib". The second kind is "loss for hastening (the period)".[127] This is controversial and we will describe it in what follows.

The jurists unanimously agreed about *ribā* in sales that it is of two kinds, delayed (*nasīʾa*)[128] and stipulated excess (*tafāḍul*),[129] except what has been narrated from Ibn ᶜAbbās about his denial of *ribā* in excess because it is narrated from the Prophet (God's peace and blessings be upon him) that he said, "There is no *ribā* except in delay (*nasīʾa*)". The majority of the jurists, however, maintained that *ribā* runs in these two types, as it has been established from the Prophet (God's peace and blessings be upon him).

The discussion of *ribā* is covered in four sections:

Section 1: things in which neither excess nor delay is allowed, along with their corresponding underlying cause (ᶜ*illa*);
Section 2: things in which excess is allowed, but delay is not;
Section 3: those in which both are allowed;
Section 4: things that are considered as one category and those that are not.

24.2.2.1 *Section 1: Identification of Things in which neither Excess nor Delay is Allowed and the Explanation of the Underlying Cause*

We say: The jurists agreed that excess and delay, neither of them is permitted in any category, from among the categories mentioned in the tradition of ᶜUbāda ibn al-Ṣāmit,[130] except what is narrated from Ibn ᶜAbbās. The

[127] This is *da*ᶜ *wa ta*ᶜ*ajjal*. The author explains it later as a discount granted for early payment of outstanding debt, before the expiry of the stipulated period. *See infra* note 134 and accompanying text.

[128] The reader must be cautioned about the distinction made by modern writers between *nasīʾa* and *nasāʾ*. They apply the term *nasīʾa* to mean *ribā* of the period of *jāhiliyya* and *nasāʾ* to mean delay in barter. The explanations of Ibn Rushd have influenced modern opinions, but he himself makes no such distinction and uses *nasīʾa* and *nasāʾ* interchangeably to mean "delay". The same application of the terms is found in the works of all earlier jurists.

[129] The two kinds of *ribā* are called *ribā al-faḍl* and *ribā al-nasīʾa* or *al-nasāʾ*.

[130] That is when two commodities of the same prohibited genus are exchanged.

tradition of ʿUbāda is that he said, "I heard the Messenger of Allāh (God's peace and blessings be upon him) prohibiting the sale of gold for gold, silver for silver, wheat for wheat, barley for barley, dates for dates, salt for salt, except through equal measure and immediate exchange. Thus, one who increases or causes to be increased has taken *ribā*". This tradition is explicit in the prohibition of excess in (exchange of) the same category of these things. With respect to the prohibition of delay (*nasīʾa*) in these (categories), it is established through more than one tradition and the best known among these is the tradition of ʿUmar ibn al-Khaṭṭāb who said, "The Messenger of Allāh (God's peace and blessings be upon him) said, 'Gold for gold is *ribā* except from hand to hand (when exchanged immediately), wheat for wheat is *ribā* except from hand to hand, dates for dates is *ribā* except from hand to hand, barley for barley is *ribā* except from hand to hand' ". The tradition of ʿUbāda includes the prohibition of excess in (exchange within) one category (of a thing) and also includes prohibition of delay in (the exchange of) two (different) categories out of these with the permission of excess (*tafāḍul*) in them. This is laid down in some of the authentic versions (of this *ḥadīth*) where after the prohibition of excess in these six it is stipulated, "Sell gold for silver as you like (but) from hand to hand and sell wheat for barley as you like but from hand to hand". All this is agreed upon by the jurists except (the case of) wheat for barley.

They disagreed about what is besides these expressly mentioned six categories Some, including the Ẓāhirites, said, "Excess is prohibited only in each one of these six species and what is besides these, in it excess is not prohibited within the species". They also said that delay is prohibited in these six species irrespective of the species being similar or different. This is a matter agreed upon, that is, the prohibition of delay (*nasīʾa*) in them together with a difference of species, except what is narrated from Ibn ʿUlayya who said, "When the species differ, delay and excess are both permitted, except in gold and silver". Thus, they have considered the proscription to be related to the essence of these six categories and as being a particular prohibition not extendable to other things.

The majority of the jurists of the provinces agreed that although it is a particular prohibition, it is extendable to other things generally, but they differed about the underlying general meaning on the basis of which these species were prohibited—that is the meaning of the *ʿilla* of prohibition of excess and prohibition of delay. The cause finally agreed upon by the astute among the Mālikites in the prohibition of excess, in four (out of six) species, is the exchange of the same species of food that can be stored. It is further said that it should be in the same storable category even if it is not food. The meaning of being stored is that it should be stored quite often. Some said that *ribā* also applies in rarely stored commodities. The *ʿilla* according to them in gold and silver for the prohibition of excess is the exchange of the same commodity as well as their being the most representative currencies and measure of value for non-durable property. This is the *ʿilla* that according to them is called deficient (*qāṣira*), as it is not applicable to things other than gold and silver. The *ʿilla* of the prohibition of delay (*nasīʾa*) according to the Mālikites in the four expressly mentioned commodities is being tasteful food and the characteristic of being stored, even though they are not of the same category. If, therefore, the categories are different, excess is permitted, but not delay (*nasīʾa*) and excess (*tafāḍul*) is permitted according to them in perishable food—that is, even when the category is the same—but delay is not permitted. The permission of excess is because of the characteristic of not being stored and it is said that storability is a condition for the prohibition of *tafāḍul* within the same species. The prohibition of delay in it (food) exists because it is a food that can be stored and we have said that the characteristic of food is always an *ʿilla* for the prohibition of delay in eatables.

The *ʿilla* of the prohibition of excess in the four species, according to Shāfiʿites, is only the characteristic of food along with being of the same category, while the *ʿilla* of prohibition of delay is the characteristic of food even though the species is different, as in Mālik's opinion. The *ʿilla* according to the Ḥanafites is the same in all six species and it is either measure or weight along with equivalence of species. The *ʿilla* of delay in these species is the difference of species except in brass and gold as there was consensus on the point that delay is permitted in them. Al-Shāfiʿi agreed with Mālik about the *ʿilla* of the prohibition of excess and delay in gold and silver, that is, that they are fundamental currencies and a measure of value for non-durable property which is the *ʿilla* according to them for the prohibition of delay when the species is different. When the species is the same excess is prohibited. The Ḥanafites for purposes of measure consider a quantity which is measured customarily. The *aḥkām* specific to *dīnārs* and *dirhams* will be taken up in the Book of *Ṣarf*. Here, however, the purpose is the elaboration of the various schools of thought of the jurists about the underlying causes of *ribā* proper in these species and the discussion of the evidence relied upon by each group.

We say: Those who restricted *ribā* to these six species belong to either of two groups: those who rejected analogy, that is the derivation of underlying causes from words and these are the Ẓāhirites; and those who rejected *qiyās al-shabah*. Because, in this case whosoever has linked the cases not expressly covered has done so by means of *qiyās al-shabah* not *qiyās al-ʿilla*, except what is related of Ibn al-Mājishūn that he considered here the value and said that the underlying cause of *ribā* is the protection of wealth, meaning thereby corporeal property. Qāḍī Abū Bakr al-Bāqillānī, on the other hand, considered *qiyās al-shabah* as weak and the *qiyās al-maʿna* as strong. He, therefore, used the latter, not finding *qiyās al-ʿilla* as useful. He linked only raisins with these six categories as he found raisins to be similar in meaning to dates. Each one of them, I mean, the users of analogy, has evidence for the derivation of the semblance (*shabah*) that he has taken into account for linking the species not expressly covered by the text with one of the (expressly mentioned) four species

The Shāfiʿites said about establishing the *ʿilla* of semblance (used by them) that when the *ḥukm* rests on a derived word (or noun) it indicates that this root meaning from which the word has been derived is the *ʿilla* of the *ḥukm*, as in the words of the Exalted, "As for the thief (*sāriq*), both male and female, cut off their hands".[131] Since the *ḥukm* rests on a derivative *sāriq*, then the *ḥukm* seems to be related to theft (*sariqa*) itself. Bearing in mind and taking into account the tradition of Saʿīd ibn ʿAbd Allāh in which he said, "I used to hear the Messenger of Allāh (God's peace and blessings be upon him) saying, 'food for food, like for like' "—it becomes evident that it is the characteristic of food upon which the *ḥukm* is based. The Mālikites, however, added to (the characteristic of) food, for the rule of *ribā*, either one more characteristic, the characteristic of being stored, according to *al-Muwaṭṭaʾ*, or two characteristics, that of being stored and of being an essential nutrient and that is what was preferred by the jurists of Baghdad. Their argument in the derivation of this last *ʿilla* is that had it been the purpose (of the lawgiver) to stipulate food only as the *ʿilla* it would have been sufficient to indicate only one of these four catagories in the text. As a number of them have been mentioned, the intention is to indicate the meaning implicit within each one of them and the meaning found in all is the characteristic of being stored and of being basic essential foods. The lawgiver indicated through wheat and barley all food grains that can be stored and indicated through dates all sweet things that can be stored like sugar, honey and raisins and indicated through salt all condiments that can be stored and used for curing food. They also said that as the underlying meaning of *ribā* is that there should be no misappropriation and that property should be protected, it becomes imperative that this be in the means of sustenance and these are the essential foods.

The reliance of the Ḥanafites in the consideration of measure and weight is that the Prophet (God's peace and blessings be upon him) tied permissibility to a similarity in kind and a similarity in quantity and he tied up prohibition to a similarity in kind and a difference in quantity. This is evidenced in his (God's peace and blessings be upon him) directive to his official to Khaybar, as in the tradition of Abū Saʿīd and others, "except measure for measure, from

[131] Qurʾān 5 : 38.

hand to hand". They were, therefore, of the view that quantity, that is measure and weight, is effective in the *ḥukm* like the effectiveness of kind. Perhaps, they argued on the basis of traditions that were less well known, but in which there was a strong emphasis on the consideration of measure and weight. Among these *ḥadīths* thus narrated, there are some which included the catagories occurring in the *ḥadīth* of ʿUbāda, but it has an addition stating that these are likewise measured and weighed. In some other traditions they narrated it is stated: 'measuring and weighing are likewise'. This matter, then, is explicit only if the traditions are authentic. However, when the matter is pondered over from the aspect of meaning, it becomes evident, Allāh knows best, that the underlying cause determined by them is the best of causes. This is because the aim of prohibiting *ribā* is (to avoid) the excessive injustice implicit in it and that justice in transactions demands an approximate equivalence. And therefore, when it became difficult to achieve equivalence in things of differing natures, *dīnārs* and *dirhams* were set up for their valuation, that is, assessment of their values. The things differing in nature—that is, those which cannot be (accurately) weighed or measured with fairness—are related to each other proportionately, I mean, the ratio of the price of a thing to its own genus and the ratio of the price of the other to its respective genus should be equal. The example of this fairness is that if a person exchanges a horse with dresses, then, the ratio of the price of this horse to horses should be the ratio of the price of the dress to dresses. Thus if the price of the horse is fifty then the price of the garment should also be fifty. It is so even if the number of a commodity is to be a multiple, like, for example, the number of garments priced as fifty is ten, the difference in number of these goods with respect to each other is then a necessity in a fair transaction, that is a fair equivalence of one horse must be ten dresses.

The case of things measured and weighed is not so, because they are not exactly dissimilar (in characteristics) and their uses are similar and there is no real necessity for one having one species to exchange it for the same species except by way of luxury. Fairness is achieved by equivalence in measure and weight, there being no preferences in utility. Prohibition of excess (*tafāḍul*) in these things prevents transaction in them as their benefits are not different and transaction is necessitated only when benefits differ. Therefore, two *ʿillahs* prohibited excess in these measured and weighed things: first, to ensure fairness in them; and second, to prevent extravagant transactions. In the prohibition of excess in *dīnārs* and *dirhams* the underlying cause is readily apparent; their purpose is not profit, but the valuation of other things that have necessary benefits. Mālik has related from Saʿīd ibn al-Musayyib that he used to consider the underlying cause of *ribā* in these (six) species as measure and the characteristic of food and that is an excellent meaning as food is a necessary ingredient of the essential commodities of human beings. It appears that the preservation of property and the prevention of *ṣaraf* (extravagance) is more important in what is an essential commodity than in what is not. It is related from some of the disciples of the Companions that he used to apply the prohibition of *ribā* to those species in which *zakāt* is imposed; and according to others it is utility, that is value (being *māl*) and that is the opinion of Ibn al-Mājishūn.

24.2.2.2. *Section 2: Identification of Things in which Excess is Permitted, but Delay is Not*

It follows from the above that, according to Mālik and al-Shāfiʿī, the underlying cause of prohibition in usurious commodities is food. In non-usurious commodities, which are not food, the underlying cause for prohibition of *nasīʾa*, according to Mālik, is similarity in kind and identical benefits along with *tafāḍul*. For al-Shāfiʿī there is no prohibited delay (*nasīʾa*) in non-usurious commodities. For Abū Ḥanīfa, the underlying cause for the prohibition of delay (*nasīʾa* or *nasāʾ*) is measure in usurious commodities and in others sameness of kind irrespective of accompanying excess. Ibn al-Qāsim has preferred an opinion related from Mālik that he prohibited delay in these (exchanges of similar kinds) as it was, according to him, from the category of loans carrying benefits.

24.2.2.3. *Section 3: Identification of Property in which Both (excess and delay) are Permitted Simultaneously*

Those in which both things are permitted simultaneously, I mean, excess and delay, are non-usurious commodities according to al-Shāfiʿī. According to Mālik it is that which is not usurious, unless it is the same species and an exactly similar kind. According to Abū Ḥanīfa, it is permissible, unless they are of the same species, whether similar or not. Mālik prohibits transactions involving excess in usurious commodities and the *ḥukm* of delay in other commodities for him depends on the similarity of benefits and their disparity. If the benefits differ he considers them (two) separate kinds even though the name is the same, while Abū Ḥanīfa takes into consideration the name and so also al-Shāfiʿī. For al-Shāfiʿī, however, sameness of kind is not effective except only in usurious commodities, that is, he prohibits excess in them and it is not for him the essential underlying cause of delay. This, then, is the gist of the opinions of these three jurists in three sections.

The things in which delay is not permitted are of two kinds: those in which excess is not permitted and their explanation has preceded; and those in which excess is permitted. With respect to the things in which excess is not permitted, the underlying cause of the prohibition of delay is food, according to Mālik. According to al-Shāfiʿī it is food alone. According to Abū Ḥanīfa, it is measurable and weighable food. Thus, if similarity in kind is combined with food, excess is prohibited according to al-Shāfiʿī and if a third characteristic is added, that of being stored, excess is prohibited according to Mālik. When the kind is dissimilar, excess is permitted but delay is prohibited.

Things in which excess is not prohibited are of two kinds according to Mālik: edible and non-edible. Delay is not permitted according to him in edible commodities and the underlying cause is food. Delay, according to him, is not permitted in non-edible commodities if the benefits are identical and when (the transaction is) accompanied by excess. Thus, one goat cannot be exchanged with a delay for two goats, except when one is meant for milking (is lactiferous) and the other for eating. This is his well-known opinion. It is said that he considered similarity of benefits and not excess. Accordingly, it would not be permitted to exchange a lactiferous goat for another lactiferous goat with accompanying delay. When the benefits differ then both excess and delay, according to him, are permitted even though the kind is one. It is also said that he considered similarity in names along with a similarity in benefits, but it is better known that he did not, then again it is said that he did.

According to Abū Ḥanīfa, what is taken into account for the prohibition of delay, besides that in which excess is not permitted, is similarity in kind irrespective of the benefits being identical or different. Thus, a goat cannot be exchanged for a goat nor for two along with accompanying delay even though the benefits are different. According to al-Shāfiʿī, on the other hand, all that in which excess is not permitted for the same kind, delay is permitted in it. Thus he permits (the exchange of) a goat for two goats exchanged with a delay or immediately, so also a goat for a goat. The evidence of al-Shāfiʿī is the tradition of ʿAmr ibn al-ʿĀṣ that "the Messenger of Allāh (God's peace and blessings be upon him) ordered him to acquire through the contracts of *ṣadaqa* (*zakāt*) a camel for two toward *ṣadaqa*". He said this is excess in the same genus along with delay. The Ḥanafites argued on the basis of the tradition of al-Ḥasan related from Samura, "that the Messenger of Allāh (God's peace and blessings be upon him) proscribed the sale of an animal for an animal". He said that this indicates the effectiveness of genus for identical categories in the case of delay.

Mālik's reliance in the consideration of the prohibition of delay, when the purposes (benefits) are identical, is the closing of the means (*sadd al-dharīʿa*) (of *ribā*); there is no use in such a transaction except that it is from the category of prohibited loans which carry benefits. It is said that this is an independent principle with him. The Kūfīs, it is said, believed that the sale of an animal for animal is not permitted with delay whether the genus is the same or is different, on the apparent meaning of the tradition of Samura. Thus it appears that al-Shāfiᶜī formed his opinion basing it on the tradition of ᶜAmr ibn al-ᶜĀṣ, while the Ḥanafites followed the tradition of Samura after placing their interpretation on it, as the apparent meaning demands that the exchange of an animal for an animal is not permitted with a delay, irrespective of whether the genus is the same or different. Mālik appears to derive his opinion through reconciliation, limiting the tradition of Samura to a similarity of purposes (benefits) and applying the tradition of ᶜAmr ibn al-ᶜĀṣ to the situation when they are different. The narration of al-Ḥasan from Samura is controversial though al-Tirmidhī has declared it *ṣaḥīḥ*. Mālik seeks support from the tradition related by al-Tirmidhī from Jābir who said, "Two animals for one is not proper with delay (*nasīᵓa*) and there is no harm if it is from hand to hand". Ibn al-Mundhir said that it is established that "the Messenger of Allāh (God's peace and blessings be upon him) purchased a slave in exchange for two black slaves and purchased a female slave for seven heads". On the basis of this tradition, the prohibition of a delayed sale of an animal for an animal appears to be a principle independent in itself and not based on the blocking of the means (*sadd al-dharīᶜa*). The jurists disagreed in the case of sale involving usurious commodities, whether actual delivery within the session of sale (*majlis*) before separation is a requisite condition for that the sale of which is not permitted with a delay (*nasāᵓ*); although they agreed about the stipulation of this as a condition in the case of currencies. The basis was the saying of the Prophet (God's peace and blessings be upon him), "Do not sell anything not present for that which is present". Those who have stipulated delivery during the session as a condition, considered it similar to *ṣarf*, while those who did not stipulate it said: "possession before parting is not a condition in sales except when there is legal evidence to support this and as there is evidence only in the case of *ṣarf*, the remaining usurious commodities retain the original rule".

24.2.2.4. *Section 4: Identification of Property Considered a Single Species and that which is not*

Under this topic they disagreed on a large number of issues about what can be considered a single species, within which there can be no excess (*tafāḍul*) and what cannot be considered a single species. Of these we will mention the best known. Similarly, they disagreed about the characteristics of a uniform species within which excess is prohibited and whether it matters if it is good or bad quality, or dried or fresh.

Among the things disputed, whether they are a single species or two different commodities, are wheat and barley. Some said they are one species of food, while others said they are two species The first opinion is that of Mālik and al-Awzāᶜī and it is related by Mālik in *al-Muwaṭṭa*ᵓ on the authority of Saᶜīd ibn al-Musayyib. The second is that of al-Shāfiᶜī and Abū Ḥanīfa and their reliance is on transmission and analogy. The transmission is the saying of the Prophet (God's peace and blessings be upon him), "Do not sell wheat for wheat, barley for barley, except like for like (in similar quantities)". Thus he considered them two categories. Similarly, in some of the narrations of the tradition of ᶜUbāda ibn al-Ṣāmit, it is said, "Sell gold for silver as you like, wheat for barley as you like and salt for dates as you like, but from hand to hand". It is related by ᶜAbd al-Razzāq and Waqīᶜ from al-Thawrī and considered *ṣaḥīḥ* by al-Tirmidhī. According to analogy they are two different things with different names and benefits and thus it is necessary that they be two separate species. The basis (of the analogy) is gold and silver and all other things with different names and benefits. The reliance of Mālik is on the practice of his ancestry (*Shaykhs*) in Medina. His disciples also relied on transmission and analogy. The transmitted text is that the Prophet (God's peace and blessings be upon him) said, "Food for food, like for like". They maintained that the term "food" includes wheat and barley, but this is a weak argument. It is a general term elaborated by *ṣaḥīḥ* traditions. By way of analogy, they reckoned a large number of things to have identical benefits and excess (*tafāḍul*) by agreement is not permitted in those having identical benefits. *Sult* (barley without shell) and barley according to Mālik are one species. Lentils are all one category according to him for purposes of *zakāt*, but about sales there are two narrations from him: first, they are one category; second, they are different categories. The reason for the difference is the conflict of the similarities and benefits and their disparity. Those who were inclined toward similarity said they are one species, while those who were inclined toward disparity said they are two kinds or more. Thus rice, millet and *jawār* are one category for him (Mālik).

24.2.2.4.1. Issue 1: Disagreement about the single category of meat in which excess is not permitted

They disagreed regarding the single category of meat in which excess is not permitted. Mālik said meats are of three kinds. The meat of all four-footed animals is of one species; the meat of those in the sea is one species; and the meat of birds is one species too. Among these three different species excess is permitted. Abū Ḥanīfa said each one of these represents many different species and excess is permitted in them, but not within a specific single species. Al-Shāfiᶜī had two opinions, one of which was like that of Abū Ḥanīfa and the other that they are all one species. Abū Ḥanīfa permitted the exchange of mutton with beef with excess, but Mālik did not permit it. Al-Shāfiᶜī did not permit the exchange of bird meat with mutton with an excess, but Mālik did. The reliance of al-Shāfiᶜī is on the saying of the Prophet (God's peace and blessings be upon him), "Food for food, like for like" and on the argument that with the departure of life the qualities of distinction are done away with and then the term "meat" applies equally to all these species. The reliance of the Mālikites is on the fact that these are separate genera which necessitates that they be separate kinds of meat. The Ḥanafites considered the difference within one genus out of these and said that: "(ignoring) the difference between different kinds (of meat and) animals, that is within one genus, is as if you would say that the difference in birds is commensurate with the difference that exists between fruit, wheat and barley". On the whole each group claims that the relative difference that exists between the things expressly covered (by the text) is the same difference it establishes for meat. The Ḥanafites are on stronger ground about meaning, as the prohibition of excess exists because of the similarity of benefits.

24.2.2.4.2. Issue 2: Disagreement about the sale of a living animal with a slaughtered animal

Within this discussion they also disagreed about the sale of an animal (living) with a carcass (slaughtered), into three opinions. First, it is not permitted at all; this is the opinion of al-Shāfiᶜī and al-Layth. Second, it is permitted in different genera in which excess is permitted, but it is not permitted in similar genera, that is in usurious commodities, because of the uncertainty by way of excess and this is in those the purpose of which is consumption. This is the opinion of Mālik. Thus, it is not permitted to exchange a slaughtered goat with a living animal meant for consumption. This is so according to him in consumable animals, so much so that he does not permit the exchange of a living animal with another if the intention is to consume one of them. This falls under this head, that is, its prohibition is in view of *ribā* and *muzābana*. The third opinion is that it is permitted absolutely. This is the opinion of Abū Ḥanīfa.

The reason for their disagreement is the conflict between principles underlying this topic and a *mursal* tradition traced to Saᶜīd ibn al-Musayyib. Mālik related from Zayd ibn Aslam from Saᶜīd ibn al-Musayyib that "the Messenger of Allāh (God's peace and blessings be upon him) proscribed the sale of an animal for meat". Those for whom the tradition does not clash with any of the principles of sale that impose prohibition adopted the tradition's view, while those who view that the principles oppose it are obliged to follow one of two courses: to prefer the tradition and make it an additional principle independent in itself; or to reject it because of its conflict with the principles. Al-Shāfiᶜī preferred the tradition, while Abū Ḥanīfa preferred the principles. Mālik reconciled it with the sale principles and considered sale in it under the category of *ribā*, that is, the sale of usurious commodities with their sources, like sale of oil for olives. The discussion of this principle will come later. This is what the jurists define as *muzābana* and it touches *ribā* from one aspect and *gharar* (hazard, uncertainty) from another. It is prohibited in usurious commodities from the aspect of *ribā* and *gharar* and in other commodities from the aspect of *gharar* alone, the cause of which is uncertainty external to the original commodity.

24.2.2.4.3. Issue 3: Sale of flour for wheat

Within this discussion is the sale of flour for wheat, like for like. The preferred opinion of Mālik grants its permission and it is found in his *al-Muwaṭṭaʾ*. It is also narrated from him that it is not permitted and that is the opinion of al-Shāfiʿī, Abū Ḥanīfa and Ibn al-Mājishūn from among the disciples of Mālik. Some of the disciples of Mālik said that this does not depict a real conflict in his opinions. The narration of prohibition applies when the consideration of likeness is by measure and the narration of permissibility applies when the consideration is by weight. Mālik considers measure and weight in those that are customarily measured and weighed and count in what is not customarily measured and weighed.

They disagreed under this discussion about that which involves workmanship and is originally usurious, like bread for bread. Abū Ḥanīfa said there is no harm in the sale of this with excess and like for like as it is no longer usurious. Al-Shāfiʿī said it is not permitted even like for like, not to say excess, as workmanship has converted it in a manner that renders uncertain its measures through which likeness can be assured. The preferred opinion of Mālik about bread is that it is permitted like for like and it is said that it is permitted with excess and equality. However, dough for dough is permitted, according to him, like for like. The reason for disagreement is whether workmanship transfers (a thing) from the genus of usurious commodities and if it does not transfer it, does it enable (the measurement of) exact likeness. Abū Ḥanīfa said it does transfer it while Mālik and al-Shāfiʿī said it does not. The latter two disagreed about the possibility of likeness in it. Mālik used to permit the consideration of likeness in bread and wheat through estimation in addition to weight. However, when workmanship did not affect one of the usurious commodities, but did the other, Mālik was of the view in most of them that workmanship transfers them from the genus, that is, from the same genus, thus permitting excess.

In others he does not hold this view and the details of his opinion in it are difficult to distinguish. Thus roasted and cooked meat are from the same genus, according to him and baked and unbaked wheat are two separate genera. His disciples have sought to make distinctions in this, but apparently there is no underlying rule in it, in his school, under which his opinions can be gathered. Al-Bājī has tried to gather them in *al-Muntaqā*. Similarly, it is difficult to gather all benefits that, according to him, obligate a similarity between individual things within a genus that is traded and to distinguish them from those benefits that do not (obligate such similarity), that is between animals, goods and plants (vegetables). The reason for the difficulty is that when a person is questioned about similar things at different times and there is no rule that he is applying for distinction except what a preliminary examination yields to him immediately, he comes up with different answers. When someone coming after him desires that these answers be reconciled under one rule and principle it becomes difficult for him. You can ascertain this from their books. These, then, are the most important (examples) in this topic.

24.2.2.5. *Section 5: Sale of a Usurious Moist (fresh) Commodity for a Dry One of its own Genus*

In their disagreement about the sale of a usurious (fresh) moist commodity for a dry one within its own genus with similarity of quantity and immediate exchange, the cause is what has been narrated by Mālik from Saᶜd ibn Abī Waqqāṣ that he said, "I heard the Messenger of Allāh (God's peace and blessings be upon him) being asked about the purchase of dried dates with fresh dates. The Messenger of Allāh (God's peace and blessings be upon him) said, 'Do the fresh diminish (in weight or volume) when they dry up?' They said, 'Yes'. He then prohibited this (sale)". Most of the jurists, including Mālik, al-Shāfiᶜī and others, followed this and said the sale of dry dates with fresh dates is not permitted at all. Abū Ḥanīfa said it is. His two disciples Muḥammad ibn al-Ḥasan and Abū Yūsuf disagreed with him. Al-Ṭaḥāwī had the same opinion as Abū Ḥanīfa.

The reason for their disagreement is the conflict of the apparent meaning of the tradition of ᶜUbāda and others with this tradition, as well as their disagreement about authenticating it. The tradition of ᶜUbāda stipulates, for permissibility, only the existence of similarity and equality and this apparently deals with the immediate mode of the contract, not with the ultimate condition. Those who have preferred the tradition of *ribā* and paid more attention to this apparent meaning, reject this tradition, while those who have considered this tradition as a principle independent in itself said that it is an additional rule explanatory of the traditions of *ribā*. The tradition is also disputed by scholars about its authenticity and it has not been recorded by the two *Shaykhs* (al-Bukhārī and Muslim). Al-Ṭaḥāwī said ᶜAbd Allāh was contradicted as Yaḥyā ibn Kathīr has related it from him, saying "that the Messenger of Allāh (God's peace and blessings be upon him) proscribed the sale of fresh dates for dried, with a delay". He (al-Taḥāwī) said that the person who has related this tradition from Saʾd ibn Abī Waqqāṣ is unknown (*majhūl*). The majority of the jurists, however, inclined toward acting according to it. Mālik has said in his *al-Muwaṭṭaʾ*, on the basis of analogy and the underlying cause of this tradition, that trading every fresh thing with a dried one of its genus is prohibited; that is, the prohibition of similarity as in dough for flour or dried meat with fresh. This according to Mālik is one of the kinds of prohibited *muzābana*, while the contract of *ʿariyya* is an exception from this principle. The same is said by al-Shāfiʿī. Prohibited *muzābana*, according to Abū Ḥanīfa, is the sale of dried dates on the ground with those on tree tops because of the uncertainty about the equality of the quantity of each, that is about their equivalence. Al-Shafiʿī extended this *ʿilla* to the case of sale of two fresh things, thus he does not allow the sale of fresh dates for other fresh dates in equal quantities, nor dough for dough with equivalence. He believed that excess (in one) would be found when they dried up. He was opposed in this by most of those who favoured this tradition.

Their disagreement about the sale of a thing of good quality for another of bad quality within the usurious species is conceived as the sale of a thing of medium quality with two others, one of a higher and the other of an inferior quality. For example, two measures (*mudd*) of dry dates of medium quality are exchanged for two measures of other dates, one of which is better than the medium and the other of a lesser quality. Mālik rejects this as there is a suspicion that two measures of medium quality are being exchanged for a measure of good quality only, while the measure of bad quality is being added to make permissible what is not. Al-Shafiʿī agrees with him in this, but the prohibition according to him is not because of suspicion as he does not attach importance to it. It appears that he considers excess (*tafāḍul*) in quality. There is no equivalence in quality as the excess of the good quality over the medium is not the same as the deficiency in the bad compared to the medium. Related to this subject is their disagreement about the permissibility of the sale of a usurious commodity with a commodity like it plus goods or *dīnārs* or *dirhams*, as the commodity to which goods are added is of a lesser quality than the other individual commodity, or there are with each one of them goods and two kinds of commodities in different quantities. The example of the first is the sale of two measures of dates with one measure (of dates) and *dirhams* while that of the second is the sale of two measures of dates and a dress with three measures of dates and *dirhams*. Mālik, al-Shāfiʿī and al-Layth said that this is not permitted while Abū Hanīfa and the Kūfīs said it is. The reason for disagreement is whether the usurious commodity and the opposing goods must be equivalent in value or whether the consent of the parties is sufficient. Those who considered equivalence in value said it is not permitted due to uncertainty, as if the goods are not equal in value to the difference of one usurious commodity over the other, excess (*tafāḍul*) would be the necessary consequence. The example of this is the exchange of two measures of dates with one measure of dates and a dress in which it is necessary that the value of the dress be equal to one measure, otherwise excess is the necessary outcome. Abū Ḥanīfa deems sufficient the consent of the parties. Mālik considers prevention of the means in these, as one of the parties has made this a means of selling one commodity with an excess. These are their well-known discussions in this category.

24.2.3. Sub-chapter: Sales through Usurious Means

Here is a situation which the parties confront when one of them stipulates excess or loss, through a negotiated rescission. The parties may enter unintentionally into an injurious sale, if one of them purchases from his companion something that he is selling with an excess, or with a loss. For example, a person sells to another goods for ten *dīnārs* in cash and then purchases the same goods from him for twenty *dīnārs* on credit. When the the second sale is related to the first, it becomes apparent that one of them has paid ten *dīnārs* in exchange for twenty with a delay. Such transactions are called deferred sales (*buyū*ᶜ *al-ājāl*). We shall mention, out of these, only the issue of the negotiated rescission (*iqāla*) as related to the issue of delayed sales for the purpose of this book is the extraction of principles not detailed opinions.

24.2.3.1. Issue: Negotiated rescission between buyer and seller

The jurists did not disagree about the case of a person who sells, for example, his slave for a hundred *dīnārs* on credit and then regrets the sale and asks the buyer to return the sold property in lieu of which he gives the buyer ten *dīnārs* cash or credit. All the jurists said that this is permitted and that there is no harm in it. The reason is that *iqāla* involving increase or decrease, according to them, is an independent transaction and there is no harm if a person sells a thing for a certain sum and then buys it back for a greater value. In this transaction the original seller purchased the slave for one hundred (units), that were due and ten units extra,[132] cash or credit. On the other hand, if the buyer, in this example, regrets the sale and demands *iqāla* so that he gives to the seller ten units cash or credit for a period greater than that in which a hundred (*dīnārs*) are due, then in this the jurists disagreed. Mālik said that it

[132] The term being used by the Author here is *mithqāl*—a unit of measure for gold.

is not permitted, while al-Shafiʿī said that it is. The reason why Mālik disapproved it is that it is a means to an end in which the intention is the exchange of gold for gold with a delay and the sale of gold plus property for gold—the buyer having paid ten units and the slave for the hundred for which he was liable. An element of a loan also enters this transaction; it is as if the buyer has sold the slave to him for ninety and considered as a loan the extra ten *dirhams*, possession of which had to be taken by him from himself, on his own behalf. Al-Shafiʿi considered all this as permitted, as it is an independent sale. There is no difference, according to him, between this issue and the issue in which an individual is a creditor to another for a hundred *dīnārs* and he buys from the debtor a slave worth ninety *dīnārs* taking immediate payment of ten *dīnārs* that are due. He said that suspicion is not to be cast on the acts of people.

If the first sale was for cash, then, there is no dispute that it is permitted as it does not amount to a sale of gold for gold with a delay. Malik, however, disapproved it for those who practice *ʿīna* (dual sale)—that is granting of loans to people—as it becomes a means for money lending in most of the cases and the parties reach it through what is beyond sale and is not genuine. The sales that are defined as delayed sales are those in which one individual sells goods for a price with a delay and then purchases them back for a different price either for cash or for credit.

24.2.3.2. Nine issues, two of which are disputed

The person who sells a thing with a delay and then purchases it, will purchase it with delay of a period ending at the same time (as the sale), or prior to it, or later. In each of these three cases, he will purchase the thing for the same price for which he has sold it, or for a lesser price, or higher. Two out of these (nine) cases are disputed and these are when he purchases during the period, for cash, at a price that is less than the price taken, or that he purchases it for a higher price with a period of delay lengthier than that of the sale. According to Mālik and the majority at Medina, this is not permitted. Al-Shafiʿī, Dawūd and Abū Thawr said it is permitted. The reasoning of those who disallowed it is based upon the consideration of the relation between the two sales. They suspected that the intention is to pay a greater amount for the sake of a delay and this is prohibited *ribā*. A false form (of the transaction) was, therefore, concocted so that the parties could obtain *harām* and it is the same as a person saying to another, "Lend me ten *dīnār*s for one month and I will repay you twenty", to which he replies, "This is not permitted, but I will sell you this donkey for twenty *dīnārs* on credit for one month and then buy it back from you for ten *dīnārs* cash". In the rest of the cases of the problem there is no suspicion (of an underlying intention). There is no allegation if he pays more than the sale price for a period shorter than the first, or if he pays less than the sale price for a lengthier period. The proof of those who hold this opinion is the *hadīth* of Abū al-ʿĀliya from ʿĀʾisha that "I heard her, when a slave-woman—who bore a child of Zayd ibn al-Arqam—said to her 'O *Umm al-Muʾminīn,* I purchased from Zayd a slave of his at the time of *'aṭā'* (the periodic governmental payment) for eight hundred. He then needed his money so I bought the debt back from him before the termination of the period for six hundred [cash]". ʿĀʾisha said, "Evil is what you sold and evil is what you bought. Convey this (my words) to Zayd that his (participation in) *jihād* with the Messenger of Allāh (God's peace and blessings be upon him) is nullified unless he repents". She (the woman) said, "Do you think it will be proper if I relinquish the second sale and just take back the six hundred?" ʿĀʾisha then replied, "Yes—He unto whom an admonition from his Lord cometh and (he) refraineth (in obedience thereto), he shall keep (the profits of) that which is past'."[133] Al-Shafiʿi and his disciples said that the *ḥadīth* of ʿĀʾisha is not established and Zayd himself contradicted her and when the Companions differ among themselves, our method is to resort to analogy (*qiyās*). An opinion similar to that of al-Shāfiʿī is also attributed to Ibn ʿUmar.

If a defect develops in the subject-matter of sale in the possession of the first buyer, then al-Thawrī and a group from among the Kūfīs permitted its seller to have a period of delay for buying it with cash at a lesser price. There are two narrations from Mālik on this. The form that Mālik considers in these sales is that they may be misused to take the shape of "postpone it for me and I will increase (the amount) for you", or sale that is not allowed with an excess, or sale not permitted with a delay (*nasīʾa*), or sale with a loan, or gold in exchange for gold, or loss (discount) for hastening (the period), or sale of food before possession, or sale and *ṣarf.* All these are the bases of *ribā.*

In relation to this is also discussed their disagreement about the person who sells food before he has taken possession of it. This was prohibited by Mālik, Abū Ḥanīfa and a group of jurists. It was permitted by al-Shāfiʿī, al-Thawrī, al-Awzāʿī and a group. The proof of those who disapproved of it is that it resembles the sale of food for food with a delay (*nasīʾa*). Those who permitted it did not view it as such in view of the absence of an intention to do so. Within this is also the disagreement about one who purchases food for cash to be delivered after a fixed period. When the period expires the seller does not have the food that he was to deliver, so he buys food from the purchaser for a price that he pays him in place of the food that he was under an obligation to deliver. Al-Shāfiʿī permitted this saying, "There is no difference in buying food, that he was under an obligation to deliver, from someone other than the buyer, or from

[133] Qurʾān 2 : 275

the the buyer himself". Mālik disallowed this, viewing it as a means to the sale of food before its possession is taken. As he (the seller) delivered food to him (the buyer), for which he was liable, it amounts to sale before possession is taken.

The form of *dharīʿa* (means) in this is that a person purchases food from another for a fixed period (of delivery) and when the period expires the seller says, "I do not have food, but I will purchase from you the food I owe you". The other says, "This is not proper as it is the sale of food before possession, but buy food from me (as a separate sale) and I will deliver it to you". This, then, develops into what we have mentioned, that is, he delivers the food that he acquires from him and the price he pays is the price of the food that he owed. Al-Shāfiʿī, as we have said, does not give weight to allegations (of using sales as a means), but looks at what is prohibited and what is permitted out of sales according to the stipulations of the parties and what they express through their own words and acts. This is based on the consensus (*ijmaʿ*) of the jurists, that is, if he says, "I will sell to you these *dirhams* for similar *dirhams* postponed for a period of a month or a year", it is not permitted. If he says, "lend me *dirhams* and allow me a certain period", say a month, it is permitted. Thus there is no disagreement among them except the form (*sīgha*) of words of sale and accompanying intention and the form of the words of *qarḍ* (loan) with the accompanying intention.

As the bases of *ribā*, mentioned earlier, are five—grant me postponement and I will increase the amount; excess (*tafaḍul*); delay (*nasīʾa*); loss for hastening (the period); sale of food before possession—it is thought that this sale falls under these categories, as the person entering it pays some *dīnārs* and takes back more, without any formality or a liability for compensating (loss). It is, therefore, necessary that we mention these two (remaining) bases here.

Daʿ wa taʿajjal (or loss for hastening the period of payment) was permitted by Ibn ʿAbbās out of the Companions and Zufar out of the *fuqahāʾ*. It was prohibited by a group, among them are Ibn ʿUmar from the Companions and Mālik, Abū Ḥanīfa, Al-Thawrī and a group from among the *fuqahāʾ*. Al-Shāfiʿī has different opinions in this. Mālik and most of those who reject *daʿ wa taʿajjal* consider its form[134] to be that a person who has a debt outstanding for a certain period, hastens the period by taking payment even though the amount paid is less than what was due to him. The reliance of those who did not permit hastening for loss is that it resembles excess with a period which is prohibited, by agreement. The basis of this resemblance is that he has rendered a part of the price equivalent to and in exchange for the period on

[134] *See supra* note 127 and accompanying text. It may be noted that this transaction resembles the all too familiar discounts given by traders to their debtors these days for making early payments. Another example may be the concessions given by banks for the recovery of bad debts, both in interest and capital.

two counts, that is, when he increased the period he increased the price proportionately and when he reduced the period he reduced the price proportionately. The reliance of those who permit it is what is related from Ibn ᶜAbbās "that some people came to the Prophet (God's peace and blessings be upon him) from Banū Naḍīr, when he ordered their expulsion and said, 'O Prophet of Allāh, you have ordered our expulsion, but we have debts outstanding against people with remaining periods'. The Messenger of Allāh (God's peace and blessings be upon him) said, 'Decrease and hasten' ". The reason for disagreement is the conflict of *qiyās al-shabah* with this tradition.

24.2.4. Proposition: Sale of Food before Possession

The jurists are in agreement over the disapproval of the sale of food before possession,[135] except what is related from ᶜUthmān al-Battī. The jurists agreed on this because of the establishment of its proscription from the Messenger of Allāh (God's peace and blessings be upon him) through the narration of Mālik, from Nāfiᶜ from ᶜAbd Allāh ibn ᶜUmar, that the Messenger of Allāh (God's peace and blessings be upon him) said, "He who purchases food must not sell it till he takes possession of it". They disagreed over this issue on three points. First is property about which possession is stipulated; second are benefits for the sale of which possession is stipulated; third is the difference between what is sold from food in heaps (by estimate) and that sold by measure. In this, then, there are three sections.

24.2.4.1. *Section 1: Subject-Matter of Sale for which Possession is Stipulated*

There is no dispute in Mālik's school about the permission of selling things, other than food, before possession and there is also no dispute in his school about usurious food that possession is a condition for its sale. Mālik has two opinions about non-usurious food. First, that it is disallowed (without prior possession). This is better known and is also the opinion of Aḥmad and Abū Thawr, though these two authorities stipulated that food should be measured and weighed. Second, that it is permitted. For Abū Ḥanīfa possession is a condition for all kinds of sold property, except immovable property like houses and real estate. For al-Shāfiᶜī, possession is a condition for all kinds of property. This is also an opinion of al-Thawrī and is related from Jābir ibn ᶜAbd Allāh and Ibn ᶜAbbās. Abū ᶜUbayd and Isḥāq said that every thing that is not measured or weighed may be sold without harm before possession and they

[135] The implications of this discussion have a direct bearing on the transactions of the commodity exchanges, especially "futures" transactions.

stipulated possession for weighable and measurable commodities. This was also the view of Ibn Ḥabīb, ʿAbd al-ʿAzīz ibn Abū Salama and Rabīʿa, however, they added counting to measure and weight. Thus, for the stipulation of possession, seven opinions are available. First, in usurious food only; second, in all food without qualification; third, in measurable and weighable food; fourth, in each movable thing; fifth, in every thing; sixth, in all measurable and weighable things; and seventh, in measurable, weighable and countable things.

The reliance of Mālik in disapproval, besides those commodities expressly covered by the text, is upon the indirect indication of the text (*dalīl al-khitāb*) in the foregoing tradition. The reliance of al-Shāfiʿī, for generalizing possession for all sales, is the generality of the saying of the Prophet (God's peace and blessings be upon him), "It is not permitted: to sell with a loan; to profit without a corresponding liability (for loss); or to sell what you do not possess". This relates to the topic of sale without liability for loss and is based on his opinion that possession is a condition for the subject-matter of sale to enter into the liability of the buyer. He also argued on the basis of the tradition of Ḥakīm ibn Ḥizām, who said, "I said, O Messenger of Allāh, 'I am involved in sale transactions, what is permitted to me in them and what is prohibited?' He said, 'O son of my brother, when you buy something, do not sell it till you take possession of it' ". Abū ʿUmar said that "the tradition of Ḥakīm ibn Ḥizām has been related from Yaḥyā ibn Abū Kathīr from Yūsuf ibn Mahak and ʿAbd Allāh ibn ʿAsmaʾ and he said that 'I do not know of a fault in Yūsuf ibn Mahak and ʿAbd Allāh ibn ʿAsmaʾ, except that only a single person relates from them' ". This, in fact, is not a fault even though it has been looked down upon by a group of traditionists. From the aspect of analysis, sale without possession raises a doubt of *ribā*. Abū Ḥanīfa exempted what is movable and transferable, in his view, from what is immovable and non-transferable, for transfer of possession, according to him, is possible by making the property available. Those who considered measure and weight did so because of their agreement that measurable and weighable things do not move out of the liability of the seller to that of the buyer except by actual measuring and weighing and the sale of that for which he (the seller) is not liable is not permitted.[136]

[136] This is based on the well-known principle of Islamic law: *al-kharāj biʾl-ḍamān*, which means that entitlement to profit or gain depends upon the corresponding liability for loss. If a person has no liability for bearing a loss in a transaction, he cannot have the profits arising from such a transaction. He becomes liable for loss only when the subject-matter moves into his possession. Thus, he is not allowed to sell the commodity before it moves into his possession. This principle plays a major role in the Islamic law of contract.

24.2.4.2. *Section 2: Benefits for the Sale of which Possession is Stipulated and those for which it is not*

For the consideration of this distinction contracts are divided first into two kinds. First are the contracts of *muʿāwaḍa* or the commutative contracts and second are those that do not have an *ʿiwaḍ* (counter value), like gifts and charity. The commutative contracts are divided into three kinds. First are those that have as their object the determination and measurement (of the subject-matter) and these are sales, hire, dower, settlements and compensation of property because of *taʿaddī* (tort; delict; wrongful act). The second kind does not involve the intention of mutual exchange, but is undertaken by way of compassion and this is *qarḍ* (charitable loan). The third kind involves both aspects, that is, the intention of mutual exchange as well as compassion and includes partnership (*sharika*), negotiated rescission (*iqāla*) and resale at cost price (*tawliya*). The result of the opinions of the jurists on this topic is as follows.

There is no dispute about the stipulation of possession in commutative sales and these are of those things for which each individual jurist has stipulated possession. Those that are purely by way of compassion, I mean *qarḍ,* there is no dispute about them also that possession is not a condition, as it is permitted to an individual to sell a *qarḍ* before possessing it. Abū Ḥanīfa has also exempted those that are due to the compensation of dower or due to *khulʾ*. He said, "Their sale before possession is permitted". I do not know of any dispute in this (Mālik's) school about contracts that are ambivalent between the intent of compassion and mutual exchange and these are *tawliya, sharika* and *iqāla,* that they are permitted before possession as well as after it.

Abū Ḥanīfa and al-Shāfiʿī said *sharika* and *tawliya* are not permitted before possession. *Iqāla* is permitted, according to them, as it is a rescission of sale before possession and not a sale. The proof of those who stipulated possession in all commutative contracts is that it amounts to a prohibited sale. Mālik, however, exempted *tawliya, iqāla* and *sharika* on the basis of *āthār* and legal analysis. The *athar* is what is related as a *mursal* from Saʿīd ibn al-Musayyib, that the Messenger of Allāh (God's peace and blessings be upon him) said, "He who purchases food must not sell it, till he takes possession of it", except what is by way of *sharika, tawliya,* or *iqāla.* Legal analysis indicates that it is compassion that is the intention in these and not mutual exchange, as excess or loss is not involved. Abū Ḥanīfa exempted from these dower, *khulʿ* and *jiʿāla*, as compensation in these is not evident, being undetermined.

24.2.4.3. *Section 3: Distinction between Food Sold by Measure and that Sold in Heaps (by estimate)*

Mālik made an exception about the stipulation of possession in the sale of food in heaps allowing it (to be sold without the condition of possession); that was also the opinion of al-Awzāʿī. Abū Ḥanīfa and al-Shāfiʿī did not permit it. One of their proofs is what is related from Ibn ʿUmar, that he said, "In the time of the Prophet (God's peace and blessings be upon him), we used to buy food in heaps, so he sent someone to us who ordered us to transfer it from the spot where we had purchased it, to a spot besides it, before we sold it". Abū ʿUmar said: "Though Mālik does not narrate from Nāfiʿ the occurrence of heaps in this recension, it has been narrated by a group; ʿUbayd Allāh ibn ʿUmar, along with others, has recited it and he has precedence in the retention of traditions from Nāfiʿ ". The reliance of the Mālikites is that there is no right to be discharged in heaps, as they are transferred to the liability of the buyer by the contract itself. This pertains to the category of the restriction of the generality by analogy, whose underlying cause is deduced. The consensus of the jurists, on the prohibition of sale by a person of that which he does not own, is also subsumed under this category and it is called *ʿīna*, according to those who consider it as a progression from the category of the means (*dharīʿa*) toward *ribā*. Those who view it from the aspect that its transfer is unlikely, maintain that it belongs to the category of uncertain sales (*buyūʿ al-gharar*). The form it acquires as a means toward prohibited usury is that a person says to another, "Give me ten *dirhams* and I will return its double to you after a period' ". The other replies, "This is not proper, but I will buy from you goods (in return) for other goods". These goods he designates, but they are not equivalent in value (to the goods bought). He then undertakes this sale and purchases the goods, delivering possession of the goods sold (in return), after the conclusion of the contract. The value of the goods (delivered) is equivalent to the amount in *dirhams* that he (the first person) had asked for as a loan, to be doubled on return. The detail exists in the school (of Mālik), but this is not the occasion for narrating it. There is, however, no disagreement in the school about the form we have mentioned that it is not permitted, I mean, their agreement about the price by which (undetermined) goods are to be purchased before the sale is actually transacted.

The Muslim jurists agreed upon the prohibition of (the sale of) a debt for a debt. They disagreed on (various) issues, though, irrespective of whether they formed part of it. As, for example, Ibn al-Qāsim did not permit a creditor to acquire from his debtor, against the debt, ripe dates, or residence in a house, or a slave-girl for service. Ashhab used to permit this, saying that this is not an exchange of a debt for a debt, but it amounts to that when he (the creditor) has not stipulated taking anything from him. This amounts to *qiyās* according to the Mālikites and is also the opinion of al-Shāfiʿī and Abū Ḥanīfa. Among the things related to this, which Mālik permitted and in which he was opposed by the majority of the jurists, is what he said (in *al-Mudawwana*) that "People used to sell meat at a fixed price delaying payment till the date of governmental *'aṭā'* and the buyer used to take a known quantity every day". He said, "The People saw no harm in this or in the other things sold in the market". Ibn al-Qāsim relates that this is not permitted except when there is fear of decay, if the entire quantity is taken at once. There is no permission for wheat and other commodities like it.

These are the fundamentals of this category. The category has been prohibited in law because of the existence of misappropriation which is voluntary and intentional.

24.2.5. Chapter 3: Sales Proscribed on Account of Misappropriation the Cause of which is *Gharar*

These are sales that are proscribed on account of misappropriation the cause of which is uncertainty (*gharar*). *Gharar* is found in sales from the aspect of *jahl* (lack of knowledge) in various forms: (1) from the aspect of *jahl* caused by the failure to identify the subject-matter of the contract, or failure to determine the contract; (2) from the aspect of *jahl* about the attributes of the price, or the priced commodity, or about the quantity, or the deferred period (of delivery), if there is one; (3) from the aspect of *jahl* about its existence or the impossibility of its acquisition; and this relates to the obstacles to delivery; (4) from the aspect of its sound existence, that is its continued existence. And then there are sales that combine in themselves most or some of these attributes.

Among the sales in which these categories of *gharar* are to be found, there are those that are expressly prohibited in the *shar*ᶜ and those about which there is silence. Most of those expressly prohibited are agreed upon, it is only the meanings of their names that are disputed. Those about which there is silence are disputed. We shall first discuss those sales that are expressly prohibited in the law and in *fiqh* and those which relate to them. After that, we will discuss, from amongst those not mentioned in the law, sales about which the disagreement of the *fuqahā*ʾ of different regions became well-known, so as to render it a rule of *fiqh*: that is, guidelines to help in referring things to their origins.

Among those that are expressly mentioned are: proscription by the Prophet (God's peace and blessings be upon him) of the sale of the foetus in the stomach of a conceiving animal (*ḥabl al-ḥabla*); his proscribing the sale of that not yet created; prohibition of sale of fruits before they are ripe; of the sales of *mulāmasa* and *munābadha*; and of sales by throwing stones (*bay*ᶜ *al-ḥaṣāt*). Among them are also his proscription about: *mu*ᶜ*āwama*; two sales in one; conditional sale; sale linked to a loan; sale of grain ears before they whiten; the sale of grapes before they blacken; and the sales of foetuses and sperm of animals (*maḍāmīn* and *malāqīḥ*).

The sale of *mulāmasa* in *jāhiliyya* took the form that the buyer could only feel a dress and not spread it out (for examination), or he would buy something on a dark night not knowing what was within. This is unanimously agreed upon for prohibition and the reason is *jahl* about attributes. In the sale of *munābadha*, each party to the sale used to fling a dress at the other, without determining the reciprocity of either, deferring the matter to their subsequent agreement. With respect to sale by throwing a stone, its form with them was that the buyer would throw a stone and say, "Any dress on which the stone falls belongs to me". It is said that they also used to say, "If the stone falls from my hand, the sale would be binding". This amounts to gambling. There are two interpretations of the sale of *ḥabl al-ḥabla*. First, that these were sales they postponed till the she-camel, for example, would deliver its offspring and then the offspring would yield an offspring. Uncertainty of period in this is evident. It is also said that it was the sale of the foetus of the she-camel. This, in fact, relates to the category of the proscription of the sale of *maḍāmīn* and *malāqīḥ*. *Maḍāmīn* are the foetuses and *malāqīḥ* are what exists in the spines of stallions (sperm). These are all sales of *jāhiliyya* that are prohibited by agreement. They are prohibited because of the reasons we have mentioned.

The sale of fruit (or crops) is established from the Prophet (God's peace and blessings be upon him) that "he proscribed its sale till it began to ripen and was in full bloom". To this are related well-known issues, out of which we shall discuss the core.

The sale of fruit can take place either before or after it sprouts. Once it comes into existence, the sale can take place either after it is picked, or before that. If it occurs before picking, it can either be before it ripens or subsequently; and each one of these (two) can be an unqualified sale, or sale with the condition of letting the fruit stay on the trees, or sale with the condition of participation in picking. All the jurists agree on the prohibition of the first kind, which is the sale of fruit before it comes into existence, for it belongs to the proscribed category of sale before creation and to that of the sale of *sinīn* and *muᶜāwama* (yearly sales). It is related from the Prophet (God's peace and blessings be upon him) that "He proscribed the sale of *sinīn* and the sale of *muᶜāwama* and these are the sales of trees for (several) years", except what has been related from ᶜUmar ibn al-Khaṭṭāb and Ibn al-Zubayr that they used to permit the sale of fruit on the basis of *sinīn*. There is no dispute about the permissibility of its sale after picking. With respect to its sale after creation, most of the jurists favour permission, with details that we shall mention; except what is related from Abū Salama ibn ᶜAbd al-Raḥmān and from ᶜIkrima, that it is not permitted except after picking.

If we accept the view of the majority that it is permitted before picking, then, it will be either before ripening, or after it. We have said that this would be either an unqualified sale, or a sale with the condition of picking, or sale with the condition of leaving (the fruit) on the trees. There is no dispute about the permissibility of sale before ripening with the condition of picking, except what is related from al-Thawrī and Ibn Abī Laylā, who disallowed it and this is a weak recension. There is no dispute, however, that sale before ripening, with the condition of leaving it on the trees, is not allowed, except what is related from al-Lakhmī about its permission, based on deduction from the principles of the school. About an unqualified sale before ripening, the jurists of different regions, disagreed. The majority—Mālik, al-Shāfiᶜī, Aḥmad, Isḥāq, al-Layth, al-Thawrī and others—said it is not permitted. Abū Ḥanīfa said it is permitted on the condition that the buyer pick the fruit (immediately), not because it is a sale of what has not yet been created, but because it is an essential condition, according to him, for the sale of fruit—as will follow later.

The evidence of the majority for disallowing an unqualified sale of fruit before ripening is the established tradition of Ibn ᶜUmar that "The Messenger of Allāh (God's peace and blessings be upon him) proscribed, for both the buyer and seller, the sale of fruit till it begins to ripen". The distinction, between what is before ripening and what is after it, was thus known. The proscription includes the unqualified sale with the condition of leaving the fruit on the trees. When it became obvious to the majority that the underlying reason in this prohibition—which is based on the saying of the Prophet (God's peace and blessings be upon him) coming after the proscription of sale before ripening, from the tradition of Anas ibn Mālik "What if Allāh were to deny the fruit; for what, then, would you be taking your brother's wealth?"—is the apprehension of diseases that will usually infect the fruit before it ripens, they did not assign an absolute meaning to the proscription, that is, the proscription of sale before ripening. They were, on the other hand, of the view that it applies to sale with the condition of leaving it (the fruit) on the trees till it ripens. Thus, they allowed its sale, before ripening, with the condition of picking. They disagreed about an unqualified sale, in this context, whether it should be interpreted to mean (immediate) picking, which is permitted, or being left on the trees, which is prohibited. Those who interpreted the unqualified sale as implying the leaving of fruit (on the trees), or considered the unqualified sale to be included in the generality of the proscription, said it is not allowed. Those who interpreted it to indicate picking said that it is allowed. Mālik's renowned opinion is that unqualified sales imply leaving the fruit on trees, yet another opinion is that they imply picking.

The proof of the Kūfīs, in permitting the sale of fruit generally before ripening, is the tradition of Ibn ᶜUmar that the Messenger of Allāh (God's peace and blessings be upon him) said "He who sells date-palms that have fertilized (must know that) the fruit is for the seller, unless the buyer has stipulated a condition (to include the fruit)". They said, "Since it is permitted to the buyer to stipulate (this condition), it is likewise permitted to sell the fruit separately". They interpreted the tradition imposing the proscription, about sale of fruit before ripening, to mean a recommendation. They argued about this using a tradition related from Zayd ibn Thābit, who said, "In the time of the Messenger of Allāh (God's peace and blessings be upon him), the people used to trade in fruit before it had ripened. When the time of payment drew near and demands were made, the buyer would say, 'the fruit has been affected by the vicissitudes of time and damaged by diseases'. As their disputes, reaching the Prophet, increased, he said, as an advice extended to them, 'Do not sell fruit till it begins to ripen' ". Perhaps they understood the meaning indicated by the tradition through the words, "till it begins to ripen", as the blossoming of the fruit—on the evidence of the saying of the Prophet, "What if Allāh were to deny the fruit; for what, then, would you be taking your brother's wealth?" It was analytically consistent for those among the Kūfīs who held this opinion and who did not share the opinion of Abū Ḥanīfa about the requirement of immediate picking in the sale of fruit, to permit its sale before the commencement of ripening with the condition of leaving it on trees. The majority, then, apply the permissibility of the sale of fruit, with a condition before ripening to a particular case—that is, when the fruit is sold with its *aṣl* (the trees).

There is no dispute about the permissibility of the purchase of fruit after ripening. The general meaning of the tradition, according to the majority of the jurists, implies that the fruit is left on trees, on the evidence of the saying of the Prophet (God's peace and blessings be upon him), "What if Allāh were to deny the fruit; for what, then, would you be taking your brother's wealth". The wisdom behind the evidence is that disease normally infects fruit before it begins to ripen; and after ripening it is rare. If the condition of leaving it on trees is not stipulated in the sale, there would be no expectation of disease. The condition is therefore invalid. According to the Ḥanafites, the stipulation of leaving fruit on trees is not permitted and the generality occurring in the tradition implies picking. This is against the implication of the tradition. Their argument is that sale of a thing itself requires (immediate) delivery, otherwise it involves uncertainty (*gharar*). It is, therefore, not permitted to sell things with (delayed) periods. The majority maintain that the sale of fruit is exempted from the rule of delayed sales, as it is not possible for fruit to become ripe all at once. The Kūfīs, then, went against the majority on two counts: first, in the permission of sale of fruit before ripening; and second, in the denial of leaving ripe fruit on trees—by stipulating it as a condition, or by making an unqualified contract. Their disagreement in the first case is more sound than it is in the second, that is, in stipulating picking even when the fruit is ripe. Their disagreement in the first case is sound as it belongs to the category of reconciliation of the two preceding traditions of Ibn ᶜUmar and because this is also related from ᶜUmar ibn al-Khaṭṭāb and Ibn al-Zubayr.

The commencement of ripening, beyond which the Messenger of Allāh (God's peace and blessings be upon him) permitted sale, takes place when the unripe dates turn yellow and the grapes turn black, if they are the type that turn black. On the whole, the attributes of ripening should appear in the fruit. This is the opinion of a group of jurists, of different regions, because of what is related by Mālik from Ḥumayd from Anas, "He (the Prophet) was asked about his words—'till it ripens'—and he said, 'till it turns red' ". It is also narrated from the Prophet (God's peace and blessings be upon him) that "He proscribed the sale of grapes till they turn black and grain till it hardens". Zayd ibn Thābit in a narration of Mālik from him, did not sell his fruit till the rise of the *Thurayya* (Pleiades) and this was when twelve nights of *ayyār*, that is May, had passed. It is also the saying of Ibn ᶜUmar, "He was asked about the saying of the Messenger of Allāh (God's peace and blessings be upon him) that proscribed the sale of fruits till they were safe from disease and ᶜAbd Allāh Ibn ᶜUmar said, 'That is the time of the ascension of Pleiades' ". It is related from Abū Hurayra from the Prophet (God's peace and blessings be upon him) that he said, "When the star ascends in the morning the diseases are removed from the residents of the land". Ibn al-Qāsim related from Mālik that there is no harm in selling an orchard even though it is not yet ripe, if the orchards around it have ripened and when it is time of safety from disease, intending thereby, Allāh knows best, the ascension of the *Thurayya*. His well-known opinion, however, is that the orchard is not to be sold till it begins to ripen. It is also said that he did not take into account, along with ripening, (the condition of) the ascension of the *Thurayya*. The resulting opinions from the jurists about the commencement of suitability (for sale) are three: one, that it is ripening; second, that it is the ascension of the *Thurayya*, even if at the time of sale there is no ripening; third, that it is both things taken together. Mālik said, in his well-known opinion, about ripening that when there are in a single orchard itself fruits of different species with different stages of ripening, no species is to be sold unless ripening commences in the species itself. He was opposed in this by al-Layth. Sale of some species in similar stages of ripening is permitted, according to him, by ripening in others.

Commencement of ripening acceptable to Mālik in one species of fruit is the start of ripening in parts of it, not necessarily in the whole of it, when such ripening occurs in it, it occurs prematurely long before the ripening of the rest, a successive process, because the time when fruits are generally secure from diseases is the commencement of ripening in succession without interruption. According to Mālik, if ripening begins in a date-palm of a grove it is permitted to sell it and to sell the groves adjacent to it, provided the date-palms of the groves are of the same species. Alshafi said, it is not permitted to sell except the grove in which ripening has commenced. Mālik considered the time of security from disease as being the same for similar species. Al-Shāfiʿī based his view on the deficiency in the coming into (proper) existence of the fruit, that is, if it did not ripen it would be the sale of that which is not created, because the criterion of ripening in it at the time of purchase is not created yet; but what he al-Shāfiʿī says is not stipulated for all fruits, only for some fruits in the same garden—it is an opinion not held by anyone else. The above is the gist of what is well known of their disagreement about the sale of fruit.

Among the transmitted traditions relevant to this heading, which they also disputed, is that which is related from the Prophet (God's peace and blessings be upon him) about the proscription of the sale of ears (of grain) till they become white and of grapes till they become black. This is because the jurists agreed that it is not permitted to sell wheat in the ear without the ear itself, as it is the sale of a thing whose characteristics are not known, nor is its quantity. They disagreed about the sale of the ear itself along with the grain. The majority permitted this, including Mālik, Abū Ḥanīfa, the jurists of Medina and the jurists of Kūfa. Al-Shāfiʿī said: it is not permitted to sell the ear itself even if it is fully mature, as first, it involves *gharar* (hazard) and, secondly, (it is prohibited) on the analogy of (the prohibition of) its sale mixed with straw after threshing. The proof of the majority is in two things: transmission and analogy. The transmission is what is related from Nāfiʿ from Ibn ʿUmar "that the Messenger of Allāh (God's peace and blessings be upon him) proscribed the sale of a date-palm till it is ripe and of an ear till it whitens and is safe from disease—prohibiting both the seller and the buyer". This tradition (contains) a significant addition over what has been related by Mālik of the same tradition; and an addition reported by a trustworthy transmitter is acceptable. It is reported that al-Shāfiʿī withdrew his opinion when he heard of this addition, because (the use of) analogy according to him is not correct with the existence of a *ḥadīth*.

The sale of an ear, when it is green and has not grown, is not permitted according to Mālik except with the condition of cutting. About the sale of ears, which have not been harvested, it is said that it is permitted according to Mālik, while it is also said that it is not permitted unless they are in a sheaf. Its sale in threshed straw is not permitted, without any disagreement. This is so when it is (sold) in heaps (by estimate), but when it is sold by weight it is permitted according to Mālik, while I am not aware of the opinions of others in this.

Those who permitted the sale of ears, when fully mature, disagreed as to who is to be responsible for harvesting and threshing. The Kūfīs said, it is up to the seller who is to undertake it and deliver clean grain. The others said that it is the responsibility of the buyer. A theme relevant to the subject of this chapter is in the tradition affirming "that the Messenger of Allāh (God's peace and blessings be upon him) proscribed two sales in one", according to the *ḥadīth* of Ibn ᶜUmar and those of Ibn Maṣᶜūd and Abū Hurayra. Abū ᶜUmar said that all these have been transmitted by the trustworthy authorities. The jurists, therefore, agreed generally on the implication of this *ḥadīth*, but differed over the details—I mean the form to which the term is applied and that to which it is not. They also agreed on some of its forms. This sale may take one of three ways: one is exchange of two priced commodities for two prices, another is exchange of a priced commodity for two prices and a third is exchange of two priced commodities for one price, in which case one of the two sales becomes binding. The (sale of) two priced commodities for two prices is visualized in two ways: first, that one says to the other, "I will sell you this commodity for such a price on the condition that you sell me that house for such price"; and second, that he says to him, "I will sell you this thing for a *dīnār* or this other commodity for two *dīnārs*". The sale of a single commodity for two prices is also visualized in two ways: first, that one of the prices is in cash while the other on credit, like one saying to the other, "I will sell you this dress in cash at such price on the condition that I buy it from you (on credit) with such period and at such price". The (sale of) two commodities for a single price is like one saying to the other, "I will sell you one of these two for such and such price".

In the first case, when one says to the other, "I will sell you this house for so much on the condition that you sell me this slave-boy for so much", al-Shāfiᶜī stipulates that it is not permitted, because the price in both cases is unknown for the two things (being sold), if they are separated the parties would not agree to the price to which they are agreeing in a single contract. The basis of al-Shāfiᶜī, in rejecting two sales in one, is the ignorance of the price or the priced commodity. As to the second case, which is when he says, "I will sell you this thing for a *dīnār*, or this other commodity for two *dīnārs* on the condition that the sale is binding in one of them", it is not permitted according to all, irrespective of the currency being the same or different. ᶜAbd al-ᶜAzīz ibn Abī Salama differed in this. He permitted it whether the currencies were the same or different. The underlying cause (*ᶜilla*) according to all is *jahl* (lack of knowledge), while according to Mālik it relates to the category of blocking of the means (*sadd al-dharāʾiᶜ*) for it is possible that he would select for himself one of the dresses and, therefore, would have sold a dress plus a *dīnār* for another dress plus a *dīnār* and this is not permitted on Mālik's principles. In the third case, which occurs when he says, "I sell you this dress for so much on cash or for so much on credit", if the sale in it is binding then there is no dispute that it is not permitted, however, if the sale is not binding in one of them then Mālik permitted it, while Abū Ḥanīfa and al-Shāfiʿī prohibited it for they (the parties) separated with an unknown price. Mālik regarded it as a case of option (*khiyār*). When he has an option the possibility of regretting the conversion of one currency into the other is not visualized, which is the (real) obstacle according to Mālik. The underlying cause of prohibition of this third case, then, according to al-Shāfiʿī and Abū Ḥanīfa, is from the point of view of ignorance about the price, which according to them is one of the sales of hazard (*gharar*). The underlying cause of its prohibition according to Mālik, is the plugging of the channels (*sadd al-dharāʾiʿ*) that may lead to usury (*ribā*). This is because of the possibility that the one who has an option may choose initially the performance of the contract, in his mind without disclosing it, with one price, immediate or deferred and then change his mind when the other appears better to him. He then gives up one price for the other; it is as if he sold one of the prices for the other, admitting the sale of a price for a price with a delay, or with delay and excess. This is the case when the price is a currency. When the price is not a currency but food, it becomes another (forbidden) situation, which is the sale of food for food with excess.

If, however, he says, "I will buy from you this dress on cash for so much on the condition that you buy it from me (on credit) with a period", it is not permitted unanimously (by *ijmāʿ*), according to them (the jurists), as it is one category of *ʿīna*, which is the sale by a person of what he does not have and it also involves the prohibiting cause of *jahl* about the price. If he says to him, "I will sell to you one of these two dresses for a *dīnār*" and one becomes binding on him, whichever he chooses and they part before the (exercise of) option, then if the two dresses are of different kinds that can be exchanged for each other, there is no dispute between Mālik and al-Shāfiʿī that it (the sale) is not permitted. ʿAbd al-ʿAzīz ibn Abī Salāma said it is permitted. The underlying cause of prohibition is uncertainty and *jahl*. If the dresses are of the same kind it is permitted according to Mālik, but not according to Abū Ḥanīfah and al-Shāfiʿī. Malik permitted it, however, as he permits an option in sales of similar kinds after the contract, because there is minimal *gharar* in this according to him. Those who did not permit it did so because they do not permit *gharar* at all, as they (the parties) separated with an uncertain sale.

On the whole, the jurists agreed that excessive *gharar* is not permitted, while minimal *gharar* is. They disagreed about things as to the kinds of *gharar* (in them). Some link them to excessive *gharar*, while others link them to permissible minimal *gharar* due to its vacillation between slight and excessive. If we adopt the opinion of Mālik's school for permissibility with the buyer having to choose between taking possession of (one out of) the two dresses and one of them is destroyed or becomes defective, then who is to suffer the loss? It is said that the loss is (shared) between them and it is said that the buyer is entirely liable unless evidence of (the agent of) its destruction is established. It is (also) said that a distinction is to be made in the dresses as to what is obvious to him (about the agent of destruction) and what is not obvious to him, as in the case of the slave and he is liable for what he was oblivious to while he is not liable for that to which he was not oblivious. Is it, then, binding on him to accept the residue? It is said that it is binding and it is said it is not binding. This belongs to the rules of sales.

We should bear in mind that the issues included in this topic are all related to the problems of *gharar* for the jurists of the provinces; but for Mālik there are among them some that he forbids as they might lead to usury (*ribā*) and there are others that he relates to the problem of *gharar*.

These, then, are the issues that relate to the expressly mentioned *aḥkām* in this topic. It is proper if we discuss, when dealing with the topic of sales (declared) void on the basis of (spurious) conditions, his (Mālik's) prohibition of sale with a double condition and sale with a condition, even though their cause is *gharar*.

24.2.5.1. *Section 1: Issues not Expressly Covered (by the texts)*

The issues under this topic, not expressly covered (by the texts) and which are disputed among the jurists of different regions, are many, but we shall choose for discussion the best known hoping that their analysis may provide inspiring guidelines for the *mujtahid*.

24.2.5.1.1. Issue 1: The subject-matter of sales is of two kinds

The things sold are of two kinds: things present and visible, there being no dispute about (the validity of) their sales; and things absent or impossible to see (or examine), in these there is disagreement among the *fuqahā*ʾ.

Some said, the sale of an absent thing (*mabī*ᶜ) is not permitted in any circumstances, whether described or not described. This is the better-known opinion of al-Shāfiᶜī and is recorded by his disciples, I mean that the sale of an absent *mabī*ᶜ is not permitted by description. Mālik and most of the jurists of Medina said that it is permitted to sell an absent commodity (*mabī*ᶜ) by description as long as it is of a kind in which the description is not likely to change prior to the taking of possession. Abū Ḥanīfa said that it is permitted to sell an absent commodity without description, but the buyer has an option, when he actually sees it, whether to maintain the sale contract or to rescind it. Similarly, they permitted sale by description, on the condition of the option of examination (*khiyār al-ru*ʾ*ya*), even when the thing conforms with the description. According to Mālik, if the thing conforms with the description the sale becomes binding. According to al-Shāfiʿī the sale does not take effect *ab initio*, in both cases. It is said in the school (of Mālik) that the sale of an absent commodity without description is valid on the condition of an option, the option of examination. This has been stated in the *Mudawwana*, but is rejected by ʿAbd al-Wahhāb, who said, "It is against our principles".

The basis of disagreement is whether the fact that the degree of knowledge gained through description being less than the degree of knowledge attained though sensory perception constitutes *jahl* (lack of knowledge) adversely affecting the sale of a commodity, as it amounts to excessive uncertainty (*gharar*), or that it is not effective being uncertainty of a minimal degree that is tolerable. Al-Shāfiʿī viewed it as excessive *gharar*, Mālik as minimal. Abū Ḥanīfa was of the view that if the buyer has the option of (later) examination then there is no *gharar* even though he did not see it at the time of the contract. Mālik held that *jahl* consequent upon the absence of a description is adversely effective in the validity of the contract. It is not a matter of contention with Mālik that description stands as a substitute for an examination of the *mabīʿ*, because of its absence or because of hardship involved in its display or the risk it is likely to be exposed to through repeated display. He, therefore, permitted sale through the listing of the description. He did not permit the sale of a weapon in the scabbard, or a folded dress in a cover, unless displayed or examined in the sheath. Abū Ḥanīfa argued on the basis of what is related from Ibn al-Musayyib, who said "that the Companions of the Prophet (God's peace and blessings be upon him) said, 'We wished that ʿUthmān ibn ʿAffān and ʿAbd al-Raḥmān ibn ʿAwf would contract a sale so as to know who had greater acumen for business and then ʿAbd al-Raḥmān bought from ʿUthmān ibn ʿAffān a mare that he had on a different (distant) land of his for forty thousand or four thousand' ", and he (Ibn al-Musayyib) related the entire report from which it is evident that the sale of an absent thing is valid. The stipulation of species, however, is a necessary condition according to Abū Ḥanīfa. Sale by description or through the option of examination of an absent *mabīʿ* admits of another kind of *gharar*, whether the thing exists at the time of the contract or is non-existent. They, therefore, stipulated that the absence of the commodity should be recent except when it is safe from destruction like immovable property. On the basis of this, Mālik allowed sale through prior examination, I mean, if it is so recent that he is assured the commodity is unlikely to change with the passage of a short time. Let it be noted.

24.2.5.1.2. Issue 2: Agreement that it is not permitted to sell things with a (delayed) period

They agreed that the sale of things is not permitted with a delayed period and one of its conditions is the delivery of the *mabīʿ* to the buyer, immediately, following the conclusion of the contract. Mālik, Rabīʿa and a group of the jurists of Medina, however, permitted the sale of a high-priced slave-girl at a mutually agreed discounted price (with the seller retaining the delivery of the girl till the termination of the period and payment of the reduced price), but they did not permit a cash sale in this just as Mālik did not permit it in the sale of an absent *mabī*ʿ. The majority prohibited this in so far as it looks like the sale of a debt for a debt and because of the inability to deliver. It appears that the prohibition of sale of a debt for a debt here belongs to the prohibition based upon *gharar*, owing to the lack of delivery from both parties, not to a case of *ribā* and we have already discussed the underlying cause of the prohibition of (the exchange of) a debt for a debt. In this topic is also the taking by a person from his debtor, in exchange of the debt he owes him, dates that have begun to ripen, which Ibn al-Qāsim viewed as not permitted as he held it to be (an exchange of) a debt for a debt. Ashhab used to permit this on the ground that (the exchange of) debt for debt occurs only when he has not begun to take possession of any part of the commodity, I mean, he used to hold the view that the possession of the first instalments stands in the place of the possession of the last instalments. This is analogy according to many of the Mālikites and is also the opinion of al-Shāfiʿī and Abū Ḥanīfa.

24.2.5.1.3. Issue 3: Crops growing in a single phase and those growing more than once

The jurists of the provinces regions agreed on the permissibility of the sale of fruit, which grow only once when a part has ripened, even though the rest have not ripened as yet. They disagreed about those, which produce different crops, even when the first crop has begun to ripen. The summary of the (opinions in the) school of Mālik in this is that the yields are either consecutive with no interruption or they are not so. If they are not consecutive the sale of those (crops) that are not created as yet is not to be included in those that are, like the fig tree which has the first yield and the later prime pick. Again, if they are consecutive, without interruption, it is possible either to distinguish the crops or it is not. An example of the distinction is the husk of winter barley which is yielded time after time. An example of those which cannot be distinguished is melons, egg plants, cucumbers and pumpkins. About those which can be distinguished and separated there are two narrations: one of permissibility and the second of prohibition. About those which are consecutive and cannot be distinguished there is (just) one opinion of permissibility.

He (Mālik) was opposed in all this by the Kūfīs, Aḥmad, Isḥāq and al-Shāfiʿī, who said that one crop cannot be sold on the basis of (the ripening of) another. Mālik's proof of the permissibility of the sale of indistinguishable things is that the containment (delay in selling the ripe part) is not possible (especially if perishable), so it is permitted to sell that which is not created from among them along with what is created and has begun to ripen. Its basis is the sale of that which is not ripe, from among crops, along with that which is ripe, as Mālik considered *gharar* in description similar to *gharar* in the thing itself. It is as if he held that the exemption here must be considered analogous to the sale of crops, I mean, sale of that which is ripe with that which is not ripe for the occasion of necessity. The principle, according to him, is that within (the categories of) *gharar* is that which is permitted at the time of necessity; and he, therefore, prohibited according to one of his reports the sale of more than one yield of winter barley because there was no necessity here if they were distinguishable. The aspect of permissibility of winter barley on its similarity with that which is not distinguishable is weak. According to the majority, all this belongs to the forbidden sale of that which has not been created and to the prohibited category of annual sale of fruit.

The sale of turnips, carrots and cabbage is allowed, according to Mālik, when they have begun to ripen and that being their suitability for consumption. Al-Shāfiʿī did not allow this except when (they are) harvested, otherwise it is from the category of the sale of that which is absent. In the same category is the sale of walnuts, almonds and legumes in their shells, which Mālik permitted and al-Shāfiʿī disallowed. The basis for their disagreement is their different views whether it belongs to (the category of) *gharar* which affects sales. This is so as they agreed that *gharar* is divided into these two kinds and that which does not affect sale is either minimal, or the sale is based upon necessity, or is a combination of these two factors. Another similar question relates to the sale of fish in a stream or a pond, over which they differed too. Abū Ḥanīfa said it is permitted, but Mālik and al-Shāfiʿī prohibited it, so far as I know. Prohibition is what his (Mālik's) principles lead to. Within this is also the sale of a runaway slave, which is permitted absolutely by some, prohibited by others including al-Shāfiʿī. Mālik said that if his description and location are known both to the buyer and the seller, it is permitted, but I believe, he then stipulated that his running away should also be known, in which case there should be mutual delay, that is, the seller does not take possession of the price till the delivery of the slave to the buyer, because it is a case of vacillation, at the time of the contract, between a sale and a loan. This is one of Mālik's principles through which he prohibits cash (payment) in the postponed sale, in the sale of the unreliable delivery and in all that is of the same genus. Among those who permitted the sale of the runaway slave and the stray camel is ʿUthmān al-Battī. The proof of al-Shāfiʿī is the *ḥadīth* of Shahr ibn Hawshab from Abū Saʿīd al-Khudrī "that the Messenger of Allāh (God's peace and blessings be upon him) proscribed the sale of a runaway slave, (the sale) of what is in the bellies of cattle till delivered, the sale of what is in their udders and the sale of booty till it is apportioned".

Mālik permitted the sale of milk of cattle for a limited number of days, if the amount milked from them was generally known in practice, but he did not permit this in a single (particular) goat. The rest of the jurists said this is not permitted except by a known measure after milking. In this topic is also the prohibition by Mālik of the sale of meat in its skin. Similarly prohibited is the sale of the diseased, but Mālik permitted it, unless the disease was incurable. It was prohibited by al-Shāfiʿī and Abū Ḥanīfa, which is also another narration from him (Mālik). Within this topic is also mineral dust and the dust from goldsmiths. Mālik permitted the sale of mineral dust for cash from another metal or for a commodity, but he did not permit the sale of dust from a goldsmithery. Al-Shāfiʿī prohibited the sale in both cases, while others allowed it in both, which was the opinion of al-Ḥasan al-Baṣrī. These, then, are the sales that are disputed from the aspect of lack of knowledge of their quality.

About the consideration of quantity, they agreed that it is not permitted to sell a thing that is (usually) measured by size or by weight or by count or by length, except when its quantity is known to the buyer and the seller. They agreed that the knowledge of these things by way of known measure or known scales is effective in the validity of sale and in things whose measure and weight is not known to the buyer or seller, out of all things measured, weighed, counted or measured by area. They also considered whether knowledge is insufficient if quantification is arrived at by way of appraisal and assessment; it is permitted in some and prohibited in others. The principle in Mālik's school in this is that it is permitted in all things the utilization of which is in bulk and not in single units. These are of different kinds, according to him: among them are those that are primarily measured but are permitted as *juzāf* and these are those measurable in size as in weight; among them are those that are primarily *juzāf* but may be measured, these are like land and dresses that are measured by area through length; among them are those in which measure and weight are basically not allowed but counting is allowed in them and their sale is not allowed as *juzāf*. It is these (last) that have utility in their separate units, as we said. According to Mālik the *juzāf* sale of gold nuggets and silver, not minted, is permitted, but it is not permitted in *dirhams* and *dīnārs*. Abū Ḥanīfa and al-Shāfiʿī said it is permitted with disapproval (*makrūh*). It is permitted, according to Mālik, to sell a heap, the total quantity of which is unknown, by means of measure at an agreed rate, that is, each measure of it for a certain (price). When its total measure has been found, its total value at the agreed rate is to be settled. Abū Ḥanīfa said that it (the *juzāf* sale) is valid only in a single measure that we have named (probably that which is in bulk). Mālik permitted this kind of sale (i.e., by estimate) in slaves, dresses and food. Abū Ḥanīfa prohibited it in slaves and dresses, while others, I think, prohibited it in everything because of the uncertainty of the price.

It is permitted, according to Mālik, that the buyer accept as true the seller's claimed measurement when the sale is not on credit, as such a sale on credit might be a way to induce the buyer to accept the seller's claim. According to the others, this is not permitted unless the buyer ascertains its measure, owing to proscription of the Prophet (God's peace and blessings be upon him) of the sale of food till it has been duly measured. Others permitted it unconditionally. Among those who prohibited it are Abū Ḥanīfa, al-Shāfiʿī and Aḥmad, while among those who permitted it without reservation are ʿAṭāʾ ibn Abī Rabāḥ and Ibn Abī Malīka. It is not permitted, according to Mālik, that the seller, who knows exactly the quantity of the commodity but does not inform the buyer of it and (then) sells this measurable commodity by estimate (*juzāf*) to a buyer who does not know the exact measure, because of uncertainty as far as the buyer is concerned. It is not permitted by al-Shāfiʿī and Abū Ḥanīfa (also). According to Mālik, the proscribed (sale of) *muzābana*, which is the sale of an uncertain quantity for an uncertain quantity, belongs to this principle. In the case of usurious commodities, this prohibition is due to excess (*tafāḍul*) and in non-usurious commodities it is due to the lack of quantitative determination.

24.2.6. Chapter 4: Sales with Conditions and Provisos

The irregularity found in these sales is from the aspect of *gharar*, however, because the traditions have dealt with them, it is necessary to render them separately as an independent category of sales. The basis for the disagreement of jurists in this issue consists of three traditions. The first of these is the tradition of Jābir, who said, "The Messenger of Allāh (God's peace and blessings be upon him) bought a she-camel from me and stipulated, as a condition, riding it to Medina". This tradition is found in the *saḥīḥ* compilations. The second tradition is that of Barīra that the Messenger of Allāh (God's peace and blessings be upon him) said, "Any condition that is not in (accordance with) the Book of Allāh is void, though it be a hundred conditions". The tradition is agreed upon (by Muslim and al-Bukhārī) for its soundness. The third is the *ḥadīth* of Jābir, who said, "The Messenger of Allāh proscribed *muḥāqala, muzābana, mukhābara, muʿāwama and thaniyyā* (proviso) and exempted the *arāya*". This too is found in Muslim's *Ṣaḥīḥ*. Related to this issue is what is reported by Abū Ḥanīfa that it is related "that the Messenger of Allāh (God's peace and blessings be upon him) proscribed sale with a condition" (that is, sale dependent upon a condition). In view of this apparent contradiction in these traditions regarding conditional sales, the jurists disputed sale with a condition. Some said, the sale is void and the condition (too) is void. Among those who held this opinion are Abū Ḥanīfa and al-Shāfiᶜī. Some said that both the sale and the condition are valid. Among those who held this opinion is Ibn Abī Shubrama. Some other (jurists) said that the sale is valid, but the condition is void. Among those who held this opinion is Ibn Abī Laylā. Aḥmad said that the sale is valid with one condition, but not with two (or more).

Those who nullify sale with a condition adopt the generality of his (the Prophet's) proscription of sale with a condition and his proscription of provisos (*thaniyyā*). Those who permitted the sale while nullifying the condition adopted the generality of the *ḥadīth* of Barīra. Those who did not permit two conditions, but permitted one, argued on the basis of the tradition of ᶜAmr ibn al-ᶜĀṣ, recorded by Abū Dāwūd, who said, "The Messenger of Allāh (God's peace and blessings be upon him) said, 'Loan with a sale is not permitted, nor are two conditions with a sale and there is no (entitlement to) profit without a (corresponding) liability for loss, nor should there be a sale in what you do not have' ".

In Mālik's view, the conditions are divided into three kinds: conditions that are nullified along with the sale; conditions that are permitted along with the sale; and conditions that are nullified, but the sale is valid. It is believed that there is, for him, a fourth category of such conditions, which if insisted upon by the stipulator nullifies the sale, but when it is given up by him the sale is valid. The expounding of clear distinctions within his school, among these four categories, is difficult, though many of the jurists have desired to do so. In fact, the distinction should be based upon the degree of *ribā* and *gharar* implicit in the conditions—the two categories of *fasād* that disturb the validity of a sale—or to what leads to a deficiency of ownership. If the degree of implied *gharar* or *ribā* is excessive, he (Mālik) nullifies the sale and nullifies the condition; when it is insignificant, he permits the sale and permits the condition with it, but when it is midway, he nullifies the condition and permits the sale. Mālik's followers are of the view that his opinion is the best, as it accommodates all the traditions and such accommodation, according to them, is better than making preference (*tarjīḥ*). The later Mālikite generations have made some similar distinctions in these; among them are Jiddī, al-Māzirī and al-Bājī. To explain the details, it may be said that a condition pertaining to the subject-matter of sale falls into one of the two primary categories. First, that which is stipulated as effective after the termination of ownership, like one who sells an *ama* or a slave boy and stipulates that when freed he (the seller) will be the *mawlā* and not the buyer. In this kind (of transaction) it is said that the contract is valid, but the condition is void due to the *ḥadīth* of Barīra. Second, to stipulate a condition that is effective within the duration of ownership. This they said is divided into three kinds: either to stipulate a benefit of the subject-matter (*mabīʿ*) for himself; or to restrict the buyer's general or particular (power of) disposal; or to assign a particular meaning to the subject-matter and this too is divided into three kinds with one of the meanings being that of magnanimity while the other is not.

When he stipulates for himself a minor benefit that does not amount to a prevention of disposal in the subject-matter itself, like selling the house stipulating residence in it for a short period, like one month—and it is said of a year—this is permitted on the basis of the tradition of Jābir. If, however, he stipulates prevention of disposal, particular or general, then this is not permitted as it involves *thaniyyā* (proviso), like selling an *ama* with the condition that he (the buyer) will not cohabit with her or will not sell her. When he stipulates some kind of magnanimity like manumission, then the stipulation of prompt (compliance) is permitted according to him, but when it is delayed it is not permitted due to the immensity of *gharar* in it. Mālik permits the sale with the condition of prompt manumission. Al-Shāfiʿī considers it to be prohibited as it is from the category of sale with a condition and the tradition of Jābir is ambiguous according to him as in some narrations he (the Prophet) sold it and stipulated riding it to Medina while in others he sold it and asked for the ride by way of *ʿāriya* (loan). Mālik viewed all this as a kind of minimal *gharar* and permitted it for short period, but not for a lengthy duration. In terms of Abū Ḥanīfa's principles, however, it is prohibited.

His (the seller's) stipulation of conditions that do not involve magnanimity, like the condition of not selling it, is not permitted according to Mālik; it is said that he held the sale to be rescinded and it is also said that only the condition was cancelled. For the person to whom the seller says, "When I bring the price (back) to you, return the *mabīʿ* to me", it is not permitted according to Mālik as it is ambivalent between being a sale and a loan. If he brings back the price it amounts to a loan, if he does not it is a sale. They disagreed about this in the school (of Mālik), whether it is permitted in a negotiated rescission (*iqāla*). Those who view *iqāla* as a sale, nullify it by the factors that nullify sales, while those who consider it as rescinding of a sale, distinguish it from sales. They also disagreed about one who sells a thing with the condition that it is not to be sold until the price is paid. Mālik is reported to have permitted this, as its *ḥukm* is like the *ḥukm* of a pledge (*rahn*) there being no distinction in a pledge whether the thing is a property sold or something else. Ibn al-Qāsim is reported to have said that this is not permitted, as it is a condition that prevents the buyer from the benefit of the sale for a long period in which the seller cannot stipulate a benefit (for himself), therefore, it is necessary to invalidate the sale. It is for this reason that Ibn al-Mawwāz said that it is permitted if it is for a very short period.

One of the narrations in this topic is his (the Prophet's) proscription of sale with a loan, about which the jurists agreed that it is a void sale. They disagreed about the validity of a sale when he (the seller) relinquishes the condition before taking possession. Abū Ḥanīfa, al-Shāfiᶜī and all the jurists prohibited it, but Mālik and his disciples permitted it, except for Muḥammad ibn al-Ḥakam. An opinion like that of the majority is also related from Mālik. The proof of the majority is that the proscription implies the *fasād* of the prohibited action and, further, the price of the *mabī*ᶜ here is uncertain due to its association with a loan. It is related that Muḥammad ibn Aḥmad ibn Sahl al-Barmakī (who held the view of the majority) enquired about this issue from Ismāʾīl ibn Isḥāq al-Mālikī, saying to him, "What is the difference between a loan with a sale and between a person who sells a slave for a hundred *dīnārs* and a skin of wine, who when he contracts the sale says, 'I forgo the skin?' He then said, "This (latter) sale is annulled by agreement of the jurists". Ismāᶜīl answered this question with a reply that is not legally persuasive, saying, "The difference between them is that the stipulator of a loan has a choice between relinquishment an non-relinquishment, while the problem of the skin of wine does not involve this". This reply is, in fact, the same as the question, which is: "How can he have a choice here and did not have one there so that he may forego the skin and validate the sale?" It is better to say that the prohibition here is not due to a thing inherently prohibited, that is a loan, as a loan in itself is permissible, but it has been imposed due to its association, I mean, the association of sale with it. Likewise, sale in itself is permitted, but is prohibited here because of the association of the condition with it. In the other case, the sale has been prohibited due to its association with a thing inherently prohibited and not for the of stipulation (of a condition). The point at issue is whether *fasād* arising in a sale, because of a condition, is removed when the condition is revoked, or is not removed—just like the *fasād* arising from an otherwise permissible sale owing to its association with a thing inherently prohibited. This too is based upon another principle and that is whether this *fasād* is revelational or is rational. If we say it is legal, it is not removed by the revocation of the condition. If we say it is rational, it is removed by the revocation of the condition. Mālik views it as rational, while the majority view it as non-rational. The *fasād* that is found in usurious sales and in those with *gharar* is based primarily upon revelation and, therefore, these sales are not valid, according to them, even if *ribā* is relinquished after the sale, or *gharar* is removed. They disagreed about its *ḥukm* if transacted, as will be explained in the *aḥkām* of the vitiated sales.

Within this topic is the sale of the ᶜ*urbān* (sale with earnest money). The majority of the jurists of different regions hold that it is not permitted, but it is related from a group of the *Tābi*ᶜ*ūn* that they permitted it, among them are Mujāhid, Ibn Sīrīn, Nāfiᶜ ibn al-Ḥarth and Zayd ibn Aslam. The form it takes is that a person purchases a thing and delivers to the seller part of the price on the condition that if the sale is executed between them this earnest money will form part of the price of the goods, if it is not executed the buyer will forgo it. The majority inclined toward its prohibition, as it is from the category of *gharar*, *mukhāṭara* and the devouring of wealth of others without compensation. Zayd used to say, "The Messenger of Allāh (God's peace and blessings be upon him) permitted it". The *Ahl al-Ḥadīth* said that this is not known from the Messenger of Allāh (God's peace and blessings be upon him).

Under the *istithnā*ʾ (provisos) are well-known issues about which the jurists have differed, I mean, whether they are included within the proscription of provisos. Among these is the case of the person who sells a pregnant (female) and exempts what is in the foetus. The majority of the jurists of the provinces, including Mālik, Abū Ḥanīfa, al-Shāfiʿī and al-Thawrī, are of the view that it is not permitted. Aḥmad, Abū Thawr and Dāwūd said that it is permitted and it is also related from Ibn ʿUmar. The reason for disagreement is their difference whether the exempted (thing) is part of the *mabīʿ*, from which it has been exempted, or it is not a part of the *mabīʿ*, but still remains in the seller's ownership. Those who considered it as part of the *mabīʿ* said, (exempting) it is not permitted and it is among the proscribed exemptions on the ground that they contain uncertainty of description as well as uncertainty of safe delivery. Those who said that it still remains in the ownership of the seller permitted it. The summary of opinions in Mālik's school about one who sells an animal and exempts part of it, depends on whether this part is defined proportionately, or specifically or by measure. If it is stated proportionately, there is no dispute about the permissibility of its sale, like his selling a slave except (say) one-fourth share in him. If it is specifically denoted, it can either be internal (invisible), like a foetus, or visible. If it is invisible, it is not permitted. If it is visible, like the head, arms, or legs, it can either be part of an animal whose slaughter is permitted or one whose slaughter is not. If it is one whose slaughter is not permitted, the sale is not permitted, as it is not permitted to sell a salve and exempt his legs, for that which is exempted is indistinct (thus entailing *gharar*) and cannot be divided. There is no dispute about this. If it is an animal whose slaughter is permitted and he sells it and exempts part of it, that has a value, with the condition of slaughtering, then in the school there are two opinions. First, that it is not permitted and this is better known. Second, that it is permitted and that is the opinion of Ibn Ḥabīb who permitted the sale of a goat exempting the feet and the head. If, however, the exempted part has no value, there is no dispute in the school about its permission. The basis for Mālik's opinion is that if he exempts it with the skin then what is under the skin is unknown and if he does not exempt it with the skin, he does not know how it will come out having been skinned. The basis for Ibn Ḥabīb's opinion is that he is exempting a determined and known limb and the existence of skin over it does not harm it, just like the purchase of grain in its ear and of walnut in its shell. For the exemption from an animal on the condition of slaughter, either by custom or expressed, a part determined by measure, like some *arṭāl* (pounds) from a slaughtered camel, there are two narrations from Mālik. First is prohibition and this is the narration of Ibn Wahb. Second is permission in a few *arṭāl* only and this is the narration of Ibn al-Qāsim.

They agreed, under this topic, about the permissibility of a person selling the fruit of his palm-grove exempting from it certain determined date-palms on the analogy of the permissibility of their fruit purchased separately. They also agreed that it is not permitted to him to exempt from his palm-grove an unspecified number of date-palms to be determined by the buyer after the sale, as it would amount to the sale of a thing not seen by the parties. They disagreed about the man who sells a palm-grove and exempts from it a number of date-palms after the sale. The majority disallow this because the quality and the description of date-palms vary, while its permissibility is related from Mālik. Ibn al-Qāsim rejects his (Mālik's) verdict in the case of date-palms, but allows it in the case of sheep. Similarly, they disagreed when the buyer exempts a measure from the sale of the palm-grove. Abū ᶜUmar ibn ᶜAbd al-Barr said, "The jurists of different regions, whose verdict is accepted and according to whose opinions books have been recorded, disallowed this because of his (the Prophet's) proscription of provisos in sales and because it is exemption of a measure in a sale by estimate (*juzāf*)". Mālik and his predecessors from among the jurists of Medina permitted this, if exemption was less than a third and disallowed it in more than that, interpreting the proscription of exemption to apply to what was more than a third. They compared the sale of what is besides the exempted part to the sale of a heap, the exact amount of whose measures is not known, being sold by estimate exempting a defined measure from it. This principle is also disputed, I mean, sale by estimate, exempting a certain measure from it.

The jurists disagreed within the same topic about sale and hire in the same individual contract. Mālik and his disciples permitted this, but the Kūfīs and al-Shāfiᶜī did not permit it, as they held that the price would then be unknown. Mālik said if the rent or wage is specified, it would not remain unknown. Perhaps those who disallowed it saw it as two sales in one. They agreed that loan and a sale are not allowed, as we have said, but the opinion of Mālik differed about the permission of a loan and partnership (*sharika*), he permitted it once and disallowed it another time.

Disagreement among the jurists over all the above questions arises from their differences on the degree of the prohibiting causes stated textually. Those for whom a prohibiting cause appeared to be strongly involved in a particular transaction prohibited it, while those to whom it appeared to carry only a little weight allowed it. This actually depends on the discretion of the *mujtahid*, who in reflecting over such issues is pulled equally by the opposing probabilities. In such cases of dispute it is fairer to hold each of the disputing jurists to be correct. It is for this reason that some say that in issues like these we may choose any of the conflicting opinions.

24.2.7. Chapter 5: Sales Proscribed because of Harm or Fraud

The transmitted (injunctions) in this chapter are those that are established through the (Prophet's) prohibition: that an individual sell countering the sale of his brother; that he make an offer countering the offer of his brother; that trade caravans be received (outside the city limits); that a settler sell on behalf of an inhabitant of the desert; and that bids be raised (*najsh*). The jurists differed about the details of the meanings of these traditions, a disagreement that is not wide apart.

Mālik said that the meaning of his (God's peace and blessings be upon him) words, "Do not sell counter to the sale of others" and of the proscription about one making an offer countering his brother's offer, is the same. It is a situation when the buyer is inclined toward the offeror when there was nothing left between them (the buyer and the seller before concluding the sale), except minor formalities like the choice of gold, or the stipulation of defects or absolution from them. Abū Ḥanīfa interpreted the tradition in the same way as Mālik. Al-Thawrī said that the meaning of his (the Prophet's) words, "Let not some of you sell over the sale of others", is that a person should not come upon the parties to the sale and say that I have goods better than these. He did not determine the time of inclination or any other matter. Al-Shāfiʿī said that the meaning is that when the oral agreement is concluded, but they have not parted, a person comes presenting him (the buyer) with goods that are better than those being sold. This is based upon his view that a sale becomes binding through parting. He and Mālik, then, are in agreement that the proscription implies the state when the sale is close to becoming binding, but they are in disagreement as to what this state is; because of their disagreement as to what it is that makes a sale binding, as we shall explain later. The jurists of the provinces hold that this sale is despicable (*makrūh*), but if it takes place it is valid, as it constitutes an offer upon an inconclusive sale. Dāwūd and his disciples said that if it takes place it is to be rescinded, whatever the manner in which it takes place, abiding by the generality (of the tradition). Its rescission is (also) related from Mālik and some of his disciples unless they part, but Ibn al-Mājishūn denied this in a sale and said that this is what Mālik said about marriage (*nikaḥ*), which has already preceded.

They disagreed about the inclusion of a *dhimmī* (non-Muslim subject of the Islamic state) in the proscription of one's offer countering the offer of another. The majority said that there is no difference between a *dhimmī* and another in this. Al-Awzāᶜī said that there is no harm in an offer against the offer of a *dhimmī*, as he is not a Muslim's brother and the Prophet (God's peace and blessings be upon him) has said, "None should offer counter to the offer of his brother". It is on this basis that some prohibited auction (*muzāyada*), although the majority favoured its permissibility. The basis for the disagreement among them was whether the proscription here is to be interpreted as disapproval or as prohibition and if it is to be interpreted as prohibition, is this so in all situations or in some cases to the exclusion of others?

24.2.7.1. *Section 1: Going Out to Meet (trade) Caravans*

They disagreed over the meaning of the proscription of going out to receive the caravans (*rukbān*) for sale. Mālik was of the view that it is aimed at the people of the market (shopkeepers), so that the one who meets them should not benefit alone from the inexpensiveness of goods, to the exclusion of other shopkeepers. He held that it was not permitted for one to buy goods till the goods have reached the market. This prohibition applies when the meeting is at a point near the market; otherwise it is all right. The limit of nearness according to the school (of Mālik) is within six miles. He held that if the sale went through it is permitted, but then the shopkeepers should share (participate in) the goods, which are saleable in the market. Al-Shāfiᶜī said that the factor behind the proscription is the protection of the interests of the seller so that the advance buyer does not deceive him, as he does not know the market price in the city. Al-Shāfiᶜī said: "If the sale goes through, the seller will have the option of rescinding the sale or keeping it". The opinion of al-Shāfiᶜī is manifest in the tradition related by Abū Hurayra, in which the Prophet (God's peace and blessings be upon him) said, "Do not intercept the goods on the way to the market; if one obtains something from these, at an unjust price and buys it, the seller has an option on reaching the market". It is recorded by Muslim and others.

24.2.7.2. *Section 2: Sale by a Settler on behalf of the Inhabitant of the Desert*

The jurists disagreed about the meaning of the Prophet's proscription of sale by a settler for a nomadic desert-dweller. Some said, in absolute terms, that the settler is not to sell for the inhabitant of the desert. He (Mālik) differed about the purchase of the settler for the Bedouin. He permitted it once—and that was the opinion of Ibn Ḥabīb—and prohibited it on another occasion. The settlers according to him (Mālik) are the residents of the cities. It is said of him that he disallowed the sale of residents of villages for the pilgrims in transit. Similar to the opinion of Mālik here are those of al-Shāfiʿī and al-Awzāʿī. Abū Ḥanīfa and his disciples said that there is no harm if a settler sells for an inhabitant of the desert and informs him of the rate. Mālik held it to be disapproved, that is, informing the Bedouin of the rates, but al-Awzāʿī permitted it.

Those who prohibited this sale agreed that the aim of this proscription is the affluence of the urbanites, as things with the ruralists are cheaper than they are with urbanites; they are inexpensive, in fact most of them are *gratis*, without a price. It was as if they held that (the act of) an urbanite advising a ruralist (on rates) was despicable, but this is in conflict with the saying of the Prophet (God's peace and blessings be upon him), "*Dīn* is advice" and on which Abū Ḥanīfa relied for support. The proof of the majority is the tradition of Jābir, recorded by Muslim and Abū Dāwūd, who said, "The Messenger of Allāh (God's peace and blessings be upon him) said, 'The urbanite is not to sell for the ruralist, leave the people alone so that Allāh may provide for some of them through others' ". This addition is unique with Abū Dāwūd, so far as I know. It belongs, more likely, to the category of protection of the Bedouin from deception, for he arrives not knowing the market price, unless this addition is established, in which case the meaning of the tradition would be the same as the proscription of going out to meet the caravans, as interpreted by al-Shāfiʿī and as it appears in an established tradition.

They disagreed when it took place. Al-Shāfiʿī said if it goes through then it is concluded and permitted on the basis of the words of the Prophet (God's peace and blessings be upon him), "Leave the people alone so that Allāh may provide for some of them through others". The disciples of Mālik disagreed about this. Some of them said that it should be rescinded, while others said that it is valid.

24.2.7.3. *Section 3: Prohibition of Raising Bids*

The jurists agreed on the prohibition of the Prophet's proscription of *najsh* (raising bids). *Najsh* occurs that when one raises (the price of) a commodity having no intention to buy it, but to benefit the seller and harm the buyer. They disagreed when such a sale takes place. The Ẓāhirites said that it is void, while Mālik said that it is like selling a defective commodity, in which case the buyer has a choice to rescind it if he likes or to maintain it if he so desires. Abū Ḥanīfa and al-Shāfiʿī said that if it takes place he (who raises the bid) has sinned, but the sale is valid. The reason for disagreement is whether the proscription implies voidability of the proscribed sale itself or of something external to the contract. Those who said that it implies rescission of the sale itself did not permit it, while those who said that it does not, permitted it.

The majority are of the opinion that if the proscription is because of one aspect of the proscribed act, it leads to its voidability, like the proscription of *ribā* and *gharar*, but if it is because of something external, it does not lead to voidability.

It appears that included in this category is the proscription by the Prophet (God's peace and blessings be upon him) of the sale of water, because of his words, some of which indicate that "he proscribed the sale of surplus water to prevent thereby (thirsty) cattle from approaching the pasture area (close to the water)". Abū Bakr ibn al-Mundhir said that it is established "that the Messenger of Allāh (God's peace and blessings be upon him) proscribed the sale of water to protect through it the pasture area". He said that the remaining water in a well should not be denied, nor should the water be sold. The jurists disagreed about the meaning of this proscription. A group of jurists interpreted it in its generality and said that the sale of water is not permitted in any circumstances, whether it is a well or pond or a spring in the ground, owned or not owned, except that when it is owned he (the owner) has a prior right to use the amount he needs. Yaḥyā ibn Yaḥyā had the same opinion and said that access (for free use) cannot be denied to four things: water, fire, firewood and pasture.

Some restricted these traditions because of their conflict with the recognized principles; namely, that one's wealth is not permissible, as has been affirmed by the Prophet (God's peace and blessings be upon him), without the good will of that person and there is consensus (*ijmā*ᶜ) on this point. Those who restricted its meaning put forward different interpretations of restriction. Some said that this is so when a well is shared between co-owners, one of them watering on one day and the other on the next. If the field of one is irrigated in part of his day, but that of his co-sharer is not irrigated in his allotted one day, then the former should not prevent him from using the water in the remainder of his day. Some said that the interpretation is: that one irrigates with his own water, but if his well suffers damage, while his neighbour has surplus water, then his neighbour is not to deny him water till his well is restored (or repaired). Both interpretations are similar and the point of the interpretations is that they qualified the indeterminate meaning in these two traditions, as the proscription of the sale of water is absolute and then there is prohibition of denying the surplus water. They qualified the absolute meaning in this tradition and said it is the surplus water, (the sale of) which is prohibited in the two traditions, that is, at first he (the Prophet) prohibited the sale of water generally and then prohibited denial of surplus water. Thus, they (the jurists) applied the general term in the tradition to the restricted one. The basis of Mālik's opinion is that when the source of water is in privately owned land, it is for the owner to sell it or deny it, unless he is approached by destitute people who are likely to die (of thirst). Further, he (Mālik) interpreted the *ḥadīth* (prohibiting the sale of water) to apply to the wells of the desert, which are dug in unowned land. He was, therefore, of the view that the owner—that is, one who dug it—has the prior right and when his animals have been watered he leaves the rest for other people. It is as if he held that a well cannot be owned by digging (revival of land).

Within this category is the rule governing the separation between the mother and her child (by the sale of the mother alone), which is unanimously prohibited on the basis of the words of the Prophet (God's peace and blessings be upon him), "As to one who causes separation between a mother and her child, Allāh will cause separation between him and his loved ones on the Day of Judgment". They disagreed, however, in this on two points: on the time of the permissibility of separation; and on the legal effect of the sale when it takes place. About the effects of the sale, Mālik said that the sale is to be rescinded, while al-Shāfiʿī and Abū Ḥanīfa said it is not to be rescinded, but the buyer and seller (are considered to) have sinned. The cause of disagreement is whether the proscription requires the invalidity of the proscribed act, when it is caused by (an) external (factor). About the time at which prohibition converts into permissibility, Mālik said its (minimum) limit is the time of teething. Al-Shāfiʿī said it is the age of seven or eight years, while al-Awzāʿī said it is over ten years, as then he (the child) recognizes his benefit and can be independent of his mother.

Related to this category is the conclusion of a sale carrying fraud (*ghabn*), but a sort of *ghabn* that is normally practised. Is the sale to be rescinded? The well-known opinion in the school (of Mālik) is that it is not rescinded. ʿAbd al-Wahhāb said that if *ghabn* involves over one-third of the value it is to be returned and he attributes it (his opinion) to some of the disciples of Mālik, basing it also on the rendering of an option by the Prophet (God's peace and blessings be upon him) for the bearer of goods when met outside the city, on the basis of *ghabn*. In addition, he finds a basis in the granting of an option to Munqidh ibn Ḥayyān for three days when it was mentioned to him that he was defrauded in sales. Some among the early predecessors were of the view that the *ḥukm* of the father is the same as that of the mother, while a group of jurists maintained this for all brothers (that is, they should not be sold separately while still young).

24.2.8. Chapter 6: Proscription (of Sale) because of the Time of Prayer

This is laid down in law only for the time of the obligation of proceeding for *jumuʿa* prayer because of the words of the Exalted, "When the call is heard for the prayer of the day of congregation, hasten unto remembrance of Allāh and leave your trading".[137] This is a matter unanimously agreed upon as far as I know, I mean, the prohibition of sale at the commencement of *adhān* (call for prayer), which takes place after the declining (of the sun) when the *imām* is at the pulpit. They disagreed about its legal effects after it takes place, whether it is to be rescinded. If it is rescinded, then for whom and also whether all other contracts are linked to sale. It is well-known from Mālik that it is rescinded and it is said (in another opinion) that it is not rescinded, which also is the opinion of al-Shāfiᶜī and Abū Ḥanīfa. The reason for disagreement, as we have said more than once, is whether the proscription laid down because of an external factor leads to the invalidity of the thing proscribed. And for whom is it rendered void? According to Mālik, voidability is for one on whom *jumuᶜa* is obligatory, not for one on whom it is not. The principles of the Ẓāhirites require its rescission for both parties to the sale.

It is possible that all other contracts be linked to sale, as in them there is the same meaning of occupation found in indulgence in sale instead of walking toward the *jumuᶜa*. It is also possible that they should not be linked with it, as their conclusion at such a time is rare as against sale. It is possible to link all other prayers, on the whole, with *jumuᶜa* by way of recommendation, in the anticipated prayer time. If it is missed then it is by way of prohibition, though no one has said this in the entirety of my knowledge. It is for this reason that Allāh has praised those relinquishing sale for the sake of prayer and the Exalted says, "Men whom neither merchandise nor sale beguileth from remembrance of Allāh and constancy in prayer and paying to the poor their due".[138]

As the general causes of vitiation of sale have been established, we move to study the reasons and conditions of its validity and that is the second division in the general examination of sales.

24.3. Part 3: Reasons and Conditions Validating Sales

The causes and conditions validating sales are, on the whole, the opposite of causes vitiating them and are confined to three areas (of study): first, the study of the contract (*ᶜaqd*); second, the study of the subject-matter (*maᶜqūd ᶜalayh*); and third, the study of the parties to the contract. In this part, then, there are three chapters.

[137] Qurʾān 42 : 9
[138] Qurʾān 24 : 37

24.3.1. Chapter 1: The Contract (ʿ*Aqd*)

24.3.1.1. Element 1: The Form of the Contract

The contract (of sale) is not valid except by the use of the words "sale" and "purchase", used in the past tense. The seller says, "I have sold to you" and the buyer (thus) says, "I have bought from you". If he says, "Sell me your commodity for such and such price" and the seller says, "I have sold it (to you)", then according to Mālik, the sale is valid and binding on one who can comprehend, unless he comes up with a (valid) excuse. According to al-Shāfiʿī, sale is not concluded until the buyer says, "I have bought". Similarly, when the buyer says to the seller, "For how much will you sell your goods?" and the seller says, "For so much", to which he replies, "I have bought it from you".

It is disputed whether sale becomes binding until he (the buyer) says, "I have bought them from you". According to al-Shāfiʿī, sale is concluded both by unequivocal words and an alluding expression and I do not remember an opinion from Mālik about this. Gestures are not sufficient for this, according to al-Shāfiʿī, to the exclusion of words. There is no dispute, as far as I know, that offer and acceptance effective for a binding sale are not to be delayed till after the parting from the session—I mean, when the seller says, "I have sold my goods to you for so much" and the buyer remains silent not accepting the offer till they part. If he later comes back and says, "I have accepted", it would not be binding on the seller.

They disagreed about the (exact) moment when it becomes binding. Mālik, Abū Ḥanīfa, their disciples and some of the jurists of Medina said that it becomes binding through acceptance during the session even though they have not parted. Al-Shāfiʿī, Aḥmad, Isḥāq, Abū Thawr, Dāwūd and from among the Companions (God be pleased with them all) Ibn ʿUmar, said that sale is binding through parting after the session and that as long as they have not parted, sale is neither binding nor is it concluded. This is the opinion of Abū Dhiʾb among a group of jurists of Medina, of Ibn Mubārak, Qāḍī Sawār, Qāḍī Shurayḥ and of a group the successors to the Companions (*Tābiʿūn*) among others. This is also related from Abū Barza al-Aslamī from among the Companions and there is no opposition to it from the Companions.

The reliance of those who stipulate the option of the session (*khiyār al-majlis*) is the tradition of Mālik from Nāfiʿ from Ibn ʿUmar that the Messenger of Allāh (God's peace and blessings be upon him) said, "The (two) parties to the sale, each one of them has an option (*khiyār*) against his counterpart, as long as they have not parted, except in the sale with an option". In some of the narrations of this tradition, it is recorded, "Except when one of them says to the other—'choose' ". The *isnād* of this tradition is most reliable and authentic, according to all *ḥadīth* authorities, so much so that Abū Muḥammad thought that *isnād* like this should lead to *yaqīn* (certainty), even if related by way of *āḥād* (individual narration). The meaning of the tradition became confusing for the contenders, because of their method of denying to act according to it. The reliance of Mālik in the denial to act according to it is that it does not correspond to the practice of the people of Medina, although he was confronted with the implication of the tradition of Ibn Masᶜūd, which he related as *munqaṭi*ᶜ (with an interrupted *isnād*), where he said, "Whoever the two parties to a sale, the final word is that of the seller, or they should retract". It is as if he assigned to it its general meaning, which implies that it (the option) can be during the session and after it. If the (duration of the) session itself is stipulated as a condition for the conclusion of the contract, there would be no need in it for the explanation of the ruling about disagreement during the session, as the sale would not as yet have been concluded or become binding, which it will through parting after the session. This tradition is (in any case) *munqaṭi*ᶜ and cannot contradict the first one. It especially does not contradict the former except by stressing its general implication. It is better, however, that the meaning of the latter should be fixed in the light of the former. This latter tradition has not been related by a *ḥadīth* authority with a complete *isnād*, in so far as I know. This, then, is what Mālik (God bless him) relied upon in relinquishing to act on the other tradition.

Mālik's disciples relied on the narrated sources and on analogy. The most significant source related to this issue exists in the words of the Exalted, "O ye who believe, fulfil your undertakings (*ᶜuqūd*)".[139] *ᶜAqd* consists of offer and acceptance and the command here implies the obligation (to fulfil). The option of the session (*khiyār al-majlis*), however, gives rise to the relinquishment of fulfilment because it grants, according to them, a party (to sale) the right to retract prior to parting after having consented. On the basis of analogy, they said, "It is a commutative contract, therefore, the option of the session is not effective in it, the basis being all other contracts like *nikāḥ*, *kitāba*, *khul*ᶜ, pledge and settlement (*ṣulḥ*) on the bloodwit of intentional bodily injury (including murder)". When it is said to them that the textual sources relied upon by you were restricted by the cited tradition and you are only left with analogy in the face of the tradition, it consequently becomes binding on them to be one of those who give precedence to analogy over tradition. That is a practice abhorred by the Mālikites—though the preference of analogy over transmission has been related from Mālik, similar to the practice of Abū Ḥanīfa. They respond to this by saying that this is neither rejection of a tradition in favour of analogy nor is it preference. It belongs to a category of

[139] Qurʾān 5 : 1

interpretation differing from the obvious meaning and interpretation through analogy is unanimously acceptable to the *uṣūliyyūn*. They say that they have two interpretations for this tradition. First, that the two parties to the sale are still haggling and the sale is not concluded between them. It is said to them, in such a case the tradition has no use as it is well-known that they can retract the contract not being made by mere discussion. In the second interpretation, they said that the parting is indirectly meant to be parting through words and not physical parting, as the Exalted has said, "But if they (the disputing husband and wife) separate, Allāh will compensate each out of His abundance".[140] The objection, however, to this is that it is a figurative not the original use (of the word). In its original application the word means physical separation. The basis of preference here is to compare the apparent meaning of the word with analogy and to prefer whichever is stronger. The wisdom behind this right of option is to give the parties opportunity to mitigate the chances of remorse. These, then, are the principles of the first element, which is contract (*ʿaqd*).

24.3.1.2. **Element 2: The Subject-Matter of the Contract**

This is the *maʿqūd ʿalayh* (the subject-matter). In it is stipulated absence of *gharar* (uncertainty) and *ribā* and the discussion of their different kinds, both agreed upon and disputed and the causes of dispute have already preceded; there is no point in repeating them here. *Gharar* is removed from a thing by its becoming known with respect to: existence; description; quantity; readiness for delivery, of both commodity and price; and period (of delivery), if it is a credit sale.

24.3.1.3. **Element 3: Parties to the Contract**

It is stipulated for them that they be full owners or lawful agents, both of age and, along with this, neither of them should be subject to interdiction, whether on the basis of idiocy—according to those who subject the idiot to interdiction—or because of the right of another like a slave, unless the slave is authorized (*maʾdhūn*) to trade.

They disagreed in this about the unauthorized agent (*fuḍūlī*), whether his sale is effective. The form it takes is that a person undertakes a sale, of someone else's property, on the condition that if the (assumed) principal ratifies the sale it will become effective, otherwise it will be rescinded. Similarly, in the purchase for a principal without his permission on the condition that if he agrees the purchase will be valid, otherwise it will be void. Al-Shāfiʿī prohibited it in both its forms while Mālik permitted it in both. Abū

[140] Qurʾān 4 : 130

Ḥanīfa made a distinction between sale and purchase. He said it is permitted in sale, but not in purchase.

The reliance of the Mālikites is on the narration that "the Messenger of Allāh gave a *dīnār* to ᶜUrwa al-Bāriqī and said, 'Buy for us out of this incoming flock, a goat'. He said, 'I bought two goats with a *dīnār* then sold one of them for a *dīnār* and came back with a goat and a *dīnār*'. I said, 'O, Messenger of Allāh, here is your goat and your *dīnār*'. He said, 'O Lord, bless him in his lawful transactions' ". The point of the argument in this is that the Prophet (God's peace and blessings be upon him) did not authorize him to deal in the second goat, either for its sale or its purchase. This forms the proof against Abū Ḥanīfa in purchase for another person and against al-Shāfiᶜī on both counts. The reliance of al-Shāfiᶜī is on the proscription laid down in the sale by a person of what he does not have. The Mālikites interpret that to mean sale for himself and not that for another (who has the commodity). They said that the evidence for this is that the proscription was laid down in the case of Ḥakīm ibn Hizām and his famous case, as he used to sell what he did not possess. The basis for disagreement is the famous issue, whether the proscription related to a cause is to be confined to it or is to be generalized.

These then are the fundamentals of this part. On the whole the examination in this part is to be potentially included in the first part; however, the technical legal approach requires that it be dealt with separately. Now that we have discussed this part, in accordance with our purpose, let us traverse the third part, which is the discussion of the *aḥkām* of valid sales.

24.4. Part 4: Discussion of the General *Aḥkām* of Valid Sales

The principles of this part, which have a direct relationship to the transmitted bases, are confined to four units. The first unit is about the *aḥkām* concerning the existence of defects in the subject-matter of sales. The second unit is about the liability for compensation (*ḍamān*) (in case of destruction) of the subject-matter, when it shifts from the ownership of the seller to the ownership of the buyer. Third is the distinction of things that follow the subject-matter, within which they exist at the time of sale, from those which do not follow it. Fourth are the disputes between the parties to the contract, though their discussion would have been more suitable in the Book of Judgments. Similar is the case of the categories of the *aḥkām* of sales like restitution (*istiḥqāq*) and so is pre-emption (*shufᶜa*) a category of *aḥkām* contingent upon sales; however, it is customary to devote individual books to them.

[141] Qurʾān 4 : 29

24.4.1. Unit 1

In this unit there are two chapters. The first chapter is on the *aḥkām* concerning the existence of defects in absolute sales. The second chapter is on the *aḥkām* of defects in sales with the condition of absolution (*barāʾa*).

24.4.1.1. Chapter 1: The *Aḥkām* of Defects in Absolute Sales

The basis for rescission due to defects are the words of the Exalted, "[E]xcept it be a trade by mutual consent",[141] and the well-known tradition of the goat not milked for some time before sale (*musarrāt*) (so as to enhance its value). The subject-matter bearing the defect, forms the basis of the contract either with the likelihood of rejection or without such likelihood. Again, when it forms the basis of the contract and is liable to rejection, it may give rise to a *ḥukm* or it may not give rise to a *ḥukm*. When it does give rise to a *ḥukm*, it is also possible that the subject-matter of sale has changed after the sale or it has not. What is its *ḥukm* when it does not change? If it does change, then, how many kinds of changes take place and what is their *ḥukm*?

The sections covering the fundamentals of this chapter are, therefore, five. Section one is about the identification of contracts in which a *ḥukm* is invoked due to defects, as distinguished from those in which it is not. The second section is about the identification of defects, which give rise to a *ḥukm* and about the conditions generating such a *ḥukm*. The third (section) concerns the identification of the *ḥukm* of the causative defect when the subject-matter of the sale is not altered. Fourth is the section for the identification of the categories of alterations taking place in the possession of the buyer and their *ḥukm*. The fifth section is about the adjudication of the *ḥukm* in case of dispute between the parties to the sale, though this was more suitable for the Book of Judgments.

24.4.1.1.1. *Section 1: Distinction of Contracts that Give Rise to a* Ḥukm, *by Virtue of Defects, from those that do not*

The contracts in which a *ḥukm* becomes obligatory without dispute, because of defects, are the contracts whose purpose is the exchange of counter-values. Similarly, in contracts whose primary aim is not mutual compensation there is no dispute that defects have no effect in them whatsoever. These are like gifts (*hiba*) for purposes other than charity and spiritual reward. About those contracts that fall between these two categories, I mean, those that combine magnanimity with compensation like a gift for a (spiritual) reward, the

[141] Qurʾān 4 : 29

apparent ruling of the school is that there is no *ḥukm* for them because of defects. It is also said, however, that a *ḥukm* can be invoked if the defect renders the transaction void.

24.4.1.1.2. *Section 2: Identification of Defects that Give Rise to a* Ḥukm *and the Conditions Necessitating the* Ḥukm

This section has two aspects: first, defects that give rise to a *ḥukm*; and second, conditions necessitating the *ḥukm*.

24.4.1.1.2.1. Aspect 1

Among these are defects in character (of the sold commodity, like a slave) and those present in the body. Of these there are those whose opposites are stipulated in the subject-matter of sale and are called defects by virtue of conditions, as well as those that invoke a *ḥukm* even if the existence of their opposites is not stipulated in the subject-matter. These are qualities whose absence constitutes an inherent deficiency. The opposites of other defects are merely perfections whose absence does not amount to a real defect, such as a professional skill (like a slave knowing carpentry or tailoring etc.). Such inherent defects are mostly found in character, but can also exist in the body. Among physical defects are those that exist in the body of a commodity as well as of an inanimate commodity.

The defects that have an effect on the contract are, according to all authorities, natural deformities or legal deficiencies, which have an adverse effect on the price of the subject-matter. These differ in accordance with the times, customs and individuals. Perhaps a deficiency in the created body is an advantage in law, like meekness in female slaves and circumcision in male slaves. Due to the interdependence of these meanings and gradually through the practice of people, disagreements arose between the jurists in these matters. Out of these issues, we shall discuss those in which controversies among the *fuqahā*ʾ became prominent, so that what is derived from them by the mind of the jurist serves as a rule and a guideline for that in which no text can be found or where the text cannot be extended to another case.

Among these is the existence of (the habit of) indulging in unlawful sexual intercourse (*zinā*) in slaves. The jurists differed about this. Mālik and al-Shāfiʿī said that it is a defect. Abū Ḥanīfa said that it is not, rather it is a deficiency in the legal requirement, which is chastity. Marriage (in a slave-girl), according to Mālik, is a defect as it is an impediment against utilization. Similarly, in the case of a debt. This is so, as a defect on the whole is that which hinders a mental or physical act and such a defect is sometimes inherent in the thing or is external. Al-Shāfiʿī said, as far as I know, that neither a debt nor marriage is a defect. Pregnancy in an attractive (slave-girl) is a defect according to Mālik and about its being a defect in an ugly slave-girl there is a disagreement among the jurists.

Taṣriya is a defect according to Mālik and al-Shāfiʿī and that is the blocking of milk in the udder for a few days so that it may give the impression that the animal yields a substantial quantity of milk. Their proof is the well-known tradition of *muṣarrāt*. It is the saying of the Messenger of Allāh, "Do not block the milk of camels and cows (to cheat in sale). If one does this, then, the buyer has two options, either to keep it or to return it along with a *ṣāʿ* of dates". They said that the option of returning was established for him (the buyer) in the case of *taṣriya* and this indicates that it is an effective defect. Further, they maintained that he is a swindler and they held fraud similar to all other effective defects. Abū Ḥanīfa and his disciples said that *taṣriya* is not a defect because of the common knowledge that whoever buys a goat and discovers later that its milk is not much, cannot designate it as a defect. They also said that the tradition of *muṣarrāt* does not obligate practice due to its deviation from general principles. This deviation from principles is (seen) from different aspects. Among them is its conflict with the saying of the Prophet (God's peace and blessings be upon him), "(Right to) profit is through a corresponding liability for loss". This is a principle agreed upon. Among them is also its conflict with the prohibition of selling food for food with a delay, which is not permitted by agreement (of the jurists). Further, (compensation in) perishable property is undertaken through payment of its value or its like and granting a *ṣāʿ* of dates as compensation of milk is neither of these. Moreover, there is an exchange of an uncertain quantity of food, that is estimated (*juzāf*), with one of known measure as the milk with which the seller caused a deception is of an unknown quantity and, further, it can sometimes be more and sometimes less while the compensation here is fixed. It is, however, necessary (according to Ibn Rushd) to exempt this case (of *muṣarrāt*) from all these principles because of the authority of the tradition. It may be said that it does not fall in this category at all, but is a specific *ḥukm* and this has been a digression, so we now return to what we were discussing and say:

There is no disagreement, among them, that being one-eyed, blind, or amputated in hand or foot are effective defects. Similarly, a disease in a limb or the entire body. Grey hair in a beautiful (slave-girl) is a defect within the school and it is said that there is no harm if it is slight. Similarly, unhealthy blood-discharge (non-menstruating) is a defect in a slave-girl, beautiful or ugly and so is menopause according to the well-known opinion of the school. Being thin-haired is a defect as are, by agreement, all diseases of the senses and limbs.

On the whole, then, the principle in the school is that all that has an effect on the value, I mean, in lowering it, is a defect. Bed-wetting is a defect, which is also the opinion of al-Shāfiʿī. Abū Ḥanīfa said that the (slave) girl is to be returned because of it, but not a (male) slave. Femininity in (slaves sold as) males and masculinity in females is a defect. All this is held by the school except that in which we have narrated disagreement.

24.4.1.1.2.2. Aspect 2

The condition of a defect invoking a *ḥukm* is that it (the defect) should have existed prior to the time of sale or it should occur during the period of contractual obligation (*ʿuhda*), according to those who uphold such a period. Mālik was unique in the maintenance of the *ʿuhda* to the exclusion of the rest of the jurists. He was preceded in this by the seven jurists and others from among the jurists of Medina. The meaning of *ʿuhda* is taken to be a post-sale period, during which defects occurring are held to be the responsibility of the seller. It is actually, according to those who uphold it, two periods: a period of three days, for all defects arising in it in the possession of the buyer; and a period of a year concerning the three defects of *judhām* (leprosy), *baraṣ* (disease similar to leprosy) and insanity. Anything of the latter which strikes the subject-matter within a year is the responsibility of the seller, but anything other than these three is the liability of the buyer, according to the principle.

The period of three days, according to the Mālikites, is on the whole like the (three) days of *khiyār* (option) and like the days of a slave-girl's waiting period; maintenance in these days and the liability for compensation belong to the seller. As to the period of a year, maintenance and liability for compensation are on the buyer except for the three diseases. This period (related to diseases), according to Mālik, applies to slaves, but also occurs in all those categories of sale the purpose of which is mutual market contention and would be treated as (immediate) sale without being deferred. There is no dispute in this (within Mālik's school), however, there is disagreement in other things. The period of a year, according to him, is calculated in months after the end of the three-day period. The period of *muwādaʿa* (place of stay of a slave mutually agreed to by the parties) runs concurrently with the three-day period, if that period is longer than three days. The period of a year does not run concurrently with the period of waiting by a slave-girl. This is the best-known opinion of the school over which there is a disagreement. The seven jurists said that none of the periods coincides with another; the period of *istibrāʾ* runs first, then the three-day period and then the period of a year. Narrations differ from Mālik whether the period is binding in every land even when the people have not been accustomed to it or made to accept it. Two points of view are narrated from him in this. If it is said that it is not binding on the people of a certain land except when made to accept the condition, then is it necessary that the people of all lands be made to accept it? There are two opinions on this also.

Cash payment is not required in the three-day period, even if stipulated in the contract, but it is necessary in the one-year period. The underlying cause in this is that the delivery of the price, if deferred, will be incomplete and it will look like (the transaction of) a loan and a sale. These, then, are the well-known *aḥkām* of the *ʿuhda* in the school of Mālik and they are all derived opinions based on the validity of the *ʿuhda*, so we must refer to the statement of the proofs establishing it and those nullifying it.

The reliance of Mālik (God bless him), in the case of *ʿuhda* and the proof on which he depended, is on the practice of the people of Medina. His later followers argued on the basis of what is related by al-Ḥasan from ʿUqba ibn ʿĀmir from the Prophet (God's peace and blessings be upon him), that he said, "The *ʿuhda* of the slave is three days". It is also related (that he said), "There is no *ʿuhda* after four (days)". The latter tradition is also related from Samura ibn Jundub al-Fazārī (God be pleased with him). Both traditions are defective (*maʾlūl*) according to the *ḥadīth* scholars, as they differed about the transmission to al-Ḥasan from Samura even though al-Tirmidhī has declared it as *ṣaḥīḥ*. The rest of the jurists of the provinces did not consider the traditions on *ʿuhda* as *ṣaḥīḥ* and were of the view that even if they were proved authentic they conflicted with general principles. This is so as the Muslim jurists are in agreement that any damage striking the subject-matter of sale prior to its possession by the buyer is on (account of) the seller. A restriction of this settled principle is only possible through an established text. It is for this reason that one of the two narrations from Mālik, demanding the application of *ʿuhda* in each land unless it is already a usage in that land or is stipulated (as a condition), particularly the period of one year, is regarded as weak, for there is no tradition in it. Al-Shāfiʿī has related from Ibn Jurayj, who said, "I asked Ibn Shihāb about the *ʿuhda* of one year and that of three (days) to which he said, 'I do not know of a precedent in this' ".

As the discussion of the distinction of defects, which give rise to a *ḥukm* and those which do not, has been completed and the condition in this—namely, that the defect must arise before the sale or within the *ʿuhda* (according to those who uphold it)—is established, let us now proceed to the remaining (discussions).

24.4.1.1.3. *Section 3:* Ḥukm *of the Causative Defect when the Subject-Matter of Sale is not Altered*

When defects are found, even though the subject-matter of sale has not altered at all in the possession of the buyer, they can either be in immovables, in goods, or in animals. In case they are in animals, there is no dispute that the buyer has an option either to return the subject-matter of sale and redeem the price, or to keep the *mabīʿ* without compensation (for the defects). When such defects are found in immovables, then, Mālik distinguishes between slight and major defects. He says, if the defect is slight, return (of the property) is not necessitated, but the value of the defect, called *arsh*, is to be paid. If the defect is major, return is obligatory. This is what is found in the well-known books of his disciples, while the jurists of Baghdad (his disciples) have not gone into details. About goods, the well-known opinion in his school is that there is no *ḥukm* in this like that for landed property. On the other hand, it is said that it is of the same nature as landed property according to the school (Mālik). Here is what was preferred by the jurist Abū Bakr ibn Rizq, Shaykh of my grandfather, may Allāh have mercy on both of them. He used to say, "There is no difference, in this issue, between landed property and goods". His opinion has to be upheld by those who distinguish between slight and major defects in landed property, that is, they have to make the same distinction in the case of goods too. The principle is that anything which lowers value necessitates a return. That is the opinion of the jurists of different regions. It is for this reason that the jurists of Baghdad did not make the distinction I have referred to concerning landed property. Their opinion was not different even in the case of animals and they did not distinguish between slight and major defects.

24.4.1.1.3.1. Subsection: Agreement between the buyer and seller that the buyer will retain the *mabī*ᶜ and the seller will pay him the value of the defect

We said that the buyer has an option either to return the *mabī*ᶜ and redeem the price or to retain it without any compensation (for defects). If, however, they agree that the buyer will retain the goods and the seller will pay him the value of the defect then the majority of the jurists of the provinces permit this, except for Ibn Surayj from among the followers of al-Shāfiᶜī. He said that they cannot do this for it is an option in wealth (*māl*) and he has no right to annul its return for compensation, as is the case of the option in pre-emption (*shuf*ᶜ*a*). Qāḍī ᶜAbd al-Wahhāb said that this is not correct as it is a right of the buyer and it is up to him to discharge it—that is to return it and have a recourse to the price or to relinquish it for compensation—and what he has said, about the option in pre-emption, is evidence favouring us as we permit its relinquishment exchange for compensation. There is no dispute in this. In this discussion there are two well-known issues for purposes of distinction.

24.4.1.1.3.1.1. Issue 1: Several items in a single contract, one of which is defective

If the buyer purchases different kinds of things in a single contract and finds one of them to be defective, should he return all of them or just the one which he found to be defective? Some said that he only has the right to return all or retain them. This was the opinion of Abū Thawr and al-Awzāʿī; unless a separate value had been specified for each of the different things in which case there is no dispute that the particular defective subject-matter (*mabīʿ*) will be returned. The dispute arises when the price of each unit has not been specified. Some said that the defective commodity is to be returned in exchange for its proportion of the price, which is to be estimated. Among those who held this opinion were Sufyān al-Thawrī and others besides him. Both opinions are related from al-Shāfiʿī. Mālik made a distinction and said that the defective thing is to be examined. If it was the prominent part of the contract and its major object, all the things are to be returned. If it was not the major part of the contract then it is to be returned in exchange for its value. Abū Ḥanīfa made another distinction and said that if the defect occurred before possession then everything is to be returned, but if it occurred after possession the defective part is to be returned for a proportionate part of the price. In this issue, then, there are four opinions. The argument of those who prohibited division for return is that the commodity returned had no value agreed upon by the buyer and the seller. Similarly, what is retained has a value that was not agreed upon by both of them. It is possible that had it been divided it would not have sold for the value now determined for it. The argument of those who viewed the return of the defective part through division is that it was a must as it was an occasion of necessity. The valuation and estimate is substituted for consent on the analogy that the part of the *mabīʿ* which is lost has no other solution except valuation.

The distinction drawn by Mālik, whether it is the object of the contract, is *istiḥsān* on his part as he held that this defective part, if it was not the object of the sale, will not cause too much harm in so far as its valuation does not conform with the price intended by the buyer and the seller. When it is the object, however, or overwhelms the *mabīʿ* the harm in it is immense. There are different narrations from him whether the effect of the defect is to be considered only on the price of the whole or for the defective part only. With respect to the distinction drawn by Abū Ḥanīfa between possessing and not possessing, the taking of possession is a condition for the completion of the sale according to him. As long as it is not possessed, the liability for loss, in his view, is on the seller. The *ḥukm* of restitution in this issue is return on the basis of a defect.

24.4.1.1.3.1.2. Issue 2: Two men buying the same thing in a single contract

They disagreed about two men buying a single thing in the same contract and finding a defect in it, one of them desiring a return (of the property) while the other refuses. Al-Shāfiʿī said, he who wishes to return (his share of the property) may do so. This is also the narration of Ibn al-Qāsim from Mālik. It is also said that he is not allowed to return it. Those who made return obligatory, deemed it to be two separate contracts as two parties joined in it. Those who did not obligate it, deemed it to be a single contract, in which the buyer wishes to return a portion of the subject-matter on the basis of a defect (he has to return it all or keep it).

24.4.1.1.4. *Section 4: Identification of the Kinds of Alterations taking place in the Possession of the Buyer*

In case of alteration of the *mabī*ᶜ in the possession of the buyer, who does not discover the defect till after the occurrence of the alteration, the *ḥukm* changes in the opinion of the jurists of different regions according to the nature of the alteration. In case of change (in a slave) by death, disease, or manumission, the jurists of different regions maintain that it is a total loss and the buyer will have recourse to the seller for the value of the defect. 'Aṭā' ibn Abī Rabāḥ said that he cannot have recourse in the case of death or manumission. Similar is the case, according to them, of one buying a slave-girl and discovering that she had conceived from her seller. So is the case of *tadbīr*, which is based upon the analogy of *kitāba*.

There is a disagreement among the jurists about changes taking place because of (further) sale. Abū Ḥanīfa and al-Shāfiᶜī said that if he sells the subject-matter, he cannot have recourse to the buyer for anything. Al-Layth had the same opinion. Mālik had a detailed opinion in case of sale. He can either sell it to the person who had sold it to him or to someone else and he can either sell it to him for the same price, or for less, or for more. If he sells it to the person who had sold it to him, for the same price for which he had bought it then he cannot have recourse on the basis of defect. If he sells it to him at a lesser price, he can have recourse for the recovery of the value of the defect. If he sells it to him at a higher price, he will examine the issue. If the first buyer had made a misrepresentation, that is he was aware of the defect, then the first will not have recourse to the second for anything. If he had not made a misrepresentation, the first will have recourse to the second for the price and the second will have recourse against the first also. The two sales will be rescinded and the *mabī*ᶜ will revert to the ownership of the first. If he sells it to the person he bought it from, then Ibn al-Qāsim says that he has no recourse for the value of the defect, like the opinion of Abū Ḥanīfa and al-Shāfiᶜī. Ibn al-Ḥakam says that he has a recourse for the defect. Ashhab said that he will have recourse for the lesser of the value of the defect or for the value of the price, this is so when he has sold for less than he bought it for. On this basis, he does not have a recourse if he sold it for the same price or more. This was also the opinion of ᶜUthmān al-Battī.

The reason for Ibn al-Qāsim's, al-Shāfiᶜī's and Abū Ḥanīfa's opinions is that if he has alienated (the property) through sale, then he has taken the compensation in it without considering the effectiveness of defect in this compensation, which is the price. Therefore, when the buyer demands from him the compensation of the defect he has recourse to the first seller without dispute. The reason for the second opinion is seen through the similarity of the sale with manumission. The reason for the opinion of Ashhab and ʿUthmān (al-Battī) is that if the *mabīʿ* was in his possession, he could do nothing but retain it or return the whole of it; however, if he has sold it he has taken compensation through the price, so he has a right only to what is deficient unless it is more than the value of the defect. Mālik said that if he gifts it or donates it alienating ownership without compensation, he has recourse for the value of the defect. Abū Ḥanīfa said he has no recourse, as his *hiba* or *ṣadaqa* is alienation of ownership to which he has consented seeking a reward. His consent to relinquishing the right to (compensation) for the defect is more appropriate and suitable in this case. Mālik, however, made an analogy in case of gift upon manumission. Analogy reveals that he should have no recourse for any part of it if he alienates it with no possibility of return, as they are in agreement that if it is in his possession he has no other option but to return it or retain it, which is evidence that a defect has no influence in discharging any part of the price, the only effect it has is in the rescission of the sale.

About contracts in which the return (of property) is consequential, as in pledges and hire, the disciples of Mālik differed. Ibn al-Qāsim said this does not prevent return because of a defect when he returns the subject-matter to him. Ashhab said if the time when it will pass out of his hands is not distant, he has a right to return it because of a defect. The opinion of Ibn al-Qāsim is better. *Hiba* for a (spiritual) reward, according to Mālik, is like sale in so far as there is alienation in it. These then are the *aḥkām* of the situations that befall a *mabīʿ* in contracts undertaken in it.

24.4.1.1.4.1. Subsection: The occurrence of a loss in the subject-matter

If a deficiency occurs in the subject-matter, it can either be in value, in the *corpus*, or in character. A deficiency in value, because of the fluctuation of the market, is not effective, by consensus, in causing return on the basis of defect. If the deficiency occurring in the *corpus* is slight, not affecting the value, it does not cause return on the basis of defect; its *ḥukm* is as if it had not occurred. This is the stipulation of Mālik's school and of others beside it. About the deficiency occurring in the *corpus*, which affects the value, the jurists are divided into three opinions. First, that he (the buyer) has no option except for the value of the defect and he cannot do anything besides this if the seller refuses the return (of the *mabīʿ*). This was the latest opinion of al-Shāfiʿī and it was also the opinion of Abū Ḥanīfa. Al-Thawrī said that he has no option but to return the subject-matter and compensate the defect which occurred in his possession. This was also the prior opinion of al-Shāfiᶜī.

The third opinion is that of Mālik, who said that the buyer has the option to hold on to the subject-matter with the seller reducing the price in proportion to the defect, or he returns it to the seller and pays him the price of the defect that occurred in his possession. If the seller and the buyer disagree, however, the seller saying to the buyer, "I will take possession of the *mabī*ᶜ and you pay me the value of the defect that occurred in your possession", while the buyer says, "No, in fact, I will hold on to the *mabī*ᶜ and you pay me the value of the defect, which occurred in your possession". Here the buyer's opinion will prevail and it is he who has the choice. It is, however, maintained in the school that the opinion of the seller will prevail and this appears correct according to the view of one who maintains that he has no choice but to retain the *mabī*ᶜ or to return it compensating the defect occurring in his possession. Abū Muḥammad ibn Ḥazm had an entirely different opinion. He said, "He has to return it and there is no liability on him".

The proof of those who said that the buyer has no choice but to return it and to repay the value of the defect, or to retain it, is their consensus that if no defect occurs in the possession of the buyer he has no option but to return it. This necessitates the maintenance of the (latter) *ḥukm* (*istiṣḥāb ḥāl*) even though the defect has occurred in the buyer's possession and he has paid the compensation for the defect occurring during his possession. The proof of those who are of the view that he does not return the *mabī*ᶜ, but has the right to the value of the defect occurring in the seller's possession, is analogy on manumission (*ᶜitq*) and death, because the principle is not agreed upon, ᶜAṭā having opposed it.

Whenever the seller's and the buyer's rights clash, Mālik deems the right of the buyer as predominant and grants him an option. This is so, as the seller may be doing one of the two (following) things: he has been negligent in so far as he did not seek out the defect and inform the buyer about it; or he knew about it, but has swindled the buyer. According to Mālik, if it is found that he has misrepresented a defect, the return (of the *mabī*ᶜ) becomes obligatory without the buyer paying him the value of the defect, which occurred in his possession. If the *mabī*ᶜ is lost by death or otherwise, the liability (for the loss) is on the seller, unlike the case in which it is not established that he has misrepresented. Abū Muḥammad (ibn Ḥazm)'s proof is based on the reason that it was an act of Allāh and it could even have occurred in the possession of the seller. The return of the *mabī*ᶜ on the basis of defect indicates that the sale has not taken place in reality, but only in apparent form. Further, there is no evidence in the Book or in the *sunna* that holds the *mukallaf* (subject) liable for a loss in which he was not instrumental, except when it is by way of an exemplary penalty for the usurper (*ghāṣib*), according to those who hold him liable for what is lost in his possession through an act of God. This is the *ḥukm* of defects occurring in the *corpus* of the *mabīᶜ*.

About the defects of character, like running away and theft (in slaves), it is said in the school that they elude return as in the case of defects of *corpus*. On the other hand, it is said they do not. There is no dispute that the defect arising in the possession of the buyer, if it is cured after its occurrence, is not instrumental in restoration, unless its adverse effect is feared. They disagreed within this issue about the buyer having had intercourse with the (bought) slave-girl. Some said that if he has intercourse with her he cannot return her, but has recourse for the value of the defect, whether she was a virgin or a non-virgin. This was the opinion of Abū Ḥanīfa. Al-Shāfiᶜī said that he has to pay the value of the decrease in her price through the intercourse in the case of the virgin, but not in the case of the non-virgin. Others said that he has to pay even this and also dower according to her status (*mahr al-mithl*). This was the opinion of Ibn Abī Shubrama and Ibn Abī Laylā. Sufyān al-Thawrī said that if she is a non-virgin he pays one-twentieth of her price (*niṣf al-ᶜushr*), while he pays one-tenth of it if she is a virgin. Mālik said there is no claim on him for intercourse with a non-virgin as it was a gain (*ghalla*) that accrued to him by virtue of bearing the liability for loss. In case of the virgin, it amounts to a defect that establishes, according to him, for the buyer an option as in his opinion that has preceded. A similar opinion is related from al-Shāfiᶜī. ᶜUthmān al-Battī said that intercourse is considered in this case of the slaves according to custom, if it is effective in (causing a decrease in) value the seller compensates the deficiency; if it is not effective he (the buyer) has no right to any compensation. This, then, is the deficiency that can occur in things sold.

The jurists disagreed about increase occurring in the *mabīᶜ*, I mean, that which is reproduced and is separable from it. Al-Shāfiᶜī was of the opinion that it is not effective in causing return and belongs to the buyer, because of the generality of the Prophet's saying, "(Right to) revenue is by a corresponding liability (for bearing loss)". Mālik exempted offspring from this and said that it belongs to the seller and the buyer has no choice except to restore the increase with its source or to retain (both). Abū Ḥanīfa said that all increases prevent restoration and necessitate valuation of the defect except for revenue and service. His proof is that what has been given birth to by the *mabīᶜ* is already included in the contract, as its return and the return of its offspring is not possible, it amounts to an alienation (of property) that requires a valuation of the defect, except for what has been stipulated by the law about revenue and service. As to the increase resulting within the *mabīᶜ* and which is not separable from it, if it is like the (change in the) colour of a dress, or a fraying of the dress, then it generates an option according to the school; either for retention with a recourse for defect or the return (of the *mabī*ᶜ) and his becoming a co-sharer with the seller in the value of the increase. About the development in the body, like corpulence, it is maintained in the school that it establishes an option for the buyer and it is also said that it does not. Similarly, in the case of reduction, like emaciation. This, then, is the discussion of the alterations (in the *mabī*ᶜ).

24.4.1.1.5. *Section 5: Judgment on the* Ḥukm *Varying with the Disagreement of the Parties.*

In relation to the nature of the judicial decision rendered in accordance with these *aḥkām*, (it is said that) if the seller and the buyer settle upon one of the situations out of those mentioned above, the *ḥukm* specific to that situation becomes applicable. If the seller refutes the denies the claim of the plaintiff, he will either be denying the defect or he will deny its occurrence in his possession. If he denies the existence of a defect in the *mabī*ᶜ, when the defect is such that all (prudent) men are equal in its discernment, then two ᶜ*adl* (morally upright) witnesses who are selected from among the people are sufficient. If the defect is of a nature whose knowledge is particular to people of some trade, then witnesses having this trade render testimony; who it is maintained by the school should be two and morally upright and it is also held that neither ᶜ*adāla* (moral probity) nor number, nor Islam is stipulated as a condition for such witnesses. The same is the case when they disagree about its being instrumental in (causing change in) value and also about its occurring prior to the time of the sale or after it. If the buyer has no evidence, the seller will take an oath that it did not take place in his possession. If he has evidence about the existence of the defect itself in the *mabī*ᶜ, no oath is to be administered to the seller.

When the existence of the defect is to be estimated no oath from the seller is required, rather the demand of the *ḥukm* in this is that the valuation be made in its defect-free form and also in its defective form, the buyer then takes back the difference of these two values. If there is an option, three types of valuation are to be undertaken: valuation in defect-free form, valuation with defect occurring in the possession of the seller and valuation with defect occurring in the possession of the buyer. The seller then refunds the price reducing from it an amount equivalent to the difference between the valuation in defect-free form and valuation in defective form. If the buyer refuses to return (the property) and prefers to retain it, the seller refunds out of the price the difference between the original value and the value with the defect occurring in his possession.

24.4.1.2. Chapter 2: The Sale of *Barāʾa* (Absolution)

The jurists differed about the permissibility of this sale. The form it takes is that the seller imposes a condition on the buyer for bearing the liability of all defects occurring in general in the *mabīʿ*. Abū Ḥanīfa said that the sale of absolution from all defects is permissible irrespective of the seller having a knowledge of the defects, of having conveyed (their existence) to the buyer, of having mentioned them to the buyer and of having pointed them out. Abū Thawr had the same opinion. Al-Shāfiʿī in his better-known opinion, which is supported by his disciples, said, "The seller is not absolved (of liability) of a defect unless he points it out to the buyer". Al-Thawrī had the same opinion. According to the well-known narration from Mālik, *barāʿa* is permitted in the defects known to the seller. This is particularly so in the case of slaves, except for absolution from pregnancy in the sale of an attractive slave-girl, which is not permitted according to him due to the immensity of *gharar* in it, but is permitted in the case of an ugly slave-girl. There is a second narration from him that it is permitted in slaves and animals. In the third narration from Mālik, he holds the same opinion as that of al-Shāfiʿī. It is related from him that the sale of absolution is permitted only in sale by the *sulṭān* and it is said in the sale of inherited property, without even stipulating absolution.

The proof of those who permitted *barāʿa* absolutely is that freedom from defects is the right of the buyer in sales; if he chooses to relinquish it, it is his privilege to forgo what is due. The proof of those who did not permit it absolutely is that it belongs to a category of *gharar* pertaining to defects the seller is not aware of and to the category of fraud and cheating in the case of defects he knows. It is for this reason that Mālik stipulated the lack of knowledge of the buyer. On the whole, the reliance of Mālik is on what he has related in the *Muwaṭṭaʿ* that " ʿAbd Allāh ibn ʿUmar sold a slave that he had for eight hundred *dirhams* and sold it on the condition of absolution. The buyer later came back to ʿAbd Allāh ibn ʿUmar and told him, 'The slave has a disease that you did not indicate to me'. They then took their claims to ʿUthmān and the man said, 'He sold to me a slave who has a disease which he did not indicate to me'. ʿAbd Allāh (ibn ʿUmar) said, 'I sold to him with absolution'. ʿUthmān ruled that ʿAbd Allāh ibn ʿUmar take an oath that he knew he was selling the slave with no disease known to him'. ʿAbd Allāh ibn ʿUmar refused to do so and took back the slave". It is also related that Zayd ibn Thābit used to permit the sale of *barāʾa*. Mālik singled out the slaves for this as their defects are mostly hidden.

On the whole, the option of returning (the sold commodity) on the basis of defects is a right established for the buyer. As this (identification of the defect) varies greatly, like the variance in the description of the things sold, it inevitably follows that if the two parties agree on the lack of knowledge of it that it should not be permitted; the basis of which is their agreement on the lack of knowledge about the characteristics of the *mabīʿ*, which influence the price. It is for this reason that Ibn al-Qāsim has related from Mālik in the *Mudawwana* that his last opinion was the rejection of the sale of *barāʾa*, except what is exempted by the *sulṭān* and particularly in the discharge of debts (foreclosures). Al-Mughīra out of the disciples of Mālik held that *barāʾa* is permitted in that in which the (value of the) defect does not exceed a third of (the value of) the *mabīʿ*.

The sale of *barāʾa* is on the whole binding with a condition, according to one who permits it, except for the sale by the *sulṭān* and of the sale of the estate of the deceased (inheritance) in the opinion of Mālik alone. The discussion of *barāʾa*, generally, is about its permissibility and about the condition of its permissibility. It is also about the kinds of contracts, kinds of *mabīʿ*, varieties of defects and its absolute and conditional permissibility, all of which has been implicitly present in our discussion, so keep it in mind.

24.4.2. Unit 2: Time of Liability of Compensation of the Subject-Matter

They disagreed about the time at which the buyer is liable for the *mabīʿ* so that it will be his loss if it is destroyed. Abū Ḥanīfa and al-Shāfiʿī said that the buyer is not liable until after taking possession. Mālik has details in this, as the things sold in relation to this topic are of three kinds: sales in which the seller is obliged to satisfy the buyer about weight, measure, or counting; sales in which these do not arise and these are *juzāf*; or those that are not weighed, measured or counted. Those in which there is the right to such satisfaction, the buyer is not liable except after taking possession. About those in which there is no right of satisfaction, the goods being present, there is no disagreement in the school that they are within the liability of the buyer even though he has not taken possession. There are three narrations from Mālik about the absent *mabīʿ*. The best known is that the liability is that of the seller unless he imposes it as a condition on the buyer. Second, that it is the liability of the buyer, unless he stipulates it to be that of the seller. The third makes a distinction between things that are not secure from perishing till the time of demand, like animals and eatables and those that are likely to survive. The disagreement in this issue is based upon the question whether possession is a condition of the contract or is a *ḥukm* among the *aḥkām* of the contract, the contract being binding without possession. Those who said that possession is a condition of the validity of the contract or of its being binding, or in whichever way you wish to convey this meaning, the liability is, according to them, that of the seller till such time that the buyer takes possession. Those who maintained that it is a binding *ḥukm* among the *aḥkām* of the *mabīᶜ* and sale has been concluded and become binding said, "The contract is now within the liability of the buyer".

The distinction of Mālik between the absent and present (*mabīᶜ*), between that in which there is a right of satisfaction (about weighing etc.) and that in which there is not, is *istiḥsān*. The meaning of *istiḥsān* in the majority of the cases is recourse to *maslaḥa* and equity.

The Ẓāhirites were of the opinion that the property is within the liability of the buyer by virtue of the contract and as far as I know the reliance of those who hold this view is that revenue belongs to the buyer even before possession. The Prophet (God's peace and blessings be upon him) has said, "(Right to) revenue is dependent upon a (corresponding) liability for loss". The reliance of the contenders is the tradition of ᶜAttāb ibn Usyad "that the Messenger of Allāh (God's peace and blessings be upon him) when he sent him to Mecca said, 'Prohibit them the sale of that which they have not possessed and the profit of that for which they are not liable' ". We have already discussed the condition of possessing the *mabīᶜ* in what has preceded. There is no disagreement among the Muslim jurists that it is within the liability of the buyer after the taking of possession, except in the case of *ᶜuhda* (period) and diseases. As we have already discussed the *ᶜuhda*, it is necessary that we now discuss the diseases.

24.4.2.1. Chapter 1: Discussion of Diseases

The jurists disagreed about the foregoing claims in the case of diseases in fruit. Mālik and his disciples gave a positive ruling in this, while Abū Ḥanīfa, al-Thawrī, al-Shāfiᶜī in his latest opinion and al-Layth denied it. The reliance of those who forgo damages is the tradition of Jābir that the Messenger of Allāh (God's peace and blessings be upon him) said, "One who sells fruit that is (later) affected by disease should not charge anything from his brother, for what reason will anyone of you take his brothers wealth?"—recorded by Muslim as the narration of Jābir. It is also related from him that he said, "The Messenger of Allāh (God's peace and blessings be upon him) commanded that the (charges for) diseased fruit be forgone".

The reliance of those who permitted (relinquishment of payment) for diseases are these two traditions of Jābir, along with *qiyās al-shabah* as they said, "It is a *mabīᶜ* in which the right of satisfaction (about weighing etc.) against the seller still remains, on the evidence of his watering it till ripening. It is, therefore, necessary that the liability should be his, the basis being all the other *mabīᶜ*s in which the right of satisfaction remains". The difference, according to them, between this sale and all the other sales is that this sale has been explicitly mentioned in the law and the *mabī*ᶜ has not ripened yet. It is as if he (the lawgiver) exempted it from the sale of what has not been created yet. It thus follows that its liability should be his, unlike all other sales.

The reliance of those who did not favour it is on the comparison of this sale to all other sales and (on the fact) that vacation (by the seller) in this sale amounts to possession (by the buyer); and they agreed that liability of the buyer is after taking of possession. There is also, by way of transmission (of tradition), the tradition of Abū Saᶜīd al-Khudrī, who said, "Fruit bought by a man was struck by disease and his debt mounted. The Messenger of Allāh (God's peace and blessings be upon him) then said, 'Grant him out of the *ṣadaqa*'. He was granted *ṣadaqa*, but it was not sufficient to meet his debt, so the Messenger of Allāh (God's peace and blessings be upon him) said, 'Take (out of his wealth) what you find and you will have nothing more than that' ". They said that he (the Prophet) did not render judgment about disease here. The reason for disagreement here is the conflict of traditions in it and the clash of the different analogies of resemblance. Each one of the parties desired to turn away the conflicting tradition with the tradition which formed the basis for him and said about the prohibition (relinquishing payment) in case of disease: "It appears that the command about diseases was laid down in connection with the proscription about the sale of fruit before it begins to ripen". They also said: "This is supported by the fact that when the complaints about diseases became numerous, they were ordered that they should not sell fruit until it began to ripen". This was in the well-known tradition of Zayd ibn Thābit. Those who permitted it in the face of the tradition of Abū Saᶜīd, said, "Perhaps the seller in that case was destitute, so he (the Prophet) did not rule for the relinquishment on the basis of disease, or the quantity affected by disease was such that it was not binding to invoke the ruling of disease, or that the time in which this happened was not the time of infection by disease, like infection after cutting or after ripening".

Al-Shāfiᶜī related the tradition of Jābir, from Sulaymān ibn ᶜAtīq from Jābir and used to consider it weak (*ḍaᶜīf*) saying, "The mentioning of relinquishment in it is ambiguous". He said, however, that "If the tradition is established, relinquishment (of payment) is a must, both in small and large quantities".

There is no dispute among them about the ruling for diseases when it occurs because of lack of water and those who uphold it generally deemed this agreement a proof for its (general) acceptance. The discussion about the fundamentals of disease, in the school of Mālik, is covered in four sections. First is the identification of the causes leading to diseases. Second, the location of the disease in the subject-matter. Third is the quantity of it that is to be forgone. Fourth is the time of relinquishment.

24.4.2.1.1. *Section 1: Identification of the Causes Effective in Calamities*

About events that strike fruit as an act of God like cold, drought, flood and decay, there is no dispute in the school that these are calamities. Shortage of water (thirst) is, as we have said, a calamity. Some of Mālik's disciples viewed that which strikes it as an act of man as a calamity, while others did not. Those who viewed it as a calamity are divided into two types. Some of them viewed as a calamity that which is irresistible like (the descending of) an army, though they did not consider (as a calamity) that which can be guarded against, like theft. Others deemed all that struck fruit through the act of man as a calamity, whatever its nature.

Those who considered it only in the acts of God relied on the apparent meaning of the saying of the Prophet (God's peace and blessings be upon him), "What do you think, if Allāh were to prevent the fruit (from maturing)". Those who considered it to be in the acts of man, compared it to the acts of God. Those who exempted the thief from it said that it is possible to protect it from him.

24.4.2.1.2. *Section 2: The Objects of Calamities*

The objects of calamities are fruits and vegetables. There is no dispute about fruits in the school and for vegetables the better-known opinion is the application of (the rulings of) calamities to them. They differed about vegetables in their comparison to the basis, which is fruit.

24.4.2.1.3. *Section 3: The Quantity Necessary for Relinquishment*

The quantity in which calamities apply is one-third for fruit. In the case of vegetables, it is said that it applies to all quantities, while it is also said that it applies to a third. Ibn al-Qāsim considers a third of fruit through measure, while Ashhab considers it a third of the value. According to Ashhab, if fruit amounting to a third of the value through measure is lost, he will forgo one-third of the price, irrespective of the third (in value) amounting to a third in measure. When a third measure of the fruit is lost Ibn al-Qāsim, however, would lower the price by a third if the fruit is of the same kind and the price of its differing stock is the same. If the fruit is of several different kinds, also with differing values, or of different stocks of different values, he would compare the value of the lost third with the total value and reduce it accordingly. So, at times he would consider measure only when the value of the different parts and stock of the fruit was the same, at other times he would consider both things (that is measure and value) when the value was different.

The Mālikites in their derivation about relinquishment for calamities argue on the basis of quantification, although the tradition is absolute. This is so as a small quantity, being well-known through practice, is lost from every yield of fruit. The buyer, then, agreed to this condition on the basis of practice though not expressly. So also the calamities on which the *ḥukm* is based demand a distinction between small and large quantities. They said, "When this distinction becomes obligatory, it is a necessary to consider a third, as the law has given it consideration on many occasions". The school, however, is not clear about this principle, sometimes rendering a third from the realm of larger, as in the case here and at other times considering it from the realm of lesser (quantity). About the distinction between less and more they were not confused at all. Quantities are difficult to establish, according to the majority of the jurists, on the basis of analogy. It is for this reason that al-Shāfiᶜī said, "If I had upheld an opinion about calamities, I would have distinguished between less and more and the consideration of a third as a criterion for less and more is laid down as a text in *waṣiyya* (bequest), as the Prophet (God's peace and blessings be upon him) said, 'A third and a third is more than enough' ".

24.4.2.1.4. *Section 4: The Time at which the Relinquishment is Made*

With respect to time, the school (of Mālik) agreed on the obligation of discharging (payment) because of calamities at the time in which there is need for leaving the fruit on top of the trees so that its ripening is achieved. They disagreed when the buyer makes the seller keep the fruit (on the trees) so that he may sell it fresh in small quantities. It is said that the (rule of) calamities is applicable here also due to its similarity with the agreed-upon time. It is also said that (the rule of) calamities would not apply because of the difference between this and the agreed-upon time in which remittance for calamities is obligatory. This is so as this time-period is similar to the agreed-upon time from some aspects while it is not from other aspects. Those who think that the time-periods coincide made (remittance because of) calamities obligatory, while those who inclined toward the distinction did not make it obligatory. I mean by this that those who thought freshness (of fruit) is required in purchase as is ripeness, made (remittance because of) calamities obligatory, while those who did not view the issue to be the same said that the (rule of) calamities would not apply. Hence, they disputed the obligation of calamities in vegetables.

24.4.3. Unit 3: Things Accompanying the Subject-Matter

Among the issues of this discussion there are two that are well-known.

24.4.3.1. Issue 1: Sale of date-palms carrying fruit

The question is when will the fruit go with the date-palm and when it will not? The majority of the jurists maintain that if a person sells a date-palm carrying fruit prior to pollination the fruit is for the buyer. If the sale takes place after pollination, then the fruit belongs to the seller, unless the buyer stipulates it for himself. All other fruit fall within the meaning of the date-palm due to the confirmed tradition of Ibn ᶜUmar from the Messenger of Allāh (God's peace and blessings be upon him), who said, "(When) one sells a date-palm that has pollinated, the fruit is for the seller unless the buyer has stipulated it (for himself)". They said that when the Prophet (God's peace and blessings be upon him) ordered that the price, after pollination, was for the seller, we came to know by implication of the text that it belonged to the buyer before pollination in the absence of stipulation. Abū Ḥanīfa and his disciples said that it belongs to the seller both before and after pollination and they did not deem the understanding here to be an implication of the text, but from the category of the explicit and primary. They said: "This is so as the fruit if it belongs to the seller after pollination, it is more appropriate that it belong to him before pollination". They compared the blossoming of fruit with the birth of offspring. Just as one sells an *ama*, who has a child, the child belongs to the seller unless stipulated for himself by the buyer, similarly in the case of fruit. Ibn Abī Laylā said that irrespective of pollination, when the tree is sold the fruit belongs to the buyer, whether he stipulates it for himself or not. He rejected the tradition in opposition to analogy, as he was of the view that the fruit is a part of the *mabīᶜ*. This view has no meaning, unless the tradition is not considered authentic by him. Abū Ḥanīfa did not reject the tradition, but he opposed the implied meaning in it.

The reason for disagreement, then, in this issue between Abū Ḥanīfa, al-Shāfiᶜī and Mālik, along with those who upheld their opinions, is the conflict of the implication of the text with the explicit and primary meaning, which is also called the signification of the communication (*faḥwā al-khiṭāb*), but it is weak here though originally it is stronger than the implication of the communication. The cause of Ibn Abī Laylā's opposition to them is the conflict between analogy and transmission, which is weak as we indicated.

Pollination, according to the jurists, is the meeting of the spadix of the date-palm with the spathe and the inflorescence in the rest of the tree. Masculinity in a tree is the spadix within the meaning of pollination. The pollination of crops is disputed within the school. Ibn al-Qāsim related from Mālik that its pollination takes place by rubbing (cross pollination?) on the analogy of the rest of the fruits. Is then the obligating cause of this *ḥukm* actual pollination or the time of pollination? It is said that it is the time and it is also said that it is pollination. It is on this basis that a disagreement arises when some trees in an orchard are pollinated while the rest are not. Does that which has not pollinated follow (take the *ḥukm* of) that which has? They agreed, as far as I know, that when the fruit is sold and it is the time of pollination, the part that has not pollinated takes the *ḥukm* of that which has.

24.4.3.2. Issue 2: Sale of the wealth of the slave

This relates to the disagreement about the sale of a slave's wealth, as they disagreed whether the slave's wealth accompanies him in sale and manumission. There are three opinions. First is that his wealth in sale and manumission belongs to his master. This was the opinion of al-Shāfiᶜī and the Kūfīᶜs. Second, that his wealth goes with him in sale and manumission, which is the opinion of Dāwūd and Abū Thawr. Third, that it goes with him in manumission, but not in sale unless the buyer stipulates it. This was the opinion of Mālik and al-Layth.

The proof, of those who were of the view that his wealth is for his master in sale unless the buyer stipulates it, is the well-known tradition of Ibn ᶜUmar from the Prophet (God's peace and blessings be upon him) that he said, "(When) one sells a slave who owns wealth, then the wealth is for the one who sells him unless the buyer stipulates it (for himself)". Those who deem it to belong to the master in manumission, do so through analogy on sale. The proof of those who were of the view that it follows the slave in all cases is based on their own verdict that the slave was the owner. This is an issue on which the jurists have disagreed considerably, I mean, on whether or not the slave can own (wealth). It appears that these (jurists) have attached more weight to analogy over transmission, as the tradition of Ibn ᶜUmar is one in which Nāfiᶜ has contradicted Sālim. Nāfiᶜ related it from Ibn ᶜUmar, while Sālim has related it from Ibn ᶜUmar from the Prophet (God's peace and blessings be upon him). Mālik, however, attached more weight to analogy in manumission and to transmission in sale. Mālik says in the *Muwaṭṭā*ʾ: "The matter that is agreed upon is that if the buyer stipulates the wealth of the slave—whether cash, goods, or debt—then it is for him".

It is related from the Prophet (God's peace and blessings be upon him) that he said, "(If) one frees a slave then his wealth belongs to him, unless his master exempts it". It is permitted, according to Mālik, that the slave may be purchased along with his belongings with *dirhams*, even when the belongings of the slave are *dirhams* or include *dirhams*. Abū Ḥanīfa and al-Shāfiᶜī opposed him when the wealth of the slave consists of cash. They said: "The slave and his wealth are like two things sold by someone and only that which is permitted in the rest of the sales is permitted in them". The disciples of Mālik disagreed about the stipulation by the buyer of some of the slave's wealth in the single transaction of sale.

Ibn al-Qāsim said that this is not permitted, while Ashhab said that it is permitted that he stipulate some of it. Others made a distinction and said: "If the thing with which the slave is being purchased is corporeal property (*ᶜayn*) (as opposed to *dayn*; debt) and the property of the slave also contains corporeal things, it is not permitted, as it amounts to exchanging *dirhams* with goods and *dirhams*, but if he is being purchased with goods, or there are no *dirhams* in his wealth, it is permitted".

The reason for the opinion of Ibn al-Qāsim, that it is not permitted to him to stipulate part of the slave's property, is its similarity with the (sale of the) fruit of the date-palm after pollination. The basis for the opinion of Ashhab in permitting it is the similarity between a part and its whole. In this topic there are many other issues not mentioned as they do not belong to our objective.

Among the best-known issues in this topic is the increase and decrease that may occur in the price, on the basis of which sale has been transacted, after the sale has been consented to by the parties to the contract. I mean that the buyer increases the price, on which sale has been transacted, for the seller after the sale or the seller reduces the price. Does this (increase or decrease) follow the *ḥukm* of the price? The usefulness of the distinction is that those who said that it is a part of the price obligate its return as detinue or as restoration due to defect or whatever is similar to it. Similarly, those who deem it as within the *ḥukm* of the original price if the sale was void and those who do not consider it a part of the original price, do not obligate any thing. Abū Ḥanīfa said that it is a part of the price, except that it is neither established in favour of the pre-emptor nor in the sale of *murābaḥa* and the *ḥukm* is for the original price. Mālik and al-Shāfiʿī said that increase or decrease are not essentially associated with the price and bear the *ḥukm* of a gift (*hiba*).

Those who associated the increase with the price argued on the basis of the words of the Exalted, "And there is no sin for you in what ye do by mutual agreement after the duty (hath been done)".[142] They said that if the increase in *ṣadāq* (dower) is associated with *ṣadāq* it would be associated with the price in a sale. The others argued on the basis of their agreement that it is not associated in pre-emption. On the whole, those who hold that the contract is settled said that the increase is *hiba*, while those who maintain that it amounts to a rescission of the sale, counted it as a part of the price in the second contract.

24.4.4. Unit 4: Agreement of the Parties on Sale and Disagreement on Price

If the parties to the sale agree on the sale and disagree on the quantity of the price, without there being any evidence, then the jurists of different regions agree on the whole that they should both take oaths and cancel the sale. These

[142] Qurʾān 4 : 24

jurists, however, disagree in details; I mean, about the time when verdict is to be given about the oaths and cancellation. Abū Ḥanīfa and a group of jurists, said that they take the oaths and cancel the sale as long as the substance of the goods has not been converted. If it has changed then the prevalent claim is that of the buyer along with his oath. Al-Shāfiʿī, Muḥammad ibn al-Ḥasan (al-Shaybānī) the disciple of Abū Ḥanīfa and Ashhab the disciple of Mālik said that they can take oaths at any time. From Mālik there are two narrations. First, that they take oaths and cancel prior to (delivery of) possession and after possession the prevalent claim is that of the buyer. The second narration is like the opinion of Abū Ḥanīfa, which is the narration of Ibn al-Qāsim and the other is the narration of Ashhab. Conversion (in the subject-matter), according to him, is through the fluctuation in the market and by any increase or decrease in the *mabīʿ*. Abū Dāwūd and Abū Thawr said that the prevailing claim is that of the buyer in every situation. Zufar had the same opinion, unless they disagreed about the species of the price, in which case they would cancel and take oaths. There is no dispute that if they disagreed about the species of the price or of the priced commodity the *ḥukm* is to cancel and take oaths.

The jurists of the provinces generally came to an agreement about cancellation and oath-taking in case of a dispute about counting of the price, because of the tradition of Ibn Masʿūd that the Messenger of Allāh (God's peace and blessings be upon him) said, "Whenever two merchants contracting a sale (disagree), the claim of the buyer is to be granted, or they (are to) retract". Those who interpreted this tradition to mean the obligation to rescind generally, said that they take oaths in any case and rescind. The underlying cause in this, according to them, is that each one of them is a plaintiff and a defendant. Those, however, who maintained that the tradition is obligatory in the case where the claims of the buyer and the seller are equipoised, said that if the goods have been delivered or have been converted then possession provides evidence on behalf of the buyer that he is most likely truthful. Oath, on the other hand, is obligatory for the apparently stronger claimant. This is the principle of Mālik in oaths and it is for this reason that he makes oath obligatory for the plaintiff on some occasions and for the defendant on others. This is so as oath is not obligatory on the defendant through the texts in so far as he is the defendant, but becomes obligatory on him as in all probability he appears more truthful. If the plaintiff, at times, has the stronger claim it is obligatory that the oath be in his domain. Those who maintain that the prevailing claim is that of the buyer hold that the seller is content about the purchase by the buyer and is a claimant only for the disputed count of the price. Dāwūd and those who upheld his opinion, rejected the tradition of Ibn Masʿūd as it is *munqaṭiʿ*, for which reason it has not been recorded by the two Shaykhs al-Bukhārī and Muslim, however, Mālik did record it.

About the refusal of the parties to take oath, there are two narrations from Mālik. First is rescission while the second is the preference of the claim of the seller. There is also a disagreement as to who is to commence oath-taking. The well-known view is that it is the seller as it occurs in the tradition. There is then the question, if cancellation has taken place is it permitted to one of the parties to accept the claim of the other party? There is a dispute about this in the school.

24.5. Part 5: A General Look at the Effect (*Ḥukm*) of the Vitiated Sale after it has taken place

The jurists agreed that in *fāsid* sales that have taken place, as long as the *mabīᶜ* has not been converted—through new contracts, growth, decrease, or the fluctuation of the market—its *ḥukm* is restoration, I mean, the seller returns the price and the buyer the priced commodity. They disagreed, when after possession, it is disposed of through manumission, gift, sale, mortgage, or through other means of disposal, whether it is an alienation of the *mabīᶜ* necessitating (return of) value. Similarly when there is growth in it or there is some deficiency. Al-Shāfiᶜī said that all this is neither alienation nor the semblance of ownership (*shubhat al-milk*) in a vitiated sale and the obligation is restoration. Mālik said that all this is disposal that necessitates (return of value), except what has been narrated from him by Ibn Wahb in (the section on) *ribā* that it is not disposal. A similar opinion was held by Abū Ḥanīfa.

The vitiated sales are divided, according to Mālik, into prohibited and disapproved. The prohibited, if they change, are passed on in value. The disapproved, if converted, become valid according to him. Perhaps some of the vitiated sales were held valid by him through possession, because disapproval in them is slight. The Shāfiᶜites compare the *mabīᶜ* in a void sale to *ribā* and *gharar*, because of the prohibition of its essence like in the sale of *khamr* and *khinzīr*. There is no such category as conversion according to them.

Mālik is of the view that the prohibition in these matters, I mean, the sales of *ribā* and *gharar*, is due to the lack of justice in them. If the goods have been converted (in a void sale), fairness requires that they be restored in value. As he (the buyer) takes possession of the goods when they are probably valued at (say) one thousand and he restores them when they may have a value of five hundred, or *vice versa*. It is for this reason that Mālik views the fluctuation of markets as the conversion of the subject-matter in a void sale. In sale with a loan, Mālik views that if the subject-matter is converted and the seller is the one who has granted the loan, the buyer will return the value as long as it does not exceed the price, for the buyer had already raised the price because of the loan and it is, therefore, not fair that he pay more than that. In case it was the buyer who had made the loan, then the seller had discounted the price because of the loan and on an obligation to return the value the buyer will not pay less than the price. The reason is that in these sales prohibition was caused by invoking compensation against the loan, which is the subject of mutual assistance among people. Mālik in this issue is more profound than all the rest.

They disagreed when the condition was dropped before possession, I mean, the condition of loan. Would the sale become valid? Abū Ḥanīfa, al-Shāfiᶜī and the rest of the jurists said that the sale is rescinded. Mālik and his disciples said that the sale is not rescinded, except for Ibn ᶜAbd al-Ḥakam who maintained that the sale is to be rescinded. An opinion like that of the majority has also been related from Mālik.

The proof of the majority is that the proscription implies vitiation of the prohibited thing. If the sale has occurred in a vitiated form it cannot be validated at all by the removal of the condition, because of which the vitiation occurred, just as removing the cause of corruption in things perceptible through the senses (tangible), after the corruption has occurred, does not return the thing to its original wholesomeness, so keep it in mind. It is related that Muḥammad ibn Aḥmad ibn Sahl al-Barmakī enquired about this problem from Ismāᶜīl ibn Isḥāq al-Mālikī, who said to him: "What is the difference between a loan and a sale and between a man who sells a slave for a hundred *dīnārs* and a skin of *khamr*? When the sale between them had taken place he said that he would drop the skin. This sale is vitiated, according to the jurists, by agreement. It is, therefore, necessary that sale and loan be like that too". He (al-Barmakī) provided an answer for this which is not persuasive and the discussion of which has already preceded.

As the discussion of the principles of vitiated sales, the principles of valid sales and the fundamental *aḥkām* of vitiation common to and general for all sales or most of them is now over, let us cover what is specific to each one of these four categories by listing those that are in the nature of principles.

XXV
THE BOOK OF *ṢARF* (EXCHANGE)

As two conditions are specific to this sale—first the absence of delay (*nasīʾa*), that is, immediate delivery and second, the absence of excess (*tafāḍul*), which is the stipulation of similarity—the study of this book is to be undertaken in (the following) five parts. First is the delineation of that which is delayed from that which is not. Second is the delineation of that which is similar from that which is not. (As these two divisions are divided into a number of sections, the disagreement (of the jurists) will be presented there.) Third, which also falls within this topic in a disputed form, is whether it is a means (*dharīʿa*) to one of the two (conditions), I mean excess and delay, or to both, according to those who uphold the principle of means (*dharāʾiʿ*), that is, Mālik and his disciples. This is also divided into two kinds like the division of its source (and includes the fourth part). The fifth relates to the *aḥkām* of this sale from the aspect of invoking one of these conditions—that is, the absence of delay or excess—or both, because this sale differs from other sales in a number of *aḥkām* by virtue of these two conditions.

When you examine the books written about the detailed cases of this topic, which they designate as the Book of *Ṣarf*, you will find all issues referred back to these five categories, or to what is consequential to them, except for the issues that they (the authors) assimilate in this single book when they do not relate to this book, like the insertion by the Mālikites into *ṣarf* of issues that actually pertain to the category of the demand of loans. They included them in this book as the vitiating element in them refers back to one of these two bases, I mean to *ṣarf* with delay or with excess, just as they discussed other independent issues jointly or separately.

As our purpose is to record the issues that are expressly covered by the law or are very close to those expressly covered, we thought it desirable to record in this book seven well-known issues, which are like principles, or models for the guidance of the (would be) *mujtahid* in whatever he may encounter of the issues of this book. We have designed the book in such a way that with the help of its methodology he may attain the status of *ijtihād*, if he has acquired what is sufficient for him of *ʿilm al-nahw*, language and the methodology of *uṣūl al-fiqh*—and out of these it is sufficient to know what is proportionate to the requirements of this book or even less. It is by learning the relevant issues and being equipped with these tools, that he deserves to be called a *faqīh*, not by merely learning too many details of *fiqh*, even if he has memorized the maximum that is possible for a human being. We find the (so-called) jurists of our times believing that the one who has memorized the most opinions has the greatest legal acumen. Their view is like the view of one who thought that a cobbler is he who possesses a large number of shoes and not one who has the ability to make them. It is obvious that the person who has a large number of shoes will (some day) be visited by one whose feet the shoes do not fit. He will then go back to the cobbler who will make shoes that are suitable for his feet. This is the position of most of the *faqīh*s of these times.

We have deviated from the path we were treading and now return to it in so far as we had promised to discuss the (seven) issues.

25.1. Issue 1: Sale of gold for gold, silver for silver and their *ḥukm*

The jurists agreed that the sale of gold for gold and silver for silver is not allowed, except from hand to hand and like for like (in similar quantity and quality). The exception is what is related from Ibn ʿAbbās and those who followed him from among the Meccans. They permitted the sale with excess and disallowed it with delay alone. Ibn ʿAbbās adopted this opinion because of what he related from Usāma ibn Zayd from the Prophet (God's peace and blessings be upon him) that he said, "There is no *ribā* except in *nasīʾa* (delay)". This is an authentic tradition. Ibn ʿAbbās took the apparent meaning and did not render as *ribā* anything besides *nasīʾa* (delay). The majority of the jurists followed what is related by Mālik from Nāfiʿ from Abū Saʿīd al-Khudrī that the Messenger of Allāh (God's peace and blessings be upon him) said, "Do not sell gold for gold except like for like and do not devour some of it with the rest, do not sell silver for silver except like for like and do not devour some of it with the rest and do not sell a thing absent for one that is present". This is one of the most authentic traditions of this topic. The tradition of ʿUbāda ibn al-Ṣāmit is another authentic tradition within this topic. The majority accepted these traditions as they are explicit about the issue. The tradition of Ibn ʿAbbās, however, is not explicit about the issue and has been narrated in two versions. First is that he said: "*Ribā* is in *nasīʾ*a alone". The permission of (dealing with) excess is not understood from this except by the indirect indication of the text (*dalīl al-khiṭāb*), which is weak especially when contradicting an explicit text. The second version is "There is no *ribā* except in *nasīʾa*", which is stronger than the first version as its apparent meaning implies that what is besides *nasīʾ*a is not *ribā*. It is probable that he (the Prophet) intended by his saying, "There is no *ribā* except in *nasīʾa*", that it occurs more often. If this is the likely meaning and the other text is explicit, it is necessary that they be interpreted in a way that reconciles the two.

The majority agreed that coins, ore, or moulds (of gold or silver) are the same for the purposes of prohibition of sale, one with the other, with excess, due to the generality of the preceding traditions, except for Muʾāwiya who used to permit excess in the exchange of ore and fabrications due the excess (value) of crafting. So also what is related from Mālik, who was asked about a person who came to a mint with silver and took in exchange *dīnārs* and *dirhams* equal in weight to the silver or (the value of) its weight in *dirhams* paying the cost of fabrication. He said: "If it is due to necessity for the departure of a company, I would say that there is no harm in it". This was also the opinion of Ibn al-Qāsim from among his disciples, while Ibn Wahb, one of his disciples, ʿĪsā ibn Dīnār and the majority of the jurists rejected this. Mālik also permitted the exchange of a deficient *dīnār* with one of standard weight, or two for one, over which there is disagreement among his disciples regarding the number that is customarily exchanged.

25.2. Issue 2: Ornamented swords and *muṣḥaf* exchanged for silver or gold

The jurists differed about an ornamented sword, or *muṣḥaf*, when it is sold for silver as it has silver ornamentation or for gold as it has gold ornamentation. Al-Shāfiʿī said that this is not permitted, because of the stipulated similarity in the sale of silver for silver and gold for gold being unknown. Mālik said that if the value of the gold or silver in it is a third or less (than the value of the whole) the sale is permitted—I mean, (sale) for silver if the ornamentation is in silver and (sale) for gold when the ornamentation is in gold—otherwise it is not permitted. It is as if he were of the view that the value of the silver in it being little it is not the object of the sale and amounts to a gift.

Abū Ḥanīfa and his disciples said that there is no harm in the sale when the silver (paid for it) is more than the silver in the sword. Same is the case with the sale of a sword ornamented with gold. They were of the opinion that the silver or gold in it is equivalent to (part of) the silver agreed upon while the excess is for the value of the sword.

The proof for al-Shāfiʿī is in the generality of the tradition explicitly laid down in this issue from the narration of Fuḍāla ibn ʿAbd Allāh al-Anṣārī, who said, "The Messenger of Allāh, when he was at Khaybar, was brought a necklace in which there was gold and pearls and it belonged to the spoils that were being sold. The Messenger of Allāh ordered that the gold be separated and then he said: 'Gold for gold, weight for weight' ". It is recorded by Muslim. Muʿāwiya, as we have already said, allowed this sale absolutely. Abū Saʿīd rejected his view and said, when the tradition was narrated, "I will not reside in the land in which you live".

25.3. Issue 3: The conditions of *ṣarf*

The jurists agreed that among the conditions of *ṣarf* is that it should be immediate (*nājiz*), however, they disagreed about the time in which this meaning is realized. Abū Ḥanīfa and al-Shāfiʿī said that *ṣarf* is immediate if it takes place before the two parties to *ṣarf* separate, irrespective of possession being prompt or delayed. Mālik said that if possession is delayed within the session *ṣarf* is void, even if they have not parted, so much so that he disapproved the fixing of a time in it.

The cause of disagreement is their divergence over the meaning of the saying of the Prophet (God's peace and blessings be upon him), "Except 'here you are', 'here you are' (i.e. immediate (spot) delivery)". This is so as it differs in measure through a long or short separation. Those who were of the view that these words are valid for one who has not withdrawn from the session, I mean, that it can be said of him that he has sold through spot delivery, said that delay is permitted within the session. Those who were of the view that the words are not realized unless possession has been taken immediately by the parties to *ṣarf*, said that if possession is delayed within the session after the (oral) contract *ṣarf* is void. It is because of their agreement on this meaning that they did not allow endorsement, surety and option within the contract of *ṣarf*, except for what is narrated from Abū Thawr that he allowed option in it. They disagreed (within Mālik's school) about delay that is compelling, occasioned by circumstances involving both parties or one of them. At times it is said that this is like the case which occurs out of choice, while at other times it is said that it is not like that. They have details in this, but it is not within our purpose to record them in this book.

25.4. Issue 4: Exchange of *dīnārs* with *dirhams* when there is a counterfeit (coin) in them

The jurists disagreed about one who exchanges, by way of *ṣarf*, *dirhams* with *dīnārs* and then finds a counterfeit coin in them and wishes to return it. Mālik said the *ṣarf* (here) is void. If the *dīnārs* are in excess, one *dīnār* is to be reduced in place of a *dirham* or what is more for the exchange value of the *dīnār*, if the *dirhams* are (now) more than the *dīnārs* another *dīnār* is to be reduced and so on till the value of the exchange *dirhams* is equal to the *dīnārs*. He said, however, that if he agrees to accept the counterfeit *dirham*, the exchange is not rendered void.

Abū Ḥanīfa said that *ṣarf* is not void because of the counterfeit *dirhams* and it is permitted to substitute them, unless the counterfeit *dirhams* are half or more of the total *dirhams*. If he returns these, *ṣarf* is void in the rejected coins. Al-Thawrī said that if the counterfeit coins are returned, he has a choice to substitute them or he becomes his partner in the *dīnārs* in proportion to their value, I mean with the owner of the *dīnārs*. Aḥmad said that *ṣarf* is not annulled by return, whether of less or more. Ibn Wahb from among the disciples of Mālik permits substitution in *ṣarf*. This is based on the fact that compelled postponement in *ṣarf* has no effect, especially in some parts and this is preferable. From al-Shāfiʿī, there are two opinions about the annulment of *ṣarf* due to counterfeit coins.

In summary, four opinions are derived from the (views of the) jurists of the provinces in this issue: one opinion annuls *ṣarf* absolutely in case of return; another opinion views the validity of *ṣarf* and the obligation of substitution; one opinion distinguishes between large and small quantities; and another provides a choice between substitution and becoming a partner of the other party.

The reason for disagreement in all this is whether the imposed delay is effective in *ṣarf*. If it is effective, then is it effective in large or in small quantities?

There is disagreement in (Mālik's) school about the existence of a deficiency. He (Mālik) maintained once that if he agrees to the loss, *ṣarf* is permitted. If he demands substitution, *ṣarf* is incompatible on the analogy of counterfeit coins. At other times he maintained that *ṣarf* is void even if he agrees to the loss, but this is weak.

They also disagreed when possession of some of the exchanged gold and silver is taken and the rest is delayed, that is, when the *ṣarf* is contracted with immediate delivery. It is said that the entire (contract of) *ṣarf* is void and this was the opinion of al-Shāfiʿī. It is also said that only the delayed part is void and this is the opinion of Abū Ḥanīfa, Muḥammad and Abū Yūsuf. Both opinions exist in the school (of Mālik). The cause of disagreement is the dispute whether the entire transaction is to be annulled or the prohibited part only, when permissible and impermissible things are mixed in a single contract.

25.5. Issue 5: Exchange of the same species by weight (*murāṭala*)

The jurists agreed that *murāṭala* is permitted in gold for gold and silver for silver with equality of weight, even though the number is different. This is so when the quality of the gold is the same. They disagreed about *murāṭala* in two cases. First is that when the quality of the gold is different. The second is that when one of the counter-values (of gold) is less than the other and the party desires to increase it with goods or *dirhams* when *murāṭala* is in gold, or with gold when the *murāṭala* is in *dirhams*.

According to Mālik, in the first case where the quality of the exchanged species is different, when one of the parties presents a single quality of gold whereas the other presents two kinds, one of a quality better than the single quality and the other of a lower quality, this is not permitted. When the single kind of gold, which is offered by one of the parties, is better than the two kinds taken together or worse than them, or it is similar to one of them and better than the other kind *murāṭala* is permitted according to him (i.e. Mālik). Al-Shāfiʿī said that when the two kinds are different it is not permitted. Abū Ḥanīfa, all the Kūfīs and all the Baṣrīs said that all this is allowed.

The reliance of the school of Mālik in the prohibition of this is uncertainty, which leads to the course of *sadd al-dharāʾiʿ*, as there is suspicion that the person exchanging by way of *murāṭala* intended the exchange of gold through *tafāḍul*. It is as if he gave a part of medium quality for an excess of bad quality or for a lesser amount of better quality and through that passed on to the sale of gold for gold with excess. An example of this is that an individual says to another: "Take from me twenty-five *mithqāls* of medium quality for twenty of a higher quality". The other says to him: "This is not permitted to us, but I will give you twenty of a higher quality and another ten of a lower quality than yours, while you will give me thirty of a medium quality. The ten of a lower quality will be equivalent to five of your gold, while twenty of a medium quality will exchange for twenty of a higher quality".

The reliance of al-Shāfiʿī is on the excess (*tafāḍul*) that exists in the counter-value. The basis for Abū Ḥanīfa is the consideration of weight in both values and the rejection of the doctrine of *sadd al-dharīʿa*.

Similar to of their disagreement about *ṣarf* undertaken by weight is their disagreement about it when undertaken by count, I mean, when the quality of gold on the two sides is different. Their disagreement about deficiency in weight, where one of the parties wished to increase the amount by something where there was *ribā* or even where there was no *ribā*, is quite similar to their dispute here. For example, one of the parties exchanges gold for gold by weight with another person and the gold on one side is found to be less than that on the other. The person whose gold is less desires to compensate the deficiency with *dirhams* or goods, then, Mālik, al-Shāfiʿī and al-Layth said: "This is not permitted and the *murāṭala* is void". Abū Ḥanīfa and the Kūfīs allowed all this. The basis for the Ḥanafites is the estimation of the existence of similarity in the gold with the excess becoming an equivalent for the goods. The basis for al-Shāfiʿī is the absence of similarity arrived at through measure, weight, or counting owing to excess. In the same way they disagreed when the exchange is made through counting.

25.6. Issue 6: Exchange of debts when one is in *dirhams* and the other in *dīnārs*

They disagreed about two individuals with one of them having a claim on the other in *dīnārs* and the other having a claim on the first in *dirhams*: Is it permitted to them to exchange these when they are liabilities? Mālik said that this is permitted if both are due at the same time. Abū Ḥanīfa said that it is permitted irrespective of their becoming due simultaneously. Al-Shāfiʿī and al-Layth said that this is not permitted whether they are due or they are not due. The proof of those who do not permit it is that it is an exchange of an absent thing with an absent thing, when an absent thing cannot be exchanged with a thing present it is more appropriate that (exchange of) two absent things should not be permitted. Mālik considered the time of payment as a substitute for their being present. He, therefore, stipulated that they should be due at the same time so that it does not amount to a sale of a debt for a debt. The opinion of Ibn Wahb and Ibn Kināna, from among the disciples of Mālik, was the same as that of al-Shāfiʿī.

Similar to this is their disagreement about the permissibility of *ṣarf* when the parties do not have what they exchange, but one party delivers it to the other before parting from the session; as for example, they borrow it and possess it within the session and before parting. This was permitted by al-Shāfiʿī and Abū Ḥanīfa, but was disapproved by Ibn al-Qāsim when it occurred from both sides and allowed when it was from one, that is, when only one of them borrowed. Zufar said that this is not permitted except when it is from one side.

In the same category is the disagreement about the person who has a claim for *dirhams* on another after a period: is he permitted to take gold from him after the termination of the period or *vice versa*? Mālik inclined toward its permissibility if possession is taken before parting. Abū Ḥanīfa had the same opinion, except that he permitted this even when the period had not terminated. A group of jurists did not permit this irrespective of the termination of the period.

This was also the opinion of Ibn ʿAbbās and Ibn Masʿūd. The proof of those who permitted this is the tradition of Ibn ʿUmar, who said, "I used to sell camels at Baqīʿ, selling in *dīnārs* and taking *dirhams* and selling in *dirhams* and taking *dīnārs*. I asked the Messenger of Allāh (God's peace and blessings be upon him) about this and he said, 'There is no harm in this if it is at the rate of that day' ". It is recorded by Abū Dāwūd. The proof of those who did not permit this is what is narrated in the tradition of Abū Saʿīd and others: "Do not sell anything absent for things present".

25.7. Issue 7: Sale with *ṣarf*

They disagreed, in Mālik's school, about sale with *ṣarf*. He said that this is not permitted unless one of them is a major part and the other is secondary, irrespective of whether *ṣarf* is for one *dīnār* or in more. It is said that if *ṣarf* is for one *dīnār* it is permitted whatever form it takes, but if it is in more the fact of one of them being subsidiary to the other is to be considered for purposes of permissibility. If both are intended together, it is not permitted. Ashhab permitted *ṣarf* and sale and this is to be preferred as there is nothing in it that leads to *ribā* or *gharar*.

XXVI
THE BOOK OF *SALAM* (ADVANCE PAYMENT)

In this book there are three chapters. The first chapter is on the subject-matter and its conditions. The second chapter is on what can lawfully be demanded from the *muslam ilayh*[143] as a substitute for subject-matter agreed to in the contract of *salam* and on the issues arising in it regarding *iqāla*,[144] premature payment, and delay. The third chapter covers the disputes (of the parties) over *salam*.

26.1. Chapter 1: Subject-Matter and its Conditions

With respect to the subject-matter, they (the jurists) agreed about the permissibility of *salam* in everything that is measured and weighed, as has been established through the well-known tradition of Ibn ᶜAbbās that he said, "The Prophet (God's peace and blessings be upon him) arrived in Medina and they used to undertake *salam* in dates for a period of two or three years. The Messenger of Allāh said, 'He who undertakes a debt (of *salam*) should do it through a determined price, a determined weight, and for a determined period' ". They agreed about its prohibition in everything that cannot be a debt, and these are houses and structures. They disagreed about other categories of goods and animals. Dāwūd and a group of the Ẓāhirites prohibited this (i.e. *salam* in these goods), inclining toward the apparent meaning of the tradition. The majority permitted it in goods that can be determined by description and number, but within this they disagreed as to what goods can or cannot be determined with description. Among these are animals and slaves. Mālik, al-Shāfiᶜī, al-Awzāᶜī and al-Layth were of the view that *salam* is permitted in them, and this is also the opinion of Ibn ᶜUmar from among the Companions. Abū Ḥanīfa, al-Thawrī, and the jurists of Iraq said that *salam* is not permitted in animals, and this is also the opinion of Ibn Masᶜūd, while from ᶜUmar there are two opinions on this.

[143] The person to whom the advance payment is made.

[144] Negotiated recission of the contract.

The reliance of the jurists of Iraq in this (prohibiting *salam* in animals and slaves) is on what has been related from Ibn ʿAbbās "that the Prophet (God's peace and blessings be upon him) prohibited incurring a debt (of *salam*) in the case of animals". This tradition is weak according to the first group. Perhaps, they also argued on the basis of the prohibition by the Prophet (God's peace and blessings be upon him) of the sale of an animal for an animal with a period of delay. The reliance of those who permitted *salam* in animals is what has been related from Ibn ʿUmar "that the Messenger ordered him to equip a troop, when they had run out of camels, so he directed him to take an advance on the *ṣadaqa*. He then took one camel for two toward the camels of the *ṣadaqa*". They also related, in support, the tradition of Abū Rāfiʾ that "the Prophet (God's peace and blessings be upon him) transacted *salam* involving a young camel". They said that this indicates the raising of a liability in the case of animals.

The reason for their disagreement are two things. First, the conflict of the traditions on this issue. Second, the vacillation of an animal between being capable of determination by description and not being so. Those who drew distinctions between animals about inborn features and description, particularly the traits of temperament, said that they cannot be determined. Those who found similarities in them said that they can be determined.

Within this is also their disagreement about eggs, milk and other things. Abū Ḥanīfa did not permit *salam* in eggs, while Mālik did through counting. Similarly in meat, Mālik and al-Shāfiʿī permitted it, but Abū Ḥanīfa prohibited it. So also in cattle and sheep, Mālik permitted it and Abū Ḥanīfa prohibited it. In this, Abū Ḥanīfa's opinion was different from that of al-Shāfiʿī. Again in pearls and gems, Mālik permitted it, but al-Shāfiʿī prohibited it.

Our purpose in (describing) these issues was the identification of the controlling principles in the law and not the listing of detailed cases, as these are unlimited.

26.1.1. Conditions

Among these are conditions that are agreed upon and those that are disputed.

26.1.1.1. Conditions agreed upon

Those agreed upon are six in number. Among them is that the price and the priced commodity must be those things in which *nasāʾ* (delay) is permitted, thus, those in which delay is not permitted are prohibited (for purposes of *salam*). These are things that have identical benefits, in Mālik's view, a similar genus, according to Abū Ḥanīfa's opinion, and the consideration of food value with species, according to al-Shāfiʿī's opinion. One of the conditions is that the thing should capable of estimation either by measure, by weight, or by number, that is, in case it is something that requires estimation, or it should be identified through description, if it is something that requires to be described. Another condition is that it should be something that exists by the end of the period. Another condition is that the price should not be delayed through a period that is extensive, so that it does not become an exchange of a debt for a debt, that is, on the whole. They disagreed about the stipulation of two or three days, delay in the payment of the price, although they agreed that it should not be delayed for an extensive or unlimited period. Mālik permitted the delay of two or three days, and also permitted its delay without any stipulation. Abū Ḥanīfa and al-Shāfiʿī were of the view that among its conditions is possession within the session like *ṣarf.* This is a practice agreed upon.

26.1.1.2. Disputed Conditions

They disagreed about four conditions. First is the period of delay, whether it is a condition in it. Second, whether the species of the *muslam fīh* (that is, the subject-matter of the contract) should be in existence at the time of the contract of *salam.* Third is the specification of the place of delivery of the *muslam fīh.* Fourth, that the price should be determined either by measure, weight, or counting and that it should not be *juzāf* (approximate).

26.1.1.2.1. Condition 1

The period of delay is definitely a condition of its validity according to Abū Ḥanīfa. The preferred and well-known narration from Mālik is that it is a condition of *salam.* It is said that there are some narrations in which he permitted immediate *salam.* Al-Lakhmī made a distinction in this and said, "*Salam* in the school (of Mālik) is of two types: immediate *salam*, which is the sale of ready goods; and delayed *salam*, the purpose of which is not the sale of ready goods".

The reliance of those who stipulated a period of delay are two things: first, the apparent meaning of the tradition of Ibn ʿAbbās; and second, that if the period of delay is not stipulated in it, it would amount to the sale of a thing that the buyer does not have, which is prohibited. The reliance of al-Shāfiʿī (who does not stipulate delay) is on the fact that if it is permitted with delay its permissibility for immediate delivery is more appropriate, as there is the least amount of *gharar* in this. Perhaps, the Shāfiʿites also argued on the basis of the tradition "that the Prophet (God's peace and blessings be upon him) purchased a camel from a Bedouin for a load of dates. When he entered his house he did not find the dates. The Prophet (God's peace and blessings be upon him) then borrowed the dates and gave the same to him". They said that this is immediate sale with dates as a liability. For the Mālikites, by way of interpretation, *salam* has been permitted for compassion as one making an advance payment is inclined to proffer the price for facilitating the (delivery) of the *muslam fīh*, while the *muslam ilayh* is inclined toward it due to the existence of a delay (*nasīʾa*). Thus, if the period of delay is not stipulated, this meaning vanishes.

They disagreed about the period of delay on two points. First, whether it can be determined by naming the seasons (or events) rather than periods in days and months, like cutting, picking, harvesting, and season. Second, about the number of days (when the *ajal* is in days). The conclusion in Mālik's school about the number of days is that the *muslam fīh* is of two types: that which is required from the land in which the contract takes place, and second, that which is not required from the land where the contract took place. If it is required from the same place, then, according to Ibn al-Qāsim the period to be considered is that in which the markets are likely to change, and this is about fifteen days. It is related by Ibn Wahb from Mālik that he permitted two or three days. Ibn ʿAbd al-Ḥakam said that there is no harm even if it is one day. That, however, which is required from another land, the period of delay in it is the time taken to travel to and from that land, whether it is short or long. Abū Ḥanīfa said that the period of delay cannot be less than three days. Those who deemed the period of delay as a condition without an underlying cause, stipulated for it the minimum period to which the name is applied, while those who considered it as dependent on the fluctuation of the markets, stipulated days in which the markets normally change. Mālik permitted the period of delay, extending it till picking, cutting, and other similar events, but Abū Ḥanīfa and al-Shāfiʿī prohibited it. Those who saw that the uncertainty of the dates of these events makes an insignificant difference permitted it, as slight *gharar* is overlooked in the law. They compared it to the difference that arises in the case of months, which can be of thirty days or twenty-nine days each. Those who considered it as a major difference of time, unlike the case of months, which vary only by one day, did not permit it. (In case of fixation of dates by events, the difference in the period can be greater.)

26.1.1.2.2. Condition 2

About the condition whether the species of the *muslam fīh* should be in existence at the time of the contract, Mālik, al-Shāfiʿī, Aḥmad, Isḥāq, and Abū Thawr did not stipulate this and said that *salam* is permitted for a thing out of its season. Abū Ḥanīfa, his disciples, al-Thawrī and al-Awzāʿī said that it is not permitted unless it is the season of the *muslam fīh*. The proof of those who did not stipulate the season is what occurred in the tradition of Ibn ʿAbbās that the people used to contract *salam* for dates for a period of two or three years, this was approved and not rejected. The reliance of the Ḥanafites is upon the tradition related by Ibn ʿUmar that the Prophet (God's peace and blessings be upon him) said, "Do not contract *salam* in date-palms until they (the dates) begin to ripen". It is as if they viewed that *gharar* would be more if the species did not exist at the time of the contract, and as if this resembled more the sale of an absent thing, even though this is present and the other is a liability. In this way *salam* is distinguished from the sale of a thing which does not exist.

26.1.1.2.3. Condition 3

This relates to the place of taking possession. Abū Ḥanīfa stipulated this due to its similarity with (the condition of) time, but no one besides him stipulated this and they are the majority. Al-Qāḍī Abū Muḥammad held the view that it is better to specify the place of delivery, but Ibn al-Mawwāz said that it is not needed.

26.1.1.2.4. Condition 4

The price should be determined by way of measure, weight, count, or measured by length and should not be an approximate estimation. Abū Ḥanīfa stipulated this, but al-Shāfiʿī did not, nor did the two disciples of Abū Ḥanīfa, Abū Yūsuf and Muḥammad. No ruling is recorded from Mālik in this, although sale by estimate is permitted according to him except when excessive *gharar* is involved as explained earlier.

It is necessary to know that determination of the *muslam fīh* in *salam* is undertaken by weight in goods usually weighed, by measure in those usually measured, by length for those customarily measured by a standardized length, and by counting in countable goods. If none of these methods is applicable to it, it is determined by description of the desired attributes of the species along with the identification of the species if it is of different kinds, or without it if it is only one species.

They did not disagree on the point that *salam* is always undertaken as a liability and is not undertaken in things present. Mālik permitted it when present in a specified, safe village (i.e. in a place different from the place of contract) and when they are not likely to perish. It was as if he considered it to be a liability.

26.2. Chapter 2: Substitute for the Subject-Matter

There are a large number of cases falling under this chapter, but we will mention out of these the well known.

26.2.1. Issue 1

The jurists disagreed about the person who contracts *salam* for some kind of fruit and when the period is over its delivery becomes difficult, so much so that the subject-matter (*muslam fīh*) becomes non-existent due to the passage of its season. The majority said that when this happens the *muslim* (person making the payment) has an option to take back the price or to postpone the performance till the next season. This was the opinion of al-Shāfiʿī, Abū Ḥanīfa and Ibn al-Qāsim, and their argument is that the contract created a liability for the described thing, which still remains applicable, and it is not a condition that the fruit should be of that very year, but it was a condition stipulated by the *muslim*, therefore, he has an option. Ashhab, from among the disciples of Mālik, said that *salam* (in this case) is rescinded by necessity and postponement is not permitted. It was as if he considered it to be a sale of a debt for a debt. Saḥnūn said that he has no right to take back the price and has to transfer it to the forthcoming (season). Mālik's opinion is ambiguous in this. The reliable opinion here is that which was held by Abū Ḥanīfa, al-Shāfiʿī and Ibn al-Qāsim. It was this opinion that was preferred by Abū Bakr al-Ṭarṭūshī. The exchange of a debt for a debt is prohibited when it is the main object, not when it is undertaken due to necessity.

26.2.2. Issue 2

The jurists disagreed about the sale of the subject-matter when the period is over and possession has not been taken from the *muslam ilayh*. There are jurists who did not permit this at all. They are of the view that no sale is allowed before possession for anything. This was the opinion of Abū Ḥanīfa, Aḥmad and Isḥāq. Aḥmad and Isḥāq relied for this on the tradition of ʿAṭiyya al-ʿAwfī from Abū Saʿīd al-Khudrī, who said: "The Messenger of Allāh (God's peace and blessings be upon him) said, 'He who contracts *salam* for a thing should not dispose it of for another thing' ". Mālik prohibited the sale of the *muslam fīh* in two cases. First, when the *muslam fīh* is food. This is based on his opinion that the thing for which possession is stipulated before sale is food, and about which texts of the tradition were quoted. Second, when the *muslam fīh* is not food and the *muslim* accepts as compensation that which is not permitted as payment in *salam*. For example, when the *muslam fīh* consists of goods and the payment is in goods different from these, the *muslim* takes from the *muslam ilayh*, at the end of the period, goods belonging to the species of the payment, then, this amounts to a loan with an excess if the goods acquired are more than the payment of the *salam*, or it amounts to a guaranty with a loan if the goods acquired are equal to it or less. Similarly, if the payment (*raʾs al-māl*) of *salam* consists of food, it is not permitted to take in exchange for it other food in excess, whether of the same or of a different species. According to Ibn Wahb, if it is the same kind of food with respect to species, measure, and description, it is permitted, as he deems it the same as goods. It is also permitted according to him to take food of the same description as that of the *muslam fīh*, even if it is of inferior quality, as it belongs, according to him, to the category of substitution for *dīnārs*. *Iḥsān* occurs, for example, when he has a claim on him for wheat and takes the same measure of barley. In all this it is a condition, according to Mālik, that possession should not be delayed; otherwise it amounts to an exchange of a debt for a debt. If the capital of *salam* is a thing present (*ʿayn*) and the *muslam fīh* is also an *ʿayn* of the same species, it is permitted as long as it is not in excess of it. It will not be regarded as a sale of an *ʿayn* for an *ʿayn* with a delay, if it was equal to it or less than it. Similarly, if he takes *dirhams* for *dīnārs*, it will not be a case of delayed *ṣarf*. It is the same if he takes *dīnārs* of a kind different from those of the capital of *salam*. The sale (of the subject-matter) of *salam* to someone other than the *muslam ilayh* is permitted in exchange for anything that can be sold, as long as it (the subject-matter) is not food, for if it were food, it would amount to sale of food before possession.

In the case of *iqāla*, it is a condition with Mālik that no increase or deficiency should result in it for otherwise it would amount to a sale, and all that is associated with a sale will be applicable to it, I mean, it will be rescinded, according to him, through that by which credit sales are rescinded. For example, it can lead to a sale with a loan, or to discount for premature payment, or to the sale of *salam* when it is not allowed. The example of its falling under a sale with a loan is that when the period comes to an end he enters into *iqāla* with him to take back part of it and leave some parts, this is not permitted according to him, as it leads to (the combining of) sale with a loan. It is, however, permitted according to al-Shāfiʿī and Abū Ḥanīfa as they do not prohibit sales that employ evasive means.

26.2.3. Issue 3

The jurists disagreed about purchase of a thing from the *muslam ilayh* with the capital (*raʾs al-māl*) of *salam* after *iqāla* (has been contracted) through a method that is not permitted before *iqāla*. There are jurists who do not permit it at all and are of the view that *iqāla* is a means of making permissible that which is not permitted. This was the opinion of Abū Ḥanīfa and his disciples, and of Mālik and his disciples, except that according to Abū Ḥanīfa it is not permitted at all, just as the sale of the *muslam fīh* is not permitted at all, according to him, before possession. Mālik, however, prohibits it on occasions where the sale of *salam* is prohibited before possession, as we have elaborated earlier (regarding his opinion). Among jurists are those who permitted it, and this was the opinion of al-Shāfiʿī and al-Thawrī. Their argument is that through *iqāla* the *muslim* has become the owner of his capital. As he owns it now, it is permitted to him to purchase with it what he likes as casting suspicion over (the acts of) Muslims is not permitted. They also said that the prohibition in the tradition of Abū Saʿīd applies to the stage prior to *iqāla*.

26.2.4. Issue 4

They disagreed about the buyer who regrets the (contract) of *salam* and says to the seller: "Enter into *iqāla* with me and I will postpone (claiming) the price that I have paid you". Mālik and a group said that this is not permitted. Another group said that it is. Mālik considered it erroneous because of the fear that when the period is over and the buyer has a claim on the seller for food he will delay taking it so that the seller may enter into *iqāla* with him, and this would amount to a sale of food with delay before taking possession. Others found it erroneous for purposes of prohibition as it is the rescission of a debt with a debt. Those who considered it permitted held that it is from the category of *maʿrūf* and *iḥsān*, which Allāh has commanded. The Messenger of Allāh (God's peace and blessings be upon him) said, "He who agrees to relieve a Muslim from a burdensome contract, Allāh will forgive his shortcomings on the day of judgment, while he who postpones his claim from one in (financial) difficulty, Allāh will cover him with His shade on the day when there will be no shade besides His".

26.2.5. Issue 5

The jurists agreed that if a person has a claim on another for *dirhams* or *dīnārs* after a certain period and the other person remits them at the end of the period or later, then he (the claimant) is bound to accept them. They disagreed about goods due after a period in *salam* and other cases. Mālik and the majority said: "If he brings them before the termination of the period, he is not bound to accept them". Al-Shāfiʿī said: "If it is a thing that does not change (alter or decay) and does not require care, like iron and copper, it is binding on him to accept it. If, however, it is a thing that requires care, like fruit, it is not binding on him".

When he delivers the goods after the termination of the period, then, the disciples of Mālik differ on this. It is narrated from him that it is binding on him to take possession, for example, when *salam* was contracted for the winter picking and he delivers them in the summer. Ibn Wahb and a group said that it is not binding on him.

The proof of the majority, in maintaining that possession of the goods is not binding before the termination of the period, is based on the fact that it is within his liability (in case of destruction) till the appointed period and there is a burden on him in this. This is not the case with *dīnārs* and *dirhams* as there is no burden in that. Those who do not obligate him to accept the goods brought later than the time of termination of the period, argue that the purpose served by the goods was at the appointed time and not at other times. Those who permitted this in both cases, that is, after the period and before it, hold them similar to *dīnārs* and *dirhams*.

26.2.6. Issue 6

The jurists disagreed—about the person who enters into a contract of *salam* with another, or buys food from him, on the basis of a measure and the seller or the *muslam ilayh* brings the food and informs the buyer that it has already been measured—whether the buyer can take possession from him without further measuring, acting in trust upon his statement. Mālik said that this is permitted in *salam* and in a cash sale, otherwise there would be fear that it belongs to the category of *ribā*: perhaps, he displayed trust in him so that he may delay payment of the price. Abū Ḥanīfa, al-Shāfiʿī, al-Thawrī, al-Awzāʿī and al-Layth said that this is not allowed unless the seller measures for the buyer a second time. Their argument is that as it is not for the buyer to sell it except after he has measured it, he cannot take possession unless the seller measures it for him. If measuring is a condition of sale, so is possession. They drew support from the tradition that the Prophet (God's peace and blessings be upon him) prohibited the sale of food before two measures had passed through it: the measure of the seller and the measure of the buyer.

They disagreed about the dispute of the parties over the measure when the food is destroyed in the hands of the buyer before measuring. Al-Shāfiʿī said that the prevalent view would be that of the buyer. This was also the opinion of Abū Thawr. Mālik said that the prevalent statement is that of the seller as the buyer believed him (about measure) when taking possession of it. This, according to him, is based on his opinion that sale is permitted by the very belief (in the seller).

26.3. Chapter 3: Disputes of the Parties over *Salam*

The parties in *salam* can differ over the price or over the priced commodity, either in their genus or about the period of delay or the place of delivery. With respect to their dispute over the quantity of the *muslam fīh*, the prevalent assertion is that of the *muslam ilayh* if his claim seemed contextually true; otherwise it is that of the *muslim* if his claim looks like the truth. If they make highly divergent statements, then analogy dictates that they take oaths and retract from the contract. If they dispute over the kind of *muslam fīh*, they take oaths and retract from the contract. For example, if one of them says that he made an advance payment for dates, while the other says that it was for wheat.

If their dispute about the period relates to its termination then the prevalent assertion is that of the *muslam ilayh*. If it is about the duration of the period, even then the assertion of the *muslam ilayh* prevails, unless he makes an unbelievable claim, in which case the view of the *muslim* prevails. For example, the *muslim* claims it to be the season of the *muslam fīh*, while the *muslam ilayh* claims it to be some other time.

The preferred opinion in their dispute about the place of delivery of possession is that one who claims it to be the place of the conclusion of the contract has the say. If none of them claims this then the opinion favoured is that of the *muslam ilayh*. Saḥnūn opposed the former position and said that the prevailing view is that of the *muslam ilayh* even when the other claims it to be the place of contract. Abū al-Faraj opposed the latter position and said that if none of them claims it to be the place of contract, then, they take oaths and withdraw from the contract. The *ḥukm* in their disagreement over price is the same as that of the dispute between parties to a sale before delivery of possession, (the discussion of) which has preceded.

XXVII
THE BOOK OF *KHIYĀR* (SALE WITH AN OPTION)

The discussion of the principles of this book first relates to (the question) whether it (sale with an option) is permitted. If it is, then, for what duration. Is cash payment stipulated in it? Who is liable for the *mabīʿ* (in case of destruction) during the period of the option? Can options be inherited? For whom is *khiyār* permitted and for whom it is not? What acts have the same status as words and constitute *khiyār*?

Permissibility of option is upheld by the majority, except for al-Thawrī and Ibn Shubrama, as well as a group of the Ẓāhirites. The reliance of the majority is on the tradition of Ḥibbān ibn Munqidh, which contains the words "and you have an option for three days", and also what has been related of the tradition of Ibn ʿUmar: "The parties to sale have an option as long as they have not parted, except in sale with an option". The reliance of those who prohibit it is (on the argument) that it constitutes *gharar* and that the basis of sale is that it is binding, unless definitive evidence is produced for the permissibility of sale with an option from the Qurʾān or the authentic *sunna* or *ijmāʿ*. They also said that the tradition of Ḥibbān is either not authentic or it is specific to the case of the person who complained to the Prophet (God's peace and blessings be upon him) that he was deceived in sales. They said that the tradition of Ibn ʿUmar and the words in it, "except sale with an option", have been interpreted through another version of this tradition in which the words "that he says to his counterpart: 'Choose', " have been recorded.

With respect to the extent of the duration, according to the opinion of those who permit it, Mālik was of the view that it does not have a determined limit in itself, but is determined by the demands of need in the various sales, and it therefore varies depending on the nature of the commodity. He said: "For example, it is a day or two for the choosing of a dress, a week or five days in the selection of a slave-girl, and a month or thereabouts in the choosing of a house". On the whole, it is not permitted according to him to have a longer duration than that required for choosing the *mabīʿ*. Al-Shāfiʿī and Abū Ḥanīfa said that the period of *khiyār* is three days; and more than that is not permitted. Aḥmad, Abū Yūsuf and Muḥammad ibn al-Ḥasan said that *khiyār* is permitted for any period that is stipulated. This was also the opinion of Dāwūd.

They differed about unlimited *khiyār* as distinguished from an option with a fixed duration. Al-Thawrī, al-Ḥasan ibn Jinniyy and a group permitted the stipulation of an absolute *khiyār*, in which the party will have an option forever. Mālik said that an absolute option is permissible, but the *sulṭān* should fix a reasonable period for it. Abū Ḥanīfa and al-Shāfiʿī said that an absolute option is not permissible and it renders the sale void. Abū Ḥanīfa and al-Shāfiʿī disagreed about the case where the option is exercised within three days of an absolute *khiyār*. Abū Ḥanīfa said that if it is exercised within three days it is permissible, but if three days pass the sale becomes void. Al-Shāfiʿī said that it is void in any case.

These, then, are the opinions of the *fuqahāʾ* about the duration of the *khiyār*, namely: Is it permitted without restriction or it is to be restricted? If it is permitted in a restricted form, then, what is its duration? If the unrestricted form is not permitted, then, is it a condition that it should be exercised within three days, or is it not permitted in any case even when exercised within three days?

Regarding their sources, the proof of those who do not permit *khiyār* is what we have already mentioned. The reliance of those who did not permit it except for three days is that essentially *khiyār* is not permissible, thus, it is not permitted beyond what has been laid down in the text of the tradition of Munqidh ibn Ḥibbān or Ḥibbān ibn Munqidh, which is like all the rest of the exemptions (*rukhaṣ*) from the general principles, like the exemption of *ʿarāyā* from (among the cases of) *muzābana* and others besides it. They said that the fixation (of the period of option) for three days was laid down in the tradition of the *muṣarrāt*, that is, the words of the Prophet (God's peace and blessings be upon him), "One who purchases a *muṣarrāt* has an option for three days". The best unbroken chain of the tradition of Munqidh is that related by Muhammad ibn Isḥāq from Nāfiʿ from ʿUmar that the Messenger of Allāh (God's peace and blessings be upon him) said to Munqidh, who was deceived in sales, "When you buy say, 'No deception', and you have an option for three days".

The reliance of Mālik's disciples is (on the argument) that the purpose of an option is the selection of the *mabīʿ*. If that is the case, then, it is necessary that it should be limited by a duration in which such selection is possible, which varies from *mabīʿ* to *mabīʿ*. It is as if the text is laid down as a reminder of this meaning, and it is for them from the category of *khāṣṣ* (particular) by which *ʿāmm* (general) is meant, but according to the first group it belongs to the category of the particular by which the particular is intended.

The stipulation of cash is not permitted, according to Mālik and all his disciples, because of its vacillation between sale and a loan, which is weak. They disagreed about who will be liable (in case of destruction) during the period of the option. Mālik, his disciples, al-Layth and al-Awzāʿī said that (liability for) a calamity is on the seller, while the buyer is a trustee irrespective of whether both have an option or only one of them. It is, on the other hand, said in the school that if it is destroyed in the hands of the seller, then, there is no dispute that he will compensate it, but if it is destroyed in the hands of the buyer, the *ḥukm* is the same as the *ḥukm* of *rahn* (pledge) and *ʿāriya*—if it was due to his negligence, the liability is on him, but if it was not due to his negligence, the liability is on the seller. Abū Ḥanīfa said that if the stipulation of option is for both of them, or for the seller alone, then, the liability is that of the seller, as the *mabīʿ* remains in his ownership; however, if the stipulation is for the buyer alone, the *mabīʿ* shifts from the ownership of the seller but has not as yet entered the ownership of the buyer, remaining suspended till the exercise of the option. It is also related from him that (in the latter case) the buyer has to pay the price and this indicates that the *mabīʿ* has moved to the ownership of the buyer. For al-Shāfiʿī there are two opinions. The better known is that the liability is that of the buyer, whoever possesses the option.

The argument, of those who hold that the liability is that of the seller in each case, is that sale with a *khiyār* is not a binding contract (as yet) and, therefore, the ownership of the seller is not transferred. It is as if the seller says: "I have sold it to you", but the buyer has not as yet said, "I have accepted". The argument of those who hold that the liability is that of the buyer, is based on the analogy of the binding sale, but this is weak due to its being an analogy drawn a disputed point from a settled point. Those who fix the liability to be that of the stipulator of the option, when one has stipulated it and the other has not, argue that if the seller is the stipulator then the option is for him with the *mabīʿ* remaining in his ownership, but if the buyer is the only stipulator then the seller has transferred it from his ownership and vacated it, and it must now move into the ownership of the buyer, if it was the buyer only who stipulated it. He (Abū Ḥanīfa) said: "It moved from the ownership of the seller, because he did not stipulate the option for himself, but it is not necessary that it enter the ownership of the buyer because he stipulated the option to return it to him". This opinion, however, prevents the *ḥukm* (from taking effect), as it is necessary that the liability be on one of them. The dispute refers back to whether option is stipulated for rescinding the sale or for completing it. If we say that it is for rescission of the sale, then, it (the *mabīʿ*) shifts from the liability of the seller, but if we say that it is for its completion, it remains within his liability.

The fifth issue is whether the option for the *mabīʿ* can be inherited. Mālik, al-Shāfiʿī, and their disciples said that it is inherited and if the possessor of the option dies his heirs have the same option as he had. Abū Ḥanīfa and his disciples said that the option is nullified with the death of the person who had it and the sale is concluded. The same is his opinion regarding options in pre-emption, accepting bequests, and *iqāla*. Abū Ḥanīfa conceded them (the other jurists) the option of rejection due to defects, I mean, that he said that it can be inherited. Similarly, in the cases of the right to spoils before division, option of *qiṣāṣ* (retaliation), and the option in *rahn* (pledge). Mālik conceded to them (the Ḥanafites) the case of revocation of what the father gifted to his son, that is, he did not grant the heirs of the deceased the option to reject what the father had gifted to his son according to what the law permitted him, I mean, to the father. Similarly, in the case of *kitāba*, divorce, and *liʿān*. The meaning of the option of divorce is that a man says to another, "Divorce my wife whenever you want", and this man to whom the option was given dies, then, his heirs do not step into his shoes according to Mālik. Al-Shāfiʿī conceded from the options to the Ḥanafites what the Mālikites had conceded, and in addition he conceded the option of *iqāla*, and acceptance of a bequest, saying that they are not inherited.

The reliance of the Mālikites and the Shāfiʿites is (on the argument) that in the first instance rights and wealth are inherited, unless evidence is proffered alienating the right in this context. The argument of the Ḥanafites is that primarily wealth is inherited to the exclusion of other rights, except when evidence is proffered linking rights to wealth. The point of dispute, then, is whether rights are inherited like wealth. Each one of the parties judges by what the rival has not conceded out of these options and what he has conceded, and then argues against the rival. The Mālikites and the Shāfiʿites use as an argument against Abū Ḥanīfa, his conceding the option of rejection due to defects, and hold similar all other options that can be inherited. The Ḥanafites, on the other hand, use as an argument against the Mālikites and the Shāfiʿites what they have disallowed. Each of the parties tries to adduce a justifying distinction where his opinion differs from his main consistent view, and desires to treat the opinion of the rival in the opposite way, that is, making the distinction (applicable) where the rival has a main coherent view and agreeing where the rival makes an exception. For example, the Mālikites say: "Indeed, we have said that the option of the father revoking his gift is not inherited, as that is an option related to an attribute of the father himself and that is not found otherwise, which is paternity, and not an attribute of the contract. It is, therefore, necessary that it should not be inherited". This, then, is the reason for their disagreement in the inheritance of options, I mean, when a thing appeals to one as an attribute of the contract, he allows inheritance, and one to whom it appeals as a specific attribute of the possessor of the option denies inheritance.

The sixth issue is about the person whose option is valid. They agreed about the validity of the option of the parties to the sale, but disagreed about the stipulation of the option for a stranger. Mālik said that it is permitted and that the sale is valid. Al-Shāfiʿī in one of his opinions said that it is not permitted, unless he who has the right to stipulate an option appoints him as an agent. Option is not permitted, according to him, on the basis of this opinion for someone other than the contracting party. It is also the opinion of Aḥmad. Al-Shāfiʿī has another opinion like that of Mālik and Mālik's opinion is also held by Abū Ḥanīfa.

The school agreed on an option for a stranger when both parties to the sale grant it, and his word is substituted for theirs. The school disagreed, however, when one of them grants it and then the seller and the person to whom he granted an option disagree, or the buyer and the person to whom the buyer granted an option disagree. It is said that the verdict is for the conclusion of the sale and the rejection of the opinion of the stranger, whether the seller or the buyer granted him the option. The opposite of this view is upheld by those who consider the option of the stranger as consultation. It is also said that a distinction is to be made between the seller and the buyer, that is, the opinion concluding the sale is to be accepted, and the view of the seller is to be rejected, not that of the stranger, or the opinion of the stranger is rejected and not that of the buyer, if it is the buyer who has stipulated the option. It is also said that the prevailing view is of that person who desires conclusion (of the sale). If the seller desires conclusion and the stranger to whom the seller granted the option desires rejection, with the buyer agreeing with him, then, the prevailing opinion is that of the seller favouring conclusion. If the seller desires rejection and the stranger desires conclusion, the buyer agreeing with him, then, the prevailing opinion is that of the buyer. Similarly, when the buyer stipulates the option for a stranger, then, the prevailing view among them will be of the person who desires conclusion. Likewise is the case of the buyer; yet it is said that a distinction is to be made in this between the seller and the buyer, that is, if the seller stipulates it, the prevailing opinion will be of the person who desires conclusion, but when the buyer stipulates it, then, the prevailing view is that of the stranger, and that is the apparent view in the *Mudawwana*. All this is devoid of strength.

They disagreed about the (case of the) person who stipulates something impermissible along with the option. For example, he stipulates an unknown period or an option over and above three days, according to one who does not permit an option beyond three days, or the option for a person who is far away from the location (of the contract) itself, that is, for a stranger. Mālik and al-

Shāfiʿī said that the sale is not valid (in such a case), even when the irregular condition has been expunged. Abū Ḥanīfa said that the sale is valid after the irregular condition has been expunged. The basis of the disagreement is whether the irregularity occurring in the sale, because of the condition, extends to the contract itself, or is confined to the condition alone. Those who say it extends to the contract nullify it even with the dismissal of the condition, but those who say it does not extend to it, hold that the sale is valid if the irregular condition is expunged, as the sale itself is sound.

XXVIII
THE BOOK OF *MURĀBAḤA* (SALE AT STATED COST PRICE)

The majority of the jurists agreed that sale is of two kinds: *musāwama*, and *murābaḥa*. *Murābaḥa* takes place when the seller declares the price for the buyer at which he had bought the goods, and then stipulates some profit in *dīnārs* or *dirhams*. They (the jurists) disagreed, on the whole, over this on two points. First, over that which the seller can count, and which he cannot count, as a part of the capital of the goods out of the expenditure he made on the goods, after purchase. Second, when the seller lies to the buyer and informs him of a higher price than that for which he bought the goods; or if he mistakenly informs him of a lesser price than that at which he bought the goods and it later appears to him that he bought them for more.

In this book, then, there are two chapters in accordance with the disagreements of the *fuqahāʾ* of different regions. Chapter one is on what is included, and what is not included, in the capital (*raʾs al-māl*), and on the description of the *raʾs al-māl* upon which profit is permitted to be charged. The second chapter is about the *ḥukm* of the excess and shortcoming in the statement of the seller about the cost.

28.1. Chapter 1: Things Counted and those not Counted in the Capital, and the Characteristics of Capital on which Profit can be based

The conclusion of Mālik's school about that which is included in the price, is that whatever the seller is entitled to for the goods over and above the cost is divided into three categories: one of the categories is that which is to be included in the cost and which also has a right to earn a profit; another may be included in the price, but has no share in the profit; and a third category is not to be included in the cost, and also has no share in the profit. Acts that are considered a part of the capital and have a share in the profit are factors that are effective in the essence of the goods, like tailoring and dyeing. Acts that are considered a part of the capital, but have no part of the profit, do not affect the essence of the goods and are those which the seller is not capable of undertaking himself, like transporting the goods from town to town and the renting of stores in which they are stocked. Those which do not fall under either case are acts that neither affect the essence of the goods nor is the seller able to undertake them himself, like brokerage, negotiation, and bargaining.

Abū Ḥanīfa, on the other hand, said that (the cost of) all that is undertaken with respect to the goods is added to the cost of the goods. Abū Thawr said that *murābaḥa* is not permitted except on the basis of the price for which he bought the goods and unless he distinguishes (between the cost and the profit), otherwise it is annulled, according to him, when it takes place as it amounts to falsehood; because the seller says to the buyer that the cost of my goods is so much, when that is not the case. It amounts to misrepresentation (*ghishsh*) according to him.

In the case of characteristics of capital, which are to be communicated, Mālik and al-Layth said about the person who purchases the goods with *dīnārs*, on a day when the exchange rate (*ṣarf*) is known, and then sells them for *dirhams*, when the exchange rate has changed and is now higher, that he has no right to communicate the rate of the day when he bought them for *dīnārs*, as this amounts to falsehood and breach of trust. Similarly, when he has bought with *dirhams* and is selling for *dīnārs*. In this context, the disciples of Mālik disagreed about one who has purchased goods with goods, whether it is permitted to him to sell them by way of *murābaḥa*. If we permit this, then, is it permitted in lieu of the value of the goods or with the goods themselves? Ibn al-Qāsim said that it is permitted to him to sell them for the goods with which he bought, but it is not permitted with value. Ashhab said that it is not permitted to one who has bought goods with any other kind of goods to sell them by way of *murābaḥa*, as he would be demanding goods of the same description from the buyer, who would generally not have such goods and it would result in the sale of a thing not possessed.

Mālik and Abū Ḥanīfa disagreed about the person who bought goods for *dīnārs*, but paid in place of such *dīnārs* other goods or *dirhams*. Is it permitted to such a person to sell them by way of *murābaḥa* without informing him (the buyer) of the form of payment? Mālik said that it is not, unless he informs him of the form of payment. Abū Ḥanīfa said that it is permitted to him to sell by way of *murābaḥa* the part of the goods he bought for *dīnārs* and not those for which he paid with goods or *dirhams*. Mālik also said about the person who bought goods for credit for a period and sold them by way of *murābaḥa*, that it is not permitted to him unless he discloses the period. Al-Shāfiʿī said that if this takes place, the buyer would have a period (of credit) similar to his. Abū Thawr said that it is like a defect and he has the choice of returning the goods. There are under this heading a number of cases, which it is not our purpose to recount.

28.2. Chapter 2: About the *Ḥukm* of Discrepancies Occurring in the Statement of the Seller

They disagreed about the person who bought goods by way of *murābaḥa* at a price that was stated, but it later became evident through acknowledgement or by evidence that the price was less; the goods still being intact. Mālik and a group said that the buyer has an option either to accept the goods at the adjusted price (or to reject them). It is not binding on the buyer to take the goods at the amended price as the seller had not made it binding for him. If, however, the seller had made it binding on him then it is necessary for him to accept them. Abū Ḥanīfa and Zufar said that the buyer has an absolute option and he does not have to accept the goods even if the sale was made binding. Al-Thawrī, Ibn Abī Laylā, Aḥmad and a group of jurists said that the sale remains binding on both of them after the excess has been removed from the price. From al-Shāfiʿī there are two opinions: an absolute option and another making the sale binding after the reduction of the price.

The argument of those who hold the sale to be binding after reduction of the excess is that the buyer has merely profited over the price at which he bought the goods and not beyond that. When a price different to what he had stated became evident it is necessary to revert to what is now true. It is just as if he had taken possession through a determined measure and the measure turned out to be different; it is obligatory that he utilize this true measure. The argument of those who uphold an absolute option is grounded on falsehood in this issue with a defect, that is, the way in which an option is imposed in case of defect is also imposed here in the case of falsehood.

When the goods are consumed (destroyed), however, al-Shāfiʿī said that the excess amount of the price is to be reduced along with the profit due to him. Mālik said, in a disputed narration from him, that if the value of the goods on the day of possession or the day of sale is the same as or less than that weighed by the buyer then the buyer has no recourse to him for anything. If the value is less the seller is given an option to return the value to the buyer, or to return the price, or to go through with the sale at the correct price. When a person sells his goods by way of *murābaḥa* and then produces evidence that the price was more than that stated and he was confused and made an error in this, the goods being in existence, al-Shāfiʿī says that such evidence is inadmissible as he lied, while Mālik says that it is admissible and the buyer is to be compelled to pay that price. This, however, is far-fetched as it amounts to a new sale. Mālik says in this issue, where the goods are consumed, that the buyer has an option between paying the value of the goods on the day of possession or accepting them at the adjusted price. These, then, are the well-known issues under this topic.

The knowledge of the *aḥkām* of this kind of sale are structured, within the school (of Mālik), upon the knowledge of the *aḥkām* of three issues and what is consequential to them: the *ḥukm* of the issue of falsehood; the *ḥukm* of the issue of deception; and the *ḥukm* of the issue of the existence of defects. The discussion of the issue of falsehood has preceded, and the *ḥukm* of return due to defects is the same as that in absolute sales. The *ḥukm* in the case of deception is the granting of an absolute option to the buyer and it is not for the seller to bind him to the sale even when he reduces the price by the extent of the deception, as was the case in the question of falsehood. This is the view of Ibn al-Qāsim. According to Ashhab, deception is divided into two kinds: a kind that affects the price and another that does not. The kind that does not affect the price has no *ḥukm* according to him, while that which affects the price has the same *ḥukm* as that of falsehood.

Things that are consequential are arranged into four issues: falsehood and deception, falsehood and swindling, deception and swindling through defects, and falsehood, deception, and swindling with defects. The principle in the view of Ibn al-Qāsim is to go by the *ḥukm* of that which remains when the *ḥukm* of the other is eliminated, or by the *ḥukm* of that which is preferable according to him when the others are not eliminated, either by granting an option if that is possible or through reconciliation where that is possible. The details of this are suited to the books of cases (*furūʿ*), that is about the opinions of Ibn al-Qāsim and others.

XXIX
THE BOOK OF THE ʿ*ARIYYA* (ADVANCE SALE)

The jurists differed about the meaning of ʿ*ariyya* and about the exemption stipulated for it in the *sunna*. The Mālikī *qāḍī*, Abū Muḥammad ʿAbd al-Wahhāb, related that ʿ*ariyya* in Mālik's school is the donation of fruit of a date-palm or of date-palms by a person, from his grove, to a specified individual. It is permitted to the donor to purchase from the donee the estimated equivalent in dried dates (*tamr*) with four conditions. The first is that the fruit should have fertilized. Second, that it should amount to five *awsuq* or less; it is not permitted if it exceeds this. Third, that the donee should deliver the dates at the time of cutting; if he delivers them on the spot, it is not permitted. Fourth, that the dates delivered should be of the same species as the dates of ʿ*ariyya*. In Mālik's school, the exemption exists only for the donor.

The concession found in it is an exemption from the (the prohibition of) *muzābana*, which is the sale of moist (fresh) dates for dry dates in respect of which prohibition has been stipulated. The exemption also relates to the two kinds of *ribā*, that is, *tafāḍul* and *nasāʾ*, because it is the sale of fruit determined by a known weight for another estimated for equivalence. This involves the sale (exchange) of the same species with a probable excess. It is also the exchange of fruit for fruit with a delay. This, then, is the opinion of Mālik as to what constitutes ʿ*ariyya*, the exemption in it, and for whom the exemption exists.

The application of the exemption in al-Shāfiʿī's view does not relate to the donor alone, but to any person who intends to purchase such a quantity of *tamr* with its estimated equivalent, that is, five *awsuq* or less. It is related that the exemption is dependent on this particular quantity of *tamr* due to the needs of individuals for consuming moist dates. This for the person who does not have moist dates but has *tamr* with which he can buy moist dates. Al-Shāfiʿī stipulates for the delivery of moist dates, with which ʿ*ariyya* is being contracted, that they be delivered immediately. He maintains that if they part before possession, the contract is vitiated.

ᶜAriyya is permissible, according to Mālik, in all things that can be dried and stored, but for al-Shāfiᶜī, it is only permitted in dates and grapes (raisins). There is no dispute about quantities that are less than five *awsuq* for al-Shāfiᶜī and Mālik, but a disagreement is related from them when the quantity is five *awsuq*; both permission and prohibition are related from them, but the well-known opinion of Mālik is about permissibility. Al-Shāfiᶜī, therefore, opposes Mālik in *ᶜariyya* on four counts. First, in the cause of the exemption as we have stated. Second, that *ᶜariyya*, which has been exempted, is not *hiba* (gift), but has been called so metaphorically. Third, in the stipulation of immediate delivery at the time of sale. Fourth, about its subject-matter, for it is permitted according to him, as we have said, only in dates and grapes (raisins) and for Mālik in all things dried and stored.

Aḥmad ibn Ḥanbal agrees with Mālik in so far as he considers *ᶜariyya* to be a gift (*hiba*), but he opposes him in that the exemption is made for the donee, that is, the *muᶜarra lahu* and not the *muᶜarrī*, because he is of the view that it is for the donee to buy from anyone he likes and not the donor specifically, as is the view of Mālik. Abū Ḥanīfa agrees with Mālik that *ᶜariyya* is *hiba*, but opposes him about the nature of the exemption. The exemption, according to him, is not from the category of an exception to *muzābana* nor does it belong on the whole to sale as such, but the exemption relates to the revocation of the gift by the donor as long as the donee has not taken possession of it and is not related, for him, to sale. It is a revocation of a gift of a specific nature in which the donee delivers a counter-value in *tamr* by estimate.

The basis for Mālik's opinion in *ᶜariyya* is that it follows the practice well known in Medina. They said the origin of this is that a person used to give away as a gift date-palms in his grove, but the breaking in by the donee became unbearable for him; so it was permitted to him to sell the date-palms for an estimated equivalent in *tamr* at the time of cutting. His proof about the exemption being specific for the donor is the tradition of Sahl ibn Abī Ḥathma that "the Messenger of Allāh (God's peace and blessings be upon him) prohibited the sale of *tamr* for moist dates, except that he made an exemption in the case of *ᶜariyya* that it be purchased for an estimated equivalent so that the owners may consume moist dates". The Mālikites, however, said that the words "the owners may consume moist dates" are an indication that the exemption is specifically for the donors for it is they who are the owners according to the apparent meaning. It is possible to say that the owners are those who purchased them, whoever they may be, but the word *ruṭab* (wet) does not conform with the situation of the donor. It does conform though according to the opinion of al-Shāfiᶜī, for it is those persons who neither have *ruṭab* nor *tamr* with which they buy them (the date-palms). The argument, therefore, lies with al-Shāfiᶜī.

ᶜ*Ariyya* being *hiba*, according to him (Mālik), the argument is based on literal construction. The experts said that ᶜ*ariyya* is *hiba*, but they disagreed about its denotation with this term. Some said it is so because it is stripped of the connotation of the term price, while others said it relates to the idea of asking for charity, as it occurred in the words of the Exalted: "*Wa at*ᶜ*imu*ʾ*l-qāni*ᶜ*a wa*ʾ*l-mu*ᶜ*tarra*".[145] Mālik stipulated that the delivery of the price should be at the time of cutting, that is, its delay till such time, because it is *tamr* and the law had ordained its return through an estimated equivalent, then it is the practice that it be delayed till cutting as in *zakāt*. This is weak, as it clashes with the analogy from the rule in the *sunna*. According to him, if he delivers earlier, voluntarily, after the conclusion of the contract, it is permitted. The basis for his stipulating its permissibility in five *awsuq* or less is what has been related from Abū Hurayra "that the Messenger of Allāh (God's peace and blessings be upon him) made an exemption in the sale of the ᶜ*arāyā* in less than five *awsuq* or in five *awsuq*". There are two narrations from Mālik about ᶜ*arāyā* in five *awsuq* due to the doubt about the narrator in this tradition. The stipulation of its being of the same species, when it dries up, is based on what is related from Zayd ibn Thābit, as recorded by Muslim, "that the Messenger of Allāh (God's peace and blessings be upon him) made an exemption for the possessor of ᶜ*ariyya* to sell it for an estimated equivalent of *tamr*". Al-Shāfiᶜī's reliance is on the tradition of Rāfiᶜ ibn Khadīj and Sahl ibn Abī Hathma from the Prophet (God's peace and blessings be upon him) "that he prohibited *muzābana* exchanging *tamr* for *tamr*, except in the case of ᶜ*arāyā*, for he permitted them to undertake that", as well as on the words "the owners may consume moist dates". For them (the Shāfiᶜites) ᶜ*ariyya* is limited to less than five *awsuq* of *tamr*, as it was customary, in their view, that a person usually gives away only this amount or even less from his date-palms, and therefore this amount became specific as it was the amount usually given as *hiba* so that the amount of gift should conform with it. He argued for his opinion on the basis of a tradition related through a *munqati*ᶜ chain (i.e. with a missing link) from Maḥmūd ibn Labīd, who himself said to one of the Companions of the Messenger of Allāh, either Zayd ibn Thābit or someone else, "What are these ᶜ*arāyā* of yours?" He (Zayd or the other Companion) said naming some needy persons from among the Anṣār, who complained to the Messenger of Allāh (God's peace and blessings be upon him) that the *ruṭab* season was around but they did not have cash at hand with which to purchase it and enjoy it along with the other people, while they had a surplus of *tamr*. He (the Prophet) made an exemption for them to buy ᶜ*arāyā* with an estimated equivalent of *tamr* that they possessed so that they may consume *ruṭab*. He (al-Shāfiᶜī) did

[145] "Eat thereof and feed the beggar and the suppliant". Qurʾān 22 : 36

not allow delay in the delivery of *tamr* as it amounted to the sale of food for food with a delay.

The basis for Aḥmad's opinion is the apparent meaning in the foregoing traditions that the Prophet made an exemption in ᶜ*arāyā* and did not differentiate the donor from the others. For Abū Ḥanīfa, as *muzābana* was not permissible and if it (ᶜ*ariyya*) was considered a sale it would be a category of *muzābana*, he considered the specification of ᶜ*ariyya* for the donor not as a category of sale, but as the recourse of the donor in what he had gifted to an estimated equivalent of *tamr*. The designation of ᶜ*ariyya* as sale is metaphorical for him. In some of the narrations from Mālik, he also inclined toward such a meaning and did not allow its sale for *dirhams* or for any other thing beside an estimated equivalent, though his well-known opinion is that he permitted this. It is said that this opinion of Abū Ḥanīfa is due to his practice of preferring *qiyās* over tradition that is not *mashhūr*. In this case too he went against the implications of the traditions in different respects; he did not call it *bay*ᶜ whereas the Lawgiver has explicitly called it *bay*ᶜ. And, unlike the text of the tradition here stated "that he (the Prophet) prohibited *muzābana* and made an exemption in the case of *arāyā*", in Abū Ḥanīfa's opinion ᶜ*ariyya* is not an exemption from *muzābana* as *muzābana* is a sale, and he regarded ᶜ*ariyya* as a revocation of *hiba*. It is surprising that it was easy for him to treat it as an exemption from the proscription of revocation of the gift, though no such exemption is recorded from the Lawgiver. But it was difficult for him to exempt it from that in which the Lawgiver has made an exemption, which is *muzābana*. Allāh knows best.

XXX
THE BOOK OF *IJĀRA* (HIRE)

The discussion in this book resembles the discussion in (the Book of) Sales, that is, its fundamental principles are covered through a discussion of its different kinds, their conditions of validity (*siḥḥa*) and vitiation (*fasād*), and through a discussion of its *aḥkām*, those that are specific to one of its kinds and those that are more general being related to more than one kind. The book is, therefore, divided initially into two parts. Part one relates to its kinds and the conditions of validity and vitiation, while part two deals with the identification of the *aḥkām* of *ijāra*. All this, however, is to be discussed after establishing the proof (*dalīl*) of its legality. We shall mention first the disagreement related to this and then move on to the discussion of the well-known issues in these two parts. The intention is to discuss those issues that relate to fundamentals and these are the ones in which disagreement became well known.

We say: *Ijāra* is permissible according to the jurists of all the regions and those of the first period. Its prohibition is related from al-Aṣamm and Ibn ʿUlayya. The proof of the majority are the words of the Exalted, "He said: Lo! I fain would marry thee to one of these two daughters of mine on the condition *that thou hirest thyself* to me for (the term of) eight pilgrimages",[146] and His words, "Lodge them where ye dwell, according to your wealth, and harass them not so as to straiten life for them. And if they are with child, then spend for them till they bring forth their burden. Then, if they give suck for you, *give them their due payment* (*ujūrahunna*) and consult together in kindness".[147] (The proof) from the *sunna* is what has been recorded by al-Bukhārī from ʿĀʾisha, who said, "The Messenger of Allāh (God's peace and blessings be upon him) and Abū Bakr (God be pleased with him) hired a man of Banū al-Dayl, who professed the faith of the *kuffār* of Quraysh, as a professional guide. They delivered to him their riding camels and agreed to meet him at the cave of *Thawr* along with their camels after three nights". Further, there is the

[146] Qurʾān 28 : 27. Emphasis added.
[147] Qurʾān 65 : 6. Emphasis added.

tradition of Jābir "that he sold a camel to the Prophet (God's peace and blessings be upon him), and stipulated riding it to Medina as a condition". And whatever is admissible through a condition is admissible through hire.

The doubt arises, for those who prohibit hire, (by looking at) the contracts of exchange (commutative) in which the delivery of the price becomes necessary through the delivery of the subject-matter (*ᶜayn*), as in corporeal things, while the benefits of hire are non-existent at the time of the contract. This amounts to *gharar* (uncertainty) and the sale of uncreated things. We say: even though they are uncreated at the time of contract, they are usually retrievable; the law has acknowledged those benefits from among these that are mostly retrievable or (the chances of) whose recovery and non-recovery are equal.

30.1. Part 1: Kinds of *Ijāra* and the Conditions of Validity and Vitiation

In this part the discussion is about the species of *thaman* (lit. price, but wages or rent in this context) and the species of *manfaᶜa* (benefits, utility), for which the *thaman* is a counter-value and an attribute. The *thaman* must be something the sale of which is permitted, and a comprehensive discussion of this has preceded in the Book of Sales. Benefits, however, must comprise that which has not been declared unlawful by the law. In all of these issues there are points on which the jurists agreed and disagreed.

30.1.1. The Species of *Manfaᶜa* (Benefits, Utility)

Among those (benefits) on which they agreed as nullifying *ijāra* are: each benefit arising out of a thing prohibited in itself; each benefit prohibited by the law, like female mourners and singers; and each benefit that is a *farḍ ᶜayn* (universal obligation) imposed on man by the law, like prayers and others. They agreed on the hiring of houses, animals, and men for permissible (*mubāḥ*) acts, as well as on the hiring of clothes and rugs.

They disagreed about renting land and water springs, hiring of a *muʾadhdhin* and instruction for learning the Qurʾān, and about the hiring of animals for mating. They disagreed extensively about the renting of land. Some of them did not allow this at all, but they are few. This was the opinion of Ṭāwūs and Abū Bakr ibn ᶜAbd al-Raḥmān. The majority permitted it, but disagreed about the thing with which it could be rented. A group said that renting it is not permitted, except with *dirhams* and *dīnārs*. This was the opinion of Rabīᶜa and Saᶜīd ibn al-Musayyib. Another group said that it can be rented with anything except food whether it grows out of this land or from another land, or with any vegetation in it whether food or something else. This was the opinion of

Mālik and most of his disciples. Some others said that renting of land is permitted with anything other than food. Some permitted the renting of land with all kinds of goods, food, and other things as long as they did not form part of food grown in such land. Those who held this opinion include Sālim ibn ᶜAbd Allāh and others from among the earlier jurists. It is also the opinion of al-Shāfiᶜī and the preferred opinion of Mālik in *al-Muwaṭṭa*ᶜ. A group said that renting it is permitted with anything, including a part of that which grows in it. This was the opinion of Aḥmad, al-Thawrī, al-Layth, Abū Yūsuf and Muḥammad the disciples of Abū Ḥanīfa, Ibn Abī Laylā, al-Awzāᶜī and a host of others.

The reliance of those who did not permit renting of land in any circumstances is what has been narrated by Mālik with its *sanad* (chain) from Rāfiᶜ ibn Khadīj "that the Messenger of Allāh (God's peace and blessings be upon him) proscribed renting through *muzāri*ᶜ (tenancy in land)". They said this has a general (*ᶜāmm*) implication, but they did not refer to the qualification of the narrator related by Mālik. Ḥanẓala is reported to have said: "I asked Rāfiᶜ ibn Khadīj about renting it with gold and silver and he said there is no harm in it". This was related from Nāfiᶜ by Ibn ᶜUmar, who accepted its generality. Ibn ᶜUmar used to rent out his land before this, but gave it up (on hearing this). This is based on the opinion of those who do not think that a general implication can be restricted by the opinion of the narrator. It is related from Rāfiᶜ ibn Khadīj, from his father that "the Messenger of Allāh (God's peace and blessings be upon him) proscribed the renting of lands". Abū ᶜUmar ibn ᶜAbd al-Barr said that they also argued on the basis of the tradition of Ḍumra from Ibn Shawdhab from Maṭar from ᶜAṭāʾ from Jābir, who said, "The Messenger of Allāh (God's peace and blessings be upon him) addressed us and said, 'He who has land should cultivate it or have it cultivated, but should not rent it out' ". These are all the traditions relied upon by those who do not allow the renting of land. They also said, from the aspect of the underlying reason, that letting out on rent is not allowed as it involves *gharar*, because it is possible that a calamity like fire, famine, or flood may hit it and payment of rent would be obligatory even though the tenant has not benefited from it at all. Al-Qāḍī (the author) said it is likely that the underlying reason is compassion for human beings by preventing sale of what Allāh created in abundance, like abundance of land, as in the case of water; an aspect of resemblance between them is that both are natural sources of survival.

The reliance of those who did not permit it except for *dirhams* and *dīnārs* is the tradition of Ṭāriq ibn ᶜAbd al-Raḥmān from Saᶜīd ibn al-Musayyib from Rāfiᶜ ibn Khadīj from the Prophet (God's peace and blessings be upon him) that he said, "Three persons cultivate the land: a man who owns the land and cultivates it himself; a man who has been granted (gifted) the land, and cultivates what he has been granted; and a man who rents it with gold or silver". They said that it is not allowed to go beyond what has been stipulated in this tradition. The other traditions are absolute (*muṭlaqa*), while this is qualified (*muqayyad*), and it is obligatory to qualify the absolute in the light of the qualification.

The reliance of those who permit renting with anything except food, irrespective of whether the food can be stored, is the tradition of Yaᶜlā ibn Ḥakīm from Sulaymān ibn Yasār from Rāfiᶜ ibn Khadīj, who said, "He who has land should cultivate it (himself), or his brother should cultivate it for him, and he should not rent it out for a third or fourth (share) nor for a determined (quantity of) food". They said that this is the meaning of *muḥāqala*, which was prohibited by the Prophet (God's peace and blessings be upon him), and mentioned the *marfūᶜ* tradition of Saᶜīd ibn al-Musayyib in which it is stated that *muḥāqala* is the renting of land for wheat (*ḥinṭa*). They said that it also amounts to the sale of food for food with a delay.

The basis for those who do not allow renting of land with food, or with any other thing drawn from the land, is the same as the basis of those who do not permit renting with food. The proof of prohibition (of renting) with any kind of produce of the land is found in the proscription of the Prophet (God's peace and blessings be upon him) laid down for *mukhābara*. They said that it is the renting of land with some of its produce. This is the opinion of Mālik and all his disciples.

The reliance of those who permitted the renting of land with all kinds of goods, food, and other things produced from it, was on the basis that it is the renting of a determined benefit with a determined thing, and this was permitted by analogy (*qiyās*) on the permission of hiring all other benefits. It was as if they considered the traditions of Rāfiᶜ as weak (*ḍaᶜīf*). It is related from Sālim ibn ᶜAbd Allāh and others about the tradition of Rāfiᶜ that they said, " Rāfiᶜ himself rented out (land)." They said that in some narrations a tradition is reported from him, which should be preferred over all others; he said, "We, the people of Medina, most of us were occupied with agriculture. One of us would rent out his land saying, 'This part is for me and that part for you'. Sometimes one part would yield something, while the other would not, therefore, the Prophet (God's peace and blessings be upon him) prohibited (it for) them". It is recorded by al-Bukhārī.

Those who did not allow renting it for what was produced from it rely on rational arguments and on tradition (*athar*). The tradition is that in which is found the proscription of *mukhābara*. This is in addition to the tradition of Ibn Khadīj from Ẓuhayr ibn Rāfiᶜ, who said: "The Messenger of Allāh (God's peace and blessings be upon him) forbade us a practice that we thought was convenient for us". I said: "What the Messenger of Allāh (God's peace and blessings be upon him) said is right". He said: "The Messenger of Allāh called me and said: 'In what way do you transact the fields?' We said: 'We rent it out on a fourth (share) and for some *awsuq* of *tamr* and barley'. The Messenger of Allāh (God's peace and blessings be upon him) said: 'Do not do this. Cultivate it or have it cultivated or hold on to it' ". This is a tradition that is agreed upon for its authenticity by the two *imāms* al-Bukhārī and Muslim.

Those who permit renting of land with what is produced from it, their reliance is on the established tradition of Ibn ʿUmar "that the Messenger of Allāh (God's peace and blessings be upon him) gave to the Jews of Khaybar the palm-groves and the land of Khaybar on the condition that they work on them with their own resources for half the produce and fruit". They said that this tradition is better than the traditions of Rāfiʿ as their texts are conflicting, and even if the traditions of Rāfiʿ are deemed authentic, we interpret them to indicate mere disapproval, not prohibition. This is so on the basis of what has been recorded by al-Bukhārī and Muslim from Ibn ʿAbbās, who said, "The Prophet (God's peace and blessings be upon him) did not prohibit it, but he said: 'If one of you grants it to his brother, it is better for him than that he should take something from him' ". They said that when Muʿādh ibn Jabal reached Yemen, on being sent there by the Messenger of Allāh (God's peace and blessings be upon him), and found the people practising *mukhābara*, he confirmed it.

30.1.1.1. Hiring a *muʾadhdhin* and hiring for the teaching of the Qurʾān.

A group of jurists did not see any harm in the hiring of a *muʾadhdhin*, while another group considered it reprehensible. Those who deemed it reprehensible and prohibited it argued on the basis of what is related from ʿUthmān ibn Abī al-ʿĀṣ, who said, "The Messenger of Allāh (God's peace and blessings be upon him) said, 'Take that person as *muʾadhdhin* who does not take wages for his *adhān*' ". Those who considered it permissible, held it as analogous to other non-obligatory acts, and that is the reason for the disagreement, that is, whether it is obligatory (*wājib*).

They also differed about hiring for Qurʾānic instruction. Some disapproved it, while others permitted it. Those who permitted it compared it to all the other acts, and argued on the basis of what has been related from Khārija ibn al-Ṣāmit from his uncle, who said, "We returned from a visit to the Messenger of Allāh (God's peace and blessings be upon him) and reached one of the villages of the Bedouin. They said, 'You have come from this man. Do you possess a medicine or a charm, for we have an idiot possessed'. We said to them, 'Yes'. So they brought him and I started reciting over him the *Fātiḥat al-Kitāb* for three days, morning and evening, and collected my saliva and then spitted it out on him. It was as if he had been released from a fetter. They brought me a reward, but I refused saying, 'Not until I ask the Messenger of Allāh (God's peace and blessings be upon him)'. I asked him and he said: 'Take it. Upon my life, there are those who consume on the basis of false charms, while you would be consuming for a legitimate charm' ". They also argued on the basis of what has been related from Abū Sa^cīd al-Khudrī "that the Companions of the Messenger of Allāh (God's peace and blessings be upon him) were on an expedition when they passed by a village of the Arabs, and the people said: 'Do you possess a charm, as the chief of the village has been stung or has been possessed". He said, "One of the men recited the *fātiḥat al-Kitāb* as a charm and the person recovered. He was given cattle (as a reward), but refused to accept them. He asked the Messenger of Allāh (God's peace and blessings be upon him), who said: 'What did you use as a charm?' He said: 'The *Fātiḥat al-Kitāb*'. The Prophet said: 'And what told you that it is a charm?' He later added, 'Accept the cattle and set aside a share for me' ".

Those who disapproved of rewards for teaching of the Qur'ān, said that it belongs to the category of rewards for teaching prayers. They also maintained that the rewards mentioned (in the traditions) do not relate to the teaching of the Qur'ān, but to voicing charms; wages for charms are permitted in our view, whether they are through the Qur'ān or some other means, as they are like other medical treatment. They also maintained that issuing charms is not obligatory on people, while the teaching of the Qur'ān is.

30.1.1.2. Hiring of animals for mating

In the hiring of animals for mating from among camels, cattle, and riding beasts, Mālik allowed that a man may give his animal on hire for impregnating a specified number of animals. It was not permitted by Abū Ḥanīfa nor by al-Shāfiʿī. The proof of those who did not permit it is the prohibition of (charging wages for) the copulation of animals. Those who allowed it, held it similar to all other benefits, but this is weak as it is the preference of *qiyās* (analogy) over transmitted texts. The hiring of a dog is also related to this category, and it is not permitted either by Mālik or by al-Shāfiʿī. Al-Shāfiʿī lays down as a condition for hiring of benefits that they should have an independent inherent value. Thus it is not allowed to rent out fruit for its smell, nor food for decorating a shop, as these benefits cannot be valued independently. This is not permitted by Mālik or by al-Shāfiʿī.

Within this category is the disagreement over the hiring of *dirhams* and *dīnārs*, and on the whole every thing that is not identified by its own essence. Ibn al-Qāsim said that the letting out on hire of this species is not permitted, but this is a loan (*qarḍ*). Abū Bakr al-Abharī and others used to think that it is valid and payment of wages is binding in this. Those who disallowed rent in this, did so as they could not conceive of a utility in this except by consumption (destruction of their essence), while those who permitted it could visualize such a utility, like using them as units of weight and measure or other uses that can be conceived in this regard. These are the well-known disputed issues related to the genus of utility.

30.1.2. The Species of *Thaman* (Rent; Wages)

The disputed issues about the species of the *thaman* are the issues related to what is valid as *thaman* in sales and what is not. Among the prohibitions laid down in this category is the tradition that "the Prophet (God's peace and blessings be upon him) prohibited (wages for) the copulation of animals, for the profession of cupping (bloodletting), and the *qafīz* (cafiz, a dry measure) of the miller". Al-Ṭaḥāwī said that the meaning of the prohibition by the Prophet of the *qafīz* of the miller is that they used to give wheat to the miller to grind in return for a part of the flour that he would produce. They said that this was not permitted in their opinion, as it amounts to hiring of the worker with something that is not possessed, nor is it something that exists as a liability. Al-Shāfiʿī agreed with him (al-Ṭaḥāwī) in this and his disciples said that if a skinner is hired for the skin or a miller with bran or a measure of flour, it is void due to the prohibition of the Prophet about the *qafīz* of the miller. This is permitted in Mālik's opinion, as hiring is for a known quantity of food, and the wages of the miller are a part that is also determined.

Regarding the work of the cupper, a group were inclined toward prohibition, while others opposed them, saying that his work is simply lowly, looked down upon (but not *ḥarām*). Others said that it is permissible. The reason for their disagreement is the conflict of *āthār* (traditions) in this connection. Those who considered it prohibited argued on the basis of what is related from Abū Hurayra, who said, "The Messenger of Allāh (God's peace and blessings be upon him) said, 'The earning of the bloodletter is illegal' ", and also on the basis of what is related from Anas ibn Mālik, who said, "The Messenger of Allāh (God's peace and blessings be upon him) prohibited the work of the bloodletter". It is related from ʿAwn ibn Abī Juḥayfa, who said, "My father hired a cupper and destroyed his cup. I said: 'Father, why have you destroyed it?' He said, 'The Messenger of Allāh (God's peace and blessings be upon him) prohibited the wages of blood' ".

Those who upheld its permissibility, argued on the basis of what is related from Ibn ʿAbbās, who said: "The Messenger of Allāh (God's peace and blessings be upon him) submitted to cupping and paid the cupper his wages". They said that if it had been prohibited he would not have paid him; the tradition of Jābir "that the Messenger of Allāh (God's peace and blessings be upon him) called for Abū Tayba, who cupped him, and asked him, 'What are your wages?' He replied: 'Three *ṣāʿs*'. He then reduced a *ṣāʿ* "; and also from

Jābir "that he (the Prophet) ordered a *ṣāʿ* of food for the cupper and asked his clients to be generous to him".

Those who deemed it reprehensible relied on the tradition which says that Rafāʿa ibn Rāfiʿ or Rāfiʿ ibn Rafāʿa came to a gathering of the Anṣār and said, "The Messenger of Allāh (God's peace and blessings be upon him) prohibited the earning of the cupper and ordered us to feed it to our water-carrying beast". They also relied on what is related from a man from Banū Ḥāritha who had a cupper, and he asked the Messenger of Allāh (God's peace and blessings be upon him) about his work. The Prophet prohibited it. He asked him again and he prohibited it (again). He kept on persisting till the Messenger of Allāh (God's peace and blessings be upon him) said, "Feed his earning to your water-carrying beast and feed your slave on it".

In this category is also their disagreement about renting a house in exchange for residence in another house. Mālik permitted this, but Abū Ḥanīfa disallowed it, perhaps he viewed it as a category of (the exchange of) a debt for a debt, which is weak. These were the well-known issues related to the genera of *thaman* and *manfaʿa*. We shall, however, relate their best-known attributes.

30.1.3. The Attributes of *Manfaʿa* and *Thaman*

The majority of the jurists of different regions—Mālik, Abū Ḥanīfa, and al-Shāfiʿī—agreed on the whole that among the conditions of *ijāra* is that the *thaman* should be known and the *manfaʿa* should be of a determined quantity. This is either accomplished through the purpose, like the sewing of a dress and manufacturing of a door, or by the fixation of time if there is no determined purpose like the work of a labourer. It is also determined by fixing the period, if it is a service, and (by fixing) the derivation of utility associated with the thing, like the renting of houses and shops, or by destination, as in the renting of camels.

The Ẓāhirites and a group of the earlier jurists permitted *ijāra* in unknown things, for example, a person gives his donkey to another who carries water and firewood on it for half of what he earns. The basis for the majority (who prohibited such *ijāra*) is that *ijāra* is a sale and, therefore, uncertainty is prohibited in it for reasons of risk as it is prohibited in sales. The other party rely on the analogy comparing *ijāra* to *qirāḍ* (*muḍāraba*, *commenda*) and *musāqāh* (share-cropping). The majority, however, maintain that *qirāḍ* and *musāqāh* have been exempted by *sunna*, therefore, analogy cannot be constructed on them as they have been excluded from the *uṣūl* (bases of analogy). Mālik and al-Shāfiʿī agreed that if the two parties stipulated benefits that do not have a fixed period of time, but they determined the commencement of the period, which is to follow the contract immediately, then, this is permitted. They disagreed, however, when the commencement of the period is not determined or it is determined but does not follow the contract. Mālik said that it is permitted if the period is determined, but not its commencement, for example, one says to the other, "I have rented from you this house for a period of one year for so much, or for a month with so much", but he does not mention the beginning of the month nor the commencement of the year. Al-Shāfiʿī said that this is not permitted. The commencement of the period for Mālik becomes the time of the conclusion of the contract, but al-Shāfiʿī prohibited it as it amounts to *gharar*; Mālik permitted it as it is known through practice. Similarly, al-Shāfiʿī did not permit it when the commencement of the period was delayed after the contract, but Mālik permitted it. The opinions of his (Mālik's) disciples differed about the leasing of unproductive land, and about subsequent changes in the period of time.

Mālik and al-Shāfiʿī also differed about the period of time to which the benefits are to be limited. Mālik permits this for periods extending over a number of years, for example, a person rents a house for ten years or more, a period in which the house is not likely to change in shape. Al-Shāfiʿī said that this is not allowed for a period of more than one year. The opinions of Ibn al-Qāsim and Ibn al-Mājishūn differed about rain-fed land, land irrigated by natural springs, and land irrigated by wells and streams. Ibn al-Qāsim permitted their leasing for any length of time, even for periods extending over several years. Ibn al-Mājishūn made a distinction saying that the leasing of rain-fed land is permitted for up to a year (at a time), that of land irrigated by natural springs for up to three or four years, and that irrigated by wells and streams for up to a fixed period of ten years. The disagreements here are on three points: the fixation of the time of commencement; the length of the period; and the gap between the time of the contract and commencement.

Mālik and al-Shāfiʿī also disagreed when the duration is not determined, but the rate per unit of time is fixed, for example, a person says to another that he will rent his house for so much per month without limiting the total duration of the period. Al-Shāfiʿī said that this is not permitted. Mālik and his disciples said that it is permitted on the basis of the analogy: "I will sell you the substance of this pile at (the rate of) a *qafīz* for a *dirham*". This, however, is not permitted by others. The reason for the disagreement is the uncertainty resulting in these things and whether it amounts to tolerable *gharar*.

In this category is also their disagreement about (the association of) sale and *ijāra*. Mālik permitted this while al-Shāfiʿī and Abū Ḥanīfa disallowed it. Mālik, however, did not allow anything else to be associated with sale except *ijāra*. Within this category is also their disagreement about the *ijāra* of joint property. Mālik and al-Shāfiʿī said that this is permitted, while Abū Ḥanīfa said that it is not as he considered the utilization of joint property (with other owners) as not being feasible. According to Mālik and al-Shāfiᶜī such utilization is possible with co-owners just like the utilization of the person renting out his share, that is, the *rabb al-māl*. In the same category is the hiring of a labourer for food and clothing; similarly, wet-nursing. Al-Shāfiᶜī declared it to be prohibited absolutely, while Mālik granted absolute permission, I mean, for all types of labour. Abū Ḥanīfa permitted this for wet-nursing alone. The reason for their disagreement is whether it is uncertain *ijāra*. These, then, are the conditions pertaining to the *thaman* and the *mathmūn* (the object of the price).

30.1.4. The Kinds of *Ijāra*.

The jurists consider the kinds of *ijāra* to be of two categories: *ijāra* of the benefits of corporeal property; and the *ijāra* of benefits existing as a liability, on the analogy of *bay*ᶜ. Those that are a liability have description as a condition, while those that are related to a (corporeal) thing have examination or description as conditions, as is the case with sales. According to him (Mālik), the required description is by mentioning of the species and its category for a thing whose benefits are derived directly, while for the thing whose benefits are derived indirectly, for example a loading animal, it is necessary to describe the nature of the mount and the load through which the benefits of the mount are to be derived. In Mālik's opinion a rider may not be described, but according to al-Shāfiᶜī such a description is required. In Ibn al-Qāsim's opinion, if a shepherd is hired for a determined number of cattle, the validity of the contract requires the mentioning of a succession (of cattle), but according to others the whole is implied without stipulation.

One of the conditions of *ijāra* through liability, according to Mālik, is that payment should be immediate so that it is excluded from the category of (the exchange of) a debt for a debt. Similarly, in the *ijāra* of land with uncertain sources of irrigation, he does not stipulate payment till after irrigation. They differed about renting, whether its different kinds involve an option (*khiyār*). Mālik said that option is valid in both kinds of renting, determined and that of liability. Al-Shāfiᶜī said that it is not permitted.

These are the well-known issues falling under the first part of this book, which treats of the subject-matter of the contract, its attributes, and kinds. These are things that resemble the basic elements of the contract. It is through them that the contract is described with respect to the legal conditions of validity and vitiation when it does not conform with them. It remains to discuss the second part, which relates to the *aḥkām* of the contract.

30.2. Part 2: The *Aḥkām* of *Ijāra*

The *aḥkām* of *ijāra* are many, but they are covered in two sections. The first section is about the requisites of the contract and its necessities without the occurrence of other contingencies. The second section is about the contingent *aḥkām*. This section is divided, according to the well-known practice, into the identification of the requisites of restitution and their absence, the identification of the requisites of rescission and their absence, and the identification of the *ḥukm* relating to dispute.

30.2.1. *Section 1: The Requirements of the Contract*

Among the well-known issues of this section is when does it become binding on the tenant to pay the rent if the contract was made general and the possession of *thaman* was not stipulated? According to Mālik and Abū Ḥanīfa, the payment of the *thaman* becomes due gradually in parts in proportion to the gradual acquisition of the benefits, unless this is stipulated (that is, complete payment), or there is reason for prior payment, as for example there is a determined benefit or the rent exists as a liability. Al-Shāfiʿī said that the payment of the *thaman* becomes obligatory on the conclusion of the contract itself. Mālik was of the view that the entitlement to *thaman* arises in proportion to the derivation of the benefit, while for al-Shāfiʿī it was as if he excluded it from the category of the exchange of a debt for debt.

Within this category is their dispute about a person who hires an animal or a house or whatever is similar, whether he has a right to let it out on hire for more than he paid. Mālik permitted this, as well as al-Shāfiʿī and a group of jurists, on the analogy of *bayʿ*. Abū Ḥanīfa and his disciples prohibited this as it amounts to gaining profit without a corresponding liability, and as the liability of the property is being borne by the owner, and also because it belongs to the category of sale of that which is not possessed. Some of the jurists permitted this when the hirer has provided some additional service. Among those who did not consider this reprehensible when it actually occurred in this form are Sufyān al-Thawrī and the majority of the jurists. They were of the view that *ijāra* in this form resembles sale. The renting of a house to a person from whom it was rented, belongs to this category. Mālik said that it is permitted; Abū Ḥanīfa said it is not, and it was as if he viewed the excess in the rent to be of the category of false devouring of wealth. Among these is also the renting of agricultural land for growing wheat, but instead of the original intention he wants to sow barley or that whose burden (on the land) is the same as burden of wheat or less than it. Mālik said that he has the right to do so, while Dawūd (al-Ẓāhirī) said that he cannot do this. Among the issues is also the sweeping of the toilets of the rented house. The well-known opinion of Ibn al-Qāsim is that it is the duty of the owners of the house, but it is also related from him that it is the duty of the hirer, which was also the opinion of al-Shāfiʿī. Ibn al-Qāsim, however, excluded from this the case of inns where the public came and went, and he said that cleaning in this case is the duty of the owner of the house. Within these is also the minor damage to the house: is it binding on the owner of the house to repair it, or is not binding, or is the rent to be reduced accordingly? Ibn al-Qāsim said that this is not binding, while some other disciples of his (Mālik's) said that it is. The cases under this category are many and it is not our intention to elaborate the various cases.

30.2.2. *Section 2: The* Aḥkām *of Contingencies*

30.2.2.1. Chapter 1: Rescission

We say: The *fuqahāʾ* differed about the contract of *ijāra*. The majority were of the view that it is a *lāzim* (binding) contract. It is related from a group, however, that it is a *jāʾiz* contract (terminable at the will of the parties) resembling *jiʿāla* and partnership. Those who said that it is a binding contract disagreed about its mode of revocation. A group of the jurists of the provinces—Mālik, al-Shāfiʿī, Sufyān al-Thawrī, Abū Thawr and others—held that it is revoked by those acts with which all the other binding contracts are revoked, like the existence of a defect or the destruction of the source of the derivation of benefits. Abū Ḥanīfa and his disciples said that the contract of *ijāra* may be revoked due to a disaster suffered by the tenant, as when he hires a shop for trading, but his goods get burned or stolen.

The reliance of the majority is on the words of the Exalted: "O ye who believe! Fulfil your undertakings (*ʿuqūd*)".[148] As hiring is a contract for benefits, it resembles marriage (*nikāḥ*), and because it is a contract of exchange, its essence comprising sale is not revoked. The basis for Abū Ḥanīfa is that he compared the destruction of the means of benefits with the destruction of the thing (*ʿayn*) comprising the benefits.

Mālik's opinion differs when hiring is not of a particular (property), but the benefits are to be derived from a particular species generally. ʿAbd al-Wahhāb said that the preferred opinion of our jurists is that the source of the benefits may not be determined in *ijāra*. If it is, then it becomes a particular attribute and (its contract of hire) is not revoked by its sale or loss, as against the destruction of the hired property. He says that the example is that of shepherding a particular herd of cattle or tailoring a particular shirt; if the

[148] Qurʾān 5 : 1

cattle and the shirt are destroyed, the contract is not revoked and it is up to the hirer to get similar cattle for shepherding or a shirt for stitching. It is also said that these things become particularized by specification and the contract is then revoked if the subject-matter is destroyed. Some of the later jurists said that this is not a dispute in the school, rather they are two cases. The first is that where the source of the benefit in itself may be the object, or it may not be the object in itself. If a particular thing is intended in itself, the contract is revoked if the object is destroyed, as in the case of wet-nursing when the infant dies. If a particular thing is not intended in itself, *ijāra* is not revoked by its destruction, as in the case of shepherding a number of cattle or the selling of food in a shop and in other similar cases. Ibn al-Qāsim stipulated in *al-Mudawwana* that if a person hires for the shepherding of a particular group of cattle, it is not permitted unless the succession (of cattle) is also stipulated. This is an inclination on his part toward the fact that the contract is revoked by the loss of a determined subject-matter. As the opinion on destruction leads to revocation, he held that (such a stipulation) amounts to *gharar*, therefore, he did not permit it without the stipulation of succession.

Similar to this is their disagreement over whether the hire (contract) is revoked by the death of one of the parties, that is, the hirer and the owner. Mālik, al-Shāfiʿī, Aḥmad, Isḥāq and Abū Thawr said that it is not revoked and the contract is inherited. Abū Ḥanīfa, al-Thawrī and al-Layth said that it is revoked. The reliance of those who do not declare it to be revoked is that it is a contract of exchange (commutative), therefore, it is not revoked by the death of one of the parties as its basis lies in sale. The reliance of the Ḥanafites is (on the argument) that death causes the transfer of the actual property from one kind of ownership to another, it is, therefore, necessary that its original basis in sale be invalidated in the property itself with respect to a long duration, that is, it is not permitted. As the assimilation of two contracts is not possible, the transfer of ownership is predominant, otherwise the ownership (rights) shall subsist without there being an heir, which is against consensus (*ijmāʿ*). Perhaps, they held *ijāra* to be similar to *nikāḥ* as both pertain to the derivation of utility and *nikāḥ* is terminated with death. This, however, is far-fetched. They probably argued against the Mālikites only in so far as the rent becomes due in parts in proportion to what is possessed from the benefits. They said that if this so and the owner dies and the *ijāra* subsists, then, the hirer derives a right in the ownership of the heir by virtue of the contract in something that no longer belongs to the contracting party. This is incorrect. On the other hand, if the hirer dies, and the rent remains due after his death, it conflicts with the rule that debts cannot be established against the deceased after his death on the basis of *ijmāʿ*. This (objection) is not valid against the Shāfiʿites, as the entitlement to the rent becomes due, in their view, by the contract itself, as has preceded earlier.

In Mālik's opinion, if rain-fed land is leased and famine prevents its cultivation or sowing so that nothing grows in it due to the existence of famine, then, the lease is revoked. Similarly, when it is flooded by rain till such time that the season of sowing has lapsed and the lessor is not able to cultivate it. All the other calamities that affect the land do not cause a reduction in the rent. According to him (Mālik), in the case of hiring that relates to a fixed time, with the time being the purpose, like the hiring of camels during the days of *ḥajj*, the disappearance of the hirer will rescind the contract. If time is not of major consequence, the contract is not revoked. All this, according to him, relates to the hiring of corporeal things (*aʿyān*). The hiring related to the raising of obligations, however, is not revoked, in his view, by the loss of the thing possessed by the hirer for the derivation of benefits, as hiring has not taken place for a particular thing in itself, rather the contract has taken place by description as an obligation. The cases in this chapter are many, and its fundamental principles are those that we have mentioned.

31.2.2.2. Chapter 2: The Discussion of *Ḍamān* (Compensation; Damages)

According to the jurists, compensation has two aspects: *taʿaddī* (tort, wrongful act, *delict*) and the protection of the interest (*maṣlaḥa*) or the protection of property. Compensation becomes obligatory upon the hirer by agreement in case of a wrongful act. The disagreement is about the kinds of tort that give rise to this, and about the extent of compensation. Among these is the disagreement of the jurists over the verdict for a person who hires an animal for a particular location and commits a wrongful act by driving it to a location beyond that agreed to in the contract of hire. Al-Shāfiʿī and Aḥmad said that he is obliged to pay the rent that is binding on him for the stipulated distance and in addition a fair rent for the distance wrongfully covered. Mālik said that the owner of the animal has an option whether to charge the rent for the distance wrongfully covered or to charge the value of the animal. Abū Ḥanīfa said that there is no rent due from him for the additional distance, but there is no dispute that if the animal perishes in the wrongful journey he is liable for it.

The basis for al-Shāfiʿī is that he has committed a tort on the benefits and is, therefore, obliged to pay fair rent—the rule being the (same as that for) torts in all other benefits. Mālik held that when he (wrongfully) deviated the animal from its proper path he transgressed against the animal itself and thus became a usurper (*ghāṣib*), but this is weak. Abū Ḥanīfa's opinion is absolutely remote from what is required by legal principles. The closest to them, in this case, is the opinion of al-Shāfiʿī. According to Mālik, if the animal should stumble owing to the wrongful act of the owner of the animal, he will be liable for what may happen to the load; similarly, if the ropes are worn. The cases under this category are many.

The jurists who differed about compensation, without there being a wrongful act, did so on account of the interest (*maṣlaḥa*) of the artisans. There is no disagreement, according to them, that the worker is not liable when what he is hired to work on is destroyed, unless he commits a wrongful act. The exceptions are the cases of the carrier of food and the miller, and Mālik holds them liable for what is destroyed in their possession, unless evidence is adduced that the destruction was caused by factors beyond their control. They disagreed about the liability of artisans charged with destruction of articles delivered to them. Mālik, Ibn Abī Laylā and Abū Yūsuf said that they are liable for what is destroyed in their possession. Abū Ḥanīfa said that one who works without wages as well as a personal employee (*ajīr khāṣṣ*), does not compensate, while one who works independently (*ajīr mushtarak*) and for (piece) wages does. There are two opinions from al-Shafiʿī about the independent worker.

The *ajīr khāṣṣ*, according to them, is one who works on the premises of the hirer, and it is said that he is one who does not serve the public, which is Mālik's opinion about the employee and who, according to him, is not liable. The net result of Mālik's opinion is that an independent artisan is liable, irrespective of whether he works for wages. The fixation of liability for the artisans was upheld by ʿAlī and ʿUmar, though ʿUmar differed with ʿAlī on this.

The reliance of those who do not uphold the liability of the artisans is that the artisan is similar to the custodian, the partner, the agent, and the hirer of cattle. Those who hold them liable have no evidence, except from one aspect of *maṣlaḥa* and *sadd al-dharīʿa*. Those who made a distinction between working for wages and not working for wages did so because the worker without wages takes possession of the articles for the benefit of his employer only and, thus, resembles the custodian. If he takes possession for wages, then, the benefit accrues to both of them and the benefit of one in possession dominates. The basic principle is derived from *qarḍ* and *ʿāriya*, according to al-Shāfiʿī. Similarly, in the case of one who did not take due care, there is no (justification in) *sadd al-dharīʿa* in holding him liable. The worker, according to Mālik, as we have said, does not compensate, except that he (Mālik) determined the liability of the carrier of food, and whoever is similar to him through *istiḥsān*; similarly, the miller. All those beside them do not compensate without transgression. The owner of a public bath does not compensate, according to him; this is what is well known from him, but it is said that he does. Ashhab adopted a distinct opinion and held the artisans liable as long as evidence was furnished about the destruction of property in their possession, without there being a tort on their part or negligence, but this is absurd. There is no dispute that the artisans are not liable, unless they have taken possession in their own establishments.

Mālik's disciples differed when the evidence relating to the destruction of the article was established and the liability was discharged, as to whether the artisans were entitled to wages, especially when the destruction was after the completion of the whole work or part of it. Ibn al-Qāsim said that there were no wages for them, while Ibn al-Mawwāz held that they were entitled to wages. The reason for the opinion of Ibn al-Mawwāz was that if the calamity struck a worker his work should not go waste. The reason for Ibn al-Qāsim's view was that the wages are due in lieu of work, and the case resembles destruction because of the negligence of the worker. The opinion of Ibn al-Mawwāz is based upon a better analogy, while the opinion of Ibn al-Qāsim is more inclined toward collective *maṣlaḥa*, as he was of the view that they should share the loss. Within this category is their disagreement over the liability of the owner of a ship. Mālik said that there is no liability for him. Abū Ḥanīfa said that he is liable, except in the case where damage is caused by natural phenomena, like a storm.

The rule in Mālik's opinion is that the artisans compensate all that is caused at their hands like fire, breakage of the article, or cutting, when they are working in their own shops, even if the owner is standing next to them, except where the risk is inherent in the work. For example, in the piercing of jewels, inscribing of gems, flattening of swords, and like the burning of bread by the baker, and the death of the patient through the doctor's treatment; similarly, the veterinarian unless he is negligent, in which case he compensates. If the doctor, and those in similar professions, is qualified and makes a mistake, there is no liability on him for loss of life and the reparation (*diya*) beyond one-third is to be paid by the *ʿāqila*, while less than one-third is to be paid by him. If he is unqualified, he is to be punished with stripes, imprisoned, and made to pay the *diya* from his wealth. It is, however, said that in this case too liability for *diya* is on the *ʿāqila*.

31.2.2.3. Chapter 3: The *Ḥukm* of Disputes

This chapter covers the discussion of disputes and includes several issues. One of these is their disagreement about the dispute between the artisan and the owner of the manufactured article about the shape of the article. Abū Ḥanīfa said that the prevailing statement is that of the owner of the article. Mālik and Ibn Abī Laylā said that the statement of the artisan prevails. The disagreement arises from the dispute as to who is the plaintiff and who is the defendant.

Another issue is where the artisans claim the delivery of the article and the one placing the order denies this. Mālik is of the view that the statement of the customer prevails and the artisans have to produce evidence, as they (the artisans) are liable for what is in their possession. Ibn al-Mājishūn maintains that the prevalent statement is that of the artisans, if the article was delivered to them without evidence (*bayyina*), but if it was delivered with evidence they shall not be absolved without the production of evidence (about delivery to the owner).

If the artisan and the owner of the article disagree about the payment of wages, the well-known opinion in Mālik's school is that the prevailing statement is that of the artisan along with his oath, if he undertakes to do this. If, however, he prolongs matters (and hesitates to swear an oath), then, the prevailing statement is that of the owner of the article. Similarly, if there is a dispute between the lessor and lessee (about rent). It is said, however, that the prevailing statement is that of the artisan and the lessor even when they choose to prolong matters, which is the (correct) principle.

If the lessor and the lessee, or the worker and the hirer, disagree about the part of the period in which the benefits were to be derived, having agreed that benefits cannot be derived in the entire stipulated period, the well-known opinion in the school (of Mālik) is that the prevailing statement is that of the lessee and the hirer as they are the debtors—the principle being that the prevailing statement is that of the debtor. Ibn al-Mājishūn said that the prevailing statement is that of the lessor and the hirer, if the thing from which benefits are to be derived is in their possession, but where the thing is not in their possession, like the worker, then, the prevailing statement is that of the worker.

Among the well-known issues under this chapter are the disputes of the parties in the hiring of loading animals and riding beasts. In these cases the disputes may be over the extent of the journey or its nature, or about the amount of rent or its nature. If their dispute is about the nature of the journey, or about the nature of the rent, then there should be oath-taking resulting in rescission, as in the case of the disputes of the parties to sale about the price. This is so, according to Ibn al-Qāsim, irrespective of the conclusion of the contract. According to others, the prevailing statement is that of the owner of the animal when the contract was concluded and what he had said was probable. If their dispute is about the extent of the journey and it arises before mounting or after covering a short distance, the (dispute is to be resolved) through oath-taking and rescission. If it occurs after covering a great distance or after completion of the distance claimed by the owner of the animal, the prevailing statement is that of the owner of the animal. This is so when he objected and his statement was likely, however, when he did not object and his statement was possible, then, they resort to oath-taking and rescission of the contract of hire as regards the longer journey claimed. The distance covered in the journey as claimed by the owner of the animal is then to be paid to him. Similarly, when he objected and his statement was not probable. If they disagreed about the amount of wages and agreed about the journey, irrespective of his having been paid, the prevailing statement is that of the person hiring, as he is the *muddaʿā ʿalayh* (defendant).

If they disagreed about both things, the journey and the wages, for example, if the owner of the animal says at Cordova, "I rented it out to you up to Carmona for two *dīnārs*", while the person hiring replies, "On the contrary, it was till Seville for a *dīnār*", then, if the dispute occurs before mounting or after a distance where revocation would not harm them, the dispute is resolved through oath-taking and rescission. If (the dispute arises) after travelling a considerable distance or after completion of the journey, which is claimed by the owner of the animal, and the hirer has not paid anything, then, the prevailing statement is that of the owner of the animal about the extent of the journey, and that of the hirer about the price and he is to be held liable for the wages due from Cordova to Carmona as if the contract of hire was up to Seville. This is so as the statement of the hirer was likely. If what he said was not so, while the statement of the owner of the animal was probable, he is liable for two *dīnārs,* even though the hirer claimed to have paid the wages for the longer journey and the statement of the owner of the animal was credible, the prevailing statement is that of the owner of the animal, who can retain the wages that he took possession of and nothing is to be recovered from him as he is the *muddaʿā ʿalayh* for part of it. If he insists that this is his right and more, his statement is accepted to this extent as he has taken possession of it, but not for the excess, while he is absolved of the distance not covered by him, irrespective of the credibility of his statement. If his statement is not credible, the wages are allocated proportionately to the entire distance acknowledged by the hirer out of which the owner of the animal takes what corresponds with the distance claimed by him. This is sufficient under this chapter.

XXXI
THE BOOK OF *JUᶜL* (WAGES)

Juᶜl is *ijāra* in which the acquisition of benefits is probable, like the stipulation of recovery (of the patient) in the case of the doctor, proficiency in the case of the teacher, and the existence of the runaway slave in the case of the seeker (bounty-hunter). The jurists disagreed over its prohibition or permissibility. Mālik said that it is permitted in minor cases with two conditions. First, that a period should not be determined (for the work). Second, that the wages should be known. Abū Ḥanīfa said that it is not permitted, while there are two opinions from al-Shāfiᶜī.

The reliance of those who permitted it are the words of the Exalted. They said: "We have lost the king's cup, and he who bringeth it shall have a camel-load, and I (said Joseph) am answerable for it".[149] They also relied on the consensus of the majority about its permissibility in the case of the runaway slave and requests and also what has been narrated in the traditions about charging wages for using the *Fātiḥat al-Kitāb* as a charm, the discussion of which has preceded. The reliance of those who prohibit it is upon the existence of risk (*gharar*) in it on the analogy of all other kinds of *ijāra*.

There is no disagreement in Mālik's school that the entitlement to *juᶜl* is not established without the completion of the task and that it is not a binding contract. Mālik and his disciples differed, however, under this category, about the renting of a ship whether it is *juᶜl* or *ijāra*. Mālik's opinion that the owner of a ship has no right to rent unless he reaches the destination, which is also the opinion of Ibn al-Qāsim, is based on the argument that it bears the *ḥukm* of *juᶜl*. Ibn Nāfiᶜ, from among his disciples, said that he is entitled to rent to the extent of the distance covered by him, and he associated its *ḥukm* with that of hire. Aṣbagh said that if he is adamant it is *juᶜl*, otherwise it is *ijāra* and he is entitled to wages in proportion to the destination reached.

The discussion under this topic relates to its permissibility, subject-matter, conditions, and *aḥkām*. The subject-matter consists of acts that the *jāᶜil* (person making the offer of *jiᶜāla*) cannot utilize in part. The partial utilization by the *jāᶜil* of the benefits, which are provided by the person responding to the offer, would mean that all the benefits for which *juᶜl* has been contracted

[149] Qurʾān 12 : 72

have not been furnished. We have already said about the *ḥukm* of *juʿl* that if the person does not deliver all the benefits he is not entitled to anything and in such a case utilization by the *jāʿil* of undetermined work without compensating the other person for his work would be unjust. It is for this reason that the jurists have differed about many issues whether they relate to *juʿl* or *ijāra*, like the foregoing example of the ship irrespective of *juʿl* being permitted in it or, for example, *jiʿāla* for the digging of wells. About planting they said that it resembles *juʿl* from one aspect and sale from another. According to Mālik, it is the giving out by a person of his land to another so that he may plant in it a known number of fruit trees. If the trees bear fruit the planter is entitled to an agreed upon part of the plantation.

XXXII
THE BOOK OF *QIRĀḌ* (SPECULATIVE PARTNERSHIP)

There is no disagreement among the Muslim jurists about the permissibility of *qirāḍ*; it used to exist in (the days of) *jāhiliyya* (the pre-Islamic times), and was acknowledged by Islam. They (the jurists) agreed about its form that it is the giving of wealth by one person to another so that he may trade with it (in return) for a defined ratio of the profit that the worker (*ʿāmil*) earns, that is, a part that is agreed upon by both as a third, fourth, or half. (They also agreed) that it is an exemption from the prohibition of the unknown *ijāra* and that the exemption is provided to make things easy for mankind. There is no liability for the worker for what is lost out of the capital (*raʾs al-māl*), as long as he does not transgress, though they did disagree about what amounts to transgression and what does not. Similarly, they agreed generally about not stipulating conditions that may add to the uncertainty of the profit or to the risk (*gharar*) that is found in it, though they did disagree about the conditions that give rise to such additions. They also agreed that it is valid with *dīnārs* and *dirhams*, but differed about things other than these. On the whole, the discussion is about its description, subject-matter, conditions, and *aḥkām*, and we shall note the well-known issues in these in three chapters.

32.1. Chapter 1: The Subject-Matter

The discussion of its form has preceded and they agreed upon it. On the other hand, they agreed about the permissibility of the subject-matter being *dīnārs* and *dirhams*, but differed about goods (*ʿurūḍ*). The majority of the jurists of different regions maintained that *qirāḍ* is not permitted with goods, but it was allowed by Ibn Abī Laylā. The argument of the majority is that when capital is composed of goods it involves *gharar*, as the person takes over the goods when they have a certain value and returns them when they may have another. Thus, capital and profit may be rendered uncertain.

If the capital is composed of that for which goods are sold (i.e. he gives the worker goods that he sells and the capital is formed by the proceeds plus the value of the service that he has rendered in selling them), Mālik disallowed it and so did al-Shāfiʿī, but Abū Ḥanīfa permitted it. Mālik's argument is that he enters into *qirāḍ* with another on the basis of that with which goods are sold (service for selling) and also on the capital resulting from the sale of goods, and this amounts to *qirāḍ* and the utilization of services. In addition, the thing with which goods are sold (service) is uncertain and it is as if he has contracted *qirāḍ* with him for an indeterminate capital. It also appears that he (Mālik) disallowed *qirāḍ* based on the value of goods because it burdens the *muqāriḍ* with sale and because the capital of *qirāḍ* fluctuates. Similar is the case when he gives him goods on the basis of the price for which he bought them, but he (Mālik) is more inclined toward permission and, perhaps, it was this that was permitted by Ibn Abī Laylā. In fact, this appears to be so from their opinions as they related from him that he allowed a man to give to another a dress to be sold on the condition that whatever the profit it will be shared between them; and this amounts to their considering the capital as the price for which he bought the dress. It also appears that if he renders the price as the capital, the *muqāriḍ* can be accused of (readily) confirming the statement of the *rabb al-māl* due to his eagerness to acquire the *qirāḍ* from him.

Mālik's opinions differ about *qirāḍ* formed on the basis of unminted gold and silver. Ashhab has related its prohibition from him, while Ibn al-Qāsim related its permission and also its prohibition in moulded (gold and silver). Al-Shāfiʿī and al-Kūfī[150] also disallowed this. Those who prohibited *qirāḍ* formed on the basis of precious metals associated it with *ʿurūḍ*, while those who permitted it compared it with *dirhams* and *dīnārs* due to the negligible disparity in their market values. The disciples of Mālik also differed about *qirāḍ* with *fulūs* (copper coins). Ibn al-Qāsim disallowed it, while Ashhab permitted it, as did Muḥammad ibn al-Ḥasan (al-Shaybānī).

The majority of the jurists—including Mālik, al-Shāfiʿī and Abū Ḥanīfa—maintain that if a man has a claim for a debt on another, he is not to contract *qirāḍ* with the debtor (for it) unless he takes possession of the debt (amount). The *ʿilla* (underlying reason) according to Mālik is the fear that the debtor might be in financial straits and the creditor desires to delay recovery so as to increase the amount, thus, it amounts to the taking of *ribā*, which is prohibited. The *ʿilla* according to al-Shāfiʿī and Abū Ḥanīfa is (derived from) the rule that what exists as a liability cannot be transformed into a trust (*amāna*).

They disagreed about the person who asks another to recover his debt from a third person and then to use it as capital of *qirāḍ*. Mālik, and his disciples, did not permit this. He was of the view that it increases the burden on the

[150] The reference is apparently to Abū Ḥanīfa.

worker, which is the (added) burden of recovering the loan. This is in accordance with Mālik's principle that the stipulation of an additional benefit in *qirāḍ* renders it *fāsid*. But this was permitted by al-Shāfiʿī and al-Kūfī, who said that he appointed him an agent for recovery and not that he stipulated recovery as a condition for *muṣārafa*. This, then, is the discussion of its subject-matter. Its description is the same as that we have presented earlier.

32.2. Chapter 2: Issues Pertaining to Conditions

On the whole, conditions that are not permitted according to all (jurists) are those that lead to *gharar* or to greater uncertainty. There is no disagreement among the jurists that if an additional profit is stipulated by one of the parties for himself, beyond that on which *qirāḍ* has been contracted, it is not permitted. This is so as it renders the ratio of profit over which *qirāḍ* has been concluded uncertain. This is a basic principle according to Mālik, which maintains that no sale, hire, loan, (additional) work, or facility be stipulated with *qirāḍ* by one party for the other. This is all that they have agreed upon, though they differed in some details.

Among these is the disagreement when the worker stipulates all the profit for himself. Mālik said it is permitted, while al-Shāfiʿī said it is not. Abū Ḥanīfa said that it amounts to *qarḍ* and not *qirāḍ*. Mālik was of the view that it was a favour granted voluntarily by the *rabb al-māl*, as it is permitted to him to take a small part out of a large amount. Al-Shāfiʿī was of the view that it involved *gharar*, because any loss would be the liability of the *rabb al-māl*, and that is where it is distinguished from *qarḍ*, while there would be nothing for the *rabb al-māl* in case of profit.

Another disagreement arises in the case where the *rabb al-māl* stipulates liability for loss on the worker. Mālik said that such a *qirāḍ* is not permitted and it is *fāsid*. Al-Shāfiʿī held the same opinion. Abū Ḥanīfa and his disciples said that the *qirāḍ* is valid, but the condition is void. Mālik's reliance is on the fact that the stipulation of liability is an addition to the *gharar* in *qirāḍ* and it, therefore, becomes *fāsid*. Abū Ḥanīfa associated it with the *fāsid* condition in sale on the basis of his opinion that sale is valid while the condition is void on the basis of the tradition of Burayra, which has preceded.

They also disagreed over the case of the worker (*muqāraḍ*) for whom the owner of capital (*muqāriḍ*) lays down specific requirements, for example, if he should stipulate for him a particular species of goods (for trade), or a particular kind of sale, or a particular location for trade, or a particular kind of people with whom to trade. Mālik and al-Shāfiʿī said about specification of one kind of goods that this is not permitted, unless this kind of goods does not vary at any time throughout the year. Abū Ḥanīfa said that what is stipulated is binding on him and if he trades in other goods besides those stipulated, he compensates the loss. Mālik and al-Shāfiʿī were both of the view that this amounts to a restriction on the worker due to which there is an increase in *gharar*. Abū Ḥanīfa lessened the risk of *gharar* implicit therein. This happens when he stipulates that he should not purchase a particular category of goods, which is binding upon him because of *ijmāʿ*.

Delayed *qirāḍ* is not permitted according to the majority, but Abū Ḥanīfa permitted it, unless they (the parties) rescind it. Those who did not permit it were of the view that such delay is a restriction on the worker, which leads to additional *gharar*, as the goods may accumulate with him and he may be constrained to sell close to the end of the period, thus exposing himself to harm. Those who permitted a period of delay compared *qirāḍ* to *ijāra*.

Within this category is also their disagreement over the permissibility of the stipulation by the owner of capital of the payment of *zakāt* by the worker out of his share of profits. Mālik stated in *al-Muwaṭṭaʾ* that it is not permitted and Ashhab also related it from him. Ibn al-Qāsim said that this was permitted and he too related it from Mālik. Al-Shāfiʿī has the same opinion as Mālik. The argument of those who did not permit this is that it renders the distribution of the shares of the worker and the *rabb al-māl* uncertain, as it is not known what the amount of wealth will be at the time of the obligation of *zakāt*. Further, it can be compared to the stipulation of the *zakāt* of the principal amount on him, I mean, on the worker, and this is not permitted by agreement. Ibn al-Qāsim's argument is that it reverts to a part whose ratio is known even if the amount is not known, as *zakāt* is a known ratio with respect to the wealth of the remitter. It is as if he (the owner of capital) has stipulated for him (the worker) a third of the profits less a quarter of one-tenth, or half less a quarter of one-tenth, or a fourth less a quarter of one-tenth. This is permitted and it is not like the stipulation of the *zakāt* on the capital, as that is known in amount and not in percentage, in which case it is possible that it would cover the entire profit, thus, rendering the work of the *ʿāmil* futile. Is it possible for the worker to stipulate this for the *rabb al-māl*? In the school (of Mālik) there are two opinions. It is said that a distinction should be made between the worker and the *rabb al-māl*, and it is also said that it is permissible that the worker stipulate this for the *rabb al-māl* and it is not permitted that the *rabb al-māl* should stipulate it for the worker. The opposite, however, is also maintained.

About the stipulation by the worker for the *rabb al-māl* of a specified servant (slave or employee), who would have a share in the profits, they differed. Mālik, al-Shāfiʿī and Abū Ḥanīfa permitted it, while Ashhab, from among the disciples of Mālik, said that it is not permitted. Those who permitted it compared it with the case where a person contracts *qirāḍ* with two persons (in one contract). Those who did not permit it consider it as an addition imposed on the *rabb al-māl* by the worker. If the worker stipulates (the inclusion) of his own servant (slave), then, al-Thawrī says this is not allowed and the servant shall have fair wages for the work he has done. This is so as the share of the worker according to him is uncertain.

32.3. Chapter 3: The Discussion of the *Aḥkām* of *Qirāḍ*

The *aḥkām* consist of those which relate to a valid *qirāḍ* and those which relate to a void *qirāḍ*. In the *aḥkām* of the valid *qirāḍ* are those that are the requirements of the contract, I mean, they are dependent on the requirements of the contract, what is disputed is whether they are dependent. Among them are the *aḥkām* of the contingencies occurring in the contract, which are not the requirements of the same contract, like torts, disputes and so on. We shall mention out of these the attributes that have gained prominence among the jurists of different regions.

We begin, from among these, with the requirements of the contract and say: the jurists are in agreement that the contract of *qirāḍ* is not inherently binding and each party has the right to terminate it as long as the *ʿāmil* has not commenced work through *qirāḍ*. They differed when he has begun work. Mālik said it is binding in such a case, and (he also held that) it is a contract that is inherited. If the worker dies and he has trustworthy sons they would be like their father with respect to the *qirāḍ*. In case they are not trustworthy, it is up to them to bring a trustworthy person. Al-Shāfiʿī and Abū Ḥanīfa said that each one of them possesses the right of termination whenever he likes (even after the worker has begun work), and it is not a contract that is inherited. Mālik considered it binding after the commencement of work, as there is harm in it, and he viewed it as a one of the inheritable contracts, while the other party (of jurists) considered the stages before and after commencement of work as the same.

There is no dispute among them that the *muqāraḍ* takes his share of the profits after the entire capital has been employed. (They also agreed that) if he suffers a loss (initially) and then enters into trade making a profit, the profit makes up for the losses. They disagreed about the person who gives to another capital by way of *qirāḍ*, and some of it is lost before the commencement of work, but he uses it in trade and subsequently makes a profit. The worker (now) desires that the part which remained after loss may be considered as capital (so that the profit may not be considered as compensation for the loss). Does he have a right to do this? Mālik and the majority of the jurists said (yes) if the *rabb al-māl* confirms this. If, however, he (the *rabb al-māl*) gives wealth to someone by way of *qirāḍ* and part of it is lost before the commencement of work and then the worker communicates this to the *rabb al-māl*, who confirms it saying that "the remaining is now with you by way of *qirāḍ* on the same conditions", it is not permitted, unless he separates the two, recovers the capital from him, and terminates the first *qirāḍ*. Ibn Ḥabīb, from among the disciples of Mālik, said that it is binding on him (the *rabb al-māl*) to give his approval and the remaining becomes capital by way of *qirāḍ*. This issue belongs to the *aḥkām* of contingencies, but we have discussed it (here) due to its relationship with the time of the obligation to divide (profits), which is one of the *aḥkām* of the contract.

They differed, into three opinions, over whether the *muqāriḍ* has the right of maintenance from the contributed capital. Al-Shāfiʿī said, in one of his better-known opinions, that there is no maintenance for him, except when the *rabb al-māl* permits this. A group said that he has a right to maintenance. This was the opinion of Ibrāhīm al-Nakhaʿī and al-Ḥasan. It was also one of the opinions of al-Shāfiʿī. Some other jurists said that he has maintenance to the extent of food and clothing during travel, but nothing when he is not travelling. This was the opinion of Mālik, Abū Ḥanīfa, al-Thawrī and the majority of the jurists. Mālik, however, said that this is so when the capital is sufficient to bear the burden. Al-Thawrī said that he may charge expenses while proceeding (on the journey) not on his way back. Al-Layth said that he can charge for lunch, but not for dinner. It is related from al-Shāfiʿī that he may have maintenance during illness; however, his well-known opinion is like that of the majority that there is no maintenance for him during illness.

The argument of those who do not permit this is that it is an additional benefit over *qirāḍ* and, therefore, not permitted, the basis being (the analogy of all) benefits. Those who allowed it argued that it was the rule in earlier times. Those who permit it in settlements compare it to a journey.

The jurists of various regions agreed that it is not permitted to the worker to take his share of the profits except in the presence of the *rabb al-māl*, and the presence of the *rabb al-māl* is a condition for the division of profits and the worker's acquisition of his share. It is not sufficient to divide the shares in the presence of witnesses or otherwise.

32.3.1. *Discussion of the* Aḥkām of *Contingencies*

They disagreed (in the case) where the *muqāraḍ* takes his share (of the profits) in the absence of the *rabb al-māl* and then the capital or part of it is lost. Mālik said that if the *rabb al-māl* had permitted him to do this then he is to be believed in what he claims about the loss. Al-Shāfiʿī, Abū Ḥanīfa and al-Thawrī said that he returns what he has taken, which is added to the capital; the excess (profit), if any, is then divided by them.

They also disagreed when the capital of the *qirāḍ* is lost after the worker has purchased goods with it, but before payment is made to the seller. Mālik said the sale is binding on the worker, while the *rabb al-māl* has an option. If he likes, he can pay for the goods a second time and the *qirāḍ* will continue between them on the conditions they had stipulated; or if he likes he may withdraw from it. Abū Ḥanīfa said that this sale is binding on the *rabb al-māl* as in the case of the agent (*wakīl*). He said, however, that the capital of this *qirād* would be equivalent to the two prices (payments), and the profits would not be divided until this (amount) is acquired, I mean, the price of the goods that was destroyed initially and the price that became obligatory on him after that.

They differed about sale by the worker of some goods of the *qirāḍ* to the *rabb al-māl.* Mālik considered it reprehensible, while Abū Ḥanīfa permitted it without qualification. Al-Shāfiʿī permitted it on the condition that they contract the sale in a manner that would not indicate cheating indulged in by people. Mālik's reason for considering it reprehensible is that he (the worker) would make a concession to him in the goods as he (the *rabb al-māl*) has contracted *qirāḍ* with him. It would be as if the *rabb al-māl* has acquired a benefit from the worker beside the stipulated profit.

I do not know of any disagreement among the *fuqahāʾ* of different regions when the worker hires (transport) for goods up to a town and the rent absorbs the entire value of the goods leaving an excess, that this would be the liability of the worker and not the *rabb al-māl*, as the *rabb al-māl* has given him his wealth for trade and any loss in the wealth would be on him, so also whatever exceeds the wealth and absorbs it. They disagreed about the worker who borrows money and trades with it along with the wealth of the *qirāḍ*. Mālik said that this is not permitted. Al-Shāfiʿī and Abū Ḥanīfa said that it is permitted and the profit would be shared between them as stipulated. Mālik's argument is that just as it is not permitted to loan out the (wealth of the) *qirāḍ*, it is not permitted to take loans for it.

They differed over whether the worker is permitted to sell on credit, if the *rabb al-māl* has not allowed him to do so. Mālik said that he has no right to do this; if he does it he is liable. This was also the opinion of al-Shāfiʿī. Abū Ḥanīfa said that he has the right to do so. All of them agreed that it is obligatory on the worker to act under the contract of *qirāḍ* as people generally do in the majority of the cases. Thus, those who were of the view that selling on credit is beyond the ambit of what people generally do, did not permit it, while those who consider it within the usual practice permitted it.

Mālik, al-Shāfiʿī, Abū Ḥanīfa and al-Layth disagreed about the worker who mixes up his own wealth with that of the *qirāḍ*, without the permission of the *rabb al-māl.* All of them, except Mālik, said that it amounts to a transgression and he is to be held liable. Mālik said that it is not wrongful. These well-known jurists of different regions did not differ about the worker who gives out the wealth of the *qirāḍ* to another worker (*muqāraḍ*) and held that he is liable in case of loss, but if there is a profit it is shared (first) as stipulated and then the worker who entered the contract as the third person gets his share out of what remains with him. Al-Muzanī relating from al-Shāfiʿī says that he (the third person) gets nothing except fair wages, as he was working under a void agreement.

32.3.2. *Discussion of the Void* Qirāḍ

The *ḥukm* of the void *qirāḍ*, they agreed, is revocation and the return of the wealth to its owner, unless it has been used in the work. They disagreed into different opinions about what is due to the worker for his work, when the capital is consumed in work. First, that it reverts to a "reasonable" *qirād* (for purposes of distribution of profits). This is the narration of Ibn al-Mājishūn from Mālik. It is also his own opinion and that of Ashhab. Second, it reverts entirely to a reasonable contract of hire. This is the opinion of al-Shāfiʿī, Abū Ḥanīfa and ʿAbd al-ʿAzīz ibn Abī Salama one of the disciples of Mālik; it is related by ʿAbd al-Wahhāb that it is also a narration from Mālik. Third, it reverts to a similar *qirāḍ*, unless it is in more than what was agreed upon. He gets less than what was agreed upon or less than what is determined through a similar *qirāḍ*, if it was the *rabb al-māl* who stipulated the conditions for the *muqāraḍ*, but if it was the *muqāraḍ* who stipulated the condition by virtue of which the *qirāḍ* was annulled, then he gets more than a similar *qirāḍ* or he gets the share that was stipulated for him. This opinion is derived from a narration from Mālik. Fourth, it reverts to a similar *qirāḍ* for each benefit that was stipulated by one of the parties for their mutual benefit and which is not specific to one of them, and it reverts to a reasonable *ijāra* for each benefit that was stipulated by a party for himself and that does not relate to *māl* and also in the case of a *qirāḍ* becoming void by virtue of risk and uncertainty. This is the opinion of Muṭarrif ibn Nāfiʿ, Ibn ʿAbd al-Ḥakam and Aṣbagh; it was preferred by Ibn Ḥabīb.

Ibn al-Qāsim's opinions differ about void *qirāḍs*. In some cases, which form the majority, he said that in it there are fair wages, while in others he said that it becomes a reasonable *qirād*. The jurists differed in the interpretation of his opinions. Among them are those who interpreted the conflict of his opinions to indicate the distinction drawn by Ibn ʿAbd al-Ḥakam and Muṭarrif, which was also preferred by Ibn Ḥabīb and is the preferred view of my grandfather (God bless him). Among them are those who did not derive an underlying reason for his opinions and said that his opinion is that there are fair wages in each void *qirāḍ*, except in those cases where it was explicitly stated that there is reasonable *qirāḍ*, which are seven: *qirāḍ* with goods, with liability, with a period of delay, *qirāḍ* with ambiguity, where he asked him (the worker) to act along with other partners in the wealth, where the parties differed and came with clear claims due to which they were asked to take oaths, and where he was given money to buy on credit but he bought with cash or was asked to buy particular goods or non-existent goods and he acted contrary to what was required. All these issues can be referred to a common underlying cause, otherwise it amounts to a conflict in the opinions of Ibn al-Qāsim.

ʿAbd al-Wahhāb related a distinction drawn by Ibn al-Qāsim that if the (cause of) *fasād* is in the the contract, it reverts to a reasonable *qirāḍ*, but if it is due to an addition stipulated by one party against the other, it reverts to fair wages. It appears, however, that the reverse is correct. The difference between fair wages and reasonable *qirāḍ* is that wages are linked to the liability of the *rabb al-māl* irrespective of the existence of profit, while reasonable *qirāḍ* follows the customary practice of *qirāḍ*; if there is profit in it the worker will get something otherwise there is nothing for him.

32.3.3. ;.*Discussion of Disputes of the Parties to* Qirāḍ

The jurists differ about the dispute of the worker and the *rabb al-māl* over the amount of share for which they contracted *qirāḍ*. Mālik said that the worker's claim should be accepted as he is trusted by virtue of the contract. Likewise, all his claims that appear to be credible. Al-Layth said that it is to be converted to a reasonable *qirāḍ*, which is also the opinion of Mālik when the claim he brings does not arouse suspicion. Abū Ḥanīfa and his disciples said that the acceptable statement is that of the *rabb al-māl*, which was also the opinion of al-Thawrī. Al-Shāfiʿi says that they take oaths and revoke (the contract), and for the worker there are fair wages.

The reason for the disagreement of Mālik and Abū Ḥanīfa is their dispute over the basis for the stipulation of the obligation of oath for the defendant in the text; is it because he is a defendant or because he has a stronger claim. He who said that it is so because he is a defendant gave preference to the statement of the *rabb al-māl*, while he who said that he is one who generally has a stronger claim maintained that the acceptable statement is that of the worker, as he is to be trusted. Al-Shāfiʿī compared their dispute with that of the parties to sale over the price of goods. This suffices under the chapter.

XXXIII
THE BOOK OF *MUSĀQĀH* (CROP SHARING)

The discussion of *musāqāh* deals first with its permissibility; second, with the identification of (the causes of) its vitiation and validity; and third, with its *aḥkām*.

33.1. Chapter 1: Discussion of its Permissibility

The majority of the jurists—Mālik, al-Shāfiʿī, al-Thawr, Abū Yūsuf and Muḥammad ibn al-Ḥasan, the disciples of Abū Ḥanīfa, Aḥmad, and Dāwūd—are in favour of its permissibility. It is, for them, an exemption based on *sunna* from the prohibition of the sale of uncreated things and from uncertain *ijāra*. Abū Ḥanīfa said that *musāqāh* is not permitted at all.

The reliance of the majority for its permissibility is the established tradition of Ibn ʿUmar "that the Messenger of Allāh (God's peace and blessings be upon him) gave to the Jews of Khaybar the palm-groves and land of Khaybar on the condition that they would work on it with their wealth, and for the Messenger of Allāh (God's peace and blessings be upon him) would be a share of its produce". This is recorded by al-Bukhārī and Muslim. In some of its narrations it says "the Prophet (God's peace and blessings be upon him) transacted *musāqāh* with them on the basis of half the produce of land and fruit". (Their reliance is also on) what has been related by Mālik from the *mursal* of Saʿīd ibn al-Musayyib that the Messenger of Allāh (God's peace and blessings be upon him) said to the Jews of Khaybar on the day Khaybar was occupied: "I allow you to settle where Allāh has settled you on the condition that the dates (*tamr*) are to be shared between us". He said that the Messenger of Allāh used to send ʿAbd Allāh ibn Rawāḥa, who used to estimate the division between him and them and then say: "If you like, this is for you and if you like, this is for me". So also his *mursal* from Sulaymān ibn Yasār to the same effect.

The reliance of Abū Ḥanīfa, and of those who held a similar opinion, is upon the clash of this tradition with the principles, along with the fact that it comprises a *ḥukm* specific to the Jews. Further, the permission for the Jews to stay could be interpreted to mean that they were (now) slaves or it could be interpreted to mean that they were *dhimmīs*. (They said that) even if we concede that they were *dhimmīs*, it still clashes with the principles, because it amounts to the sale of uncreated things, and it belongs to (the category of) *muzābana*, which is the sale of dates for dates with an increase, as division by estimate is an estimated sale. They adduced the evidence that it is a sale that opposes principles on the basis of what has been related in the tradition of ʿAbd Allāh ibn Rawāḥa, who used to say to them at the time of estimating the division: "If you like, this is for you, but you guarantee the share of the Muslims, and if you like, it is for me and I guarantee your share". This (they said) is *ḥarām* by consensus (*ijmāʾ*). Perhaps, they said that the prohibition of *mukhābara* is related to the occurrence of this transaction at Khaybar, while the majority are of the opinion that *mukhābara* is the renting of land with part of its produce. They said that the indication of the abrogation of this tradition, or that it is specific to the Jews is in the authentic tradition of Rāfiʾ, and others, about the "prohibition of the renting of land for what is produced in it". This is so as *musāqāh* implies its legality. Further, it is specific (to the Jews) in some of the narrations of the tradition of *musāqāh*. The addition, therefore, has not been reported by Mālik or by al-Shāfiʿī, I mean, the report that "the Prophet (God's peace and blessings be upon him) transacted *musāqāh* with them on the basis of half the produce of land and its fruit". It is, however, an authentic addition as confirmed by the Ahl al-Ẓāhir.

33.2. Chapter 2: Discussion of the Validity (*Ṣiḥḥa*) of *Musāqāh*

The examination of its validity is the examination of its integral elements, its time, and its conditions stipulated within the elements. It has four elements: the subject-matter specific to it; the part (of the produce) for which it is transacted; the nature of the work that is agreed to; and the period for which it is permitted and agreed upon.

33.2.1. Element 1: The Subject-Matter of *Musāqāh*

They disagreed about the subject-matter of *musāqāh*. Dāwūd said that *musāqāh* is valid only in date-palms, while al-Shāfiʿī said it is valid in date-palms and grape-vines alone. Mālik said that it is valid in deep-rooted trees like pomegranates, figs, olives, and what is similar to them with no stipulation of necessity. It is also valid in others that are not deep-rooted (shrubs) like water melons, if the owner is unable to care for them. Similarly, in crops. It is not permitted in any kind of vegetables, according to all of them, except Ibn Dīnār who permitted it at the time of sprouting before plucking.

The reliance of those who restricted it to date-palms is that it is an exemption; it is, therefore, necessary that it should not be extended beyond the subject-matter mentioned in the *sunna*. Mālik was of the view that it is an exemption in which a general purpose can be found and it must be extended to other things. According to a group of jurists, it is possible to draw analogies from exemptions if underlying causes, more general than the things with which exemptions are linked, can be understood. Another group disallowed *qiyās* on the basis of exemptions. Dāwūd disallows *qiyās* (analogy) in its entirety, therefore *musāqāh* on the basis of his principles is limited. Al-Shāfiʿī permitted it in vineyards due to the fact that the *ḥukm* in *musāqāh* is based on estimate. It is stated in the tradition of ʿAttāb ibn Usayd that the *ḥukm* requires estimation in date-palms and grape-vines, though that was for purposes of *zakāt*. It was as if he compared *musāqāh* to *zakāt*. The tradition that came down from ʿAttāb ibn Usayd was "that the Messenger of Allāh (God's peace and blessings be upon him) sent him and ordered him to estimate the grapes and pay their *zakāt* in raisins, just as the *zakāt* of date-palms is paid in dates". The tradition of ʿAttāb ibn Usayd was rejected by Dāwūd as it is *mursal*, and was related through ʿAbd al-Raḥmān alone, who is not reliable.

When there is with the date-palms uncultivated or crop-bearing land, they differed whether it is permitted to water the land along with the date-palms (in exchange) for a section of the date-palms or for a section of the date-palms and a part of the produce of the land. A group was inclined toward its permissibility, which was the opinion of the disciples of Abū Ḥanīfa and of al-Layth, Aḥmad, al-Thawrī, Ibn Abī Laylā and a group of jurists. Al-Shāfiʿī and the Ahl al-Ẓāhir said that it is not permitted except in the case of *tamr*. Mālik said that if the land is dependent on the fruit, and the fruit is the major part of it, there is no harm in including it in the *musāqāh* irrespective of the stipulation of a share external to it. This share was limited by him to a third or less than it, I mean, that the amount of rent should be a third of the fruit or less than it. He also did not permit that the owner of the land should stipulate that he should cultivate the barren land for himself, as it is an additional stipulation. Al-Shāfiʿī said that this is permissible.

The proof of those who permitted *musāqāh* in both collectively, I mean, for the land for a part of its produce, is the tradition of Ibn ʿUmar that has preceded. The proof of those who did not permit it is what is related of the prohibition about renting land for a part of its produce in the tradition of Rāfiʾ ibn Khadīj. This too has preceded. Aḥmad ibn Ḥanbal said the the text of the tradition of Rāfiʾ is confused and the tradition of Ibn ʿUmar is more authentic. Its restriction by Mālik to a third is weak, and it is *istiḥsān* based on extraneous sources as the sources require that no distinction be made between the permitted and prohibited or between more or less in the same genus.

Among these (issues) is their disagreement about *musāqāh* in vegetables. Mālik, al-Shāfiʿī and his disciples, Muḥammad ibn al-Ḥasan and Al-Layth said that *musāqāh* is not allowed in vegetables. The majority allowed it as the worker, though he does not have to water them, has other tasks to do like grafting and so on. Al-Layth was of the view that watering is the act for which the contract of *musāqāh* is concluded, and because of which the exemption was laid down.

33.2.2. **Element 2: The Nature of the Work**

The jurists on the whole are in agreement that the obligation of the worker is watering and grafting for fertilization. They differed as to who was responsible for harvesting, the making of fences, cleaning of pools, and the (maintenance and operation of the) irrigating water-wheel. Mālik stated in *al-Muwaṭṭaʿ* that according to the practice in *musāqāh* it is permitted to the owner of the grove to stipulate the building of fences, cleaning of springs, watering and grafting for fertilization, the cutting of palm-boughs, clipping of fruit, and all other similar things for the worker. This is a statement from which it is understood that these things are included in *musāqāh* when stipulated, though it is possible to comprehend their inclusion through the (basic) contract itself. Al-Shāfiʿī said that the building of fences is not his responsibility, as it is not something that affects the fruit harvest, like watering and irrigation. Muḥammad ibn al-Ḥasan said that the cleaning of water-wheels and streams is not his responsibility. Mālik and al-Shāfiʿī maintained that cutting is the responsibility of the worker, though Mālik said that if the worker stipulates it for the *rabb al-māl* it is permitted, while al-Shāfiʿī said that this is not allowed and the *musāqāh* is vitiated if he does. Muḥammad ibn al-Ḥasan said that cutting is shared equally between them. The systematizers among the disciples of Mālik said that the work in a palm-grove is of two types: work that is not effective in the growth of fruit, and work that is effective. The work that is effective in growth of fruit includes the kind that is permanent and continues after the maturity of fruit. It also includes that which does not persist after the fruit. The kind that is not effective in the growth of fruit does not form part of *musāqāh* either through the contract itself or by stipulation, except for minor things. Anything which is effective in the growth of fruit and continues after it is included by stipulation, according to Mālik, and not by the contract itself, like the digging of a well, the making of reservoirs of water, undertaking plantation, making of boxes in which plucked fruit is gathered. Anything which is effective in the growth of fruit and is not permanent is binding through the contract itself. This is like digging, watering, trimming of grapevines, pruning of trees, fertilization, uprooting, and what resembles these.

They agreed that the worker has no right to whatever is part of the orchard, like animals or slaves. They differed if the worker were to stipulate this in the agreement with the owner. Mālik said that this is permissible in case of those things that were present in the orchard before the (conclusion of) *musāqāh*, but if he stipulates it for those not there it is not permitted. Al-Shāfiʿī said that there is no harm in this even when they are not present in the grove. This was also the opinion of Ibn Nāfiʾ from among the disciples of Mālik. Muḥammad ibn al-Ḥasan said that it is not permitted to the worker to stipulate this for the *rabb al-māl*, but if the *rabb al-māl* stipulates this for the worker it is permitted. The reason for his disapproval of this is the uncertainty that is associated with the share of the *rabb al-māl* because of it. Those who permitted it viewed it as insignificant and minor. It was because of the vacillation of the *ḥukm* between these two principles that Mālik permitted, through *istiḥsān*, the stipulation of slaves who were already working in the grove, but disallowed it in the case of additional slaves as the stipulation of an extra benefit through this is apparent. Muḥammad ibn al-Ḥasan, however, made a distinction in the stipulation of both things for the worker as they belong to the category of work that is obligatory in *musāqāh*, which is working with his hands. The upholders of *musāqāh* are in agreement that if the entire expenditure is borne by the owner of the orchard and the worker is to work with his hands alone, this is not permitted, as it amounts to *ijāra* for uncreated things. These, then, are the attributes of the first element and the distinction between the conditions permitted and those not permitted.

33.2.3. **Element 3: The Share Agreed upon**

They agreed that *musāqāh* is permitted with whatever they agree upon as the share of the fruit. Mālik allowed that all the fruit be for the worker, as he did in *qirāḍ*. It is said that this is a grant and not *musāqāh*. It is also said that it is not permitted. It is agreed that it is not permitted to stipulate in it any additional benefit, like the stipulation by one of the parties for the other an addition in terms of *dirhams* or *dīnārs*. Nor is it permitted to stipulate anything outside the ambit of *musāqāh*, except for minor things like the building of fences and repairing of water reservoirs. It is also not permitted, according to Mālik, to water two orchards at the same time, each for a different share. He argued on the basis of the act of the Prophet (God's peace and blessings be upon him) in the matter of Khaybar, where he gave out different groves for watering for the same share. In this there is dispute.

Most of the jurists maintained that the division of the fruit between the worker and the owner cannot take place except by measure, just as in *sharika* (partnership), and that it is not permitted to do it by estimate, but a group permitted its division by estimate. The disciples of Mālik differed in this, and the narrations from him also differ. It is said that it is permitted, but it is also said that it is not permitted in usurious fruit and is permitted in others. Again, it is said that it is permitted without qualification, in accordance with the varying needs of the parties. The argument of the majority is that it involves vitiation from the aspect of *muzābana*, and it is related to the sale of fresh dates for *tamr*, and to the sale of food for food with a delay. The argument of those who permitted its division by estimate is its similarity with *ʿariyya*, and with estimation in *zakāt*, which is weak. The strongest evidence on which they relied for this is what is laid down about estimation in the *musāqāh* at Khaybar in the *mursal* tradition of Saʿīd ibn al-Musayyib and ʿAṭāʾ ibn Yasār.

33.2.4. **Element 4: The Element of Time**

The stipulation of time in *musāqāh* is of two types: time that is a condition for its permissibility, and time that is a condition for the validity of the contract, which determines its duration. With respect to time that is a condition for the permissibility of its contract, the jurists are agreed that it is the time before ripening. They disagreed about its permissibility after ripening. The majority of those who uphold *musāqāh* maintained that it is not permitted after ripening. Saḥnūn from among the disciples of Mālik said that there is no harm in it. The opinion of al-Shāfiʿī differed on this. On one occasion he said that it is not permitted, while on another he said it is. It is reported from him that he said it is not permitted once the fruit comes into existence.

The reliance of the majority is on the argument that there is nothing to do once the fruit has ripened, and there is no necessity for *musāqāh*, as that is the time when it can be sold. They said that it then amounts to *ijāra*, if it does take place. The argument of those who permitted it is that if it is permitted before the existence of fruit, its permission after ripening lies on firmer ground. It is due to this that *musāqāh* is not permitted in vegetables, because it is then saleable, according to them, I mean according to the majority.

The majority maintain that (stipulation of a) time (period) that is a condition for the duration of the *musāqāh* should not be left uncertain, that is, for an undetermined period. A group, and among them are the Ẓāhirites, permitted it for an unlimited period. The reliance of the majority is on the argument that it involves *gharar* on the analogy of *ijāra*. The reliance of the Ahl al-Ẓāhir is on what is stated in the *mursal* of Mālik about the saying of the Prophet (God's peace and blessings be upon him): "I allow you to settle where Allāh has settled you".

Mālik disapproved the *musāqāh* that extended over an unspecified number of years, in which the termination of the years is based on periodical cutting not on determined periods. They differed over the stipulation of special terminology for this contract. Ibn al-Qāsim maintained that among the conditions of its validity is that it should not be concluded without the word '*musāqāh*,' and that it is not concluded with the word '*ijāra*', which was the opinion of al-Shāfiʿī. Others said that it may be concluded by the use of the term *ijāra* and this is similar to the opinion of Saḥnūn.

33.3. Chapter 3: Discussion of the *Aḥkām* of Validity

Musāqāh, according to Mālik, is one of those contracts that become binding merely through words (agreement) not with (the commencement of) work, unlike the case of *qirāḍ* in his view, which is concluded through work not words. It is also, in Mālik's view, an inheritable contract and it is the responsibility of the heirs of the worker, if they are not trustworthy themselves, to bring a trustworthy person to work, who shall be responsible for the work if the heirs refuse to accept his estate. Al-Shāfiʿī said that if he has not left an estate, the *rabb al-māl* will pay wages to the heirs for the work he had done and the contract will be revoked, but if he has left an estate, *musāqāh* will be binding on him. Al-Shāfiʿī said that the contract is revoked in the case of inability; however, he did not elaborate. Mālik said that if he is incapacitated and the time of sale is near, the owner does not have the right to make a contract with another person, rather it is obligatory on him to hire someone who will do the work. If he is penniless, the hiring shall be done from the worker's share of fruit.

If the worker is found to be a thief or is dishonest, the contract is not rescinded according to Mālik. It is related from al-Shāfiʿī that he said that it is binding on him (the owner) to appoint someone else for the work. Al-Shāfiʿī also said that if the worker runs away before the completion of work, it is for the *qadī* to hire someone who will do his work. It is permitted, according to Mālik, that each one of them stipulates, unlike *qirāḍ*, the payment of *zakāt* and their *niṣāb* (scale for computation), according to him, is like the *niṣāb* of a single person as against his opinion in the case of partners (*shurakāʾ*). If the *rabb al-māl* and the worker differ about the amount of fruit yielded by the *musāqāh*, then, in Mālik's view, the acceptable statement is that of the worker along with his oath, if he comes forth with a credible claim. Al-Shāfiʿī said that both take oaths and revoke the contract, and for the worker there are wages similar to those in sale. Mālik made the oath obligatory in the case of the worker as he is a trusted party, and it is a principle with him that oath is obligatory on the stronger claimant.

The details of this chapter are many, but those in which the disagreement of the jurists became well known are the ones we have mentioned.

33.4. Chapter 4: The *Aḥkām* of the Void *Musāqāh*

They agreed that once *musāqāh* has been concluded in a manner that is not lawful, it is revoked, as long as it is not invalidated through (after) work. They disagreed, when it is invalidated through work, about what is obligatory in it. It is said that it reverts to a "reasonable" *ijāra* in each kind of invalidation, which is the analogical opinion of al-Shāfiʿī and is also one of the narrations from Mālik. It is also said that it reverts to a "reasonable" *musāqāh* without qualifications, which is the opinion of Ibn al-Mājishūn as well as his narration from Mālik.

Ibn al-Qāsim held that in some of the cases it reverts to "reasonable" *musāqāh*, while in others it reverts to "reasonable" *ijāra*. His interpretation in these cases, as reported, has differed. It is said that it reverts, in his opinion, to fair wages except in four issues, in which it reverts to a reasonable *musāqāh*. The first is the case where in a grove there were dates that were allowed to be consumed. Second is the case where the worker stipulates that the *rabb al-māl* should work with him. Third is the case of combining *musāqāh* with sale in a single contract. Fourth, when they agree to vary the share, for example, to contract a *musāqāh* in a grove for one-third of the produce for one year and one-half the other year. It is said that his principle in this is that when *fasād* is associated with *musāqāh* due to a void *ijāra* or because of the sale of the fruit prior to ripening, or when an addition is stipulated by one of the parties for the other, it reverts to fair wages. For example, when the owner agrees with the worker that one of them pay to the other, as an addition, *dīnārs* or *dirhams*. If this addition is from the owner of the grove it amounts to a void *ijāra*, and if it is from the worker it amounts to a sale of fruit before it has come into existence. The *fasād* arising due to *gharar*, like the *musāqāh* of different groves, reverts to a "reasonable" *musāqāh*. All this is *istiḥsān* deviating from analogy. In the issue there is a fourth opinion which is that it reverts to "reasonable" *musāqāh* as long as it does not exceed the share that is stipulated, if it is for the worker, or is less than it if stipulated for the owner. This is sufficient for our purposes.

XXXIV
THE BOOK OF *SHARIKA* (PARTNERSHIP)

The study of the *aḥkām* of *sharika* covers its kinds, and the requisite elements of its validity. We shall discuss, out of these, the views that are agreed upon and those in which disagreement became well known, as is our purpose in this book.

Sharika on the whole, according to the jurists of the provinces, is of four kinds: *sharikat al-ʿinān*, *sharikat al-abdān*, *sharikat al-mufāwaḍa*, and *sharikat al-wujūh*. One of these is agreed upon, which is *sharikat al-ʿinān*, though some of the jurists did not designate it with this term, and they also differed about some of its conditions, as will be described in what follows. The other three kinds are disputed, and there is disagreement about some of their conditions among those who agreed about them generally.

34.1. Chapter 1: The Discussion of *Sharikat al-ʿInān*

The elements of this partnership are three: first, its subject-matter from among the varieties of wealth (capital); second, the determination of the ratio of profit with respect to the common capital; and third, the identification of the proportion of work by the partners with respect to the common capital.

34.1.1. Element 1: The Subject-Matter (Capital) of Partnership

Some of the kinds of subject-matter in a partnership are agreed upon while others are disputed. The Muslim jurists agreed that *sharika* is permitted in one kind of corporeal property, that is, *dīnārs* and *dirhams*, which is, in fact, a sale where the two categories (*dirhams* and *dīnārs*) are not being exchanged immediately, and it is a condition in the sale of gold or *dirhams* that the counter-values be present. This condition, however, has been restricted by consensus (*ijmāʾ*) for purposes of partnership. Similarly, they agreed, as far as I know, that in a partnership (constituted) with goods it is required that the goods be of the same description, while they differed about (partnership constituted with) different kinds of goods or things, as in the case of partnership through *dirhams* proffered by one party and *dīnārs* by the other. They also disputed the case of usurious food (offered in partnership) when it is of the same single species. Three (disputed) issues, therefore, arise here:

34.1.1.1. Issue 1

Partnership with two kinds of goods—or with goods and *dirhams* or *dīnārs*—is permitted by Ibn al-Qāsim. This is also Mālik's opinion, though it is said that he did not approve of it. The reason for such disapproval is the combination in it of partnership and sale. As the goods differ, it is as if each one of them sold a part of his goods for a part of the goods of the other.

Mālik takes into account the value (*qīma*) of the goods when partnership is constituted with them, while al-Shāfiʿī says that partnership cannot be constituted except on the basis of the price (*thaman*) of the goods. Abū Ḥāmid has reported that the preferred opinion of al-Shāfiʿī indicates that partnership is like *qirāḍ*; it is, therefore, not valid except in *dirhams* and *dīnārs*. He said that analogy dictates the substitution of mixing (*khalṭ*) by joint ownership.

34.1.1.2. Issue 2

If the two kinds (of capital) consist of those things in which delay (*nasāʾ*) is not permitted, as in partnership with *dīnārs* contributed by one and *dirhams* by the other, or with different kinds of food, then, the opinion of Mālik differs in this. He permitted it once and disallowed it another time, because a partnership with *dīnārs* contributed by one and *dirhams* by the other involves partnership and monetary exchange (*ṣarf*) at the same time, just as the exchange of two kinds of food in partnership results in the lack of immediate exchange. Ibn al-Qāsim, therefore, disallowed it. Those who did not take these reasons into consideration, permitted it.

34.1.1.3. Issue 3

Ibn al-Qāsim permitted partnership constituted with one kind of food, on the analogy of its unanimous permissibility in one kind of gold or silver. Mālik disallowed it in his well-known opinion, due to the implicit lack of immediate exchange. He argued on the basis of the unanimous principle that analogy is inoperative in a case of exemption. It is also said that the reason for Mālik's disapproval lies in the fact that partnership requires equality in value, and sale requires the similarity of measure. Thus, a partnership in food of the same species requires a similarity in value and in measure, which rarely occur. Mālik disapproved of this saying that this is the very similarity in value and measure that is rarely possible. He disapproved of it and that is where their disagreement lies: in the species of the subject-matter of partnership.

They disagreed whether it is a condition for the capital of the partnership that it must be mixed either physically or legally, that is, for example, that both (capitals) be in one box with both (partners) having access to it. Al-Shāfiʿī said that partnership is not permitted unless the two capitals are mixed to such an extent that the capital of one is not distinguishable from that of the other.

Abū Ḥanīfa said that partnership is valid even if each one of them retains his capital in his possession. Abū Ḥanīfa was satisfied with the conclusion of the partnership through words (offer and acceptance), while Mālik stipulated in addition to this the joint ability to employ the wealth. Al-Shāfiʿī added *ikhtilāṭ* (actual mixing) to these two conditions. The point being that with *ikhtilāṭ* the participation of the partners is fuller and more effective, as each one of them will be as honest with the other as he is to himself. This, then, is the discussion pertaining to the (first) element and its conditions.

34.1.2. **Element 2: Division of Profits**

They agreed over the validity of the partnership when the parties stipulated that the profits were to be in proportion to the capital (contributed) by each party, so that if original capital was contributed equally the profits would be divided among them equally. The jurists disagreed over whether it was permitted to share the profits equally when the capital contributed was unequal. Mālik and al-Shāfiʿī said that this is not permitted, while the jurists of Iraq said that it is allowed.

The reliance of those who disallowed this was on the fact that sharing of profits is to be compared with the sharing of losses. Just as the stipulation by one of them for bearing a part of the loss would not be allowed, the stipulation of profit, out of proportion with his capital, would not be permitted. Perhaps, they compared the profits here with the rent of landed property owned jointly by two persons, that is, the *manfaʿa* is shared by them in the ratio of co-ownership. The basis for the jurists of Iraq is the similarity of partnership with *qirāḍ*. As it is permitted to the worker in *qirāḍ* to share profits as stipulated by the parties, when the worker is not contributing anything but only his work, it is more appropriate in partnership to give the worker a part of the wealth when the partnership consists of capital as well as work from both. The (surplus) part of the profit would be in return for the surplus work he does as compared to his partner. Human beings differ with respect to work just as they differ in other things.

34.1.3. **Element 3: Work**

According to Mālik, work, as we have said, is to be in proportion to capital, and is not to be taken into account independently. According to Abū Ḥanīfa, it is to be considered along with capital. I believe there are among the jurists those who do not permit partnership unless the capitals of the partners is equal, keeping in view the work. They are of the view that work is usually equal, therefore, if the capital between them is not equal it amounts to injustice done to one of them in work. It is for this reason that Ibn al-Mundhir has said that the jurists unanimously agreed on the permissibility of the partnership in which each party contributes the same as his partner, and in the same kind, that is, *dirhams* or *dīnārs*, after which they mix them till they become a single indistinguishable capital, which they can both use to buy and sell any kind of goods as they deem fit, and whatever excess it yields is shared between them equally as is the loss. (He adds that) this is the case if each one should trade in the presence of his partner. The stipulation of this condition by him indicates that there is a dispute about it. It is well known that, according to the majority, it is not a condition that each one should trade in the presence of his partner.

34.2. Chapter 2: The *Mufāwaḍa* Partnership

They disagreed about *sharikat al-mufāwaḍa*. Mālik and Abū Ḥanīfa agreed, on the whole, about its permissibility, though they disagreed about some of the conditions. Al-Shāfiʿī said it is not permitted. The meaning of *sharikat al-mufāwaḍa* is that each partner delegates to the other to undertake transactions in his wealth, both in his presence and absence, and this takes place, according to them (Mālik and Abū Ḥanīfa), in all of their possessions.

The reliance of al-Shāfiʿī is on the argument that the term *sharika* is applied to the mixing of wealth, while the profits are an outcome, and it is not permitted that the outcome be common except by the joining of the sources. If each one of them stipulates, out of his own wealth, a share of the profits for the other, it amounts to *gharar*, which is not permitted, and it is an attribute of the *mufāwaḍa* partnership. Mālik is of the view that each partner has bought a part of the other's wealth with a part of his own wealth, after which each one of them has appointed the other as an agent to supervise the wealth that is under his control. Al-Shāfiʿī maintains that partnership is not a combination of agency and sale. Abū Ḥanīfa, on the other hand, is true here to his principle, which does not permit in *sharikat al-ʿinān* anything except cash.

Mālik and Abū Ḥanīfa differ over some of the conditions of this partnership, as Abū Ḥanīfa holds equality of capital to be a condition in this partnership, while Mālik said that this is not necessary on the analogy of *sharikat al-ʿinān*. Abū Ḥanīfa said that whatever any of them earns is considered a part (income) of the partnership. His argument is that the term *mufāwaḍa* requires these two things, that is, the equality of wealth and the totality of their possessions.

34.3. Chapter 3: *Sharikat al-Abdān*

Sharikat al-abdān is permitted, on the whole, by the Ḥanafites and the Mālikites. Al-Shāfiʿī disallowed it. The argument of the Shafiʿites is that partnership is specific to wealth and not work as it is variable, which amounts to *gharar* according to them, because the work of each is unknown to his partner. The argument of the Mālikites is (based on) the participation of warriors in booty and they become entitled to this due to work on the basis of the report that Ibn Masʿūd participated with Saʿd on the Day (battle) of Badr. Saʿd secured two mares, while Ibn Masʿūd did not get anything. This (partnership) was not denied by the Prophet (God's peace and blessings be upon him). Also, *muḍāraba* is agreed to on the basis of work, it is, therefore, valid that partnership be constituted on the same basis. Al-Shāfiʿī advances the argument that *muḍāraba* is an exemption and an analogy cannot be constructed on it; similarly, it is possible that the *ḥukm* of *ghanīma* lies outside the pale of *sharika*. Among its conditions, according to Mālik, is the similarity of trades and the location. Abū Ḥanīfa, however, said that it is permitted with a dissimilarity in trades. Thus, a tanner and a bleacher can become partners, according to him, but they cannot according to Mālik. The basis for Mālik is the increase in *gharar*, which arises due to a difference in trade or location. The reliance of Abū Ḥanīfa is on the permissibility of partnership in work.

34.4. Chapter 4: *Sharikat al-Wujūh*

Sharikat al-wujūh, according to Mālik and al-Shāfiʿī, is void. Abū Ḥanīfa said that it is permitted. This is a partnership based on the joining of liabilities (credit), without contributing work or wealth. The argument of Mālik and al-Shāfiʿī is that partnership is related to wealth or work, and both are lacking in this issue besides the presence of *gharar*, because each has delegated (authority) to his partner without qualification of a particular skill or work. Abū Ḥanīfa believes that it is a kind of work and, therefore, it is valid to contract partnership with it.

34.5. Chapter 5: Discussion of the *Aḥkām* of the Valid Partnership

It is a revocable contract, not a binding one, that is, it is the right of (any) one of the partners to withdraw from the partnership whenever he likes. It is a contract that is not inheritable. The maintenance and clothing of the partners is from the wealth of the partnership if they have almost similar obligations and when they do not exceed what is reasonable for them for maintenance. It is permitted to each partner to invest in goods, borrow, and make deposits whenever it is necessary, but it is not permitted that he gives gifts from the wealth of the partnership, nor is he to make a transaction that requires their joint participation. He is liable, however, for negligence or a wrongful act. For example, in the case where he gives away the wealth of the partnership without witnesses and the possessor denies his claim. He has to compensate as he has been negligent in not taking witnesses. He has the right to accept a defective thing in purchase. The acknowledgement by one of the partners of a financial claim for the other is not valid. *Iqāla* and *tawliya* on his part are valid. One of the partners (alone) is not liable for the losses in trade that has been undertaken by agreement. It is not permitted to a partner in *mufāwaḍa* to enter into a transaction of loan without the permission of his partner. Each partner stands in the position of his partner with respect to rights and liabilities (that is, liability is joint). The details under this topic are too many.

XXXV
THE BOOK OF *SHUFʿA* (PRE-EMPTION)

The examination of *shufʿa* is initially taken up in two parts. The first part is about the validity of this *ḥukm* and its elements. The second is about its *aḥkām*.

35.1. Part 1: The Legal Validity of *Shufʿa* and its Elements

The Muslims agreed about the obligation of the *ḥukm* of pre-emption on the basis of what was stipulated for it in established traditions, except those who do not consider the sale of a jointly owned piece of land as valid. It has four elements: the pre-emptor (*shafīʿ*), the buyer (*mashfūʿ ʿalayh*), the property (*mashfūʿ fīh*), and the mode of acquisition through *shufʿa*.

35.1.1. Element 1: The Pre-emptor

Mālik, al-Shāfiʿī, and the Ahl al-Madīna maintained that there is no right of pre-emption for anyone except the joint owner, as long as partition has not taken place. The Ahl al-ʿIrāq maintained that pre-emption has an order of priority. The first priority is for the co-owner, before partition, followed by the joint owner after partition, as long as a joint ownership exists in the (common) street (drive way) or in the courtyard. The next order of priority is for the adjacent neighbour. The Ahl al-Madīna, however, said that there is no right of pre-emption for the adjacent neighbour or even for the co-owner after partition.

The reliance of the Ahl al-Madīna is on the *mursal* report of Mālik from Ibn Shihāb from Abū Salama ibn ʿAbd al-Raḥmān and Saʿīd ibn al-Musayyib that "the Messenger of Allāh (God's peace and blessings be upon him) issued a verdict in the case of co-owners before partition. However, when boundaries have been demarcated between them (their properties), they have no (mutual) right of pre-emption". They also rely on the tradition of Jābir that "the Messenger of Allāh (God's peace and blessings be upon him) issued a verdict for pre-emption before partition. However, when the boundaries are demarcated there is no (right of) *shufʿa*". This is recorded by Muslim, al-Tirmidhī and Abū Dāwūd. Aḥmad ibn Ḥanbal used to say that the tradition of Maʿmar from al-Zuhrī from Abū Salama ibn ʿAbd al-Raḥmān is the most authentic out of those narrated about *shufʿa*. Ibn Maʿīn used to say that the *mursal* of Mālik is dear to me as Mālik reported it from Ibn Shihāb as *mawqūf*,[151] but some people considered this dispute over Ibn Shihāb in his *isnād* as weakening this *isnād*. It is related from Mālik, in sources other than *al-Muwaṭṭā*ʾ, from Ibn Shihāb from Abū Hurayra.

The point of their argument in this tradition lies in the fact that if the boundaries are drawn there is no right of pre-emption. Thus, if there is no right of pre-emption in the case of a co-owner after partition, it is more appropriate that it should not be obligatory in the case of a neighbour. Further, the co-owner after partition is also a neighbour once partition takes place.

The reliance of the Ahl al-ʿIrāq is on the tradition of Abū Rāfiʿ from the Prophet (God's peace and blessings be upon him) that he said, "The (immediate) neighbour has a prior right to that which is adjacent to him". This is a tradition that is related both by al-Bukhārī and Muslim. Al-Tirmidhī and Abū Dāwūd have recorded a tradition of the Prophet (God's peace and blessings be upon him) in which he said, "The neighbour of a house has a prior right to the house of his neighbour". It has been declared authentic by al-Tirmidhī.

They also maintain as a rational argument that as the aim of pre-emption is the repelling of harm inherent in co-ownership, and in so far as this meaning exists in the case of the neighbour it is necessary that the right should vest in him too. The Ahl al-Madīna would say that the harm involved in co-ownership is greater than that sustained by the neighbour. On the whole, the argument of the Mālikites, as a matter of principle, is that none be deprived of ownership except by his consent, and that he who buys a thing should not lose it without his consent, unless an evidence indicates such an exemption. The traditions are in conflict on this topic and it is, therefore, necessary to have recourse to that for which the principles bear evidence. For both opinions we find support from earlier authorities from among the *Tābiʿūn* in Iraq and the Companions among the Ahl al-Madīna.

35.1.2. **Element 2: The Property (*mashfūʿ fīh*)**[152]

The Muslim jurists agreed that *shufʿa* applies in real estate, properties such as houses and land, but they differed about other properties. The summary of views in Mālik's school is that it applies to three kinds (of property). The first is the primary property, namely, real estate such as houses, shops, and orchards. The second is what is attached to real estate, and is fixed, neither transferable nor movable, like springs and areas surrounding palm-groves, as

[151] That is, the words are those of Ibn Shihāb al-Zuhrī about the Prophet's acts, and are not the Prophet's own words.

[152] It may be observed here that the Author did not follow the order laid down in his introduction of the topic.

they subsist in a state to which *shufʿa* is applicable. This means that the original property, like land, be jointly owned by him (the pre-emptor) and his partner without partition. The third is what relates to these things, like fruit, about which there are different narrations from Mālik. There are also different narrations from Mālik about the leasing of land for cultivation and the contract of *kitāba* in the case of the *mukātab* slave. Narrations from him differ about public baths and grinding-mills. There is no *shufaʿ* in all other things besides these, including goods and animals, according to him, and the same is the case with driveways and courtyards of a house.

The narrations from him (Mālik) differ about the cases of rented houses, of *musāqā*, and debt, whether the debtor (or the tenant) has a prior right; similarly, in the case of *kitāba* (whether the *mukātib* has a prior right). ʿUmar ibn ʿAbd al-ʿAzīz was in favour of this and it is related that "the Messenger of Allāh (God's peace and blessings be upon him) decided in favour of (the right of) *shufʿa* in the case of debt". This was the opinion of Ashhab from among the disciples of Mālik, while Ibn al-Qāsim said that there is no *shufʿa* in the case of debt. These two jurists did not differ about its obligation in the case of *kitāba*, due to the significance of manumission.

The jurists of the provinces deny the application of *shufʿa* in things other than real estate. On the other hand, it is related from a group that there is *shufʿa* in everything except those weighed and measured. Abū Ḥanīfa did not permit *shufʿa* in springs or in male animals, but he did permit it in courtyards and driveways. Al-Shāfiʿī agreed with Mālik on courtyards, springs, and driveways, but everyone opposed him in the case of fruit.

The reliance of the majority in restricting *shufʿa* to real estate is what is related in the confirmed tradition of the Prophet (God's peace and blessings be upon him), "*Shufʿa* is valid in what has not been partitioned, but once boundaries have been drawn and driveways made, there is no *shufʿa*". It is as if he said that *shufʿa* is valid in that in which partition is possible, as long as it has not been partitioned. This amounts to a proof through the indirect indication of the text (*dalīl al-khiṭāb*). The jurists of the provinces unanimously agreed on this, despite their disagreement over the extent of its validity as evidence. The reliance of those who permitted it in all things is what has been recorded by al-Tirmidhī as a narration from Ibn ʿAbbās "that the Messenger of Allāh (God's peace and blessings be upon him) said, 'The co-owner is a *shafīʿ* (pre-emptor) and *shufʿa* is valid in everything". This is so, as the implication of harm in co-ownership and in the case of a neighbour exists in each thing,[153] though it is more apparent in real estate. On observing

[153] It is unlikely that the concept of neighbourhood implies harm. The reference here is to sharing property with a stranger to whom the co-owner may sell without the approval of his partner

this, Mālik deemed what resembles landed property to fall in the same category.

Abū Ḥanīfa argued for the prohibition of *shufʿa* in springs on the basis of the report that "there is no *shufʿa* in springs". Mālik interpreted this tradition to mean the springs in the deserts that are used to revive barren lands (*mawāt*), not those that are in privately owned land.

35.1.3. Element 3: The Buyer (*Mashfūʿ ʿAlayh*)

They agreed about the *mashfūʿ ʿalayh* that he is one to whom the property is transferred through purchase from a co-owner of an unpartitioned property or from a neighbour, according to those who view the validity of *shufʿa* for a neighbour. They disagreed about the person to whom the property is transferred without purchase. The well-known opinion of Mālik is that *shufʿa* arises when the transfer of ownership is for compensation as in sale, settlement, dower (*mahr*), *arsh* (damages) for torts and so on. This was also the opinion of al-Shāfiʿī. There is a second opinion from him (Mālik) that it is valid in each transfer of ownership whether it is for compensation or is without compensation, as in a non-charitable gift, except in the cases of inheritance as there is no *shufʿa* in that by unanimous agreement.

Shufʿa in the opinion of the Ḥanafites is only valid in the case of sale. Their reliance is on the apparent meaning of the traditions, the general import of which is that it arises from sale; in fact, it is so explicitly stated in all (the traditions) and not only in some. He (the co-owner) is not to sell till his co-owner permits him. The Mālikites are of the opinion that anything transferred for compensation is within the meaning of sale, and the underlying reason of the second narration (from Mālik) is merely the consequential harm. There is no *shufʿa* in a gift seeking spiritual reward (*thawāb*), according to Abū Ḥanīfa and according to al-Shāfiʿī; for Abū Ḥanīfa, it is because *shufʿa* is valid in sales only, and for al-Shāfiʿī because a reward-seeking gift is void in his opinion. There is no dispute about it in Mālik's view or that of his disciples, that is that *shufʿa* is valid in it.

The jurists agreed that in the case of a sale with an option, where the option is stipulated for the seller, *shufʿa* does not arise until the sale becomes binding. They disagreed when the option is (stipulated) for the buyer. Al-Shāfiʿī and the Kūfīs said that *shufʿa* is valid as he has severed the land from his ownership and alienated it. It is said that *shufʿa* is not valid against him as he is not liable. This is the opinion of a group among the disciples of Mālik. They disagreed about *shufʿa* in the case of *musāqāh*, where it is the exchange of land for land. There are three narrations from Mālik about it: permission, prohibition, and the third is that it is not valid when it involves co-sharers and valid when strangers are involved.

35.1.4. Element 4: Acquisition through Pre-emption

The discussion under this element relates to the amount with which the pre-emptor acquires the property, how much he acquires, and when. They agreed that in the case of sale he acquires with the sale price if it is immediate. They disagreed when the sale is for a delayed period, whether the pre-emptor acquires it for the price in the same delayed period, or with the sale price on immediate payment, or whether he has an option. Mālik said that he acquires it on the basis of the price of a delayed sale if he is well-to-do or he comes up with a rich guarantor. Al-Shāfiʿī said that the pre-emptor has an option, if he likes he can go through with it immediately or he can delay it to the end of the period. This is like the opinion of the Kūfīs. Al-Thawrī held that he cannot acquire it except by immediate payment, as it has entered the liability of the other person. He said that there are among us some who say that it should stay in the possession of the seller and when the period is over the pre-emptor can acquire it.

Those who maintain the validity of pre-emption in all contracts of exchange other than sale, held that he (the pre-emptor) exercises the right of pre-emption in the value of the share if the compensation is something that cannot be easily estimated, as in the case of something given away in *khulʿ*. If he pays with a thing the value of which can be determined, but it is not *dīnārs* or *dirhams* or on the whole anything that can be measured or weighed, then he acquires it with the value of the thing given in exchange for the share. If the value of the thing is determined by law, he acquires the share with that value, as in the case of *mūḍiḥa* for which he is liable or *munaqqala*, (both injuries), he acquires with the *diya* (reparation) fixed for them.

In answering the question how much he acquires, (the assumption is that) the pre-emptor is one or more than one, and the buyer is also one or more. When the pre-emptor is one and the buyer is one, there is no disagreement that the pre-emptor has either to take the entire property or leave it. When the buyer is one and the pre-emptors are more than one, they disagreed about it on two points. First, about the mode of partitioning the pre-empted property between them and second, when the bases of their ownership are different, are some to be excluded by the others in the pre-emption? For example, if some of them are co-owners in property that they have inherited, on equal or the same basis (like two sisters sharing their assigned portion), while the others did not inherit on the basis of a fixed share, having a single share, or because some of them are residuaries.

35.1.4.1. Issue 1: Mode of distribution of property (among pre-emptors)

Mālik, al-Shāfiʿī, and the majority of the jurists of Medina were of the opinion that the property is to be divided among them according to the proportion of their shares (in the disputed partition). Thus, one whose share in the portion of the wealth is a third acquires a third of the portion with a third of the price, and one whose share is a fourth acquires a fourth. The Kūfīs said that it is to be divided per head in equal shares, irrespective of whether there is one among them who has the largest share and one who has the smallest.

The argument of the Medinites is that *shufʿa* is a right that is to be exercised in accordance with the prevailing ownership. It is, therefore, necessary that it be distributed in accordance with the original property, the origin being rents in jointly rented things and profit in *sharikat al-amwāl.* In addition, *shufʿa* is intended to eliminate harm, and the harm is suffered by each in unequal measures and it affects each in accordance with his share. Thus, it is necessary that their entitlement to the extent of repelling it be in proportion to this ratio. The argument of the Ḥanafites is that the validity of the *shufʿa* arises by ownership itself and the possessors of different shares derive this right equally by mere ownership. Perhaps, they held it similar to co-owners in a slave in unequal shares. If one of them sets his share free, he bears equally the share of those who did not free him.

35.1.4.2. Issue 2: Residuaries

The jurists differed about the effect of co-ownership where some are residuaries while others have a (fixed) share. Mālik said the possessors of a prescribed fixed share (*farḍ*) have a prior right to *shufʿa* when one of them sells to the heirs among their co-owners. The residuaries do not have the right of *shufʿa* in case of sale by one of those with fixed shares, but the sharers have the right of *shufʿa* in sale by the residuaries. For example, if a person dies leaving behind real estate inherited by two daughters and two sons of his (the deceased) uncle. If one of the daughters sells her share, the other daughter, according to Mālik, is the one who exercises the right of pre-emption for the property her sister is selling and not the sons of the uncle. If a son of the uncle sells his share the daughters and the other son (of the uncle) exercise the right. This is also the opinion of Ibn al-Qāsim. The Kūfīs said that the sharers do not participate with the residuaries nor the residuaries with the sharers, but the sharers exercise the right of pre-emption within themselves only. This was also the opinion of Ashhab. Al-Shāfiʿī said in one of his opinions that the sharers participate with the residuaries and the residuaries with the sharers, which is the opinion preferred by al-Muzanī; it was also the opinion of al-Mughīra from among the disciples of Mālik.

The basis of al-Shāfiʿī's opinion is the generality of the decision of the Prophet about the right of *shufʿa* among co-owners where he did not distinguish the sharers from the residuaries. Those who distinguished the sharers from the residuaries were of the view that the co-ownership arose from different causes, that is, between the sharers and the residuaries, and they compared the co-ownership arising from different causes with different partnerships based on differences in capital, which is the sharing of wealth on the basis of capital. Those who allowed the participation of the sharers in the *shufʿa* of the residuaries, but did not allow the participation of the residuaries in the case of the sharers, decided on the basis of *istiḥsān* as a breach from analogy. The reasoning through *istiḥsān* is that the sharers have a priority over the residuaries.

If the buyers are two or more and the pre-emptor desires to exercise the right against one of them and not the other, then, Ibn al-Qāsim is of the opinion that he acquires the whole or relinquishes (his right). Abū Ḥanīfa, his disciples, and al-Shāfiʿī said that he may exercise the right against any of them he pleases. This was also the opinion of Ashhab. If, however, a person buys from two individuals and the pre-emptor desires to exercise the right with respect to one of them and not the other, Abū Ḥanīfa prohibits it, while al-Shāfiʿī permits it. If the pre-emptors are more than one, that is, the co-owners and some of them decide to exercise the right while the rest surrender it, then, the majority are of the opinion that the buyer should ask the co-owner to acquire the whole property or relinquish his right; he does not have the right to pre-empt according to the extent of his share, unless the buyer permits this, thus, he does not have the right to divide the *shufʿa* with respect to the buyer if he does not agree to such division. Aṣbagh, one of the disciples of Mālik, said that if some of them surrender their right out of concern for the buyer, the pre-emptor can only exercise his right to the extent of his share.

There is no disagreement in Mālik's school that when some of the pre-emptors are absent and some are present and those present wish to exercise the right to the extent of their shares, they cannot do so. They have to take the whole or relinquish; when those absent return they have the right to exercise their right or surrender it. They agreed that a condition for acquisition through pre-emption is the existence of co-ownership prior to the sale. They disagreed whether it was a condition that the co-ownership should exist during the sale and should be established before the sale.

35.1.4.3. Issue 3: When the seller is not a co-owner at the time of the sale

This is visualized when a person delays the acquisition of the property through pre-emption due to some reason till he sells his share because of which he was a co-owner. Ashhab relates that the opinion of Mālik differs in this. He said once that he has the right to acquire through *shufʿa*, and said another time that he does not. Ashhab preferred the opinion that he has no right, which is also the opinion of al-Shāfiʿī and the Kūfīs on the basis of *qiyās* as the object of pre-emption is the elimination of harm resulting from co-ownership and this person is no longer a co-owner. Ibn al-Qāsim said that he has the right if he decides to exercise it soon. He is of the opinion that a right acquired by him cannot be negated by the sale of his share by him.

35.1.4.4. Issue 4: Co-ownership prior to sale

This takes the form that a person becomes entitled to a share in a land out of which another share is being sold, but before the actual time of the entitlement, does he have the right to acquire it through pre-emption? A group said that he has this right as it accrues to him through the precedence of the co-ownership to the sale and it does not matter if he is in possession of his share or not. Another group said that he has no right of pre-emption as the right of co-ownership will be established on the day of delivery. They said, "Do you not see that he does not collect the produce from the buyer". Mālik said that if a long time passes there is no *shufᶜa*, but if such time has not passed then the right exists. This is based on *istiḥsān*.

With respect to (the time) when he exercises it in order that his right may subsist, there are two cases of persons having the right of pre-emption, one of them absent and the other present. The jurists are in agreement, about the person absent, that his right subsists as long he is not aware of the sale by his co-sharer. They disagreed when he is absent, but aware of the sale. Some said that his right of pre-emption is annulled, while others said that it is not, which is Mālik's opinion. His proof is what is related from the Prophet (God's peace and blessings be upon him) in the tradition of Jābir, that he said, "The neighbour has a greater right to the property adjacent to him", or he said, "(he) has a stronger right in his *shufᶜa*, which is to be delayed if he is absent". Further, the person absent is restrained from acquisition through *shufᶜa* and his excuse is justified. The basis for the (argument of the) other group is that his silence after awareness of the sale is circumstantial proof of his consent to the relinquishment of his right.

The jurists disagreed about the time of validity of *shufᶜa* in the case of one present. Al-Shāfiᶜī and Abū Ḥanīfa said that it is valid immediately, as he knows and is able to make the demand. If he knows and is able to make the demand, but still does not, his *shufᶜa* is invalidated; Abū Ḥanīfa, however, said that if he takes witnesses about his intention to acquire, the right is not annulled even if it is delayed. The right is not immediate according to Mālik, but has an extended duration. His opinion differed about the limit of such a duration. He said once that it is unlimited and is not terminated at all, unless the buyer adds to the building or makes substantial changes while he is present, knowing and silent. On another occasion, he limited this time-period to one year, which is the better-known opinion, but it is said that he allowed it for more than a year. It is sometimes related from him that the right of *shufʿa* remains valid up to five years. Al-Shāfiʿī argued on the basis of what is related from the Prophet (God's peace and blessings be upon him), "*Shufʿa* is like the unwinding of the *ʿiqāl*". It is also related from al-Shāfiʿī that its duration is three days.

Those who do not annul the right of pre-emption on the basis of silence argue that silence does not annul the right of a Muslim, unless his behaviour indicates its relinquishment. This, it appears, is similar to the principles of al-Shāfiʿī for, according to him, no express statement can be attributed to one who is silent even when the accompanying circumstances indicate his consent. I believe, however, that in this case he relied on the traditions.

This, then, is the discussion about the elements of *shufʿa* and its validating conditions; what now remains is the discussion of the *aḥkām*.

35.2. **Part 2: The Discussion of the *Aḥkām* of**

These *aḥkām* are numerous, but we shall discuss only those in which the disagreement of the jurists of the provinces became well known. Among these is their disagreement over the inheritance of the right of pre-emption. The Kūfīs maintained that it cannot be inherited, just as it cannot be sold. Mālik, al-Shāfiʿī, and the jurists of Hijāz held that it is inheritable on the analogy of all kinds of wealth. The discussion of the reason for disagreement on these issues has preceded in the discussion of the reason for the return (of the *mabīʿ*) due to defects.

They also disagreed about the contractual obligation[154] with respect to the pre-emptor; does it lie on the buyer or the seller? Mālik and al-Shāfiʿī said that it is on the buyer, while Ibn Abī Laylā said it is on the seller. The reliance of Mālik is on the argument that the right of pre-emption for the co-owner arose after the acquisition of ownership by the buyer, and after such acquisition became effective. Therefore, it is necessary that the contractual obligation should be on him (the buyer). The reliance of the other party is on the fact that the right of pre-emption arose out of the sale itself and the imposition of *shufʿa* on the sale amounts to its revocation, and its conclusion in favour of the possessor of the right of *shufʿa*.

They agreed that *iqāla* (negotiated rescission) does not annul the right of pre-emption, on the view that it is a sale and also on the view that it is revocation, I mean, *iqāla*. The disciples of Mālik disagreed as to who was liable for the contractual obligation in the case of *iqāla*. Ibn al-Qāsim said it is the buyer, while Ashhab said that he (the pre-emptor) has an option.

In the case where the buyer undertakes construction or plantation or what resembles it, in the land before the demand of the pre-emptor and the

[154] That is, who is to satisfy the claim of the pre-emptor.

pre-emptor makes his demand later, Mālik said that there is no *shufʿa*, unless the buyer is given the value of what he has constructed or planted. Al-Shāfiʿī and Abū Ḥanīfa said that he is a trespasser and the pre-emptor has the right to give him the value of his construction demolished or to take it from him after this reduction. The reason for their disagreement is the vacillation of the act of the buyer, who is aware of the entitlement of the *shufʿa*, between the likelihood that it is the invalid act of the usurper and between the act of the buyer who is facing a claim of restitution. He has constructed and planted in the land and his position vacillates between the two. Those who considered the case of restitution as predominant said that he should not take their value, but those whose views were dominated by the likelihood of trespass said that the pre-emptor has a right to acquire it after demolition or by reducing the price accordingly (down to the demolished value of the structure).

When the buyer and the pre-emptor differ about the price (paid by the buyer for the share in the property), the buyer saying that he bought the land for a certain sum, and the pre-emptor saying that he bought it for less, without any of them having evidence, the majority of the jurists say that the admissible statement is that of the buyer, as the pre-emptor is the claimant and the buyer is the defendant. Some of the later jurists opposed this saying that the acceptable statement is that of the pre-emptor, as the buyer has acknowledged the validity of the *shufʿa* and has made a claim for a certain sum as price, which the other has not acknowledged.

Mālik's disciples differed over this issue. Ibn al-Qāsim said that the acceptable statement is that of the buyer, along with his oath, when he makes a credible claim. If he brings up an incredible claim, then, the acceptable statement is that of the pre-emptor. Ashhab said that if he brings up a credible claim, the statement of the buyer is accepted without an oath, and in the case of an incredible claim he has to swear an oath. It is related from Mālik that he said that if the buyer is a person of authority, who is known to increase the amount of the price, his (the pre-emptor's) statement is accepted without oath. It is said that if the buyer comes up with an exaggerated claim the pre-emptor is asked to have recourse to value; the same is the case, as far as I think, when each one of them comes up with an exaggerated claim.

They disagreed when each one of them comes up with evidence that is equally reliable about *ʿadāla* (moral probity). Ibn al-Qāsim said that both are to be set aside and they revert to the original basis where the acceptable statement is that of the buyer along with his oath. Ashhab said that the acceptable evidence is that of the buyer as it is based on better knowledge.

XXXVI
THE BOOK OF *QISMA* (DIVISION; PARTITION)

The source for this law are the words of the Exalted, "And when kinsfolk and orphans and the needy are present at the division (of the heritage) bestow on them therefrom and speak kindly unto them",[155] and "Whether it be little or much—a legal share".[156] (Its source is) also the words of the Messenger of Allāh (God's peace and blessings be upon him), "Any house that was partitioned in the days of *jāhiliyya* is to be retained on that division and any house established after Islam that has not been partitioned will be partitioned according to Islam".

The discussion in this book is about the *qāsim*, the *maqsūm ʿalayh*, and about *qisma*. The discussion of *qisma* is undertaken in several chapters. The first chapter is about the kinds of *qisma*. The second is about the identification of the subject-matter of each of its kinds, that is, things amenable to partition and those that are not; the method of *qisma* in them, and their conditions, I mean, of the things amenable to *qisma*. The third is about the identification of the *aḥkām*.

36.1. **Chapter 1: The Kinds of *Qisma***

The discussion of *qisma* is first divided into two parts: division of inherited wealth, and the benefits of such wealth.

36.1.1. **Part 1: Division of Inherited Wealth**

The division of property that is neither weighed nor measured is classified, on the whole, into three types: division through lots after valuation and equalization of (shares); division by consent after valuation and equalization; and division by consent without valuation and equalization. With respect to those that are measured and weighed, their division is by measure and weight. Property, on the other hand, is divisible into three types. First is that which

[155] Qurʾān 4:8
[156] Qurʾān 4:7

is fixed and immovable, that is, houses and real estate. The second is movable (property) and is divided into two kinds: that which is not measured or weighed, and consists of animals and some types of goods; and that which is measured and weighed. Thus, in this chapter there are three sections: first, about landed property; second, about non-measurable goods; and third about things measured and weighed.

36.1.1.1. *Section 1: Landed Property*

The division of landed property is permissible through consent and (partition into) lots on the basis of value. The jurists are all in general agreement over this, though they differed about the subject-matter and the conditions. Partition can either be of one property alone or of many. There is no disagreement about its division, and when there is one property it can be partitioned into sections with similar attributes with no decrease in the utility of each section due to partition. The sharers are to be forced to accept this. When the property can be divided only into sections having no utility, Mālik and his disciples differ. Mālik said that it is (still) to be divided among them when the sharers demand it, even if the portion allotted to each has no utility, like (land covering) the area of the human foot. This opinion was upheld only by Ibn Kināna, from among his disciples, and it is also the opinion of Abū Ḥanīfa and al-Shāfiʿī. Their reliance in this is upon the words of the Exalted, "Whether it be little or much—a legal share".[157]

Ibn al-Qāsim said that it is not to be divided unless each one of them gets as a share that from which he can benefit, without incurring any harm in its utilization as a result of the partition. He did not, however, take into account the effect on its price. Ibn al-Mājishūn said that it is to be divided if each one of them gets what he can utilize, though it may not be a benefit of the same category as that which could be derived through co-ownership, and it may even be less. Muṭarrif, out of the disciples of Mālik, said that unless each one of them gets as a share that which he can utilize it is not to be divided, but if the shares of some of them can be utilized while those of the others cannot, it is to be divided and they are to be forced to accept it whether the demand is made by the owner of the larger or the smaller share. It is said, however, that they are to be forced if the demand is made by the owner of the smaller share and not if it is made by the owner of the larger share. The opposite is also maintained by some, but that is weak.

They differed, under this topic, when the utility of the property partitioned is converted to a different benefit, like that of a public bath. Mālik said that it is to be partitioned if one of the co-owners demands this, which was also

[157] Qurʾān 4:7

the opinion of Ashhab. Ibn al-Qāsim said that it is not to be divided, which is also the opinion of al-Shāfiʿī. The reliance of those who prohibited this is on the words of the Prophet (God's peace and blessings be upon him), "No harm (is to be borne) and none is (allowed) to harm". The reliance of those who upheld partitioning is on the words of the Exalted, "Whether it be little or much—a legal share".[158] Among the proofs for those who do not uphold division is the tradition of Jābir from his father, "There is to be no *taʿḍiya* (dismemberment) of the heirs, (divide) only that which bears partitioning". *Taʿḍiya* is disunion, which means here that there is to be no partition.

If the properties are more than one, then, they can either be homogeneous or be different. When they are homogeneous, the jurists of the different regions differ about them. Mālik said that if they are homogeneous, they are to be divided by valuation, equalization, and by drawing lots. Abū Ḥanīfa and al-Shāfiʿī said that each property is to be partitioned separately. The reliance of Mālik is on the belief that it involves the least amount of harm for the co-owners in the partition. The reliance of the other party is on the fact that each property is to be identified separately as it may (later) involve *shufʿa* (pre-emption).

The disciples of Mālik differ, into three opinions, when differing properties have similar market values, even when they are in different locations. If the properties are different, for example, when some are houses, some orchards, and others land, there is no dispute that they are not to be combined for distribution by lots. A condition for the partition of fruit-bearing orchards is that they are not to be partitioned, by agreement in the school, when the fruit has begun to ripen, as this would amount to the sale of food for food on the trees, which is *muzābana*. There is disagreement in the Mālik's school about their partition before the ripening of fruit. Ibn al-Qāsim does not permit this before pollination in any circumstances. He is cautious about it as it leads to the sale of food for food with an excess. It is thought for this reason that Mālik did not allow the sale, delayed or immediate, of food that had not ripened with food. If it is after pollination, it is not permitted, according to him, except on the condition that one of them stipulates for the other that whatever fruit is obtained through his share is also to be divided and they are to be partners in that which does not come out of his share. The *ʿilla*, according to him, in this is that a buyer can stipulate the inclusion of fruit after pollination, but it is not permitted before it. It is as if one of them has purchased the share of his co-owner from all the fruit that is reaped by him through partition with his share in the fruit reaped by his co-owner, when he had stipulated (the inclusion) fruit.

[158] Qurʾān

The method of partition by lots is that the inheritance be divided, verified, and adjusted to whole numbers if there is a fraction in the shares, so that the shares are reduced to wholes, then, each location and each kind of plantation should be valued, and thereafter adjusted on the basis of the smallest share with respect to value. It is possible that a section in one location is equal to three in another on the basis of the value of the land and the location. Once they are divided and adjusted in this way, the names of the co-owners be written on slips along with the different sections. The person whose name comes out matching a section takes it. It is suggested that names be dropped into the various sides, and the person whose name is found in a section takes it. If his share exceeds this, it is done again for him till his entitlement is completed.

This is the position on drawing lots in inherited property. The jurists introduced the drawing of lots in partition for the satisfaction of the persons participating in the partition, and it is present in the *sharᶜ* in different contexts. Among them are the words of the Exalted, "And then [he] drew lots and was of those rejected",[159] and "Thou wast not present with them when they threw their pens (to know) which of them should be the guardian of Mary".[160] Related to this is also the established tradition in which it is reported "that a man, close to his death, freed six unnamed slaves and the Messenger of Allāh (God's peace and blessings be upon him), drew lots among them, thus freeing a third of the slaves". Division through agreement, irrespective of whether it is after valuation and adjustment or without it, is permitted in similar and differing properties as it is a kind of sale, but whatever is prohibited in sale is prohibited here.

36.1.1.2. *Section 2: Division of Goods*

The jurists agreed about animals and goods that division is allowed in none of them due to the *fasād* (corruption) involved. They differed, however, when the co-owners covet one particular thing and are not willing to utilize it jointly, with one of them proposing to sell it out. Mālik and his disciples said that he is to be compelled to agree. If one of them wishes to acquire it on the basis of the value assigned to it he may do so. The Ẓāhirites said that he is not to be compelled, as the principles require that none is to be dispossessed of his property except on the basis of an evidence from the Qurʾān, *sunna*, or *ijmāᶜ*. Mālik's argument is that with no compulsion the other party may be harmed. This is based on *qiyās* that is *mursal* (that is, related *maṣlaḥa mursala*), which, as we have said on more than one occasion, none besides Mālik, from among

[159] Qurʾān 37:141
[160] Qurʾān 3:44

the jurists of different regions, upholds, but it becomes necessary in certain things.

When the goods have more than one species, the jurists agree about their division through consent. They disagree about dividing the variety of goods through adjustment and drawing lots. Mālik and his disciples permitted it in a single category, but ᶜAbd al-ᶜAzīz ibn Abī Salama and Ibn al-Mājishūn disallowed it. Mālik's disciples, however, differed about the distinction of the single category in which the drawing of lots is permitted from that in which it is not permitted. Ashhab held it to be that in which a part cannot be taken as (delayed) payment for another part. Ibn al-Qāsim's opinion wavered. On one occasion he permitted division through drawing of lots in a thing in which a part can be used to pay for another part, considering division less involved than *salam*, but on another occasion he disallowed division in a thing in which *salam* is disallowed. It is said, though, that he considered division as less involved than *salam* in such a case (with respect to permissibility). His decisions in cases because of which it is thought that division in his view is more serious than *salam* (advance payment) may be interpreted on the basis of his second principle. Ibn Ḥabīb, on the other hand, held that similar goods like silk and silk fabrics, cotton and cotton fabrics may be combined as one category for the purpose of division. Ashhab permitted the combination of two kinds for division for drawing lots with the consent (of the parties). This is weak, however, as the involved *gharar* is not acceptable (even) on the basis of consent.

36.1.1.3. *Section 3: Rules Pertaining to Things Measured and Weighed*

Drawing of lots is not permitted, by agreement, for dividing things measured and weighed, except what is related from al-Lakhmī. Things measured can be one heap, two, or more. If they are of the same kind, their division can take place through equal measure or weight when one of the co-owners demands this. There is no disagreement about the permissibility of their division on the basis of consent even with apparent excess (in some), irrespective of whether they are usurious or non-usurious, that is, those in which *tafāḍul* is not permitted. This is permitted with an accepted measure or even with a different measure, but it is not permitted through estimate, without a measure or weight. If the division is through examination, it is said that this is not allowed in things measured, but is permitted in those weighed. The disagreement here is the same as that related to sale through examination.

If the division is not in heaps of one kind, but there are two (kinds), then, if these are things in which excess *tafāḍul* is not allowed, they cannot be divided by way of combining; (they can only be divided) through a determined measure for those measured, and a determined weight for those weighed. If they are divided by way of an undetermined measure it will not be known how much has been received of one quantity when they vary (in value) with respect to a determined measure. All this is according to the opinion of Mālik, as the principle underlying it is that excess is prohibited in similar things when their utility is similar, as in wheat and barley.

In case the commodities are those in which excess is allowed, their division is permitted by way of adjustment, through combining, even when they are two different kinds, with the existence of apparent excess that is customary through the use of determined measure or weight. Such permission in the school is granted in the case where there is consent. The obligation arising from the *ḥukm* is that each heap is to be divided separately. When each pile is divided separately, the division is allowed with a determined or an undetermined measure.

All this is the *ḥukm* of the division that takes place in inherited wealth.

36.1.2. **Part 2: Division of Benefits**

The division of benefits is not permitted, according to the opinion of Ibn al-Qāsim, through the drawing of lots, and the person who refuses to accept it is not to be compelled. This is in view of the fact that division of benefits is not to be undertaken through drawing lots. Abū Ḥanīfa and his disciples were of the opinion that the parties are to be compelled in the division of benefits. The division of benefits, according to all (jurists), is through the joint sharing of the usufruct, which takes place over time or by (the use of) things. The division of benefits over time takes place when each person has the chance to use the thing for an equal duration. In its division through the utilization of things, the *ʿayn* is allocated to both and is used for a fixed duration, the *ʿayn* still being retained in joint ownership.

In (Mālik's) school there is disagreement about division of benefits over time, regarding the duration for which the division is permitted for certain things as compared to others for purposes of yield or utilization, like the service of a slave or the riding of an animal or the cultivation of land. The disagreement was also influenced by things movable and immovable. It is not permitted in those which are movable, according to Mālik and his disciples, for a lengthy duration, but is allowed for short durations; and this is for purposes of revenue and utilization. With respect to immovables, it is permitted for long durations and distant periods, for yield and utilization. They differed about the short duration. It is said that it is for a day or so, and it is also said that this is not permitted in the case of a slave or a riding animal. With respect to (personal) service, it is said that this is permitted for a period of five days, and it is said for a month or a little more than that.

About the usufruct of things, like one of them using a house for a duration and the other for a similar duration, it is said that it is permitted for residence in a house and the cultivation of land, but it is not permitted for earning revenue through renting, except for short durations. It is also said that it is permitted on the analogy of things used on the basis of time. Similar is the opinion about the service of a slave or animal where the discussion takes place on the basis of the division of time.

This, then, is the discussion about the division of inherited wealth, benefits, and the validating and invalidating conditions. What remains in this book is the discussion of the *aḥkām*.

36.2. Chapter 2: The Discussion of the *Aḥkām*

Qisma is one of the binding contracts, which the parties to the division cannot revoke nor can they withdraw from, except in the case of a contingency. Such contingencies are three: cheating, existence of a defect, and the right of a third party (*istiḥqāq*). Revocation is not allowed in cases of cheating, unless it has occurred in the drawing of lots, by agreement of the school. An exception, however, is made by those who make an analogy from its effectiveness (that is, of cheating) in sale and, therefore, hold it necessary even in division.

With respect to return due to defect, in Ibn al-Qāsim's view, the defect may be found in a major part of an individual's share or in a small part. When it is found in most of the share, it is possible that the share of his co-sharer has been consumed or not consumed. If it has been consumed, the finder of the defect returns part of his share to the co-ownership and acquires from his co-owner half the value of his share, as it existed on the day of possession. If the (co-owner's) share is not consumed, the division is revoked and the co-ownership is restored to its original position. If the defect was in a small part of the share, this small part alone is returned to the co-ownership, irrespective of whether the share of the co-owner is consumed. He has recourse to his co-owner for half the value of the excess and does not claim anything for what is in his possession, even if it is defective. Ashhab said: the thing which precludes return has preceded in the Book of Sales.[161] ᶜAbd al-ᶜAzīz ibn al-Mājishūn said that the existence of a defect revokes the division based on the drawing of lots, but not that which is through consent, as the one based on consent amounts to sale, while that based on the drawing of lots is the separation of rights; if it is revoked due to cheating it must be revoked and returned for defects.

The *ḥukm* of third-party rights (*istiḥqāq*), according to Ibn al-Qāsim, is the same as the *ḥukm* for the existence of defects, in case the claimed part is the major portion and the share of the co-sharer has not expired; he again becomes

[161] This is how it appears in the text. Perhaps, it should read: "What Ashhab said, about the factor that precludes return, has preceded in the Book of Sales".

a co-sharer for whatever is in his possession. If the share has expired, he has recourse to half the value of whatever is left in his possession. If the claim is very small, he has recourse to half its value. Muḥammad said that if a claim has been made on what is in the possession of one of them, division is annulled in the case of drawing of lots, as it has become obvious that the division was not fair, as was the case in the opinion of Ibn al-Mājishūn in defects.

When a claim is made on wealth, like the claim of a debt on the estate (inheritance) after division, or the claim of a bequest (*waṣiyya*), or the claim of an heir, Mālik's disciples differ. If a debt is claimed, it is said in the well-known view of the school, which was held by Ibn al-Qāsim, that the division is cancelled unless the heirs agree to pay the debt themselves, irrespective of whether their shares are still in their possession, or destroyed by a natural calamity. It is said that the division is cancelled with respect to the shares that are still in their possession and have not been destroyed by a natural calamity; there is no recourse for the debt to the person whose share has been destroyed by a natural calamity, nor does he have a recourse to the other heirs for what is left in their possession after payment of the debt. It is also said that the division is cancelled, as it must be, as a right of Allāh, on the basis of the words of the Exalted, "[A]fter any legacy he may have bequeathed, or debt (may have been paid)".[162] Again, it is said that the division is cancelled, except with respect to one who has been paid a debt that he (the deceased) had intended to pay. This is the *ḥukm* for the claim upon the heirs by the legatee (*mūṣā lahu*).

The division is not cancelled because of the claim of the heir on the co-ownership after the division, but before the expiry of the share of each one of them, and he takes his share from each, if it is something that is measured or weighed; if it is an animal or goods, the division is set aside. Does each one of them compensate that which perishes in his possession, without any fault of his? It is said that he does and it is also said that he is not liable.

[162] Qur'ān 4:11

XXXVII
THE BOOK OF *RAHN*[163] (SECURITY FOR A DEBT; PLEDGE; MORTGAGE)

The source for this book are the words of the Exalted, "If ye be on a journey and cannot find a scribe, then a pledge in hand (shall suffice)".[164] The discussion in this book is about the elements (*arkān*), conditions and *aḥkām*.

37.1. Chapter 1: The Elements (*Arkān*)

The *arkān* deal with the *rāhin* (pledgor, mortgagor) and the *marhūn* (the pledged property), the *murtahin* (pledgee, mortgagee), the thing in return for which the pledge is made, and the nature of the contract of *rahn* (pledge, or mortgage).

37.1.1. Element 1: The Pledgor (*Rāhin*)

There is no dispute that one of the attributes (of the legal capacity) of the pledgor must be that he is not interdicted by those having the authority to interdict. The *waṣī* (executor) pledges on behalf of one under his authority, when it is judicious in case of necessity, according to Mālik. Al-Shāfiʿī said that he pledges for his obvious interest (*maṣlaḥa*). The *mukātab* and the *maʾdhūn* (authorized) slaves can also pledge, in the opinion of Mālik. Saḥnūn said that if he pledges borrowed wealth, it is not permitted. Mālik and al-Shāfiʿī agreed about the insolvent person (*muflis*) that his pledge is not permitted. Abū Ḥanīfa said that it is. Mālik's opinion differed about a person whose liabilities had surpassed his assets, as to whether his pledge was allowed, that is, whether it was binding. The well-known opinion narrated from him is that it is allowed,

[163] The term *rahn* has generally been translated into English as pledge or mortgage, by modern writers, both Muslim and Western. The *rahn* transaction is somewhat different from pledge or mortgage. The contract of *rahn* as explained by the author here is merely a security for a debt that exists, for whatever reason, before the *rahn* is transacted; the pledge is made when the payment of the loan becomes due. It does not involve pledging, pawning, or mortgaging where something is submitted as a collateral and some value, money or other, is raised as a loan to be returned later. Such a contract would amount to a sale, according to Muslim jurists, which is revocable at the termination of the agreed period, with the buyer having the right to dispose of the property during this period. This kind of contract (pledge or mortgage) would, perhaps, be permissible under Ḥauafite law (e.g. *bayʿ al-wafāʾ*), but certainly not according to the description of *rahn* by the author. It appears, however, that Mālik did permit this transaction. Please note his opinion as against that of al-Shāfiʿī discussed at the end of the third element.

[164] Qurʾān 2:283

that is, before he becomes insolvent. The disagreement refers to the question whether an insolvent is interdicted. Any person who is qualified to be a pledgor is also qualified to be a pledgee (*murtahin*).

37.1.2. Element 2: The Pledge (*Rahn*)

The Shafiᶜites said that it is valid with three conditions. First, that it should be an *ᶜayn* (corporeal present property) and it is not permitted to pledge a *dayn* (claim for a debt). Second, that the pledgor should not prevent the pledgee from having access to it, as in the case of the *muṣḥaf* (written copy of the Qurʾān). Mālik permits the pledge of the *muṣḥaf* with the condition that the pledgee does not use it. The disagreement is based on the saleability of the *marhūn*. Third, that the pledge should be capable of being sold after the termination of the period (of the pledge). It is permitted, according to Mālik, to pledge things whose sale is not permitted at the time of the pledge, like crops and fruit that have not ripened. These are not to be sold, according to him, for discharging a debt before they have begun to ripen even if the period of the pledge has expired. Two opinions are narrated from al-Shāfiᶜī about fruit that has not begun to ripen. These, in his view, are to be sold at the time of the termination of the period with the condition of immediate picking. Abū Ḥāmid said that the preferred opinion is about its permissibility.

The pledging of things not physically specified is permitted according to Mālik, as in the case of stamped *dīnārs* and *dirhams*. It is also not a condition in *rahn* that the property should be owned by the pledgor, either according to Mālik or according to al-Shāfiᶜī; in fact, it is permitted by them that it be a borrowed thing. They agreed that among its conditions is the acknowledgement by the pledgor of the possession of the pledgee over it. They disagreed when the possession of the pledgee is the result of *ghaṣb* (usurpation) and the pledgor later ratifies it as a pledge. Mālik said that it is permitted to allow the conversion of a liability of usurpation to that of a pledge, and the person from whom the property is usurped may declare the thing usurped to be a pledge in the hands of the usurper before repossessing it. Al-Shāfiᶜī said that this is not permitted and it stays as a liability of the usurper unless he (the pledgor) repossesses it. They disagreed about pledging the *res nullius* (property not owned by anyone), with Abū Ḥanīfa disallowing it and Mālik and al-Shāfiᶜī permitting it. The reason for disagreement being whether it can be owned.

37.1.3. Element 3: The Consideration for the *Rahn*

The principle in Mālik's school is that it is permitted to accept collateral in return for all those things that can serve as a price (*thaman*) in all kinds of sales, except (when the exchange would amount to) *ṣarf* or the advance payment of *salam* that is related to liability. This is so, as a condition of *ṣarf* is (immediate) mutual possession; it is, therefore, not permitted in the contract of *rahn*. Similarly, the advance payment of *salam*, though according to Mālik it differs from *ṣarf* in this regard. Some of the Ẓāhirites said that accepting a pledge is not permitted, except in the specific case of *salam*, that is, as a security for the object of *salam*. They upheld this due to the verse of *rahn*, which was revealed in the context of debts arising from sales, which is *salam* according to them. It was as if they considered this to be a condition for the validity of *rahn* as the verse of *rahn* begins with the words, "O ye who believe!! When ye contract a debt for a fixed term, record it in writing",[165] and this is followed by the directive: "If ye be on a journey and cannot find a scribe, then a pledge in hand (shall suffice)".[166]

Thus, in Mālik's view, it is permitted to accept a pledge in the case of *salam*, loan, usurpation, compensation for destroyed property, damages in torts against property, and in (damages for) intentional injuries in which there is no retaliation (*qawad*), like the (injuries called) *mā*ʾ*mūma* and *jā*ʾ*ifa*. Regarding intentional murder and bodily injuries for which retaliation is prescribed, two opinions have been derived for the acceptance of a pledge in place of *diya* (composition, reparation) when the *walī* (one who possesses the right of retaliation) has forgiven (the offender). The first is that it is permitted, which is based on the view that the *walī* has an option between retaliation and *diya* in intentional murder (ʿ*amd*). Second, that it is not permitted, which is also based on an opinion that the *walī* has no option, but to retaliate when the offender refuses to pay the *diya*.

It is also permitted to accept a pledge in the case of manslaughter (*qatl al-khaṭa*ʾ) from a member of the the ʿ*āqila* after a year. It is permitted in ʿ*āriya* (borrowing), for which there is liability for compensation, but is not valid in those with no liability. It is permitted in hire, and in *ju*ʾ*l* after the completion of work, but not before it. It is permitted in the case of *mahr* (dower). *Rahn* is not permitted in *ḥudūd* or in *qiṣāṣ* (probably, as bail for release) or in *kitāba*, and, on the whole, in those things where surety (*kafāla*) is not permitted.

The Shāfiʿites said that there are three conditions for the thing for which a pledge may be made. First, that it should be a loan (*dayn*), a pledge is not allowed for an ʿ*ayn*. Second, that it should have accrued, and it is not permitted before accrual, like demanding a pledge for a loan requested;[167] this is permitted by Mālik. Third, that its becoming binding (*luzūm*) should not be something likely to happen, and it should not be binding like the *rahn* in *kitāba*. This view is closer to that of Mālik.

165 Qurʾān 2:282

166 Qurʾān 2:282

167 This would apply to the raising of loans by offering collateral.

37.2. Chapter 2: The Discussion of Conditions

The conditions of *rahn* expressly stated in the *sharᶜ* (law) are of two kinds: conditions of validity, and the conditions of *fasād*. The conditions of validity, expressly stated, for *rahn*, that is, for its being (constituted as) *rahn*, are two. The first, which is agreed upon generally, and disputed from the aspect of its being a condition, is possession. The second is disputed about its stipulation.

They agreed, on the whole, about possession that it is a condition in *rahn* due to the words of the Exalted, "Then a pledge in hand (shall suffice)".[168] They differed whether it is a condition of completion or a condition of validity. The purpose of the distinction is that those who say it is a condition of validity, maintain that until possession is delivered, *rahn* is not binding for the *rāhin* (pledgor). Those who maintain that it is condition of completion consider it binding through the contract itself and compel the pledgor for the delivery of possession, unless the pledgee has delayed the claim to such an extent that the pledgor has become insolvent, has fallen ill, or has died.

Mālik held that it is a condition of completion, while Abū Ḥanīfa, al-Shāfiᶜī, and the Ẓāhirites maintained that it is a condition of validity. The reliance of Mālik is upon the analogy of conclusion through offer and acceptance in all the other binding contracts. The reliance of the others is on the words of the Exalted, "Then a pledge in hand (shall suffice)".[169] Some of the Ẓāhirites said that *rahn* is not allowed (in this case) in the absence of a scribe, because of the words of the Exalted, "[A]nd cannot find a scribe, then a pledge in hand shall suffice".[170] The Ẓāhirites do not permit the depositing of a collateral with a trustworthy (third party).

According to Mālik, a condition for the validity of *rahn* is continuous possession of the pledgee. When it reverts to the possession of the pledgor, with the consent of the pledgee, by way of *ᶜāriya* or *wadīʾa* (deposit) or some other way, it is no longer remains binding. Al-Shāfiᶜī said that continued possession is not a condition of validity. Mālik generalized the condition on the basis of the apparent meaning, interpreting the words of the Exalted, "a pledge in hand", to mean the existence of continued possession, which he deemed a condition. Al-Shāfiᶜī said that when possession is found *rahn* is valid and concluded, and it is not altered by loaning or by any other means of disposal, as is the case in sale. It would have been appropriate, however, for those who stipulate possession for the validity of the contract to lay down continuity as a condition, and for those who do not stipulate it as a condition of validity not to impose continuity as a condition.

[168] Qurʾān 2:283
[169] Qurʾān 2:283
[170] Qurʾān 2:283

They agreed upon its permissibility during a journey, but disagreed about it when the parties are resident. The majority permitted this, but the Ẓāhirites and Mujāhid said that it is not permitted in residence, because of the apparent meaning of the words of the Exalted, "If ye be on a journey and cannot find a scribe . . . ".[171] The majority sought support from what has been laid down that "the Prophet (God's peace and blessings be upon him) made a pledge when he was not travelling". The derivation of the prohibition of *rahn* in a settlement from the verse is based on the indirect indication of the text (*dalīl al-khiṭāb*).

The prohibited condition, proscribed by the text, is the stipulation that he (the pledgor) should redeem the *rahn* at the end of the period, otherwise the collateral is his (the pledgee's). They agreed that this condition makes rescission obligatory and it is the meaning of the words of the Prophet (God's peace and blessings be upon him), "Do not forfeit the pledge".

37.3. **Chapter 3: The Discussion of the *Aḥkām***

This chapter is divided into the identification of the rights and liabilities of the pledgor, the rights and liabilities of the pledgee, and the identification of the *ḥukm* in case of their disputes, which relate either to the contract itself or to contingencies affecting the pledge. From among these, we shall discuss the well-known agreements and disagreements of the jurists of different regions.

The right of the pledgee in the *rahn* is to keep it in his possession till the pledgor pays what is due from him. If he does not redeem it by the end of the period, the pledgee has the right, if the pledgor has not given him the right to sell it, to file a claim with the *sulṭān*, who will sell it and give the pledgee his due. This is also the case when the pledgor is missing. It is also permissible for the pledgor to appoint the pledgee as his agent for the sale of the pledge on the termination of the period. Mālik, however, disapproved of it and preferred that the case be referred to the *sulṭān*, always.

The *rahn* is linked with its consideration (the *marhūn fīh*) as a whole and in parts. This means that if the pledge has been made in consideration of a number of things, and the pledgor has repaid some, the pledge shall remain with the pledgee in its entirety, till he has recovered all that is due. Some held that, on the contrary, the pledge remains with the pledgee in proportion to the remaining dues. The argument of the majority is that the collateral is tied up in its entirety due to a right, and it follows that it should be restrained due to each part, the basis being the seisin of the estate with respect to the heirs till

[171] Qurʾān 2:283

they pay the debt owed by the deceased. The argument of the other party is that all of it is tied up for the entire payment, it is, therefore, necessary that parts of it be tied up for parts of that, the basis being surety (*kafāla*).

One of the well-known issues of this topic is their disagreement about mesne profits that are separable, like the fruit on the mortgaged trees, like revenue, and like offspring. They disagreed whether these are included in the collateral. A group maintained that separable mesne profits are not to be included as part of the pledge, that is, such profits as accrue in the possession of the pledgee. Among those who held this opinion is al-Shāfiʿī. Others maintained that the entire increase is included in the *rahn*. Those who held this opinion are Abū Ḥanīfa and al-Thawrī. Mālik drew a distinction and said that whatever separable increase is of the same nature and form is included in the *rahn*, like the child of a slave-girl; but that which does not have the same nature or form is not included, irrespective of whether it is produced by it, like the fruit of a tree, or is not produced by it, like the rent of a house or the earning of a slave.

The reliance of those who were of the view that the mesne profits of a *rahn* and its revenue are for the pledgor (*rāhin*) are the words of the Prophet (God's peace and blessings be upon him), "The *rahn* is to be milked and ridden". They said that this cannot be interpreted to give a right to the *rāhin* to ride it and milk it, as this would mean it is not delivered, which is contrary to the existence of the *rahn* in which delivery is a condition. On the other hand, it cannot be interpreted to mean that the pledgee may milk it and ride it. Thus, the only remaining meaning is that the wages for riding it (and for its other produce) are for its owner and the liability of its maintenance is upon him. They also argued on the basis of the general meaning of the words of the Prophet (God's peace and blessings be upon him), "Those who pledged it, for them is its revenue and upon them its liability". They also added that it is an additional development over that which he agreed to pledge, and it should belong to the pledgee only with an additional stipulation.

Abū Ḥanīfa's reliance is on the fact that the *furūʿ* (offshoots) are dependent upon the *uṣūl* and must, therefore, follow the *ḥukm* of the *aṣl*. It is for this reason that the *ḥukm* of the child of a slave-girl is dependent upon the *ḥukm* of the mother in the contracts of *tadbīr* and *kitāba*. Mālik argued that the child of a slave-girl has the *ḥukm* of the mother in sale, that is, it is dependent upon her, but he distinguished between a child and fruit on the basis of a *sunna*. Thus, fruit does not depend upon the sale of its *aṣl* (the tree) except with a condition, whereas the child of a slave-girl does without a condition.

The majority maintain that the pledgee has no right to benefit in any way from the pledged property. A group, however, said that if the pledge is an animal, the pledgee has the right to milk it or ride it to the extent that he feeds it or spends on it. This is the opinion of Aḥmad and Isḥāq, who argued on the basis of the apparent meaning of what has been related by Abū Hurayra from the Prophet (God's peace and blessings be upon him), who said, "The *rahn* is to be milked and ridden".

Within this topic is their disagreement about the perishing (of the pledge) in the possession of the pledgee, as to who is liable. A group said that a *rahn* is merely an *amāna* (trust) in the hands of the pledgee and the pledgor is liable. The claim of the pledgee, along with his oath, that he was not negligent nor did he transgress is to be accepted. Among those who held this opinion are al-Shāfiʿī, Aḥmad, Abū Thawr, and the majority of the traditionists. Another group said that the *rahn* is the liability of the pledgee and anything befalling it is upon him. Among those who held this opinion are Abū Ḥanīfa and the majority of the Kūfīs. Those who made the pledgee liable are divided into two opinions. Some of them said that the pledge is to be compensated by the lesser of its value or the amount of debt. This was the opinion of Abū Ḥanīfa, Sufyān, and a group. Others said that it is to be compensated by its value, whether less or more, and if there is a surplus over and above the debt, the pledgor takes it from the pledgee. This is the opinion of ʿAlī ibn Abī Ṭālib, ʿAṭāʾ and Isḥāq. One group made a distinction between visible things about which he can be aware, like an animal or real estate, and those that are not apparently visible, like goods. They said that he is liable for that which is concealed from view, but a trustee for that which is visible. Those who held this opinion are Mālik, al-Awzāʿī and ʿUthmān al-Battī, except that Mālik said that if witnesses testify to the perishing of things hidden without any negligence or wastage on his part, he is not liable. Al-Awzāʿī and ʿUthmān al-Battī said that he is liable anyway, irrespective of the availability of evidence. Mālik's opinion is followed by Ibn al-Qāsim, while Ashhab follows the opinion of al-Awzāʿī and ʿUthmān al-Battī.

The reliance of those who rendered it a non-compensatory trust is the tradition of Saʿīd ibn al-Musayyib from Abū Hurayra that the Prophet (God's peace and blessings be upon him) said, "Do not constrain the *rahn*, those who pledged it, for them is its revenue and upon them its liability". That is on him is its fodder and for him its revenue, and upon him is its perishing and injury. They said that the pledgor agreed to its being a trust and, therefore, resembles the depositor, in their view. Al-Muzanī, from among the disciples of al-Shāfiʿī, arguing for him said that Mālik and those who followed him held that the animal and whatever leads to its loss are a trust, it is necessary that it should be so as a whole, while Abū Ḥanīfa maintained that whatever is surplus from the value of the pledge over the debt is a trust.

The meaning of the words of the Prophet, "upon them is its liability", according to Mālik and those who followed him, is its maintenance, and they said that the meaning of the words of the Prophet, "The *rahn* is to be ridden and milked", is that the rent from riding is for the owner, while its maintenance is upon him. Abū Ḥanīfa and his disciples interpreted the words of the Prophet (God's peace and blessings be upon him), "for them its booty and on them its liability", to mean its yield is what is left as surplus over debt, while its liability is what is deficient.

The reliance of those who view that the pledgee is liable for it is (on the argument) that it is an *ᶜayn* to which is initially related the right of satisfying a claim, which should be discharged when it perishes; the basis being the perishing of the sold commodity in the possession of the seller when he holds on to it till the price is paid. This is agreed upon by the majority, though according to Mālik, it is like a *rahn*. Perhaps, they argued on the basis of what is related from the Prophet (God's peace and blessings be upon him) "that a man pledged a horse with another, but it perished in his possession. The Prophet (God's peace and blessings be upon him) said to the pledgee, 'Your right is extinguished' ".

The distinction made by Mālik between what is visible and what is not is based on *istiḥsān*. It means that suspicion arises in the case of what is not visible and not in the case of what is visible. They differed about the meaning of *istiḥsān*, which was often used as a basis by Mālik, declaring it as weak and saying that it resembles the *istiḥsān* used by Abū Ḥanīfa. They defined *istiḥsān* as an opinion that is not based on a valid source. The meaning of *istiḥsān*, in Mālik's view, however, is the combining of conflicting evidence (*adilla*). If this is so, it is not a ruling without evidence (*dalīl*).

The majority maintain that the pledgor has no right to sell the pledge or give it away. If he sells it, the pledgee has the right to ratify (grant *ijāza*) or rescind it. Mālik said that if he lets it out on rent and claims that it is for the early satisfaction of his right, his claim is to be accepted with an oath. A group, however, said that its sale is permitted. When the pledge is a male slave or a slave-girl and the pledgor frees him or her, then, according to Mālik, if the pledgor is well off the manumission is accepted as valid and he must make an early settlement of the right of the pledgee, but if he is hard up manumission is disallowed and the slave is to be sold to settle the right of the pledgee from the price. From al-Shāfiᶜī, there are three opinions: the rejection of manumission; its ratification; and the third is like the opinion of Mālik.

The jurists disagree about the disagreement of the pledgor and the pledgee over the extent of the claim met by the pledge. Mālik said that the acceptable opinion is that of the pledgee as to the extent of the claim satisfied by the pledge, unless the value of the pledge is not less than his claim; for whatever is surplus over the value of the pledge, the accepted opinion is that of the pledgor. Al-Shāfiᶜī, Abū Ḥanīfa, al-Thawrī, and the majority of the jurists of the provinces said that the accepted opinion is that of the pledgor. The argument of the majority is that the pledgor is the defendant (*muddaʿa ʿalayh*), while the pledgee is the claimant. It is, therefore, necessary that the oath be on the pledgor, due to the apparent meaning of the well-known *sunna*. The reliance of Mālik, here, is on the argument that though the pledgee is a claimant in this case there is a ground for the transfer of the oath in his favour, in view of the existence of the pledge which supports him. One of his principles is that the oath is to be taken by the litigant whose claim appears to be stronger. This, however, is not so for the majority, as the pledgor may have offered a collateral whose value is more than the corresponding claim.

When the pledge perishes and they differ about its description, the accepted statement, according to Mālik, is that of the pledgee as he is the defendant and is acknowledging part of what is claimed from him. This is based upon his principles, as the pledgee is also liable for what is concealed from view. According to the principles of al-Shāfiʿī, the oath for the pledgee is inconceivable, unless the pledgor denies the very perishing of the pledge. For Abū Ḥanīfa, the accepted statement is that of the pledgee with respect to the value of the pledge, and he is in no need of a description, whereas for Mālik the oath is about the description and valuation on the basis of the description.

When they differ about both things, I mean, about the description of the pledge and about the extent of the claim, the accepted statement is that of the pledgee about the description, and about the claim it is whatever the deposed description of the pledge supports it to be. This is weak. Does the claim indicate the value of the pledge when they agree about the claim and differ about its value? There are two opinions about it in the school, the more appropriate is to demand a witness; if the (value of the) debt is proved through the pledge, then the (value of the) pledge is to be proved through the debt.

The cases under this topic are many, and what we have mentioned suffices for our purposes.

XXXVIII
THE BOOK OF *ḤAJR* (INTERDICTION)

The discussion in this book is covered in three chapters. The first chapter is about the categories of persons interdicted. The second deals with the question as to when they are released from interdiction, when they are placed under it, and on what conditions they are released. Chapter three is about the identification of the *aḥkām* related to their acts with respect to revocation and ratification.

38.1. **Chapter 1: The Categories of Persons Interdicted**

The jurists agreed unanimously about the obligation of interdiction in the case of orphans, who have not attained puberty (*ḥulum*), on account of the words of the Exalted, "Prove orphans till they reach the marriageable age; then if ye find them of sound judgment, deliver unto them their fortune; and devour it not by squandering and in haste lest they grow up. Whoso (of the guardians) is rich, let him abstain generously (from taking of the property of orphans); and whoso is poor let him take thereof in reason (for his guardianship). And when ye deliver up their fortune unto orphans, have (the transaction) witnessed in their presence. Allāh sufficeth as a Reckoner".[172]

They disagreed about mature and sane persons with respect to interdiction, when they indulge in the squandering of their wealth. Mālik, al-Shāfiʿī, the jurists of Medina, and many of the jurists of Iraq upheld the permissibility of the initiation of interdiction against them with the order of the ruler. This is done when their prodigality is proved after they are asked to show cause, but have no defence. This is also the opinion of Ibn ʿAbbās and Ibn al-Zubayr. Abū Ḥanīfa and a group from Iraq maintained that interdiction cannot be initiated against majors, which is also the opinion of Ibrāhīm and Ibn Sīrīn. These jurists are divided into two opinions. Among them are those who said that interdiction is not permitted against them, in any circumstances, after they have attained puberty, even if they exhibit prodigality. Others held that if they persist in being prodigal from the age of minority, interdiction is to

[172] Qurʾān 4:6

continue, even when they have displayed discretion (*rushd*) temporarily after puberty, but subsequently revert to their prodigal ways. They do not, however, initiate interdiction against them (once they have displayed *rushd* on attaining majority). Abū Ḥanīfa sets a limit for the removal of (continued) interdiction, even when prodigality is exhibited, as the age of twenty-five years.

The argument of those who initiate the imposition of interdiction on majors, is that interdiction is obligatory in the case of minors due to prodigality, which is usually found in their case; it is, therefore, necessary that *ḥajr* be imposed on those who exhibit the same meaning in their acts, even though they are not minors. They said that it is for this reason that the existence of discretion, along with the attainment of majority, is stipulated for the removal of *ḥajr*. Allāh, the Exalted, says, "[T]hen if ye find them of sound judgment, deliver unto them their fortunes". This indicates that the cause requiring interdiction is prodigality. The reliance of the Ḥanafites is upon the tradition of Ḥibbān ibn Munqidh in which he says that "it was brought to the notice of the Messenger of Allāh (God's peace and blessings be upon him) by a person that he was cheated in sales. The Messenger of Allāh (God's peace and blessings be upon him) decreed, in his case, the stipulation of an option for three days, but did not interdict him". Perhaps, they regarded minority to be the cause of the prohibition of undertaking transactions in wealth, on the evidence of its effectiveness in the discharge of religious obligations.

Minority has been given importance as it is a state in which prodigality is a common feature, just as deficiency of reason is common in it. It is also for this reason that puberty has been fixed as a sign of (attaining mental maturity, making the person subject to) the obligation of legal liability (*taklīf*) and a sign of discretion. Both are found in such a person, that is, reason and discretion. Just as exceptional early mental maturity is not taken into account for the purposes of legal liability, similarly, exceptions of prodigality have not been considered, that is, the existence of prodigality after puberty with respect to interdiction. They said that the words of the Exalted, "Give not unto the foolish (what is in) your (keeping of their) wealth, which Allāh hath given you to maintain; but feed and clothe them from it, and speak kindly unto them",[173] do not contain more than the requirement of keeping their hands away from their wealth, which does not necessitate the revocation and invalidation of their sales.

Those placed under interdiction are six, according to Mālik: the minor, the foolish, the slave, the insolvent, the sick, and the wife. The discussion of each follows in the appropriate place.

[173] Qur'ān 4:5

38.2. Chapter 2: Removal of Interdiction, Time of Imposition and Conditions of Removal

The discussion in this chapter takes place from two aspects: the time of release of minors from *ḥajr*, and the time of release for the prodigal. We say: minors, on the whole, are of two kinds: males and females. Each one of them either has a father or an executor (*waṣī*), or they may be *muhmal* (neglected), that is, those who have attained majority, but have neither a father nor an executor.

They agreed about male minors having fathers that they do not move out of interdiction, until they have reached the age of legal liability and have attained discretion; though they disagreed as to the nature of discretion. This is on the basis of the words of the Exalted, "Prove orphans till they reach the marriageable age; then if ye find them of sound judgment, deliver unto them their fortune".[174]

They disagreed about the female. The majority maintained that her *ḥukm* is the same as that for the males, that is, (interdiction is lifted with) the commencement of menstruation and the attainment of discretion. Mālik said, in the well-known opinion from him, that she stays under the guardianship of her father till such time that she marries and her marriage is consummated and discretion is found in her. The opinion of the majority is also related from him. The disciples of Mālik have other opinions in this. They said that she is under the guardianship of her father till one year after the consummation of her marriage; some of them said till two years have passed, and it is also said till seven years have passed. Mālik's argument is that discretion is not visible till after their first dealings with men. The opinions of his disciples, however, are weak and conflict with the text and analogy. They did not stipulate discretion, in accordance with the text, nor do their views agree with analogy, as the appearance of discretion is conceivable prior to this fixed period.

If we uphold Mālik's opinion and not that of the majority that the consideration in the case of males having fathers is puberty and the appearance of discretion, then Mālik's opinion differs. One opinion is that when he (the child) attains puberty, but his foolishness cannot be distinguished from his discretion, the child is to be treated as a *safīh* till discretion becomes obvious. This is his well-known opinion. It is also related from him that he is to be considered as having *rushd* till he exhibits foolishness.

The person having an executor (*waṣī*) does not move out of interdiction, according to Mālik's well-known opinion, except by the release from interdiction given to him by his executor, that is, he says about him that he possesses discretion. This is so, without dispute, when he (the executor) has

[172] Qur'ān 4:6

been appointed by the father, but (it takes place) with the permission of the judge (*qaḍī*) along with that of the executor, when he has been appointed by someone other than the father, about which there is dispute. It is said about the executor appointed by the father that his word (alone) that the child is a *rashīd* is not acceptable till his discretion is made manifest, while it is also said that his (the child's) position *vis-à-vis* the executor is the same as that with the father: he is released from interdiction on the appearance of discretion even when the executor has not taken witnesses to the effect. The *ḥukm* of the person, in this case, whose state is undetermined is the same as that of the person with an undetermined state with respect to the father.

Ibn al-Qāsim, however, holds an opinion that establishment of guardianship (*wilāya*) cannot be considered with the appearance of discretion, nor is it discharged when foolishness is evident. This is also related from Mālik, but that is his opinion in the case of an orphan not a virgin. The difference between the opinions is that those who accept guardianship say that all his acts are to be invalidated, even if discretion had appeared, till such time that he is released from guardianship, but this is a weak opinion, because the effective factor is *rushd* not the order of the judge (*ḥākim*).

In their disagreement over the nature of *rushd* (discretion), Mālik is of the view that it is only (financial), that is, his ability to make profitable investment of wealth and to improve it, while al-Shāfiʿī stipulates along with this sound religious behaviour. The basis for their disagreement is their dispute whether the term *rushd* may apply to the non-righteous.

The position of the virgin with respect to the executor is the same as the position of the male in so far as she does not move out of guardianship except through a release, unless she advances in age without marriage, though this is disputed. It is also said that her position with respect to the executor is the same as that with the father, which is the opinion of Ibn al-Mājishūn. Their disagreement about the appearance of her discretion was not so intense as in the case of the orphan.

The well-known opinion about the neglected male is that his acts are valid when he reaches puberty, irrespective of his attaining majority in a state of *safah*, which may have been continuous, declared, or undeclared. Ibn al-Qāsim, on the other hand, considers each act in itself when it takes place. If it is based on discretion, he permits it, otherwise he rejects it. With respect to the female orphan, who neither has a father nor an executor, there are two opinions about her in the school. First, that her acts are valid when she begins to menstruate. Second, that her acts are rejected, unless she stayed unmarried for a long time, and this is the better-known opinion.

38.3. Chapter 3: Legality of Acts with Respect to Rejection and Ratification

The discussion in this chapter relates to two things. First, what kind of acts of the different categories of persons under interdiction are permitted? If they undertake those acts, what is their *ḥukm* with respect to rejection or ratification? Similarly, what is the *ḥukm* of the acts of those neglected; namely, the children who attain puberty without having a father or an executor? All these individuals, as we have said, are either minors, who have not attained puberty, or are majors under continued interdiction since minority, or are majors under reimposed interdiction.

There is no dispute in the school that acts of charity like *hiba* (gift), *ṣadaqa* (charity), *ʿaṭiyya* (bestowal), and *ʿitq* (manumission) are not permitted to male minors, who have not attained puberty, and to women who have not begun to menstruate, even with the permission of the father or the executor. If something moves out of their hands without (a corresponding) compensation, it is suspended subject to the consideration of the guardian, if they have a guardian. If he finds it to be based on sound discretion, he ratifies it, otherwise he annuls it. If they do not have a guardian, a guardian is to be appointed to examine the action; even when he continues to transact till such time as a guardian is appointed, the ratification and rejection depend upon the guardian.

They disagreed when his (the minor's) act is so appropriate and sound that it should be ratified by the guardian, but the final outcome is contrary to the expectations of the market, or of the (expected) profit in what he sold, or of the discount in what he bought. Does the guardian have a right to cancel it? The well-known opinion is that he has the right to do so, while it is also said that he does not have such a right.

The minor is held liable for damage he may cause to any property not entrusted to him. They disagreed about that which he ruined and broke when it was entrusted to him. The oath he took and subsequently broke during his minority, like setting free slaves is not binding on him after he has attained puberty and discretion. They disagreed about the oath he had sworn during his minority but broke upon attaining majority. The well-known opinion is that it is not binding upon him. Ibn Kināna said that it is. He is not obliged to take an oath for a claim (he denies). They disagreed when he had only one witness, whether he takes an oath with him. The well-known opinion is that he does not, but it is related from Mālik and al-Layth that he does. The position of the virgin, having a father and an executor, is the same as the male, as long as she has not turned into a spinster, in the opinion of those who attach weight to this.

About the *safīh*, who is a major, the majority of the jurists, except Ibn Abī Laylā and Abū Yūsuf, maintain that a person interdicted, if he divorces his wife or transacts *khulʿ* with her, both his divorce and *khulʿ* are void. Ibn Abī Laylā differed in the case of manumission and said that it is to be given effect. The majority said that it is not to be given effect. In the case of his bequest (*waṣiyya*), I am not aware of a disagreement about its execution, but his *hiba*, *ṣadaqa*, *ʿaṭiyya*, *ʿitq*, and other acts recommended by religion are not binding on him, unless he emancipates his *umm al-walad* (female slave bearing his child), for her liberation is binding on him. All this is maintained in the school. Do her (the *umm al-waladʾ's*) possessions go with her? There is disagreement in this. It is said that they do, and it is said that they do not; while a distinction is also made by some between smaller and bigger things. What he (the *maḥjūr*) transacts for a counter-value is also subject to scrutiny by his guardian, if he has one; and one is appointed for him if he does not. If the guardian rejects his sale, but he has consumed the price taken, the rejection cannot be pursued; similarly, when he has destroyed the property bought.

The acts of those under interdiction and those neglected are divided, in Mālik's school, into four kinds: those to be completely rejected, even when discretion was displayed; the opposite of these, that is, all the acts are considered to be based upon discretion, though a degree of prodigality is involved; acts that are all considered to be based upon *safah*, unless discretion is exhibited; and the opposite of these too, that is, the acts are all considered to be based upon *rushd* till *safah* is evident.

Acts that are to be rejected entirely as acts of *safah* are those of the minor who has not attained puberty, though he exhibits some discretion, or those of the virgin having a father and an executor, unless she has turned into a spinster, on the opinion of those who consider *taʿnī*s, and they differed extensively about the age of *taʿnī*s as being below thirty to the age of sixty.

The case where the *ḥukm* assigned is *rushd*, even when some degree of prodigality is visible, is that of the *safīh*, when no guardianship has been established by his father, nor by the *sulṭan*, according to Mālik's well-known opinion. This is opposed by Ibn al-Qāsim, who considers *rushd* itself and not guardianship. This category includes the neglected virgin orphan, in Saḥnūn's opinion.

The person who is assigned the *ḥukm* of *safah* is the male child after the attainment of puberty, during the lifetime of his father, unless *rushd* is exhibited, and the virgin having a father, but not an executor, when she is married and her marriage is consummated, unless *rushd* is exhibited or the determined age is reached, according to those who consider such a limit. Similarly, the female orphan, who does not have an executor, in the opinion of those who consider her acts to be rejected.

The situation in which the *ḥukm* of *rushd* is assigned, till the appearance of *safah*, includes the virgin spinster, according to those who consider *taʿnīs*, and the married female whose marriage stands consummated and the fixed number of years after consummation having passed, according to those who consider such a period. It also covers the son with a father who has attained puberty, but his state of *rushd* is unknown, according to one of two narrations. It also includes the virgin daughter after puberty, on the basis of the narration that does not take into account consummation through marriage.

This, in general, is all that is to be covered in this book, though the cases are many.

XXXIX
THE BOOK OF *TAFLĪṢ* (INSOLVENCY; BANKRUPTCY)

The discussion in this book, in so far as it relates to *taflīs* (insolvency), is about the *aḥkām* of the *muflis* (insolvent).

We say: the term *iflās*, in the law, is applied in two meanings. First, when the debts completely cover the assets of the debtor, and his wealth does not suffice to pay his debts. Second, when he does not have any known wealth at all. In both cases of *iflās*, the jurists have differed about the *aḥkām*.

In the first case, that is, when his insolvency is brought to the notice of the judge (*ḥākim*), as we observed, the jurists differ whether the judge has the right to interdict him from disposing of his wealth, till he sells it for him and divides it among the creditors in proportion to their debts; or whether he is to imprison him, till he pays to them all his wealth in any proportion that they agree, or to those among them who agree. This disagreement can be conceived in the case of one who has wealth that meets the claims of debts, but refuses to satisfy his creditors. Does the judge sell his property for him and distribute it, or is he to imprison him till he distributes it among them with his own hands? The majority maintain that the judge is to sell his property for him and from it (the sale proceeds) he is to satisfy his creditors or creditor, in case he is well off, or he issues the verdict of insolvency against him, if his wealth does not equal the debts, and interdicts him with respect to transactions in it. This is Mālik's opinion and al-Shāfiʿī's, while the other view was upheld by Abū Ḥanīfa and a group of the jurists of Iraq.

The proof of Mālik and al-Shāfiʿī is the tradition of Muʿādh ibn Jabal "that his debts mounted in the time of the Messenger of Allāh (God's peace and blessings be upon him) and his creditors did not increase before he delivered to them his wealth", and the tradition of Abū Saʿīd al-Khudrī "that in the period of the Prophet a man suffered a loss through a calamity, in fruit that he had bought. His debts increased and the Messenger of Allāh said, 'Give him something as *ṣadaqa*'. People gave him charity, but it was not enough to meet his debts, so the Messenger of Allāh (God's peace and blessings be upon him) said, 'Take what you can find of his wealth and that is all you will have' ". (They also relied on) the tradition about the verdict of ʿUmar in the case of an insolvent whom he had imprisoned. He said, "O Men! Verily al-Usyaf, Usyaf Juhayna, has been content with not meeting his debts and trusts, and has been postponing. He raised loans and refused to meet them and they are now double that of his wealth, so he who has a claim for a debt against him should come to us". They also relied on a rational argument that if a person suffering from a fatal-illness is interdicted for the interests of the heirs, it is more appropriate that a debtor should be interdicted in the interests of the creditors. This opinion is more agreeable, as it is more just; Allāh knows best.

The proof of the other party, who uphold the view that the debtor should be imprisoned till he pays what is due from him or dies in that condition so that the judge may then sell his property and divide it among the creditors, is a tradition from Jābir when his father died as a *shahīd* (martyr) at Uḥud while he was under debt. When the creditors made a demand on him, Jābir says, "I went up to the Messenger of Allāh (God's peace and blessings be upon him) and related the matter to him. He asked them if they would accept my palm-grove and discharge the claim against my father, but they refused. The Messenger of Allāh, therefore, did not give them my palm-grove and said, 'I will come over to your place tomorrow'. He came over in the morning and went around the grove praying for abundance in its fruit". He (Jābir) says, "When I (finally) cut the fruit, I paid off their claim and (yet) something was left over". (They also rely upon) what was related about the death of Usayd ibn al-Ḥudayr when he was under a debt of ten thousand *dirhams*. "ᶜUmar ibn al-Khaṭṭāb summoned his creditors and presented his land to them for a period of four years in exchange for their claims upon him". They said that in all these traditions there is nothing that indicates the sale of the corpus (principal property) in satisfaction of debts. They maintained that the imprisonment of the debtor is indicated by the words of the Prophet (God's peace and blessings be upon him), "Undue postponement by one with means makes legal (an action against) his integrity and (also legitimizes his) punishment". They said that punishment here means his imprisonment. Perhaps they held similar the retrieval of his permission to the restitution of the principal property.

If we were to say that the insolvent should be interdicted, the discussion then relates to the questions: For what types of activities is he to be interdicted? For what kind of debts is there to be an apportionment (*muḥaṣṣa*) of shares? What types of property are to be apportioned? How is (all) this to be carried out?

There are two kinds of status for the insolvent (*muflis*): his status at the time of insolvency, before interdiction; and his status after interdiction. With respect to his status before interdiction, he is not permitted to do away with anything without (a corresponding) compensation, if it is not something that is binding upon him or is an act common in practice. The exemption in the case of things not binding upon him is made because he is to do that which is binding upon him by law, even if there is no compensation, like the maintenance of his needy parents and of his children. And the stipulation of not being customary was added as he is entitled to a reasonable consumption of his property without compensation, like sacrifice and expenditure on the ʿĪd (celebration) and payment of small charity. Similarly, practice permits his expenditure in cases where there is (a kind of) compensation, like marriage and his expenditure on his wife. His sale and purchase are also permitted as long as it does not involve the making of favours. Likewise, is his acknowledgement of a debt in cases that do not arouse suspicion. Mālik's opinion differed about the satisfaction of some of his creditors to the exclusion of others and also about (the redemption of) his pledges.

Those, among the majority, who upheld interdiction said that before the verdict of interdiction, he is just like ordinary people. The majority upheld this opinion as in principle all acts are valid till the imposition of interdiction. Mālik, on the other hand, took into account the actual fact of debts exceeding his assets, but he did not do so in each case as he permitted his sale and purchase when it did not involve favouritism, while he does not permit this for one who is interdicted.

In Mālik's view, his status after interdiction does not permit him to sell or purchase, nor to acquire or donate. His acknowledgement of a liability for a debt is not valid, either for a relative or for someone distant, unless one of them, it is said, has supporting evidence, or, it is also said, someone is known to have made a demand from him. They differed in the school about his acknowledgement of determined property as (belonging to) the capital of *qirāḍ* or a deposit, into three opinions: validity; rejection; and the third is to make a distinction whether there exists, for the capital of *qirāḍ* or deposit, (supporting) evidence. It is said that if it exists (that is, evidence), his claim is to be accepted as truthful, otherwise not.

They disagreed under this topic whether the debts of the insolvent with different (repayment) periods become immediate. Mālik maintained that insolvency, in this case, resembles death (and, therefore, such debts become immediate), while the others held a contrary opinion, though the majority held that deferred debts become immediate on death. Ibn Shihāb said that there has been a practice (*sunna*) that the debt becomes due as soon as he dies. The evidence is that Allāh, the Exalted, has not permitted (the distribution of) inheritance except after the satisfaction of debts. The heirs are in one of two positions. They may not wish to delay (the satisfaction of) their rights in the estate till the expiry of the period of the debt, thus making the prompt satisfaction of the debt necessary, or they may consent to the delay of (the distribution) of the estate till the debts become due, with the debts being the liability of the estate and not that of the heirs as against the situation before death, when they were a liability of the deceased, which is appropriate with respect to the rights of the creditors. Some, for this reason, maintained that if the creditors consent to the carrying of the liability by the heirs, the debts will remain postponed till their respective periods. Among those who held this opinion is Ibn Sīrīn, while Abū ʿUbayd, from among the jurists of the provinces, preferred it. Insolvency, however, does not resemble death completely, though in both the capacity to bear liabilities is gone, because the revival of the capacity of the insolvent, unlike that of the deceased, is to be hoped for.

The discussion of the property of the insolvent to which the creditors have recourse depends on the species and quantity. If the corpus of the thing itself, because of which the creditor has a claim against the insolvent, has expired, the debt exists as a liability of the insolvent. If, however, the thing exists and has not expired, but the creditor did not take possession of the price (*thaman*), the jurists of the provinces differ about it into four opinions. The first is that the owner of the goods has a prior right to it, unless he relinquishes it and participates in the liquidation. This was the opinion of al-Shāfiʿī, Aḥmad, and Abū Thawr. The second opinion takes into account the value of the goods as it was on the day of the verdict of insolvency. If it was less than the price, the owner is given a choice between taking them and participating with the creditors in liquidation. If it is more than or equal to the price, he takes the goods. This was Mālik's opinion and that of his disciples. The third opinion considers the average of the value of the goods in both kinds of insolvency (before and after the verdict); if the value equals the price or is less than it, they are delivered to him, that is, the seller, but if it is more, he is paid the price and the remaining is to be included in the liquidation. This opinion was held by a group of traditionists. The fourth opinion is that he shares it along with the creditors in all circumstances. This was Abū Ḥanīfa's opinion and that of the Kūfan jurists.

The basis in this issue is the confirmed tradition from Abū Hurayra that the Messenger of Allāh said, "If a person becomes insolvent, and another man finds his property among his wealth, he has a prior right to it to the exclusion of others". This tradition has been recorded by Mālik, al-Bukhārī, and Muslim, in similar words; the words quoted here are from Mālik. Among them (the jurists) were those who interpreted it in its general meaning. These were the jurists who hold the first opinion. Some restricted it by means of analogy, saying that the underlying meaning is the support for the owner of the goods due to the existence of his goods. The most he can do is to take the price for which he sold it. To participate with the creditors and be paid more than the price is not permitted according to the principles of the law, particularly when the creditors have the right to purchase the goods for the price, as is stated by Mālik. The jurists of Kūfa, on the other hand, rejected this tradition as a whole, as it is their method to reject traditions with single *isnād* (*kahbar al-wāḥid*) when they oppose universally transmitted sources (*mutawātir*), the individual narration being *zannī* (probable) while the universally transmitted sources are definitive (*qatᶜī*), as did ᶜUmar when he said in the tradition of Fāṭima bint Qays, "We cannot forgo the Book of Allāh and the *sunna* of our Prophet for the narration of a woman". It is related from ᶜAlī that he gave a verdict in favour of the insolvent in the case of goods, which is the opinion of Ibn Sīrīn and Ibrāhīm from among the *Tābiᶜūn*. Perhaps they argued that the tradition of Abū Hurayra was disputed, as al-Ẓuhrī related from Abū Bakr ibn ᶜAbd al-Raḥmān from Abū Hurayra that the Messenger of Allāh said, "If a man dies or becomes insolvent and if one of the creditors finds his specific goods among his property, it is to be shared among the creditors". This tradition is superior as it corresponds with the established sources of the law. They said that there is a way of reconciliation between the two traditions if interpreted for purposes of deposits and borrowed items (*ᶜāriya*). The majority, however, turned down such an interpretation on the basis of that in some versions narrated from Abū Hurayra the term sale is used.

All the above, according to all jurists, relates to the case when the buyer (the insolvent) has taken possession of the goods. The jurists, those of Hijāz and Iraq, are in agreement about the case prior to possession that the owner of the goods has a prior right to them as the liability (for loss) is his. The supporters of this opinion differed when the seller takes possession of part of the price. Mālik said that if he likes he can return what he took and take all the goods, or if he likes he can participate with the creditors in the liquidation of what is left of his goods. Al-Shāfiᶜī said that he takes what is left of the goods in proportion to the remaining price. A group of jurists—Dāwūd, Isḥāq, and Aḥmad—said that if he has taken possession of part of the price, he is to share it with the creditors. Their proof is what is related by Mālik from Ibn Shihāb from Abū Bakr ibn ᶜAbd al-Raḥmān that the Messenger of Allāh (God's peace and blessings be upon him) said, "If a man sells goods and the person he sold to becomes insolvent when the seller has not taken possession of anything, he has a prior right to the goods on finding them. If the purchaser dies, then the owner of the goods shares with the creditors". Though this tradition is recorded as a *mursal*[175] by Mālik, its (full) chain has been provided by ᶜAbd al-Razzāq, and it has been related through al-Zuhrī from Abū Hurayra in a version with an additional text, which is, "If he takes possession

[175] In the *isnād* of which the name of the Companion has been dropped.

of something of his price, it is to be shared with the creditors". It is recorded by Abū ʿUbayd in his book on *fiqh*.

Al-Shāfiʿī's argument is that the goods as a whole or a part of them take the same *ḥukm*. They did not disagree when the buyer consumes (or destroys) part of the goods, the seller has a prior right to the quantity that he finds, except for ʿAṭā who said that if the buyer has consumed some of them, the seller shares with the creditors.

Al-Shāfiʿī and Mālik differed about death, whether the *ḥukm* for it is the same as the *ḥukm* of insolvency. Mālik said the (seller) in the case of death shares with the creditors but not so in insolvency. Al-Shāfiʿī said the situation in both cases is the same. Mālik's reliance is on what is related by Ibn Shihāb from Abū Bakr, which is explicit in this context and also on the rational argument that differentiates between liability in insolvency and death, as the insolvent may gain wealth and the creditors would be able to claim what is left of their dues against him, which is not conceivable in case of death. Al-Shāfiʿī's reliance is on what is related by Ibn Abī Dhiʾb through his *sanad* from Abū Hurayra, who said, "The Messenger of Allāh (God's peace and blessings be upon him) said, 'If a man dies or becomes insolvent, then the owner of the goods has a prior right' ". Thus, he treated, in this tradition, death and insolvency as the same. He (al-Shāfiʿī) said that the tradition of Ibn Abī Dhiʾb is superior to that of Ibn Shihāb as the tradition of Ibn Shihāb is *mursal* while this is *musnad*, and also by way of reason it is wealth in which the owner cannot transact, except after paying off what is due from him, thus resembling the wealth of the insolvent. Mālik's analogy is stronger than that of al-Shāfiʿī, and his tradition (that related by Ibn Shihāb) is preferred over the tradition of Ibn Abī Dhiʾb as it supports the stronger *qiyās*. This is so as among the conflicting traditions, the one which agrees with *qiyās al-maʿnā* is stronger than the tradition which agrees with *qiyās al-shabah*. The analogy that corresponds with the tradition quoted by al-Shāfiʿī is *qiyās al-shabah*, while that corresponding with Mālik's tradition is *qiyās al-maʿnā*. In addition, the tradition quoted by Mālik, though a *mursal* has been recorded by ʿAbd al-Razzāq (with a complete *sanad*). So the reason for disagreement here is the conflict of traditions in this context, and of analogy. Further, the principle supports Mālik's opinion in the case of death, I mean, that one who sells a thing does not have recourse to it. Thus, Mālik comes out stronger in this issue, although al-Shāfiʿī considers Mālik's opinion here as weak, because of his reliance on a *mursal* tradition, which according to al-Shāfiʿī is not to be acted upon (except those of Saʿīd ibn al-Musayyib).

Mālik and al-Shāfiʿī differ about the person who finds his specific property with the insolvent, who has added something to it; for example, he had (agricultural) land in which he planted or a vacant lot in which he constructed.

Mālik said that an addition leads to loss (of a specific right of the seller in it) and he becomes a co-owner in it with the other creditors. Al-Shāfiʿī maintained that, on the contrary, the seller is to be given a choice between paying the value of what the buyer added and taking back the property or taking the principal property and participating with the creditors in the addition. What constitutes a loss (of a right) and what does not in Mālik's school is stated in their well-known books.

The summary of Mālik's opinions about one creditor having a right prior to that of the other creditors, in cases of death and insolvency, or in insolvency to the exclusion of death, is that things sold on credit, for purposes of insolvency, are divided into three kinds: specific goods, disputed things, specified or not, and work that is not determined. If the goods are in the hands of the seller and he does not deliver them till he (the buyer) becomes insolvent, he has a prior right both in the case of death and of insolvency. In this there is no disagreement. If he had delivered them to the buyer, who then became insolvent while they were in his possession, he has a prior right over the creditors in insolvency, and not in the case of death, but they have a right to buy his goods by paying the price. Al-Shāfiʿī said that they have no such right, while Ashhab said that they do not take it, except with the addition for which they pay the insolvent. Ibn al-Mājishūn said that if they like, the price can be paid by them or out of the wealth of the insolvent. Ibn Kināna said that it has to be paid by them. He (the seller) has a prior right to the thing itself in case of death, if it is in the hands of the insolvent, but they disagreed when the buyer gives it back to the seller and then he becomes insolvent or dies, and it still exists identified in the hands of the seller. It is said that he has a prior right to it as in the case of goods in insolvency, but not in the case of death. This is Ibn al-Qāsim's opinion. It is also said that he has no right to it and it is to be shared by the creditors. This is Ashhab's opinion. Both opinions spring from the disagreement about the determination of the *ʿayn*. If it is not determined, it belongs to the common sharing by the creditors.

With respect to work that has not been specified, if the hirer becomes insolvent before the acquisition of the services of the worker, the worker has a prior right to his services both in the case of death and of insolvency, as in the case of goods that are in the hands of the seller at the time of insolvency. If he becomes insolvent after he had fully secured the services of the worker, the worker participates in the liquidation for the creditors for his wages that he (the insolvent) stipulated for him, in the case of insolvency as well as in death, on the basis of the preferred opinion, unless he has in his hands the goods upon which work was to be done, for he then has a prior right to them in both insolvency and death. This is so as they are like a pledge with him. If he delivers them, he shares with the creditors, unless he has produced something out of them to which he then has a prior right in insolvency, but not in death. It is the same with him (Mālik) in the case of insolvency related to one renting animals, if he rents out he has a right to the goods loaded on them in both death and insolvency. Similarly, for one renting out a boat. All this, for Mālik, has a similarity with *rahn* (pledge).

On the whole, there is no disagreement in his (Mālik's) school that the seller has a prior right to what is in his hands in case of insolvency as well as death, and a prior right to his goods existing out of his possession in the case of insolvency, but not in death, and he participates with the creditors in the liquidation if his goods are lost. The case of the worker, according to Mālik's disciples, may resemble that of the seller of a benefit, and may sometime resemble that of the seller of the corpus. They once compared *manfaʿa* (utility) to the work done on the goods, not taken possession of by the buyer, saying that he has a prior right both in the case of insolvency as well as death. On another occasion they compared it to the goods left in his possession that have not expired, saying that he has a prior right to it in insolvency and not death. On yet another occasion they compared it to the case of death where it (the goods) has expired, saying that he participates with the creditors. An example of this is the case of the person hired for watering a palm-grove. He watered it till the fruit grew, but then the hirer became insolvent. It is in this case that they expressed their three opinions.

The comparison of the sale of benefits, under this topic, with the sale of the corpus itself is something that is original, as far as I think, to Mālik's school as compared to the jurists of the provinces. It is, however, weak as *qiyās al-shabah* derived from a distinctive factor in the sources is considered weak. It is for the same reason that analogy constructed upon cases of exemptions is considered weak by some. Yet *qiyās al-ʿilla* is more legitimate here and is stronger. Perhaps the Mālikites claim the existence of this meaning in analogy, but (further discussion of) all this is not suitable for a precis like this.

To this topic also belongs their disagreement about the insolvent slave authorized (*māʾdhūn*) to trade. Is the debt (created by him) to be met from the sale of his person? Mālik and the jurists of Hijāz maintained that the claim for the debt is to be satisfied from what he possesses, and not through his sale. Then, if he should be freed, the remaining is to be claimed. A group was of the view that he is to be sold, while another group held that the creditors are to be granted an option of selling him or making him work for what remains of the debt. This was the opinion of Shurayḥ. A group said that what he owes is the liability of his master, even if he did not stipulate this. Those who did not favour his sale said that he transacted with people on the basis of what he possessed and, therefore, resembles a freeman. Those who upheld his sale compared his acts with the offences he commits. Those who maintained a recourse to his master, for whatever debt he owes, held his wealth to be similar to the wealth of his master, as he has a right to whatever he holds. The reason for disagreement here is the conflict in analogies of *shabah* in this issue.

A relevant question here is the issue of a slave and his master when they become insolvent at the same time; from whom should the claim be made first? Is it to be commenced with the debt of the slave or with the debt of the master? The majority said that it is (to commence) with the debt of the slave, as those who granted credit to the slave did so on seeing the wealth possessed by him; whereas those who gave credit to the master did not rely on the wealth of the slave. Those who uphold commencement with the master argued that the wealth of the slave is in fact that of the master. The reason for the disagreement is the vacillation of the slave's wealth between taking the *ḥukm* of a stranger's wealth or the *ḥukm* of the master's wealth.

It is maintained in the school with respect to the amount of wealth that is to be left with the insolvent that it should be a sum with which he, his family, and his minor children can survive for some days. It is stated in *al-Wāḍiḥa* and *al-ᶜUtbiyya*: (that it should be sufficient for) a month or so, and (an amount sufficient for) clothing, in conformity with his status, is (also) to be left for him. Mālik suspended judgment about his (the insolvent's) wife's clothing due to the question whether her clothing is incumbent with compensation or without compensation. Saḥnūn said that the cost of her clothing is not to be left for him. Ibn Rāfiᶜ related from Mālik that nothing is to be left with him (for clothes) except what will cover his modesty, which was also the opinion of Ibn Kināna. They disagreed about *sharīᶜa* books into two opinions based on whether it is *makrūh* (disagreeable) to sell books of *fiqh*.

For the identification of debts, because of which liquidation for distribution among the creditors is undertaken, as against those for which there is no liquidation in Mālik's opinion, they (the debts) are divided first into two kinds. First, those that are due in return for a counter-value. Second, those that are due without any counter-value. Those due for a counter-value are divided into debts in which the counter-value has been taken possession of, and those in which the counter-value has not been possessed. With respect to debts in which the counter-value has been possessed, whether it is wealth or damages for an offence, there is no disagreement that liquidation for the creditors is obligatory due to them.

Those (debts) that are for a counter-value, which is not possessed, are divided into five kinds. First, when it is not possible to pay the counter-value in any circumstances, as in the case of maintenance of wives, that is, carried over from an earlier period. Second, when the payment of a counter-value is not possible, but something in return is, from which it can be recovered. For example, a person hires a house for cash, when the customary practice is to pay cash for it, and he (the hirer) subsequently becomes insolvent before he has resided in the house or after he has resided in it for a short while, but prior to the payment of rent. Third, when it is possible to pay the counter-value and it is binding, like the payment of the capital of *salam*, but the *muslam ilayh* becomes insolvent before the payment of the capital. Fourth, when it is possible to pay the counter-value, but is not binding, like goods, if they are bought and the buyer becomes insolvent before the seller has delivered them. Fifth, when there is no requirement of immediate delivery of the counter-value, for example, a man makes an agreement to make an advance payment to another (*salam*) in *dīnārs* for goods deliverable after a period, but the *muslim* becomes insolvent before he has made the payment and prior to the termination of the period.

The debts in which the payment of the counter-value is not possible in any circumstances, there is no liquidation in them, except in the case of dowers of wives if the husband becomes insolvent prior to consummation. About those in which the payment of the counter-value is not possible, but it is possible to deliver something in return from which it can be recovered, like the hirer becoming insolvent prior to the payment of rent (in *dīnārs*), it is said that the person letting out on hire can participate in the liquidation for the entire rent after giving possession of the house to the creditors, while it is also said that he has no more than participation for the period of residence and he takes possession of his house; if the person did not reside at all he gets nothing and just takes possession of his house.

In the case where it is possible for him to pay the counter-value and it is binding on him, which happens when the counter-value is an *ᶜayn*, it is said that the creditors participate with him in its liquidation and he delivers it, while it is said that he has a prior right to it and on that basis he is not obliged to deliver the counter-value. In the case where it is possible to deliver the counter-value, but is not binding, he has an option to participate or to keep it, this also happens when the counter-value is an *ᶜayn*. In the case where there is no requirement for immediate delivery of the counter-value, like the insolvency of the *muslim* before he has paid the capital and prior to the termination of the period of the *salam*, if the *muslam ilayh* consents to make prompt delivery and to participate with the creditors for the capital of *salam*, it is permitted if the creditors also agree. If one of the creditors refuses, the creditors participate in the liquidation of the capital that is due to him, as far as the debtor has wealth, and also in the goods that are due from him if the period is over for they belong to the insolvent; if they wish to sell them for cash and then share in the liquidation they have a right to do so.

In the case of the obligatory rights arising without a counter-value, those among them that are not obligatory under the law, but are so by contract (voluntary commitment), like gifts and charities, there is no liquidation because of them. Regarding the rights obligatory under the law, like the maintenance of parents and children, there are two opinions. First, that liquidation is not obligatory due to them, which is the opinion of Ibn al-Qāsim. Second, they render liquidation obligatory if they have been made binding by the order of the *sulṭān*, which is Ashhab's opinion.

The fifth point in the discussion is the mode of liquidation. The *ḥukm* in this is that the wealth of the debtor be liquidated in accordance with the species of the creditors' claims, irrespective of the fact that the wealth of the creditors was composed of a single or of different species, for what is required must be of the same species as that of the debt, unless they agree to accept it in another permissible thing.

Within this topic, they disagreed about unexpected contingencies, like the destruction of the interdicted wealth, after interdiction and prior to possession by the creditors, as to who is liable for (the loss from) the calamity. Ashhab said that the liability is on the insolvent. Ibn al-Mājishūn said that the liability is on the creditors, if it (the liquidation) was suspended by the sulṭān. Ibn al-Qāsim said the portion that needed to be sold is the liability of the debtor, as it was being sold through his ownership, while that which did not require sale is the liability of the creditors, for example, when the wealth constitutes an *ᶜayn* and the debt constitutes an *ᶜayn*. All of them related their opinions from Mālik. Aṣbagh distinguished between death and insolvency, saying that in case of a calamity after death, the liability is on the creditors, while in insolvency it is on the insolvent.

All this is the discussion about the insolvent, who has wealth to meet his debts. About the insolvent who does not have any wealth at all, the jurists are agreed that the absence of wealth is effective in the discharge (postponement) of debts till the time of his sufficiency, except what is related from ᶜUmar ibn ᶜAbd al-ᶜAzīz that they have the right to hire his services. Aḥmad, among the jurists of the provinces, held this opinion.

All of them agree that when the debtor feigns insolvency, the truth of which is not known, he is to be imprisoned till his veracity is established or his insolvency is acknowledged by the creditors, in which case he is released. It is related from Abū Ḥanīfa that the creditors have the right to follow him around wherever he goes. All of them agreed about the validity of imprisonment in the case of debts, though no authentic tradition is available for it, but it is something necessary for securing the people's rights from each other. This is evidence for those who uphold the principle of *maṣlaḥa*, which has been called *al-qiyās al-mursal*. It is related that the Prophet (God's peace and blessings be upon him) imprisoned someone on suspicion. It has been recorded, as far as I recall, by Abū Dāwūd. Those interdicted, according to Mālik, are the prodigal, the insolvents, slaves, the (seriously) ill, and the wife if she made a bequest for more than one-third, as the husband has a right in (her) wealth, but the majority have opposed him in this.

This suffices in pursuance of our purposes in this book.

XL
THE BOOK OF *ṢULḤ* (SETTLEMENT; NEGOTIATION)

The source for this book are the words of the Exalted: "*Ṣulḥ* (Peace) is better",[176] and what has been related from the Prophet (God's peace and blessings be upon him) as *marfūʿ*[177] and *mawqūf*[178] up to ʿUmar: "Making a settlement between Muslims is permitted, except the settlement that legalizes a prohibited thing or prohibits a legal thing." The Muslim jurists agreed over its permissibility (validity) in the case of acknowledgement (or confession), but they disagreed about its permissibility in the case of denial. Mālik and Abū Ḥanīfa said that it is permissible even in the case of denial, while al-Shāfiʿī said that it is not permitted in case of denial as it amounts to the (endorsement of the) unjust devouring of wealth without compensation. The Mālikites say that it does carry compensation, and leads to the suspension of litigation and the removal of the obligation for an oath from the person (denying).

There is no dispute in Mālik's school that for the settlement, which occurs in the case of acknowledgement, the same conditions that are required in sale are to be observed. It is invalidated by the same factors that invalidate sale, from among the kinds of *fasād* specific to sales, and it becomes valid with the same conditions of validity. The examples for this are a person (who first) makes a claim on another for *dirhams* and then settles with him after he has acknowledged the claim in *dīnārs* with a delay as well as whatever resembles it from among sales invalidated due to the implication of *ribā* or *gharar*.

The well-known narration from Mālik and his disciples about settlement in the case of denial is that the conditions of validity of sales are observed in it (otherwise settlement is not valid). For example, a person makes a claim against another in *dirhams* and upon his denial settles with him in *dīnārs* with a delay. This is not permitted according to Mālik and his disciples. Aṣbagh said it is permitted, as the reprehensible act in it is only from one party, the claimant, as he admits the taking of *dīnārs* with a delay in place of *dirhams* that

176 Qurʾān 4:128

177 Attributed to and raised up (in the chain) to the Prophet.

178 This means that the *isnād*, through which a *ḥadīth* is related, stops at the Companion.

were permissible for him. He maintains about the person paying that it is a gift from him.

If there is a commission of a reprehensible act from both sides, as for example each one of them claims *dirhams* or *dīnārs* from the other and each denies it, but subsequently settle that each will delay whatever the other party claims for a period, then, this is *makrūh*, according to them. The abomination is due to the fear that each one of them may be truthful and each has delayed his claim in exchange for delay by the other, thus, entering the (prohibited) transaction "you delay for me and I will delay it for you". The reason for its permissibility, on the other hand, is the claim by each one of them that what he had done was a gift from him and there was nothing due from him. Such sales, it is said, are permissible if they occur. Ibn al-Mājishūn said that they are to be rescinded if they occur, immediately after the contract, but if prolonged for a long time they take effect.

The settlement that incorporates what is not permissible in sales is, in Mālik's school, divided into three kinds: settlement that is rescinded by agreement (of the jurists); settlement that is rescinded with some disagreement; and settlement that is not rescinded if prolonged, there being a disagreement when it is not prolonged.

XLI
THE BOOK OF *KAFĀLA* (SURETY)

The jurists disagreed about the kinds of *kafāla*, its duration, the *ḥukm* that is binding due to it, its conditions, the description of its obligations, and (the description of) its subject-matter. It has different names: *kafāla, ḥamāla, ḍamāna*, and *zaʿāma*.

It has two kinds: *ḥamāla biʾl-nafs* (bail, surety for the person), and *ḥamāla biʾl-māl* (surety for wealth, property). *Ḥamāla biʾl-māl*, is established through *sunna* and is agreed upon among the first generation and also among the jurists of the provinces. It is related from a group that it is not binding due to its resemblance with *ʿidda*, but this is an isolated opinion. The *sunna* on which the majority relied in this respect were the words of the Prophet, "The *zaʿīm* is liable (for the loss)". The majority of the jurists agree about the legality of *ḥamāla biʾl-nafs*, which is also known as *ḍamān al-wajh*[179] when it occurs due to a financial claim. It is related from al-Shāfiʿī, in his latest opinion, that it is not permitted, which was also the view of Dāwūd.

Their proof is the words of the Exalted, "Allāh forbid that we should seize save him with whom we have found our property".[180] They also argued that *kafāla biʾl-nafs* resembles (that is, amounts to) a surety for *ḥudūd* (penalties). The proof of those who permitted it is the general (unrestricted) implication of the words of the Prophet (God's peace and blessings be upon him), "The *zaʿīm* is liable (for the loss)". They also argued that an interest (*maṣlaḥa*) is secured through it, and that its validity is said to have been held by the first generation.

About its binding effect, the majority, who uphold surety of the person, agree that if the principal dies within the jurisdiction where surety is furnished the surety for his person is not liable, yet it is narrated that some have upheld the obligation for loss. Ibn al-Qāsim distinguished between the cases when the principal dies being present (in the jurisdiction) and when he is absent (from this area). He said that if he dies when present, the surety is not liable at all. If he dies in absence, the case is to be examined further. When the distance

[179] *Wajh* literally means 'face'. It is used figuratively to denote the person as it is the most respected part of the individual. Thus, it signifies his credit worthiness.

[180] Qurʾān 12:79

between the two towns is such that it is possible for the surety to deliver the person, in the stipulated period like two or three days, if he (the surety) is negligent, he is liable otherwise not.

They disagreed about the *ḥukm* of the surety for the person in the absence of the principal, maintaining three opinions. First, that it is binding on him to deliver him, otherwise he bears the loss. This is the opinion of Mālik, his disciples, and the jurists of Medina. The second opinion is that the surety is to be imprisoned till he arranges to deliver him or till the death of the principal becomes known. This is Abū Ḥanīfa's opinion and that of the jurists of Iraq. The third opinion is that he has no option but to deliver the principal, if he knows his whereabouts. This implies that he is not to bear the burden of delivering the principal, except with the condition of knowing his whereabouts and having the ability to deliver him. If the claimant alleges that the surety knows his whereabouts, when the surety denies this, the burden of proof is on the claimant. They said that the surety is not to be imprisoned, unless the whereabouts of the principal are known, in which case he is to be compelled to deliver him. This opinion is related by Abū ʿUbayd al-Qāsim ibn Sallām, in his book on *fiqh*, attributing it to a number of jurists, and he has preferred it.

Mālik's proof is that since the principal is liable to the owner of the right (the aggrieved person), the surety is, therefore, to be liable for the loss when he disappears. Perhaps they (Mālik and his supporters) argued on the basis of what is related from Ibn ʿAbbās, "A man asked his debtor to pay him his money or provide him with a surety. He was unable to do either till the matter was brought up for arbitration to the Prophet (God's peace and blessings be upon him). The Prophet (God's peace and blessings be upon him) stood surety for him and then paid the amount due". They said that this indicates liability in *ḥamāla* without any restrictions.

The jurists of Iraq said that it is obligatory on him to deliver the principal, as that for which he stood surety was his person and he is under no obligation to convert this into a financial liability, unless he had committed himself to do so, as the Prophet (God's peace and blessings be upon him) has said, "The Believers (should) abide by their conditions". It is, thus, obligatory on him to deliver him (the principal) or to be imprisoned in return, just as when he stands surety for property, he delivers it or is imprisoned for it; the situation is similar in the case of surety of the person. The reliance of the other party (jurists) is on the fact that it is binding upon him to deliver him, if delivering him is possible for him, for he will be imprisoned if he does not do so. If it is known that delivering him is not possible, such delivery is not obligatory on him, just as if the principal were to die, it would not be obligatory on him to deliver him. They said that it is more likely for one who stands surety for the person and incurs financial liability to be a victim of deception rather than being the deceiver himself. If, however, he has stipulated surety of the person and not a financial liability, having expressly said so, then Mālik says that he is not liable financially; and there is no dispute in this, as far as I know, for that would amount to an obligation contrary to what he had stipulated. This is all about the *ḥukm* of surety for the person.

The jurists are in agreement about the *ḥukm* of surety for property that in the absence or disappearance of the principal the surety is liable. They disagree over the case in which the surety and the principal are present and both are financially stable. Al-Shāfiʿī, Abū Ḥanīfa and his two disciples, al-Thawrī, al-Awzāʿī, Aḥmad and Isḥāq said that it is up to the claimant to hold either the surety or the principal liable. Mālik said, in one of his opinions, that he has no right to hold the surety liable in the presence of the principal; and he has another opinion like that of the majority. Abū Thawr said that surety for the person and surety for property are the same and one who stands surety for property on behalf of an individual is liable for it; the principal is absolved and it is not permitted that a single claim be split into two. This was also the opinion of Ibn Abī Laylā and Ibn Shubrama. The proof of those who maintain that the claimant is allowed to claim from the surety, whether the principal is absent or present, is rich or in financial straits, is the tradition of Qabīṣa ibn al-Mukhāraqī, who said, "I stood surety (for someone) and came up to the Prophet (God's peace and blessings be upon him) to ask him about it. He said, 'We shall take it out of the camels of the *ṣadaqa* on your behalf. It is not allowed except in three cases . . .' and he mentioned the case of a man who stands surety for someone till he pays it off. The point of the argument in this is that the Prophet (God's peace and blessings be upon him) permitted the demand (from the *ṣadaqa*) without taking into account the situation of the principal.

The subject-matter of *kafāla* is wealth, according to the majority of the jurists, due to the words of the Prophet (God's peace and blessings be upon him), "The surety is liable (as a debtor)", that is, surety for property as well as surety for the person. This is so irrespective of whether the wealth is claimed due to property or arises due to the *ḥudūd*, like the payment due in case of manslaughter (*qatl khaṭaʾ*) or composition in intentional murder or theft, in which the liability is not for amputation, being the case of theft of a lesser value than the *niṣāb*, or for something else. The permission for bail in *ḥudūd* and *qiṣās* is related from Abū Ḥanīfa, or in *qiṣāṣ* to the exclusion of the *ḥudūd*. This is also the opinion of ʿUthmān al-Battī, that is, about surety for the person.

The jurists agreed that the time of obligation of the insured amount, that is, of asking him to produce a surety, arises after the establishment of the right against the principal, either by acknowledgement or by evidence. With respect to the time of obligation in bail, they disagreed whether it is binding before the establishment of the right. A group said that it is binding prior to the establishment of the right for any plausible reason. This is the opinion of Shurayḥ, the *qāḍī* and of al-Shaʿbī; it was also upheld by Saḥnūn from among the disciples of Mālik. A group said that it is obligatory at the time of the establishment of the charge, but they differed as to when exactly and for what duration, it is binding. A group said that if he comes up with a strong defence, like a witness, it is necessary that he be asked to provide a bail till his claim is clarified otherwise granting of bail is not binding, unless he mentions evidence to be found in the (same) province, in which case he is granted bail for five days to a week. This is the opinion of Ibn al-Qāsim; from among the disciples of Mālik.

The jurists of Iraq said that bail is not to be accepted prior to the establishment of the charge against him unless he claims the existence of evidence within the province, as in the opinion of Ibn al-Qāsim; however, they limited the duration to three days saying that if he comes up with a good defence it is necessary that bail be granted to him till such time that his claim is accepted or dismissed. They denied any distinction between the person who claims the existence of evidence that is available and between the person who claims it about missing evidence. They said that bail is not to be accepted for anyone except in the case of evidence that will lead to the truth of his claim or its falsity. The reason for this disagreement is the disparity of fairness between the two litigants. If he is not asked to provide bail on the mere lodging of the complaint, there is no guarantee that he will not disappear thus causing hardship for the claimant and if he is asked to provide bail there is no guarantee that the complaint will be be found to be false causing a hardship for the defendant. It is for this reason that they made a distinction between a claim for evidence that is available and that in which it is missing.

It is related from ʿArāk ibn Mālik, who said, "A group of Bedouins with some saddle-beasts came in. Two men had accompanied them (on the way) staying the night with them. On waking up in the morning, they found a number of camels missing. The Messenger of Allāh (God's peace and blessings be upon him) said to one of the (two) men, 'Go and find them' and he confined the other person. He, then, came back with what was missing. The Messenger of Allāh (God's peace and blessings be upon him) said to one of the men, 'Pray for my forgiveness'. The man said, 'May Allāh forgive you' . He replied, 'And you, may Allāh forgive you and make you strive in His way' ". This tradition has been recorded by Abū ʿUbayd in his book on *fiqh*. He said, "It does not appeal to me, as confinement is not necessary by the mere lodging of a complaint. It is, it seems to me, from the category of surety for a claim that is not due when there is doubt due to their staying with them (for that reason)".

There is very little disagreement over the categories of principals. They disagreed about the surety for the deceased who was under debt and did not leave enough for its satisfaction. Mālik and al-Shāfiʿī permitted it, but Abū Ḥanīfa said it is not allowed. Abū Ḥanīfa argued that surety is not to be associated with someone not present, which is unlike the case of the insolvent. Those who were of the view that surety is necessary argued on the basis of the report that the Prophet (God's peace and blessings be upon him) in the early period of Islam did not perform (pray) the funeral service of the deceased who had left a debt, till an undertaking was given. According to the majority the surety of one imprisoned or absent is valid, it is not valid according to Abū Ḥanīfa.

Under the conditions of *kafāla*, Abū Ḥanīfa and al-Shāfiʿī stipulate the consent of the principal in order for the surety to have a recourse to him for demanding a refund for what he had paid on his behalf. Mālik does not stipulate this. According to al-Shāfiʿī, surety for an unknown person (or a thing) is not allowed nor for a claim that is not yet due. All this, however, is binding and permitted according to Mālik and his disciples. In response to the question in what things *ḥamāla* is permitted, as against that in which it is not, Mālik and his disciples said that it is permitted in everything that can be established as a liability, except *kitāba*, that in which delay is not allowed and that in which the dues accrue in parts like the maintenance of wives and what resembles it.

XLII
THE BOOK OF *ḤAWĀLA* (TRANSFER OF DEBT; ENDORSEMENT)

Ḥawāla is a valid transaction, exempted from (the prohibition of) exchange of a debt for a debt, due to the words of the Prophet (God's peace and blessings be upon him), "Procrastination by the wealthy is unjust, and when one of you is transferred (the claim for his debt) to a wealthy person he should accept (the transfer)". The discussion here relates to an examination of its conditions and its *ḥukm*.

Related to the conditions is their dispute about the consent of the *muḥāl* (original creditor) and the *muḥāl ʿalayh* (transferee). Among the (disputing) jurists is one who took into account the consent of the creditor, but not the endorsee, and he is Mālik. Among them is he who stipulated the consent of both at the same time; and then there is one who did not take into account the consent of the transferor, but considered the consent of the transferee, which is the opposite of Mālik's opinion. This was Dāwūd's opinion.

Those who considered it as a bilateral transaction, took into account the consent of both, but those who considered the transferee in the same position as the transferor (debtor or *muḥīl*) did not take into account his consent, just as they did not take into account (the consent of) the transferor along with the creditor, if he should demand from him his due before its transfer to anyone. The proof in Dāwūd's view is the apparent meaning of the words of the Prophet (God's peace and blessings be upon him), "When one of you is transferred (the claim) for his (debt) to a wealthy person, let him follow (agree)". The command here indicates obligation (*wujūb*) (for the other two), while the transferee has been left in his original position, which is the stipulation of his consent.

Among the conditions, which they generally agreed upon, is that what is due from the transferee should be the same as that due from the transferor, both in amount and description. There are those among them (the jurists), however, who permitted it (*ḥawāla*) in gold and *dirhams* alone and disallowed it in food. Those who prohibit it (in food) are of the view that it amounts to the sale of food before taking possession, as the transferor here sells the food that was due to him from his debtor (before receiving it) for the food due to his creditor from him. Mālik allowed this when the two kinds of food are both loans (with a period), when the debt of the creditor is immediate. If, however, one of them is (the debt of) *salam*, it is not allowed, unless the two debts are immediate. According to Ibn al-Qāsim, and others from among Mālik's school, this is permitted if the debt of the transferee is immediate. Al-Shāfiʿī did not make these distinctions as it is like sale through the liability of the debtor. Mālik made an exemption in the case of *qarḍ*, as the sale of a *qarḍ* is permitted, according to him, prior to possession. Abū Ḥanīfa, on the other hand, permitted *ḥawāla* in food, comparing it to *dirhams* (money), and rendered it as exempt from the *general* principles as in the exemption of *ḥawāla* in *dirhams*. The issue turns on whether analogy can be constructed upon what is exempt from the principles. The issue is well known in *uṣūl al-fiqh*.

Ḥawāla has three conditions according to Mālik. First that the debt of the creditor (*muḥāl*) should be due immediately; if it is not due immediately, it amounts to the exchange of a debt for a debt. Second, that the debt being transferred should be similar to the debt to which it is transferred in amount and description. If they differ in either (way), it amounts to sale, not *ḥawāla*, for it has then moved out of the category of an exemption to the category of sale; when it moves to the category of sale, it becomes an exchange of a debt for a debt. The third condition is that the debt should not be in food related to *salam*, (either both) or one of them, and according to the opinion of Ibn al-Qāsim the delay of a transferred debt is not permitted. When both debts belong to *salam*, *ḥawāla* of one for the other is not permitted irrespective of whether the periods have terminated, or whether one of them is terminated and not the other, as it amounts to the sale of food prior to possession, as we indicated. Ashhab, however, says that if their capitals are equal, *ḥawāla* is permitted and it amounts to *tawliya* (friendly sale), but Ibn al-Qāsim does not uphold this, as in the case when they are unequal.

The creditor occupies the position of the debtor (transferor) in the debt to which his claim has been transferred, along with his position in his claim because of which it has been transferred. This is for purposes of what he desires to take as a counter-value for it, or to sell it for something else, I mean, it is not permitted to him to take other than what was permitted to him with respect to the transferor and what was permitted to the transferor with respect to the transferee. An example of this is when his claim for food, due to him from a *qarḍ*, is transferred to food due from *salam*—or for food due from *salam* to food due from *qarḍ*; it is not permitted to him to sell it to another before taking possession of it. If his claim is transferred to a claim for *qarḍ* due to a claim from *salam*, he descends into the position of the debtor in so far as it was not permitted to him to sell anything that was due from his debtor before taking possession of it, as it is food related to sale. If his claim has been transferred to food due on account of *salam* for food due on account of *qarḍ* he moves into the position of the transferee with respect to the transferor, I mean, just as it was not permitted to him to sell food that was still with his debtor, the transferor, prior to taking possession, similarly, it is not permitted to him to sell the food to which his claim has been transferred, even when it was from *qarḍ*. All this is held in Mālik's school and the evidence for these distinctions is rather weak.

The majority of the jurists maintain, about its *aḥkām*, that *ḥawāla* is the opposite of *ḥamāla*, to the extent that when the transferee becomes insolvent, the creditor has no recourse to the *muḥīl* for anything. Mālik and his disciples maintain that this is so unless the debtor has deceived him (by transferring his claim) to someone destitute. Abū Ḥanīfa said that the creditor has recourse to the debtor if the transferee dies an insolvent or denies the *ḥawāla*, even when he does not have proof. This was also the opinion of Shurayḥ, ʿUthmān al-Battī and a group of jurists. The reason for their disagreement is the similarity of *ḥawāla* with *ḥamāla*.

XLIII
THE BOOK OF *WAKĀLA* (AGENCY)

In this book there are three chapters. The first chapter is about the elements of agency, which covers the study of the subject-matter and the principal. The second is about the *aḥkām* of agency. The third is about the differences (which may arise) between the principal and the agent.

43.1. Chapter 1: The Elements of Agency

This relates to the study of the subject-matter of agency, the principal, and the agent.

43.1.1. Element 1: The Principal (*Muwakkil*)

They agreed about the constitution of agency by someone absent, the sick, and a woman, who exercises authority over their own affairs. They disagreed about the constitution of agency by a male who is present and has full capacity. Mālik said that agency by a male who is present and has full capacity is valid. This was also al-Shāfiʿī's opinion. Abū Ḥanīfa said agency by a person with full capacity who is (himself) present is not permitted, nor is agency constituted by a woman, unless she is an outgoing person.

Those who were of the view that in principle the acts of a person are no substitute for those of another, unless required by necessity—upon which there is consensus (*ijmāʿ*)—held that representation of someone, about whose representation there is disagreement, is not permitted. Those who maintained that this is originally permitted said that agency is permitted in each legal transaction, except in those things about which there is agreement that agency in them is not valid, like the *ʿibādāt* (ritual worship) and whatever resembles them.

43.1.2. Element 2: The Agent (*Wakīl*)

The condition for the agent is that he should not be legally prohibited from disposal of the thing for which he has been constituted an agent. Thus, it is not permitted to appoint as agent a minor or an insane person; likewise, appointment of a woman is not valid according to Mālik and al-Shāfiʿī for the contract of marriage. Al-Shāfiʿī added that it is neither valid directly nor indirectly, that is, when she appoints someone who would conclude the contract of marriage. According to Mālik, it is permitted through a male (with full capacity).

43.1.3. **Element 3: The Subject-Matter of Agency**

The condition for the subject-matter of agency is that it should be suited to delegation, like sale, *ḥawāla*, compensation (*ḍamān*), all other contracts and revocations, partnership, agency, *ṣarf*, *jiʾāla*, *musāqah*, divorce, marriage, *khulʿ*, and composition (*sulḥ*). It is not permitted in physical (acts of) worship, but is allowed in worship involving finances, like *ṣadaqa*, *zakāt*, and *ḥajj*. It is permitted, according to Mālik, in litigation involving acknowledgement and denial. Al-Shāfiʿī said, in one of his opinions, that it is not permitted in acknowledgement, which he compared with testimony and oath. *Wakāla* is permitted, according to Mālik, for securing satisfaction in penalties, while al-Shāfiʿī allows it in the presence of the principal in one of his opinions. Those who said that *wakāla* is valid in acknowledgement differed about absolute *wakāla* in litigation whether it includes acknowledgement. Mālik said it is not included, while Abū Ḥanīfa said it is.

43.1.4. **Element 4: The Contract of**

Wakāla may become a binding contract through offer and acceptance, like the rest of the contracts; however, it is not a binding contract but is a permissible (terminable) contract in the light of what we are going to explain in the chapter on the *aḥkām* of this contract. It (*wakāla*) is of two types according to Mālik: general and special. General agency is constituted, according to him, through a general delegation in which nothing specific is mentioned, but if it is it would not convey generality and delegation in his view. Al-Shāfiʿī said that general agency is not valid as it involves *gharar*, but whatever is specifically mentioned and distinguished is valid. This is better analogy as the basis in it is prohibition, except that on which there is consensus.

43.2. Chapter 2: The *Aḥkām* of Agency

Among the *aḥkām* are those related to the contract and those related to the acts of the agent. The contract, as we have said, is not a binding contract. It is for the agent to terminate the agency whenever he likes, according to all, but Abū Ḥanīfa stipulates in this the presence of the principal. It is for the principal to remove him (the agent) whenever he likes, except when it is a *wakāla* for litigation, they said. Aṣbagh said that he may do this except when the final verdict is about to be issued. The agent may not dismiss himself in a situation where it is not permitted to the principal to dismiss him. The presence of the contestant is not necessary for the conclusion of this contract, according to Mālik and al-Shāfiʿī, but Abū Ḥanīfa said that it is a condition. Similarly, the presence of the principal for the confirmation of agency before the judge is not a condition according to Mālik. Al-Shāfiʿī said that it is.

Mālik's disciples differed, into two opinions, on whether *wakāla* is terminated by the death of the principal. If we say that it is terminated by (his) death as it is by dismissal, then, at what time does the agent stand dismissed and the agency terminated, according to the school, with respect to the rights of the person who deals with him? There are three opinions. First, it is revoked with respect to everyone through death and dismissal. Second, it is terminated with respect to each depending on (the communication of) knowledge (of death or dismissal). Thus, for the person who has come to know about it, it is terminated as far as he is concerned, but it is not if he does not know. Third, it is terminated with respect to the person who deals with the agent, by knowledge reaching the agent, even if he does not know about it himself. It is not terminated with respect to the agent, by virtue of the knowledge of the person who deals with him, as long as the agent does not come to know, but he who delivers something to him after knowledge of dismissal is liable for it as he has delivered it to one whom he knows not to be the agent.

The *aḥkām* for the agent include widely known issues. The first arises when he has been constituted an agent for sale—is it permitted to him to buy for himself? Mālik said it is permitted, but it is also related that he said it is not. Al-Shāfiʿī said it is not permitted. Mālik holds the father and the executor to be in the same position (neither should buy for himself a property belonging to the child under his guardianship). An issue arises when he is appointed through an absolute agency. According to Mālik, it is not permitted to him to sell, except at the current rate and for the currency prevalent in the land. It is not allowed if he sells on credit, or for currency other than that used in the land, or at a rate that is not current. The same is the ruling, according to him, in the case of purchase.

Abū Ḥanīfa made a distinction between sale and purchase of a specified commodity. He said that it is permitted in sale that he sell at a rate that is not current, and also on credit. He did not permit it, however, when he is made an agent for the purchase of a particular slave, that he buy at a rate other than the one current or on credit. It appears that Abū Ḥanīfa made a special distinction in the case of agency for the sale of a particular thing; his argument is that just as a man may sell a thing at a rate lower than the current rate and on credit for a good reason that he recognizes in it all, the same should be the *ḥukm* for the agent, as he has occupied his position. The opinion of the majority, however, is clearer.

The agent must compensate any damage caused by his transgression, according to those who consider it a transgression. When the agent purchases a thing, intending the purchase for the principal, the ownership is transferred to the principal instantly. Abū Ḥanīfa said that it is transferred to the agent first and then to the principal. If the agent pays a debt on behalf of the principal and has not taken evidence, the agent is liable when the creditor denies settlement.

43.3. Chapter 3: The Disputes of the Principal and the Agent

The disagreement of the agent with the principal can arise in the case of loss of the property remaining with the agent, or about its return to the principal, or about the price at which he has sold or purchased when he was ordered to sell at a fixed price, or it could be about the commodity (*mathmūn*) itself, or it could be about the identification of the person whom he had instructed to make payment, or it could be due to a claim from a tort.

When they disagree about the loss of property, with the agent saying that he has lost it, and the principal saying it is not lost, the acceptable statement is that of the agent if he had taken possession of it without evidence. If the property was acquired from one of the debtors of the principal and the debtor did not take witnesses, he will not be absolved through the acknowledgement of the agent, according to Mālik, and will be held liable once again. Does the debtor in this case have recourse to the agent? There is disagreement over it. If, however, it was acquired with evidence, he is absolved and the agent is not liable for any of it.

When they disagree about delivery—the agent saying "I have delivered it to you" and the principal says, "No!"—it is said that the acceptable statement is that of the agent, and it is said that the acceptable statement is that of the principal, while it is also said that if the two statements were widely different, the acceptable statement is that of the agent. In the case of their disagreement about the price at which he was ordered to sell, Ibn al-Qāsim said that if the goods are not lost, the acceptable opinion is that of the buyer, but if they are lost the statement is that of the principal. It is also said that both take oaths, then the sale is revoked and they withdraw—on the basis of value when the goods are lost. If their disagreement is about the price at which he was ordered to sell, then, according to Ibn al-Qāsim, the acceptable statement is that of the principal, as he considered the payment of the price equivalent to the loss of goods in purchase.

When they disagree about the person to whom payment was to be made, there are two opinions in the school. The well-known opinion is that the acceptable statement is that of the person ordering, while it is said that the acceptable statement is that of the person ordered. When the agent has committed an act that amounts to a tort, claiming that the principal asked him to do it, the well-known opinion is that the acceptable statement is that of the principal, while it is also said that the acceptable statement is that of the agent that the principal ordered him to do it, because he is a trusted agent.

XLIV
THE BOOK OF *LUQṬA* (FOUND PROPERTY)

The discussion of *luqṭa* is undertaken in two chapters. The first is about its elements and the second about its *aḥkām*.

44.1. Chapter 1: The Elements of *Luqṭa*

It has three elements: *iltiqāṭ* (taking into custody), *multaqiṭ* (the finder) and *luqṭa* (found property).

The jurists disagreed whether taking into custody was to be preferred over relinquishment. Abū Ḥanīfa said that it is better to possess it, as it is obligatory on a Muslim to preserve the property of his brother Muslim. This was also the opinion of al-Shāfiʿī. Mālik and a group of jurists maintained the abomination of taking into custody, which is attributed to Ibn ʿUmar and Ibn ʿAbbās and is also Aḥmad's opinion. This is based on two factors. First, on the report that the Prophet (God's peace and blessings be upon him) said, "(Taking the) stray animals of a believer is (to lead to) burning in fire". Second, the fear of failure to announce it and declare publicly that it is in his keeping, as well as the fear of transgression. Those who preferred taking into custody interpreted the tradition saying, "He meant the intention to benefit from it and not for purposes of public notification". A group of jurists said that, on the contrary, taking (such things) into custody is obligatory.

It is said that this disagreement arises when the property is found in the territory of trustworthy people and the ruler is just. They said that even when the property is found among an unreliable people, but the ruler is just, taking into custody is obligatory. If the property is among reliable people and the ruler is an oppressor, it is better not to take into custody. If it is found among a people who are unreliable and the ruler is unjust, he (the finder) has an option in accordance with what he feels to be more likely of the two probabilities for the safety of the found property.

All this is about property found outside of the *ḥajj* season. The jurists agreed that it is not permitted to take custody of property found in the vicinity of the *ḥajj* area due to its prohibition by the Prophet. The taking into custody of found property in Mecca is also not allowed, except by the proclaimer (crier), because of the occurrence of a text about this. Two versions are reported in this. First, that it is not to be taken to someone other than the crier. The second is that it is not to be taken by anyone except the crier. Mālik said that these two kinds of found property are to be proclaimed publicly.

The *multaqiṭ* (the finder) can be any free Muslim major, as this is a case of *wilāya* (guardianship). From al-Shāfiᶜī there is a disputed opinion about the permissibility of custody by a non-believer. Abū Ḥāmid said that the preferred opinion is its permissibility in the *dār al-Islām*. He said, "About the legal capacity of the slave and the *fāsiq* there are two opinions from him, the reason for prohibition is the absence of the capacity of *wilāya* and the reason for permissibility is the generality of the traditions of *luqṭa*".

Luqṭa, in general terms is the property of any Muslim that is exposed to loss, whether it is in inhabited or in a waste area; inanimate objects and animals are the same for this purpose, by agreement (of the jurists), except camels. The basis for found property is the tradition, which is agreed upon for authenticity, of Yazīd ibn Khālid al-Juhanī, who said, "A man came to the Messenger of Allāh (God's peace and blessings be upon him) and asked him about found property. He said, 'Make known its tying ropes and strings and continue to do so for one year, either the owner comes or you may do what you like with it'. Yazīd asked, 'If it should be stray sheep, O Messenger of Allāh?' He replied, 'They are either for you or your brother or for the wolves'. He said, 'Stray camels?' He replied, 'What have you to do with them? They have their own water skins and their shoes! (Leave them alone) to go around drinking from pools and eating tree-leaves till their owner meets with them' ". This tradition includes the identification of what is to be taken into custody and what is not and the identification of the way of dealing with what is taken into custody for a year and after it and how the claimant is to establish a right to it. They agreed that camels are not to be taken into custody and they agreed about sheep (*ghanam*) that they are taken into custody. They wavered about cows. The textual report from al-Shāfiᶜī is that they are like camels, while that from Mālik is that they are like sheep, though there is disagreement (reported) from him.

44.2. Chapter 2: Public Proclamation

With respect to the *ḥukm* of notification, the jurists agreed about the notification of that which has a value for a year, as long as it was not cattle. They disagreed about its *ḥukm* after (the passing of) one year. The jurists of the provinces—Mālik, al-Thawrī, al-Awzāᶜī, Abū Ḥanīfa, al-Shāfiᶜī, Aḥmad, Abū ᶜUbayd and Abū Thawr—agreed that when the year had passed he (the person taking them into custody) had a right to consume it if he was poor and to give it as charity if he was not so. If the owner turned up, he had the option to ratify the charity and gain its spiritual reward or to hold him liable for it. They disagreed in the case of the rich person, whether he had the right to consume it or give it away after one year. Mālik and al-Shāfiʿī said that he had the right (to do either), while Abū Ḥanīfa said that he has no option but to give it in charity; opinions like his have also been attributed to ʿAlī, Ibn ʿAbbās and to a group of the *Tābiʿūn*. Al-Awzāʿī said that if the wealth is considerable, he remits it to the treasury (*bayt al-māl*). Opinions like those of Mālik and al-Shāfiʿī have been related from ʿUmar, Ibn Masʿūd, Ibn ʿUmar and ʿĀʾisha. All of them, except for the Ahl al-Ẓāhir, agreed that if he consumes it, he has to compensate its owner (if the latter turns up).

Mālik and al-Shāfiʿī argued on the basis of the words of the Prophet, "you may do what you like with it", without distinguishing between the rich and the poor. Among their proofs is what has been related by al-Bukhārī and al-Tirmidhī from Suwayd ibn Ghafla, who said: "I met Aws ibn Kāʿb, who said, 'I found a purse containing a hundred *dīnārs*. So I went up to the Prophet (God's peace and blessings be upon him) who said, "'Proclaim it for a year'". I proclaimed it for a year, but did not find anyone. I then went to him thrice and he said, "'Preserve the purse and its string, in case its owner emerges, otherwise enjoy it'". Al-Tirmidhī and Abū Dāwūd recorded the words, "Spend it".

The reason for disagreement is the conflict between the apparent meaning of the traditions of *luqṭa* and the principle of the *sharʾ*, which is that the wealth of a Muslim is not permissible (*ḥalāl*) for anyone else to use or consume without his voluntary consent. Those who assigned more weight to this principle over the apparent meaning of the tradition—which are the words of the Prophet after notification of a year, "Do what you like with it"—said that its disposal is not permitted except by way of charity alone, on the assumption that if the owner of the *luqṭa* turns up and does not ratify the charity he will indemnify it. Those who assigned more weight to the apparent meaning of the tradition over the principle, considering it an exemption from that principle, said that it is permissible to him after a year and it is then regarded as a part of his wealth; he will not indemnify it even if the owner appears. Those who found a middle course said that he can dispose of it after a year even if it is an *ʿayn*, on the condition of indemnification.

They agreed about the *ḥukm* of delivery of found property, to the person who claims it, that it is not be delivered to him unless he identifies the tokens (ropes and strings). They differed when he identifies these, as to whether he needs additional evidence. Mālik said that he has a right to it by (the description of) the tokens and is not in need of evidence. Abū Ḥanīfa and al-Shāfiʿī said that he is not entitled to it except through evidence.

The reason for disagreement is the conflict between the principle of stipulating evidence for the validity of the claim, on the one hand, and the apparent meaning of the tradition on the other. Those who preferred the principle said that evidence is a must; whereas those who preferred the tradition said that he is not in need of evidence. The stipulation of evidence by al-Shāfiʿī and Abū Ḥanīfa is due to their interpretation of the words of the Prophet (God's peace and blessings be upon him), "Know (or keep) the ropes and strings, either the owner appears or you may do what you like with them". They said that these are simply distinctive signs of the found property so that it does not get mixed up with others in his custody, or they imply that he asked him to deliver it to the owner along with the ropes and strings. (In other words, the purpose of the *multaqiṭ*'s knowing them is not by way of proof to facilitate identification by the claimant). Thus, when ambiguity arises recourse to the original principle is necessary. The principles cannot be challenged by opposing probabilities, unless an addition is authenticated, which we shall mention later.

According to Mālik and his disciples, the owner of the *luqṭa* has to describe, along with the bags and strings, the description of the *dīnārs* and their number. They said that this is present in some of the versions of the tradition, which read, "If the owner appears and describes the bag and the string and their number, then deliver it (the property) to him". They maintained that ignorance as to their number does not go against him if he has correctly described the bag and string; similarly, it does not if he mentions a greater number. They disagreed, into two opinions, when he mentions a lower number, or when he is ignorant of the description (of the *dīnārs*), but describes the bag and the string. If, however, he makes an error in the description (of the bag and string), there is nothing for him. When he makes an error in one of the two tokens mentioned in the text, but is ignorant of the other, it is said that there is nothing for him unless he mentions them together, while it is also said that he delivers it to him after declaring himself absolved; it is said that if he acknowledges ignorance, he is absolved, but when he makes an error, nothing is to be delivered to him. There is disagreement in the school when he mentions the entitling tokens, whether to deliver to him (the found property) with an oath or without an oath. Ibn al-Qāsim said that it is (to be delivered) without an oath, while Ashhab said that it is with an oath.

The jurists agreed about stray *ghanam* that their finder in a deserted spot, away from settlement, is entitled to consume them on the basis of the words of the Prophet, "They are for you, or your brother, or for the wolves". They disagreed whether he is to compensate their owner (if he should appear) for their value. The majority of the jurists said that he is liable for the value, while Mālik said in the best-known opinion of his that he is not liable. The reason for the disagreement, as we have said, is the conflict of the apparent meaning of the tradition with a known principle of the *sharīʿa*, except that Mālik in this case preferred the apparent meaning and pursued the *ḥukm* of the apparent meaning. Similarly, he did not permit disposal of the found property which must be proclaimed (even) after a year, due to the strength of the tradition here. There is another narration from him that he is liable, as in the case of perishable food about which he is afraid that it will be destroyed if left. The conclusion from the opinions of Mālik, according to his disciples, is that it (found property) is of three kinds: a kind that is likely to be secure in the hands of the *multaqiṭ*, but in which there is fear of loss if left, like things (*ʿayn*) and goods; a kind that is not in his custody, but is (also) going to perish if left, like goats in deserted places or food that will decay; and a kind in which there is no fear of loss.

The first kind that is secure in the hands of the possessor and is likely to be lost if abandoned, is divided into three types. First, that which is trivial having no significance and is of negligible value and it is obvious that the owner will not care for it due to its triviality. This is not to be notified, according to him (Mālik) and it belongs to the finder. The basis for this is the report "that the Messenger of Allāh (God's peace and blessings be upon him) passed by dates lying on the road and said, 'Had they not belonged to the *Ṣadaqa*, I would have eaten them'. He did not mention notification in this case". This category consists of things like a walking-stick and a whip, though Ashhab preferred their notification. Second, are those that are trivial, though they have some significance and utility. There is no dispute in the school about their notification. They disagreed about the duration of such notification. It is said that it is made for a year and it is said that it is for some days. Third, is that which is substantial or has value. There is no dispute about the necessity of its notification for a year.

With respect to the second kind, which will not subsist in the hands of the *multaqiṭ* and is bound to perish if left, the finder can consume it whether he is rich or poor. Does he compensate (if the owner claims it)? There are two narrations in this, as we have said, the well known being that there is no liability. They disagreed when he finds that which is likely to be overcome by decay (even) within the town. It is said that there is no liability in this and it is said that there is liability in it. A distinction is also made between giving it as charity—in which case there is no liability—and between consuming it, for which there is liability. In the third kind, which includes camels, (Mālik's) preference in it is that they be left alone due to the relevant text, but if he takes them into custody, notification is obligatory. The preference is relinquishment and it is maintained in the school that this (ruling) is general for all times, while it is said that it applies to times of justice. It is better, however, to take such things into custody in times of injustice.

In the indemnification of that which is notified, the jurists agreed that the person who takes custody in the presence of witnesses does not have to compensate if the thing perishes in his custody. They disagree when he does not take witnesses. Mālik, al-Shāfiʿī, Abū Yūsuf and Muḥammad ibn al-Ḥasan said that there is no liability on him when there is no negligence on his part, even if he did not take witnesses. Abū Ḥanīfa and Zufar said that he is liable if he did not take witnesses. Mālik and al-Shāfiʿī argued that *luqṭa* is a deposit (*wadīʿa*) and the absence of witnesses does not move it from (the category of) trust to liability. They said that it is a deposit on the basis of what is related in the tradition of Sulaymān ibn Bilāl and others, who said that "if the owner comes (deliver it) otherwise let it be a deposit with you". Abū Ḥanīfa and Zufar argued on the basis of the tradition of Muṭarrif ibn al-Shikhīr from ʿIyāḍ ibn Ḥimār, who said, "The Messenger of Allāh (God's peace and blessings be upon him) said, 'He who takes custody of a *luqṭa* must take two reliable (*ʿadl*) witnesses and should not conceal it or cause hardship. If the owner appears he has a right to it, otherwise it is wealth from Allāh and He may give it to whom he wishes".

The conclusion in the school about this is that the finder of a *luqṭa*, according to Mālik, may be motivated to take custody by one of three reasons: first, that he takes it for the purpose of *ightiyāl* (devouring, conversion); second, that he takes it for *iltiqāṭ*; third, that he takes neither for *iltiqāṭ* nor for conversion. If he takes custody by way of *iltiqāṭ*, it is a trust with him and he is obliged for its safe custody and notification. If he returns it after taking custody, then, according to Ibn al-Qāsim, he is liable. Ashhab says that he is not liable if he leaves it at the same spot, but if he leaves it at another spot, he is liable as in the case of a deposit. His statement is acceptable about its loss, without an oath, unless he is suspected. If he takes it with the intention of conversion he is liable, but in this case his intention is known only to him (and to Allāh). The third aspect relates to cases like finding a dress and taking it thinking that it belongs to his own people. In this case, if none of his people recognizes it or claims it, it is for him to return it where he found it without any liability on him, by agreement among Mālik's disciples.

Related to this topic is an issue over which the jurists disagreed. It is the case of a slave who destroys a *luqṭa*. Mālik said that it is related to the property rights over him, either the owner surrenders him in return for it or redeems him by paying its value. This is the case when the loss occurs before the end of the year (*ḥawl*), but if he destroys it after one year it becomes a debt on him and is not related to the property rights over him. Al-Shāfiʿī said that if the owner knows about this, he is liable, but if he does not know about it, it is related to property rights over him (the slave).

They disagreed whether the *multaqiṭ* has recourse to the owner for what he has spent over the *luqṭa*. The majority said that the custodian of the *luqṭa* is providing a voluntary service and thus has no recourse to the owner for anything. The Kūfīs, on the other hand, said that he does not have a recourse for what he incurred, unless it is with the permission of the judge (*ḥākim*). This issue is among the *aḥkām* of *iltiqāṭ*. This exposition is sufficient for our purposes under this topic.

44.3. Chapter 3: The *Laqīṭ* (Foundling)

The discussion is about the *aḥkām* of *iltiqāṭ*, the *multaqiṭ* and about the *laqīṭ* (foundling) and its *aḥkām*. Al-Shāfiʿī said that taking custody of everything exposed to waste, with no one to secure it, is a collective (communal) obligation (*farḍ kifāya*). About the obligation of taking witnesses, out of fear that it may lead to enslavement, there is a dispute. The dispute is based upon the differences about the taking of witnesses in the case of *luqṭa*.

The *laqīṭ* (foundling) is a minor child, who has not attained puberty. When the child is a discriminating minor (*mumayyiz*), there is vacillation about it in al-Shāfiʿī's school. The *multaqiṭ* in this case may be any free, reliable and sane person, who is not a slave or a *mukātab*. A non-believer may only take charge of a non-believer to the exclusion of a Muslim, as he cannot be a guardian over him, but a Muslim can take charge of a non-believer. A foundling is to be retrieved from the custody of a *fāsiq* and a spendthrift. Wealth is not a required condition for taking custody, nor is the (proper) maintenance by the custodian binding on him, if he has spent there is no recourse for him.

With respect to the *aḥkām*, he is assigned the *ḥukm* of a Muslim, if taken into custody within the *dār al-Islām*. A child follows the religion of his father if he is a Muslim in Mālik's view and according to al-Shāfiʿī the child is a Muslim when the religion of either of its parents is Islam. This was also the opinion of Ibn Wahb from among Mālik's disciples.

They disagreed about the status of the foundling. Some said that he is the slave of one who takes him into custody, while it is said that he is free with his *wilāya* belonging to the person who takes custody. It is also said that he is free with the *wilāya* belonging to the Muslims, which is Mālik's opinion and for which the sources bear out unless there be a restricting source like the words of the Prophet (God's peace and blessings be upon him), "A woman inherits from three persons: her foundling, her manumitted slave and her child who is free from blame".

XLV
THE BOOK OF *WADĪ^cA* (DEPOSIT; BAILMENT)

Some of the outstanding issues discussed by the jurists of different regions in this book are related to the *aḥkām* of *wadī*ʿ*a*. Among them is their agreement that it is a trust not subject to liability, except what has been related from ʿUmar ibn al-Khaṭṭāb.

The Mālikites said that the proof of its being a trust is that Allāh has commanded the restoration of trusts without requiring the taking of witnesses. It is, therefore, necessary to accept the claim of the bailee (trustee) about the return of the deposit along with his oath when the bailor (depositor) denies it. They said that unless he has made the deposit in the presence of witnesses, the statement accepted cannot be that of the bailor (depositor). They maintained that if he delivers it to him in the presence of witnesses, it is as if he has trusted him for safe-custody and not for its return, he (the trustee) will, therefore, be believed in his claim of loss rather than in his claim of returning it. This is what is well known from Mālik and his disciples.

It is said, on a report from Ibn al-Qāsim, that the acceptable statement is that of the bailee, even if he (the bailor) has delivered it to him in the presence of witnesses. This was also the opinion of Abū Ḥanīfa and al-Shāfiʿī and it is based on *qiyās* (analogy) as a distinction is made between a claim for loss and the claim of restoration, and it is not likely that a trust can be split up (into parts). All this relates to the delivery of the trust (back) to the person who made the deposit.

With respect to the delivery of the trust to a person other than one who made the deposit, he (the trustee) is to procure evidence, which is the same as that required of the guardian of an orphan, according to Mālik, otherwise he is liable. The words of the Exalted require: "And when ye deliver up their fortune unto orphans, have (the transaction) witnessed in their presence". If the person (allegedly) taking possession denies the possession, the trustee is not to be believed without evidence, according to Mālik and his disciples. It is said that the derived opinion in the school is that he is to be believed, and it is the same for Mālik whether or not the owner of the deposit ordered the delivery of the trust to whom it was allegedly delivered. Abū Ḥanīfa said that if he claims to have delivered to one to whom he was ordered to deliver, the acceptable statement is that of the trustee with his oath.

If the person to whom delivery was made acknowledges the deposit (delivery), that is, if he is someone other than the depositor and he claims loss (of the deposit), the trustee has either delivered to him on trust, when he is the agent of the trustee, or on his own responsibility. If the acceptor is a reliable person, the opinion of Ibn al-Qāsim differs. He said once that the person making the delivery is absolved through the acknowledgement of the acceptor, and the liability is on the person giving the order and his agent for possession. He said another time that the person delivering the possession is not absolved except by adducing evidence of delivery or by the possessor coming up with the property.

When he delivers it to him on his responsibility, for example a man says to the trustee, "Deliver it to me as an exchange for goods or something similar". If he retains his credit worthiness the person delivering is absolved, in the opinion of the school without dispute, but when the legal capacity in terms of credit has become defective, there are two opinions in it.

The cause of all this disagreement is that a trust strengthens the claim of the plaintiff so that his statement is accepted along with his oath. Those who considered the *amāna* of the depositor equivalent to the *amāna* of the person for whom the depositor ordered delivery, that is, the agent, said that the acceptable statement is his in his claim as is the case with the claim of the trustee. Those who considered this *amāna* to be weaker said that the person making the delivery is not absolved through the confirmation of the person taking the delivery in a claim for loss.

Those who consider that the person giving the order is in the same position as the one receiving it, said that the acceptable statement is that of the person making the delivery to the *maʾmūr*, just as his statement was accepted with respect to the person giving the order. This is the opinion of Abū Ḥanīfa. Those who consider him (the agent) as weaker than the principal said the trustee is liable unless the person taking possession produces the property.

When he makes a deposit with the condition that he will be liable, the majority maintain that he is not liable, while others hold that he is. On the whole, the jurists collectively maintain that the trustee is not liable, unless he transgresses, and they differed in different cases whether the act amounted to transgression. A well-known issue in this topic is when he utilizes the deposit and then returns something identical, or utilizes it for his expenditure and then restores it. Mālik said that liability is removed from him, in the case of identical property, when he returns it, while Abū Ḥanīfa said that if he returns the property itself before spending it, he does not compensate, but if he returns something identical, he is liable. ʿAbd al-Mālik and al-Shāfiʿi said that he is liable in both cases. Those who portray the act as wrong hold him liable for it just for moving it with the intention of spending it, while those who made an exemption do not hold him liable when he returns something identical.

A point of disagreement is travelling with the deposit. Mālik said that he has no right to travel with it unless he has been given the deposit on a journey. Abū Ḥanīfa said that he may do so if the road is safe and the depositor has not prohibited him from doing so. Another issue is that the trustee does not have the right to entrust the deposit of another to someone else, without an excuse, if he does this he is liable. Abū Ḥanīfa said that if he entrusts it to someone for whom maintenance is obligatory on him, he is not liable as they are the same as his family. According to Mālik, he has a right to entrust what has been entrusted to him to members of his family, those whom he trusts and who are under his authority like his wife, child, *ama*, and those who resemble them.

On the whole, by collective agreement, it is obligatory on him to protect the deposit in accordance with the practice of the people in protecting their properties. They agreed upon what was obviously the right manner of protection, but disagreed about that which was not so obvious, like their disagreement about the person who put the deposit in his pocket and it was lost. The well-known opinion is that he is then liable for it. According to Ibn Wahb, one who was given a deposit in the mosque and he placed it upon his shoes and it was lost, there is no liability for him. They disagree about his liability arising due to forgetfulness, like forgetting where he kept it or forgets who deposited it with him, like two persons claiming the same thing. It is said that they take oaths and it is divided between them. It is also said that he compensates each one of them. When he desires to go on a journey, according to Mālik, he has to deposit it with a trustworthy person in the land and there is no liability for him irrespective of his being able to deposit it with the judge. The disciples of al-Shāfiʿī differed in this. Some of them said if he deposited it with someone other than the *ḥākim*, he is liable.

Acceptance of a deposit, according to Mālik, is not obligatory at all, but there are jurists who hold that it is obligatory when the depositor cannot find anyone else with whom he can make the deposit. There is no compensation for the trustee, according to him (Mālik), for safeguarding the deposit, but whatever he requires with respect to residence or expenditure, it is the responsibility of the depositor.

They disagreed under this topic about a well-known issue regarding the person who is given a deposit and he transgresses in it, using it for trade and making a profit. Is this profit permitted (*ḥalāl*) or prohibited (*ḥarām*)? Mālik, al-Layth, Abū Yūsuf, and a group said that if he returns the property, the profit is proper for him, though he was a usurper besides being a trustee. Abū Ḥanīfa, Zufar, and Muḥammad ibn al-Ḥasan said that he is to pay back the principal and give away the profit as charity. A group said that both the principal and the profit belong to the owner of the deposit. Another group said that he has an option between the principal and the profit. Yet another group said that the sale occurring in this trade is void. They made charity of the profit obligatory in the case of his death. Those who took into consideration the transaction said that the profit is for the person undertaking the transaction, while those who considered the principal said that the profit is for the owner of the capital. It is for this reason that when ᶜUmar, may Allāh be pleased with him, ordered his sons, ᶜAbd Allāh and ᶜUbayd Allāh, to return the money which Abū Muṣā al-Ashᶜarī had loaned out of the *bayt al-māl* with which they traded and made a large profit, it was said to him, "If only you had given it as *qirāḍ*". He complied with this, as one part of the profit would go to the worker and the other part to the owner of the capital, and this was fair.

XLVI
THE BOOK OF ʿ*ĀRIYA* (COMMODITY LOAN)

The discussion of *ʿāriya* (commodity loan) relates to its elements and *aḥkām*. It has five elements: *iʿāra* (lending), *muʿīr* (lender), *mustaʿīr* (borrower), *muʿār* (thing lent), and *ṣīgha* (the form of the contract: offer and acceptance).

Iʿāra is a benevolent act that is recommended. A group from among the earliest ancestors emphasized it vigorously. It is related from ʿAbd Allāh ibn ʿAbbās and ʿAbd Allāh ibn Masʿūd, both saying about the words of the Exalted, "yamnaʿūn al-māʿūn", that these are utensils in the house that people exchange among themselves like hatchets, buckets, ropes, pots and what is similar to them. There is no other condition for the *muʿīr* (lender) other than that he should be the owner of the thing lent (*ʿāriya*), either its corpus or its usufruct. The preferred view is that it is not proper on the part of the borrower, that is, to lend it.

Commodity loans are granted in houses, land, animals, and in anything that can be identified by its substance as long as it has a permissible utility. It is, therefore, not permitted to allow the lending of slave-girls for sexual gratification, and borrowing of a woman's services are considered abominable, unless the person is a consanguine relation (*maḥram*).

The form (*ṣīgha*) of *iʿāra* consists of any word that indicates consent. It is a permissible (*jāʾiz*: terminable at will) contract according to al-Shāfiʿī and Abū Ḥanīfa, that is, it is for the lender to recall his loan whenever he likes. Mālik said in his well-known opinion that he does not have right to withdraw it prior to utilization. If he stipulates a duration, such a duration is binding on him. If he does not stipulate a duration, a duration that is considered reasonable by people for such a loan is binding on him. The reason for this disagreement is its similarity to the binding and permissible contracts.

There are many *aḥkām* related to it. The best known of its problems is whether it is a liability or a trust. Among them (the jurists) were those who said that it is a liability even when evidence can be adduced for its loss. This is the opinion of Ashhab, al-Shāfiʿī and one of the opinions of Mālik. Among them are those who held the opposite of this, that is, it is not a liability at all. This is Abū Ḥanīfa's opinion. Some said that he is liable for what is concealed from him, when there is no evidence for proving loss, but he is not liable for what is not concealed from him, nor in that for which evidence is adduced showing loss. This is Mālik's opinion, as well as the opinion of Ibn al-Qāsim and of the majority of his (Mālik's) disciples.

The reason for disagreement is the conflict of traditions on the issue. It has been related in a confirmed tradition that the Messenger of Allāh (God's peace and blessings be upon him) said to Ṣafwān ibn Umayyah: "But it is an ʿ*āriya*, a liability to be returned". In some versions he said: "But it is an ʿ*āriya* to be returned". It is also related from him (God's peace and blessings be upon him) that he said: "There is no liability on the borrower". Those who preferred and accepted this dropped liability from it, while those who adopted the tradition of Ṣafwān ibn Umayyah held him liable. Those who attempted to the reconcile them made a distinction between what is concealed from view and what is visible. The tradition, however, which says that "There is no liability on the borrower", is not widely known (*mashhūr*), while the tradition of Ṣafwān is *saḥīḥ*.

Those who did not favour liability, compared ʿ*āriya* to *wadīʿa*, while those who made a distinction said that *wadīʾa* is accepted for the benefit of the person making the deposit; whereas ʿ*āriya* is for the benefit of the recipient. They agreed—I mean al-Shāfiʿī, Abū Ḥanīfa and Mālik—about *ijāra* (hire) that it carries no liability (for loss). Al-Shāfiʿī having held that there is no liability in hire, must accept that there should be no liability in ʿ*āriya*, especially when it is accepted that the basis of liability is utilization of benefits; because if he was not liable when he took possession for the mutual benefit of both lender and beneficiary, it is appropriate that he should not be liable when he takes possession for his own benefit alone, if the (deletion of the) benefit of the person making the delivery is effective in negating liability.

They disagreed when liability is stipulated as a condition. A group of jurists said that it makes him liable, while another group said that he is not liable and the condition becomes void. It is deduced from Mālik's opinion that if he stipulates liability as a condition on an occasion when liability is not imposed on him, it necessitates the payment of a reasonable rent for the ʿ*āriya*, as this condition removes ʿ*āriya* from the *ḥukm* of ʿ*āriya* and moves it to that of a void *ijāra*, the owner not having consented to loan it with the exclusion of liability. It amounts to an unknown compensation and must, therefore, revert to a known rule.

The opinions of Mālik and al-Shāfiʿī differ when the borrower plants or constructs (in the land) and the term of the loan expires. Mālik said that the owner has an option, he can ask the borrower to uproot his plantation and demolish the construction, or he may give him the value that his work will have after demolition. It makes no difference, according to Mālik, whether the duration is terminated by condition, by custom, or by practice. Al-Shāfiʿī said that if he did not stipulate uprooting, he cannot demand it; on the contrary, the lender has an option to let it stay after making payment to him or to destroy with damages or to possess with a *badal* (counter-value); whatever the lender chooses to do the borrower will be compelled to comply. If he refuses, he will be required to vacate the property. The borrower, in his view, does not have the right to demolish the addition for sale of the rubble as he opposes demolition; and the borrower's demand to destroy the addition without damages amounts to injustice. Mālik held that the vacation of the place is his responsibility, and that what is customary is to be regarded as a condition.

According to Mālik, if he uses the loaned property in a way that reduces its value, he is liable for the reduction (caused). They disagreed under this topic about a person who asks his neighbour to lend him his wall so that he may insert a beam in it (for his roof) in a way that does not injure the neighbour; and generally, anything by which the borrower benefits and it does not injured the lender (is valid). Mālik and Abū Ḥanīfa said that this is not to be enforced by the court, as ʿ*āriya* is not subject to judicial action, while al-Shāfiʿī, Aḥmad, Abū Thawr, Dāwūd and a group of the traditionists said that it may be imposed by the court.

The proof of the latter is what has been recorded by Mālik from Ibn Shihāb from al-Aʾraj from Abū Hurayra that the Messenger of Allāh (God's peace and blessings be upon him) said: "None of you should prevent his brother from laying a beam on his wall". Abū Hurayra added: "What is this that I see you opposing it, by Allāh, it will be thrust between your shoulder blades". They also argued on the basis of what has been related by Mālik from ʿUmar ibn al-Khaṭṭāb that al-Daḥḥāq ibn Qays wanted to run a canal through land. They decided that it should pass through the land of Muḥammad ibn Maslama, so he asked him to let him through, but Muḥammad still refused. Al-Daḥḥāk said to him: "You forbid me when it is beneficial for you too, you can be the first and the last to water from it and it will not harm you. Muḥammad still refused. So al-Daḥḥāk spoke to ʿUmar ibn al-Khaṭṭāb about it. ʿUmar summoned Muḥammad ibn Maslama and ordered him to let him through. Muḥammad said: 'No!' ʿUmar said to him: 'Do not forbid your brother what benefits him and does not harm you'. Muḥammad said: 'No!' ʿUmar, then, said to him: 'By Allāh we will run it through even if it is over your (dead) body'". Umar asked him to go through with it and al-Daḥḥāk complied. Similar is the tradition of ʿAmr ibn Yaḥyā al-Māzinī from his father that he said: "In the grove of my grandfather there was the harvest for ʿAbd al-Raḥmān ibn ʿAwf, so he decided to move it toward the side of the next grove, but the owner of the grove forbade him. He talked to ʿUmar ibn al-Khaṭṭāb, who decided in favour of ʿAbd al-Raḥmān ibn ʿAwf for moving it".

Al-Shāfiʿī blamed (*ʿadhala*) Mālik for including these traditions in his *al-Muwaṭṭaʾ* and not using them. The reliance of Mālik and Abū Ḥanīfa is on the words of the Prophet (God's peace and blessings be upon him): "The wealth of a Muslim cannot become lawful (for use), except by his voluntary consent". According to the others the generality of this has been restricted by these traditions, particularly by the tradition of Abū Hurayra. According to Mālik it is to be interpreted as a recommendation (not an obligation) and whenever a tradition is capable of restricting (the general) and it also consists of a recommendation, interpreting it to mean recommendation is better, because assigning the particular meaning to the general is necessary when reconciliation and removal of conflict is not possible. Aṣbagh has related from Ibn al-Qāsim that the ruling of ʿUmar in the case of Muḥammad ibn Maslama about the canal is not to be followed, but his ruling in the case of ʿAbd al-Raḥmān ibn ʿAwf for moving the harvest may be followed. He was of the view that moving of the harvest was more tolerable as compared to making a path that was not there before. This suffices for our purpose.

XLVII
THE BOOK OF *GHAṢB* (USURPATION)

In this book there are two chapters. The first is about liability (*ḍamān*), which has three elements (*arkān*). First, the causes giving rise to liability. Second, things in which liability arises. Third, the obligation. The second chapter is about the unexpected contingencies affecting the usurped property.

47.1. Chapter 1: Liability in Usurpation

47.1.1. Element 1

The cause of liability is the commission of the act of acquiring the usurped property or of causing its destruction or loss, or it is the bringing about of the cause that leads to loss, or it is the establishment of possession over the property.

They disagreed about the cause, the bringing about of which, leads to liability, when loss has occurred through another (direct) cause. Does it lead to liability? This, for example, is like opening the cage of a bird, which flies away after it is opened. Mālik said he is liable irrespective of his shooing it away. Abū Ḥanīfa said that he is not liable in any circumstances. Al-Shāfiʿī made a distinction between whether he shooed it away or he did not. He said that he is liable if he shoos it away, but he is not if he did not. Within this issue is also the digging of a well so that something falls in it and perishes. Mālik and al-Shāfiʿī said that if he dug it in a manner that amounts to a tort, he is liable for what is lost in it, otherwise he is not liable. It appears through the principle of Abū Ḥanīfa, in the case of the bird, that he is not liable.

Is intention stipulated as a condition for the commission of the act? The well-known opinion is that wealth is to be compensated whether destroyed intentionally or by mistake, though they did differ in the subsidiary issues under this topic. Is it also stipulated that his act be voluntary. It is known about al-Shāfiʿī that he stipulated voluntary conduct and, therefore, imposed liability on the coercer, I mean the coercer causing loss.

47.1.2. **Element 2**

Things in which compensation is obligatory include each thing whose substance he destroys, or perishes in the possession of the usurper due to a natural calamity, or passes into the possession and ownership of another. This, by agreement, is in things that are movable and transformable. They disagreed about things that are immovable and cannot be transformed like real estate. The majority said they are to be compensated in case of usurpation, I mean, when a house is razed its value becomes due. Abū Ḥanīfa said they are not to be compensated. The reason for their disagreement is whether the possession of the usurper over immovables is the same as his possession over movable and transformable things. Those who rendered their *ḥukm* as one said that they are compensated, while those who did not consider it the same said that there is no compensation.

47.1.3. **Element 3**

This relates to the obligation (*liability*) in usurpation. The obligation of the usurper, when the property exists with him in substance without mesne profits or loss, is its restitution. There is no disagreement in this. When the substance has perished, they agreed that if it is (property that is) measured or weighed, the usurper is liable for identical property, I mean identical to what has perished in description and weight.

They disagreed about chattel (*ᶜurūḍ*). Mālik said that the verdict assigned in the case of chattel including animals and other things is to be nothing but the value on the day of destruction. Al-Shāfiᶜī, Abū Ḥanīfa and Dāwūd said that the liability in this is for identical property. Recourse to payment of value is made only when the an identical property is non-existent. Mālik's reliance is upon the well-known tradition of Abū Hurayra from the Prophet (God's peace and blessings be upon him), which reads: "If one who sets free a slave in whom he has a share, he is obliged to pay the value of the remainder through fair valuation". The point of the argument in this is that he (the Prophet) did not oblige him for identical property, but for its value.

The reliance of the other group is upon the words of the Exalted, "Whoso of you killeth it of set purpose he shall pay its forfeit in the equivalent (*mithl*) of that which he hath killed, of domestic animals"[181] and also on the argument that it is the utility of a thing that is the desire of one transgressed upon. Among their proofs is what is recorded by Abū Dāwūd of the tradition of Anas and others "that the Messenger of Allāh (God's peace and blessings be upon him) was with some of his wives and one of the Mothers of the Believers sent a maid with a large bowl of hers in which there was food". He said, "She

[181] Qurʾān 5:95

(one of the wives) struck it with her hand and the bowl broke. The Prophet (God's peace and blessings be upon him) took the two pieces and pressed them against each other and placed all the food in it saying, 'Your mother is jealous, eat! eat!' till such time that her sound dish was brought from her house. The Messenger of Allāh (God's peace and blessings be upon him) kept the bowl till they had finished eating when he delivered the sound dish to the maid. He kept the broken one in his house". In another tradition it is said "that ʿĀʾisha was the one who felt jealous and broke the utensil and it was she who said to the Messenger of Allāh, 'What is the penalty for what I have done?' He said, 'A utensil identical to that utensil and food identical to that food' ".

47.2. Chapter 2: Contingencies

The unexpected happenings affecting the usurped property and causing an increase or loss, are either from creatures or from the Creator. In case of loss occurring through a natural calamity, the owner can either take it back with the loss or hold him liable for the value as on the day of usurpation. It is said that he has a right to take it back and hold the usurper liable for the value of the defect (caused). If the loss is caused through a wrongful act of the usurper, the person wronged has an option, in Mālik's school, to hold him liable for the value as it was on the day of usurpation or to take it with the value of the defect with Ibn al-Qāsim saying that the value of the defective property is what it was on the day of the tort and Saḥnūn saying it is the value of the defect on the day of usurpation. Ashhab held that he has an option to hold him liable for the value or to take it with the defect and there is nothing for him on account of defect caused through a natural calamity. This was also the opinion of Ibn al-Mawwāz.

The reason for this disagreement is that those who considered the usurped property a liability of the usurper on the basis of value as it was on the day of usurpation considered any resulting increase or decrease in it as if it had taken place under valid ownership, thus, holding him liable for revenue, but not for loss whether it was caused by him or was an act of God. This is deduced from the opinion of Abū Ḥanīfa and, generally, from the opinion of those who hold him liable for value on the day of usurpation only. Those who hold the usurped property to be a liability of the usurper and consider it be his as long as he has possession over it, impose upon him the highest value and make him liable for the restitution of revenue and compensation of loss, irrespective of whether it is caused by his act or by an act of God. This is the opinion of al-Shāfiʿī or a deduction from his opinion. Those who distinguish between a damage caused by the usurper and the damage resulting from an act of God, which is Mālik's well known opinion and also of Ibn al-Qāsim—

and his reliance is upon *qiyās al-shabah*—maintain that the wrongful act of the usurper upon the thing usurped is a second usurpation repeated by him, as if he committed a tort upon it when it was in the possession of its owner. This is the point of disagreement under this topic, so let it be known.

If the tort is committed when it is in the possession of the usurper, but is not the act of the usurper, the owner of the property has an option either to hold the usurper liable for the value as it was on the day of usurpation, with the usurper prosecuting the offender, or to let go the usurper and to prosecute the offender under the rules of torts. This is the *ḥukm* of a tort committed on the property in the possession of the usurper.

Torts committed upon things, when the tortfeasor has usurped them, are divided in Mālik's view into two types. First, torts that do away only with a negligible utility, with the major function of the thing subsisting. The liability in this is for compensating the loss with its value on the day of the tort. This is done by valuation in its sound state and its valuation after the tort, the difference being paid. If the tort destroys the major purpose of the thing, the owner has the option to deliver it to the offender and charge its value, or to charge the value of the damage caused by the offender. Al-Shāfiʿī and Abū Ḥanīfa said that he has nothing besides the value of the damage caused. The cause of disagreement is the comparison with the case of the usurper and holding similar the loss of the major function as the loss of the thing itself.

Growth is divided into two types. First, when it is an act of God, like a minor growing into maturity or the weak becoming stronger or the defect being removed. Second, when it is brought into being by the usurper. With respect to the first, it involves no loss. The growth that is brought into being by the usurper, however, is divided, as reported by Ibn al-Qāsim from Mālik, into two types: first, when he adds to it from his own wealth something tangible, like dyeing a dress or decorating a building or what resembles it; second, when his addition costs him no money but only labour, like stitching, weaving, or milling wheat and hay, making flour out of it and making a wooden case from a piece of wood.

In the first case when he adds something tangible costing him some of his wealth, it is divided into two types: first, when the thing can be restored to its original shape like a swamp on which he erected a building or what resembles it; second, when it cannot be restored to its original shape, like a dress he has dyed or flour he has turned into dough. In the first instance, the owner has an option to require the usurper to restore the plot to its original shape and remove what he has accumulated in it of debris and other material, or to give the usurper what would be the value of the debris after reducing the cost of demolition from it, that is, when the usurper is not ready to do this himself or to have it done by someone else, but is going to hire someone to do it. It is said, though, that he is not to reduce the cost of demolition from it. This takes place when such rubble has value, but when it has no value the usurper has no claim upon the owner for it, as it is a right of the owner to require the usurper to restore it to its original shape. If he does not ask him to do this, the usurper has no cause of complaint. In the second instance, he has the option to pay for the value of the dyeing and to take back his dress or to hold him liable for the value of the dress on the day of usurpation. This is not possible in flour that he has converted into dough with fat, or in similar food, where he has no option in so far as it involves *ribā*. It is a loss and the usurper is obliged to return identical food for it, or value when identical food is not available.

The second type in the first main division, that is, when the usurper does not add anything to it beside labour, is also divided into two types. First, when it is minor and the name of the thing does not change to something else as in mending a dress or trailing it. Second, when the labour is considerable and transforms the name of the usurped property, like wood by making it into a box, or wheat by turning it into flour, or yarn through weaving, or silver by moulding it into jewellery or into *dirhams*. In the first case, the usurper has no right to anything and the owner takes the usurped item with the labour done on it. In the second case, it is a loss and the usurper is obliged to pay the value of the thing as it was on the day of usurpation, or its *mithl* where it is available.

All this is according to the opinion of Ibn al-Qāsim in this context, while Ashhab assigns it entirely to the owner, the basis being the issue of construction. He says that the usurper has no right in that which he cannot separately acquire out of dyeing, darning, spinning, weaving and milling. It is related from Ibn ᶜAbbās that dyeing amounts to loss (of the item) that makes the usurper liable for the value as on the day of usurpation. It is also said that both, the owner and usurper, become joint owners, the former in the value of dyeing and the latter in the value of the dress, that is, when the owner of the dress refuses to pay the value of dyeing or when the usurper refuses to pay the value of the dress. This opinion was rejected by Ibn al-Qāsim in *al-Mudawwana* while discussing the topic of *luqṭa*. He said that joint ownership does not occur, except in cases of manifest doubt. The opinion of al-Shāfiᶜī in the case of dyeing is the same as that of Ibn al-Qāsim, except that he permits joint ownership between them saying that the usurper is to be ordered to bleach the dress if that is possible even if the dress is reduced in value, the owner being liable for the extent of the loss.

The principles of the law (*sharᶜ*) require that the wealth of the usurper should not become permissible due to his usurpation, whether it is a utility or a thing (*ᶜayn*); except when the contender argues on the basis of the words of the Prophet (God's peace and blessings be upon him), "No right ensues from the share (ᶜ*irq*) of the usurper (*ẓālim*)". This, however, is ambivalent and implies in the first meaning that no benefit is generated between his wealth and the thing that he usurped, I mean, his wealth related to the usurped property. This is the *ḥukm* obligatory in a thing usurped, irrespective of its being altered.

They disagreed in the school about the *ḥukm* of mesne profits into two opinions. First, that the *ḥukm* of the mesne profits is the same as the *ḥukm* of the thing itself. Second, that their *ḥukm* is different from the usurped property. Those who held that their *ḥukm* is the same as that of the usurped property, which is the opinion of Ashhab from among the disciples of Mālik, said that he (the usurper) is liable for the mesne profits from the day of usurpation; or is liable for the highest value they have reached—according to those who maintain that the usurper is to be made liable for the highest value attained and not the value of the usurped property on the day of usurpation. Those who hold that the *ḥukm* of the mesne profits is different from that of the usurped property, differed extensively about their *ḥukm* after agreeing that if they are lost with supporting evidence there is no liability on the usurper. If he merely claims that they are lost, he is not to be believed, when the property is that which is not concealed from his view.

The summary of the opinions of these jurists about the *ḥukm* of mesne profits is that mesne profits are divisible into three kinds. First, that they are mesne profits generated from the usurped property, being of the same species and nature, that is, an offspring. Second, mesne profits that are generated by the thing, but do not have the same form, like fruit and milk of animals. Third, mesne profits that are in the nature of benefits like rents and produce and what resembles them.

There is no dispute, that I know of, about things having the same nature and form that the usurper returns them, as in the case of a child with its abducted mother, even if it is the child of the abductor. They differed about it when the mother dies. Mālik said that he has an option between the child and the value of the mother. Al-Shāfiᶜī said that he returns the child and the value of the mother, which is analogy. When the mesne profits generated are of a different nature and form, there are two opinions about it. First, that these mesne profits are for the usurper. Second, that it is binding on him to return it with the usurped property if it exists, or its value if he claims to have lost it, there being no other support for his statement. If the usurped property perishes he has an option to hold him liable for the value, there being nothing for him from the mesne profits, or to take it with the mesne profits, there being no compensation of value.

They disagree about mesne profits that are not born, forming five opinions. First, that he is not liable for its return as a whole without distinction. Second, that he is liable for its return as a whole without distinction. Third, that return is binding on him if he rented it out, but no return is binding on him if he just utilized it or let it stay idle. Fourth, return is binding on him if he rented it or used it, but not if he let it stand idle. Fifth, that there is distinction between animals and real estate, I mean, he returns the benefits derived from real estate, but he does not return the benefits derived from animals. All this relates to what he earns from the usurped property through its substance and with its existence.

In the case of the amount he earns by transacting in it and by converting its substance, like *dīnārs* that he appropriates and trades with making a profit, the profit is for him through the unanimous opinion of the school. A group of jurists, however, said that the profits are also considered usurped. This is the case when he also intended the appropriation of the capital, but when he intended the appropriation of the profits and not the capital, he is liable for the profits without qualification. There is no dispute about this whether he let it stand idle, utilized it, or rented it, or did something with it through which it is reduced.

Abū Ḥanīfa said that in the case of the person who commits a tort against a man's animal, riding it or carrying loads on it, there is no liability for rent on him for riding it or for carrying loads on it, as he is liable for it if it perishes through his tort. This is his opinion in all things that are movable and can be transformed. He maintains that when he became liable for it through his tort, its profit became permissible to him. This is just what the Mālikites maintain in the case of trading with usurped wealth though the difference between them is that whatever is utilized in trade changes its form, but in this case the form did not change.

The reason for their disagreement, whether the usurper is to return the usufruct, is based on their disagreement about the generality of the words of the Prophet (God's peace and blessings be upon him), "Entitlement to revenue is through a corresponding liability (for loss)" and his words, "No right ensues from the investment of the usurper". The words of the Prophet were recorded for a reason. It was the case of a slave where the person using him wished to return the income from his earnings to the buyer. (The question is) when a general tradition relates to a specific cause, is it to be confined to that cause or is to have a general application? There is a well-known dispute about it among the jurists of different regions. Those who confined it in this case to its cause said that (payment of) revenue becomes obligatory as a liability in whatever comes to a person in doubtful circumstances, like buying a thing and deriving revenue from it thus (giving rise to) an entitlement. The revenue of that which comes to him in circumstances that are not doubtful is not permissible to him as he is a usurper and the investment of the usurper does not lead to a right. The application of this tradition extended to capital and profits, I mean, the generality of the tradition, while the other was restricted.

Those who treated the matter in the opposite way and made the words of the Prophet (God's peace and blessings be upon him), "Entitlement to revenue is through corresponding liability (for loss)", applicable to cases having a cause other than its specific cause for which it was prescribed, while they restricted the saying of the Prophet (God's peace and blessings be upon him), "No right ensues from the investment of the usurper", by making it applicable to the corpus and not the usufruct, said that the usurper does not have to return the usufruct. The general rule of analogy, as we have said, requires that benefits and reproduced things should be given the same treatment in assigning liability or in not assigning it. All other opinions that fall in between these two are based on *istiḥsān*.

The jurists agreed unanimously that one who plants date-palms and cultivates crops generally or vegetation in another's land is to be ordered to uproot it due to what is established through the tradition of Mālik through Hishām ibn ʿUrwa from his father that the Messenger of Allāh (God's peace and blessings be upon him) said: "One who revives barren land, it is for him, but no right ensues from the investment (*ʿirq*) of the usurper". *ʿIrq* of the usurper, according to them, is what he plants in another's land. Abū Dāwūd has reported this tradition with the following addition: ʿUrwa said that the one who related this tradition to me said, "Two men brought their dispute to the Prophet (God's peace and blessings be upon him), one of whom had planted date-palms in the other's land. The Prophet gave his decision returning the land to its owner and ordered the owner of the date-palms to uproot them from it". He said, "I saw them when their roots were being cut with hatchets and they were date-palms fully grown when they were uprooted from it". The exception is what is widely related from Mālik: "In the case of the person who sows crops in another's land when the sowing season has passed, the owner of the land is not to uproot the crops and the cultivator is obliged to pay rent for the land". It is sometimes reported from him and it resembles the opinion of the majority, that anything that is of no use to the usurper, once he uproots and removes it, belongs to the owner who pays the cost of sowing to the cultivator.

A group of jurists distinguished between crops and fruit trees. They said that one sowing in another's land is entitled to maintenance and the cost of sowing. It is the opinion of a large number of the Ahl al-Madīna and was upheld by Abū ʿUbayd. It is related from Rāfiʿ ibn Khadīj that the Prophet (God's peace and blessings be upon him) said, "One who sows in other people's land without their consent is entitled to maintenance, but does not get any share of the produce".

The jurists disagreed in regarding what is ruined by domestic and loading animal into four opinions. First, that in the case of the unleashed animal, the owner is liable for what it ruins. Second, that he is not liable. Third, that the liability rests on the owners of animals (let loose by them) at night, but there is no liability on them for what they destroy during the day. Fourth, imposition of liability in the case of those that did not break loose, there being no liability for those that cut loose. Among those who said that there is liability during the night, but none during the day are Mālik and al-Shāfiʿī. Those who said that there is no liability at all are Abū Ḥanīfa and his disciples. Al-Layth upheld unqualified liability, except that he said that the liability extends to the value of the animal. The fourth opinion is related from ʿUmar (God be pleased with him).

The sources of reliance for Mālik and al-Shāfiʿī are two, in this issue. First are the words of the Exalted, "And David and Solomon, when they gave judgment concerning the field, when people's sheep had strayed and browsed therein by night; and We were witnesses to their judgment".[182] *Nafsh*, according to the experts of the language, does not take place except by night. This is a proof according to the opinion of those who view that we are bound by the law of those before us (earlier Scriptures). The second is his (Mālik's) *mursal* report from Ibn Shihāb "that al-Barāʾ ibn ʿĀzib's camel entered someone's grove and caused damage in it. The Messenger of Allāh (God's peace and blessings be upon him) decided that the grove's owners have to guard it during the day, but what the animals destroy during the night their owners have to bear". Abū Ḥanīfa's reliance is on the words of the Prophet (God's peace and blessings be upon him), "Dumb (animals)! Their injuries are waived". Al-Ṭaḥāwī says that the actual opinion of Abū Ḥanīfa is that if they are guarded while loose, there is no liability, but if they are let loose without a guard there is liability. The Mālikites said that their statement is contingent upon the fact that the cattle be in grazing land; if they are in cultivated land that has no pasture in it they (the owners) are liable during the day as well as night. The reliance of those who maintain liability for damage during the day as well night is the evidence of the principles that goes in their favour, that is, it is a tort through things let loose and the principles say that the tortfeasor is liable. The basis for those who distinguish between those that break loose and those that are let loose is obvious, as that which breaks loose cannot be controlled.

The reason for the disagreement in this topic is the conflict of principles with traditions and the conflict of traditions *inter se*, I mean, the principle opposes, "Damage by the dumb (animals) is waived (as a waste)". It also

[182] Qurʾān 21:78

opposes the distinction made in the tradition of al-Barāʾ. Similarly, the distinction in the tradition of al-Barāʾ opposes the words of the Prophet, "Damage by the dumb (animals) is waived (as a waste)".

Among the well-known issues in this topic is their disagreement about the *ḥukm* of injuries to the limbs of animals. It is related from ʿUmar ibn al-Khaṭṭāb that he gave a decision about the eye of an animal awarding a fourth of its price. He wrote to Shurayḥ and ordered him to award damages accordingly. The Kūfīs upheld this and ʿUmar ibn ʿAbd al-ʿAzīz also gave similar decisions. Al-Shāfiʿī and Mālik said that the award of damages for an injury to an animal is binding to the extent of the reduction in its price, on the analogy of torts against property. The Kūfīs relied in this on the opinion of ʿUmar (God be pleased with him) saying that if a Companion expresses an opinion and none of the other Companions opposes him, but his opinion is contrary to analogy, it is obligatory to act upon his opinion as it is known that he adopted the opinion on the basis of *tawqīf*, that is, *naql* or a precedent from the Prophet. The reason for the disagreement is, then, the conflict of analogy with the opinion of a Companion.

Within this topic is their disagreement about killing an (attacking) violent camel and all cases of self-defence and what resembles them. When a person is afraid for his life and kills the assailant, is he to be held liable? Mālik and al-Shāfiʿī say that there is no liability on him if it turns out that he was afraid from him for his life. Abū Ḥanīfa and al-Thawrī said that he pays his value (that is, *diya*) in all circumstances. The reliance of those who do not view liability (in this case) is analogy on the case where a man aims at another intending to kill him and the person defending himself kills the assailant, there being no retaliation against him. If this is the case for retaliatory liability (in killing a human being) (*nafs*) it is appropriate that this be the case for financial liability, as life has a greater priority for protection than wealth. In addition, there is the analogy on the case of the permissibility to kill the animal prohibited for hunting when it attacks. The astute among the disciples of al-Shāfiʿī held on to this. The reliance of Abū Ḥanīfa is that wealth is to be compensated even when damage is by necessity, the principle lies in the case of one under duress through starvation, in need for food belonging to another and there is no special regard for the camel in comparison with a human soul.

Under this topic is also their disagreement about the female victim in rape. Is the coercer to be held liable, along with *ḥadd*, for *ṣadāq* (dower)? Mālik, al-Shāfiʿī and al-Layth said that he is liable to *ḥadd* as well as payment of her dower. Abū Ḥanīfa and al-Thawrī said that he is liable for *ḥadd*, but there is no liability for dower, which is also the opinion of Ibn Shubrama. The reliance of Mālik is on the fact that claims for two kinds of rights are made against him, the right of Allāh and the right of the individual; one does not annul the other. The basis for this is the case of theft (*sariqa*) due to which both liability for property and amputation of the hand is imposed, according to them. Those who do not make the payment of dower obligatory linked it to two principles. First, when two rights gather in one case, the right of Allāh and the right of creatures, the right of creatures is annulled in favour of the right of Allāh. This is the opinion of the Kūfīs, in so far as they do not assimilate two rights in the case of the thief, financial liability and amputation. The second principle is that *ṣadāq* is not a counter-value for sexual gratification, but a type of an *ʿibāda* (worship) when the marriage is in accordance with the *sharīʿa*. This being the case, there is no dower in a *nikāḥ* (copulation) that is contrary to the *sharīʿa*.

Among their well-known issues in *ghaṣb* is the case of the *usṭuwāna* (column) on which the usurper makes a construction the value of which is in multiples of the *usṭuwāna*. Mālik and al-Shāfiʿī said that the usurper is to be ordered to demolish it and the owner takes back his *usṭuwāna* from him. Abū Ḥanīfa said that it is considered lost in exchange for its value, as in Mālik's opinion about the usurper who alters the usurped property by erecting that which has considerable value. According to al-Shāfiʿī, nothing is lost with an addition to it. Here this book ends.

XLVIII
THE BOOK OF *ISTIḤQĀQ* (RESTITUTION; THIRD-PARTY RIGHTS)

The major discussion in this book is about the *aḥkām* of *istiḥqāq*. The summary of the fundamental *aḥkām* of this topic is that a thing in the hands of a person to which entitlement is claimed (by another), by virtue of those things that establish such a claim for the claimant in the law, if it was acquired by this man (the possessor) through purchase, then, the claim is either for a small part, the whole, or for most of it. Further, when the claim is for the whole of it or for a major part, it has either been altered in the hands of the possessor with an addition or a decrease or has not been altered. Again, it may either have been purchased by the person, from whom it is claimed, through a price or with another commodity (*mathmūn*).

If the claim is for a small part, the claimant, according to Mālik, can demand only the value of what he is claiming and he cannot claim the whole of it. If he is entitled to the whole or most of it, and it has not been altered, the claimant takes it from the possessor, who in turn has recourse to the seller for its price, if he had bought it with a price. If he had bought it with another commodity (*mathmūn*), he has recourse to the seller for the commodity itself, if that has not been altered. If it has been altered in a manner that changes its value, he has recourse for its value as it was on the day of the purchase. If the property claimed has been sold, the claimant has a right either to let the sale proceed and take its price or to take the property itself. This is the *ḥukm* of the claimant and the person from whom the claim is made as long as the property has not been altered.

If the thing has been altered, it is either altered through an addition or a decrease. In case it is altered with an increase, the increase may be due to the act of the possessor or due to a natural growth. If the growth is natural, the claimant takes it, like a slave-girl growing healthier or a slave boy attaining maturity. In the growth attributable to the possessor, like constructing further in a house he purchased and which is later claimed, he (the claimant) has an option either to pay for the addition and take his claim or to take the value of the claim from the possessor or to become a joint owner with the claimant owning to the extent of the value of his claim and the possessor to the extent of what he has added. This is the decision of ʿUmar ibn al-Khaṭṭāb. When the addition is due to an act of reproduction on the part of the possessor, for example, he buys an *ama* and has a child from her, and she is then claimed, or marries her off as a free person, but she turns out to be an *ama*, they agreed that the claimant cannot take away the child and disagreed over whether he can charge their value. About the mother it is said that he can take her and it is also said that he charges her value. If the child is born through a *nikāḥ* and the mother is claimed as a slave, there is no disagreement that the claimant takes her and the husband has recourse for the dower to the person who deceived him. If he (the husband) is obliged to pay the value of the child, he cannot have recourse for it to the person who deceived him, as the deception did not relate to the child.

If he (the possessor) was liable for the usufruct of the claimed property through a semblance of ownership (*shubhat al-milk*), there is no disagreement that the usufruct belongs to the possessor. I mean, by liability, that it would have been his loss had it perished in his possession. If he is not deemed liable, for example, when he is an heir and another heir appears and claims part of what is in his hands, he then returns the usufruct. When he is not liable, though he can claim its price, like the case of a slave (he bought) who turns out to be emancipated, so that he may have recourse for the price even if he dies in his possession, there are two opinions in this. First, he is not liable when he cannot find a person to whom he can have recourse (for the price). Second, he is liable if he can find a person to whom he can have recourse for the price.

With respect to the time after which the usufruct is valid for the claimant, it is said that it is the day of decision, and it is said that it is the day of the establishment of the claim, and it is said that it is from the day of its suspension. If we say that the usufruct becomes due to the claimant in any of these three timings, and in case these (the property in question) are trees bearing fruit and the fruit has appeared in the relevant time and has not been picked, it is said that it belongs to the claimant as long as it has not been picked, and it is said that as long as it has not dried up, and it is also said as long as the fruit has not ripened; the possessor has recourse to the claimant for (expenses of) watering and caring. This is the case when he (the possessor) bought them prior to pollination (fertilization). If he bought them after pollination, the fruit is for the claimant, according to Ibn al-Qāsim, if it was cut, and the possessor has recourse for (expenses) of watering and caring. Ashhab said that they are for the claimant unless it has been cut. When a right to land is claimed, the rent is for the claimant if the entitlement is established during the period of sowing, but if the time of sowing has passed the rent is due to the possessor.

When the property is altered with a decrease and it is not caused by the possessor, there is no liability on the possessor. In case he (the possessor) has charged a price for it, for example, a house collapses and he sells the debris, after which the house is claimed by another man, this man has a right to recover the price for which he sold the debris. Al-Qāḍī (Ibn Rushd) said: "I have not come across a disagreement, in this topic, that can be relied upon, in all that I have transmitted from Mālik and his disciples, which are their principles in this subject. But it can be deduced from the principles of others that if the claimed thing was bought with goods and the goods have been lost, he should have recourse (to the seller) for identical goods and not the value. They are the ones who uphold the taking of identical goods in all cases of destruction. It is also deduced from the principles of others that he (the claimant) should have recourse in a similar way to the buyer, whether the claimed right is small or large, as his right does not extend to the rest and no sale has taken place in it (between him and the buyer) nor has consent been given.

The book of *istiḥqāq* is completed, with praise for Allāh.

XLIX
THE BOOK OF *HIBĀT* (GIFTS)

The discussion of *hiba* (gift) covers its elements, its conditions, its kinds, and its *aḥkām*. We shall mention in these genera those issues that are well known.

49.1. **Chapter 1: The Elements of *Hiba***

We say: The elements are three: the *wāhib* (donor), *mawhūb lahu* (donee) and *hiba* (gift). They agreed about the donor that his gift is valid if he is the owner of the donated property through a legally valid ownership, is in good health, possesses legal capacity and has a valid power of disposal. They disagreed in the cases of (death) illness, prodigality and insolvency. In the case of fatal illness, the majority said that it is valid up to the extent of a third (of his property) on the basis of its similarity to *waṣīyya* (bequest), that is, the gift in which all conditions are fulfilled. A group of the earlier jurists and one group of the Ẓāhirites said that the gift is to be drawn entirely from his capital if he dies. There is no dispute among them that if he recovers from his illness his gift is valid.

The reliance of the majority is on the tradition of ᶜImrān ibn Ḥuṣayn from the Prophet (God's peace and blessings be upon him) "in the case of the person who manumitted six of his slaves close to his death. The Messenger of Allāh (God's peace and blessings be upon him) ordered him so that he emancipated a third of them and kept the remaining enslaved". The reliance of the Ẓāhirites is on *istiṣḥāb al-ḥāl*, that is, the continued application of the consensus (*ijmāᶜ*) on this point, which is that as they agreed to the validity of his gift in health the *istiṣḥāb* of the *ḥukm* of consensus is extended to illness, unless evidence from the Book or the explicit *sunna* indicates the contrary. The tradition (above) is applicable, according to them, to cases of *waṣiyya* (bequest).

The illnesses in which gift is restricted (to a third), according to the majority, are cases of serious illnesses. According to Mālik, serious situations are like serious illnesses, such as being between fighting forces, a pregnant (woman) approaching the time of delivery and travelling in a stormy sea, although there is disagreement over this. There is no interdiction in prolonged incurable illnesses, as has preceded in the Book of *Ḥajr* (interdiction). With respect to the mentally weak and insolvents, there is no disagreement among those who uphold their interdiction that their gifts are not to be given effect.

The property that may be donated is anything that legitimately comes into his ownership. They agreed that a man has the right to donate his entire wealth to a stranger, but they disagreed about a person preferring some of his children over others or in donating all his wealth to some of them to the exclusion of others. The majority of the jurists of different regions held this to be abominable for him, but if it takes place, it is valid. The Ẓāhirites said that no preference is permitted, not to speak of his donating all his wealth to some of them. Mālik said that preference is allowed, but he may not donate his entire wealth to some of them to the exclusion of others.

The evidence of the Ẓāhirites is the tradition of al-Nuᶜmān ibn Bashīr, which is agreed upon for its soundness, though there is a difference in words (in different versions). The tradition is that he said "that his father, Bashīr, came up to the Messenger of Allāh (God's peace and blessings be upon him) and said, 'I have gifted to this son of mine a slave that I had'. The Messenger of Allāh asked, 'Have you made such a donation to each of your children?' He said, 'No!' The Messenger of Allāh said, 'Then retract it' ". Mālik, al-Bukhārī and Muslim agree upon this version. They said that retraction means cancellation of the *hiba*. In some of the versions of this tradition the Prophet (God's peace and blessings be upon him) is reported to have said, "This is injustice". The reliance of the majority is on the fact that according to a consensus a person has a right to give away all his wealth to a stranger to the exclusion of his children and if that is the case for a stranger it is more appropriate if he gives it away to one child to the exclusion of others. They argued on the basis of Abū Bakr's well-known tradition that "he gifted to ᶜĀʾisha twenty *awsuq* of the yield of al-Ghāba wilderness. When he approached death, he said, 'O, my daughter, there is none among mankind I would prefer to see rich after me than you and none whom I would love to see free from poverty after me than you. I gifted to you twenty *awsuq*. If you have harvested and taken possession of it, it is for you, for it is today the wealth of the heirs' ". They said that the tradition (of al-Nuᶜmān) indicates merely a recommendation and the evidence of that is the occurrence in some of its versions of the words, " 'Do you not wish that they be equal in loving you and in treating you well?' He said, 'Yes!' He said, 'Then take as witness someone beside me' ". Mālik, on the other hand, was of the view that the prohibition about a man gifting his entire wealth to one of his children is more appropriate when construed as an obligation. He thus considered the meaning of this tradition as a prohibition obligatory against a man favouring one of his children exclusively with all his wealth.

The reason for the disagreement is the conflict of analogy with the words of the reported prohibition, because prohibition, according to most, should be couched in prohibiting terms, just as a command indicates an obligation. Those who upheld a reconciliation between a traditional text and analogy, interpreted the tradition as a recommendation, or restricted it to some forms as is done by Mālik. There is no disagreement among the upholders of analogy (as a principle of law) that it is permitted to restrict the generality of a *sunna* through analogy. Similar is the case in redirecting its apparent meaning, I mean, to interpret the prohibiting term to mean disapproval. As analogy is not permitted by the Ẓāhirites, they relied on the apparent meaning of the tradition upholding the prohibition of favouring some of the children in *hiba*.

They disagreed in this topic about the permissibility of gifting a share in an undivided common property. Mālik, al-Shāfiʿī, Aḥmad and Abū Thawr said it is valid. Abū Ḥanīfa said it is not valid. The reliance of the former group is on the fact that possession in *hiba* is as valid as possession in sale. Abū Ḥanīfa's argument is that possession in it is not valid, unless it is separated as in the case of *rahn*.

There is no disagreement in the school (Mālik's) about the permissibility of donating an undetermined thing or a non-existent thing that is likely to come into existence. On the whole, each thing whose sale is valid in the law (*sharʿ*) with the existence of *gharar* (can be gifted). Al-Shāfiʿī said that all things whose sale is allowed, their donation is allowed, as in the case of a debt, and a thing whose sale is not allowed, its donation is not allowed. According to al-Shāfiʿī, anything whose possession is not allowed, its donation is not allowed, as in debts and *rahn*.

Offer and acceptance is a must in a gift, according to all. Among the conditions for the donee is that he must be one whose acceptance and possession is valid. One of the best known is possession, that is, the jurists disagreed whether possession is a condition for the validity of the contract. Al-Thawrī, al-Shāfiʿī and Abū Ḥanīfa agreed that possession is among the conditions of validity of *hiba* and as long as he (the donee) has not taken possession, it does not become binding on the donor. Mālik said that the contract is concluded with acceptance and he is to compelled to take possession as in sale. If the donee delays the demand for possession till such time that the donor becomes insolvent or falls (seriously) ill, the gift is annulled. He (the donor) has the right to sell it, and if the donee neglects this after knowing it he may only claim the price, but if he claims immediately, he will get the gifted property. Possession, according to Mālik, is a condition of completion of *hiba* and not a condition of its validity, while it is a condition of validity according to al-Shāfiʿī and Abū Ḥanīfa. Aḥmad and Abū Thawr said a gift is valid through the contract and possession is not one of its essential conditions, neither of completion nor of validity, which is also the opinion of the Ẓāhirites. It is, however, related from Aḥmad ibn Ḥanbal that possession is a condition in things measured and weighed.

The reliance of those who stipulate possession as a condition in *hiba* is due to its similarity to sale. The principle in contracts is that possession is not prescribed as a condition for their validity, unless evidence is proffered for the (specific) stipulation of possession. The reliance of those who stipulate possession is on the fact that it is related from Abū Bakr (God be pleased with him) in the tradition of his gift to ᶜĀᵓisha that has preceded, which is explicit in the stipulation of possession as a condition for the validity of *hiba*. It is also related from ᶜUmar that he said, "What is the matter with some men who make gifts to their sons and then hold on to them. When the son of one of them dies he says that my wealth is in my hands, I did not give it to anyone. If his (own) son is dead he would say I had given this to my son. He who makes a gift and then does not permit it to the donee, retaining it till such time that he dies so that it is given to the heirs, then, such a gift is void". This is also ᶜAlī's opinion. They said that this amounts to a consensus of the Companions, as no one has related a disagreement on this from them. Mālik relied on both things, that is, analogy and what is related from the Companions, reconciling the two. Thus, in so far as it is a contract like the other contracts, possession is not a condition for its validity and because of the way it is stipulated as a condition by the Companions, for *sadd al-dharīᶜa* mentioned by ᶜUmar, possession is a condition of completion and a right of the donee, but if he delays it till possession is lost through illness or insolvency of the donor, his right is annulled.

The majority of the jurists of different regions maintain that a father may permit for his minor son who is in his guardianship and for a prodigal who is a major what they have gifted, just as he may permit to them what is gifted by others to them. It is sufficient for him in possession to take witnesses for the gift and to proclaim it. This is the case in things other than gold and silver and those which are not determined. The source in this, according to them, is what is related by Mālik from Ibn Shihāb from Saᶜīd ibn al-Musayyib from ᶜUthmān ibn ᶜAffān, who said, "One who makes a gift to his son who is not a major so that he may take possession of the gift, he should make it public and take witnesses over it. This amounts to possession even though he is his guardian". Mālik and his disciples said that it is necessary to take possession in things resided in and worn. If it is a house meant for residence he (the donor) should move out of it. Similarly, in things worn, if he wears it the gift is annulled.

In the case of goods, they held the same opinion as the other jurists, that is, it is sufficient to proclaim them and to have it witnessed. The narration from Mālik about gold and silver differs. It is related from him that it is not permitted, except when the father removes them from his possession and passes them on to another. It is also related from him that it is permitted if he places them in a container or a utensil and places a seal over it and witnesses witness the fact. There is no disagreement among Mālik's disciples that the *waṣī* stands in the father's position in this. They disagreed about the mother, Ibn al-Qāsim said that she cannot be a substitute for the father, and he related this from Mālik; others from among his disciples said that she does. This was also the opinion of Abū Ḥanīfa. Al-Shāfiʿī said that the grandfather is a substitute for the father. The grandmother, mother's mother, according to Ibn Wahb stands in the position of the mother and the mother, according to him, stands in the position of the father.

49.2. Chapter 2: The Discussion of the Kinds of Gifts

A gift may be a gift of the corpus or the gift of the usufruct. Among the gifts of the corpus are those whose aim is the gaining of reward (*thawāb*) and among them are those whose aim is not reward. Those intended for reward may be for seeking favour with Allāh, or for seeking the favour of the creatures. There is no disagreement about the permissibility of gifts devoid of reward, the disagreement is about their *aḥkām*.

They disagreed about the gifts seeking reward. Mālik and Abū Ḥanīfa permitted them, while al-Shāfiʿī disallowed them, which was also the opinion of Dāwūd and Abū Thawr. The basis for the disagreement was whether they amount to a sale for an undetermined price. Those who considered them as sale for an undetermined price said that they are like the sales of *gharar* that are not permitted. Those who did not consider them as undetermined sales said they are permitted. It was as if Mālik considered custom as (a sufficient) condition in them, which is the gaining of a similar reward. It was for this reason that their opinions differed when the donor did not agree to the *thawāb*. What then was the *ḥukm*? They said that it is binding on him if the donee paid him its value, while it is said that it is not binding on him unless it satisfied him. This is ʿUmar's opinion as will be seen in what follows. If consent is stipulated as a condition in it, then there is no sale. The first view is well known from Mālik. If, however, he is made to accept its value, sale does take place. Mālik construes a gift to be for *thawāb* when there is disagreement about it, especially when a poor man makes a gift to a rich person, or any one in whose case it can be seen that he intends the attainment of *thawāb*.

Included in the gifts of the usufruct are those that are deferred and they are called *ʿāriya* or a grant or what resembles them. Among them are those in which the stipulation is the duration of the lifetime of the donee and these are called *al-umrā*, like a person gifting to another residence in a house for his lifetime. The jurists disagreed about this into three opinions. First, that this is a definitive gift, that is, it is the gift of the corpus. This was the opinion of al-Shāfiʿī, Abū Ḥanīfa, al-Thawrī, Aḥmad and a group. The second opinion is that the only thing in it that is for life is the utility; if he dies the corpus reverts to the donor or to his heirs. This was Mālik's opinion and that of his disciples. In case he stipulates succession, according to Mālik, it reverts to the donor or his heirs when the succession terminates. The third opinion is when he says that this is for you and your successors, the corpus passes to the ownership of the donee, but if he does not mention successors the corpus reverts on the death of the donee to the donor or his heirs. This is the opinion of Dāwūd and Abū Thawr.

The cause of disagreement in this issue is the conflict of the traditions and the conflict between conditions and practice, on the one hand, and the traditions, on the other. The traditions are two. First is that which is agreed upon for its authenticity. It is what is related by Mālik from Jābir that the Messenger of Allāh (God's peace and blessings be upon him) said, "If any of you institutes a *waqf* for the life of a person and his successors, it belongs to the person for whom it is made, not reverting to the person who made it, ever". This is because he made a grant in which inheritance is now involved. The second tradition is that of Abū Zubayr from Jābir, who said, "The Messenger of Allāh (God's peace and blessings be upon him) said, 'O community of the Anṣār, hold on to your wealth and do not grant it for life. One who grants it for his life, it is for him in his life and on his death'". It is related from Jābir in a different version, "Do not grant it for life and do not turn it to a *ruqbā* (*waqf* with the condition that it will revert to the donor). One who grants it for life or turns it into a *ruqbā*, it belongs to his heirs".

The tradition of Abū Zubayr is opposed to the condition of the donor. The tradition of Mālik from him is also opposed to the condition of the donor, but it appears that in it the opposition is less, as the mentioning of successors gives the impression of perpetuity of the grant. Those who preferred the traditions over the condition argued on the basis of the tradition of Abū Zubayr from Jābir and also the tradition of Mālik from Jābir. Those who gave preference to the condition held on to Mālik's opinion. Those who held that the *ʿumrā* reverts to the donor if successors are not mentioned and to the donee if successors are mentioned went by the apparent meaning of the tradition. The tradition of Abū Zubayr from Jābir is disputed, I mean, the narration of Abū Zubayr from Jābir.

If he (the donor) uses the word residence, saying, "I make you a resident of this house for your life" the majority maintain that the word residence or service is different from the word *al-ᶜumrā* even when accompanied by the expression successors. Mālik considered the words *al-taᶜmīr* and *al-iskān* as similar. Al-Ḥasan, ᶜAṭāʾ and Qatāda used to hold *suknā* and *taᶜmīr* as synonymous as they do not indicate the house itself in perpetuity, according to the opinion of the majority in *al-ᶜumrā*. The truth is that *iskān* and *taᶜmīr* have the same meaning and it is necessary that the *ḥukm* with the expression "successors" be the opposite of that where the term "successors" is not mentioned, as has been upheld by the Ahl al-Ẓāhir.

49.3. **Chapter 3: The Discussion of the *Aḥkām***

Among the well-known issues in this topic is the permissibility of *iᶜtiṣār*, which is the retraction of a gift. Mālik and the majority of the jurists of Medina held that the father has a right to retract what he has gifted to his son as long as the son has not married or procured loans, that is, as long as no outside right is claimed from him. The mother too has the right to retract what she has gifted, if the father is alive. It is also related from Mālik that she does not have a right to retract. Aḥmad and the Ahl al-Ẓāhir said that no one has the right to retract what he has gifted. Abū Ḥanīfah said that it is permitted to every person to retract what he has gifted, except what he has gifted to those in the prohibited degrees. They agreed that the gift that is called *ṣadaqa* (charity), seeking nearness to Allāh, no one has a right to retract.

The reason for disagreement is the conflict of traditions. Those who did not view retraction as a principle argued through the generality of the established tradition, that is, the words of the Prophet (God's peace and blessings be upon him), "The person retracting his gift is like a dog lapping up what it has vomited". Those who exempted the parents argued on the basis of the tradition of Ṭāwūs that the Prophet (God's peace and blessings be upon him) said, "It is not permitted to the donor to retract his gift, except for the father". The mother was included through analogy of the father. Al-Shāfiᶜī said that if the tradition of Ṭāwūs had a complete chain I would have followed it, while others said that the chain is complete through the channel of Ḥusayn al-Muᶜallim, who is reliable. Those who permitted retraction, except in the case of the prohibited degrees, relied upon what has been related by Mālik from ᶜUmar ibn al-Khaṭṭāb, may Allāh be pleased with him, who said, "He who makes a gift to those in the prohibited degrees or makes a *ṣadaqa* cannot retract it, while he who has made a gift with a view to seeking a reward (*thawāb*), he has the right to retract his gift if he is not satisfied". They also said, the principle is that he who makes a gift without compensation is not to be adjudged as if he had made a (contractual) promise, except what has been agreed upon in a gift by way of *ṣadaqa*.

The majority of the jurists maintain that one who grants a *ṣadaqa* to his son and the son dies after taking possession, inherits it. One among the *mursal* traditions of Mālik is: "A man from the Anṣār of al-Khazraj granted a *ṣadaqa* to his parents, who subsequently died. Their son inherited the property consisting of a palm-grove. He asked the Prophet (God's peace and blessings be upon him) about it, who said, 'You have been rewarded for your *ṣadaqa*, now take it as your inheritance' ". Abū Dāwūd has recorded from ʿAbd Allāh ibn Burayda from his father about a woman who came to the Messenger of Allāh (God's peace and blessings be upon him) and said, "I gave to my mother as *ṣadaqa* a female infant. She died and left this infant girl. The Prophet (God's peace and blessings be upon him) said, 'Your reward has been assured and she has now returned to you through inheritance' ".

The Ẓāhirites said that it is not permitted to any one to retract due to the generality of the words of the Prophet (God's peace and blessings be upon him) to ʿUmar about horses that he had given as *ṣadaqa*, "Do not buy them, the person who retracts his gift is like a dog lapping up what it vomited". The tradition's authenticity is agreed upon. Al-Qāḍī said that retraction of a gift is not an approved ethical norm. The Lawgiver (God's peace and blessings be upon him) was sent to perfect the ethical norms. This discussion is sufficient for this book.

L
THE BOOK OF *WAṢĀYĀ* (BEQUESTS)

The discussion of bequests is first divided into two kinds: first, the discussion of the elements; second, the *aḥkām*. We shall talk about those well-known issues that became prominent.

50.1. Chapter 1: The Discussion of the Elements

The elements are four: *mūṣī* (testator), *mūṣa lahu* (legatee), *mūṣa bih* (bequeathed property), and *waṣiyya* (testament or will).

They agreed that the testator could be any owner with a legally valid ownership. According to Mālik the bequest of a *safīh* (prodigal) or of a minor approaching majority is valid. Abū Ḥanīfa said that the bequest of a minor (*ṣabī*), who has not attained puberty, is not allowed. Both opinions are related from al-Shāfiʿī. The testament of non-believer is also valid according to them, as long as it is not for a forbidden thing.

In the case of the legatee, they agreed that a bequest is not valid for an heir, due to the words of the Prophet (God's peace and blessings be upon him), "No bequest for an heir". They differed whether it is valid for other than the close relations (*qarāba*). The majority of the jurists said that it is valid for other than the close relatives, but is considered reprehensible. Al-Ḥasan and Ṭāwūs said that it is to be returned to close relatives, which was also the opinion of Isḥāq. The proof of these jurists is in the words of the Exalted, "It is prescribed for you, when one of you approacheth death, if he leave wealth, that he bequeath unto parents and near relatives in kindness. (This is) a duty for all those who ward off (evil)".[183] They are of the opinion that the article "*al*" (prefixing the word "will") implies comprehensiveness restricted to those mentioned and exclusion of others. The majority argued on the basis of the well-known tradition of ʿImrān ibn Ḥuṣayn that "a man manumitted six slaves that he had during his illness, and he had no wealth besides them. The Messenger of Allāh drew lots between them and freed two keeping the other four enslaved". Those slaves were not relatives (of the deceased).

[183] Qurʾān 2:18

They agreed that a bequest is not permitted for an heir, if the other heirs do not give their consent. They disagreed as we have said when the heirs agreed. The majority said it is permitted, while the Ahl al-Ẓāhir and al-Muzanī said it is not permitted. The reason for the disagreement is whether the prohibition relates to the underlying cause of (the right of) heirs or of non-rational (revealed) guidance. Those who maintained that it is revealed guidance said that it is not permitted even if the heirs permit it. Those who prohibited it due to the right of the heirs said that it is permitted when the heirs grant permission. The wavering on this issue refers to the vacillation about the meaning of the words of the Prophet (God's peace and blessings be upon him), "No bequest for an heir", whether they have an underlying meaning (cause) or are to be accepted as revealed teaching without the need for rationalization?

They disagreed about a bequest for a deceased person. A group, and they are the majority, said that it is annulled by the death of the legatee. Another group said it is not annulled. They also disagreed about the bequest for a killer, both for murder and manslaughter. Within this topic is also a well-known sub-issue, that is, if the heirs permit (prior to his death) a bequest for a deceased person, do they have the right to retract it after his death? It is said that they have the right, while it is said that they do not. Others make a distinction whether the heirs are from the family of the deceased. If they are from his family they have the right of retraction. All three opinions exist in the school (of Mālik).

50.2. Chapter 2: The Bequeathed Property

In the discussion of genus, they agreed about the permissibility of the bequest of the corpus, but disagreed about usufruct. The majority of the jurists of different regions said it is permitted. Ibn Abī Laylā, Ibn Shubrama, and the Ahl al-Ẓāhir said that a bequest of the usufruct is void. The argument of the majority was that usufruct carries the meaning of wealth. The argument of the other group was that the usufruct stands transferred to the heir and the deceased now has no ownership, thus, a bequest of what lies in the ownership of another is not permitted to him (the testator). This was also the opinion of Abū ᶜUmar ibn ᶜAbd al-Barr.

Regarding the amount (extent), the jurists agreed that a bequest is not valid for more than a third of the estate in the case of the person who has heirs. They disagreed about the person who has not left heirs, and also about the extent whether it is a third or less than it. All of them adopted the opinion that a bequest is not permitted for more than a third for one who has heirs according to what is established from the Prophet (God's peace and blessings be upon him), "that he visited Saʿd ibn Abī Waqqāṣ and he said to him, 'O Messenger of Allāh, my ailment has overcome me as you can see and I have wealth, but no one inherits me except a daughter that I have. Do I, then, bequeath two-thirds of my wealth?' The Messenger of Allāh (God's peace and blessings be upon him) said, 'No!' Saʾd said to him, 'Half?' He said, 'No!!' The Messenger of Allāh (God's peace and blessings be upon him), then said, 'A third, a third is (more than) enough. If you leave your heirs rich, it is better than leaving them indigent, dependent on people' ". The jurists, due to this tradition, adopted the opinion that a bequest should not exceed a third.

They disagreed about the recommended rate. A group maintained that it is whatever is less than a third due to the words of the Prophet (God's peace and blessings be upon him) in the tradition, "A third is a lot (*kathīr*)". A large number of the earlier jurists held this opinion. Qatāda said that Abū Bakr made a bequest of a fifth, and ʿUmar of a fourth, but a fifth is preferable for me. Those who said that the recommended rate is a third relied upon what is related from the Prophet (God's peace and blessings be upon him) that he said, "Allāh has rendered for you in bequest a third of your wealth as an addition (supplement) to your (good) deeds". This tradition is weak according to the traditionists. It is established from Ibn ʿAbbās that he said, "If the people came down in bequest from a third to a fourth, it would be dearer to me, as the Messenger of Allāh (God's peace and blessings be upon him) said, 'A third, a third is more than enough".

With respect to their disagreement about the permissibility of *waṣiyya* for more than a third, for one who has no heirs, Mālik does not permit it, nor does al-Awzāʿī, while the opinion of Aḥmad differed in it. Abū Ḥanīfa and Isḥāq permitted it, and it is also the opinion of Ibn Masʿūd. The reason for the disagreement is whether this *ḥukm* is specific to the underlying cause stated by the lawgiver or is not specific, that is, not to leave heirs dependent on people, as the Prophet (God's peace and blessings be upon him) said, "If you leave your heirs rich, it is better for you than leaving them indigent, dependent on people". Those who consider this cause specific must remove the *ḥukm* with the removal of the cause, while those who considered it as an *ʿibāda* (non-rational ruling), even if associated with a cause, or considered all the Muslims included as heirs in this meaning, said that a bequest exceeding a third is not permitted at all.

50.2.1. The Implication of the Term *Waṣiyya*

Waṣiyya, generally, is the gift by a man to another or to several, after his death, or is manumission of a slave, whether he has expressly stated the term *waṣīyya* or not. This contract, according to them, is *jāʾiz* (revocable) by agreement (of the jurists), I mean, the testator has the right to retract what he has bequeathed, except in the case of the *mudabbar* (slave declared to be free at his master's death), about whom they differed as will be stated in the book of *tadbīr*. They agreed that it does not become due to the legatee, except after the death of the testator. They disagreed about the acceptance of the legatee, whether it is a condition for its validity. Mālik said that acceptance by the legatee of the bequest is a condition for its validity. It is related from al-Shāfiʿī that it is not a condition for its validity. Mālik compared it to *hiba* (gift).

50.3. Chapter 3: The Discussion of the *Aḥkām*

The *aḥkām* relate either to the use of terms, or numerical calculations, or the law.

Among the well-known legal issues is their disagreement about the *ḥukm* of the testator who bequeaths a third of his wealth to a man and specifies what he bequeaths out of his wealth as a third. The heirs then say that what has been specified for him by the testator is more than a third. Mālik said that in such a case the heirs have an option to give the man what the testator specified or to give him a third from the entire wealth of the deceased. He was opposed in this by Abū Ḥanīfa, al-Shāfiʿī, Abū Thawr, Aḥmad and Dāwūd. Their argument is that the bequest, by agreement, has become due to the legatee by the death of the testator and by its acceptance by the legatee. How then can a thing that has become his due be transferred from his ownership without his voluntary consent or without the alteration of the bequest? Mālik's argument lies in the likelihood of the veracity of the heirs in what they claim. Abū ʿUmar ibn ʿAbd al-Barr has an outstanding opinion in this issue. He said that if the heirs claim this the burden is on them to prove it. If it is proved the legatee takes his one-third from the specified thing and shares it with the heirs, but if it is a third or less, the heirs are to be compelled to deliver it.

If they do not disagree that the bequeathed property is less than a third, then according to Mālik, the heirs have a choice in giving him what has been bequeathed to him or in giving him a third of the entire wealth of the deceased comprising either the same property or (a third of) the entire property, in accordance with the differing narrations from Mālik. Abū Ḥanīfa and al-Shāfiʿī said he gets a third of this (specified) thing and he becomes a joint owner (for the residue) with the heirs in the entire estate left by the deceased till his entire third is acquired.

The reason for the disagreement is that as the deceased has transgressed in making his bequest in a specified thing; is it then fair to the heirs that they be given a choice in executing the *waṣiyya* or in being lenient to him in view of the purpose that was permitted to the deceased of depriving them of his wealth, or to annul the transgression and convert the right to joint ownership. The latter is better when we say the transgression was in the specification as it was more than a third, I mean, the obligation is that the specification be invalidated. To obligate the heirs to let the specification take effect or to take out a third from the entire wealth is to place a burden upon them.

Within this topic is their disagreement about the person who was under an obligation to pay *zakāt*, but he did not make a bequest for it. If he made a bequest, is that also to be from the third or is it to be taken from the capital? Mālik said that if he did not make a bequest for it, it is not binding on the heirs to pay it. According to al-Shafiʿi, the heir must pay it from the capital. If he should bequeath it, Mālik then obliges them to pay it from the third. According to al-Shāfiʿī, it is to be taken in both cases from the capital, comparing it to a debt, on the basis of the words of the Prophet (God's peace and blessings be upon him), "The debt of Allāh has a prior right of satisfaction". The same is the case with obligatory *kaffāra* (expiation) and obligatory *ḥajj*, according to him. Mālik considers them from the genus of bequests required to be paid after death. There is no disagreement that if he had paid it during his lifetime (even on his death-bed), it would be from his capital, even if it was continuous. It is as if Mālik, places the burden on the heirs, I mean, even in the context of his death. He appears to suspect the deceased of ill-intention toward the heirs when he makes a bequest for such obligations. He said that if this is permitted it would be possible for a person to delay all his *zakāt* throughout his life and when he approaches death to make a bequest for them. When the other bequests clash with *zakāt*, it is to be given priority over those that are of lesser importance. Abū Ḥanīfa said that *zakāt* and all the other bequests are of the same order, intending thereby proportional division. Mālik and all his disciples agreed that the bequests which (collectively) amount to more than the third, if they are of equal status, are to be allotted the third proportionately, but if some of these are more important than the others the more important are to be given priority.

They disagreed about the order of priority, as is recorded in their books. Among the well-known arithmetical issues in this topic is when a man makes a bequest for one person for half his wealth and for another for two-thirds of his wealth, with the residue reverting to the heirs. According to Mālik and al-Shāfiʿī they divide the third among themselves by way of reduction (as in *ʿawl*), so that the first gets two-fifths and the other three-fifths of the third of the estate. Abū Ḥanīfa said that they are to share the third equally. The reason for the disagreement is whether the excess over the third, which is annulled, is not to be taken into account in the division, just as it is annulled itself by the rejection of the heirs. Those who said that it is annulled, but the consideration (of its ratios) is not annulled maintained that it should be shared by way of reduction, while those who maintained that its consideration is annulled, just as if it was specified, said that they divide it among themselves equally.

Among their disputes over terminology in this topic is the case when he (the testator) bequeaths a part of his wealth, and he has property that is known and also that which is unknown. According to Mālik, the bequest takes effect in that which is known to the exclusion of that which is unknown, but according to al-Shāfiʿī, it applies to both kinds. The reason for the disagreement is whether the term *māl*, which he used, applies to both known and unknown wealth, or only to the wealth known to him? In case there is a *mudabbar* and the wealth known to the deceased is insufficient to free him, the balance should be taken from the unknown wealth.

In this topic there are many cases and all of them refer to these three genera. There is no disagreement among them that a man may leave a testament for his children (to be followed) after his death as this is a minor *khilāfa*, like the greater general *khilāfa* of the *imām* for which he may leave a testament.

LI
THE BOOK OF *FARĀ'IḌ* (INHERITANCE)

The discussion in this book is about those who inherit and those who do not, and whether those who inherit do so always, or together with some heirs to the exclusion of others, and when they inherit along with others, how much they inherit. Similarly, when they inherit alone, how much they inherit. When they inherit with other heirs, does this (inheritance) vary from heir to heir?

Instruction in all this can be by different methods, most of which have been followed by the experts in inheritance. The present course in it begins by mentioning separately the *ḥukm* of each category of the heirs, when such a category exists alone (as an heir), and enumerating its *ḥukm* with each of the remaining categories. An example of this is a child, when he is the sole heir; how much is his inheritance? His position is then examined with (the existence of) each of the remaining heirs.

51.1. Chapter 1: The Different Categories of Heirs and Their Inheritance

The categories of heirs are three: *dhawū nasab* (blood relatives), *aṣhār* (relations by marriage), and *mawālī* (by contract). In blood relations, some are agreed upon and some are disputed. Those agreed upon are the *furūʿ*, that is, descendants; and *uṣūl*, ascendants, parents and grandparents, whether male or female. Then there are the *furūʿ* of the level of the deceased among the lower ascendants, that is brethren, male or female, and the distant ascendants in the same lineage, uncles and son's of uncles, specifically only the males among them.

If these heirs are enumerated, they come to ten among men and seven in women. The men are: the son, son's son howsoever low, father, paternal grandfather howsoever high, brother from whichever side, I mean, father's and mother's or of either one of them, brother's son howsoever low, uncle and uncle's son howsoever low, the husband, and the *mawlā*. As to the women, they are: daughter, son's daughter howsoever low, mother, grandmother howsoever high, sister, wife, and the *mawlā*.

Those disputed are the *dhawū l-arḥām* (distant kindred), for whom no share has been mentioned in the Book of Allāh and they are not the residuaries.

These, generally, are the sons of daughters, daughters of brothers, sons of sisters, daughters of uncles, and the father's mother's son, sons of mother's brother, father's sisters, mother's sisters, and maternal uncles. Mālik, al-Shāfiʿī, most of the jurists of different regions, and Zayd ibn al-Thābit from among the Companions maintained that they have no part in the inheritance. All the other Companions, the jurists of Iraq, Kūfa, and Baṣra, and a group of the jurists from the rest of the regions upheld their inheritance. Those who maintained their inheritance, differed about its nature. Abū Ḥanīfa and his disciples maintained their inheritance in the order of the residuaries, while all the others who grant them inheritance do so through the doctrine of substitution *tanzīl*, that is, to put them in the position of the person through whom they are related to the deceased.

The reliance of Mālik, and of those who adopted his opinion, is on the fact that as analogy has no operation in inheritance, the principle is that nothing should be established in it unless it is found in the Book or the established *sunna*, and these sources are absent in this issue. The other group believed that their evidence is in the Book, the *sunna*, and analogy. In the Book it is the words of the Exalted, "And those who are akin (*ūlū l-arḥām*) are nearer one to another in the ordinance of Allāh",[184] and "Unto the men (of a family) belongeth a share of that which parents and near kindred leave, and unto the women a share of that which parents and near kindred leave, whether it be little or much—a legal share".[185] The term *al-qarāba*, they say, applies to *dhawū l-arḥām*. The opponents are of the view that these verses are limited by the verses of inheritance. With respect to the *sunna* they argued on the basis of that which is recorded by al-Tirmidhī from ʿUmar ibn al-Khaṭṭāb, that he wrote to Abū ʿUbayda that the Messenger of Allāh (God's peace and blessings be upon him) said, "Allāh and His Prophet are the *mawlā* of one who does not have a *mawlā*, while the maternal uncle (*khāl*) is the heir of one who does not have an heir". As a rational argument, the earlier disciples of Abū Ḥanīfa said that the *dhawū l-arḥām* have a higher priority over the other Muslims, as there are gathered in them two bases, *qarāba* and Islam. They compared it to the preference of the full brother over the consanguine brother, I mean, the person who is supported on two grounds is better than the person who has one. Abū Zayd and his later followers compared inheritance with *wilāya* (guardianship) saying that as the guardianship for funeral, prayer, and burial of the deceased belongs to the *dhawū l-arḥām* in the absence of the sharers and residuaries, it is necessary that the *wilāya* for inheritance be theirs. The first group has objections to these analogies, but

[184] Qurʾān 33:6
[185] Qurʾān 4:7

they are weak. If this has been established, we shall begin by mentioning each category out of the categories of the heirs, and state those which resemble principles among the well-known issues, those agreed upon and those that are disputed.

51.1.1. Inheritance of Children

Muslims agreed that the inheritance of the child from his father or mother, if there are both males and females, is that the share of the male is equal to the share of two females. When a son inherits alone, he gets the entire wealth. In the case of daughters being sole inheritors, one alone gets half, but if there are three or more they get two-thirds. They disagreed about two daughters. The majority maintained that they get two-thirds, and it is related from Ibn ʿAbbās that two daughters get half. The reason for the disagreement is the vacillation of the meaning of the words of the Exalted, "[A]nd if there be women more than two, then theirs is two-thirds of the inheritance",[186] whether the *ḥukm* of two females not expressed is to be linked with the *ḥukm* of three or with that of one. The apparent meaning through the indication of the text is that they be linked with of one female. It is said that the better-known opinion of Ibn ʿAbbās is the same as that of the majority. It is related from Ibn ʿAbd Allāh ibn Muḥammad ibn ʿUqayl from Ḥātim ibn ʿAbd Allāh and from Jābir "that the Prophet (God's peace and blessings be upon him) gave two daughters two-thirds". Ibn ʿAbd al-Barr said, as far as I know, that a group of jurists accepted the tradition of ʿAbd Allāh ibn ʿUqayl, while others opposed him. The reason for agreement on this issue are the words of the Exalted, "[A]nd if there be women more than two, then theirs is two-thirds of the inheritance", up to the words "and if there be one (only) then the half".[187]

They agreed that the sons of sons stand in the position of the sons in their absence, inheriting as they inherit and excluding others like they exclude, except what has been related from Ibn Mujāhid. He said that the sons of sons do not exclude the husband from half, restricting him to a fourth as the son himself does, nor do they restrict the wife so as to move her from a fourth to an eighth, or the mother from a third to a sixth. They agreed that there is no inheritance for the daughters of sons with daughters, if the daughters of the deceased exhaust the two-thirds. They disagreed when there is with the daughters of the son a son of the son of their order or lower than them. The majority of the jurists of different regions said that he becomes a residuary with the daughters of the son for what is left over from the daughter, and they share it in the ratio of two shares of females for one of the male. This was

[186] Qurʾān 4:11
[187] Qurʾān 4:11

also the opinion of ᶜAlī, may Allāh be pleased with him, and Zayd ibn Thābit from among the Companions. Abū Thawr and Dāwūd maintained that if the daughters exhaust the two-thirds, the remaining is for the son of the son to the exclusion of the daughters, whether they are in the same order as he is, or are above him or below him. Ibn Masᶜūd used to say in this, "for the male a share like that of two females", except when the fraction for the women is more than a sixth, otherwise they are to be given a sixth.

The reliance of the majority is on the generality of the words of the Exalted, "Allāh chargeth you concerning (the provision for) your children: to the male the equivalent of the portion of two females", and the fact that the child of a child is included in the meaning of the term "child". In addition, since the son of the son becomes a residuary in his order for the entire wealth, it follows that he become a residuary for the residue. The reliance of Dāwūd and Abū Thawr is on the tradition of Ibn ᶜAbbās that the Prophet (God's peace and blessings be upon him) said, "Divide the inheritance among sharers according to the Book of Allāh, the Mighty and Exalted, and what is left as a residue from the shares, should go to the nearest male". As a rational argument too, it is because the son's daughter does not inherit, when alone, what remains after the two-thirds. It is appropriate that she should not inherit with another.

The reason for their disagreement is the conflict of analogy and the view on preference (*tarjīh*). Ibn Masᶜūd's opinion is based on his principle that as the daughters of the son do not inherit in the absence of a son more than a sixth, they are not entitled to inherit with another more than what is their due when alone. This is an argument that is close to Dāwūd's argument. The majority maintain that the son's son shares with them as a residuary whether he is of their order or is lower than them. Some of the later jurists, however, expressed an isolated view saying that he does not make them a residuary unless he is of the same order.

The majority of the jurists maintain that if the deceased has left behind a daughter and a son's daughter or sons's daughters, who do not have a brother, the son's daughters get a sixth in order to complete the two-thirds. The Shiᶜites opposed this saying that the son's daughter does not inherit anything with a daughter, as is the case of a son's son with a son. The disagreement about the son's daughters is in two cases: with son's sons, and with daughters in what is less than two-thirds and more than half. The conclusion about them is that when they accompany son's sons, it is said that they inherit, while it is said that they do not inherit. Those who maintain that they inherit hold that they inherit absolutely as residuaries, but some of them said that they inherit as residuaries, except when it is more than a sixth. When it is said that they inherit, it is also said that they do so if the son's son is of their order, and it is said of whatever order. The summary about their inheritance in the absence of a son's son in what is excess of the half to complete the two-thirds, it is said they inherit and it is said they do not.

51.1.2. Inheritance of Spouses

The jurists agreed that the inheritance of a man from his wife, if she does not leave behind a son or a daughter, or a son's son or son's daughter, whether male or female, is a half, except for the *mujtahid*'s dispute mentioned above. If she leaves behind a child (or a son's child), he gets a fourth. The inheritance of a woman from her husband, if the husband does not leave behind a child or a child of the son, is a fourth, but if he leaves behind a child or a son's child, then, it is an eighth. No one can exclude them from inheritance, or reduce their share except a child (or a son's child). This is based on the explicit prescription in the words of the Exalted, "And unto you belongeth a half of that which your wives leave, if they have no child; but if they have a child then unto you the fourth of that which they leave, after any legacy they may have bequeathed, or debt (they may have contracted, hath been paid). And unto them belongeth the fourth of that which ye leave, after any legacy ye may have bequeathed, or debt (ye may have contracted, hath been paid)".[188]

51.1.3. Inheritance of Father and Mother

The jurists agreed that if the father survives alone, he gets the entire wealth, and if the parents survive alone, the mother gets a third and the rest is for the father due to the words of the Exalted, "[If the deceased has no child] And his parents are his heirs, then to his mother appertaineth the third".[189] They agreed that the shares of the parents in the inheritance from their son (or their daughter), when their son has a child or a son's child, are two-sixths, that is, for each one of them a sixth due to the words of the Exalted, "And to his parents a sixth of the inheritance, if he have a child (*walad*)".[190] The majority are of the opinion that the term *walad* in this case refers to a male and not a female. They were opposed in this by some who had isolated opinions. They agreed that the share of the father cannot be reduced from a sixth, with other sharers, and that to him belongs whatever is in excess.

They agreed in this topic that the mother is excluded by the brothers from a third to a sixth due to the words of the Exalted, "And if they have brethren, then to his mother appertaineth the sixth".[191] They disagreed about the minimum number of brothers who reduce the share of the mother from a third to a sixth. ʿAlī, may Allāh be pleased with him, and Ibn Masʿūd maintained that the brothers who exclude (in this way) are two or more, which was also

[189] Qur'ān 4:12

[190] Qur'ān 4:11 The word 'son' for *walad* in pickthall's translation has been changed to 'child'.

[191] Qur'ān 4:11

Mālik's opinion. Ibn ᶜAbbās held that they were three or more, and that two do not reduce her from a third to a sixth. The disagreement is caused by a dispute over the minimum number which a plural noun indicates. Those who said that the minimum a plural noun indicates is three, said that the brothers who exclude her are three or more, while those who maintained that the minimum included in the plural noun is two, said that the brothers who exclude her are two, I mean, in the words of the Exalted, "And if he has brethren".[192] There is no dispute that males and females are included in the term "brethren" in the verse, and this is according to the majority. Some of the later jurists thought that the mother is not reduced from a third to a sixth by sisters alone, for they assumed that the term "brethren" does not include sisters, unless there be with them a brother due to the immediate masculine denotation of the term; as the term "brethren" is a plural of brother, which is masculine.

Within this topic they differed about who inherits the sixth that is reduced from the share of the mother through brethren when the deceased is survived by parents and brethren. The majority said that this sixth is for the father along with four-sixths (as the father's presence excludes brothers). It is related from Ibn ᶜAbbās that this sixth is for the brothers who excluded (the mother from it), and for the father are his two-thirds; as (Ibn ᶜAbbās says) no principal heir who excludes (reduces) and does not get what he has caused except along with the parents. Some declared weak the chain of this narration from Ibn ᶜAbbās, although the opinion of Ibn ᶜAbbās agrees with analogy.

They disagreed, in this topic, over the two cases called *al-gharrāwayn*. This occurs when a deceased leaves behind a wife and his parents, or a husband and her parents. The majority said, in the first case, for the wife is a fourth and for the mother is a third of the residue, which is a fourth of the whole capital, and for the father is the residue, which is half of the total. In the second case, they said that for the husband is a half and for the mother a sixth of what is left, which is a sixth of the entire capital, and for the father is the remainder, which is two-sixths. This is the opinion of Zayd, and the better-known opinion of ᶜAlī (God be pleased with him). Ibn ᶜAbbās said, in the first case, that for the wife is a fourth of the whole capital, for the mother a third, which is also from the whole as she is a sharer (in Qurʾanic terms), and for the father is the residue as he is a residuary. He also said in the second that the husband takes half, and for the mother is a third, being a stated sharer, and for the father is the residue. This was the opinion of Shurayḥ, the *qāḍī*, of Dāwūd, Ibn Sīrīn and a group of jurists.

[192] Qurʾān 4:11

The argument of the majority is that the father and mother when they survive alone for inheriting the wealth, the mother has a third and the father takes the residue (father gets twice the mother's share); therefore, the situation must be the same when they get the remainder of the wealth. It was as if they were of the view that if the inheritance of the mother was more than that of the father, it would be contrary to the rules of inheritance. The reliance of the other group is on the fact that the mother is an expressly mentioned sharer, while the father is a residuary, and the residuary does not have a fixed share along with the sharers, but what he gets can vary, more or less. The basis of the majority is thus based on rationalization; whereas the argument of the other group is closer to the text. I mean by rationalization here that between the mother and the father, the person to be given priority is one who was the greater cause (for the deceased's existence).

51.1.4. Inheritance of Uterine Brethren

The jurists agreed that (in the case of) uterine brethren, when one of them is inheriting alone he (or she) gets a sixth, whether male or female. If they are more than one, they share a third equally, the male among them getting the same share as the female. They agreed that they do not inherit with any of the four persons, namely, the father, father's father howsoever high, children, both male and female, and children of sons howsoever low, both male and female. All this is due to the words of the Exalted, "And if a man or a woman have a distant heir (having left neither parent nor child), and he (or she) have a brother or a sister (only on the mother's side) then to each one of them twain (the brother and the sister) the sixth, and if they be more than two, then they shall be sharers in the third".[193] This is so as there is consensus (*ijmāʿ*) that what is meant in this verse are uterine brethren only, and it has been read as "have a brother or a sister on the mother's side". Similarly, they agreed here, as far as I think, that *kalāla* means the absence of the four categories of relations that we have mentioned, that is, parents, grandparents, children, and children's children.

51.1.5. Inheritance of German and Consanguine Brethren

They agreed that german or consanguine brethren alone inherit in *kalāla* also. If the sister inherits alone, she gets a half, but if there are two they get two-thirds, as in the case of daughters. If the brethren are males and females, then the share of the male is equivalent to two shares of the female, as in the case of sons with daughters. This is because of the words of the Exalted, "They ask thee for a pronouncement. Say: Allāh hath pronounced for you concerning

[193] Qurʾān 4:12

kalāla. If a man die childless and have a sister, hers is half the heritage, and he would have inherited from her had she died childless. And if there be two sisters, then theirs are two-thirds of the heritage, and if they be brethren, men and women, unto the male is the equivalent of the share of two females".[194] They differed, however, about the meaning of *kalāla* here in part and disagreed about some, and its discussion will come up God willing.

Within this topic they agreed that the german brethren, male or female, do not inherit anything with the male child, nor with a child's child, nor anything with the father. They disagreed about what was besides this. Among them is their disagreement about the inheritance of german brethren with a daughter or daughters. The majority said that they are residuaries and are to be given what is left over from the sisters, while Dāwūd ibn ʿAlī al-Ẓāhirī and another group maintained that the sister does not inherit anything with the daughter. The reliance of the majority in this is on the tradition of Ibn Masʿūd from the Prophet (God's peace and blessings be upon him), in which he said about the daughter, son's daughter, and sister, "that for the daughter is half, for the son's daughter a sixth completing the two-thirds, and whatever is left is for the sister". Through a rational argument too, just as they agreed on the inheritance of brethren with daughters, so too on the sisters. The reliance of the second group is upon the apparent meaning of the words of the Exalted, "And if a man die childless and he has a sister, hers is half the heritage, and he would have inherited from her had she died childless".[195] (They said that) He did not allot anything for the sister, except in the absence of a child. The majority, here, interpreted the term *walad* as a male to the exclusion of females.

The jurists agree, in this topic, that the german brethren exclude the consanguine brethren from inheritance on the analogy of son's children with sons. Abū ʿUmar said that this is related as *ḥasan* through reliable individual narrators from ʿAlī (God be pleased with him), who said, "The Messenger of Allāh (God's peace and blessings be upon him) decided that the uterine brothers inherit without the german brothers". The jurists agreed that when german sisters exhaust their two-thirds, there is nothing for the consanguine sisters with them, as is the case of son's daughters with actual daughters. If there is only one german sister then for the consanguine sisters is the rest of the two-thirds, that is, a sixth. They disagreed when there was with the consanguine sisters a brother. The majority said that they become residuaries and share the wealth giving the male the equivalent of the share of two females, as is the case of the son's daughters with daughters. Mālik stipulated

[184] Qurʾān 4:177
[195] Qurʾān 4:177

that he be in the same order. Ibn Masʿūd said that when the true sisters exhaust the two-thirds, the remainder is for the male consanguine brothers to the exclusion of the sisters, which was also the opinion of Abū Thawr. Dāwūd opposed him in this issue, along with his agreement with him on the issue of sisters and the son's of children. If they have not exhausted the two-thirds, then, the male among the children of the father, according to him, gets two shares of the female, except when the share coming to the women is more than a sixth as is the case of the daughters with the son's children. The proofs of the two parties are identical in this issue.

They agreed that consanguine brethren stand in the position of german brothers in their absence, as is the case with the son's children with true children. If there is a male among them they become residuaries. After allotment to the sharers, they share the residue, with the male getting a share equivalent to the shares of two females as in the case of children, except in one case that is known as *mushtaraka*, in which the jurists disagreed. This occurs when a woman dies leaving her husband, mother, uterine brethren, and german brethren. ʿUmar, ʿUthmān and Zayd ibn Thābit used to give the husband half, the mother a sixth and to the uterine brethren a third, finishing the wealth leaving the german brothers with nothing. The german brethren (complained, and their share was recognized. They), then, used to share with the uterine brothers in the third, dividing it as a share for the male equivalent to the share of two females. Mālik, al-Shāfiʿī and al-Thawrī among the jurists of different regions upheld this participation. ʿAlī (God be pleased with him), Ubayy ibn Kaʿb and Abū Mūsā al-Ashʿarī did not make the german brothers participate with the uterine in this division, and did not give them anything. This opinion was upheld by Abū Ḥanīfa, Ibn Abī Laylā, Aḥmad, Abū Thawr, Dāwūd and a group among the jurists of different regions.

The proof of the first group is that the german brethren participate with the uterine brethren due to a reason, for which they are entitled to inheritance, and she is the mother (through whom they are related to the deceased). It is, therefore, necessary that they do not share it alone without them. If they share in the reason due to which they inherit, they must participate in the inheritance. The argument of the other group is that full brethren are residuaries, and there is nothing for residuaries if the shares of the sharers envelop the inheritance. Another argument for them is that all agree that if the deceased leaves behind a husband, a mother, a single uterine brother and ten or more german brothers, the uterine brother alone is entitled to an entire sixth, and the remaining sixth is to be shared by all the full brothers (each getting no more than a tenth of the third) even though they have the same mother. The reason for disagreement in most of the issues of inheritance is the conflict of analogies and the ambivalence of words in the cases where there is a text.

51.1.6. Inheritance of the Grandfather

The jurists agreed that the father excludes the grandfather, but he stands in the position of the father in his absence with the children, and that he is a residuary with the sharers. They disagreed whether he stands in the position of the father in excluding true brethren, or in the exclusion of consanguine brethren. Ibn ʿAbbās, Abū Bakr (God be pleased with him), and a group of jurists said that he excludes them, and this was the opinion of Abū Ḥanīfa, Abū Thawr, al-Muzanī and Ibn Surayj among the disciples of al-Shāfiʿī, Dāwūd and a group of jurists. ʿAlī ibn Abī Ṭālib (God be pleased with him), Zayd ibn Thābit and Ibn Masʿūd agreed on granting inheritance to them with the grandfather, except that they disagreed about the method, as we shall describe later.

The reliance of those who considered the grandfather of the same status as the father is upon the common meaning, that is, from the point of view that both are fathers with respect to the deceased, and also on the fact that many of the *aḥkām* are, by agreement, equally applicable to both so much so that it is related from Ibn ʿAbbās that he said, "Would that Zayd ibn Thābit had feared Allāh when he considered the son's son as a son, but did not consider the father's father as a father". They agreed that he is like the father in many other *aḥkām* besides those of inheritance, among them is that his testimony for his grandson is like the testimony of the father, and that the grandfather becomes free once he falls in the possession of the grandson just as the father would be if he is possessed by his son, and that satisfaction by way of retaliation (*qiṣāṣ*) is not to be derived from the grandfather just as it is not derived from the father. The reliance of those who make the brother inherit along with the grandfather is that the brother is closer to the deceased than the grandfather, as the grandfather is the father of the father of the deceased, while the brother is the son of the father of the deceased, and the son is closer than the father. In addition, they agreed that the son of a brother is prior to the uncle, he (the brother's son) is related through the father, while the uncle is related through the grandfather.

The reason for disagreement, therefore, is the conflict of analogies in this topic. If it is asked, which of the two analogies is stronger in accordance with the legal viewpoint? We would say it is the analogy of one who held the father and grandfather as equal, as the grandfather is a father in the second or third order, just as the son's son is a son in the second or the third order. Moreover, the son does not exclude the grandfather, while he does exclude the brothers; it follows that the grandfather should exclude him whom the son excludes. Further, the brother is neither an ascendant of the deceased nor a descendant, but is only a participant with the deceased in the ascendants; and the ascendant has a prior right to being a participant with the ascendants. In addition, the grandfather is not (merely) an ascendant through the father, he is a true ascendant, while the brother inherits because he is a descendant of an ascendant of the deceased, thus, he who is an ascendant of his ascendant is prior to one who is a descendant of an ascendant. It is, therefore, reasonable to claim that brothers are related through children whereas the grandfather is related through the father, because the brother is not the son of the deceased, but is the son of his father, while the grandfather is the father of the deceased.

(*Bunūwwa*) (sonship, filiation) is stronger than *ubūwwa* (paternity) in inheritance in the case of only one person and that is the propositus himself. In the case of *bunūwwa* that exists for the father of the propositus, it is not necessary that it be stronger in relation to the propositus than the *ubūwwa* that exists for the father of the propositus, because the *ubūwwa* that exists for the father of the propositus is some kind of *ubūwwa* for the propositus, I mean, distant *ubūwwa* for the propositus, while the *bunūwwa* that exists for the father of the propositus is not any kind of *bunūwwa*, that is, it is neither distant nor near. Thus, those who said that the brother has a better right than the grandfather, as the brother is relegated due to something because of which inheritance of *bunūwwa* exists, and who is the father, and the grandfather too is relegated because of *ubūwwa*, is an opinion that is erroneous and conjectural. The grandfather is some kind of father, while the brother is not some kind of son. On the whole the brother is an affiliate among the affiliates of the deceased, as if he was an accidental fact, while the grandfather is a cause among the causes (of his existence), and the cause has better right to assimilate ownership than an affiliate.

Those who made the grandfather inherit with the brothers, differed about the mode of such inheritance. The gist of Zayd's opinion in this is that there may either be with him, besides brothers, some sharers, or there may not be any. If there are no sharers having stated shares he is given the better of two (choices), either the third of the wealth, or he becomes like one of the male brethren, irrespective of whether the brethren are male or female or both, he divides the wealth with one brother through *muqāsama*; similarly, with two, or three, but with four brothers he takes a third. With sisters from one to four he divides it with them as a share of the male equivalent to the share of two females, but with five sisters he gets the third, as he is preferable in the division. This is the case with brethren to the exclusion of others. If, however, there are sharers with them, the division is begun with the sharers, who take their shares and whatever is left is to be given to him as the best of three situations: either the third of the remainder after the allotment to the sharers, or as a male among the brethren, or he is given a sixth of the wealth not reducing anything from it, whatever is left after that is shared by the brethren as a share of the male equivalent to the shares of two females as in al-Akdariyya, which we shall mention along with the opinions of the rest of the jurists.

ᶜAlī (God be pleased with him) used to give the grandfather whatever was better for him from two choices: either a sixth or that would not reduce him below the sixth, irrespective of their being sharers with the grandfather. As they had agreed that the sons do not reduce anything from his share, so it was appropriate that the brethren should not reduce it. The reliance for Zayd's opinion is (the argument) that as he excluded the uterine brothers, he gets the third which was due to them (if they were not excluded). Zayd's opinion was upheld by Mālik, al-Shāfiᶜi, al-Thawrī and a group, while the opinion of ᶜAlī (God be pleased with him) was adopted by Abū Ḥanīfa.

The jurists differed about the division known as *al-akdariyya*, which was the case of a woman who died leaving behind a husband, a mother, a sister and a grandfather. ᶜUmar (God be pleased with him) and Ibn Masᶜūd used to give the husband half, the mother a sixth, the sister half and the grandfather a sixth. This was done by the method of reduction (*ᶜawl*). ᶜAlī ibn Abī Ṭālib (God be pleased with him) and Zayd used to say that the husband gets half, the mother a third, the sister half and the grandfather a sixth as share. Zayd, however, used to combine the share of the sister and the grandfather and made them share on the basis of a share for the male equivalent to the share of two females. Some of them thought that this is not Zayd's opinion, and they all considered as weak the sharing upheld by Zayd in this division. Mālik adopted Zayd's opinion. It is said that the issue was called *al-akdariyya* due to the irritating opinion of Zayd.

All this is based on the opinion of those who upheld reduction (*ᶜawl*). The majority of the Companions upheld *ᶜawl* as did the jurists of different regions, except Ibn ᶜAbbās. It is related from him that he said, "The first person to apply reduction (*ᶜawl*) to inheritance was ᶜUmar ibn al-Khaṭṭāb, and by Allāh, had he preferred those whom Allāh has preferred and relegated those whom Allāh has relegated, he would not have applied reduction to inheritance". It was said to him, "Who are those whom Allāh has preferred, and those He has relegated?" He said, "Each (fixed) share that Allāh has not caused to descend, except to another (prescribed) share, that is what Allāh has preferred. Each share, that slips from its due and has nothing except the residue, that is what Allāh has relegated. The first is like a wife and mother, while the relegated is like the sisters and daughters, and when the two categories are combined it is obvious who Allāh has preferred. If something is left, it is for those relegated by Allāh, otherwise there is nothing for them". It was said to him, "Why did you not say this to ᶜUmar?" He said, "*Hibtuh* (I was afraid)".

Zayd was of the opinion that if there were, with the grandfather and german brothers, consanguine brethren, the german brethren push back the grandfather due to the consanguine brethren and prevent him, due to them, from a substantial part of the inheritance, but they do not inherit anything with the german brethren unless there is only one german sister, for she pushes back the grandfather because of her consanguine brethren who share with her so that she completes her half. If there is something in excess of the half, it belongs to the consanguine brethren who share it as one share of the male is equivalent to the shares of two females. If there is nothing in excess of the half, there is no inheritance for them. ʿAlī (God be pleased with him) did not take into account the consanguine brethren here due to *ijmāʿ* on the point that the german brethren exclude them, and also that this act is against the principles, I mean, to calculate on the basis of those who do not inherit.

The Companions disagreed in this topic about the case called *al-kharqāʾ*, into five opinions, in which there is a mother, a sister, and a grandfather. Abū Bakr (God be pleased with him) and Ibn ʿAbbās held that the mother gets a third, and the grandfather takes the residue, excluding the sister through him. This is based on the opinion that allows the grandfather to stand in the position of the father. ʿAlī (God be pleased with him) said that the mother gets a third, the sister half, and what remains is for the grandfather. ʿUthmān held that the mother gets a third, the sister a third, and the grandfather a third. Ibn Masʿūd said the sister gets half, the grandfather a third, and the mother a sixth, and he used to say, "May Allāh protect me from giving preference to the mother over the grandfather". Zayd held that the mother gets a third and the residue is shared between the grandfather and the sister as one share of the male is equivalent to the shares of two females.

51.1.7. Inheritance of Grandmothers

They agreed that the maternal grandmother gets a sixth in the absence of the mother, and for the paternal grandmother also, in the absence of the father, is a sixth. If they survive together, both share a sixth. Zayd and the jurists of Medina maintained that the maternal grandmother is assigned a sixth as a fixed share, if both exist together the sixth is to be shared between them as their proximity is the same, or the proximity of the paternal grandmother is higher. If the proximity of the maternal grandmother is higher, that is, if she is closer to the propositus, the sixth belongs to her and the paternal grandmother has nothing. It is related from him that whosoever is of a closer, the sixth belongs to her. This was also the opinion of ʿAlī (God be pleased with him).

Among the jurists of the regions, Abū Ḥanīfa, al-Thawrī and Abū Thawr, they did not combine for purposes of inheritance any other grandmothers, except these two. Al-Awzāʿī and Aḥmad used to combine the inheritance of three grandmothers, one from the mother's side, and two from the father's side, father's mother and father's father's mother, that is, grandfather's mother. Ibn Masᶜūd gave the inheritance to four grandmothers at the same time: mother's mother, father's mother, father's father's mother and mother's father's mother. This was also the opinion of al-Ḥasan and Ibn Sīrīn. Ibn Masᶜūd used to combine the shares of the grandmother, the nearest and the remotest, as long as they were not excluded by the presence of their daughters or the daughters of their daughters. It is related from him that he used to drop the remotest for the nearest if they were in the same lineage. It is related from Ibn ᶜAbbās that the grandmother is like the mother when the mother is absent, but the majority consider this isolated, but it has some validity through analogy.

The reliance of Zayd, the jurists of Medina, al-Shāfiᶜī, and whoever adopted the opinion of Zayd, is upon what has been related by Mālik that he said, "A grandmother came to Abū Bakr (God be pleased with him) asking him about her inheritance, so Abū Bakr said, 'There is nothing for you in the Book of Allāh, the Mighty and Glorious, and I do not know of anything in the *sunna* of the Messenger of Allāh (God's peace and blessings be upon him), so return till I ask some people'. Mughīra ibn Shuᶜba, then, said to him, 'I was there when the Messenger of Allāh gave her (the grandmother) a sixth.' Abū Bakr said, 'Is there someone else to support you?' He said, 'Muḥammad ibn Maslama.' He said the same thing that Mughīra had said, so Abū Bakr implemented (the rule) for her. Another grandmother came to ᶜUmar ibn al-Khaṭṭāb asking about her inheritance. He said to her, 'There is nothing for you in the Book of Allāh, the Mighty the Glorious, and there has been no decision like this before except for a different category of grandmothers. I am not one to make an addition to shares, but that sixth if both of you can share it together, it is for you, and whichever one of you takes it alone, it is for her'". Mālik has also related "that two grandmothers came to Abū Bakr, so he desired to give a sixth to the one who was from the mother's side. A man, then, said to him, 'Would you leave the one whom he would inherit, if he were alive and she died?' Abū Bakr then allotted the sixth to be shared between them". They said that it is obligatory that this *sunna* and consensus of the Companions should not be violated.

The reliance of those who made three grandmothers inherit (at the same time) is the tradition of ᶜUyayna from Manṣūr from Ibrāhīm "that the Prophet (God's peace and blessings be upon him) gave the inheritance to three grandmothers, two from the father's side and one from the mother's side". Ibn Masᶜūd's reliance is on analogy through the comparison with the paternal grandmother, but the tradition opposes him.

They disagreed whether the paternal grandmother is excluded by her son, who is the father. Zayd was of the opinion that she is excluded by him. It was adopted by Mālik, al-Shāfiᶜī, Abū Ḥanīfa and Dāwūd. Others said that the grandmother inherits with her son, which is related from ʿUmar and Ibn Masʿūd, and a group of the Companions. This was adopted by Shurayḥ, ʿAṭā', Ibn Sīrīn and Aḥmad, and it was also the opinion of the Egyptian jurists.

The reliance of those who excluded the grandmother through her son is on the fact that as the grandfather is excluded by the father, it is, therefore, appropriate that the grandmother have priority for exclusion. In addition, as the maternal grandmother does not inherit anything, by consensus, with the mother, it should be the same for the paternal grandmother with the father. The reliance of the second group is upon what is related by al-Shaʿbī from Masrūq from ʿAbd Allāh, who said, "The first grandmother whom the Messenger of Allāh (God's peace and blessings be upon him) granted a sixth was the grandmother with her son and her son was alive". They added, as a rational argument, that as the mother and maternal grandmother are not excluded by males, the same should be the *ḥukm* of all grandmothers.

It must be known that Mālik does not oppose Zayd in any issue except one, and that is in the case of a woman who dies leaving a husband, a mother, uterine brethren, german brethren and a grandfather. Mālik said that the husband gets half, the mother a sixth, and the grandfather gets the residue, which is a third, while there is nothing for the german brethren. Zayd said that the husband gets half, the mother a sixth, for the grandfather a sixth, and the residue is for the german brethren. In this issue Mālik went against his principle that the grandfather does not exclude the german brethren, nor the consanguine brethren. His (Mālik's) reason is that when the grandfather excluded the uterine brethren from a third to which they were entitled to the exclusion of the german brethren, he had a greater right to it. Zayd, on the other hand, acted on his principle by which he does not exclude them.

51.2. Chapter 2: Exclusion (*Ḥajb*)

The jurists agreed that the german brother excludes the consanguine brother, the consanguine brother excludes the children of the german brother, the children of the german brother exclude the children of the consanguine brother, the children of the consanguine brother have priority over the grandchildren of the german brother, the children of the consanguine brother have priority over the uncle, who is the father's brother, the children of the uncle, who is the father's german brother have priority over the children of the father's consanguine brother. All of these categories exclude their children, and those who exclude a category also exclude those excluded by this category.

On the whole, the brothers who are closer to the deceased exclude those who are distant. If they are equal (of the same order), those depending on two grounds, mother and father, exclude those depending upon a single ground, father only. Similarly, the uncles who are closer (to the deceased) exclude those who are distant, if they are of the same order, those linked to the deceased due to two grounds exclude those linked with a single ground, I mean, the uncle who is the consanguine brother of the deceased's father excludes the son of the uncle who is the consanguine brother of the deceased's father.

They agreed that the german brethren and the consanguine brethren exclude uncles, because the brethren are the children of the father of the deceased, while the uncles are the children of his grandfather. The children exclude their children, the fathers exclude the grandfathers, and the children and their children exclude the brethren. The grandfather excludes the grandfathers above him by consensus, while the father excludes the brethren and those whom the brethren exclude. The grandfather excludes the uncles, by consensus, and also the uterine brothers. The children of german brothers exclude the children of the consanguine brethren. The daughters and the daughters of children exclude the uterine brethren.

The jurists disagreed about the person who leaves behind two sons of uncles, one of whom was also a uterine brother. Mālik, al-Shāfʿī, Abū Ḥanīfa and al-Thawrī said for the uterine brother is a sixth and he is also a residuary in the remainder of the wealth with the son of the uncle, which they divide equally. This was the opinion of ʿAlī (God be pleased with him), Zayd and Ibn ʿAbbās. A group said that the wealth belongs entirely to the son of the uncle who is also a uterine brother. He takes a sixth as due to brotherhood and the remaining as a residuary, as he is linked (to the deceased) through two grounds. The person who held this opinion among Companions is Ibn Masʿūd, and among the jurists were Dāwūd, Abū Thawr and al-Ṭabarī. It is also the opinion of al-Ḥasan and ʿAṭāʾ.

The jurists disagreed about the *radd* (return) of what remains of the estate to the sharers, if there remains a part not covered by the shares and there is no residuary. Zayd did not uphold the doctrine of return and used to deliver the wealth to the treasury *bayt al-māl*. This was adopted by Mālik and al-Shāfiʿī. *Radd* was upheld by the majority of the Companions, that is, to the sharers, except for the husband and wife, though they did differ about its mode. This was adopted by the jurists of Iraq, the Kūfīs and Baṣrīs. These jurists agreed that *radd* takes place according to their shares (*pro rata*). The person who has a half, takes half of the remainder, and so on for each share. The reliance of these jurists is on the argument that proximity (*qarāba*) due to *dīn* and lineage is better than proximity due to *dīn* alone, that is, these people assimilated two grounds, while for the Muslims in general is a single ground.

There are some issues here, disagreement about which is well-known among the jurists. They are related to the bases of inheritance and must be mentioned here. Among these is the agreement of the Muslims that the non-believer does not inherit from the Muslim due to the words of the Exalted, "Allāh will not give the disbelievers any way (of success) against the believers",[196] and because of what is established through the words of the Prophet (God's peace and blessings be upon him), "The Muslim does not inherit from the disbeliever, nor the disbeliever from the Muslim". They disagreed about the inheritance of the Muslim from the disbeliever and the inheritance of the Muslim from the apostate. The majority of the jurists among the Companions and the *Tābiᶜūn* and among the jurists of the regions maintained that the Muslim does not inherit from the disbeliever due to this established tradition. Muᶜādh ibn Jabal and Muᶜāwiya, from among the Companions, and Saᶜīd ibn al-Musayyib and Masrūq, from among the *Tābiᶜūn*, and a group of jurists said that a Muslim may inherit from a disbeliever. They compared this to (the marriage of) their women, saying that as it is permitted to us to marry their women and it is not permitted to us to marry our women to them, same is the case with inheritance and they related for this a *musnad* tradition, about which Abū ᶜUmar said that it is not strong enough according to the majority. They also compared it to retaliation (*qiṣās*) in injuries which is not equal.

The majority of the jurists of Ḥijāz said that the wealth of the apostate, when he is executed or dies, belongs to the community of the Muslims and is not inherited by his relatives. This was adopted by Mālik and al-Shāfiᶜī, and was Zayd's opinion from among the Companions. Abū Ḥanīfa, al-Thawrī, the majority of the Kūfans and many of the Baṣrans said that it is inherited by his Muslim heirs. It is the opinion of Ibn Masᶜūd and ᶜAlī, may Allāh be pleased with them both, from among the Companions. The reliance of the first group is on the generality of the tradition, while the Ḥanafites restrict the generality through analogy. Their analogy in this is that their (the heirs') proximity is more than that of the Muslims as it is based on two grounds, Islam and *qarāba*, while the Muslims have only one ground, Islam. Perhaps, they strengthened this with the continuity of the *ḥukm* of Islam for his wealth on the evidence that it is not to be taken immediately, but remains held by him till he dies, thus, his life is given consideration for his wealth to remain in his ownership, which would not be possible if his wealth did not have inviolability under Islam, and it is for this reason that acknowledgement of apostasy is not allowed against a disbeliever. Al-Shāfiᶜī and others beside him said he is to be held liable for missing *salāh* during the period of apostasy, when he repents from it. Another group said that his wealth is suspended as it has inviolability through Islam. It is suspended in the hope that he would return to Islam, and the entitlement of the Muslims to his wealth is not by way of inheritance. One

[196] Qur᾿ān 4:141

group gave an isolated opinion saying that his wealth belongs to the Muslims as soon as he becomes an apostate, and I believe that it is Ashhab who maintains this.

They agreed about the members of a single community that they inherit from each other. They disagreed about the inheritance of (the members of) different religious communities. Mālik and a group of jurists maintained that the members of different communities do not inherit among themselves, like the Jews and Christians. This was adopted by Aḥmad and a group of jurists. Al-Shāfiʿī, Abū Ḥanīfa, Abū Thawr, al-Thawrī, Dāwūd and others said that all the disbelievers inherit (among themselves). Shurayḥ, Ibn Abī Laylā, and a group of jurists used to acknowledge three communities that do not inherit among themselves: Christians, Jews and Sabians, as one community; the Magians and those who do not have a Book as a (second) community; and Muslims as a (third) community. An opinion similar to that of Mālik is related from Ibn Abī Laylā.

The reliance of Mālik and those who adopted his opinion is on what is related by reliable narrators from ʿAmr ibn Shuʿayb from his father from his grandfather that the Prophet (God's peace and blessings be upon him) said, "The members of two communities do not inherit among themselves". The reliance of the Shāfiʿites and the Ḥanafites is on the words of the Prophet (God's peace and blessings be upon him), "A Muslim does not inherit from a disbeliever, nor a disbeliever from a Muslim". The meaning that emerges from this through the indication of the text is that a Muslim inherits from a Muslim and a disbeliever from a disbeliever. There is a weakness in an opinion based on the (implicit unspoken) indication of the text, especially here.

They differed about the *ḥumalāʾ* (immigrants), and the *ḥumalāʾ* are people who move with their children from the lands of the polytheists to the land of Islam, I mean, the children are born in the lands of the polytheists and then they move to the lands of Islam and claim that birth as effective in establishing descent (among themselves). They differed about them into three opinions. First, that they inherit according to what they assert of their descent, which is the opinion of a group among the *Tābiʿūn* and was adopted by Isḥāq. Second, the opinion that they do not inherit except through evidence establishing their descent, which was the opinion of Shurayḥ, al-Ḥasan and a group of jurists. Third, an opinion that they do not inherit at all. All three opinions are related from ʿUmar, except that the well-known opinion from him is that he did not allow to inherit except those who were born in Arab lands, which is the opinion of ʿUthmān and of ʿUmar ibn ʿAbd al-ʿAzīz.

The opinions of Mālik and his disciples differ about this. Among them are those who do not permit inheritance except through evidence, which is the opinion of Ibn al-Qāsim. Among them are those who hold that they do not inherit at all, even through reliable evidence. The person who held this opinion among the disciples of Mālik is ᶜAbd al-Malik ibn al-Mājishūn. Ibn al-Qāsim has related from Mālik about the inhabitants of a fortress who surrendered to Muslim authority, supporting each other about their inheritance. From this it is derived that they inherit without evidence, as Mālik does not permit the testimony of the disbelievers for each other. If, however, they are made captive, their claim is not acceptable. Similar details are upheld by the Kūfīs, al-Shāfiᶜī, Aḥmad and Abū Thawr, as they said that if they come into Muslim lands and no one has dominion over them, their claim about their descent is accepted, but if they are made captive and enslaved, their claim is not accepted, except through evidence. Thus, in this issue there are four opinions, two extreme and two making distinctions.

The majority of the jurists of the regions and those among the Companions, ᶜAlī, Zayd and ᶜUmar maintained that one who does not inherit does not exclude (others from inheritance by way of *ḥajb*), like a disbeliever, or a slave, or a murderer. Ibn Masᶜūd used to exclude through these three without granting them inheritance, I mean, through the People of the Book, slaves, and those guilty of intentional homicide. This was adopted by Dāwūd and Abū Thawr. The reliance of the majority is on the argument that exclusion and inheritance are close to each other and that they go together (so that when one goes away the other follows). The argument of the other group is that exclusion is not removed except by death.

The jurists differed about those who were missing in war or at sea or under a landslide, and it was not known which one of them died first before his companion, how they were to inherit from each other if they were heirs. Mālik and the jurists of Medina held that they could not inherit from each other, and their estates collectively would go to the survivors among their relatives who were heirs, or they would go to the treasury (*bayt al-māl*) if they did not have relatives who could inherit. This was al-Shāfiᶜī's opinion and also of Abū Ḥanīfa and his disciples in so far as it is related by al-Ṭaḥāwī. ᶜAlī, ᶜUmar, may Allāh be pleased with them both, the jurists of Kūfa, Abū Ḥanīfa, as quoted by (writers) other than al-Ṭaḥawī, and the majority of the Baṣrans maintained that they do inherit, and the mode of their inheritance is that each inherits from his companion on the basis of his original wealth and not what they have inherited from each other, that is, the wealth of the heir is not combined with what he inherits from others, they are made to inherit the whole as if it were one unit of wealth as is the case with those whose deaths are known to have preceded the deaths of others. An example of this is the case of a husband and wife who died in war, at sea, or through a landslide and each one of them had a thousand *dirhams*. The husband will inherit from his wife five hundred *dirhams*, while the wife will inherit a fourth out of the one thousand that the husband had excluding the five hundred that he inherited from her, which comes to two hundred and fifty.

Among the issues in this topic is the disagreement of the jurists about the estate of a child of a woman accused through the process of *liᶜān* and a child born through unlawful intercourse (*zinā*). The jurists of Medina and Zayd ibn Thābit held that the estate of the child of the *mulāᶜana* is to be inherited just like her other children and that his mother gets a third, while the remaining goes to the treasury, unless there are uterine brethren who will get a third, or the woman may be a *mawlā* in which case the remaining wealth will go to her *mawālī*, otherwise the remainder will go to the treasury. This was adopted by Mālik, al-Shāfiᶜī, Abū Ḥanīfa and his disciples, except that Abū Ḥanīfa according to his principle considers the *dhawū l-arḥām* superior to the community of the Muslims, and also following the analogy of those who uphold the doctrine of return (*radd*), the remainder will be returned to the mother. ᶜAlī, ᶜUmar and Ibn Masᶜūd held that his residuaries are the residuaries of the mother, unless she is absent (dead), and they used to substitute through the doctrine of *tanzīl* (substitution) the mother for the father. This was adopted by al-Ḥasan, Ibn Sīrīn, al-Thawrī, Ibn Ḥanbal and a group of jurists.

The reliance of the first group is the general meaning of the words of the Exalted, "And if he have no *walad* (son in this case) and his parents are his heirs, then to his mother appertaineth a sixth".[197] They said this woman is a mother and to each mother goes a third, thus, for this woman too is a third. The reliance of the second group is what has been related of the tradition of ᶜUmar from the Prophet (God's peace and blessings be upon him), "that he linked the child of a *mulāᶜana* with his mother", and also the tradition of ᶜAmr ibn Shuᶜayb from his father from his grandfather, who said, "The Prophet (God's peace and blessings be upon him) gave the estate of the child of the *mulāᶜana* to his mother and his heirs". They also relied on the tradition of Wāthila ibn al-Asqaᶜ from the Prophet (God's peace and blessings be upon him), "A woman gathers three kinds of wealth: that of her freed slave, that which she finds, and that of her child who is free of blame", and on the tradition of Makḥūl from the Prophet (God's peace and blessings be upon him) to the same effect. All of these have been recorded by Abū Dāwūd and others besides him. Al-Qāḍī said that acting according to these tradition is obligatory as they restricted the general meaning in the Book, and the majority believe that a particular *sunna* restricts the generality of the Book. Perhaps, these traditions did not reach the first group or were not proved authentic according to them. This opinion is related from Ibn ᶜAbbās and ᶜUthmān, and

[197] Qurᵓān 4:11

was well known among the First Generation. Its being well known among the Companions is an indication of the authenticity of these traditions, and such an opinion cannot depend on analogy. Allāh knows best.

Among the issues of the establishment of paternity, which is a requisite for inheritance, is their disagreement about the person who leaves behind two sons, with one of them acknowledging the existence of a third son and the other denying it. Mālik and Abū Ḥanīfa said that it is obligatory on him to give him his due in inheritance, meaning thereby the one who acknowledged, although his paternity is not established in this way. Al-Shāfiʿī said that paternity is not established in this case nor is it obligatory on the one acknowledging it to give him anything from his share of inheritance. Mālik and Abū Ḥanīfa differed about the amount for which the acknowledging brother is liable. Mālik said that the obligation is to give what would have been due to him had the other brother acknowledged him and his paternity had been established. Abū Ḥanīfa said that it is obligatory on him to pay him half of what he gets. The same is the *ḥukm* according to Mālik and Abū Ḥanīfa about the person who is survived by one son and he acknowledges the existence of another son, I mean, paternity is not established but inheritance is obligatory. From al-Shāfiʿī there are two opinions about this issue. First, that paternity is not established nor is inheritance obligatory. Second, that paternity is established and inheritance is obligatory, and this is the opinion over which there is altercation among the Shāfiʿites, among the issues of proclamation, and they render it as a question of public interest, that is, each person who is entitled to wealth may establish paternity through acknowledgement, whether he is alone or there are others besides him.

The reliance of the Shāfiʿites in the first issue and in one of his (al-Shāfiʿī's) opinions, I mean, the opinion that is not well known, is on the argument that paternity is not established except by two *ʿadl* witnesses, and as this is not established, therefore, there is no inheritance, as paternity is the primary point while inheritance is secondary, and when the primary issue is not established the secondary is non-existent. The reliance of Mālik and Abū Ḥanīfa is on the argument that the establishment of paternity is a right extendible to the brother denying it and can only be established by two *ʿadl* witnesses; however, his share of the inheritance is in the hands of the brother who has acknowledged him and the acknowledgement is effective as it is a claim that he has acknowledged against himself. The fact is that a decision against him by the judge cannot be issued except after the establishment of paternity. Yet, it is not permitted to him, between his Lord and himself, that he should deny someone whom he knows to be his co-owner in the inheritance to the extent of his share.

The reliance of the Shāfiʿites, in establishing paternity through the acknowledgement of one person who is entitled to inheritance, is based on transmission and analogy. With respect to transmission, it is the tradition of Mālik from Ibn Shihāb from ʿUrwa from ʿĀʾisha, agreed upon for its soundness, in which she said, " ʿUtba ibn Abī Waqqāṣ acknowledged in front of his brother Saʿd ibn Abī Waqqāṣ that the son of the slave-girl of Zamʿa is mine so take care of him. At the time of the conquest of Mecca, Saʿd ibn Abī Waqqās took possession of him saying, 'My brother's son, he acknowledged him before me.' ʿAbd ibn Zamʿa challenged him saying, 'He is my brother, son of my father's slave-girl, born on his bed'. They dragged him to the Messenger of Allāh (God's peace and blessings be upon him) and Saʿd said, 'O Messenger of Allāh, he is my brother's son, he acknowledged him before me'. ʿAbd ibn Zamʿa challenged him saying, 'He is my brother, the son of my father's slave girl, born on his bed.' The Messenger of Allāh (God's peace and blessings be upon him) said, 'He is yours, O ʿAbd ibn Zamʿa'. The Messenger of Allāh (God's peace and blessings be upon him), then, said, 'The child belongs to the *firāsh* (bed where it is born),[198] and to the fornicator the stone (*rajm*)'. He then said to Sawda bint Zamʿa, on seeing his resemblance with ʿUtba ibn Abī Waqqāṣ, 'Veil yourself from him'. She said, 'He did not see her till he met his God' ". Thus, the Messenger of Allāh decided to grant ʿAbd ibn Zamʿa his brother and established his paternity through acknowledgement, when there was no contending heir. For the majority of *fuqahāʾ*, the understanding of this tradition became difficult, due to its conflict with the agreed principle for establishing paternity, and they have different interpretations for this (tradition). This is so as the apparent meaning of this tradition indicates that he established his paternity simply through an acknowledgement by his brother, while the principle is that paternity is not established without two *ʿadl* witnesses, and it was for this reason that people made different interpretations in this.

A group said that the Prophet (God's peace and blessings be upon him) established his paternity through the acknowledgement of his brother, as it is possible that he knew that this *ama* had sexual relations with (her master) Zamʿa ibn Qays, and that she was his *firāsh*. They said that what confirms this is the fact that Zamʿa was related to him by marriage, and Sawda bint Zamʿa was the Prophet's wife, so it was possible that the affair was not unknown to him. This is on the assumption that the *qāḍī* does not decide on the basis of his personal knowledge. This interpretation is not suited to Mālik's opinion, as the *qāḍī*, according to him, does not decide on the basis of his personal information, but it suits al-Shāfiʿī's opinion, according to his second opinion, I mean, the one in which paternity is not established. Those who upheld this

[198] That is, the paternity of the child is attributed to the man who had legal access to the woman for sexual intercourse.

opinion said that he ordered Sawda to veil herself as a precaution due to a semblance of a doubt, not that it was obligatory. Some of the Shāfiʿites said on this basis that the husband has the right to ask his wife to veil herself from her brother. Another group said that his command to Sawda to veil herself is evidence that his paternity was not linked with the statement of ʿUtba nor with his knowledge about the *firāsh*. These jurists made a distinction about the statement of the Prophet (God's peace and blessings be upon him), "He is for you" and said he meant by this "he is your slave as he is the son of your father's *ama*". This, however, is not apparent in the indication of the cause in the command of the Prophet (God's peace and blessings be upon him) in his statement, "The child belongs to the *firāsh* and to the fornicator the stone". Al-Ṭahāwī said that he intended by his words, "he is yours, O ʿAbd ibn Zamʿa" that you have possession over him like the possession of a finder over found property. All these interpretations are weak due to the *taʿlīl* (indication of the underlying cause) by the Prophet of his *ḥukm* by saying, "The child belongs to the *firāsh* and to the fornicator the stone".

The rule upon which the Shāfiʿites rely in this opinion is that the acknowledgement of one who is entitled to inherit amounts to an acknowledgement of succession (*khilāfa*), that is, the acknowledgement of one who collects the inheritance of the deceased. According to others, it is acknowledgement of testimony (*shahāda*) and not acknowledgement of succession, meaning thereby that the acknowledgement that was due from the deceased has been transferred to the one who collects his inheritance.

The majority of the jurists agreed that children born through *zinā* cannot be attributed to their (natural) parents, except what took place in *jāhiliyya* according to what is related from ʿUmar ibn al-Khaṭṭāb with reported disagreement of the Companions. A group came up with an isolated opinion saying that the child born through *zinā* was legally attributed to the parents in Islam, I mean, one who was born through *zinā* after Islam. They agreed that a child cannot be legally associated with the *firāsh* (lawful sexual relationship) if born within a period that is less than six months, either from the time of the contract or from the time of consummation, and the period of the relationship is counted in the shortest period of gestation beginning with the time of consummation, even if the man separated from the woman or dissociated himself from her (thereafter).

They disagreed about the longest period of pregnancy through which the father can be associated with the child. Mālik said that it is five years, while some of his disciples said it is seven. Al-Shāfiʿī said that it is four years. The Kūfīs said it is two years. Muḥammad ibn al-Ḥakam said it is a year. Dāwūd said it is six months. This counting is based on practice and experience. The opinions of Ibn ʿAbd al-Ḥakam and the Ẓāhirites are closer to the normal. The rule should be based upon what is normal, not upon what is rare, which would, perhaps, be impossible.

Mālik and al-Shāfiʿī held that when a man marries a woman, but does not consummate the marriage or does so later, and the woman gives birth to a child in six months from the time of the contract not from the time of consummation, the child is not to be associated with him, unless she gave birth to it after six months or more from the time of consummation. Abū Ḥanīfa said that she is his legal wife (*firāsh*) and the child is associated with him. Mālik's argument is that she does not become a *firāsh* except through the possibility of intercourse and that is through consummation. The reliance of Abū Ḥanīfa is on the generality of the words of the Prophet (God's peace and blessings be upon him), "The child belongs to the *firāsh* (lawful marital or sexual relationship)". It was as if he considered this as a command to be obeyed without rationalization (*taʿabbud*) in giving the possibility of lawful sexual intercourse greater weight than that of unlawful sexual intercourse for purposes of associating the child with lawful sexual intercourse.

They disagreed under this topic about the establishment of paternity through physiognomy (*qāfa*). This occurs when two men have sexual intercourse with the same woman in a single period of purity, through a valid marriage or *milk yamīn*. The *ḥukm* for *qāfa* can also be conceived in the case of a foundling claimed by two men or three. *Al-Qāfa* according to the Arabs were a group of people who had the skills to identify the resemblance in the features of people. The use of *qāfa* was upheld by Mālik, al-Shāfiʿī, Aḥmad, Abū Thawr and al-Awzāʿī from among the jurists of different regions. The *ḥukm* of *qāfa* was rejected by the Kūfīs and most of the jurists of Iraq. The *ḥukm* according to them was that if two men claimed a child, it would belong to both, in case none of them claimed through *firāsh*, as in the case of the foundling, or when a woman becomes a *firāsh* for two men like an *ama* or a free woman with whom two men have intercourse in a single period of purity.[199]

According to the majority who uphold this opinion, it is permitted that there be, according to them, two fathers only for a child. Muḥammad, the disciple of Abū Ḥanīfa said that it is permitted that there be three if they claim this. All this is the mixing up and the annulment of (the rules derived from) reason and transmission.

The reliance for the deduction of those who upheld physiognomy is what was related by Mālik from Sulaymān ibn Yasār that ʿUmar ibn al-Khaṭṭāb used

[199] The only conceivable case in which this could occur in Islam is the hypothetical case of error *(shubhat al-milk)*, which is discussed in some law manuals, but it is difficult to imagine otherwise. A woman can marry a second husband only after the death of the first, or after divorce from him. In both cases she can marry the second after her *ʿidda*.

to assign the children born during *jāhiliyya* to those who were related to them, that is, those who claimed them after Islam. Two men came to him, both claiming the child of a woman. He called a physiognomist, who looked at them and said, "They have both participated in it". ʿUmar beat him with his stick. He, then, called the woman and said to her, "Tell me what you think". She said, "He belongs to one of the men, who used to visit my people regarding camels and used to associate with me, till he thought and we thought that he had made me pregnant". (She continued) that he then went away and she even made a sacrifice for him. He then assigned the other man to succeed him, and who associated with her, meaning thereby the second man, and she said that she did not know to whom the child belonged. At this the physiognomist said, "*Allāhu akbar*". ʿUmar said to the boy, "Choose whom you will".

They said that the decision of ʿUmar in the presence of the Companions about the utilization of physiognomy, without denial by any of them, amounts to *ijmāʿ* (consensus). According to Mālik, the *ḥukm* of participation in paternity, as judged by the physiognomist, is to be postponed till the child attains puberty. It is then to be said to him, "Choose whom you like". The child cannot, however, be associated with both. This was the opinion of al-Shāfiʿī. Abū Thawr said that he becomes the son of both, if the physiognomist says that both contributed to his conception. According to Mālik, he cannot be the son of both due to the words of the Exalted, "O mankind! Lo! We have made you from a male and a female".[200] The supporters of physiognomy also argued on the basis of the tradition of Ibn Shihāb from ʿUrwa from ʿĀʾisha, who said: The Messenger of Allāh (God's peace and blessings be upon him) (once) came in very pleased, his face beaming with delight, and said: "Have you not heard what Mujazziz al-Mudlijiyy said to Zayd and ʿUsāma on seeing their feet? He said, 'These feet are related to each other'". They said that this is related from Ibn ʿAbbās and from Anas ibn Mālik.

No one opposed them from among the Companions (regarding the validity of the findings of the physiognomists). The Kūfīs asserted the principle that no decision be given in favour of either of the litigants, unless there is an indication of a *firāsh* (lawful sexual relationship), due to the words of the Prophet (God's peace and blessings be upon him), "The child belongs to the *firāsh*". If the *firāsh* is absent or is ambiguous the child belongs to both. It was as if they considered this as legal *bunūwwa* (paternity, filiation) and not natural (physical). Thus, it is not necessary for one who denies that one child can have two fathers according to reason, to deny that it can be so legally. An opinion similar to theirs is related from ʿUmar, and ʿAbd al-Razzāq narrated one from ʿAlī.

[200] Qurʾān 49:13

Al-Shāfiʿī said that less than two physiognomists are not acceptable. From Mālik there are two opinions about this, the first is like the opinion of al-Shāfiʿī, and the second is that the finding of one physiognomist is accepted. The physiognomist, according to the well-known opinion of Mālik, is to be employed in the cases of *milk yamīn* only and not in the cases of *nikāḥ* (marriage). Ibn Wahb related from him an opinion similar to that of al-Shāfiʿī. Abū ʿUmar ibn ʿAbd al-Barr said that there is a *ḥasan*, *musnad* tradition in this, which has been accepted by a number of traditionists and the Ẓāhirites, and is related by al-Thawrī from Ṣāliḥ ibn Ḥayy from al-Shaʿbī from Zayd ibn Arqam, who said, " ʿAlī was in Yemen when they brought up to him a woman with whom three men had committed sexual intercourse in a single period of purity. He asked each one of them to acknowledge the child as belonging to the other, but each refused. He then drew lots between them and granted the child to the man whose name was drawn through the lot and imposed upon him two-third *diya*. This was reported to the Prophet (God's peace and blessings be upon him), who admired his decision. He was so pleased with it that he smiled widely as his front teeth shone". In this tradition we find the implementation of the *ḥukm* through physiognomy and the assignment of the child through lots.

They disagreed about the inheritance of the murderer, into four opinions. A group said that the murderer does not inherit his victim at all, while some others said that he does. Another group made a distinction between manslaughter and intentional killing, saying that he does not inherit anything in *ʿamd* (murder), but does inherit in cases of *khaṭaʾ*, except from the *diya*. This is the opinion of Mālik and his disciples. Others made a distinction between intentional homicide as an obligatory act (excusable homicide) and when it was not obligatory, as for example in the case of the person who has the task of implementing the *ḥudūd* (the executioner). They also distinguished between suspicious and unsuspicious circumstances.

The reason for disagreement is the conflict between the legal principle related to this with a view based on *maṣlaḥa*, as *maṣlaḥa* requires that he should not inherit so that people may not employ murder as a means to inheritance on the basis of the apparent meaning. *Taʿabbud* (blind obedience) requires that this should not be considered, because had this been the intention it would have been considered by the Lawgiver, as the Ẓāhirites say, "And thy Lord was never forgetful".[201]

They disagreed about the heir who was not a Muslim, but becomes a Muslim after the death of the propositus, and before the division of the estate; similarly, when the propositus professed a faith other than Islam. The majority

[201] Qurʾān 19:64

said that consideration in this is to be given to the time of death. If on the day he died his heir was not a Muslim, he cannot inherit at all, whether he converted to Islam before the division or after it. Similarly, if the propositus professed a faith other than Islam and his heir was not a Muslim, he inherits from him by necessity, whether his acceptance of Islam was prior to the division or after it. A group said, among them al-Ḥasan and Qatāda, that the thing to be reckoned is the time of division, and this is related from ʿUmar ibn al-Khaṭṭāb. The reliance of both sides is on the words of the Prophet (God's peace and blessings be upon him), "Any house or land that was divided in *jāhiliyya* stays divided according the division of *jāhiliyya*, and any house or land that was found in Islam and was not divided, then, that is to be divided according to Islam". Those who took into consideration the time of division assigned the *ḥukm* of Islam as at that time, while those who took into account the time when division becomes due assigned the *ḥukm* of Islam from the time of death. It is related from the tradition of ʿAṭā' that "a man converted to Islam at the (time of) inheritance in the period of the Messenger of Allāh (God's peace and blessings be upon him), prior to the division. The Messenger of Allāh (God's peace and blessings be upon him) gave him his share". The same is the *ḥukm*, according to them, in the case of (slave) heirs who are emancipated after the death (of the propositus) and prior to the division. These, then, are the well-known issues that are related to this book.

Al-Qāḍī (Ibn Rushd) said that as inheritance depends on one of three causes, descent, marital relations, and *walā'*, and as we have already spoken about the heirs through descent and marriage we must now discuss *walā'*, for whom it is obligatory, in whose case it is obligatory and in whose case it is not, and what are its *aḥkām*.

51.3. Chapter 3: Clientage (*Walā'*)

The discussion of entitlement to *walā'* consists of important issues that are of the nature of principles in this topic.

51.3.1. Issue 1

The jurists agreed that whoever sets free his slave on his own account, his *walā'* belongs to him and he inherits him if he does not have heirs, and he is a residuary if there are heirs who do not exhaust the wealth.

The entitlement to *walā'* for the emancipator freeing the slave on his own account is established through the words of the Prophet (God's peace and blessings be upon him) in the tradition of Barīra, "*Walā'* belongs to one who sets (him) free". They disagreed when he emancipates his own slave for the sake of someone else. Mālik said that the *walā'* belongs to the person on whose account he is set free, not the person who undertakes the emancipation. Al-Shāfiʿī and Abū Ḥanīfa said that if he sets him free with the knowledge of the person on whose account he does it, then, the *walāʾ* belongs to the other person, but if he sets him free without his knowledge, it belongs to the person who undertook the act.

The reliance of the Ḥanafites and the Shāfiʿites is on the apparent meaning of the words of the Prophet, "*Walāʾ* belongs to one who sets (him) free", and on his words, "*Walāʾ* is kinship like the kinship of descent". They said as it is not permitted that descent be linked to a free man without his approval, so is *walāʾ*. As a rational argument (they said), as his emancipation is freedom that occurs within his owned property, it follows that *walāʾ* should belong to him, the basis being the same as when he sets him free on his own account. Mālik's argument is that when he emancipates him on the other person's account, it is as if he loses ownership in him, and (himself) resembles the agent. It is for this reason that they agreed that when the other person on whose behalf emancipation is made permits him, the *walāʾ* belongs to him and not the one undertaking the act. According Mālik, a person who says to his slave, "You are free for the sake of Allāh and the Muslims", the *walāʾ* belongs to the Muslims, but according to them (al-Shāfiʿī and Abū Hanīfa) it belongs to the emancipator.

51.3.2. Issue 2

The jurists disagreed about the person who converts to Islam at the hands of a certain man, whether his *walāʾ* belongs to him. Mālik, al-Shāfiʿī, al-Thawrī, Dāwūd and a group of jurists said that there is no *walāʾ* for him. Abū Ḥanīfa and his disciples said that *walāʾ* belongs to him, if he agrees to accept him as his *mawlā*. This is so as it is their principle that it is up to an individual to consider someone else as his *mawlā* so that he will inherit him and act as his *ʿāqila*, and he has the right to transfer the *walāʾ* to someone else if he does not pay the dues of the *ʿāqila* on his behalf. Others said that he becomes his *mawlā* by the very act of conversion to Islam at his hands.

The reliance of the first group is on the words of the Prophet (God's peace and blessings be upon him), "The *walāʾ* belongs to the one who sets (him) free". This word, *innamā*, (only) when it introduces a sentence is what is they call *ḥāṣira*, "the confining tool", and the definite article prefixing *walā*, according to them, is for *ḥaṣr*. The meaning of *ḥaṣr* also implies the idea of confinement, as the the *ḥukm* is specific to the person (or the thing) for whom it is laid down and nothing else shares it with him. So according to the meaning of this tradition, *walāʾ* cannot belong to anyone except the emancipator who undertook the act. The reliance of the Ḥanafites in establishing *walāʾ*, through the contract of clientage, are the words of the

Exalted, "And unto each we have appointed heirs (*mawālī*) of that which parents and near kindred leave", and His words, "As for those with whom your right hands have made a covenant, give them their due".[202] The proof of those who said that *walāʾ* can be acquired by the act of conversion to Islam at the *mawlā's* hands alone is the tradition of Tamīm al-Dārī, who said, "I asked the Messenger of Allāh about a polytheist converting to Islam at the hands of a Muslim, and he said, 'His rights are superior to the rest of the people, and are preferable during his life and after his death'". It was also decided accordingly by ʿUmar ibn ʿAbd al-ʿAzīz. The answer of the first group is that the implications of the words of the Exalted, "As for those with whom your right hands have made a covenant, give them their due",[203] have been abrogated by the verses of inheritance, and that this was the *ḥukm* in early Islam.

They agreed that it is not permitted to sell *walāʾ* or to gift it away due to the Prophet's established prohibition of this, except in the case of *walāʾ* that is unrestrained (*sāʾiba*).

51.3.3. Issue 3

The jurists disagreed when the master says to his slave you are free without restraints (*sāʾiba*). Mālik said that his *walāʾ* and dues of the *ʿāqila* are for all the Muslims, and he considered it the same as when he sets him free categorically on account of the Muslims, unless he intends thereby the meaning of freedom alone, in which case *walāʾ* will belong to him. Al-Shāfiʿī and Abū Ḥanīfa said that his *walāʾ* belongs to the emancipator in all circumstances. This was also the opinion of Aḥmad, Dāwūd and Abū Thawr. A group of jurists said that he has the right to assign his *walāʾ* to whomsoever he likes, and if generalizes his *walāʾ*, it belongs to the Muslims. This was the opinion of al-Layth and al-Awzāʿī. Ibrahīm and al-Shaʿbī said that there is no harm in the sale of the *walāʾ* of the *sāʾiba*, or in its donation. The arguments of these jurists are the same as the proofs that are stated in the preceding issue. I do not recall at the present moment the argument of those who permitted its sale.

51.3.4. Issue 4

The jurists disagreed about the *walāʾ* of a Muslim slave, to whom it belongs, when manumitted by a Christian prior to sale. Mālik and his disciples said that his *walāʾ* belongs to the Muslims, and if his *mawlā* converts to Islam later, the *walāʾ* does not revert to him, nor does the inheritance. The majority said that

[202] Qurʾān 4:33
[203] Qurʾān 4:33

his *walāʾ* belongs to his master, and if he converts to Islam, he gets the inheritance too.

The argument of the majority is that *walāʾ* is like descent, if the father converts to Islam after the conversion of the son he inherits him, so also in the case of the slave. Mālik's reliance is on the generality of the words of the Exalted, "And Allāh will not give the disbelievers any way (of success) against the believers".[204] He says that as *walāʾ* did not belong to him on the day of manumission it is not due to him through what follows.

If, however, it belongs to him on the day of manumission and then some obstacle occurs that prevents the assignment of *walāʾ* to him, the jurists agreed that *walāʾ* will revert to him when such obstacle is removed. It is for this reason that they agreed when a Christian manumits a *dhimmī* slave of his, before either of them has converted to Islam, with the slave converting thereafter, the *walāʾ* is cancelled, but if the master converts to Islam, it will revert to him. They did disagree about the case of a *ḥarbī* (the warring enemy) who sets free a slave professing his faith and (later) both cross over to the Muslims. Mālik said he is his *mawlā* and will inherit from him. Abū Ḥanīfa said that the relationship of *walāʾ* does not exist between them, and it is up to the slave to accept whom he likes among those professing his faith for *walāʾ* and affiliation. Ashhab opposed Mālik and said that if the slave converts to Islam before, his *walāʾ* cannot revert to his master ever. Ibn al-Qāsim said that it does, which is the meaning in Mālik's opinion, as Mālik considers the time of manumission (as being effective).

All these issues are hypothetical in their opinions and do not actually take place now, as there is none among the religion of Christians who enslave each other, nor in the religion of the Jews according to what they believe today, considering it as proscribed.

51.3.5. Issue 5

The majority of the jurists agreed that women have no part in inheritance through *walāʾ*, unless they have undertaken manumission themselves on their own account or what has been caused by those whom they directly manumitted, either through *walāʾ* or through descent. For example, in the case of a manumitted slave of a manumitted slave or the children of a manumitted slave. They do not inherit from the manumitted slave of the person from whom they inherit, except what is related from Shurayḥ. His argument is that as she has the *walāʾ* of one whom she manumitted on her own account, she has the *walāʾ* of one whom the propositus manumitted on the analogy of the (entitlement) of a man. This is what they call *qiyās al-maʿnā*, which is the

[204] Qurʾān 4:141

highest category of analogy; however, it has been rendered feeble as it is isolated. The argument of the majority is that *walāʾ* became due on the basis of the benevolence of the manumitter for the manumitted, and this benevolence is found in the case of one who has directly manumitted, or is found due to a cause as strong as that, which is being a residuary.

Al-Qāḍī (Ibn Rushd) said that as it has been settled who is entitled to *walāʾ* and who is not, what remains is the gradation of the possessors of *walāʾ* in the topic of *walāʾ*.

51.3.6. Gradation in *Walāʾ*

Among the best known of their issues in this topic is what they call *walāʾ al-kubr*. An example is the case of a man who manumits his slave and then dies leaving behind two brothers or two sons. One of the brothers, or one of the sons, then dies leaving behind a son. The majority said that in this issue, the right of the dead brother about *walāʾ* is not inherited from him by his son, but it passes on to his brother as he has a right to it prior to his (brother's) son, as against (the rules of) inheritance, where exclusion is caused by the presence of the person closest to the deceased, but here it depends on being the closest to the person undertaking the manumission. This is related from ʿUmar ibn al-Khaṭṭāb, ʿAlī, ʿUthmān, Ibn Masʿūd and Zayd ibn Thābit from among the Companions. Shurayḥ and a group of jurists from Baṣra said that the right of the dead brother, in this issue, passes on to his children. The argument of these jurists is based on the similarity of *walāʾ* with inheritance. The argument of the first group is that *walāʾ* is a kind of lineage whose origin lies with the direct manumitter.

A well-known issue in this topic is the issue called *jarr al-walāʾ*. It takes the form of a slave who has children from an *ama*. The *ama* is manumitted and then the slave (her husband) is also manumitted. The jurists disagreed as to whom the children's *walāʾ* belongs when the father is manumitted. This is so as they agreed that their *walāʾ* after the freedom of the mother, whom the freed slave later marries, belongs to the *mawālī* of the mother, slavery not affecting the child when he is in its mother's womb. They disagreed when the father is freed, whether the *walāʾ* of his children passes on to his master. The majority—Mālik, Abū Ḥanīfa, al-Shāfiʿī and their disciples—maintained that it does. This was also the opinion of ʿAlī (God be pleased with him), Ibn Masʿūd, al-Zubayr and ʿUthmān ibn ʿAffān. ʿAṭāʾ, ʿIkrima, Ibn Shihāb and a group said that *walāʾ* does not pass on to him. It is also related from ʿUmar, and was decided this way by ʿAbd al-Malik ibn Marwān when Qubayṣa ibn Dhūʾayb related it to him from ʿUmar ibn al-Khaṭṭāb, though an opinion similar to that of the majority is related from ʿUmar. The argument of the majority is that *walāʾ* is like paternity, and paternity belongs to the father and not the mother. The argument of the second group is that as the question of the determination of the children's freedom is dependent on the status of their mother, they are dependent on her in the results of their emancipation also, that is, for *walāʾ*.

Mālik held the opinion that the *walāʾ* of the grandchildren passes on to the grandfather, if the father is a slave, unless the father is freed. This was also the opinion of al-Shāfiʿī. The Kūfans opposed him relying on the argument that the *walāʾ* of the grandchildren is established for the manumitter of the grandfather through the father, and if the father does not have the *walāʾ*, it is proper that the grandfather not have it either. The reliance of the second group is on the argument that the slavery of the father is like his death, in which case it is necessary that the *walāʾ* pass on to the father's father.

There is no dispute among those who say the *walāʾ* belongs to the residuaries, as far as I know, that the descendants have a right prior to the ascendants and that it does not pass on to the ascendants, except in the absence of the descendants, as against the rule of inheritance. *Bunūwwa* is stronger for purposes of residue than *ubūwwa*, and the father is the weakest as a residuary. Brethren and their children are closer, according to Mālik, than the grandfather. According to al-Shāfiʿī and Abū Ḥanīfa, the grandfather is closer than them.

The reason for the disagreement is that one who is the closest through lineage and the strongest as a residuary does not inherit *walāʾ* as a prescribed share, but as a residuary. If the *mawlāʾ* among the descendants dies without leaving any heirs, or has heirs who do not exhaust the inheritance, his residuary for *walāʾ* is the highest ascendant. Similarly, the residuaries of the highest ascendant are those who are related to the ascendant through descent, I mean, his daughters and sons and the children of his children.

Within this topic is a well-known issue. When a woman, who has *walāʾ*, dies leaving behind a son and residuaries, to whom is the *walāʾ* transferred? A group said it passes to her residuaries, as they are the ones who compose the *ʿāqila* for her, and *walāʾ* belongs to the residuaries. This is the opinion of ʿAlī ibn Abī Ṭālib. Another group said that it passes to her son, which is the opinion of ʿUmar ibn al-Khaṭṭāb and is followed by the jurists of the regions. This is opposed to this legal tradition, as a woman's son is not among her residuaries.

The book of *farāʾiḍ* and *walāʾ* is completed, praise be to Allāh, as is His due.

LII

THE BOOK OF ᶜ*ITQ*
(MANUMISSION; EMANCIPATION)

The discussion in this book relates to those (persons) whose acts of emancipation are valid and those whose acts are not, those on whom emancipation becomes binding and those on whom it does not, that is, by law. It is also about the words used for emancipation, about oaths related to it, about its *aḥkām*, and about the conditions imposed in it. We shall mention, under these headings, those well-known issues that relate mostly to the transmitted texts.

They agreed that the person whose act of emancipation is valid is the sole owner, with valid ownership, in possession of discretion, of sound body, and having sufficient resources not being destitute. They disagreed about the person whose liabilities cover his assets. They also disagreed about one who emancipates while he is sick (*marīḍ*) and about the *ḥukm* governing him.

The jurists disagreed about the permissibility of emancipation by the person whose liabilities exceeded his assets. The majority of the jurists of Medina, Mālik and others, said that it is not permitted. This was also the opinion of al-Awzāᶜī and al-Layth. The jurists of Iraq said that this is permitted till such time that he is placed under interdiction by the judge. This was the opinion of those among them who upheld interdiction. The derivation of an opinion from Mālik's principles indicates permissibility on the analogy of what is related from him in *rahn* (security for a debt) that it is permitted, even if his liabilities exceed his assets, as long as the judge does not interdict him.

The argument of those who prohibited his (act of) emancipation is that his wealth in such a state is linked with the right of the creditors, therefore, he does not have a right to dispose of anything from it without compensation. This is the underlying cause due to which the judge interdicts him with respect to disposal, and the *aḥkām* must coexist with their causes. Interdiction by the judge is not the underlying cause itself, rather it is an obligatory *ḥukm* necessitated by the underlying cause, thus, it is not to be taken into account.

The argument of the other party is that a consensus has taken place on the point that he (whose liabilities cover his assets) has the right to have intercourse with his slave girl, make her pregnant, and (to spend from his assets and) not to reimburse anything of the amount spent on himself or his family until the judge interdicts him, thus, tying down his hands. It is, therefore, necessary that the same *ḥukm* be applicable here. This is also the opinion of al-Shāfiʿī.

There is no disagreement among all of them that emancipation by a person who has not attained puberty is not valid, unless it is a part of a bequest, or by a person interdicted (*maḥjūr*), who is not permitted to emancipate any of his slaves, except that Mālik and his disciples permitted him to emancipate the slave-girl who is the mother of his child (*umm al-walad*).

In the case of the *marīḍ* (one seriously ill), the majority maintain that his act of emancipation takes effect if he recovers from his illness, but if he dies it is effective up to a third of his estate. The Ẓāhirites said that his act of manumission is the same as that of a healthy person. The reliance of the majority is on the tradition of ʿImrān ibn Ḥuṣayn about the person manumitting six slaves, which has preceded.

The persons compelled to emancipate their slaves constitute three cases of those who make a partial emancipation. One of these cases is agreed upon while two are disputed. These (two disputed cases) are: the case of one who comes to own the person who has to be legally emancipated (like owning his mother), and the person who maims his slave. Those who make a partial emancipation are of two kinds. First, is the case of the person who emancipates his slave, but does not own more than a part of him. The second is the case of a person who owns the slave in full, but chooses to emancipate him in part.

The jurists differed about the *ḥukm* of the slave owned by two men, one of whom manumits him to the extent of his share. Mālik, al-Shāfiʿī and Aḥmad ibn Ḥanbal said that if the emancipator is financially sound the share of his co-owner is evaluated fairly and he pays it to him, freeing the slave completely. In such a case the *walāʾ* belongs to him. If the emancipator is in financial straits, he is not obliged to pay anything, and the freed person remains a slave in part, and his *aḥkām* would be the those of a slave. Abū Yūsuf and Muḥammad said that if he (the emancipator) is facing financial difficulties, the slave is to work for his value for the owner who did not emancipate his share of the slave, but he is a free man the day the first person liberated his share; his *walāʾ* belongs to the first. This was the opinion of al-Awzāʿī, Ibn Shubrama, Ibn Abī Laylā and a group of Kūfī jurists, except that Ibn Shubrama and Ibn Abī Laylā stipulated that the slave has recourse to the first owner for the amount of work he has done, when his financial condition improves.

The majority maintain about the co-owner who has not emancipated his share that he has an option between setting free his share or having it evaluated. Abū Ḥanīfa said that the partner who is financially sound has three options. First, to free his share just as his partner has set free his; the *walāʿ*

would then be shared by them. There is no dispute about this among them (the Ḥanafites). The second option is that he has his share valued. Third, that he asks the slave to work for it, the *walāʾ* being shared by them. The first person who emancipated him, when he pays the valued share, may ask the slave to work for what he has paid and the *walāʾ* will belong to him completely.

The reliance of Mālik and al-Shāfiᶜī is on the tradition of Ibn ᶜUmar that the Messenger of Allāh (God's peace and blessings be upon him) said, "One who emancipates a slave in whom he has a share, and he possesses wealth that is equal to the price of the slave, he is to be asked to pay a fair valuation. He pays the co-owners their shares, and the slave is freed on his account, otherwise the slave is free to the extent he is freed". The reliance of Muḥammad and Abū Yūsuf, the disciples of Abū Ḥanīfa, and of those who uphold their opinion is the tradition of Abū Hurayra that the Prophet (God's peace and blessings be upon him) said, "One who manumits a part of a slave that he owns, may have him released with his wealth, if he has wealth, but if he does not have it the slave is to be asked to work for it without hardship". Both traditions have been recorded by the recorders of *ṣaḥīḥ* traditions, al-Bukhārī, Muslim and others besides them.

Each party has reasons for the preference of the tradition adopted by it. The Kūfīs declined the tradition of Ibn ᶜUmar on account of the fact that some of its narrators doubted the source of the final words not found in the tradition of Abū Hurayra, namely "Otherwise the slave is free to the extent he is freed", whether these are the words of the Prophet or the words of Nāfiᶜ. In addition, there is a difference of words used in its different versions. What the Mālikites consider as weak in the tradition of Abū Hurayra is that some of the narrators from Qatāda reported different words about work (by the slave). As a rational argument, the Mālikites relied on the fact that payment of the valued share is binding on the (first) owner, if he has wealth, due to the damage he has caused to his partner, while the slave has caused no harm to him, so nothing is binding on him. The argument of the Kūfīs, by way of reason, is that freedom is an indivisible legal right. If the emancipating partner is well off the entire emancipation becomes his liability, but if he is in difficult circumstances, the slave works for his (remaining) value. There is no harm in this ruling to the co-owner and no harm is done to the slave. Perhaps, they introduced *qiyās al-shabah* saying that as emancipation is found in the law in two forms—one form occurring through choice, which is the emancipation of the slave by his master seeking the favour of Allāh, and another form that is not voluntary, which is compelling the master to free a slave whom he cannot own legally—it is necessary that freedom through work be the same. The emancipation that is voluntary is through *kitāba*, while that which is not voluntary is through work.

Mālik and al-Shāfiʿī, in one of his opinions, differed when the emancipator is in difficult straits, whether the emancipation of the share of his co-owner is to be imposed upon him through a judicial decree or by the coming into effect of the *ḥukm*, that is, the obligation of (total) emancipation passes on to him by the very act of emancipation. The Shāfiʿites said that he is freed through the application of the *ḥukm*, while the Mālikites said that it is decreed. The Mālikites argued that had it been obligatory through application of the *ḥukm*, it would have been applicable in times of hardship and ease. The Shāfiʿites argued on the basis of the binding nature of the words of the Prophet (God's peace and blessings be upon him), "he is to be asked to pay a fair valuation". They argued that things that are subject to valuation are valued after their destruction, and he has destroyed the share of his co-owner by the very act of emancipation. He is, thus, obliged to pay fair valuation at the time of such destruction, even if the judge has not decreed this to be so. The co-owner, therefore, has no right to manumit his share, as manumission has become effective. This is evident.

Abū Ḥanīfa's opinion in this issue goes against the apparent meaning of the two traditions. Other isolated cases of disagreement are also reported. It is related from Ibn Sīrīn that he considered the share of the co-owner to be the liability of the *bayt al-māl* (treasury). It is related from Rabīʿa, about a person manumitting a share that he has in a slave, that the manumission is void. One group said that the whole value is not to be the liability of a person who is in financial straits and manumission is to be valid in what he has manumitted. Another group maintained that it is obligatory to hold the manumitter liable through valuation, whether he is in difficult straits or in financial ease, and the co-owner has recourse to him. In some narrations of the tradition of Ibn ʿUmar, the words "financial straits" have been dropped. All this is a disagreement based on the differences in traditions; perhaps, all the traditions did not reach them. Mālik's opinion in one issue, out of these, has differed, which is the case of a person in difficult straits. The *ḥukm* (in his case) was deferred by delaying evaluation till such time that he attained financial ease. It is said that he is liable for a fair value, while it is said that he is not.

Those who adopted these traditions agreed that if a person acquires, of his own volition, a share in a slave who is to be set free automatically, the remaining share in the slave is also set free on his account, in case he is in financial ease. If, however, he acquires the share without choice, as in the case of inheriting a share in the slave, a group said that the remaining part of the slave is set free on his account when he is in financial ease. Another group said that the manumission is not on his account, while a third group said that he is manumitted on his account with the condition of work (on the part of the slave), yet another group said that manumission does not take place at all.

If the master owns the entire slave and manumits part of him, then, the majority of the jurists of Hijāz and Iraq—Mālik, al-Shāfiʿī, al-Thawrī, al-Awzāʿī, Aḥmad, Ibn Abī Laylā, Muḥammad ibn al-Ḥasan and Abū Yūsuf—say that the entire slave is set free. Abū Ḥanīfa and the Ẓāhirites said that only the part manumitted by him is free and the slave works for the rest. This is also the opinion of Ṭāwūs and Ḥammād. The basis for the argument of the majority is that as the *sunna* has established the manumission of the share of another person in the case of a shared slave, due to the sanctity of manumission, it is appropriate that it be obligatory when he is the sole owner. Abū Ḥanīfa's argument is that the basis for the obligation of manumission on the person who divides up manumission is the harm that is likely to be caused to the co-owner, in the case of a shared slave, but when the entire ownership is his own there is no harm to others. In short, the basis for disagreement, through rational reasoning, is whether the ʿ*illa* (underlying cause) of this *ḥukm* is the integrity of manumission, that is, division should not occur in it, or it is the harm caused to the co-owner.

The Ḥanafites (Abū Ḥanīfa alone in this case) argued on the basis of what has been related from Ismāʿīl ibn Umayya from his father from his grandfather that he emancipated a part of his slave and the Messenger of Allāh (God's peace and blessings be upon him) did not disapprove such emancipation. Among the proofs of the majority is what has been recorded by al-Nasāʾī and Abū Dāwūd from Abū al-Malīḥ from his father "that a member of (the tribe of) Hudhayl emancipated part of one of his slaves, so the Prophet (God's peace and blessings be upon him) completed his emancipation saying, 'There is no partner for Allāh' ". In this way he explicitly stated the underlying cause (ʿ*illa*) adopted by the majority. This ʿ*illa* was superior, as the ʿ*illa* mentioned expressly is superior to the one that is derived. The reason for their disagreement, thus, is the conflict of traditions pertaining to this topic and the conflict of *qiyās*.

The jurists disagreed about manumission resulting from maiming. Mālik, al-Layth and al-Awzāʿī said that if a person maims his slave, he is emancipated on his account. Abū Ḥanīfa and al-Shāfiʿī said that he is not emancipated. Al-Awzāʿī gave an isolated opinion saying that if a person maims another's slave, he is set free on his account, while the majority maintain that he compensates the loss he causes in the value of the slave. Mālik, and those who adopted his opinion, relied on the tradition of ʿAmr ibn Shuʿayb from his father from his grandfather "that a person found one of his slaves in a compromising position with his slave-girl, so he cut off his penis and severed his nose. He came to the Prophet (God's peace and blessings be upon him) and mentioned this to him. He asked the man, 'What led you to do this?' He (the man) said that he did such and such a thing. The Prophet (God's peace and blessings be upon him) said to him (the slave), 'Go! You are a free man' ". The source for the other party are the words of the Prophet (God's peace and blessings be upon him), in the tradition of Ibn ᶜUmar, "One who slaps his slave or strikes him, the expiation for him is manumission".

They said that he did not consider manumission binding in this, but merely a recommendation. They maintain as a rational argument that the principle in law is that the master is not to be coerced into freeing his slave, unless (the principle) is restricted by evidence (*dalīl*). The traditions from ᶜAmr ibn Shuᶜayb are disputed as to their authenticity and did not attain the strength to restrict such a principle.

Now a question is, does a slave, who is the kin of the owner, become free automatically once he falls into the ownership of his relative? If so, then, who is (the relative) to be emancipated in this way? They differed about this. The majority of the jurists, except Dāwūd and his disciples, maintained that emancipation of a slave, who is a relative, is to take place once he is owned by him. Dāwūd and his disciples did not hold the view that a person is to be emancipated once he is owned by a close relation. Those who upheld emancipation differed about who was to be set free and who was not after agreeing that a man's parents and his children are to be set free once any of them falls into his ownership.

Mālik said that three categories of relatives are to be set free. First, the ascendants. They are fathers, grandfathers, grandmothers, mothers and their fathers and mothers. In fact, any one who is linked to the person through paternity. Second are the descendants. These are the sons and daughters and their children, howsoever low (in descent), and whether they are males of females. As a whole, all those with whom the person is linked through paternity, whether direct or indirect and whether they are males or females. Third are those who share his paternity with him through the same ascendants. These are his brethren, whether german, consanguine or uterine. He confined himself to persons related to each other through direct parenthood and did not hold the emancipation of the brethren's children as obligatory.

Al-Shāfiᶜī held an opinion similar to Mālik's with respect to the ascendants and descendants, but he disagreed with him about brethren and did not deem their emancipation as obligatory. Abū Ḥanīfa, on the other hand, held as obligatory the emancipation of all blood relatives in the lineage including paternal uncles and aunts, maternal uncles and aunts, brethren's children, and all those who resembled these categories, and who fall in the prohibited degrees for marriage.

The reason for the disagreement of the Ẓāhirites with the majority is their difference over the meaning of the established tradition, comprising the words of the Prophet (God's peace and blessings be upon him), "A son is not to be given compensation by his father, unless he found him enslaved, bought him, and emancipated him". It is recorded by Muslim, al-Tirmidhī, Abū Dāwūd and others. The majority said that it is understood from this tradition that if he buys him it is obligatory on him to emancipate him, but purchasing him is not obligatory on him. The Ẓāhirites said that the meaning of this tradition is that it is neither obligatory on him to purchase him nor to set him free, and attributing manumission to him is evidence of the validity of his ownership. If what they (the majority) say had been correct, the words would have been "if he purchases him, let him set him free". The reliance of the Ḥanafites is on what has been related by Qatāda from al-Ḥasan from Samura that the Prophet (God's peace and blessings be upon him) said, "If anyone owns a relative, he is free". This tradition was apparently not deemed authentic by Mālik and al-Shāfiʿī. Mālik viewed the brethren through the analogy of children and parents. Al-Shāfiʿī did not consider the brethren as similar to parents, but did hold children to be similar to parents.

The Mālikites aspired to argue for their school on the ground that sonship (*bunwwa*) is an attribute that is the opposite of servility (*ʿubūdiyya*) and, therefore, cannot be combined with it due to the words of the Exalted, "When it is not meet for (the Majesty of) the Beneficent that he should choose a son. There is none in the heavens and the earth but cometh unto the Beneficent as a slave".[205] This "servility" has a meaning different from the "servility" on the basis of which they argue. This servility is subject to reasoning and so is sonship, but the servility that exists between the creatures and their Master is servility stipulated by revelation and not by reason, and by stipulation I mean that which is without the influence of reason, as is assumed by them. It is a weak argument. Allāh, in fact, has deemed sonship to be the same as paternity by genus of their existence, or of kind, that is, the two in existence, one of them a father and the other a son, are very close to each other, so much so that they are either of the same genus or of the same category, while there is none among creatures who can share anything with Allāh from near or from far. In fact, the dissimilarity between them (Allāh and His creation) is the utmost possible. It is, thus, not correct that there be among the things in existence here an association with Him like that between the father and the son. On the other hand, if the relationship of the creatures with Him had been compared with the relationship of a slave with his master, it would have been closer to the truth of the matter rather than the relationship between a father and his son, as the disparity between the master and his slave is of a much more acute than that between the father and his son. The truth is that there

[205] Qurʾān 19:92-93

is no similarity between the two relationships. Yet, as there is not, in the existing realities, a relationship with a greater disparity than this, a disparity as to being noble at one end or base at the other end, that is, in the relationship of the master and his slave, it becomes exemplary. Those who saw love, mercy, sympathy and compassion in the relationship of a father and his son, permitted, according to the religion of Jesus (ᶜĪsā), the saying that some people are the sons of Allāh. These are all the issues related to emancipation that is imposed upon a person without his own volition.

They disagreed about the *aḥkām* of emancipation in an issue that relates to transmission. They disagreed about the person who freed his slaves during his illness, or made such freedom subject to his death, when he had no wealth beside them. Mālik, al-Shāfiᶜī, their disciples, Aḥmad and a group said that if he manumitted them during his illness and had no other wealth beside them, they are to be split up into three groups and one group from among them is to be freed, after his death, by drawing lots, and the same is their *ḥukm* in the case of a bequest (*waṣiyya*). Ashhab and Aṣbagh opposed Mālik in terminal manumission through illness, saying that the drawing of lots relates to bequest, while the *ḥukm* of this terminal manumission is like that of the *mudabbar* slave.

There is no disagreement in Mālik's school that if *mudabbars* are emancipated at the same time and the third of the estate is insufficient (to free them), a part of each is manumitted from the third, to the extent of the share of each in the third. Abū Ḥanīfa and his disciples maintained in this terminal manumission that if the third is insufficient, a third part of each is manumitted, while others said that a third part of the entire (number) is manumitted. Some, among them, took into account a third of the value of the entire (number), which is the opinion of Mālik and al-Shāfiᶜī, while others considered the number. According to Mālik, if there were six slaves, for example, a third of them would be manumitted by value, which may amount to two of them, or less, or more. A group said that the consideration is for number, thus, if there were six, two of them would be manumitted, and if there were seven, two and a third from among them would be manumitted—this too would be by the drawing of lots, after they had been split up into three groups.

The reliance of the jurists of Ḥijāz is what is related by the people of Baṣra from ᶜImrān ibn al-Ḥuṣayn "that a man freed six slaves close to his death and he had no other wealth. The Messenger of Allāh (God's peace and blessings be upon him) was consulted, and he divided them into three groups and then drew lots between them freeing two and keeping four enslaved". It is recorded by al-Bukhārī and Muslim with complete chains, but with a *mursal isnād* by Mālik. The reliance of the Ḥanafites, in accordance with their practice of rejecting traditions transmitted through single *isnād* (*khabar aḥād*) when they opposed established principles based on *tawātur*, is that the master made total manumission obligatory for each one of them and if he had owned (sufficient) wealth this would be implemented (*in toto*) on the basis of consensus, but when he does not possess sufficient wealth, it is obligatory that the (legal) act of the master be implemented for each one them to the extent of the permissible third. This principle, however, is not clearly applicable to this case in the rules of the law. It is possible to say that if a third of each one of them is manumitted it would be harmful for the heirs and the manumitted slaves, and the law has made it obligatory for one undertaking partial manumission to complete it, and as there is no one here to complete it, it is better to gather it in a few determined individuals, but when value is taken into account and not the number the transaction leads again to this situation of partial manumission. It is, therefore, better to consider number, which is the meaning in the tradition also. The manumitted part in each one of them is the right of Allāh and it is necessary that it be assimilated in some specified individuals, its basis being the rights of humans.

They disagreed about the wealth of the slave, when he is manumitted, as to whom it will belong. A group said that the wealth is for the master, while another group said that his wealth follows him. The first view was upheld by Ibn Masʿūd, from among the Companions, and of Abū Ḥanīfa from among the *fuqahāʾ* along with al-Thawrī, Aḥmad, and Isḥāq. The second view was that of Ibn ʿUmar, ʿĀʾisha, al-Ḥasan, ʿAṭāʾ, Mālik and the jurists of Madīna, the proof for them being the tradition of Ibn ʿUmar that the Prophet (God's peace and blessings be upon him) said, "(In the case of) one who manumits a slave, the wealth (of the slave) belongs to him (the slave), unless the master stipulates (retaining) his wealth".

The words (legal form) of emancipation may be unequivocal or indirect according to most of the jurists of the regions. Unequivocal words are like saying, "you are free" or "you are manumitted" or derivatives of the root meaning of the words "freedom" and "manumission". These words are binding for the master by the consensus of the jurists. Indirect expressions are like a master saying to his slave, "I have no hold over you" or "I have no ownership in you". In these, according to the majority, the slave elicits the intention of the master irrespective of his intention to manumit. They disagreed, however, in the case where the master addresses his slave as "my son or his slave-girl as "my daughter", or he says "O! my father" or "O! my mother". A group held, and they are the majority, that manumission is not binding on him. Abū Ḥanīfa said they are to be manumitted on his account. Zufar held an deviant opinion saying that if the master says of his slave, "this is my son", then the slave is to be freed, even if the slave is twenty years old and the master is thirty.

Within this topic is their disagreement about a person who says to his slave, "you are none, but a freeman". A group, and these are the majority, said that this is praise for him (a courtesy), while a group said that he becomes a free man, which is the opinion of al-Ḥasan al-Baṣrī. Within these issues is also the case of a person calling out to his slave by name, when another (another one of his slaves) answers and he says to him, "you are free", but he says that I had intended the other. It is said that both are to be set free, while it is said that his intention is to be elicited. They agreed that one who manumits what is in the womb of his slave-girl, he is free to the exclusion of the slave-girl (the mother). They disagreed over the case in which the master emancipates his slave-girl, but exempts what is in her womb. A group said that he has the right to make an exemption, while another group said that both are free.

They disagreed about manumission conditional upon the will of Allāh. A group said that there is no proviso in this as in the case of divorce, which is the opinion of Mālik. Another group said that provisos are effective in it, and they maintain the same in the case of divorce. I mean by this a person saying to his slave, "You are free, God willing". Similarly, they differed about the occurrence of manumission with the condition of ownership. Mālik said it takes place, while al-Shāfiʿī and others said it does not. Their proof is in the words of the Prophet (God's peace and blessings be upon him), "There is no manumission in what is not owned by the son of Adam". The argument of the second group lies in its resemblance with *yamīn* (oath).

The words in this topic resemble those in the subject of divorce and its conditions are like the conditions of divorce. So also oaths in it are similar to oaths in divorce. As to its *aḥkām*, these are many. Among these, according to the majority, is that children follow their mother in emancipation and slavery. A group differed and said, "Except when the father is an Arab". There is disagreement about manumission effective at a future date. A group said that he has no right (in this period) to have intercourse with her, to sell her, or to gift her away. This was upheld by Mālik. A group said that he has all these rights, which was the opinion of al-Awzāʿī and al-Shāfiʿī.

They agreed about the stipulation of service for a determined period (to be performed) by the manumitted person before or after manumission, but they disagreed about the person who said to his slave, "If I sell you, you are a free man". A group said that this is not effective as after he has sold him he does not have the right to manumit him. Others said that if he sells him, he is to be set free on his account, that is, from the wealth of the seller when he sells him. This is the opinion of Mālik and al-Shāfiʿī. The former was held by Abū Ḥanīfa, his disciples and al-Thawrī. The cases in this chapter are many, but this is sufficient.

LIII
THE BOOK OF *KITĀBA* (MANUMISSION BY CONTRACT)

A comprehensive examination of *kitāba* covers its elements, conditions, and *aḥkām*. The elements are three: the contract, its conditions, and characteristics; the contracting party and his attributes; and the subject-matter of the contract and its description. In each of these categories, we shall mention the issues that were well known among the jurists of the regions.

53.1. Chapter 1: Issues Related to the Contract

Among the well-known issues in this category is their disagreement about the contract of *kitāba*, whether it is obligatory (*wājib*) or recommended (*mandūb*). The jurists of the various regions said that it is recommended, while the Ẓāhirites said it is obligatory. They argued on the basis of the words of the Exalted, "And such of your slaves as seek a writing (of emancipation), write it out for them if ye are aware of aught of good in them",[206] saying that the command (*amr*) here implies an obligation. When the majority considered the principle that no one is to be forced to emancipate his slaves, they interpreted the verse to indicate a recommendation, so that it would not conflict with this principle. Further, as the slave has no right to demand a decree for his (own) sale, which amounts to the passing of his corpus from his ownership with compensation, it is appropriate that he have no right to ask for a decree for passing out of his ownership without compensation, for he is his owner and the services of the slave belong to the master. This issue is closely related to the *aḥkām* of this contract rather than to its elements.

The contract in general means that the slave purchases himself and his wealth from his master with the wealth that the slave earns. Thus, the elements of this contract comprise the price, the object of the price, the period (of payment), and the words that indicate the contract. They agreed about the price that it is valid if it can be ascertained with the (same) knowledge that is stipulated for sales. They disagreed when the form of words employed

[206] Qur'ān 24:33

contains some ambiguity. Abū Ḥanīfa and Mālik said that it is permitted if he contracts *kitāba* with his slave in consideration (payment) of a slave-girl or a male slave without describing them as long as they are considered average among slaves. Al-Shāfiʿī said that it is not permitted unless he describes clearly the slave to be presented as consideration for his freedom. Those who required examination of the slave to be offered as a price held it similar to sales, while those who viewed its object as generosity and a lack of avarice, permitted a small degree of *gharar* in it, as is the case in dower (*ṣadāq*). Mālik permits, between a slave and his master in *mukātaba*, even a certain amount of *ribā* that would not be permitted between strangers, like the sale of food before taking possession, the cancellation of a debt with a debt, and discount for early payment. Al-Shāfiʿī and Aḥmad prohibited this. Both opinions are related from Abū Ḥanīfa. The reliance of those who permitted it, saying that there is no *ribā* between a master and his slave, is (on the argument) that he and his wealth belong to the master and that *kitāba* in itself is a *sunna*.

They agreed about the period that it is permitted with a delay, but disagreed whether it could be immediate, and this, after their agreement that it is permitted immediately for the wealth that is in the possession of the slave, which is referred to as *qiṭāʿa* not *kitāba*. It is in *kitāba* that the slave stipulates to purchase himself and his wealth from his master with wealth that he will earn. The point of disagreement is whether it is permitted that he purchase himself from his master with wealth that is not in his possession. Al-Shāfiʿī said that this is futile talk and nothing is binding upon the master in this case. The later Mālikites said that the *kitāba* becomes binding upon the master and the slave has a right to take up the issue with the judge and present before him wealth in accordance with the situation of the slave. The argument of the Mālikites is that the master obliged the slave to enter into *kitāba*, except that he stipulated in it a condition, which becomes an obstacle, thus, the contract is valid and the condition is void. The argument of the Shāfiʿites is that an invalid condition leads to the vitiation of the contract, like a person selling a slave-girl stipulates that he (the buyer) will not have intercourse with her as he did not have wealth in hand; thus, it leads to an inability and is contrary to the purpose of *kitāba*. The thrust of the Mālikite opinion is that a period is one of the elements of *kitāba*, and if something contrary to this element is stipulated, the condition is void and the contract is valid.

They agreed that if the master says to his slave, "I have entered into *kitāba* with you for a thousand *dirhams*, when you pay it you are free", the slave is free if he pays it. They disagreed if he says to him, "I have entered into *kitāba* with you for one thousand *dirhams*", but remains silent about whether he would be free or not, not saying "you are free if you pay it". Mālik and Abū Ḥanīfa say that he is free as *kitāba* is a legal term and invokes all its *aḥkām*.

A group said that he is not free unless the master pronounces the words unequivocally. The opinion of Al-Shāfiʿī varied in this. Within this topic is the conflict of Ibn al-Qāsim's and Mālik's opinions about the person who says to his slave, "you are free and a thousand *dīnārs* are due from you". The school differed about this with Mālik saying that the payment is binding upon him and he is free. Ibn al-Qāsim said that he is free, but payment is not binding upon him. On the other hand, when he says, "you are free on the condition that you owe a thousand *dīnārs*", the school differed about this with Mālik saying that he is free and he owes the money like any other debtor. It is also said that the slave has an option, if he chooses freedom the payment becomes due and emancipation is effective, otherwise he remains a slave. Another opinion maintains that if he accepts, it amounts to *kitāba* and he will be freed upon payment. Both opinions are Ibn al-Qāsim's.

Kitāba is valid, according to Mālik, on the basis of specified work, and it is also permitted according to him without qualification, in which case it reverts to a reasonable *kitāba*, as is the case (of dower) in marriage (*nikāḥ*). *Kitāba* is also permitted, according to him, for the value of the slave, I mean, reasonable *kitāba* with respect to time and price. It was due to this that it was said he permitted immediate *kitāba*.

They disagreed whether it was a condition of *kitāba* that the master reduce some of the payment of *kitāba* on the completion of the payment, because of their disagreement about the meaning of the words of the Exalted, "And bestow upon them of the wealth of Allāh which He hath bestowed upon you".[207] The reason is that some of them were of the view that it is the masters who are the addressees in this verse, while others said that it is the community of Muslims to whom a recommendation has been made to assist the *mukātab* slaves. Those who held this view disagreed whether it contained an obligation or recommendation. Those who held the former opinion differed about the amount of the obligation. Some said it should be a reasonable sum, while others fixed it.

Several issues relate to the *mukātab*. Among them is whether *kitāba* with adolescents is valid, and whether in a single contract of *kitāba* more than one slave can be included. Whether *kitāba* with a slave who is partly owned is valid without the permission of the co-owner. Whether *kitāba* with a slave, who is unable to work, is valid. Whether *kitāba* with a person, who is part slave, is valid.

In the case of the adolescent, who had not attained puberty, but was strong and able to work, Abū Ḥanīfa permitted *kitāba*, while al-Shafiʿī prohibited it, except for those who had attained puberty. From Mālik both views are related.

[207] Qurʾān 24:32

The argument of those who stipulate puberty is the comparison with the rest of the contracts. The argument of those who did not stipulate it is that things are permitted between master and slave that are not permitted between strangers, and the the important factor is the ability to work, which may be present in one who has not attained puberty.

Can more than one slave be included in a single *kitāba*? The jurists disagreed about this. Further, when we uphold inclusion, are they become sureties for each other through the same *kitāba*, so that none is emancipated until all are emancipated together? There is disagreement in this too. With respect to the permissibility of inclusion, the majority uphold it, while a group prohibited it, which is one of the opinions of al-Shāfiᶜī. Do some stand surety for others? There are three opinions about this from those who upheld inclusion. A group said that this is implied by the contract of *kitāba*, that is, they will stand surety for each other. This was the opinion of Mālik and Sufyān. Others said that it is not binding by the absolute contract, but it is through a stipulated condition. This was Abū Ḥanīfa's opinion and that of his disciples. Al-Shāfiᶜī said that it is not permitted, either by the implication of the contract or by stipulation, and each is emancipated by the payment of his proportional share.

The basis for those who rejected the ruling of becoming sureties is the element of *gharar* in it, as the amounts that are due from each are unknown. The basis for those who permitted this is that minor *gharar* to be tolerated for purposes of *kitāba*, as it is a transaction between a master and his slave, and the slave and his wealth belong to the master. Mālik's argument is that as it is a single *kitāba*, it follows that the *ḥukm* for all of them be that for a single person. The argument of the Shāfiᶜites is that surety of one them for the other is just like the surety of one stranger for another, and those who held that the surety of one stranger for another is not valid said that it is not permitted on this occasion either. They denied surety in *kitāba* as in case of the inability of the *mukātab* the surety would have recourse to nothing. This does not appear to be so from the surety of the slaves, one for the other; what is apparent is that the condition is the cause, for one who is not able to work is hindered by the inability of one who is not. This is *gharar* specific to *kitāba*. It may also be said that inclusion may lead to the emancipation of those who are unable to work in order that they be free. Just as it results in the (continued) enslavement of those who can work, it causes the emancipation of those who cannot. Abū Ḥanīfa held it to be similar to the surety of a stranger for another stranger, in cases where surety is permitted, and made it binding through a condition, though he still does not permit surety in *kitāba* generally.

The jurists disagreed about two co-owners of a slave, whether one of them can contract *kitāba* for his share without the permission of his partner. Some said that he does not have this right and the *kitāba* would be void, and what he gains from it is to be shared between them according to their shares. A group said that it is not permitted to a person to contract *kitāba* for his share to the exclusion of the share of the other co-owner. One group made a distinction saying it is permitted with the permission of the co-owner, but it is not valid without his permission. The first opinion was held by Mālik, the second by Ibn Abī Laylā and Aḥmad, and the third by Abū Ḥanīfa and al-Shāfiʿī, in one of his opinions; he has another opinion similar to that of Mālik.

Mālik's argument is that if this were to be permitted, it would lead to the complete emancipation of the slave through valuation in favour of the person who contracted the *kitāba* for his share. This is not permitted, except in the division of emancipation. Those who held the view that he has right to contract *kitāba*, maintained that he is to complete the emancipation if the slave makes the payment, provided he is financially sound. Mālik's argument here is based on a principle, which is not agreed to by his opponents, but that does not affect the soundness of the principle itself. The stipulation of a condition, however, is weak. Abū Ḥanīfa maintains, about the mode of payment to the *mukātib* (master), when the *kitāba* is with the permission of his co-owner, that whatever is paid to the co-owner who contracted the *kitāba*, the other co-owner takes out of it his share and recovers the remaining from the slave who works for him till such time that the agreed payment is completed. In this there is an estrangement from the principles.

Is the *kitāba* of one who is unable to work valid? There is no disagreement, as far as I know, among them that a condition for the *mukātab* is that he should be strong enough to work, due to the words of the Exalted, "[I]f ye are aware of aught of good in them".[208] They differed about the meaning of the term "*khayr*" (good) in the text. Al-Shāfiʿī said it means work and reliability, while some of them said it means wealth and reliability. Others said that it means right conduct and the observance of *dīn*. Some denied *kitāba* for those who did not have a skill, for fear that they would start begging, while others permitted this due to the tradition of Barīra that "she was granted *kitāba* in a state when she needed to ask from others". Mālik considered as abominable the *kitāba* of a female slave, when she did not have an income through a skill for fear that it might lead her to prostitute herself. Mālik permitted the *kitāba* of the *mudabbara* and all those who were partly slaves, except the *umm al-walad*, as he (the master) had no right to use her for services.

[208] Qurʾān 24:33

53.2. Chapter 2: The Parties to the Contract

They agreed that one of the conditions for the *mukātib* (master) is that he should be the owner, with a valid ownership, should not be under interdiction, and be in possession of a sound body (not a *marīḍ*). They disagreed whether a *mukātab* could enter into *kitāba* with his slave. This discussion will come up when we consider what is permitted to the *mukātab* and what is not. Mālik did not permit that a slave authorized to trade (*mā'dhūn*) should contract *kitāba* with another slave, as *kitāba* is manumission and he is not permitted to manumit. Similarly, *kitāba* by one whose assets are immersed in debt is not permitted, except when the creditors grant permission, and the payment of *kitāba* consists of something that can be a substitute of the slave. The *kitāba* of the *marīḍ* is valid, according to him, up to a third. The whole question is to be suspended till he recovers, in which case it would be valid; but if he dies, it would take effect out of a third, being the same as manumission. It is said that if he can oblige with payment it is accepted, but if he cannot, he works for it; if he makes the payment while he (the master) is ill, it amounts to manumission. The *kitāba* of a Christian with a Muslim is valid, according to him, and he (the Muslim *mukātab*) is to be sold out as in the case of an ordinary slave (so that he does not remain a slave of the Christian).

These, then, are the well-known issues that are related to the elements, that is, the *mukātib*, *mukātab*, and *kitāba*. The *aḥkām* are many, as are the conditions, whether permissible or prohibited. It appears that the foremost *aḥkām* of this contract would be: when is the *mukātab* emancipated, when is he enslaved due to inability (to pay), what is his legal position if he dies before he is emancipated or re-enslaved, who is included with him in the *kitāba* and who is not, and the distinction between what is left out of the restrictions of slavery and what is not? We begin by mentioning the issues of the *aḥkām* in each category out of these five categories.

53.2.1 Category 1

When is he emancipated? They agreed that he is emancipated on paying the entire value of the *kitāba*. They disagreed when he is unable to pay part of it, but has paid the rest. The majority say that he is a slave as long as some part of the *kitāba* remains, and is to be enslaved if he is unable to pay it. From the earlier jurists four opinions, besides the opinion of the majority, are related. First, the *mukātab* is emancipated by the very act of *kitāba*. Second, he is free to the extent that he has made the payment. Third, he is emancipated if he has paid half or more than that. Fourth, he is free if he has paid a third, otherwise he remains a slave.

The reliance of the majority is on what has been recorded by Abū Dāwūd from ʿAmr ibn Shuʿayb from his father from his grandfather that the Prophet

(God's peace and blessings be upon him) said, "Any slave who is granted a *kitāba* for a hundred ounces and pays all except ten ounces remains a slave, and any slave who is granted a *kitāba* for a hundred *dīnārs* and he pays all except ten *dīnārs* remains a slave". The reliance of those who hold that he is emancipated by the contract itself is on its similarity with sale. It is as if the *mukātab* had purchased himself from his master and the buyer being unable to pay, the seller has no recourse to him except to share his wealth, just as one who purchased him from him on credit becomes insolvent and then dies. The reliance of those who maintained that he is set free to the extent of what he has paid is what has been related by Yahyā ibn Kathīr from ᶜIkrima from ibn ᶜAbbās that the Prophet (God's peace and blessings be upon him) said "For the *mukātab* is paid the *diya* of a free man to the extent that he has paid and the *diya* of a slave for the part that of him that is still a slave". It is recorded by al-Nasāʾī. The disagreement in it is related to ᶜIkrima, just as the disagreement in the tradition of ᶜAmr ibn Shuᶜayb is related to the fact that he related from a written *ṣaḥīfa*. This opinion was upheld by ᶜAlī, that is, the one in the tradition of Ibn ᶜAbbās. It is related from ᶜUmar ibn al-Khaṭṭāb (who said) that if he pays a part of what is owed he is emancipated. Ibn Masᶜūd used to say (he is emancipated if he pays) a third. The opinions of the Companions, though they are not a *ḥujja*, yet it is manifest that a verdict issued by them is to be interpreted as containing a *sunna*, which must have reached them.

In this issue there is a fifth opinion. If he pays three-fourths, he is emancipated and remains a debtor without means for purposes of the remaining fourth. It is said that if he has paid to the extent of his value, he remains a debtor (for the remaining and is emancipated). This is the opinion of ᶜĀʾisha, Ibn ᶜUmar, and Zayd ibn Thābit. The well-known opinion from Ibn ᶜUmar and from Umm Salama is like the opinion of the majority, and it is their opinion that the jurists of the various regions have relied upon. This is so as the narrations from them are authentic beyond doubt, and are related by Mālik in his *Muwaṭṭaʾ*. In addition, it reflects care for the wealth of the masters, and also because in sold commodities the recourse is to the corpus of the sale when the buyer becomes insolvent.

53.2.2. Category 2

They agreed that he is enslaved when he is unable to make part of the payment or the whole of it, in accordance with their disagreements we have presented earlier. They disagreed whether the slave has the right to declare his inability on his own, without any reason, or that he has no such right except for a reason. Al-Shāfiᶜī said that *kitāba* is a contract binding upon the slave, but it is not binding upon the master. Mālik and Abū Ḥanīfa said that *kitāba* is a contract that is binding on both, that is, the master and the slave. The conclusion from Mālik's opinions is that the master and the slave may either agree upon the slave's inability or they may disagree. If they differ, then it may be the master who claims the inability of the slave, while the slave denies it, or *vice versa*, that is, the master desires the existence of *kitāba*, while the slave claims inability. If they agree upon inability, the issue falls into two cases. First, that a child has entered (been born) into the *kitāba*, or it has not. If a child has entered into the *kitāba*, there is no disagreement, according to him, that inability is not permitted. If there is no child, then, there are two opinions related from him. First, that it is not permitted if he possesses wealth, which was also Abū Ḥanīfa's opinion. Second, that it is permitted to him to claim it. If, however, the slave is claiming inability and the master is denying it, the slave has no right to do so if he possesses wealth or has the capacity to work. On the other hand, if the master claims inability with the slave denying it, he cannot impose inability on him, except by the decree of the judge. This he can do by establishing that he (the slave) has no wealth nor the capacity to work.

We refer now to the reliance for their evidence on the actual point of disagreement over the issue. The reliance of Al-Shāfiʿī is on the report that "Barīra came over to ʿĀʾisha saying to her, 'I want that you should buy me and emancipate me'. She said, 'If your family (masters) are willing'. The family came and sold her while she was a *mukātaba*". It is recorded by al-Bukhārī. The reliance of the Mālikites is on the comparison with other binding contracts, and the *ḥukm* of the slave in this must be the same as that of the master, as it is in the nature of contracts that they be binding or have options equally for both parties. If they are binding for one party and not for the other, they become inconsistent with the principles. They attributed the *ʿilla* to the tradition of Barīra that what the family sold was her *kitāba* and not her corpus. The Ḥanafites say that as the predominant right in *kitāba* belongs to the slave, it is, therefore, necessary that the contract be binding with respect to the subordinate right belonging to the master; its basis being *nikāḥ*, which is not binding for the husband due to the existence of the right of *ṭalāq* that he possesses, but it is binding for the wife. The Mālikites object to this by saying that it is binding in so far as compensation has been given, for he does not have the right to recover the dower.

53.2.3. Category 3

They agreed about his *ḥukm* when he dies before paying for the *kitāba*, that is, if he dies childless without paying anything toward the *kitāba* he would be considered a slave. They disagreed when he dies leaving behind a child. Mālik said that the child's *ḥukm* is the same as his *ḥukm*. If he leaves behind wealth that can satisfy the payment of the *kitāba*, it is paid and the children are emancipated. If he does not leave behind sufficient wealth, but the children are strong enough to work, they are allowed to make the payments of their father till they express their inability to do so or are emancipated. If they neither have wealth nor the ability to work, they are to be enslaved. If something is left over from the payment of the *kitāba*, they inherit it according to the laws of inheritance applicable to free persons. Only his children, who were part of the *kitāba* are to inherit his wealth to the exclusion of the other relatives, if he had relatives other than his children, who were part of the *kitāba*. Abū Ḥanīfa said that after the payment of *kitāba* has been made, the wealth left by him is inherited by the children who were made a part of the *kitāba*, the children who were born during the period of *kitāba*, his free children, and all his heirs. Al-Shāfiʿī said that the wealth is not inherited by his free children, or by those who were made part of the *kitāba*, or those who were born during the period of the *kitāba*, and the wealth belongs to his master.

It is obligatory on his children, who have been made a part of the *kitāba*, that they work toward its fulfilment in proportion to their shares in it, and the share of the father is to be charged to them. Abū Ḥanīfa also upheld the charging of the father's share to them, as did all the jurists of Kūfa. Some, among those who upheld charging of his share, said that it is to be by value, which is the opinion of al-Shāfiʿī. It is also said that it is by price, or that it is to be per head. These jurists said that the share of the father is to be charged to the account of the sons who were part of the *kitāba*, not those who were born during the period of *kitāba*, as the children who were born during the *kitāba* take up the father's rights.

Mālik's argument is that the slaves participating in a single *kitāba* are sureties for each other, therefore, if one of them is emancipated or dies, the others are not absolved of his share. The argument of the other group is that there is no surety in *kitāba*. Mālik has also related in his *Muwaṭṭa*ʾ on the authority of ʿAbd al-Malik ibn Marwān an opinion similar to that of the Kūfīs. The reason for their disagreement is the state in which the *mukātab* dies. According to Mālik, he dies a *mukātab* and according to Abū Ḥanīfa he dies a free man, while for Al-Shāfiʿī he dies a slave. It was on these principles that they built up the *aḥkām* related to it. The reliance of al-Shāfiʿī is on the argument that between bondage and freedom there is no middle position, thus, if he dies as a *mukātab*, he is still not a free person, as freedom takes effect after he has paid for the *kitāba* and this he has not yet done. The consequence is that he dies a slave for it is not proper that a corpse be emancipated. The argument of the Ḥanafites is that freedom takes effect with his death with the existence of wealth for which he contracted *kitāba*, for it does not suit him to keep himself in bondage, and it is necessary that freedom be accessible to him with the coming into existence of the wealth, not through its actual delivery to his master. Mālik deemed his death to be a state between bondage and freedom, which is *kitāba*. In so far as his free children have not inherited from him, he is given the *ḥukm* of a slave, and if the master has not inherited from him, he is given the *ḥukm* of a free man. The issue is within the scope of *ijtihād*.

Related to this category is their disagreement of the *umm al-walad* of the *mukātab*, when the *mukātab* dies and leaves behind children who are not capable of working, and the mother decides to work on their behalf. Mālik said that she has a right to do so. Al-Shāfiʿī and the Kūfīs said that she does not have a right to do so. Their argument is that the *umm al-walad* is the property of the master when the *mukātab* dies. Mālik maintained that the protection of *kitāba* that was available to her master flows over to her and her children. There is ambiguity in Mālik's opinion that if the *mukātab* leaves behind children, who cannot work, and an *umm al-walad* who is unable to work, she is to be sold and the remaining amount of *kitāba* is to be paid. According to Abū Yūsuf and Muḥammad ibn al-Ḥasan, it is not permitted to the *mukātab* to sell his *umm al-walad*, while it is permitted according to Abū Ḥanīfa and al-Shāfiʿī.

Mālik's disciples differed about the *umm al-walad* of the *mukātab*, when the *mukātab* dies leaving behind children and has satisfied the dues of *kitāba*, whether she is to be emancipated. Ibn al-Qāsim maintained, if she has borne a child, she is to be emancipated otherwise she is kept in bondage. Ashhab said that she is emancipated at all costs. On the principles of al-Shāfiʿī, whatever the *mukātab* has left is the property of the master and the children cannot benefit from it for the payment of what he owed of the *kitāba*, whether they were with him in the *kitāba* or were born in its duration; they have to work. According to the principles of Abū Ḥanīfa they are free, by all means. The opinion of Ibn al-Qāsim appears to be based on *istiḥsān*.

53.2.4. Category 4

This relates to the question of who participates with him in the *kitāba* and who does not. They agreed under this topic that the children of the *mukātab* are not included in his *kitāba*, unless stipulated, as they are separate slaves of their master. Similarly they agreed about the inclusion of whoever is born to him in the period of the *kitāba*. They disagreed about the *umm al-walad* as has preceded. They disagreed about the inclusion of his wealth through the unqualified contract. Mālik said that his wealth is included in the *kitāba*. Al-Shāfiʿī and Abū Ḥanīfa said that it is not included. Al-Awzāʿī said that it is included if stipulated, that is, when the *mukātab* stipulates it. This issue is based on the question whether a slave can own, and whether his wealth goes with him in manumission. This has preceded.

53.2.5. Category 5

It is the examination of what is disallowed to the *mukātab* and what is not. Whatever is left of the *aḥkām* of the *mukātab*, relates to this issue.

We say: The jurists agreed under this topic that the *mukātab* does not have the right to donate anything of value from his wealth, nor does he manumit or give charity without the permission of his master. He is interdicted with respect to these and other similar things, that is, he does not have the right to dispose of anything without compensation. They differed under this topic in different cases. Among them is the case when he does not inform the master of his intentions or that he has manumitted (someone), except after he has paid the *kitāba*. Mālik and a group of jurists said that it (his action) takes effect, but others denied it. The argument of those who prohibited it is that it took place in a state when its occurrence was not permitted, therefore, it is *fāsid*. The argument of those who permitted it is that the cause of the legal obstacle is no longer there, which was the fear that the *mukātab* would be unable to pay (his dues). The basis for their disagreement is whether the permission of the master is a condition for the contract to become binding or is a condition of its validity. Those who said that it is a condition of its validity did not permit it, even if he manumitted (someone). Those who said that it is a condition of its becoming binding said that it is permitted if he manumitted someone as the contract was made in a valid manner, thus, when the requirement of permission was removed the contract became valid, as if he had granted permission; this is according to those who consider his (act of) manumission to be valid when the master grants permission. Some persons disagreed even in this after their agreement that his manumission is not valid if the master does not grant permission. A group said that it is valid, while another said that it is not, which was Abū Ḥanīfa's opinion. Mālik upheld its permission and both opinions are related from al-Shāfiʿī.

Those who permitted this disagreed about the *walāʾ* of the emancipated person, as to whom it belongs. Mālik said that if the *mukātab* dies before he is emancipated, the *walāʾ* of his slave belongs to his (*mukātab's*) master, but if he dies when he had been emancipated, the *walāʾ* would belong to him. A group from among these jurists said that the *walāʾ* in each case would belong to the master. The reliance of those who did not permit manumission by the *mukātab* is that *walāʾ* belongs to the person who manumits, due to the words of the Prophet (God's peace and blessings be upon him), "*Walāʾ* is for the person who manumits", and the *mukātab* cannot possess the *walāʾ* during his *kitāba*, therefore, his manumission is also not valid. The argument of those who held that *walāʾ* belongs to the master is that the slave of his slave is in the position of his slave. Those who tried to distinguish between these relied on *istiḥsān*.

Within this topic is their dispute about the issue whether the *mukātab* has the right to marry or to travel, without the permission of his master. The majority out of them said that he does not have the right to marry, except by the permission of his master, while some permitted him to do so. The majority permitted him to travel, while some denied this right to him, which was Mālik's opinion. Saḥnūn from among the disciples of Mālik permitted him to travel and did not permit the master to stipulate "no travelling" as a condition for the *mukātab*. Ibn al-Qāsim permitted him travel over short distances. The *ʿilla* for the prohibition of marriage is the fear that it might lead to his inability (to meet his payments), while the *ʿilla* for the permission of travel is that through it he will strengthen the means of earning and hence the means of payment. As a whole, in this issue, the jurists had three opinions. First, that the *mukātab* has the right to travel with or without the permission of his master, and it is not permitted to stipulate a condition for him that he cannot travel. This was the opinion of Abū Ḥanīfa and al-Shāfiʿī. The second opinion is that travel is not permitted to him except with the permission of his master, which was Mālik's opinion. Third that he has the right to travel by the implication of the unqualified contract, unless the master stipulates that he will not travel. This opinion was held by Aḥmad, al-Thawrī and others.

In this topic is also their disagreement whether the *mukātab* has the right to contract *kitāba* with his slave. Mālik permitted this as long as he is no granting concessions to the person; it was also the opinion of Abū Ḥanīfa and al-Thawrī. For Al-Shāfiʿī both opinions are related, one confirming *kitāba* and the other declaring it void. The argument of the majority is that it is commutative contract that has as its purpose the earning of profit, therefore, it resembles all other permitted contracts of sale and purchase. The argument of the Shāfiʿites is that *walāʾ* belongs to the person who manumits and the *mukātab* cannot possess *walāʾ* as he is not a free person.

They agreed that the master had no right to withdraw anything from his (the *mukātab's*) wealth nor could he benefit from it. They disagreed about the master having intercourse with his slave-girl, who was a *mukātaba*. The majority came to prohibit this, while Aḥmad, Dāwūd and Saʿīd ibn al-Musayyib, from among the Companions, said that it is permitted if he stipulates this as condition for her. The majority's argument was that it is intercourse that is to end in separation in the future and it, therefore, resembles a temporary marriage. The argument of the other group is based on its similarity with the position of the *mudabbara*. They agreed that if she was reduced to inability (of making payments) intercourse with her was permitted. Those who prohibited this differed about the case when he has intercourse with her, whether he is liable to *ḥadd*. The majority said that there is no *ḥadd* for him as it is intercourse in a situation of doubt (*shubha*). Some of them said he is liable to *ḥadd*. They disagreed (in this case) about her entitlement to dower. The jurists, as far as I know, maintain that the laws applicable to him, with respect to marriage, divorce, evidence, penalties, and others, are those that are specific for slaves.

In this discussion is also their disagreement about his sale (to another). The majority said that the *mukātab* is not to be sold, except with the condition that he will be allowed to retain his *kitāba* with the buyer. Some of them said that his sale is valid as long as he has not paid anything of his *kitāba*, as Barīra was sold when she had not paid anything from her *kitāba*. Some said that if the *mukātab* agrees to the sale it is valid, which is al-Shāfiʿī's opinion, as *kitāba*, according to him, is not a binding contract favouring the slave; he argued on the basis of the tradition of Barīra when she was a *mukātaba* and was sold. The argument of those who did not permit the *mukātab's* sale was based on the breach of contract involved in it, and Allāh has commanded the fulfilment of contracts. The issue turns on the point whether *kitāba* is a binding contract. Similarly, they disagreed about the sale of the *kitāba*. Al-Shāfiʿī and Abū Ḥanīfa said that it is not permitted, while Mālik permitted it, but upheld the right of pre-emption in it for the *mukātab*. Those who permitted this compared it with the sale of a debt, while those who did not allow it viewed it as a category of *gharar*. Similarly, Mālik compared *shufʿa* (pre-emption) in it to pre-emption in debts. For this there is a tradition from the Prophet (God's peace and blessings be upon him), I mean, for pre-emption in debts. The opinion of Mālik in the sale of *kitāba* is that if it is contracted for gold, it is permitted to be sold for immediate goods not delayed, due to the occurrence of sale of a debt for a debt. If the *kitāba* is for goods its purchase is to be for gold or silver or dissimilar goods. When he is emancipated the *walāʾ* would belong to the master not to the buyer. Within this topic is also the issue whether the master has the right to force his slave to accept *kitāba*?

54.3. Chapter 3: The Conditions of *Kitāba*

Among the conditions of *kitāba* are those that are legally prescribed. These are conditions essential for the contract—their discussion has preceded in the description of the elements of this contract. Among them are those that are stipulated by mutual consent, some of these (if stipulated) vitiate the contract. Among them are also those conditions the stipulation of which renders the contract vitiated, but if they are given up the contract becomes valid. Among them (finally) are those that are permissible and are not binding, while there are those that are binding. All these conditions are expounded in the books of *furūʿ* (manuals of *fiqh*), while this book of ours is not a book of *furūʿ* (manual of *fiqh*), it is a book of principles.

The conditions that generally render the contract void are those which are contrary to the conditions legally prescribed for the validity of the contract. The permissible conditions are those that do not lead to the vacation of the conditions rendering the contract valid nor do they make them binding. The jurists do not, as a whole, disagree about all these conditions, but they differ about the conditions due to their disagreement whether a condition is one of the validating conditions. They would differ depending on how close or far a condition is from vacating a validating condition. It was for this reason that Mālik determined a third category of conditions. These conditions, if adopted by the stipulator, render the contract void, but if they are not acted upon, the contract is valid. It is necessary that we understand this for all the other *sharᶜī* contracts.

Among the well-known issues in this topic is where service, travel, or the like, is stipulated in *kitāba* and the slave becomes strong enough to make the payments before the expiry of the (stipulated) period of *kitāba*. Is he to be emancipated? Mālik and a group (of jurists) said that this condition is void and he is to be emancipated on payment of all the wealth. Another group said that he is not to be emancipated till he pays the entire sum and in addition fulfils other stipulated conditions. This is based on a tradition traced to ᶜUmar ibn al-Khaṭṭāb (God be pleased with him) that he manumitted the slaves of the state and stipulated for them that they serve the Caliph for another three years. They did not disagree that the slave's manumission, if his master manumits him and stipulates for him service for a number of years, is incomplete till he serves for the stated number of years. Some deduced from this that the condition is binding. These then are the well-known issues occurring in the principles in this book.

There are other issues, which are mentioned in this book, though they belong to other books. If they are mentioned in this book, it is on the assumption that they are cases falling under the principles in this book, but when they are mentioned in other books they are presented as principles. It is for this reason that mentioning them in this book is preferable. Among these is their disagreement when the master weds his daughter to the *mukātab*, the master subsequently dies and the daughter inherits. Mālik and Al-Shāfiᶜī said that the marriage is annulled as she now owns part of him, and what the right hand of a woman possesses is a prohibited category for her by consensus (*ijmāᶜ*). Abū Ḥanīfa said that the marriage is valid for what she has inherited is wealth that is a liability of the *mukātab* not his corpus. This issue deserves to be in the Book of Marriage (*nikāḥ*).

Within this category is their disagreement when the *mukātab* dies and he owes a debt and part of the payment of *kitāba*. Does the master share with the creditors? The majority said he does not share his claim with the creditors.

Shurayḥ, Ibn Abī Laylā and a group said that the master participates with the creditors. Similarly, they disagreed when he becomes insolvent and owes debts that submerge what he possesses: do the claims extend to his corpus? Mālik, al-Shāfiʿī and Abū Ḥanīfa said that they (the creditors) have no claim over his corpus. Al-Thawrī and Aḥmad said that they take him over unless the master has him released. They agreed that if he is unable to pay the reparation for an offence, he is to be surrendered in lieu of it, unless the master pays the reparation. The discussion whether he participates in the distribution belongs to the Book of Insolvency and the discussion of offences to the Book of Offences. On the issues relating to judicial verdicts, which are cases in this book and principles in the Book of Judgments, disagreement over their *ḥukm* concerns the disputes of the master and the *mukātab* over the wealth of *kitāba*. Mālik and Abū Ḥanīfa said that the acceptable statement is that of the *mukātab*, while al-Shāfiʿī, Muḥammad and Abū Yūsuf said that they are required to take oaths and then rescind the contract on the analogy of the parties to a sale.

The cases under this topic are many, but those recalled at the moment are mentioned in the discussion we have presented. Those who come across well-known issues disputed among the jurists of the regions and they are related to transmission, must verify them in this topic. The purpose is the recording of the well-known issues over which dispute arose between the jurists of the regions together with the issues expressly stated by the *sharʿ*. This is so, and we have stated this more than once, because our intention in this book is to establish the issues expressly stated by the texts, agreed upon or disputed, and to mention those issues about which the texts are silent, but in which disagreement of the jurists of the regions has become well known.

Truly, the knowledge of these two categories of issues provides the *mujtahid* with general principles for those issues over which the texts are silent and in cases where disagreement among the jurists of the regions is not well known, irrespective of an opinion from any of the jurists having been related in it. It is likely that one who works through these issues and understands the principles of the causes that generated the disagreement of the jurists in them, will be able to derive what is required in each particular case, I mean, what is the answer for it in the opinion of each one of the *fuqahāʾ* of the regions, that is, in one particular issue itself, and will know when a jurist has opposed his own principle and when he has not. This is the case when an opinion has been related from him in that issue. If, however, a verdict has not been related from him or it has not reached the investigator of these principles, it is possible for him to come up with the answer in accordance with the principles of that jurist according to whose school he is rendering an opinion, and according to the truth to which his *ijtihād* leads him. We hope, God willing, after being free of this book, to compile a book for Mālik's school that assimilates the principles of his school and the well-known issues that work as principles for further derivation. This is what Ibn al-Qāsim did in *al-Mudawwana*. He reconciled that in which he did not have his opinion with what he possessed of the issues of Mālik in the same category and that resembled principles in so far as people (jurists) adopted them for purposes of practice and *taqlīd* in rendering *aḥkām* and verdicts. It is, however, a strength of this book that through it a person can attain, as we have said, the status of *ijtihād* as he proceeds, along with a knowledge of the Arabic language and of *uṣūl al-fiqh* that is sufficient for this purpose. It is for this reason that we thought that the most suitable title for this book would be if we name it: *Bidāyat al-Mujtahid wa Kifāyat al-Muqtaṣid*

LIV

THE BOOK OF *TADBĪR* (MANUMISSION AT THE DEATH OF OWNER)

The study of *tadbīr* covers its elements and its *aḥkām*. It has four elements: meaning, words, the *mudabbir*, and the *mudabbar*. The *aḥkām* are of two categories: *aḥkām* relating to the contract, and the *aḥkām* relating to the *mudabbar*.

54.1. **Chapter 1: The Elements**

We say: The Muslims agreed over the permissibility of *tadbīr*, and that is when the master says to his slave, "You are free when I turn my back (die)", or he does not qualify his statement and says, "You are a *mudabbar*". These, according to them, by agreement, are the two forms for *tadbīr*. The jurists are of two categories with respect to *tadbīr* and *waṣiyya*. Among them are those, who do not distinguish between the two, and there are those who made a distinction between *tadbīr* and *waṣiyya* by rendering *tadbīr* as binding and *waṣiyya* as not binding (terminable). Those who distinguished between them, disagreed over whether the unqualified form for manumission after death includes the meaning of *waṣiyya* or the *ḥukm* of *tadbīr*, that is, when he says, "You are free after my death". Mālik said that if he says "You are free after my death", and it is valid, then, it is apparent that it is *waṣiyya*, and the acceptable statement would be his (the master's) (in case of dispute). It is also possible to retract this, unless he had intended *tadbīr*. Abū Ḥanīfa said that the apparent meaning in this is *tadbīr* and he has no right to retract it. Ibn al-Qāsim adopted Mālik's opinion, while Ashhab adopted Abū Ḥanīfa's, though he added: unless there is corroborating evidence to show that it is *waṣiyya*, like his (the master's) being on a journey or being ill and what resembles it among the circumstances in which people usually write their testaments.

In accordance with the opinion of those who do not distinguish between *waṣiyya* and *tadbīr*, which includes al-Shāfiʿī and those who adopted his opinion, this form is manifestly for *tadbīr*. According to the opinions of those who do make a distinction it is either one of the allegorical forms used for *tadbīr*, or it is not an allegorical form for *waṣiyya* or for *tadbīr*. This happens when the person interprets it to mean *waṣiyya*, but it does not serve either as an explicit, or as an allegorical statement, for *waṣiyya*. When he interprets it to mean *tadbīr*, invoking the intention for *waṣiyya*, it serves as an allegorical statement for *tadbīr*.

With respect to the *mudabbar*, they agreed that the person who accepts this contract is a slave under valid (legal) bondage and that his emancipation is not automatic, and it makes no difference whether it is full or partial ownership. They disagreed about the *ḥukm* of one who is owned in part and is then granted *tadbīr*. Mālik said this is permitted, and for the person (co-owner) who has not granted *tadbīr* there are two options. First, that they subject him to mutual valuation, if the person who granted him *tadbīr* buys him (in full), he becomes a *mudabbar* completely, but if he does not purchase him *tadbīr* is revoked. The second option is that he claim the value of his share. Abū Ḥanīfa said that the co-owner, who does not grant *tadbīr*, has three options. If he likes he can hold on to his share, or if he likes he may make the slave serve him for the value of the share that he has in the slave, or he may claim the value of his share from his co-owner if he is well off, otherwise, he makes the slave serve him. Al-Shāfiʿī said that *tadbīr* is valid, and nothing else follows from it. The slave stays a *mudabbar* to the extent of the share owned by the *mudabbir*, that is, half, or a third, or whatever is his share. When the *mudabbir* dies that part of him is emancipated, and the value of the remaining part is not to be paid to his other master as is done in the case of emancipation, as the wealth (of the *mudabbir*) now belongs to others and these are the heirs. This issue, however, belongs to the *aḥkām* and not to the elements, that is, the *aḥkām* of the *mudabbar* and should be expounded there.

About the *mudabbir* (master pronouncing *tadbīr*) they agreed that a condition for him is that he be the owner with valid ownership and should not be under interdiction, whether he is in sound health or is ill. Among the conditions is also this that his debts should not have absorbed (or exceeded) his wealth, as they agreed that debts nullify *tadbīr*. They disagreed about (the *ḥukm* of) the *tadbīr* of the prodigal (*safīh*). These, then, are the elements of this legal category.

The bases of the *aḥkām* of *tadbīr* refer to five categories. First, from what kind of wealth is the (value of the) *mudabbar* debited; is it from the capital or from the third of the estate? Second, what *aḥkām* of slavery still cling to him and what do not, that is, as long as he is a *mudabbar*? Third, what follows him in his emancipation, and what does not? Fourth are the contingencies that nullify *tadbīr*, while fifth are the *aḥkām* of splitting up *tadbīr*.

54.2. **Chapter 2: The *Aḥkām* of *Tadbīr***

54.2.1. Category 1

The jurists disagreed about the part (head of account) from which the *mudabbar's* value is to be debited, when the *mudabbir* dies. The majority maintained that it is to be debited to the third (of the estate). A group, most of whom were the Ẓāhirites, said that it is to be debited to the capital. Those who held that it is to be debited from a third considered it similar to a bequest (*waṣiyya*), as it is a *ḥukm* that takes effect after death. A tradition is related from the Prophet (God's peace and blessings be upon him) that he said, "The *mudabbar* is from the third". It is, however, a weak tradition according to the traditionists, as it is narrated by ʿAlī ibn Ṭaybān from Nāfiʿ from ʿAbd Allāh ibn ʿUmar, and the traditions of ʿAlī ibn Ṭaybān are rejected by the traditionists. Those who held it to be deducted from the capital, considered it to be something that a man donates from his wealth during his lifetime, and, therefore, it resembles a gift (*hiba*). The upholders of the view of a third, disagreed in some cases. When a person declares a slave a *mudabbar* during his lifetime and emancipates another during his illness, and dies thereafter, with the third falling short of the combined value of the two, Mālik said that the *mudabbar* is to be preferred as his transaction was undertaken in the time of health, while al-Shāfiʿī said that the conclusively emancipated slave is to be preferred as his right cannot be rejected. According to his principles *tadbīr* can be withdrawn. This issue deserves to be in the Book of Bequests.

54.2.2. Category 2

The best-known issue in this is whether the *mudabbir* has the right to sell the *mudabbar*. Mālik, Abū Ḥanīfa, and a group from Kūfa said that the master has no right to sell his *mudabbar*. Al-Shāfiʿī, Aḥmad, the Ẓāhirites and Abū Thawr said that he has a right to retract and then sell his *mudabbar*. Al-Awzāʿī said that he is not to be sold, except to a person who desires to emancipate him. In this issue, Mālik and Abū Ḥanīfa differed in cases, one of which is when he sells him and the buyer manumits him. Mālik said that manumission takes effect, while Abū Ḥanīfa and the Kūfīs said the sale is cancelled, whether the buyer manumits him or he does not, which is better analogy as it (sale in this case) is prohibited by way of *ʿibāda*.

The reliance of those who permitted his sale is what is established through the tradition of Jābir "that the Prophet (God's peace and blessings be upon him) sold a *mudabbar*", and, perhaps, they also held it similar to a bequest. The reliance of the Mālikites is on the generality of the words of the Exalted, "O ye who believe! Fulfil your undertakings", as it is manumission with a delay and resembles the case of the *umm al-walad* or it resembles an unqualified manumission. The reason for the disagreement here is the conflict of analogy with the text, or of the general word with the particular.

There is no disagreement among them that the *aḥkām* for the *mudabbar* about *ḥudūd*, divorce, testimony, and all other issues are the same as those of slaves.

They disagreed in this topic about the permissibility of having sexual relations with the *mudabbara*. The majority of the jurists inclined toward the permissibility of intercourse with her, while its prohibition is related from Ibn Shihāb and its abomination from al-Awzāʿī if the master did not have it with her before. The argument of the majority is based on its similarity with the *umm al-walad*, while those who did not permit it held her case to be similar to a manumitted female slave with a delay. Those who prohibited intercourse with a female slave manumitted with a delay compared her case to that of a wife married for a period, which is *mutʿa*. They agreed that the master has the right to demand service of the *mudabbar* and to deprive him of his wealth whenever he likes as is the case with any slave. Mālik said the exception is when he falls ill contacting a threatening illness, and in this case it is reprehensible.

54.2.3. Category 3

One of the best-known issues about who (or what) goes along with the slave in *tadbīr* is their disagreement about the children of the *mudabbara*, to whom she gives birth through wedlock or through unlawful intercourse, after pronouncement of *tadbīr* by her master. The majority said that her children, born after her *tadbīr*, are in the same position as she is: they are emancipated with her or are kept enslaved with her. Al-Shāfiʿī said, in an opinion preferred by his disciples, that they are not emancipated through her emancipation. They agreed, however, that if the master emancipates her in his lifetime they are also emancipated with her.

The argument of the Shāfiʿites is that if they are not emancipated in immediate emancipation, it is appropriate that they should not be emancipated through freedom that is delayed by means of stipulation. They also argued that the jurists have unanimously agreed that in the case of a legatee through manumission the children do not participate in the manumission. The majority maintained that *tadbīr* has some kind of sanctity and, therefore, validated the manumission of children due to its similarity with *kitāba*. This opinion of the majority is related from ʿUthmān, Ibn Masʿūd, and Ibn ʿUmar, while al-Shāfiʿī's opinion is related from ʿUmar ibn ʿAbd al-ʿAzīz, ʿAṭāʾ ibn Abī Rabāḥ and Makḥūl.

The summary of the views in Mālik's school in this is that the children of each woman follow her, if she is free they too are free, if she is a *mukātaba* they are *mukātabs*, if she is a *mudabbara* they are *mudabbars*, and if she is manumitted with a delay they too are manumitted with a delay. Similarly, in the case of the *umm al-walad*, her children have the same status (as that of their mother). The Ẓāhirites disagreed with this. The person manumitted in part also falls under the same rule, according to Mālik.

The jurists agreed unanimously that each child born through marriage follows the status of its mother in freedom and bondage, as in all contracts occurring between these two stages that lead to freedom, except those in which they have differed like *tadbīr* and the one whose husband is from the Arab nation. They also agreed that each child born through a possession of the right hand (*milk al-yamīn*) is subordinate to the status of his father; if he is free the child is free too, if he is a slave, the child too is a slave, and if he is a *mukātab*, the child is also a *mukātab*. They disagreed about the *mudabbar*, when he possesses a slave and a child is born to that slave. Mālik said that its *ḥukm* is the *ḥukm* of the father, that is, he is a *mudabbar*. Abū Ḥanīfa and al-Shāfiʿī said that the child does not follow him in *tadbīr*. The reliance of Mālik is on consensus (*ijmāʿ*) on the point that the child from the possession of the right hand is subordinate to the *ḥukm* of his father, except for the *mudabbar*, which amounts to the analogy of a disputed point on a point of consensus. The argument of the Shāfiʿites is that the child of the *mudabbar* is a kind of wealth owned by him, and the wealth of the *mudabbar* belongs to the master and can be taken over by the master. It is not conceded to him that he is a kind of his wealth and, according to Mālik, his wealth follows him to freedom.

54.2.4. Category 4

We have already talked, in relation to the splitting up of *tadbīr*, about the person who pronounced *tadbīr* for the share he possessed in a slave, when his co-owner had not done the same. So, reference should be made to it. With respect to the person who pronounces *tadbīr* in part, when he owns the slave completely, the verdict issued, according to Mālik, is that of complete *tadbīr*, on the analogy of one who splits up manumission.

54.2.5. Category 5

In this topic is their disagreement over a debt nullifying *tadbīr*. Mālik and al-Shāfiʿī said that a debt annuls it, while Abū Ḥanīfa said that it does not and he (the slave) works to pay off the debt, whether the debt covers his entire value or part of it. In this topic is also their disagreement about a Christian pronouncing *tadbīr* for his Christian slave, when the slave becomes a Muslim before the death of his master. Al-Shāfʿī said that he is to be sold immediately, the very hour when he accepts Islam and his *tadbīr* is nullified. Mālik said that he should be separated from his Christian master. He is to be released in lieu of *kharāj* due from his Christian master, and is not to be sold till his master dies or the price is entirely paid; if he dies, the *mudabbar* is emancipated, unless there is a debt in excess of his wealth. The Kūfīs said that if a Christian *mudabbar* converts to Islam, his value is determined and he works for this value.

The *mudabbar*, who is declared a *mudabbar* during his master's good health, is to be preferred (for a right to the third of the estate), according to Mālik, over a *mudabbar* declared to be so during the master's illness.

LV
THE BOOK OF *UMMAHĀT AL-AWLĀD* (SLAVE-WOMEN BEARING THEIR MASTER'S CHILD)

The principles of this topic focus on whether the *umm al-walad* may be sold. If she is not to be sold, then, when does she become the *umm walad* and due to what does she become an *umm walad*? What rights are left to her master with respect to bondage? When does she become a free woman?

The earlier and the later jurists disagreed about the first issue. The established report from ʿUmar (God be pleased with him) is that he decided that she is not to be sold and is a free woman, on the death of her master, and her value is to be debited to the capital of his estate. A similar report is related from ʿUthmān, and it is the opinion of most of the *Tābiʿūn* and the majority of the jurists of the regions. Abū Bakr Siddīq and ʿAlī, may Allāh be pleased with them both, Ibn ʿAbbās, Ibn al-Zubayr, Jābir ibn ʿAbd Allāh and Abū Saʿīd al-Khudrī used to permit the sale of the *umm al-walad*. This was upheld by the Ẓāhirites from among the jurists of the regions. Jābir and Abū Saʿīd said that "We used to sell the *ummahāt al-awlād* and the Prophet being among us did not see any harm in it".

They argued on the basis of what is related from Jābir, who said, "We used to sell the *ummahāt al-walad* in the period of the Prophet (God's peace and blessings be upon him), in that of Abū Bakr, and in the early days of the Caliphate of ʿUmar. It was then that ʿUmar prohibited us from selling them". Among the grounds for the Ẓāhirites in this issue is a kind of reasoning that is known as *istiṣḥāb ḥāl al-ijmāʿ*. They said that as the *ijmāʿ* occurred on the point that she is owned before birth (of the child), it is necessary that it should be the same after birth, unless evidence indicates the contrary. The strength of this kind of reasoning has been shown in the books on *uṣūl*, and it is not valid according to those who uphold analogy (*qiyās*) being evidence only in the opinion of one who denies analogy. Perhaps, the majority argued with them in a similar way, which is known as matching one claim with another (*muqābalat al-daʿwā biʾl-daʿwā*). It occurs when they say, "Do you not know that consensus has taken place on the prohibition of her sale in the period of her pregnancy? If this so, it is necessary that this requirement of the consensus stay with her even after she has delivered". The later Ẓāhirites, however, introduced a conflicting factor. They do not accept the prohibition of her sale during the period of her pregnancy.

Among the traditions on which the majority have relied in this topic is that related from the Prophet (God's peace and blessings be upon him), who said about Māriya his slave-girl when she gave birth to Ibrāhīm, "Her child has set her free". On the same issue is the tradition of Ibn ʿAbbās from the Prophet (God's peace and blessings be upon him), who said, "Any woman who bears a child to her master is free when he dies". Both traditions have not proved sound according to the traditionists, which is stated by Abū ʿUmar ibn ʿAbd al-Barr, may Allāh have mercy on him, who was an authority this field. Perhaps they gave a rational argument that some protection is necessary for her due to her link with the child and the fact that it is a part of her. This reasoning is given by ʿUmar (God be pleased with him) when he upheld that she is not to be sold saying, "Our flesh stands mixed with theirs, as does our blood stand mixed with theirs".

When does she become an *umm al-walad*? They agreed that she becomes an *umm walad* if he owned her before she conceived from him. They disagreed when she is already pregnant from him or after she has given birth to his child. Mālik said that she does not become an *umm walad* if she gave birth to his child before he came to own her, even when she gives birth to another child of his after he has owned her. Abū Ḥanīfa said that she does become an *umm walad*. Mālik's opinion differed when he comes to own her and she is pregnant. Analogy dictates that she should become an *umm walad* in all cases for it is against all noble traits that a man sell the mother of his child. The Prophet (God's peace and blessings be upon him) said, "I was sent to perfect all noble traits".

About the question, with what does she become an *umm walad*, Mālik said it is anything that she delivers from which it can be known that it was to be a child, even if it is an embryo or a blood-clot. Al-Shāfiʿī said it is necessary that physical appearance and features be discernible in this. Their disagreement relates to the meaning of the term "birth" or what verifies the meaning of "child".

In the remaining *aḥkām* of bondage, they agreed that she is like an ordinary female slave in her testimony, penalties, bloodwit, *arsh* (estimated compensation) for her injuries. The majority of those who prohibited her sale do not foresee any contingent happening that would necessitate her sale, except what is related from ʿUmar ibn al-Khaṭṭāb that if she is commits unlawful intercourse she is to return to bondage. The opinions of Mālik and al-Shāfiʿī differed whether the master can make her serve him all his life and earn through these services. Mālik said that he does not have that right, except for her sexual favours, while al-Shāfiʿī said that he does. Mālik's argument is that as he does not own her corpus for purposes of sale, so he does not possess her for hiring, except that he permitted the hiring of her children other than his own, as their inviolability is weaker in his view. Al-Shāfiʿī's reliance is on the occurrence of consensus that he is permitted to have intercourse with her. The reason for the disagreement is the vacillation of her hiring between two rules: first, intercourse with her; and second, her sale. It is necessary that the manifestly stronger rule be preferred.

When does she become a free woman? There is no disagreement among them that this time arrives when the master dies. I know of no one up till now who has said that she is emancipated from a third of the estate. The statement of one who would say, on the analogy of the *mudabbar*, that she is manumitted from a third, is weak.

LVI
THE BOOK OF *JINĀYĀT* (OFFENCES)

Offences that have prescribed legal penalties, are four. First, offences against the body, life, or limbs, which are called *qatl* (homicide) and *jurh* (injuries, wounds). Second, offences involving sexual organs, which are called *zinā* (unlawful sexual intercourse) and *sifā* (fornication). Third, offences against wealth (property) in which acquisition is sometimes accompanied by force of arms and is called *hirāba* (brigandage), when committed without justification, and *baghy* (insurrection, rebellion), when committed with a reason, but when acquisition takes place by way of stealth from a place of safe-custody (*ḥirz*), it is called *sariqa* (theft). If the acquisition is effected through the use of high status, or through the power of the *sulṭān*, it is called *ghasb* (usurpation). Fourth, offences against reputation, which are called *qadhf*. Fifth,[209] offences that are committed through a delict resulting in making lawful what the law has prohibited from among edibles and beverages. Out of these, in this *sharīʿa*, there is a penalty for the drinking of wine (*khamr*) alone. It is a penalty that was agreed upon after the time of the lawgiver (God's peace and blessings be upon him).

We begin, from among these, with penalties that are prescribed for bloodshed and say: The obligation for causing loss of life or limb is either *qiṣāṣ* (retaliation) or financial compensation, which is called *diya* (bloodwit, reparation). The study in this book is first divided into two parts: the study of *qiṣāṣ* and the study of *diya*. The study of *qiṣāṣ* is divided to *qiṣāṣ* for loss of life and *qiṣāṣ* for limbs. The study of *diya* is also divided into the study of *diya* for loss of life and *diya* for the severance of limbs and (for inflicting) wounds. This book is, thus, divided first into two books. In the first is transcribed the book of *qiṣāṣ*, while in the second is transcribed the book of *diyāt*.

[209] The author begins by saying that there are four offences, but here he mentions a fifth category. The reason appears to be that this fifth category does not fall under the categories that "have prescribed legal penalties", by which he could mean those whose penalty is not explicitly mentioned in the Qur'ān or *sunna*. It is well known that though drinking of wine is established as an offence from the Qur'ān and *sunna*, there is some ambiguity about the exact penalty for drinking wine.

56.1. THE BOOK OF QIṢĀṢ (*LEX TALIONIS*; RETALIATION)

This book is divided into two sections. First is the study of *qiṣāṣ* for loss of life, while the second is *qiṣāṣ* for limbs. We begin with *qiṣāṣ* for life.

56.1.1. The Book of *Qiṣāṣ* for Loss of Life

The study of this book is first divided into two parts: the cause, that is, the cause of *qiṣāṣ*, and the obligation, that is, *qiṣāṣ* and its substitutes, when it has one. We begin first with the examination of the cause. The study of the cause relates to the description of homicide and the killer, which combined gives rise to the cause, and to the description of the victim in *qiṣāṣ*. Not every killer, that there may be, is liable to *qiṣāṣ*, nor is he liable for every homicide that he may have committed, nor due to any victim, who may have been killed, rather (the liability arises) for a particular killer, for a determined homicide, and due to a specific victim. As the aim in this chapter is to maintain a balance, we begin first with the discussion of the murderer, then with the act of murder, and finally the victim.

56.1.1.1. The Discussion of the Conditions of the Murderer

We say:[210] They agreed that for the murderer, who is subjected to *qiṣāṣ* (or *qawad*), it is stipulated, by agreement, that he be sane, *bāligh* (having attained puberty), and possess a free will for acting directly, without the participation of another. They disagreed generally about the *mukrah* (one coerced) and the *mukrih* (coercer): the person issuing the order (*āmir*) and one directly committing the act (*mubāshir*). Mālik, al-Shāfiʿī, al-Thawrī, Aḥmad, Abū Thawr and a group of jurists said that the liability (for *qiṣāṣ*) is on the *mubāshir* rather than on the *āmir*, but the *āmir* is to be punished (with a penalty other than *qiṣāṣ*). A group of jurists said that both are to be subjected to *qiṣāṣ*. This is the case when there is no coercion and the *āmir* has no authority over the *maʾmūr* (person given the order). When the *āmir* has authority over the *maʾmūr*, that is, the *mubāshir*, they disagree into three opinions. One group said that the *āmir* is subjected to *qiṣāṣ* and not the *maʾmūr* (who may be punished under *taʿzīr*), which is the opinion of Dāwūd and Abū Ḥanīfa and is one of the two opinions of al-Shāfiʿī. Another group said that the person coerced is to be subjected to *qiṣāṣ* and not the *āmir*, which is the other of the two

[210] The terminology used by the author in this section is somewhat indiscriminate. In particular, the use of the term "*qatl*" and its different forms. He uses the term *qatl* where he should be using the term "*qiṣāṣ*". Apparently, he is following the terminology found in the traditions on the subject. A literal translation of such use would be "is put to death", or better still "executed", but that is not the *ḥukm* in these cases. The *ḥukm* is *qiṣāṣ*, which has certain formalities before an offender can be executed or put to death. Wherever this term is used the phrases "subject to *qiṣāṣ*" or "is subjected to *qiṣāṣ*", or "retaliation", have been employed, as the context dictates.

opinions of al-Shāfiʿī. The third group said that they are both to be subjected to *qiṣāṣ*, which is Mālik's opinion.

Those who did not impose *ḥadd* on the *maʾmūr*, took into account the effectiveness of coercion in the waiving of many obligations in the law, due to the similarity of the state of the coerced with one who has no will of his own. Those who upheld *qiṣāṣ* for him, applied to him the *ḥukm* of a person with a free will and this is because the coerced person resembles, from one aspect, a person having a free will, while he resembles from another aspect a person dominated and under duress, like one falling from a height, or swept by the wind from place to place. Those who subjected both to *qiṣāṣ* did not hold coercion as an obstacle (in the way of punishment) for the *maʾmūr*, nor did they consider the absence of direct causation an obstacle for the *āmir*. Those who subjected only the *āmir* to *qiṣāṣ* compared the person given the order with a dumb instrument. Jurists applying *ḥadd* to the person who does not act directly consider the term "murderer" applicable to him metaphorically. The Mālikites relied, in murder by the coerced, on murder under threat of death, by virtue of their consensus that if a person is close to death due to starvation (duress), he has no right to kill a human being and consume him.

Homicide is intentional or by mistake, the killer has legal capacity or he does not—and we shall be discussing intentional homicide (murder) under the case of subjecting a group to *qiṣāṣ* for killing one person—but when a murderer participates with one who is making a mistake, or a person with legal capacity participates with one lacking capacity, like a murderer with a minor or an insane person and a free person with a slave in the killing of a slave, under the rules of those who do not subject a free person to *qiṣāṣ* for killing a slave, then, the jurists disagreed in this. Mālik and al-Shāfiʿī said that the murderer is subjected to *qiṣāṣ*, while the person guilty of manslaughter and the minor are liable to half of the blood money, though Mālik transfers it to the *ʿāqila*, while al-Shāfiʿī directs it to his wealth, as will be discussed in what follows. Similarly, both had the same opinion about the free man and the slave, who kill a slave intentionally, that the slave is to be subjected to *qiṣāṣ*, while the free person pays half the value (of blood-money). The same is the case for a Muslim and a *dhimmī*, who are both subjected to *qiṣāṣ*.

Abū Ḥanīfa said that when a person, who may be liable to *qiṣāṣ*, participates in the offence with another who may not be liable to it, there is no *qiṣāṣ* on either one of them and both pay the *diya*. The argument of the Ḥanafites is that this is a case of *shubha* (doubt), as *qiṣāṣ* cannot be split up and there is a possibility here that the actual loss of life was caused by the act of the person who is not liable to *qiṣāṣ*, just as there is a possibility that it was caused by the person who is liable to *qiṣāṣ*. The Prophet (God's peace and blessings be upon him) has said, "Waive the *ḥudud* on the basis of doubt". Thus, when *qiṣāṣ* cannot be imposed, its substitute becomes obligatory, which is *diya*. The argument of the second group is based on *maṣlaḥa* that requires severity for the curtailment of bloodshed. It is as if each one of them had committed the murder alone and should be awarded the same penalty, but this is weak in terms of analogy.

They agreed about the description of the act for which *qiṣāṣ* becomes obligatory that it is intentional homicide (murder). They are in agreement that homicide is of two kinds: intentional (murder) and by mistake or accident (manslaughter). They disagreed whether there was a third category between these two and that is what they called *shibh al-ʿamd* (quasi-wilful homicide). This (category) was upheld by the majority of the jurists of the regions and its denial by Mālik is well known, except in the case of a son killing his father. It is said that a different opinion is also related from him in this. ʿUmar ibn al-Khaṭṭāb, ʿAlī, ʿUthmān, Zayd ibn Thābit, Abū Mūsā al-Ashʿarī and al-Mughīra all confirmed it (quasi-wilful murder) and no one opposed them in this from among the Companions.

Those who upheld it distinguished quasi-wilful homicide from intentional homicide. This distinction refers mostly to the type of instrument with which murder is committed and also to the circumstances in which the blow was struck. Abū Ḥanīfa said that the use of an instrument not made of iron, like a stick, or fire or whatever is similar, results in *shibh al-ʿamd*, while Abū Yūsuf and Muḥammad said that *shibh al-ʿamd* is caused by that which is not usually employed for killing. Al-Shāfiʿī said that *shibh al-ʿamd* is caused by means used intentionally for beating, but not for killing, that is, the intention is to strike and not to commit homicide, but it results in homicide and *khaṭaʾ* (mistake) is that which is completely by mistake, while intentional homicide is that which is completely with intention. This is the best (distinction).

The reliance of those who deny that there is a middle category is on the argument that there is no middle ground between having an intention and not having an intention. The argument of those who uphold the middle category is that no one but Almighty Allāh is aware of true intentions, but the *ḥukm* is to be assigned (by humans) on the basis of the apparent circumstances. Thus, if a person intends something else with an instrument that is usually employed for killing he will be assigned the usual *ḥukm* and he who intends murder will be assigned the *ḥukm* of murder, without doubt. When a person intends to kill a specific person with an instrument that is not usually employed for murder, his case will vacillate between *ʿamd* and *khaṭaʾ*, but this is for our purposes only and not in the reckoning of Allāh, the Exalted.

Shibh al-ʿamd, from one aspect, is similar to the case of *ʿamd* in that there exists an intention to strike the victim and from another aspect it resembles *shibh al-khaṭaʾ* as an instrument is employed that is not normally used for killing. A *marfūʿ* tradition attributed to the Prophet (God's peace and blessings be upon him) says, "Beware! Homicide through quasi-wilful mistake, that which is committed with a whip, stick, or stone, has an enhanced *diya* of a hundred she-camels, forty of whom bear their offspring in their wombs". It is, however, a tradition lacking sufficient support of the traditionists and is not settled with respect to its chains of transmission in accordance with the statement of Abū ʿUmar ibn ʿAbd al-Barr, though Abū Dāwūd and others have recorded it. This category of homicide, according to those who do not uphold it, gives rise to *qiṣāṣ*, but according to those who uphold it, it necessitates the payment of *diya* alone.

There is no dispute in Mālik's school that a blow struck with anger or malice makes *qiṣāṣ* obligatory (in case of death). They disagreed when it would be considered intentional if struck in sport, or for disciplining, in the case of one who has a right to discipline.

The condition stipulated for the victim, by virtue of which *qiṣāṣ* becomes obligatory, is that he should be at least of the same status as the murderer. The things due to which people differ are Islam and *kufr*, freedom and bondage, being male or female and being one or more. They agreed that if the victim is equal to the killer in these four things, *qiṣāṣ* will become obligatory. They disagreed about these four categories when they did not exist together. If a free man killed a slave, the jurists disagreed about it. Mālik, al-Shāfiʿī, al-Layth, Aḥmad and Abū Thawr said that the free man is not to be subjected to *qiṣāṣ* because of a slave. Abū Ḥanīfa and his disciples said that a free man is to be subjected to *qiṣāṣ* for a slave, except when he owns the slave. A group said that a free man is subjected to *qiṣāṣ* for a slave whether he belongs to him or to someone else. This was upheld by al-Nakhʿaī.

Those who said that a free man is not subjected to *qiṣāṣ* because of a slave argued through the implication of the text in the words of the Exalted, "Retaliation is prescribed for you in the matter of the murdered; the free man for the free man and slave for the slave and the female for the female".[211] Those who said that a free man is subjected to *qiṣāṣ* for a slave argued on the basis of the words of the Prophet (God's peace and blessings be upon him), "The blood of the Muslims is equal (in status) among them, the lowest of them creates an equal liability for them, but they are superior to those beside them". The reason for the disagreement is the conflict of the general meaning with the implication of the text. The distinction, however, is weak.

There is no disagreement among them that the slave is subject to *qiṣāṣ* because of a free man and also one who has a subordinate status (with respect to the four categories) because of one having a superior status. Among the

[211] Qurʾān 2:178

proofs of those who said that the free man is subjected to *qiṣāṣ* because of the slave is also what is related by al-Ḥasan from Samura that the Prophet (God's peace and blessings be upon him) said, "We put to death one who kills his slave". As a rational argument, they said that as his killing is prohibited like that of a free man, it is necessary that *qiṣāṣ* in it should be similar to the *qiṣāṣ* of the free man.

The jurists disagreed into three opinions about the execution of a believer because of a *dhimmī*. A group said that a believer is not to be executed (subjected to *qiṣāṣ*) because of a *kāfir*. Among those who upheld this are al-Shāfiʿī, al-Thawrī, Aḥmad, Dāwūd and a group. Another group said that he is subjected to *qiṣāṣ*. Those who upheld this are Abū Ḥanīfa, his disciples and Ibn Abī Laylā. Mālik and al-Layth said that he is not to be subjected to *qiṣāṣ*, unless he kills him by way of *ghīla* (treachery, deception). *Qatl al-ghīla* is committed when he catches him unawares and slaughters him, especially for his money.

The argument of the first group is what was related in the tradition of ʿAlī when he was asked by Qays ibn ʿUbāḍa and al-Ashtar whether the Messenger of Allāh (God's peace and blessings be upon him) had conveyed to him something that he did not convey to the people. He said, "No, except what is in this, my document". He then proceeded to extract it from the sheath of his sword and it was written there: "The blood of the Muslims is equal (in status) among them, the lowest of them creates an equal liability for them, but they are superior to those beside them. Beware! A believer is not to be subjected to *qiṣāṣ* because of a *kāfir*, nor one who has made a pact in the duration of his pact. He who innovates or supports an innovator, upon him is the curse of Allāh, of the Angels and of the people, all at the same time". It is recorded by Abū Dāwūd. It is also related from ʿAmr ibn Shuʿayb from his father from his grandfather that the Prophet (God's peace and blessings be upon him) said, "A believer is not to be killed for a *kāfir*". They argued in this, in agreement, that a Muslim is not to be executed because of a *ḥarbī* (one of the enemy at war) who sought sanctuary.

The disciples of Abū Ḥanīfa relied in this upon reports, among which is a tradition related by Rabīʿa ibn Abī ʿAbd al-Raḥmān from ʿAbd al-Raḥmān al-Salmānī, who said, "The Messenger of Allāh had one of the *Ahl al-Qibla* executed because of a person from the *Ahl al-Dhimma* and said, 'I have the greatest right, among those whose covenant should be accepted' ". They related this from ʿUmar saying that it restricts the generality of the Prophet's saying, "A believer is not to be executed because of a *kāfir*, that is, he meant by *kāfir* a *ḥarbī* and not a *kāfir* under a treaty". The traditionists declared the tradition of ʿAbd al-Raḥmān al-Salmānī and also what they related from ʿUmar as weak. By way of analogy, they relied on the consensus of the

Muslims that the hand of a Muslim is cut if he steals the wealth of a *dhimmī*. They said that if the sanctity of his property is the same as that of a Muslim, it is necessary that the sanctity of his blood be the same as a Muslim's. The reason for the disagreement is the conflict of traditions with analogy.

In the subjection of a group (of killers) to *qiṣāṣ* because of one man (victim), the majority of the jurists of the provinces said that the group is to be executed for one person, whatever the number of the group. Among these jurists are Mālik, Abū Ḥanīfa, al-Shāfiʿī, al-Thawrī, Aḥmad, Abū Thawr and others. This was the opinion of ʿUmar, who went to the extent of saying, "Had the people of Ṣanʿā conspired to do it, I would have put all of them to death". Dāwūd and the Ẓāhirites said that a group is not to be put to death for a single person, which is also the opinion of Ibn al-Zubayr, al-Zuhrī and it is also related from Jābir. Similarly, according to this group the hands, of the persons in the group, are not to be severed, if two or more participated in the cutting of one person's hand. Mālik and al-Shāfiʿī said that their hands are to be cut. The Ḥanafites made a distinction between life and limbs saying that lives are to be taken for one life, but only one limb is to be amputated for a limb. This will be discussed in the section of *qiṣāṣ* for limbs.

The reliance of those who execute a group for a single person is the consideration of *maṣlaḥa*. It is understood that *qiṣāṣ* has been decreed for the elimination of murder, as is pointed out by the Book in the words of the Exalted, "And there is life for you in retaliation, O men of understanding".[212] In such a case, if a group of persons is not put to death for one victim, people would find in it a means to get away with murder by conspiring to kill one person through a group. One objecting, however, has the right to say: this would be necessary if no one out of the group is executed, but if one of them is executed, the one whose execution is believed to be a deterrent, then, it is not likely that the *ḥadd* would be negated and become a means for widespread wasting of life.

The reliance of those who execute only one person for one victim are the words of the Exalted, "And We prescribed for them therein: The life for the life and the eye for the eye and the nose for the nose and the ear for the ear and the tooth for the tooth and for wounds retaliation".[213]

Ibn al-Mundhir and others beside him, who mentioned disagreement, said about the execution of the male for the female that there is consensus (ijmāʿ) on this point, except what has been related from ʿAlī from among the Companions and ʿUthmān al-Battī, that if a man is executed for a woman, the woman's *awliyāʾ* have to pay half of the blood money. Abū al-Walīd al-Bājī,

[212] Qurʾān 2:178
[213] Qurʾān 5:45

the *qāḍī*, has related from al-Ḥasan al-Baṣrī in *al-Muntaqā* that a male is not to be put to death because of a female. This has also been related by al-Khaṭṭābī in the *Maᶜālim al-Sunan*. This is an isolated opinion, but it has strong evidence due to the words of the Exalted, "[A]nd the female for the female",[214] although the implication of the text here conflicts with the general meaning in the words of the Exalted, "And We prescribed for them therein: The life for the life".[215] The objection, however, is that the latter communication was laid down in a *sharīᶜa* other than ours, which is an issue that is disputed, that is, whether the law of those who preceded us is law for us. The reliance on the execution of a man because of a woman is on the consideration of the general interest.

They disagreed in this topic about the case of a father and his son. Mālik said the father is not to be subjected to *qawad* (retaliation), except when he catches him unawares and slaughters him (kills him in cold blood), but if he restrains him with a sword or a stick and thereby kills him, he is not to be subjected to *qiṣāṣ*. Similarly, in the case of the grandfather with his grandson. Abū Ḥanīfa, al-Shāfiᶜī and al-Thawrī said that neither the father, because of his son, nor the grandfather, because of his grandson, is to be subjected to *qiṣāṣ*, whatever the form of malice with which he killed him. This was also the opinion of the majority of the jurists. Their reliance is on the tradition of Ibn ᶜAbbās that the Prophet (God's peace and blessings be upon him) said, "The *ḥudud* are not to be applied in mosques, nor is a father to be subjected to retaliation *qawad* because of his son". The basis for Mālik is the general application of *qiṣāṣ* among the Muslims.

The reason for their disagreement is what they relate from Yahyā ibn Saᶜīd from ᶜAmr ibn Shuᶜayb that a man called Qatāda, from the tribe of Mudlij, restrained his son with a sword and struck his leg. The wound (inflammation) spread and he died. Surāqa ibn Juᶜsham went up to ᶜUmar and mentioned this to him and ᶜUmar said, "Go to (their) potable water and count a hundred and twenty camels and lead them in front of you". When they reached ᶜUmar, he selected from them thirty *ḥiqqas* (three-year-old female camels entering the fourth year), thirty *jadhaᶜs* (in the fifth year) and forty *khalifas* (pregnant camels) and then called out, "Where is the victim's brother?" He said, "Here I am". He (ᶜUmar) said, "Take them for, verily, the Messenger of Allāh said, 'There is nothing for the murderer'". Mālik interpreted this tradition to show that it did not involve pure malice and verified the category of *shibh al-ᶜamd* as related to a father and his son. The majority read in it its apparent meaning to indicate malice, due to their consensus that anyone who strikes another with

[214] Qurʾān 2:178
[215] Qurʾān 5:45

a sword and kills him is guilty of wilful homicide. Mālik, on the other hand, was of the view that as the father has authority of disciplining his son and bears love for him, the interpretation of homicide that occurs in these circumstances should not be considered intentional. He does not accuse the father, when the murder is not by way of *ghīla*, but considers the perpetrator of *ghīla* to have intended the homicide on the basis of predominant probability and strength of the accusation, for true intentions are known only to Allāh, the Exalted. Thus, Mālik does not accuse the father where he does charge a stranger, due to the strength of the love that exists between a father and his son. The majority deemed the cause of waiving the *ḥadd* penalty from the father due to his right over his son. The inference from the principles of the Ẓāhirites is that the father is to be subjected to *qiṣāṣ*. This, then, is the discussion of the cause.

56.1.1.2. The Discussion of the Consequential Obligation

They agreed that the *walī al-dam* (heir entitled to exact *qiṣāṣ*) is entitled to one of two things: *qiṣāṣ*, or *ᶜafw* (pardon)—either in return for *diya* or without it. They disagreed whether the conversion of *qiṣāṣ* into pardon by acquiring *diya* is the exclusive right of the heirs of the victim, without there being an option for the person subjected to *qiṣāṣ*; or whether the liability for *diya* is not established without the consent of both parties, that is, the heirs of the victim and the killer; and that if the killer does not wish to pay the *diya*, do the heirs have no choice but to retaliate or to pardon? Mālik said that the heir has no right to pardon for *diya*, unless the offender consents to pay the *diya*. This is a narration of Ibn al-Qāsim from him and was also the opinion of Abū Ḥanīfa, al-Thawrī, al-Awzāᶜī and a group of jurists. Al-Shāfiᶜī, Aḥmad, Abū Thawr, Dāwūd and the majority of the jurists of Medina from among the disciples of Mālik, said that the heir has an option, if he likes he can exact *qiṣāṣ* and if he likes he can impose *diya*, whether the killer agrees or he does not. This has been related by Ashhab from Mālik, though his well-known opinion is the former.

Mālik's reliance, for his well-known opinion, is on the tradition of Anas ibn Mālik about retaliation for the teeth of al-Rabīᶜ that the Messenger of Allāh said, "The decree of Allāh is *qiṣāṣ*". It was understood by the indication of the text that he had no choice but to exact *qiṣāṣ*. The reliance of the second party is on the established tradition of Abū Hurayra, "One whose kin is killed may choose one of two alternatives, whichever he may prefer: the acquisition of *diya* or pardon". Both traditions are agreed upon for their soundness, but the implication of the first is weak as it leaves him (the *walī*) no choice but the option of *qiṣāṣ*. The second is explicit in granting him options. Their reconciliation is possible if the implication of the (first) text is avoided. Since reconciliation is necessary and it is possible then the adoption of the second tradition is inevitable and the majority maintain that reconciliation is obligatory, when it is possible and it is better than preference (of one over the other). In addition, Allāh, the Powerful and Glorious says, "[A]nd kill not one another (yourselves—*anfusakum*)".[216] If a responsible agent (*mukallaf*) is presented the choice of ransoming himself for wealth, then it is obligatory on him to accept. The basis is that if he finds food in a state of duress (starvation) for an exchangeable value and he has that with which he can buy it, I mean, he is ordered (by law) to buy it, so what about buying his own life?

On the basis of this opinion, if the victim has heirs who include majors as well as minors, it is necessary to postpone retaliation till the minors grow up to exercise their option, especially when the minors exclude the adults, like children along with brothers.

The Qāḍī (Ibn Rushd) says: This case came up in Cordoba, during the time of my grandfather (God bless him) and the jurists of his time issued the verdict according to the well-known narration (from Mālik), which requires that they should not wait for the minors (to grow up), but he, may Allāh have mercy on him, issued the verdict of waiting on the basis of analogy. His contemporaries declared this as abominable, due to the intensity of their *taqlīd*, so much so that he was compelled to issue a verdict in which he supported this school and this (decision) can be found with people.

The study of this section comprises two themes: pardon and retaliation. The study of pardon relates to two things. First, as to who possesses the right of pardon and who does not and the order of priority of heirs in this. Second, whether he has the right to pardon for *diya*. We have talked about whether he has the right to pardon for *diya*.

Those who possess the right to pardon are, on the whole, those who have the right to retaliate and those who have the right to retaliate are the residuaries, according to Mālik and all the legal heirs, according to the others. This is so, as they agreed that if the person killed intentionally has sons and some of them pardon (the offender), then the right to *qiṣāṣ* is annulled and *diya* becomes the remaining choice. They disagreed when there was a dispute between daughters and sons as to whether to pardon or to claim *qiṣāṣ*. Similarly, (in a case of disagreement) between a spouse (wife or husband) and the brothers. Mālik said that the opinion of the daughters as against that of sons and the opinion of sisters as against that of brothers has no significance in the taking of *qiṣāṣ*, or in doing the opposite (that is, pardon) and that their opinion is not considered along with that of men. It is the same in the case of disagreement between a wife and her husband. Abū Ḥanīfa, al-Thawrī, Aḥmad

[216] Qurʾān 4:29

and al-Shafiʿī said that the opinion of each heir is taken into account in the waiving of *qiṣāṣ* and in the relinquishing of his share of the *diya*, as in the taking of *qiṣāṣ* or accepting the share of *diya*. Al-Shāfiʿī said that those absent and those present, the minors and the majors, are all equal in this matter.

The reliance of these jurists is on holding equivalent the exacting of *qiṣāṣ* and the right to *diya*. The reliance of the first group is on the argument that *wilāya* belongs to the males and not to females.

The jurists differed about the person killed intentionally, when he pardoned the offender before dying, whether this is valid as against the rights of the *awliyāʾ*. Similarly, in the case of the person killed by mistake, when he waives the claim of *diya*. A group said that if the person killed had pardoned the claim for his blood in the case of wilful homicide, this is implemented. Those who upheld this were Mālik, Abū Ḥanīfa and al-Awzāʿī and it is also one of the two opinions of al-Shāfiʿī. Another group maintained that his pardon is not binding and the *awliyāʾ* have the right to retaliate or pardon (the offender). Among those who held this opinion were Abū Thawr and Dāwūd and it is also al-Shāfiʿī's opinion rendered in Iraq. The argument of this group is that Allāh has granted an option to the *walī* for three things—pardon, *qiṣāṣ* and *diya*—and this has a general application for each deceased, whether or not he pardoned the claim on his blood. The argument of the majority is that the thing passing on to the *walī* is the right of the deceased and he becomes his representative or stands in his place. The deceased had a right superior to the person who now stands in his place after his death. The jurists agreed that the meaning in the words of the Exalted, "But whoso forgoeth it (in the way of charity) it shall be expiation for him",[217] convey that the subject pronoun of the verb "forgoes", which is the same as the preceding relative pronoun, refers to the deceased, who forgoes his claim by way of charity. They disagreed as to whom the pronoun in "it shall be expiation for him" applies. Some said it applies to the murderer in so far as they saw repentance in it for him, while it was said that it applies to the deceased with respect to his sins and errors.

Mālik, al-Shāfiʿī, Abū Ḥanīfa and the majority of the jurists of the provinces said about the disagreement over the pardoning of *diya* by the person killed through error that his pardon is effective to the extent of a third of the claim, unless the heirs permitted the excess. A group said that it is valid for the entire claim. Those who maintained this are Ṭāwūs and al-Ḥasan. The argument of the majority was that he was donating his wealth, effective after his death and, therefore, it was not effective, except to the extent of a third, its basis being bequest (*waṣiyya*). The argument of the other group was that if he had a right to pardon a claim for blood, he had a better right to waive a claim for wealth. This issue is particularly related to the Book of *Diyāt*.

[217] Qurʾān 5:45

The jurists differed when a wounded person forgives the offender for his wounds, but subsequently dies from them, whether the *awliyā*ʾ had the right to make a demand for *qiṣāṣ*. Mālik said that they have a right to do so, unless he had said that he forgives the injuries and what may result from them. Abū Yūsuf and Muḥammad said that if he forgives the injuries and dies from them, they have no right at all and forgoing the injuries means forgoing the right to *qiṣāṣ* for life. A group said that they have right to *diya* if he forgave the infliction of injuries without qualification. These jurists then differ with some of them saying that the offender is bound to pay the entire *diya* (for life), which was preferred by al-Muzanī from among the opinions of al-Shāfiʿī, while others said that he is bound to pay the *diya* after discounting from it (the portion of) the *diya* related to the wounds, which were forgiven and this is the opinion of al-Thawrī.

There is no dispute, in the opinion of those who said that he cannot forgo the claim for life, that it does not discharge the right of the *walī* to claim the *diya* and as his forgiveness for *qiṣāṣ* for life does not negate the right of the *walī*, it will certainly not discharge the claim for injuries. They disagreed about the murderer, who had been forgiven, whether the *sulṭān* (state) still retained a right in the matter Mālik and al-Layth said that he is to be awarded a hundred stripes and imprisoned for a year, which was also the opinion of the jurists of Medina and is related from ʿUmar. A group—al-Shāfiʿī, Aḥmad, Isḥāq and Abū Thawr—said that the sulṭān does not have to do so. Abū Thawr added that unless he is known to be a hardened criminal in which case the *imām* awards him what he deems fit. There is no evidence with the first group, except for a weak tradition, while the evidence with the second group is the apparent meaning of the law and that fixation (of punishment) cannot take place without an authoritative source and there is no confirmed source for this.

56.1.1.3. The Discussion of *Qiṣāṣ*

The study of *qiṣāṣ* relates to its description, to the person who carries it out and the time of its execution. The jurists disagreed about the description of *qiṣāṣ* for life. Among them were those who said that it is to be exacted from the murderer in the way he committed the murder. Thus, one who killed by drowning is to be drowned and one who killed by hurling a stone is to be killed in the same way. This was Mālik's and al-Shāfiʿī's opinion. They said that it is to be so unless his agony is prolonged, in which case the sword is swifter for him. The disciples of Mālik differed about the person who burned another; is he to be burned too, on the basis of their agreement with Mālik about the implementation of the same method of death? Similarly, one who kills with an arrow.

Abū Ḥanīfa and his disciples said that whatever the mode in which the offender killed the victim, he is not to be put to death by anything but the sword. Their reliance is on what is related by al-Ḥasan from the Prophet (God's peace and blessings be upon him), who said, "There is no *qawad* (retaliation) except by the sword".

The reliance of the other group is on the tradition of Anas "that a Jew crushed a woman's head with a stone and the Prophet (God's peace and blessings be upon him) similarly crushed his head with a stone", or, as in another version it is said, "between two stones", and on the words of the Exalted, "Retaliation is prescribed for you in the matter of the murdered",[218] as retaliation (*qiṣāṣ*) demands similarity.

Regarding the person who is entitled to (physically) exact *qiṣāṣ*, the apparent answer is that it is the *walī al-dam*, but it is said that this is not possible due to the enmity that exists between them and he is likely to commit excesses. The time when *qiṣāṣ* is exacted is after all its requirements have been established. Rebuttal is upon the murderer if he has not confessed. They disagreed whether it is among the conditions of *qiṣāṣ* that the location should not be the *Ḥaram*. They agreed that a pregnant woman, if she has murdered, is not to be subjected to *qiṣāṣ* until she has delivered. They disagreed about the person who has murdered by poisoning. The majority upheld the obligation of *qiṣāṣ*, while some of the Ẓāhirites said that it is not to be exacted from him due to the reason that the Prophet and his companions were poisoned, but did not retaliate against the person who poisoned them. This completes the book of *qiṣāṣ*.

56.2. THE BOOK OF *JIRĀḤ* (INJURIES)

Injuries are of two kinds: those that involve *qiṣāṣ*, *diya*, or pardon; and those that have just *diya* or pardon. We begin with those in which there is *qiṣāṣ*. The study here concerns the conditions related to the offender inflicting the injuries, the conditions related to the injury itself and those related to the injured. It also covers the consequential obligation, that is, *qiṣāṣ* and its substitutes, if it has a substitute.

56.2.1. The Offender Inflicting the Injuries

It is stipulated for the offender that he must be a *mukallaf* (must have legal capacity), as is stipulated for the murderer, which means that he should be a *bāligh* (major) and sane. *Bulūgh* (puberty) is determined, without dispute, by

[218] Qurʾān 2:178

sexual maturity (emission) and age, but they differed over the exact age. The highest is eighteen and the lowest is fifteen years. This was also al-Shāfiᶜī's opinion.

There is no disagreement that if a person severs another's limb, *qiṣāṣ* is to be exacted from him if it is a limb that entails *qiṣāṣ*. They disagreed when a group of persons sever a single limb. The Ẓāhirites said that two hands (of different offenders) cannot be amputated in lieu of one hand. Mālik and al-Shāfiᶜī said that any number of hands can be amputated because of one hand, just as many lives can be taken in because of one. The Ḥanafites made a distinction between loss of life and limbs. They said that more than one limb cannot be amputated for a single limb, but (a number of) lives can be taken for loss of one life. According to them (liability for) limbs is divisible, while (liability for) life is not.

They differed about pubescence. Al-Shāfiᶜī said that it amounts to *bulūgh* without doubt, but the school (Mālik's) differed about it in the case of ḥudūd, irrespective of whether it qualifies as absolute puberty. The basis for all this is the tradition of Banū Qurayẓa, "the Prophet (God's peace and blessings be upon him) executed those minors who were *bāligh* and on whom the razor could be applied". The basis for age is the tradition of Ibn ᶜUmar "that he presented himself (for fighting) on the day of the Battle of Badr,[219] when he was fourteen years old, but he was not accepted, while he was accepted for the battle of Uhud when he was fifteen years old".

56.2.2. The Discussion of the Injured

They stipulate for the wounded person that he should be of the same legal status as that of the offender. The things that are effective in status are bondage and *kufr*. Regarding the slave and the free man they disagreed over the occurrence of *qiṣāṣ* between them in injuries, as in the case of loss of life. Among them were those who maintained that the *qiṣāṣ* cannot be exacted from the free man because of the slave, but the slave is to subjected to *qiṣāṣ* for a free man as is the case in loss of life. Among them were those who held that each one of them is subjected to *qiṣāṣ* for the other and they did not distinguish between life and limbs, for this purpose. Among them were also those who made a distinction saying that the superior is to be subjected to *qiṣāṣ* for the inferior in life and injuries, while others said that *qiṣāṣ* is exacted for life and not for injuries. From Mālik there are two narrations. The correct position, however, is that *qiṣāṣ* is to be exacted for injuries in the manner it is exacted for life. This is the situation of the slaves with respect to freemen.

[219] The text says 'al-Khandaq' or the battle of the Trenches. Historically, this is not possible as Uhud was fought before al-Khandaq. The word Badr has, therefore, been substituted for it.

About the relationship of the slaves among themselves, the jurists have three opinions. First, that *qiṣāṣ* is applicable among them for life as well as injuries, which is the opinion of al-Shāfiʿī and a group of jurists and is also related from ʿUmar ibn al-Khaṭṭāb and is one opinion from Mālik. The second view is that there is no *qiṣāṣ* among them, either for life or for injuries and they are like chattel. This is the opinion of al-Ḥasan, Ibn Shubrama and a group of jurists. The third opinion is that there is *qiṣāṣ* among them, but for life and not injuries, which is the opinion of Abū Ḥanīfa and al-Thawrī and it is also related from Ibn Masʿūd. The reliance of the first group is on the words of the Exalted, "[A] slave for a slave". The reliance of the Ḥanafites is on what was related by ʿImrān ibn al-Ḥuṣayn "that a slave of some poor people cut off the ear of a slave of some rich people and they came up to the Messenger of Allāh (God's peace and blessings be upon him) who did not exact *qiṣāṣ* from him". This, then, is the *ḥukm* for *qiṣāṣ* among the slaves.

56.2.3. The Discussion of Injuries

It is stipulated for an injury that it be by way of malice (intent), that is, the injury in which there is liability for *qiṣāṣ*. Injuries may be caused by the destruction of the limbs of the injured person or they may not. If it is of the type where there is destruction of a limb, then intention is realized when a blow is struck in rage, in a manner that usually causes an injury. When he injures him by way of sport, or in a manner that does not usually result in injury, or by way of discipline, it appears that there is disagreement in it, of the same nature as was found in murder about the probable consequences of a blow that does not normally kill and is struck while playing or disciplining. Abū Ḥanīfa attaches considerable importance to the instrument, so much so that he says a murder cannot be committed with a blunt weapon (*muthaqqal*), which is an unusual opinion from him, that is, regarding the disagreement whether there is *qiṣāṣ* or *diya* in it if it is an injury that carries *diya*.

The condition for *qiṣāṣ* in injuries where the limb has been maimed is, without dispute, malice, but in the distinction of intentional from unintentional injuries there is a disagreement. If the offender struck at the limb itself, severing it with an instrument that is normally used for the purpose, or he had struck him in a rage, then, there is no dispute that there arises a liability for *qiṣāṣ*. If, however, he slapped him, or struck him with a whip or what resembles it, when it is obvious that he did not intend the loss of a limb, as in the case where he slaps him and his eye comes out of its socket, the majority maintain that this is quasi-wilful injury and there is no *qiṣāṣ* in it, but there is enhanced *diya* in it, charged to his wealth. This is the narration of the Iraqis from Mālik, while the well-known opinion in the school is that it is wilful and there is *qiṣāṣ* in it, except in the case of the father injuring his son. Abū Ḥanīfa, Abū Yūsuf and Muḥammad maintain that there is *shibh al-ᶜamd* in homicide only and not in injuries.

When the offender injures him by way of sport, destroying his limb, there are two opinions in this. The first makes *qiṣāṣ* obligatory while the second negates it. What follows from these two opinions are two more opinions: one fixing enhanced *diya* and the other the *diya* of mistake, that is, in those cases where *diya* is invoked. Similarly, when the injury is caused while disciplining; there is disagreement in it.

The obligation in intentional injuries, when they occur according to the conditions that we have mentioned, is *qiṣāṣ* due to the words of the Exalted, "And for wounds retaliation".[220] This applies to those cases in which the exacting of *qiṣāṣ* is possible and where the exact area of amputation can be located, without there being fear of loss of life. They adopted this opinion on the basis of the report "that the Messenger of Allāh (God's peace and blessings be upon him) waived *qiṣāṣ* in the case of the *mā'mūma,* (a head injury) *munaqqala,* (splintered bones) and *jā'ifa* (facial or other cavities)". Mālik and those who adopted his opinion maintained that this is the *ḥukm* of all injuries that are within the meaning of the stated injuries that are fatal, like the splintering of the bones in the neck, spine, chest, or thighs and whatever is similar. Mālik's opinion wavered with respect to the *munaqqala* and he ruled for *qiṣāṣ* once and for *diya* another ime. The same is the case, according to Mālik, where a similarity in *qiṣāṣ* cannot be maintained, like the partial loss of sight or hearing. *Qiṣāṣ* is also prohibited, according to Mālik, in cases where there is an initial absence of similarity, like a blind man destroying the eye of one whose sight is sound.

Within this, they disagreed about the case of the one-eyed person, who intentionally destroys the sight of one in possession of both eyes. The majority maintained that if he prefers he has the right to retaliate, but they disagreed when he forgoes retaliation. A group said that if he likes he is entitled to full *diya* of one thousand *dīnārs*, which is the opinion of Mālik. It is also said that he is only entitled to half of the *diya*, which was the opinion of al-Shāfiᶜī and is also related from Mālik. Ibn al-Qāsim held the same opinion as that of al-Shāfiᶜī, while the other opinion was adopted by al-Mughīra, from among his disciples and also by Ibn Dīnār. The Kūfīs said that the person with the sound eyes, whose eye has been destroyed, is only entitled to retaliation or composition agreed to by both. It is also said that he does not exact *qiṣāṣ* from the one-eyed person and there is full *diya* for him. This is related from Ibn al-Musayyib and from ᶜUthmān. The reliance of the jurist who maintains this opinion is on the argument that one eye of the one-eyed person is equal to

[220] Qur'ān 5:45

two eyes, thus, the person who destroys it in retaliation is taking two eyes from him instead of one. The same argument was advanced by another jurist who said that if he relinquished retaliation he is entitled to full *diya*. It is binding upon the upholder of this opinion that he relinquish *qiṣāṣ* by necessity. The jurist who insisted on *qawad* in this case and ruled for half of the *diya* is consistent with his principle, so ponder over this as it is self-evident, Allāh knows best.

Whether the injured person has a choice between *qiṣāṣ* and the taking of *diya*, or the only option he has is the exacting of *qiṣāṣ*, unless he settles for *diya* with the offender, there are two opinions in this from Mālik like his two opinions in murder and one of his opinions in the case of the one-eyed person destroying an eye of the person with sound eyes. The correct opinion is that he should be given the option to destroy the eye of the one-eyed person or to take the full *diya* of one thousand *dīnārs*—or five hundred on the basis of the disagreement.

When does he exact *qiṣāṣ* for the injury caused to him? According to Mālik, he does not exact *qiṣāṣ* till his injury is healed, but according to al-Shāfiʿī he can do so at once. Al-Shāfiʿī follows the apparent meaning, while Mālik considers what the injury may lead to fearing that it may cause loss of life.

The jurists differed when the offender subjected to *qiṣāṣ* dies from the act of exaction of *qiṣāṣ*. Mālik, al-Shāfiʿī, Abū Yūsuf and Muḥammad said that the person exacting *qiṣāṣ* owes nothing. The narration from ʿAlī and ʿUmar is the same and it was also adopted by Aḥmad, Abū Thawr and Dāwūd. Abū Ḥanīfa, al-Thawrī, Ibn Abī Laylā and a group of jurists said that if he dies the *ʿāqila* of the person exacting will pay up the *diya*. Some of them said that it will be charged to his personal wealth, while ʿUthmān al-Battī said that the value of the injury is to be discounted from the *diya* paid to him, which is the opinion of Ibn Masʿūd.

The argument of the first group is that the when the thief dies, on amputation of his hand, there is no claim upon the person who amputates his hand. The argument of the Ḥanafites is that it is a case of homicide through error (*khaṭaʾ*), which creates a liability for *diya*.

Qiṣāṣ is not to be exacted, according to Mālik, in extreme heat or extreme cold and is to be delayed lest the offender die from it. It is said that the location is also a condition for retaliation and it should be other than the *ḥaram*.

This, then, is the *ḥukm* of *ʿamd* (intention) in offences against life and in offences against the limbs of the body. It is necessary that we turn to the *ḥukm* of *khaṭaʾ* in these and we begin with the *ḥukm* of *khaṭaʾ* in loss of life.

56.3. THE BOOK OF *DIYĀT* (BLOOD-MONEY) FOR LOSS OF LIFE

The basis of this law are the words of the Exalted, "He who hath killed a believer by mistake must set free a believing slave and pay the blood-money to the family of the slain, unless they remit it as a charity".[221] The *diyāt* differ in the *sharīʿa* depending upon the person whose life is lost, on whom it becomes obligatory and also the agreement of the parties, or in the case of murder on the consent of the person who has the right to exact *qiṣāṣ*, as has been mentioned earlier in their disagreement over it.

The study of *diya* is about its cause, that is, in what kind of homicide it becomes due, about its kinds and amount, about the time when it becomes due and about the issue on whom it is obligatory.

About homicide, for which it becomes payable, they agreed that it becomes binding in manslaughter and in murder by a person who does not have full legal capacity, like an insane person or a minor. It is also binding in intentional homicide where the protection accorded to the victim is less than that accorded to the murderer, like the case of the free man and slave.

Among the categories of *khaṭaʾ* are those about which they agreed, as to their being *khaṭaʾ* and those about which they disagreed, a short description of which has preceded. We shall also take up later the imposition of liability on the rider, the driver and the guide.

They agreed about its amounts and kinds that the *diya* of a Muslim free man is a hundred camels, for those whose mode of life is closely related to camels. In Mālik's opinion it has three kinds: *diya* for *khaṭaʾ*, *diya* for *ʿamd* and *diya* for *shibh al-ʿamd*, which according to Mālik is like the act of one restraining his son. *Diya* is of two types only in al-Shāfiʿī's view: reduced (*mukhaffafa*) and enhanced (*mughallaẓa*). Reduced *diya* is for cases of *khaṭaʾ*, while enhanced *diya* is for *ʿamd* and *shibh al-ʿamd*. There are two kinds of *diyāt* in Abū Ḥanīfa's view also, for *khaṭaʾ* and for *shibh al-ʿamd*. There is no *diya*, according to him, for *ʿamd*. The obligation in *ʿamd*, for him, is composition (value arrived at through settlement (*sulḥ*)), which is payable immediately and cannot be delayed. This meaning is also found in the well-known opinion of Mālik, because there is no point in calling it *diya* if he does not make it obligatory on him, except by settlement, though it is related from him that it can be delayed like the *diya* of *khaṭaʾ*, which excludes it from the category of amount arrived at through settlement.

The *diya* of *ʿamd*, according to Mālik, has four components: twenty-five *bint makhāḍ*, twenty-five *bint labūn*, twenty-five *ḥiqqa* and twenty-five *jadhaʿ*. This is also the opinion of Ibn Shihāb and Rabīʿa. The enhanced *diya*, according to

[221] Qurʾān 4:92

him has three components: thirty *ḥiqqa*, thirty *jadhaʿ* and forty *khalifa*, which are pregnant. The enhanced *diya*, according to his well-known opinion, is paid only in an act like that of the person killing his son while restraining him. According to al-Shāfiʿī it has three components even for *shibh al-ʿamd*. This is also related from ʿUmar and Zayd ibn Thābit. Abū Thawr said that *diya* in *ʿamd*, when the *walī al-dam* has waived retaliation, is composed of five parts, like the *diya* of *khaṭaʾ*.

They disagreed about the ages of camels in the *diya* for *khaṭaʾ*. Mālik and al-Shāfiʿī said that they are composed of five parts (with respect to age): twenty *bint makhāḍ*, twenty *bint labūn*, twenty male *ibn labūn*, twenty *ḥiqqa* and twenty *jadhaʿ*. This is related from Ibn Shihāb and Rabīʿa. It is also the opinion of Abū Ḥanīfa and his disciples, that is, its five-part composition, though they substituted male *ibn makhāḍ* for male *ibn labūn*. Both opinions are related from Ibn Masʿūd. It is related from our master ʿAlī that he determined it to be composed of four components, eliminating from it twenty-five *banī labūn*. This was adopted by ʿUmar ibn ʿAbd al-ʿAzīz. There is no tradition related from the Prophet for this and, thus, it indicates permissibility (*ibāḥa*)—Allāh knows best—as is stated by Abū ʿUmar ibn ʿAbd al-Barr. Al-Bukhārī and al-Tirmidhī have recorded a report from Ibn Masʿūd from the Prophet (God's peace and blessings be upon him), who said, "In the *diya* of *khaṭaʾ* there are twenty *bint makhāḍ*, twenty *ibn makhād* (male), twenty *banāt labūn*, twenty *jadhaʿ* and twenty *ḥiqqa*". Abū ʿUmar indicated a deficiency in this tradition in so far as it had been related by Ḥanīf ibn Mālik from Ibn Masʿūd and this person is unknown (that is, Ḥanīf). He said, "The report from ʿAlī in this is dearer to me as there is no dispute about the narration from ʿAlī but it is disputed in the case of Ibn Masʿūd". Abū Dāwūd has recorded a report from ʿAmr ibn Shuʿayb from his father from his grandfather "that the Messenger of Allāh (God's peace and blessings be upon him) decided that the person who is killed by mistake, his *diya* is a hundred camels: thirty *bint makhāḍ*, thirty *bint labūn*, thirty *ḥiqqa* and ten *ibn labūn* (male)". Abū Sulaymān al-Khaṭṭābī said that this is a tradition I have never known any of the famous jurists mentioning and most of the jurists have maintained that the *diya* for *khaṭaʾ* has five components, though they did disagree about the kinds of camels. It is related from some of the jurists that the *diya* of *khaṭaʾ* has four components. These are al-Shāʿbī, al-Nakhaʿī and al-Ḥasan al-Baṣrī. These jurists stated it to be: twenty-five *jadhaʿ*, twenty-five *ḥiqqa*, twenty-five *bint labūn* and twenty-five *bint makhād*, as has been related from ʿAlī and recorded by Abū Dāwūd.

The majority inclined toward *diya* of *khaṭaʾ* that had five components: twenty *ḥiqqa*, twenty *jadhaʿ*, twenty *bint makhāḍ*, twenty *bint labūn* and twenty *ibn makhād* male. They did not agree, however, about *ibn makhāḍ* as the age had not been mentioned in them. On the basis of analogy, those who adopted the tradition of five components for *khaṭaʾ* and of four components for *shibh al-ʿamd*, if this third category is established, would say that the *diya* for *ʿamd* is composed of three parts, as has been related from al-Shāfiʿī. Those who did not accept three components held *ʿamd* similar to the other categories. These, then, are their well-known opinions about *diya* that is composed of camels and is imposed on the owners of camels.

They disagreed about what was obligatory on those who deal in gold and silver. Mālik said that those who deal in gold have to pay a thousand *dīnārs*, while those who deal in silver have to pay twelve thousand *dirhams*. The jurists of Iraq said that those dealing in silver are to pay ten thousand *dirhams*. Al-Shāfiʿī said in Egypt that what is due from people dealing in gold or silver is the value of a hundred camels, whatever this amount, but his opinion in Iraq was the same as that of Mālik. Mālik's reliance is on the valuation of a hundred camels by ʿUmar ibn al-Khaṭṭāb for those dealing in gold at a thousand *dīnārs* and for those dealing in silver at twelve thousand *dirhams*. The reliance of the Ḥanafites is also related from ʿUmar that he fixed the value of one *dīnār* at ten *dirhams* and also on their consensus in the valuation of a *mithqāl* for purposes of *zakāt*. Al-Shāfiʿī said that the basis for *diya* is a hundred camels and ʿUmar fixed it at one thousand *dirhams* for those dealing in gold and at twelve thousand *dirhams* for those dealing in silver, as they represented the value of a hundred camels in his days. His proof lies in what was related from ʿAmr ibn Shuʿayb from his father from his grandfather, who said, "The *diya* in the days of the Messenger of Allāh (God's peace and blessings be upon him) was eight hundred *dīnārs* and eight thousand *dirhams*. The *diya* for the People of the Book was half of what it was for the Muslims". He said, "This continued until ʿUmar succeeded to the Caliphate, when he addressed the people saying that 'the price of camels has risen'. ʿUmar, then, fixed it for those dealing in silver at twelve thousand *dirhams* and for those dealing in gold at a thousand *dīnārs*. For those who possessed cows, he fixed it at two hundred cows, for the owners of sheep at two thousand sheep and for the owners of dresses at two hundred dresses, but he left alone the *diya* for the *ahl al-dhimma* not changing anything in it". Some jurists argued on behalf of Mālik that if the valuation by ʿUmar was a substitute (as claimed by al-Shāfiʿī) it would amount to the exchange of a debt for a debt, due to their consensus that *diya* in *khaṭaʾ* may be delayed for a period of three years.

Mālik, Abū Ḥanīfa and a group of jurists are in agreement that *diya* is only to be taken either in camels, or gold, or silver. Abū Yūsuf, Muḥammad ibn al-Ḥasan and the seven jurists of Madīna said that those dealing in cows owe two hundred cows, while those dealing in textiles owe two hundred dresses. Their reliance is upon the tradition of ʿAmr ibn Shuʿayb that has preceded and also on what has been transmitted by Abū Bakr ibn Abī Shayba from ʿAṭāʾ

that "the Messenger of Allāh (God's peace and blessings be upon him) imposed *diya* on people according to their wealth, whatever it was: on the possessors of camels, a hundred camels, on the possessors of sheep, one thousand sheep, on the possessors of cows, two hundred cows and on the possessors of textiles, a hundred dresses". They also rely on what is related from ᶜUmar ibn ᶜAbd al-ᶜAzīz that he wrote to the military forces that the *diya* in the days of the Messenger of Allāh (God's peace and blessings be upon him) was a hundred camels. He said that if the offence is committed by one of the Bedouins, then, the *diya* is to be in camels and a Bedouin is not to be asked to pay in gold or silver, but if he does not have a hundred camels, he will pay its equivalent in sheep, a thousand sheep. The jurists of Iraq also relate as a text from ᶜUmar what is similar to the tradition of ᶜAmr ibn Shuᶜayb from his father from his grandfather. The argument of the first group, however, is that if an equivalence in sheep or cows had been permitted, it would also be possible in food for the possessors of food and in horses for the possessors of horses, but this has not been asserted by any jurist.

The study of *diya*, as I said, relates to its kinds, its amount, on whom it is imposed, for what and when. We have already discussed its kind and amount for the case of male Muslim free men. About the question, on whom is it obligatory, there is no disagreement that the *diya* of *khaṭaʾ* is imposed on the *ᶜāqila* and this is a specific *ḥukm* exempted from the general implication of the words of the Exalted, "Each soul earneth only on its own account, nor doth any laden bear another's load",[222] and from the general meaning of the words of the Prophet (God's peace and blessings be upon him) to Abū Zamna about his son: "He does not compensate offences on your behalf, nor do you pay for his". The majority maintain about the *diya* of *ᶜamd* that it is not to be paid by the *ᶜāqila*, on the basis of what is related from Ibn ᶜAbbās and none of the Companions opposed him. He said, "The *ᶜāqila* does not bear *ᶜamd* (intentional offences), nor confessions, nor composition in *ᶜamd*". The majority of them also maintain that the *ᶜāqila* does not pay when a person kills himself by mistake. Alawzai differed saying that when a person strikes the enemy and kills himself (in error), the *ᶜāqila* has to pay his *diya*. They have the same opinion in the case of severance of limbs. It is related from ᶜUmar that once a person gouged out his eye accidentally and ᶜUmar decided in his favour for the payment of its *diya* by the *ᶜāqila*.

They disagreed about the *diya* for *shibh al-ᶜamd*, the enhanced *diya*, into two opinions. They also disagreed about the *diya* of a victim attacked by an insane person or a minor, as to who would pay it. Mālik, Abū Ḥanīfa and a group of jurists said that all these are to be paid by the *ᶜāqila*, while al-Shāfiᶜī said that

[222] Qurʾān 6:165

an intentional offence of a minor is to be on his own account. The reason for their disagreement is the vacillation of the act of the minor between malice and mistake. Those who viewed *shibh al-ʿamd* possible in his case imposed *diya* on his wealth, while those who considered it similar to *khaṭaʾ* made his *ʿāqila* liable. Similarly, they disagreed about the case where a minor participates with one premeditating the offence. Those who imposed *qiṣāṣ* on the murderer and *diya* on the minor, differed as to who would pay it. Al-Shāfiʿī, on the basis of his principle, said it is to be imposed on the wealth of the minor. Mālik said it is paid by the *ʿāqila*, while Abū Ḥanīfa held that there is no *qiṣāṣ* in this case.

With respect to the time that it is due, they agreed that *diya* for *khaṭaʾ* is delayed over a period of three years, but the *diya* for *ʿamd* is immediate, unless they settle on delaying it.

Who are the *ʿāqila*? The majority of the jurists of Ḥijāz agreed that the *ʿāqila* are the close relatives on the paternal side and these are the residuaries, to the exclusion of the members of the *dīwān* (military unit). They also held that the clients bear the *diya*, in case the residuaries are unable to do so, except for Dāwūd, who did not consider clients as residuaries. There is no limit, according to Mālik, on the amount each one may have to bear. Al-Shāfiʿī said that the rich pay one *dīnār*, while the poor pay half a *dīnār*, which is imposed, in his view, in accordance with their nearness to the offender: first the children of his father, then the children of his grandfather, then the children of the children of his father. Abū Ḥanīfa and his disciples maintained that the *ʿāqila* is composed of the members of the *dīwān*, if he belonged to one. The argument of the jurists of Ḥijāz is that the people used to pay as an *ʿāqila* in the days of the Prophet and in the days of Abū Bakr and there was no *dīwān* at that time; it came into existence in the days of ʿUmar ibn al-Khaṭṭāb. The Kūfīs relied upon the tradition of Jubayr ibn Muṭʿim from the Prophet (God's peace and blessings be upon him), who said, "There is no grouping in Islam and any grouping that existed in the days of *jāhiliyya*, Islam only adds to its strength". On the whole, they accepted this in the way they accepted the obligation of clientage as a group.

They disagreed about the offence of the person who had no residuaries or clients. These are unaffiliated individuals. If they commit an offence by way of *khaṭaʾ*, do they have a liability for the payment of *diya*? If they do, then who is to pay? Those who do not assign them clients (by law) said that the unaffiliated persons do not pay *diya*. The same opinion is held by those who do not impose a duty on the clients (as members of the *ʿāqila*) to pay *diya*. These jurists were Dāwūd and his disciples. Those who assigned clientage to the person who emancipated him said that the liability is on the client, while those who assigned their *walāʾ* to the Muslims generally said that their *diya* is paid by the treasury (*bayt al-māl*). Those who said that the unaffiliated person may adopt the clientage of any person they like, assigned the liability for *diya* to the person who accepted the *walāʾ*. All these opinions have been related from the earlier Muslims.

The *diyāt* vary in accordance with the status of the victim. The factors effective in the reduction of *diya* are the feminine gender, *kufr* and bondage. They agreed about the *diya* of a woman that it is half the *diya* of a man, for loss of life only and they differed about cases of injuries and loss of limbs, as will be discussed in the section on *diyāt* for wounds and maiming. The jurists disagree into three opinions about the *ahl al-dhimma* when they are killed by way of *khaṭaʾ*. First, that their *diya* in the case of males is half of that for Muslim males, while their women have *diya* that is half of Muslim women. This was Mālik's opinion and also that of ʿUmar ibn ʿAbd al-ʿAzīz. On the same basis, the *diya* for their injuries is half that for the Muslims. The second opinion maintains that their *diya* is a third of the *diya* for Muslims. This was al-Shāfiʿī's opinion and is related from ʿUmar ibn al-Khaṭṭāb, ʿUthmān and was adopted by a number of the *Tābiʿūn*. The third opinion is that their *diya* is the same as that of the Muslims, which is the opinion of Abū Ḥanīfa, al-Thawrī and a group of jurists and is also related from Ibn Masʿūd and has been related from ʿUmar, ʿUthmān and from a number of the *Tābiʿūn*.

The reliance of the first group is on what has been related from ʿAmr ibn Shuʿayb from his father from his grandfather from the Prophet (God's peace and blessings be upon him) that he said, "The *diya* of a *kāfir* is half the *diya* for a Muslim". The reliance of the Ḥanafites is on the general implication of the words of the Exalted, "And if he cometh of a folk between whom and you there is a covenant, then the blood-money must be paid unto his folk and (also) a believing slave must be set free".[223] Their argument from the *sunna* is based on what has been related from Maʿmar from al-Zuhrī, who said, "The *diya* of a Jew, a Christian and any *dhimmī* is the same as the *diya* of a Muslim". He said that it was like this (full) in the days of the Messenger of Allāh (God's peace and blessings be upon him) and in those of Abū Bakr, ʿUmar, ʿUthmān and ʿAlī till the time of Muʿāwiya came and half of it was deposited in the treasury, the other half being given to the heirs of the deceased. It was later that ʿUmar ibn ʿAbd al-ʿAzīz fixed it at half the *diya*. About the amount that Muʿāwiya placed in the treasury, al-Zuhrī says that it appeared to him that ʿUmar ibn ʿAbd al-ʿAzīz did not recall it. He, then, informed him that the *ahl al-dhimma* were entitled to full *diya*.

If a slave kills by way of *khaṭaʾ* or ʿ*amd* and the opinion of those who do not hold him liable to *qiṣāṣ* is taken into account, a group of jurists said that

[223] Qurʾān 4:92

he is to pay his own value whatever the amount, even if that exceeds the amount of *diya* for a free man. This was the opinion of Mālik, al-Shāfiʿī and Abū Yūsuf. It was also the opinion of Saʿīd ibn al-Musayyib and ʿUmar ibn ʿAbd al-ʿAzīz. Abū Ḥanīfa and Muḥammad said that the *diya* is not to exceed the value of the slave. Some of the jurists of Kūfa said that there is *diya* in this case, but it is not to exceed the *diya* of a free man, in fact, something is to be reduced from it. The argument of the Ḥanafites is that bondage is a state of defective capacity and, therefore, the amount should not exceed the *diya* of a free man. The argument of those who imposed *diya* in this case, but rendered it less than the *diya* of the free man is that he possesses defective capacity and, therefore, the assigned *ḥukm* should be lesser in intensity, though it should be of the same category; the basis being the *ḥad* penalties in *zinā*, *qadhf*, *khamr* and *ṭalāq*. If it is said that his *diya* should be half of the free man, the assertion would have some basis, I mean, in the *diya* of *khaṭaʾ*, but none has claimed this. Mālik's argument is that he is chattel that has been destroyed, therefore, the value has to be paid, the basis being all other kinds of property. They differed in the case of the payment of *diya* for a salve, as to who is to pay it. Abū Ḥanīfa said that it is owed by the *ʿāqila* of the offender. This is also the well-known opinion from al-Shāfiʿī. Mālik said that it is paid by the killer himself. The argument by Mālik is based on the similarity of the slave with chattel, while that by al-Shāfiʿī is based on analogy drawn from a free man.

Within the topic of the various kinds of *khaṭaʾ* is the *diya* for the *janīn* (unborn child; when the woman is "quick" with child, to be exact). This is so as miscarriage caused because of a blow is not pure malice, but is malice with respect to the mother and *khaṭaʾ* with respect to the *janīn*. The study of this topic relates to: the consequential obligation for different kinds of offences; the description of the *janīn* for which this obligation arises; the person liable for payment and to whom; and the conditions attached to the obligation.

They agreed about the different kinds of *janīn* that the obligation for the *janīn* of a free woman and for that of a slave-woman bearing the child of her master, is a *ghurra*, on the basis of what has been established from the Prophet (God's peace and blessings be upon him) in the tradition related by Abū Hurayra and others "that there were two women of Hudhayl, one of whom pushed the other thereby causing her to miscarry and lose her *janīn*. The Messenger of Allāh (God's peace and blessings be upon him) awarded a *ghurra* for a *janīn* male or a female". Those who upheld that the amount of *ghurra* is fixed in value, which is the opinion of the majority, agreed that the obligatory value of the *ghurra* is five per cent of the *diya* of the (*janīn's*) mother. Those who maintained that the full *diya* upon the possessors of *dirhams* is ten thousand *dirhams* said that the *diya* of the *janīn* is five hundred *dirhams*, while those who maintained that the full amount was twelve thousand *dirhams*, determined it to be six hundred *dirhams*. The jurists who did not fix any limit to it, or they did not fix it with respect to value and permitted the determination of its value from her value, said that the obligation is to pay the value of the *ghurra*,[224] whatever the limit that it may attain. Dāwūd and the Ẓāhirites said that anything to which the term '*ghurra*' can be applied is to be paid and, as far as I know, the payment of value in this is not permitted according to him.

They disagreed about the liability for the *janīn* of a slave-girl and a *kitābiyya* (Christian or Jewish woman). Mālik and al-Shāfiʿī maintained that for the *janīn* of the slave-woman, it is a tenth of her value on the day of the offence, whether it was a male or a female. Some jurists made a distinction between a male and a female saying that if it is a female there is a tenth of the value of the slave-woman for it, but if it was a male the amount is a tenth of his value, even if the *janīn* was alive at the time. This is the opinion of Abū Ḥanīfa. There is no dispute among them that if the *janīn* of the slave-woman is alive at the time of the miscarriage, its value has to be paid. Abu Yusuf said that if the *janīn* of the slave-woman is stillborn, the decrease in the value of its mother has to be paid.

About the *janīn* of the *dhimmiyya*, Mālik, Abū Ḥanīfa and al-Shāfiʿī said that there is a tenth of the *diya* of the mother in this case, but Abū Ḥanīfa's opinion is based on his principle that the *diya* of a *dhimmī* is the same as that of a Muslim. Al-Shāfiʿī maintained his rule that the *diya* of the *dimmī* is one-third of the *diya* of a Muslim, whereas Mālik's rule is that it is one-half of a Muslim's *diya*.

In description of the *janīn*, because of which payment becomes obligatory, they agreed that among its conditions is that the *janīn* be delivered stillborn and that the mother should not die from the blow. They disagreed when the mother dies from the blow and thereafter the *janīn* is delivered stillborn. Mālik and al-Shāfiʿī said that there is nothing in this case, while Ashhab said that a *ghurra* has to be paid, which was also the opinion of al-Layth, Rabīʿa and al-Zuhrī. They disagreed in this issue about details, particularly the sign that indicates the state of being dead or alive of the *janīn* at the time of miscarriage. Mālik and his disciples maintained that the sign of life is hearing of a squall or cry. Al-Shāfiʿī, Abū Ḥanīfa, al-Thawrī and the majority of the jurists maintained that any indication of what usually signifies life, like movement, sneezing, or breathing, will be assigned the *ḥukm* of life. This is more convincing.

224 The word *ghurra* has several literal meanings, the best known being the white spot on a horse's forehead. Technically, it is the compensation paid for causing miscarriage and may be said to be the value of the foetus. The details appear in the discussion which follows.

They disagreed about the state of the foetus that creates a liability for a *ghurra*. Mālik said that anything appearing at miscarriage in the nature of flesh or a clot from which it can be determined that it would have been a child gives rise to a *ghurra*. Al-Shāfiʿī said that nothing is to be paid unless it becomes manifest that it was a child and it is better to consider the presence of spirit in it, I mean, that a *ghurra* is payable in it if the presence of life is established.

They disagreed as to who is liable for the payment. One group from among them—Mālik, al-Ḥasan ibn Ḥayy and al-Ḥasan al-Baṣrī—said that the liability is imposed on the wealth of the offender, while others said that it is upon the *ʿāqila*. Those who maintained the latter opinion are al-Shāfiʿī, Abū Ḥanīfa, al-Thawrī and a group of jurists. Their argument is based on the fact that it is an offence by way of *khaṭaʾ* and raises an obligation upon the *ʿāqila* and is also based on what is related from Jābir ibn ʿAbd Allāh "that the Prophet (God's peace and blessings be upon him) determined a *ghurra*, in the case of the *janīn*, as a liability of the assailant's *ʿāqila*, beginning with her husband and her child". Mālik compared it to *diya* in the case of *ʿamd*, when the blow was intentional.

To whom is the payment due? Mālik, al-Shāfiʿī and Abū Ḥanīfa said that it is to be made to the heirs of the *janīn* and its *ḥukm* is to be the *ḥukm* of *diya* in so far as it is inherited. Rabīʿa and al-Layth said that it belongs exclusively to the mother, for they treated the *janīn* as one of her limbs.

The obligation about which they differed in the case of the *janīn*, along with the *ghurra*, was expiation (*kaffāra*). Al-Shāfiʿī held that there is obligatory expiation in it, while Abū Ḥanīfa held that there is no such obligation. Mālik recommended it, but did not make it obligatory. Al-Shāfiʿī declared it obligatory, as expiation is obligatory, according to him, in cases of *ʿamd* as well as *khaṭaʾ*, while Abū Ḥanīfa imposed upon it the *ḥukm* of *ʿamd*, which does not carry expiation in his view. As expiation is not obligatory in *ʿamd* for Mālik, but it is in *khaṭaʾ* and this case in his view vacillates between *ʿamd* and *khaṭaʾ*, he, therefore, recommended expiation in it not making it obligatory.

Among the categories of *khaṭaʾ* that are disputed is their disagreement about holding the rider, driver (of animals) and the guide liable. The majority said that they are liable for the injuries caused by the animals. They argue in this on the basis of the decision of ʿUmar imposing *diya* in the case where a person was leading his mare and it trampled upon another. The Ẓāhirites said that there is no liability upon anyone for injuries caused by dumb animals. They relied on the established tradition in it related from the Prophet (God's peace and blessings be upon him) by Abū Hurayra that the Prophet said, "Injuries by the dumb (animals) go uncompensated, as are those during the digging of a well or in mining (for metals). In the treasure-trove there is a fifth (as revenue)". The majority interpreted this tradition to imply that the animals neither have rider nor one who is driving them, nor one leading them, as they held that if the animals had a rider, driver, or a leader, he was liable, by way of *khaṭaʾ*.

The majority disagreed about an animal when it injured someone with its hind-legs. Mālik said that there is no liability in this case, unless the owner of the animal does something that provokes it to strike with its hind-legs. Al-Shāfiʿī said the rider compensates what is hit by its fore-legs or by its hind-legs. This was also the opinion of Ibn Shubrama and Ibn Abī Laylā, who deemed equivalent what was damaged by legs or otherwise. This was Abū Ḥanīfa's opinion too, but he made an exception in the case of striking with hind legs or injuring with its tail. Perhaps, those who did not impose liability for injuries through legs, argued on the basis of what is related from the Prophet—"Injuries caused with legs go uncompensated"—but this tradition was not proved sound for al-Shāfiʿī and he rejected it.

Under the opinions of the jurists about the person digging a well (or pit) and a passer by falling in it, Mālik said that if he dug the pit in a spot where wells are usually dug, there is no liability, but if he transgresses in such digging, he is to compensate. Al-Layth said that if he digs it in land owned by him, he does not compensate, but if he digs in property not owned by him, he compensates. Compensation, according to him, is by way of *khaṭaʾ* in such a case. They also disagreed about an animal brought to a halt in a particular place. Some of them said that if he brings it to a halt in a spot where he was bound to do so, but still causes damage, there is no compensation, but if it was otherwise he is to compensate, which was al-Shāfiʿī's opinion. Abū Ḥanīfa said that he compensates in any case and is not absolved if he ties it up in a place where he is permitted to tie it, just as he is not absolved from liability while he is riding it, in case it strikes something, even when such riding is permitted.

They disagreed about two riders colliding with each other, when both die from the collision. Mālik, Abū Ḥanīfa and a group of jurists said that on each is the liability for the *diya* of the other, which is paid by the *ʿāqila*. Al-Shāfiʿī and ʿUthmān al-Battī said that on each is half of the *diya* of the other, as each died due to his own act as much as he did from the other's. They agreed that the physician (surgeon) who makes an error is liable for *diya*, like injuring the penis in circumcision, or what resembles it, as he falls under the definition of an offender at fault. There is a narration from Mālik, however, that there is no liability for him, when he belongs to the medical profession. There is no disagreement that he is liable when he does not belong to the profession as in that case he is a tortfeasor. In this there is, along with *sijma* (consensus), the tradition of ʿAmr ibn Shuʿayb from his father from his grandfather that the Messenger of Allāh (God's peace and blessings be upon him) said, "One who indulges in medicine, when he has not been known to practise medicine prior to that, is to be held liable". The *diya* in the case of *khaṭaʾ* by a physician is to be paid by the *ʿāqila*, but there are jurists who assign this to his wealth. There is no dispute that if he is not a physician (and practises medicine), the *diya* is paid from his wealth, on the apparent meaning of ʿAmr ibn Shuʿayb's tradition.

There is no disagreement among them that the *kaffāra* (expiation) ordained by Allāh in the killing of a free man in the case of *khaṭaʾ* is obligatory. They disagreed about murder (*ʿamd*), whether it entails *kaffāra* and also the case of a slave through *khaṭaʾ*. Mālik made it obligatory in the case of killing of a free man through *khaṭaʾ*, to the exclusion of *ʿamd*, while al-Shāfiʿī considered it obligatory in *ʿamd* deeming it prior and evident. According to Mālik the *ḥukm* of the slave in this is the *ḥukm* of *khaṭaʾ* (for a free man).

They disagreed about the enhancement (*taghlīẓ*) of *diya* in the prohibited month and in the protected (sacred) city. Mālik, Abū Ḥanīfa and Ibn Abī Laylā said that there is no enhancement of *diya* in this case, while al-Shāfiʿī did enhance it in the case of death and bodily injuries. It is related from Ibn al-Qāsim, Muḥammad and Ibn Shihāb that it is to be increased by a third of its amount in such cases. This is related from ʿUmar. Similarly, for al-Shāfiʿī in the case of one killing a close relative.

The reliance of Mālik and Abū Ḥanīfa is on the general meaning emerging from the limitations of time set on *diyāt*. Thus, anyone claiming a restriction of this meaning has to come up with the evidence (*dalīl),* along with the fact that there is consensus on the point that there is to be no enhancement of *kaffāra* for anyone killed in the Ḥaram. The argument of al-Shāfiʿī is on the fact that this has been related from ʿUmar, ʿUthmān and Ibn ʿAbbās. If something is related from the Companions that opposes analogy, it is necessary to interpret it as a *ḥukm* based on an evidence in a revelationary source. The aspect from which this opposes analogy is that enhancement in a case that has occurred through mistake (*khaṭaʾ*) diverges widely from the principles of the law. The other party may say that analogy in this case is based on what has been established in the law about the reverence of the Ḥaram and the solitary case of imposition of liability for hunting within it.

56.4. THE BOOK OF *DIYĀT FĪ MĀ DUN AL-NAFS* (INJURIES NOT LEADING TO LOSS OF LIFE)

The injuries in which *diya* becomes payable are head and facial injuries (*shijāj*) and loss of limbs. We begin with the discussion of *shijāj*. The study of this topic, however, relates to the subject-matter of the obligation (for payment), its conditions, the amount payable, from who it is due, when it is due and to whom.

The subject-matter of the obligation are *shijāj* and the severance of limbs. *Shijāj* are ten, in the literal sense as well as in *fiqh*. The first one is called *dāmiya*, which bruises the skin causing it to bleed. Second is the *ḥārisa*, which ruptures the skin. This is followed by *bāḍiᶜa*, which exposes the flesh, that is, cuts it up. Fourth, the *mutalāḥima*, which severs a small part of the flesh. Fifth is the *simḥāq*, which reaches the thin (fibrous) membrane between the flesh and the bones (periosteum); it is also called *malṭāʾ*. Then comes the *mūḍiḥa* that uncovers the bones, that is, exposes them. It is followed by the *hāshima*, which crushes the bones. The eighth is the *munaqqila*, which causes the bones to splinter. Then comes the *māʾmūma*, which reaches the cerebral membrane. Finally, there is the *jāʾifa*, which descends into the internal cavities. The names of these *shijāj* are exclusively applied to the injuries that occur in the area of the head and the face and not the rest of the body; the name of the injuries afflicting the body is *jirāḥ* (pl. of *jurḥ*) and these pertain specifically to the body. These, then, are the names of such injuries (to the face and the head).

About their *aḥkām*, I mean, the liability arising from them, the jurists agreed that *diya* is to be paid for an intentional *mūḍiḥa* and for what is less than *mūḍiḥa*, as well as for *mūḍiḥa* arising from *khaṭaʾ*. They agreed that in the case of *khaṭaʾ*, for what is less than the *mūdia*, there is no *diya*, but there is *ḥukūma* (estimated damages). Some of them said that this is the amount of the wages of the physician; however, it is reported from ᶜUmar and ᶜUthmān that they awarded one-half *diya* for *simḥāq*. It is reported from ᶜAli that he awarded four camels in it. It is related from Zayd ibn Thābit that he said, "In the *ḍāmiya* is a camel, in the *bāḍiya* there are two, in the *mutalāḥima* there are three camels and in the *simḥāq* four". The majority of the jurists maintain, what we have already mentioned, that the principle in injuries is *ḥukūma*, except those in which the *sunna* has prescribed a limit. Mālik stipulates in the imposition of *ḥukūma* that the injuries, less than the *mūḍiḥa*, should heal beyond any disfigurement, while the other jurists impose *ḥukūma* in them irrespective of healing beyond disfigurement. These are the *aḥkām* for what is less than the *mūḍiḥa*.

All the jurists agree about *mūḍiḥa* that when it occurs by way of *khaṭaʾ* there are five camels in it. This has been established from the Prophet (God's peace and blessings be upon him) in his letter to ʿAmr ibn Ḥazm and also from the tradition of ʿAmr ibn Shuʿayb from his father from his grandfather that the Prophet (God's peace and blessings be upon him) said, "In the *mūḍiḥa* there are five", that is, camels.

The jurists disagreed about the location of the *mūḍiḥa* in the body, after their agreement over what we have mentioned, I mean, the liability in the case of *qiṣāṣ in ʿamd* and the liability of *diya* for *khaṭaʾ*. Mālik said that the *mūḍiḥa* is not inflicted, except in the area of the head, the forehead, cheeks and the upper jaw; it is not inflicted in the area of the lower beard (chin, lower jaw), as that takes the *ḥukm* of the neck, nor is it inflicted on the nose. For al-Shāfiʿī and Abū Ḥanīfa, the *mūḍiḥa* can be inflicted in the entire area of the head and the face. The majority, however, agree that it is not inflicted on the (remaining parts of the) body. Al-Layth and a group of jurists said that it is inflicted on the sides, while al-Awzāʿī said that if it is inflicted on the body, it carries one-half of the *diya* for the head and face. It is related from ʿUmar that he said, "If the *mūḍiḥa* is inflicted on the body, it will carry five per cent of the *diya* of the limb (upon which it is inflicted)".

Some of the jurists enhanced the *diya* for the *mūḍiḥa* when it caused disfigurement. Some upheld the award of an additional amount equal to half its *diya*. This is related by Mālik from Sulaymān ibn Yasār. Mālik's opinion wavered in this, for he upheld Sulaymān ibn Yasār's opinion once and said another time that the *diya* is not to be enhanced, which was the majority's opinion. It is also related from Mālik that he said, "If the face is disfigured there is *ḥukūma* in it without restrictions of precedent". The meaning of *ḥukūma*, according to Mālik, is the amount by which the person's value would go down had he been a slave.

The majority fix the *diya* for the *hāshima* at ten per cent. This is related from Zayd ibn Thābit and no one from among the Companions opposed him. Some of the jurists deviated from this saying that the *hāshima* is (like) the *munaqqila*. There is no disagreement that there is ten per cent *diya* in it and five per cent when it is inflicted by way of *khaṭaʾ*. When it is inflicted by way of *ʿamd*, the majority of the jurists maintain that there is no retaliation in it due to apprehension (of transgression). It is related from Ibn al-Zubayr that he used to grant the verdict for retaliation in this and also in the *māʾmūma*. About the *hāshima* by way of *ʿamd*, Ibn al-Qāsim related from Mālik that there is no retaliation in it. Those who permitted retaliation in the *munaqqila* should have first permitted it in the *hāshima*. There is no disagreement about the *māʾmūma*, that there is no retaliation in it and there is one-third *diya* in it, except what has been related from Ibn Zubayr.

They agreed about the *jāʾifa* that it is an injury inflicted on the body, not on the head and there is one-third *diya* for it. It amounts to *jāʾifa* when inflicted on the back and the stomach. They disagreed when it is inflicted on another part of the body, but extends to one of the internal cavities. Mālik has related from Saʿīd ibn al-Musayyib that each injury extending to a hollow part of the body, whatever part that is, carries one-third *diya* of that part. Ibn Shihāb has related that he did not go by this opinion, though it was this that Mālik had preferred, but construction of analogy here is not justified as its basis (*sanad*) is *ijtihād* without precedent. Saʿīd ibn al-Musayyib deduced it through analogy from the *jāʾifa* in the same manner as that related from ʿUmar about the *mūḍiḥa* inflicted on the body.

For the injuries inflicted upon the rest of the body, in the case of *khaṭaʾ*, there is nothing but *ḥukūma*.

56.4.1. The Discussion of *Diyāt* for the Limbs

The principle about the limbs in the body is that if they are severed by way of *khaṭaʾ*, there is fixed compensation for them, which is called *diya*. Similarly, in the case of loss of life and injuries, as in the tradition of ʿAmr ibn Ḥazm from his father about the letter that the Messenger of Allāh wrote to him regarding *diyat*, wherein he said, "For the loss of life there are a hundred camels, for the nose, when severed completely, a hundred camels, for the *māʾmūma* one-third *diya*, for the *jāʾifa* similar to it, for the eye fifty, for the forearm fifty, for the leg fifty, for each finger, as many as there may be (on a hand), ten camels and for the teeth and the *mūḍiḥa* five". All this is agreed upon, except the teeth and the thumb; they disagreed about them, as we shall be discussing.

Among the things that they agreed upon—which are not mentioned here (in the tradition)—by way of analogy upon those that are mentioned, we say: The jurists agreed that for the lips there is full *diya*, while the majority maintained that for each one of them separately is one-half *diya*. It is related from some of the Tābiʿūn that for the lower lip is two-thirds *diya* as it prevents food and drink from dripping out and, as a whole, its function and utility are greater than that of the upper lip. This is the opinion of Zayd ibn Thābit. The majority of the jurists and the leading *muftīs* are in agreement that for each part of the human being existing as a pair is full *diya*, except for the eyebrows and a man's breasts.

They differed about the ears as to when they carry full *diya*. Abū Ḥanīfa, al-Thawrī and al-Layth said that if they are cut from the base there is full *diya* in them, but they did not stipulate loss of hearing, on the other hand, they determined independently full *diya* for loss of hearing. The well-known opinion from Mālik is that he did not determine *diya* for the ears, unless it was accompanied by loss of hearing, if that was not lost they were to be compensated through *ḥukūma*. It is related from Abū Bakr that he rendered judgment for fifteen camels for the ears saying that it does not cause loss of hearing and they (the area) can be covered by the hair or a turban. It is related from ʿUmar, ʿAlī and Zayd that they rendered judgments for ears severed from the base as one-half *diya*. As for the majority of the jurists, there is no disagreement among them that there is full *diya* for loss of hearing. There is *ḥukūma* for the eyebrows, according to Mālik and al-Shāfiʿī, while Abū Ḥanīfa said that there is full *diya*; similarly, for the eyelashes, but there is nothing but *ḥukūma* in this, according to Mālik.

The reliance of the Ḥanafites is on what has been related from Ibn Masʿūd that he said, "For each pair that a man has is full *diya*". They held them (the ears) similar to the other double organs over which they were in complete agreement. Mālik's reliance is on the argument that analogy has no role to play in this issue and the method requires transmitted precedent; if nothing is established through transmission to the effect that there is *diya* in it, it acquires *ḥukūma* as its basis. Further, the eyebrows are not limbs that have utility or function, that is, necessary for creativity.

About the eyelids it is said that for each one of the them there is one-fourth *diya*, which was also the opinion of al-Shāfiʿī and the Kūfī, for there is no survival for the eye without the eyelids. According to others beside them, there is one-third *diya* for the lower eyelids, while there is two-thirds for the upper.

They agreed that one who becomes entitled to more than a full *diya* because of the loss of his limbs has a right to it, for example, one who loses his two eyes and his nose is entitled to two full *diyas*. With respect to the testicles also, they agreed that there is full *diya* for them and all of them said that for one of them there is one-half *diya*, except what is related from Saʿīd ibn al-Musayyib, who said that for the left one there is two-thirds *diya* as the child is conceived because of it and for the right one there is one-third. These, then, are the issues related to pairs of limbs.

In the case of the single organs, the majority of the jurists agreed that for the tongue, lost by way of *khaṭaʾ*, there is full *diya*; and this is related from the Prophet (God's peace and blessings be upon him). This is the case when the whole of it is cut or, at least, a part that prevents speech. If the part cut does not prevent speech, there is *ḥukūma* in it. They disagreed about retaliation in it, when cut by way of *ʿamd*. Among them were those who did not uphold retaliation in it and made *diya* obligatory; these were Mālik, al-Shāfiʿī and the Kūfī, but al-Shāfiʿī awarded *diya* from the wealth of the offender, while the Kūfī and Mālik imposed it on the *ʿāqila*. Al-Layth and others beside him said that for the tongue, cut intentionally, there is retaliation.

They agreed about the nose that if it is cut from the base there is full *diya* in it as is laid down in the tradition. It is the same for Mālik irrespective of the sense of smell having been lost. If one of these (the nose or the sense of smell) is lost, according to him, there is *diya* in it, but if one is lost after the other the *diya* becomes full. They agreed that in the case of a physically sound penis, capable of sexual intercourse (not impotent), there is full *diya*. They disagreed about the penis of the impotent or of one castrated, just as they differed about the tongue of the dumb and the forearm of one paralysed. There were among them those who determined a (full) *diya* for these (organs) and there were those who ruled for *ḥukūma*. Some of them said that for the penis of the impotent and the castrated is one-third *diya*, but the opinion adopted by the majority favours *ḥukūma*. The minimum part of it that entails *diya*, according to Mālik, is the glans penis (*ḥashafa*), in which case there is *ḥukūma* for the remaining penis.

About the eye of a one-eyed person, the jurists have two opinions. First, there is full *diya* in it, which was upheld by Mālik and a group of the jurists of Medīna; it was also the opinion of al-Layth, the verdict of ᶜUmar ibn ᶜAbd al-ᶜAzīz and the view of Ibn ᶜUmar. Al-Shāfiᶜī, Abū Ḥanīfa and al-Thawrī said that it carries one-half *diya* as in the case of one with two sound eyes. This is related from a group of *Tābiᶜūn*. The reliance of the first group is on the argument that one sound eye for a one-eyed person is like two sound eyes for one who has them. The reliance of the second party is on the tradition of ᶜAmr ibn Ḥazm, I mean, the general meaning in the words, "For an eye one-half *diya*". They also relied on analogy from the point of their consensus that one who cuts the forearm of a person with one arm is liable for only one-half *diya*. The reason for their disagreement in this is the conflict of the general meaning of the text with analogy and also the clash of an analogy with another analogy.

One of the best opinions in the case where a person loses his sight partially, because of a blow to the eye, is what has been related from ᶜAlī (God be pleased with him). He ordered the person, whose eye had been damaged, to bandage his sound eye and then gave a shield to another person, who moved away from him while the (hurt) person kept on looking at it till such time that he could not see it. He drew a line on the ground at the spot when he first stopped seeing it. He then ordered the person to bandage his hurt eye, the sound one being uncovered now and gave a shield to the person, who passed by his eye (into the distance). He drew a line again where he first stopped seeing it and worked out the difference between the first distance and the end of the second. He awarded him *diya* in the same ratio. In order to verify the truth of his statement about the extent of his vision for the bad and the sound eye, the process is to be repeated a number of times at different locations. If the distances come out to be similar, we will know that he is telling the truth.

The jurists differed about the offence against the eye which is without vision but retains its physical appearance. Mālik, al-Shāfiʿī and Abū Ḥanīfa said that there is *ḥukūma* in it, while Zayd ibn Thābit said that in this case there is ten per cent *diya*: a hundred *dīnārs*. Al-Shāfiʿī interpreted this saying that this was valuation on the part of Zayd and not fixation of a limit. It is related from ʿUmar ibn al-Khaṭṭāb and ʿAbd Allāh ibn ʿAbbās that they issued the verdict, in each case of a blind eye retaining its appearance, an arm paralysed and a tooth dislocated (blackened), one-third *diya*. Mālik said that the *diya* becomes payable with dislocation and the extraction of a dislocated tooth leads to full *diya*.

They disagreed about the one-eyed person who damages another person's sound eye. The majority held that if he likes he can demand retaliation, but if he forgoes it there is *diya* for him. One group said it is to be full (*diya*), while another said it is one-half, which was the opinion of al-Shāfiʿī and Ibn al-Qāsim, while Mālik has both views. Al-Mughīra, from among his disciples and Ibn Dīnār upheld full *diya*. The Kūfīs said that the person whose eye has been lost has the right to retaliate only, unless they settle for some amount. The reliance of those who upheld full *diya*, in case he forgoes retaliation, is on the argument that he becomes liable for what he has allowed him to retain, that is, his sole eye, which carries full *diya* according to the majority of the jurists. The opinion of ʿUmar, ʿUthmān and Ibn ʿUmar about a solitary eye, when it is lost, is that the liability is one thousand *dīnārs*, as it is for this person equivalent to two eyes collectively, except that when the victim forgives him (the one-eyed person) the liability is for the *diya* of one eye. Their argument is that in such a case the rule reverts to its original basis, that is, for one eye there is one-half *diya*. Abū Ḥanīfa's argument is that there is no fixed *diya* in cases of *ʿamd*. This issue has been discussed in the topic of retaliation for wounds.

The majority of the jurists and the leaders of the *muftīs*—Mālik, Abū Ḥanīfa, al-Shāfiʿī, al-Thawrī and others—said that for each finger there are ten camels and the fingers for this purpose are equal and for each phalange (*unmula*) is one-third of the tenth, except for fingers that have only two phalanges like the thumb, in which case there are five camels for each phalange. Their reliance in this is on what is laid down in the tradition of ʿAmr ibn Ḥazm that the Messenger of Allāh (God's peace and blessings be upon him) said, "For each finger, as many as there may be (in the hand), are ten camels". ʿAmr ibn Shuʿayb has recorded from his father from his grandfather "that the Messenger of Allāh (God's peace and blessings be upon him) issued the verdict of one-tenth of ten camels for fingers", which is the opinion of ʿAlī Ibn Masʿūd and Ibn ʿAbbās.

According to them (the jurists), for those who deal in silver, it will come to what each views to be the *diya* in silver. Thus, it is ten per cent in the opinion of those who consider it to be twelve thousand *dirhams*. It is also ten per cent in the opinion of those who consider it to be ten thousand *dirhams*.

A difference of opinion has been related from the earlier jurists about the compensation for fingers. It is related from ʿUmar ibn al-Khaṭṭāb that he held the compensation in the case of the thumb and the index finger to be one-half *diya*, for the middle finger ten prescribed camels, for the next finger nine and for the little finger six. It is related from Mujāhid that he determined fifteen camels for the thumb, for the index finger ten, for the middle finger ten, for the next finger eight and for the little finger seven.

For the collar bone and ribs, according to the majority of the jurists, there is *ḥukūma*, while it is related from some of the earlier jurists that there is fixed compensation. It is related from Mālik that ʿUmar ibn al-Khaṭṭāb awarded a load-bearing camel for a molar tooth, a rib, or the collar bone. Saʿīd ibn Jubayr said that there are two camels for the collar bone, while Qatāda said that there are four. The argument of the majority of the jurists of the regions is that if nothing fixed is established directly from the Prophet (God's peace and blessings be upon him), there is *ḥukūma* in it.

The majority of the jurists of the regions maintain that for each tooth from among the teeth in the mouth, there are five camels, which was Ibn ʿAbbās's opinion. Mālik has related from ʿUmar that he awarded a load-bearing camel in the case of molars, when the front teeth were missing. There is no disagreement about the front teeth that they are compensated with five camels. Saʿīd ibn al-Musayyib said that for the molars there are two camels for each. It is related from ʿAbd al-Malik ibn Marwān that Marwān ibn al-Ḥakam objected to the opinion of Ibn ʿAbbās saying, "Do you consider the molars similar to the front teeth?" Ibn ʿAbbās said that if they are to be compared with the fingers, their *diya* is the same. The reliance of the majority in such cases is what has been established from the Prophet (God's peace and blessings be upon him) that he said, "For the teeth there are five (camels)" and this is from the tradition of ʿAmr ibn Shuʿayb from his father from his grandfather. The term "tooth" applies equally to all teeth, those in the front of the mouth and those at the back. Further, the teeth are compared to the fingers that have the same *diya* though their utility varies. The argument of those who differentiated between them is that such excess in terms of *diyāt* can be witnessed in the law due to the greater utility of some of the limbs. It appears, however, that those, in the earlier period, who inclined toward this opinion did so on the basis of established precedent.

All these limbs for which *diya* is established in the case of *khaṭaʾ*, there is retaliation in them too, amputation for cutting and extraction for dislocation (in the case of ʿ*amd*). They disagreed in the case of fractures, like that of the calf (bone) or the forearm, whether there is retaliation for them or not. Mālik and all his disciples maintained that there is retaliation for all fractures, except for the thigh bone and the spine. Al-Shāfiʿī and al-Layth said that there is no retaliation in bones that are fractured. This was also the opinion of Abū Ḥanīfa, except that he made an exemption in the case of teeth, which is reported from ʿUmar. Abū ʿUmar ibn ʿAbd al-Barr said that retaliation for broken teeth is established from the Prophet (God's peace and blessings be upon him) from the tradition of Anas. He said that it is related in another tradition from the Prophet where he did not permit retaliation in bones cut off; however, it does not have sufficient strength. It is related from Mālik that Abū Bakr ibn Muḥammad ibn ʿAmr ibn Ḥazm exacted *qiṣāṣ* for a broken thigh bone.

They agreed that the *diya* for a woman is one-half that for a man, in the case of loss of life. They disagreed in the case of *diyāt* for *shijāj* and limbs. The majority of the jurists of Medina said that a woman is equal to a man in the case of compensation for *shijāj* and limbs, when the amount is up to one-third *diya*, but when it exceeds this, her *diya* reverts to the rule of one-half that of a man, I mean, the *diya* for his various limbs. An example of this is that for each of her fingers is a *diya* of ten camels, for two it is twenty camels, for three thirty, but for four it is twenty. This was the opinion of Mālik and his disciples and also of al-Layth ibn Saʿd and ʿUmar ibn ʿAbd al-ʿAzīz. Another group said that the *diya* of a wound for a woman is like the *diya* of the wound of a man up to the *mūḍiḥa*, after which it is half of the *diya* for a man's wounds. This is the well-known opinion of Ibn Masʿūd; it is also related from ʿUthmān and was the opinion of Shurayḥ and a group of jurists. One group said that the *diya* for a woman's wounds and injuries is half that for a man in major and minor cases. This is the opinion of ʿAlī (God be pleased with him) and is also related from Ibn Masʿūd; however, his well-known opinion we have mentioned first. This was adopted by Abū Ḥanīfa, al-Shāfiʿī and al-Thawrī.

The reliance of the upholders of this (the last) opinion is on the principle that the *diya* of a woman be half that of a man. The adoption of this principle is, therefore, obligatory till futher evidence is furnished from the established transmission, as *qiyās* is not permitted in the case of *diyāt* (all crimes), especially in view of the fact that a distinction on the basis of more and less violates *qiyās* itself. It is for this reason that Rabīʿa said something to Saʿīd, which will be coming up in what follows. The second group, on the other hand, has nothing to rely upon except *mursal* traditions. It is related from Saʿīd ibn al-Musayyib, when Rabīʿa ibn Abī ʿAbd al-Raḥmān asked him as to what is the compensation for four fingers of a female, he said, "Twenty". "I (Rabīʿa) would say that when her wound inflamed and her affliction intensified, it decreased the compensation". He said, "Are you an ʿIrāqī?" I said, "On the contrary, I am an enquiring scholar, or an ignorant learner". He retorted, "It is a *sunna*". It is also related from the Prophet (God's peace and blessings be upon him) from the *mursal* of ʿAmr ibn Shuʿayb from his father and also from ʿIkrima. One group of jurists was of the opinion that when the opinion of a Companion opposes analogy it is necessary to act according to it, as it is known that he would not depart from analogy unless it is due to an established source, but there is weakness in this for it is possible that he may relinquish analogy as he does not uphold it or because there is another analogy for it that opposes the first, or he may be following the opinion of another person on that issue.

This, then, is the situation about the *diyāt* for injuries inflicted upon free persons and of the offences against their limbs, whether they are male or female.

The jurists differed into two opinions about the injuries inflicted upon slaves and the maiming of their limbs. Among them were those who maintained that for their injuries and maiming the compensation is the decrease in their value. Among them were also those who said that the liability in this case is the decrease in the amount of his *diya*. Thus, in the case of a *mūḍiḥa*, it will be five per cent of his value and for his eye would be half his value. This was the opinion of Abū Ḥanīfa and al-Shāfiʿī and is the opinion of ʿUmar and ʿAli. Mālik said that the consideration here is for whatever is the decrease in his price, except in the cases of the *mūḍiḥa*, the *munaqqila* and *māʾmūma*, for in these is compensation that is paid as the *diya* of a free man. The argument of the first group is based on the similarity of the slave to goods, while the argument of the second group is based on the comparison with free men, for they are Muslims and subject to the imposition of religious obligations (*taklīf*).

There is no disagreement among them that the *diya* of *khaṭaʾ*, in this case, if it exceeds a third, is to be paid by the *ʿāqila*. They disagreed about what was less than this. Mālik and the seven jurists of Medina said that the *ʿāqila* does not bear anything, in this case, a third or more. Abū Ḥanīfa said that it bears ten per cent or more of the full *diya*. Al-Thawrī and Ibn Shubrama said that the liability for the *mūḍiḥa* and beyond that is on the *ʿāqila*, while al-Shāfiʿī said that the *ʿāqila* bears the *diya* of *khaṭaʾ*, in all cases, whether more or less. The argument of al-Shāfiʿī is that the principle requires the *ʿāqila* to bear the *diya* for *khaṭaʾ* and whoever restricts this bears the burden of proof. The first group has nothing to rely upon, except the argument that it is practised and well known.

Here this book comes to an end. Praise be to Allāh as is His due.

56.5 THE BOOK OF *QASĀMA*[225] (MULTIPLE OATHS)

The jurists disagreed about *qasāma* on four issues that work like principles for the cases in this topic. The first issue is whether the *ḥukm* of *qasāma* is obligatory. Second, if we concede that it is obligatory, do *qiṣāṣ*, *diya*, or the elimination of criminal proceedings become obligatory through it? Third, do the complainants commence oath-taking or is it done by the defendant, and what is the number of the *awliyāʾ* (victim's heirs) who take oath? Fourth, what is it that constitutes *lawth* (suspicion), by virtue of which the complainants commence with oath proceedings?

56.5.1. Issue 1: The obligation of its *ḥukm*

About the obligation of its *ḥukm*, generally, the majority of the jurists of the regions—Mālik, al-Shāfiʿīh, Abū Ḥanīfa, Aḥmad, Abū Sufyān, Dāwūd, and their disciples—upheld it. A group of jurists—Sālim ibn ʿAbd Allāh, Abū Qalāba, ʿUmar ibn ʿAbd al-ʿAzīz, and Ibn ʿUlayya—said that it is not permitted to adjudicate through it. The reliance of the majority is on what has been established from the Prophet (God's peace and blessings be upon him) through the tradition of Ḥuwayyiṣa and Muḥayyiṣa, which is a tradition agreed upon for its soundness among the traditionists, except that they disagreed about its words, as will be discussed in what follows.

The reliance of the group denying the obligation of its *ḥukm* is on the argument that *qasāma* is opposed to the principles of law that are agreed upon for their soundness. Among them is the principle of law that no one is to take an oath, unless he knows about the facts with certainty or he has physically witnessed them. If that is the case, then, how can the victim's heirs swear, when they have not witnessed the homicide; in fact, they may be in one town and the homicide may have occurred in another town. It is for this reason that al-Bukhārī has related from Abū Qalāba "that one day ʿUmar ibn ʿAbd al-ʿAzīz sat on his chair outside his residence and summoned the people. When they had come he said, 'What is your opinion about *qasāma*?' The people cautiously said, 'It is said that retaliation on the basis of *qasāma* is lawful and the Caliphs have ordered retaliation because of it'. He said, 'What do you say O Abū Qalāba, while I am facing the people'. I said, 'O *Amīr al-Muʾminīn*, you have with you the Arab nobility and the leaders of the forces, what do you say if fifty of them render testimony in front of you that a man has committed unlawful intercourse in Damascus, but they did not actually see it, would you subject him to *rajm*?' He said, 'No!' I said, 'If fifty of them render

[225] *Qasāma* has been called 'a kind of compurgation' by some. The distinction is that compurgation works to clear the name of the accused or to prove his innocence, while *qasāma* is a procedure through which the guilt of the accused is established.

testimony in front of you that a man committed theft in Ḥumṣ, but they did not see it, would you amputate his hand?" He said, "No!" "In some narrations it says, "What is their position if they render testimony that a certain person killed another, while they were here with you, would you order retaliation by their testimony?" He said that ʿUmar ibn ʿAbd al-ʿAzīz, after this, had a decree recorded that if they could produce two *ʿadl* witnesses that such and such a person killed him, retaliation may be ordered, but the person is not to be subjected to *qiṣāṣ* on the testimony of fifty persons who merely swear to it.

They also maintain that one of the principles requires that "the (burden of proof) evidence is upon the plaintiff and the oath is upon the person who denies (the charge or claim) (defendant)". They also advance the argument that they do not find the Messenger of Allāh (God's peace and blessings be upon him) approving the *ḥukm* of *qasāma* in these traditions. It was a *ḥukm* of the days of *jāhiliyya* and the Messenger of Allāh gently pointed out to them how its *ḥukm* could not be binding according to the principles of Islam. It was for this reason that he said to them, that is the heirs of the victim, who were from among the Anṣār, "Will you undertake fifty oaths?" They said, "How can we swear when we did not witness it?" He said, "Then will the Jews swear for you?" They said, "How can we accept the oaths of a people who do not believe?" These jurists said that had the undertaking of oaths, without witnessing, been a *sunna* the Messenger of Allāh (God's peace and blessings be upon him) would have said to them that it is a *sunna*. They maintained that as these traditions are not explicit with respect to adjudication on the basis of *qasāma*, and as the texts are open to interpretation, it is better to refer them (the traditions) to the general principles.

Those who upheld it, particularly Mālik, maintained that the *sunna* of *qasāma* is a *sunna* independent in itself, restricting the general principles like all other restricting *sunan*. He thought that the underlying cause for it was the prevention of bloodshed, as homicide is rampant and there is very little evidence available due to the murderer having taken care to commit it in a secluded spot. The *sunna*, therefore, instituted this practise for the security of life. This *ʿilla* is rejected, however, as it can apply to highway robbers and thieves, as evidence is difficult to procure against thieves, so also the highway robber. It is for this reason that Mālik makes admissible the evidence of those plundered against the plunderers, despite its opposition to the general principles, because those plundered are complainants due to their being plundered—Allāh knows best.

56.5.2. Issue 2: The liability arising from it

The jurists who upheld *qasāma* disagreed about the liability arising from it. Mālik and Aḥmad said that it leads to the entitlement of *qiṣāṣ* in the case of *amd* and *diya* in *khaṭaᶜ*. Al-Shafiᶜī, al-Thawrī and a group of jurists said that it gives rise to the liability for *diya* only. Some of the Kūfīs said that there is no right flowing from it, except that it acts as a defence in a complaint, as the principle entitles only the defendant to take the oath. Some of them (the Kūfīs) said that the defendant takes the oath and pays up the *diya*, according to which it merely acts as a defence against retaliation. There are, thus, with respect to entitlement, four opinions.

Mālik's reliance and the reliance of those who adopted his opinion is on what has been related of the tradition of Ibn Abī Laylā from Sahl ibn Abī Ḥathma, which says, "The Messenger of Allāh (God's peace and blessings be upon him) said to them, 'You take the oath and become entitled to the blood of your comrade'". Similarly, what Mālik has related from the *mursal* of Bushayr ibn Yasār, which says, "The Messenger of Allāh (God's peace and blessings be upon him) said to them, 'Would you swear fifty oaths and be entitled to the blood of your comrade or your killer'".

The reliance of those who imposed only *diya* through it is upon the argument that oaths are effective in determining entitlement to wealth, that is, in the law, like the *ḥukm* of restitution of property through an oath and a witness and also like the obligation arising from the refusal of the defendant to take the oath or by his refusal and the transference of the oath to the plaintiff, according to those who uphold the transference of oath in case of refusal. In addition (they said), the tradition of Mālik from Ibn Abī Laylā is defective, for he is an unknown person, no one else having related from him beside Mālik. It is also said about him that he did not transmit (directly) from Sahl. The tradition of Bushayr ibn Yasār varies in its chains of transmission, Mālik transmitted it as *mursal*, while others had complete chains. The Qāḍī (Ibn Rushd) said: It appears that this was the underlying reason why al-Bukhārī did not record these two traditions. Analogy also supported them in this, because of what has been reported from ᶜUmar (God be pleased with him) that he said, "There is no retaliation through *qasāma*, but it leads to the entitlement for *diya*".

Those who said that the only right arising from it is that of defence in a complaint argue that oaths are sworn by the defendant alone. In addition, there are traditions that we shall be quoting in what follows.

56.5.3. Issue 3: The prior right to the oath

The upholders of *qasāma*, that is, those who said that it gives rise to the entitlement of *qiṣāṣ* or *diya*, disagreed as to who is to commence the swearing of fifty oaths, as is laid down in the traditions. Al-Shāfiᶜī, Aḥmad, Dāwūd ibn ᶜĀli and others said that the complainants begin taking the oaths, while the jurists of Kūfa, Baṣra and a number of the jurists of Medīna said that, on the contrary, it is the defendants who begin with the oath first. The reliance of those who commence the proceedings with the plaintiffs is on Mālik's tradition from Ibn Abī Laylā from Sahl ibn Abī Ḥathma and also on his *mursal* tradition from Bushayr ibn Yasār. The reliance of those who begin with the defendants, is on the tradition recorded by al-Bukhārī from Saᶜīd ibn ᶜUbayd al-Ṭāʾī from Bashīr ibn Yasār from a man from the Anṣār, called Sahl ibn Abī Ḥathma, which says, "The Messenger of Allāh (God's peace and blessings be upon him) said, 'Will you come up with evidence as to who killed him?' They said, 'We do not have any evidence'. He said, 'Will they undertake an oath for you?' They said, 'We cannot agree to an oath by the Jews'. The Prophet disliked that his killing should go unpunished and gave for him a hundred camels from the *ṣadaqa*". The Qāḍī (Ibn Rushd) said: This is explicit in its meaning that fifty oaths are only effective in the rebuttal of the allegation.

They also argued on the basis of what is recorded by Abū Dāwūd from Abū Salama ibn Abī ᶜAbd al-Rahmān and Sulaymān ibn Yasār on the authority of a number of men from amongst the Anṣār "that the Messenger of Allāh (God's peace and blessings be upon him) called upon the Jews and commenced with them, saying, 'Will fifty of you swear fifty oaths'. When they declined, he said to the Anṣār, 'Take the oath'. They said, 'Do we swear about the unseen, O Messenger of Allāh?' The Messenger of Allāh (God's peace and blessings be upon him) then fixed *diya* as the liability for the Jews", as he (the victim) was found among them. This tradition is relied upon by those who declared that the oath was a duty for the defendant and yet despite that they impose *diya* on him. It is a tradition with sound chains of transmission and has been related by reliable reporters from al-Zuhrī from Abū Salama. The Kūfīs relate it from ᶜUmar, that is, he issued the verdict of oaths and *diya* for the defendants. Similar traditions, about the commencement of oaths with the Jews, have also been related from Rāfiᶜ ibn Khadīj.

These jurists argued against Mālik on the basis of what has been related from Ibn Shihāb al-Zuhrī from Sulaymān ibn Yasār and ᶜArāk ibn Mālik that ᶜUmar ibn al-Khaṭṭab said to al-Juhanī (a member of the tribe of Juhayna), who claimed the blood of his *walī* (ward) from a man from Banī Saᶜd. He was leading his horse when it trampled upon the feet of another member of the tribe. (The wound) thus, spread and killed him. ᶜUmar called upon the defendants, saying, "Do you swear an oath by Allāh that he did not die from it?" They refused to take the oath and made excuses. He then said to the complainants, "Take the oath". When they refused, he awarded them part of the *diya*. They said that these traditions of ours are preferable to those related about the commencement of oaths with the complainants, as the principle supports the tradition that the oath is upon the defendant. Abū ᶜUmar said that there are many conflicting yet widely circulating traditions on this issue.

56.5.4. Issue 4: The cause invoking *qasāma*

The majority of those jurists who upheld *qasāma* said that *qasāma* does not come into operation except in the case of suspicion (*shubha*). They disagreed about what constituted *shubha*. Al-Shāfiʿī said that it comes into operation if the *shubha* is of the same kind due to which the Messenger of Allāh rendered judgment on the basis of *qasāma*, which exists when the person killed is found in the locality of a people who do not mingle with others and between these people and the people of the deceased there is enmity, like the enmity that existed between the Anṣār and the Jews. Thus, Khaybar was the exclusive residence of the Jews and the victim, one of the Anṣār, was found there. He said (it becomes obligatory) also when the person suspected of homicide is found next to, or in the vicinity of, the deceased smeared with blood, or when a group of people are found in a place with a murdered person, or any other similar suspicion that persuades the authorities that the complainants are justified in raising such a suspicion. Mālik said something similar to this, that is, *qasāma* does not become obligatory without suspicion (*lawth*).

A single *ʿadl* witness, according to Mālik along with the agreement of his disciples, is sufficient to raise the required suspicion, but they differed when this witness was not reliable (*ʿadl*) by law. He also agreed with al-Shāfiʿī about circumstantial evidence that makes it probable, like a dead man covered with his blood is found and next to him is a person holding a blood-smeared iron club. Mālik, however, was of the view that the existence of the deceased in a residential locality does not amount to *lawth* (suspicion), even when there is enmity between the people of the deceased and the residents of the locality. If this is the case, then, there is nothing left that can form the basis for the stipulation of *lawth* for the obligation of *qasāma*. It is for this reason that many jurists did not uphold it.

Abū Ḥanīfa and his disciples said that if the deceased is found in the residential locality of a people and his tracks lead up to it, then, the imposition of *qasāma* becomes obligatory upon the residents of the locality. Some of the jurists imposed *qasāma* merely on the basis of the existence of the deceased in a locality, without the imposition of all the conditions laid down by al-Shāfiʿī and without the condition of the existence of a clue that was laid down by Abū Ḥanīfa. Such an opinion is related from ʿUmar, ʿAlī and Ibn Masʿūd. It was also upheld by al-Zuhrī, a group of the Ṭābiʿūn and is the opinion of Ibn Ḥazm, who said, "*Qasāma* becomes obligatory when a murdered person is found, wherever this may be and it is not known who killed him. If the heirs of the victim accuse someone and fifty of them take oaths, retaliation is imposed if they swore that it was *ʿamd*, but if they swear that it is *khaṭaʾ*, then, *diya* is to be imposed". According to him, less than fifty persons are not sufficient to take the oath, but according to Mālik there may be two or more from among them. Dāwūd said that *qasāma* is not be invoked, except in circumstances similar to those of the cases decided by the Prophet (God's peace and blessings be upon him).

Mālik and al-Layth were unique, among the jurists of the regions in upholding *qasāma*, merely on the basis of the dying declaration of the deceased—"so and so killed me"—as *lawth* that would give rise to *qasāma*.

Each one of the jurists, that is, those among them who maintained such views, declared what constituted suspicion according to his own conviction and each maintained that the complainants should begin with the oaths because of their being suspect. According to Mālik, suspicion transfers the *yamīn* from the defendant to the complainant, as the basis in the law for assigning the defendant the oath is the existence of strong suspicion about what he is denying. It was as if he compared this to an oath plus a witness, as in the case of property.

The opinion that the complaint itself constitutes sufficient suspicion is weak and contrary to the principles and texts, due to the words of the Prophet, "If the people were to be granted their unsubstantiated claims there would be some who would make claims on the blood of men as well as their property, but (in the absence of evidence) the burden of oath (*yamīn*) is upon the defendant". This is an established tradition from among the traditions of Ibn ʿAbbās. It has been recorded by Muslim in his *Ṣaḥīḥ*. The citing of the case of the cow of the Banī Isrāʾīl, as proof by the Mālikites, is weak, as the verification in that case has been attributed to a miraculous act.

Those who imposed retaliation on the basis of *qasāma* differed whether more than one person can be executed because of it. Mālik said that *qasāma* is only valid against one person, which was also the opinion of Aḥmad ibn Ḥanbal. Ashhab said that *qasāma* can be applied against a group, but only one of them identified by the victim's heirs is to be executed. This is weak. Al-Mughīra al-Makhzūmī said that all those against whom *qasāma* has been applied are to be put to death. Mālik and al-Layth said that if two *ʿadl* witnesses testify that a person struck another and the victim survived for some days after the blow and then died and if the heirs swear that he died because of the blow, the assailant is to be subjected to *qiṣāṣ*. All this, however, is weak.

They disagreed about *qasāma* in the case of a slave. Some confirmed it, which was the opinion of Abu Ḥanīfa based on a comparison with a free man. Some of them rejected it drawing a comparison with animals, which was Mālik's opinion.

The *diya* imposed after *qasāma* is to be derived from the wealth of the killer, for which no less than fifty person take fifty oaths, according to Mālik. According to him, no less than two persons are to take the oath for the accusation of killing and no less than one for the cases of *khaṭaʿ*. If any one of the heirs refuses to take the oath, *qasāma* is rendered invalid, according to him, for purposes of *qiṣāṣ*, but remains valid for *diya* in respect of those who did not refuse, that is, their share (is due). Al-Zuhrī has said that if one of them refuses to take the oath, *diya* is invalidated with respect to all of them. The details in this chapter are many.

The Qāḍī says: The discussion of *qasāma* forms part of the ways in which homicide is proved, but it is, in fact, a part of the Book of Litigation and we have mentioned it here according to what is customary with the jurists. If a case specific to one of the categories of law is brought up, they are of the view that it is better to mention it within that category.

Litigation that pertains to more than one category of the different legal categories is to be discussed in the Book of Litigation, though you will find them doing both the things, as Mālik did in his *al-Muwaṭṭaʾ*, for he has drawn into it cases from all books.

56.6. THE BOOK OF THE *AḤKĀM* OF *ZINĀ* (UNLAWFUL INTERCOURSE)

The study of the fundamentals of this book relates to the *ḥadd* of *zinā*, [226] the kinds of fornicators, the punishments for each category of crime (within it), and the mode of proof of this immoral offence (*fāḥisha*).

56.6.1. Chapter 1: The *Ḥadd* of *Zinā*

Zinā is (defined as) all sexual intercourse that occurs outside of a valid marriage, the semblance (*shubha*) of marriage, or lawful ownership (*milk yamīn*). This is agreed upon, as a whole, among the scholars of Islam, though they did differ about what constitutes doubt that is sufficient to waive the *ḥadd* penalty. In this topic there are a number of issues, out of which we shall mention those well known.

Among these is the case of the slave-woman with whom a man has intercourse, but he has joint ownership in her. Mālik said that *ḥadd* will be waived in this case; if the slave-woman gives birth to a child, it will be ascribed

[226] The term "unlawful intercourse" is being used here to describe the offence of *ẓina*. The term "adultery" has different connotations and cannot be a substitute for the term "*zinā*". It is confined to cases of married persons. On the other hand, terms like "sex offenders" are too general and may include categories not intended by some to be part of the term "*zinā*". The term proposed to be used here for "*zānī*" is "fornicators", though this term has its problems too, as it may include the case of sexual relations with slaves.

to him and he will have to pay her value (to the co-owner for his share). This was also Abū Ḥanīfa's opinion. Some of them said that he is to be awarded *tᶜazīr*. Abū Thawr said that he is to be awarded *ḥadd* without mitigation if he was aware of the prohibition.

The legal basis, for the majority, are the words of the Prophet (God's peace and blessings be upon him), "Waive the (fixed) penalties because of doubt". Those who did waive the penalties, disagreed about the offender's obligation to pay reasonable dower (*ṣadāq al-mithl*) in proportion to his share in the (slave-woman). The reason for the disagreement was whether the *ḥukm* to be applied would be based on the share owned by him or on the share not owned by him, as the *ḥukm* of what he owned yields permissibility, while the *ḥukm* of what he does not own requires prohibition.

Another issue relates to their disagreement over the soldier who has had intercourse with a woman captured as part of the spoils. One group said that *ḥadd* is to be applied to him, while another group waived the *ḥadd*, which appears sound. The reason for disagreement in this is the same as the previous issue—Allāh knows best.

When a man permits another to have intercourse with his slave-girl, Mālik is of the view that *ḥadd* is to be waived, while the others said that he is to be awarded *tᶜazīr*. Some of them said that this is a case of a gift accompanied by delivery and the corpus (of the slave-woman) is subservient to utilization for intercourse.

One of the issues is about a man who has intercourse with his son's, or his daughter's, slave-girl. The majority said that there is no *ḥadd* in this case, because of the saying of the Prophet (God's peace and blessings be upon him), "You and your wealth belong to your father", and his saying, "A father is not subject to *qiṣāṣ* because of his son", and also because of their consensus (*ijmāᶜ*) that he is not subject to amputation of the hand for what he stole from his son. It is, however, said that he is to be asked to pay her value, irrespective of her conceiving of him, for she is now prohibited for his son, and it is as if he had "consumed" her. One of the proofs is their consensus that if the father kills his grandson, his son has no right to claim *qiṣāṣ* from him; so also in the case of the person for whom his son acts as *walī*.

Among the issues is the case of a man who has intercourse with his wife's slave-girl. The jurists differed about it into four opinions. Mālik and the majority said that he is liable to unmitigated *ḥadd*. One group of jurists said that there is no *ḥadd* on him and he is to be considered a debtor for her value, in case the slave-girl voluntarily participated in the act, but if he coerced her he is to pay her value and she is free. This was the opinion of Aḥmad, Isḥāq, Ibn Masᶜūd and the first opinion of ᶜUmar related from him by Mālik in *al-Muwaṭṭa*ʾ. Another group said that he is liable to a hundred lashes only, whether he is a *muḥṣan* or a *thayyib* (non-virgin). The fourth group said that he is liable to *tᶜazīr*.

The reliance of those who held him liable to *ḥadd* is that he indulged in intercourse without valid ownership, joint ownership, or valid marriage, therefore, *ḥadd* becomes obligatory. The reliance of those who waived the *ḥadd* is on the established tradition "that the Messenger of Allāh (God's peace and blessings be upon him) decided, in the case of a man who had intercourse with his wife's slave-girl, that if he had coerced her into it she is free and he owes, in lieu of her, a reasonable value to her mistress, but if she participated voluntarily, she belongs to him and he owes her reasonable value to her mistress". Further, they agreed that there exists a doubt (of ownership) in his case about her (his wife's) wealth, on the evidence found in the words of the Prophet (God's peace and blessings be upon him), "A woman is taken into wedlock for three things"—and he mentioned one of these as her wealth. This is supported by the principle, of those who accept it, that a woman is interdicted by the husband in what is over a third her wealth; it is Mālik's opinion.

Abū Ḥanīfa is of the opinion that the *ḥadd* from a person who has sexual intercourse with a hired woman is waived. The majority oppose this. His opinion is weak and objectionable. It is as if he held that such a benefit is similar to all other benefits for which he may hire her, thus doubt intervenes and it begins to resemble the marriage of *mutᶜa*.

Among these issues is also the waiving of *ḥadd* from a person who confines a woman and they differed about this too. On the whole, void marriages are all included in this topic and in most of them, according to Mālik, *ḥadd* is waived, except in the cases where marriage takes place within the permanently prohibited degrees, like marriage with one's mother or a similar case, in which an excuse of ignorance is not acceptable.

56.6.2. Chapter 2: The Categories of Fornicators and Their Punishments

Fornicators, for whom punishments vary according to their categories, are of four kinds: *muḥṣan* (married) or *thuyyab* (non-virgins); *abkār* (virgins); free or slave; and male or female. The Islamic *ḥudud* are of three kinds: *rajm* (stoning to death); *jald* (whipping); and *taghrīb* (exile). The Muslim jurists agreed about free *thayyib muḥṣans* that the *ḥadd* for them is *rajm*, except that a group of those who follow their own whims held that the punishment for every fornicator is a hundred lashes. The majority inclined toward *rajm* because of the authentic traditions supporting it. They restricted the (general meaning in the) Book with the *sunna*, that is, the words of the Exalted, "The adulteress and adulterer, scourge ye each one of them (with) a hundred stripes. And let not pity for the twain withhold you from obedience to Allāh, if ye believe in Allāh and the Last Day. And let a party of believers witness their punishment".[227] They differed on two points. First, whether stripes are to be awarded along with stoning. Second, about the conditions of *iḥṣān*.

56.6.2.1. Issue 1: Stripes with stoning?

The jurists disagreed whether stripes are to be awarded to the person who has become liable to *rajm*, before *rajm* is applied. The majority said that there are no stripes for a person liable to *rajm*. Al-Ḥasan al-Baṣrī, Isḥāq, Aḥmad and Dāwūd said that a *muḥṣan* fornicator is to be awarded stripes before he is subjected to *rajm*.

For the majority the legal basis is "that the Messenger of Allāh (God's peace and blessings be upon him) awarded *rajm* to Māʾiz, to a woman from Juhayna, to the Jews and a woman from (the tribe of) Ghāmid from al-Azad". All this has been recorded in the *Ṣaḥīḥs* and it is never related that he awarded stripes to any of these people. As a rational argument, the minor *ḥadd* is included in the major *ḥadd*, for *ḥadd* has been laid down as a deterrent and stripes are not effective as a deterrent along with stoning. The reliance of the other group is upon the general meaning of the words of the Exalted, "The adulteress and the adulterer, scourge ye each one of them (with) a hundred stripes", which did not distinguish between the *muḥṣan* and the non-*muḥṣan*.

They also argued on the basis of the tradition of ʿAli (God be pleased with him) as recorded by Muslim and others, that ʿAli (God be pleased with him) subjected Shurāḥah al-Hamdāniyya to stripes on Thursday and to *rajm* on Friday, saying, "I awarded her stripes by the Book of Allāh and subjected her to *rajm* by the *sunna* of His Messenger". There is also the tradition of ʿUbāda ibn al-Ṣāmit, which says "that the Prophet (God's peace and blessings be upon him) said, 'Take from me, take from me, verily, Allāh has ordained for them a way: the virgin with the virgin, a hundred stripes and exile for a year; the *thayyib* (non-virgin) with the *thayyib*, a hundred stripes and pelting with stones'".

They agreed about *iḥṣān* that it is one of the conditions of *rajm*, but differed about the conditions of *iḥṣān* itself. Mālik said that these are puberty, Islam, freedom and sexual intercourse through a valid marriage. Intercourse for this purpose should be permissible intercourse and not intercourse prohibited during menstruation or while fasting. If a person commits unlawful intercourse after having fulfilled the conditions of valid intercourse, the punishment for him is *rajm* according to Mālik. Abū Ḥanīfa agreed with Mālik about these

[227] Qurʾān 24:2

conditions, except about intercourse that is not temporarily prohibited and he also stipulated that freedom should exist on both sides, that is, the *zānī* and the *zāniya* should both be free persons. Al-Shāfiʿī did not stipulate Islam as one of the conditions.

Al-Shāfiʿī's reliance is on what has been related by Mālik from Nāfiʿ from Ibn ʿUmar, which is a tradition agreed upon for its soundness, "that the Prophet (God's peace and blessings be upon him) awarded *rajm* to the Jews, man and woman, who had committed unlawful intercourse, when the Jews referred their affair to him". Allāh, the Exalted, says, "But if thou judgest, judge between them with equity".[228] Mālik's argument, by way of reason, is that *iḥṣān* is a matter of honour and there can be no honour in the absence of Islam. It is one of his principles that intercourse in a valid marriage is recommended. This, then, is the *ḥukm* of the (free) *thayyib* (non-virgin).

The Muslim jurists agreed that the *ḥadd* for the virgin (one never married) for ẓinais a hundred stripes due to the words of the Exalted, "The adulteress and the adulterer, scourge ye each one of them (with) a hundred stripes". They disagreed about exile (*taghrīb*) along with stripes. Abū Ḥanīfa and his disciples said that there is essentially no exile whatsoever (as *ḥadd*), while al-Shāfiʿī said that exile is a must for each fornicator, male or female, free or slave. Mālik said that men are exiled, but not women, which was also the opinion of al-Awzāʿī. There is no exile for slaves according to Mālik. The reliance of those who imposed exile without qualifications is the tradition of ʿUbāda ibn al-Sāmit that has preceded, which says, "A virgin with a virgin, hundred stripes and exile for a year". The compilers of the *Ṣaḥīḥ* have likewise recorded a tradition from Abū Hurayra and Zayd ibn Khālid al-Juhanī both of whom said, "A Bedouin came up to the Prophet (God's peace and blessings be upon him) and said, 'I beseech you to decide my case by the Book of Allāh alone'. His rival, who was more knowledgeable than him, said, 'Yes, judge between us by the Book of Allāh, but permit me to plead (my case)'. The Prophet said, 'Speak'. He (the other Bedouin) said, 'My son was his servant and committed intercourse with his woman. I had been told that my son was liable to *rajm*, so I offered as ransom a hundred goats and a young slave-girl. I, then, asked the learned people, who have informed me that my son is liable to a hundred stripes and exile for a year and the woman of this man is liable to *rajm*'. The Messenger of Allāh said, 'By Him, in whose hands is my life, I will certainly decide your case according to the Book of Allāh. As for the slave-girl and the goats, they are returned to you and upon your son are a hundred stripes and exile for a year. (He added) Go, O Unays, to this man's woman, if she confesses subject her to *rajm*'. Unays went up to her and she confessed.

[228] Qurʾān 54:2

The Prophet (God's peace and blessings be upon him), then, issued the order and she was stoned (to death)".

Those who made an exemption for a woman from this general command (of exile) did so on the basis of analogy, as exile exposes a woman to greater opportunity for *zinā*. This analogy belongs to the category of *mursal*, I mean, it pertains to *maṣlaḥa*, which is often adopted by Mālik. The reliance of the Ḥanafites is upon the apparent meaning of the Book. This is based on their opinion that an addition to (the *hukm*) of the explicit text amounts to *naskh* (abrogation) of the text and the Book of Allāh cannot be abrogated through individual narrations. They also related from ᶜUmar and others that he awarded the *ḥadd*, but did not award exile. The Kūfīs related from Abū Bakr and ᶜUmar that they did award exile.

For purposes of the *ḥukm* of the slaves in this offence, the slaves are divided into two kinds: male and female. The jurists agreed in the case of females that a slave woman, if she marries and then indulges in unlawful intercourse, her *ḥadd* is fifty stripes due to the words of the Exalted, "And if when they are honourably married they commit lewdness they shall incur the half of the punishment (prescribed) for free women (in the case)".[229] They disagreed when a slave-girl was not married. The majority of the jurists of the regions said her *ḥadd* is fifty stripes. One group said that there is no *ḥadd* for her, but there is *tᶜazīr*, while another group said that there is essentially no *ḥadd* for a slave-woman. The reason for their disagreement is the equivocality of the term *iḥṣān* in the words of the Exalted (translated as), "honourably married". Those who understood it to mean "marriage" and looked at the implication of the text said that the unmarried slave-woman is not subjected to *ḥadd* at all. Those who understood the meaning of *iḥṣān* to be 'Islam' applied it generally to the married and the unmarried. Those who did not maintain *ḥadd* for the unmarried slave-woman, argued on the basis of the tradition of Abū Hurayra and Zayd ibn Khālid al-Juhanī "that the Prophet (God's peace and blessings be upon him) was asked about the slave-woman committing fornication when she was not a *muḥṣana* and he said, 'If she commits *ẓina* whip her, if she commits *ẓina* again whip her and if she does it again sell her, even if it is for a trifle' ".

The jurists of the regions maintain that the *ḥadd* of a male slave is half that of a free man on the analogy of the slave-woman. The Ẓāhirites said that, on the contrary, his *ḥadd* is a hundred stripes, as they inclined toward the general meaning of the words of the Exalted, "scourge each one of them (with) a hundred stripes", which do not distinguish a slave from a free man. There are

[229] Qurʾān 4:25

jurists who waived *ḥadd* in his case on the analogy of the (unmarried) slave woman, which is a deviant view and is related from Ibn ᶜAbbās.

This, then, is the discussion about the kinds of *ḥudud* (in the case of *zinā*), the kinds of persons liable to *ḥadd* and conditions related to each one of the *ḥudud*. To these is related the discussion of the mode of application of *ḥadd* and its time.

The best-known issue about the mode of implementation relates to the digging of a pit for the person to be subjected to *rajm*. One group said that a pit is to be made for the person and this is related from ᶜAlī in the case of Shurāḥah al-Hamdāniyya, when he ordered her to be stoned. It is also related from Abū Thawr. Part of the report says, "On Friday he brought her out and had a pit dug for her. When she had entered the pit, the people surrounded her and began to stone her. He said, 'This is not the way to execute *rajm*, I am afraid some of you will be hitting each other, but make rows as you would for prayer'. He then said that *rajm* is of two kinds: concealed from view and in the open. Out of these, in the one proved by confession, the first person to commence stoning is the *imām* followed by the public, while in the case proved by testimony, it is the witnesses who begin followed by the *imām* and then the public. Abū Ḥanīfa and Mālik said that no pit is to be dug for the person stoned, while al-Shāfiᶜī made a distinction saying that it is only dug for a woman. Their reliance is upon what has been recorded by al-Bukhārī and Muslim about the tradition of Jābir. Jābir said, "We stoned him (Māᵓiz) in the place of prayer and when the stones enveloped him, he bolted, but we took him by the stony (volcanic) area and crushed him". It is, however, recorded by Muslim that a pit was dug for him on the fourth day. The traditions generally vary on this issue. Aḥmad said that most of the traditions imply that there is no pit.

(In the case of stripes) Mālik said that the *ḥadd* is to be applied to the back and the proximate areas. Abū Ḥanīfa and al-Shāfiᶜī said that all parts of the body are to be touched; however, the sex organs and the face are to be protected. To this Abū Ḥanīfa added the skull also. The person, if male, is to be stripped of his clothes, according to Mālik, in all applications of the *ḥudud*, while the exception, according to Abū Ḥanīfa and al-Shāfiᶜī, is the case of *qadhf* (false accusation of sexual intercourse) as will be coming up in what follows. Stripes are to given in the sitting posture, not while standing, as against the opinion of those who say they are applied while standing, according to the apparent meaning of the verse.

It is considered recommended by all that the *imām* should bring as witnesses a number of people at the time of execution, due to the words of the Exalted, "And let a party of the believers witness their punishment". They disagreed about the exact implication of the term "party". Mālik said that four persons constitute a party, but (figures like) three, two, seven or more are also claimed. About the time of execution, the majority maintain that it should not be in the time of extreme heat, or of extreme cold and that it is not to be applied to a sick person. A group said that it may be (applied to a sick person), which was the opinion of Aḥmad and Isḥāq. They argued on the basis of a report from ʿUmar that he applied *ḥadd* to Qudāma, who was ill. The reason for the disagreement is the clash of the apparent meaning with the idea behind *ḥadd* that it is to be applied when there is no likelihood of the person, subjected to it, dying from it. Those who looked at the unqualified meaning of the execution of *ḥadd*, without any exceptions, said that it is to be applied to the sick person, while those who took into account the inherent meaning said that the sick person is not to be punished till he recovers. There is similar disagreement about extreme heat or cold.

56.6.3. **Chapter 3: Identification of the Methods of Proving This Offence**

The jurists agreed that *ẓina* is proved through confession and testimony. They disagreed about its proof through the appearance of pregnancy in unmarried women, when they claim to have been coerced (raped). They also disagreed about the conditions of confession and testimony.

They disagreed about a confession on two points. First, the number of confessions that give rise to the liability for *ḥadd*. Second, whether it is a condition that confession should not have been retracted till the time of the application of *ḥadd*.

56.6.3.1. Issue 1: Number of confessions.

Regarding the number of confessions giving rise to the liability for *ḥadd*, Mālik and al-Shāfiʿī said that for purposes of liability for *ḥadd* just one confession is sufficient. This was also the opinion of Dāwūd, Abū Thawr, al-Ṭabarī and a group of jurists. Abū Ḥanīfa, his disciples and Ibn Abī Laylā said that *ḥadd* is not proved except by four confessions made one after the other. This was also the opinion of Aḥmad and Isḥāq. Abū Ḥanīfa and his disciples, however, added that these should have been made in separate sessions.

The reliance of Mālik and al-Shāfiʿī is upon what is reported in the tradition of Abū Hurayra and Khālid about the saying of the Prophet (God's peace and blessings be upon him), " 'Go, O Unays to his woman and if she confesses stone her (to death)'—she confessed and he stoned her". Here the number (of confessions) were not mentioned. The reliance of the Kūfīs is on what is reported in the tradition of Saʾīd ibn Jubayr from Ibn ʿAbbās from the Prophet (God's peace and blessings be upon him) "that he turned Māʾiz away till he had confessed four times and then ordered him to be subjected to *rajm*. Regarding the other traditions, they said that what is laid down in some reports about his confessing once, twice or three times is deficient reporting and that which is deficient cannot be held up as proof against the complete report.

56.6.3.2. Issue 2: Retraction of confession

The majority of the jurists, except for Ibn Abī Laylāʾ, said that retraction is admissible. Mālik made a distinction saying that if he retracts with a supporting *shubha* it is acceptable, but when he withdraws without *shubha*, there are two opinions from him. First, that it is acceptable, which is the well-known opinion, while the second maintains that it is not. The majority inclined toward the effectiveness of retraction of confession because of the practise of the Prophet (God's peace and blessings be upon him) in the case of Māʾiz, and others of them ask time and again to reconfirm that they might retract. It is for this reason also that those who waive *ḥadd* due to retraction, do not insist that the maintenance of a confession for a long duration is a condition for the imposition of *ḥadd*. It is related through a number of narrations "that when Māʾiz was being stoned, he ran as the stones hit and with the people in pursuit he said to them, 'Take me back to the Messenger of Allāh,' but they killed him with the stones. They mentioned this to the Prophet (God's peace and blessings be upon him), who said, 'Would that you had let him go, perhaps he would have repented and Allāh would have forgiven him'". It is from here that al-Shāfiʿī made the stipulation that repentance removes liability for *ḥadd*, but the majority maintain the contrary. It is also from this that the absence of repentance becomes the third condition for the liability for *ḥadd*.

The jurists agreed about the proof of *ẓina* through testimony that it is proved through testimony and the stipulated number of witnesses is four as distinct from the testimony for the rest of the rights, because of the words of the Exalted, "And those who accuse honourable women but bring not four witnesses, scourge them (with) eighty stripes and never (afterward) accept their testimony—They indeed are the evildoers".[230] The condition for the witnesses is that they should be *ʿadl*. A condition for the quality of the testimony is that it should describe the contact of the sex organs and that it should be rendered in explicit, not figurative (insinuating), language. The majority maintain that such testimony should not be contradictory with respect to time or place, except for the well-known issue raised by Abū Ḥanīfa about the angles, which requires that each of the witnesses should have seen them

[230] Qurʾān 24:4

from a separate corner of the room (for example) and it should not be the same corner from where another witness has viewed the offence. The reason for the disagreement is whether testimony relating to different locations can be combined into one as is the testimony relating different times. They agreed that it cannot for a dissimilar location is the same as dissimilar timing and the apparent purpose of the law is to achieve greater certainty in the proof of this *ḥadd* more than any other.

Regarding their disagreement about the application of *ḥadd* due to the appearance of pregnancy along with a claim of rape, a group of jurists imposed *ḥadd* in such a case as is recorded by Mālik in his *al-Muwaṭṭa*ʾ in the tradition of ʿUmar. This was the opinion of Mālik, unless she could provide evidence of coercion, as in case she was a virgin and complained while she was bleeding, or shows on her body the signs of coercion. The case is the same, according to him, when she claims to be married; she has to prove it. The exception is the one on an unexpected visit. Ibn al-Qāsim said that when she claims marriage on a sudden visit, her statement will be accepted. Abū Ḥanīfa and al-Shāfiʿī said that *ḥadd* is not to be applied to her due to the appearance of pregnancy accompanied by the claim of coercion, or the claim of marriage, even if she does not come up with the evidence of coercion in a claim of coercion or of marriage in a claim of marriage, as she is in the position of one who has confessed and then claims coercion. One of the proofs for them is what is related in the tradition about Shurāḥa that Alī (God be pleased with him) said to her, "Were you coerced?" She said, "No!" He said, "Maybe someone came upon you while you were asleep?" They said that proof is related from ʿUmar in so far as he accepted the statement of a woman who claimed that she was a sound sleeper and a man came upon her and went away, but she did not come to know who it was.

There is no disagreement among the Muslim jurists that there is no *ḥadd* for a woman coerced. They differed about the obligation of paying dower to her. The reason for the disagreement is whether *ṣadāq* is compensation for utilization or a gift. Those who said that it is compensation for utilization, imposed it in lawful as well as prohibited cases, while those who said that it is a gift required exclusively for marriage did not impose it in this case.

This exposition is sufficient for this book and with Allāh is the granting of reward.

56.7 THE BOOK OF *QADHF* (FALSE ACCUSATION OF UNLAWFUL INTERCOURSE)

The discussion in this book is about the accuser (*qādhif*), the accused (*maqdhūf*), the punishment obligatory in this offence and how the offence is proved. The legal basis of this law is in the words of the Exalted, "And those who accuse honourable women but bring not four witnesses, scourge them (with) eighty stripes and never (afterward) accept their testimony—They indeed are the evildoers". They agreed that two attributes must be found in the accuser, as a condition. These are puberty and sanity, irrespective of whether the accuser is a male or a female, free or slave, Muslim or non-Muslim. They agreed about the accused that five attributes must be gathered in him. These are puberty, freedom, chastity, Islam and the possession of a sound sex organ. If any of these attributes is missing *ḥadd* will not become obligatory. The majority, generally, are inclined toward the stipulation of freedom as a condition for the accused. It is likely that there may be disagreement in this. Mālik takes into account the age of a woman so that she may be capable of sexual intercourse.

They agreed on two points relating to the false accusation giving rise to the liability for *ḥadd*. First, that the accuser makes a false allegation of *zinā* against the accused. Second, that he denies his descent (from his father), when his mother is a Muslim free woman. They disagreed when she was a non-believer or a slave. Mālik said that whether she is free, slave, Muslim, or a non-believer *ḥadd* becomes obligatory. Ibrāhīm al-Nakhaᶜī said that there is no *ḥadd* for the accuser if the accused's mother is a slave or a *kitābiyya*. This is analogous to the opinions of Abū Ḥanīfa and al-Shāfiᶜī.

They agreed that the accusation, when it made in either of these two ways (direct accusation or denial of parentage), creates a liability for *ḥadd*, if it is explicit. They differed when it is by way of insinuation. Al-Shāfiᶜī, Abū Ḥanīfa, al-Thawri and Ibn Abī Laylā said that there is no *ḥadd* for insinuation, but Ābu Ḥanīfa and al-Shāfiᶜī maintained that there is *ataᶜzir* in such a case. A similar opinion was expressed, among the Companions, by Ibn Masᶜūd. Mālik and his disciples maintained that there is *ḥadd* for insinuations and it is an issue that occurred in the time of ᶜUmar. ᶜUmar consulted the Companions about it, but they differed, so he upheld *ḥadd* for it.

Mālik's reliance is on the argument that metaphorical language is based on usage and such use is a substitute for explicit designation, though the word is used for something other than its normal designation by way of metaphor. The argument of the majority is that the ambiguity surrounding the use of a metaphor leads to a doubt and the *ḥudud* are waived because of doubts. The truth is that metaphorical use is sometimes similar to explicit expressions, but at other times it is not, particularly when the word is not in common use.

The liability for *ḥadd* is waived, by consensus, for the accuser if he can prove, with the help of four witnesses, the commission of unlawful intercourse by the accused. When the witnesses are fewer than four they are equally guilty, according to Mālik, of *qadhf*, but they are not according to other jurists. There is disagreement in the school about the witnesses who testify about the testimony of the original witnesses. The reason for the disagreement is whether transmission of testimony requires the same number of witnesses as prescribed for the original testimony, where their number cannot be reduced, or two witnesses are sufficient, as is the case in other matters beside *qadhf*.

The discussion of *ḥadd* pertains to its category, limitations and discharge. They agreed that eighty stripes are awarded to the accuser, who is a free man, because of the words of the Exalted, "eighty stripes". They disagreed about the *ḥadd* of the slave who accuses a free man. The majority of the jurists of the regions said that his *ḥadd* is half that of the free man, which is forty stripes and this has been related from the four Caliphs and from Ibn ᶜAbbās. A group of jurists said that his *ḥadd* is the same as that of the free man, which is the opinion of Ibn Masᶜūd, from among the Companions, of ᶜUmar ibn ᶜAbd al-ᶜAzīz and of a group of jurists of the regions—Abū Thawr, al-Awzāᶜī and Dāwūd and his disciples from among the Ẓāhirites.

The reliance of the majority, for purposes of *qadhf*, is upon the analogy of his *ḥadd* in the case of *zinā*. The *Ahl al-Ẓāhir* held on to the general meaning (of the verse) and to the consensus that the *ḥadd* for a *kitābī* is eighty stripes; it was as if the slave deserves it more.

They agreed about its limitations that if the accuser accuses the same person a number of times he is to be subjected to *ḥadd* only once if he has not been subjected to *ḥadd* before, but if he makes an accusation and is subjected to *ḥadd* for it and makes the accusation again he will be subjected to it a second time. They disagreed when he accuses a group of persons. One group of jurists said that he is liable to a single *ḥadd*, whether he made a single collective accusation or made several separate accusations. This was the opinion of Mālik, Abū Ḥanīfa, āl-Thawri, Aḥmad and a group of jurists. Another group of jurists said that he is to be awarded (a separate) *ḥadd* for each person, which was the opinion of al-Shāfiᶜī, al-Layth and a group. Al-Ḥasan ibn Ḥayy went to the extent of saying that if a person says, "Anyone who enters through this door is a fornicator", he is to be awarded (eighty) stripes as *ḥadd* (separately) for each person who enters the door. A third group said that if he addresses them collectively saying, "O, fornicators", he is to be awarded a single *ḥadd*, but if he addresses each one of them individually, calling them fornicators, he is to be awarded punishment for each individual.

The reliance of those who do not impose on an accuser of a group more than a single *ḥadd* is the tradition of Anas and others, "that Hilāl ibn Umayya accused his wife of having intercourse with Shurayk ibn Samḥāʾ. This was reported to the Prophet (God's peace and blessings be upon him) who instituted *liʿān* proceedings among them, but did not award him *ḥadd* because of (the accusation against) Shurayk". This has come to be a point of consensus among the jurists in the case of a husband who accuses his wife of having intercourse with another man. The argument of those who hold that he is liable separately for each individual is that it is a category of the rights of individuals, thus, if some of them forgive him while others do not, the *ḥadd* is not waived. Those who distinguished between collective and individual accusations, or between accusations in a single session and in several sessions, argued that it is obligatory that *ḥadd* should increase in proportion to the number of accusations, as a number of accusations made separately against a number of persons would lead to *ḥadd* being awarded the same number of times.

They differed about the discharge of liability, as to when the accused person forgives him. Abū Ḥanīfa, āl-Thawri and āl-Awzāʿ said that forgiveness is not valid, that is, the *ḥadd* is not to be waived. Al-Shāfiʿī said that forgiveness is effective and *ḥadd* is waived, irrespective of the matter having been reported to the *imām*. One group said that if the complaint is filed with the *imām* forgiveness is not permitted, but it is if the matter has not been reported to the *imām*. Mālik's opinion differed in this; he held one opinion similar to al-Shāfiʿī's and said another time, which is his well-known opinion, that it is permitted if information has not reached the *imām* and it is not if it has, unless the accused wishes to cover up his personal affair.

The reason for their disagreement is whether the offence affects the right of Allāh or the rights of individuals, or both. Those who said that it relates to the right of Allāh did not permit forgiveness, as in the case of *zinā*. Those who held that it pertains to the right of individuals permitted forgiveness. Those who said that it affects both rights, but the right of the *imām* becomes predominant when information reaches him, made a distinction on the basis of information received and not received, which in itself is based on analogy from the established tradition laid down in the case of theft (*sariqa*). The reliance of those who said that it relates to the right of the individuals, which is the outstanding opinion, is that if the accused confirms what was alleged in the accusation *ḥadd* would be waived from accuser.

There is no dispute that the person who undertakes the application of *ḥadd* is the *imām* who does this in the case of false accusation of unlawful intercourse. They agreed that along with liability for *ḥadd* the testimony of the accuser is no longer acceptable, as long as he does not repent. They disagreed when he does repent. Mālik said that in such a case his testimony would be admissible, which is also al-Shāfiʿī's opinion. Abū Ḥanīfa said that his testimony is not admissible, ever. The reason for their disagreement is whether the exception (*istithnāʾ*) (proviso) in the verse extends backwards to the entire preceding sentence or to the immediately preceding category. This refers to the words of the Exalted, "[A]nd never (afterward) accept their testimony—They indeed are the evildoers—[s]ave those who afterward repent and make amends". Those who maintained that the exception extends to the immediately preceding category said that repentance merely does away with the imputation of "evildoers (*fāsiqūn*)", but testimony is still not acceptable. Those who held that the exception includes both categories collectively said that repentance does away with the imputation and the rejection of testimony. The removal of the imputation of "evildoers" along with the rejection of testimony is (an opinion) incompatible with the *sharīʿa*, that is it is inconsistent with the principles, as the removal of the imputation of "evildoers" makes testimony admissible. They agreed that repentance does not discharge the liability for ḥadd.

How is it proved? They agreed that it is proved by the testimony of two free male *ʿadl* witnesses. There is a disagreement in Mālik's school whether it is proved with one witness and an oath, by the testimony of women and whether proof through an oath has a binding effect; or if he refuses to take the oath, is he to be awarded *ḥadd* because of his refusal supported by the oath of the complainant?

These are the principles of this topic upon which the various individual cases are constructed.

The Qāḍī (Ibn Rushd) said: If Allāh were to grant me a long life, I will compile a book about the cases in the school of Mālik ibn Anas, arranging them in an organized manner, as that is the school followed in this peninsula, the peninsula of Andalus, so that the reader may attain the status of a *mujtahid* within Mālik's school. The enumeration of all the narrations, I think, is a task in which life terminates before it (the task) can come to an end.

56.7.1 Chapter on *Khamr* (The Drinking of Wine)

The discussion of this offence relates to the cause, the obligation and the mode of proof of the offence. They agreed that the cause is the drinking of *khamr*, without coercion, in large or small quantities. They disagreed about other intoxicants. The jurists of Ḥijāz said that their *ḥukm* is the same as that of *khamr*, with respect to prohibition and the liability for *ḥadd*, upon those who consume them in large or small quantities, irrespective of intoxication. The jurists of Iraq said that in case of these (other intoxicants), only the act of intoxication is prohibited and it invokes *ḥadd*. We have already mentioned the evidences of both groups in the Book of Food and Beverages.

The consequential obligation is the application of *ḥadd* and the imputation of *fisq*, unless followed by repentance. The imputation of *fisq* is made for every person drinking *khamr*, even if he is not intoxicated, but in the case of other intoxicants it is made upon actual intoxication.

Those who upheld the prohibition of even small quantities of intoxicating beverages, differed about the consequential *ḥadd*, though most of them maintain that it becomes obligatory. They differed, however, about the magnitude of obligatory *ḥadd*. The majority said that the *ḥadd* in this case is eighty stripes, while al-Shāfiʿī, Abū Thawr and Dāwūd said that the *ḥadd* in this case is forty stripes; and this is the *ḥadd* for the free man. They differed about the *ḥadd* of the slave, with the majority saying that it is half of the *ḥadd* of the free man. The Ẓāhirites said that the *ḥadd* of the free man and the slave is the same, which is forty stripes, while according to al-Shāfiʿī it is twenty stripes and for those who upheld eighty it is forty.

The reliance of the majority is upon the consultation of ʿUmar with the Companions, when the drinking of *khamr* became excessive in his times and the observation of ʿAlī that the *ḥadd* should be fixed at eighty on the analogy of the *ḥadd* of *qadhf*. It is reported about him (God be pleased with him) that he said, "When he drinks he is intoxicated, when he is intoxicated he raves and when he raves he makes false accusations". The reliance of the other group is on the argument that the Prophet did not fix a *ḥadd* for this and he used to award unnumbered strokes with whatever was available, like shoes, and that Abū Bakr (God be pleased with him) consulted the Companions of the Prophet (God's peace and blessings be upon him) as to what were the maximum number of strokes awarded by the Prophet and they fixed it at forty. It is related from Abū Saʿīd al-Khudrī "that the Messenger of Allāh awarded forty strokes with two (pair) of shoes", thus, ʿUmar substituted a stripe for each shoe. A more authentic report is related, through another chain, from Abū Saʿīd al-Khudrī "that the Messenger of Allāh awarded forty". As this is a more authentic narration from the Prophet (God's peace and blessings be upon him) and a similar more reliable report from ʿAlī is also available, al-Shāfiʿī maintained it at forty.

They agreed the person who applies this *ḥadd* is the *imām* as is the case in all the other *ḥudud*. They disagreed about the masters applying the *ḥadd* to their slaves. Mālik said that the master applies, to his slave, the *ḥadd* of unlawful intercourse and of false accusation of intercourse, if the witnesses render testimony before him, but he does not apply it on the basis of his own knowledge and no one except the *imām* is to undertake the amputation of the hand for theft. This was also the opinion of al-Layth. Abū Ḥanīfa said that no one but the *imām* is to apply the *ḥudud* to slaves. Al-Shāfiʿī said that the master applies all the *ḥudud* to his slaves, which was also the opinion of Aḥmad, Isḥaq and Abū Thawr.

Mālik's reliance is upon the well-known tradition "that the Messenger of Allāh (God's peace and blessings be upon him) was asked about the slave-woman who committed unlawful intercourse, but was not a *muḥṣana*, to which he said, 'If the slave-woman of any one of you commits *zinā*, he should give her the stripes'". The Prophet (God's peace and blessings be upon him) also commanded, "Should the slave-girl of any of you commit *zinā*, give her the stripes". Al-Shāfiʿī relied on these traditions as well as on what is related from the Prophet (God's peace and blessings be upon him) in another tradition that he said, "Apply the *ḥudud* to those whom your right hands possess". In addition, he maintained that this point is also related from the Companions and none had opposed them; among them are Ibn ʿUmar, Ibn Masʿūd and Anas. The reliance of Abū Ḥanīfa is on the consensus stating the principle that the application of the *ḥudud* is the right of the *sulṭan*. It is related from al-Ḥasan, ʿUmar ibn ʿAbd al-ʿAzīz and others that they said, "*Jumuʿa* (Friday prayers), *zakāt*, *fayʾ* and the *ḥukm* are the right of the *sulṭan*".

56.7.1.1. *Section: Proof*

About the manner of proof of this *ḥadd*, the jurists agreed that it is established through confession or the testimony of two *ʿadl* witnesses. They disagreed over its proof through smell. Mālik, his disciples and the majority of the jurists of Ḥijāz said that *ḥadd* becomes obligatory on the basis of smell if two *ʿadl* witnesses render testimony to the effect before the judge. He was opposed in this by al-Shāfiʿī, Abū Ḥanīfa, the majority of the jurists of Iraq, a group of jurists from Ḥijāz and the majority of the jurists of Baṣrah, who said that the offence is not proved for purposes of *ḥadd* through smell. Those who permitted testimony about smell did so because of its similarity to testimony about voices and features. The reliance of those who did not permit proof by smell is on the existence of similarity in smells and that the *ḥadd* is waived because of doubt.

56.8. THE BOOK OF *SARIQA* (THEFT)

The discussion in this book relates to the *ḥadd* for theft (*sariqa*), the conditions of the stolen property, because of which *ḥadd* becomes obligatory, the attributes of the thief (*sāriq*), who is liable to *ḥadd*, the punishment and the procedures through which this offence is proved.

Theft is the taking of the property of another by way of stealth, when the thief has not been entrusted with it. We have said this as they (the jurists) agreed that there is no liability for amputation of the hand in breach of trust or in embezzlement, except for (the opinion of) Iyyās ibn Muʿāwiya, who imposed the penalty of amputation on the person guilty of *khilsa*. And, a group of jurists subjected to amputation any person who borrowed jewellery or goods and then denied taking them, because of the renowned tradition about the Makhzūmiyya woman "who used to borrow jewellery and the Messenger of Allāh ordered that her hand be amputated on the basis of her denial". This was also the opinion of Aḥmad and Isḥāq and is based on the tradition of ʿĀʾishah, who said, "A Makhzūmiyya woman used to borrow goods and then denied taking them. The Prophet (God's peace and blessings be upon him) ordered the amputation of her hand. Her family came to Usāma and talked to him about it. Usāma brought the matter up with the Prophet (God's peace and blessings be upon him), who said, 'O Usāma, I do not expect you to interfere in the *ḥudud* of Allāh'. The Prophet then began addressing the people, saying, 'Those before you were destroyed (for the reason) that if one of their élite committed theft they let him go, but when a person of low status stole something they cut off his hand. By Him, in Whose hands is my soul, had it been Fāṭima, the daughter of Muḥammad, I would surely have cut her hand'".

The majority rejected this tradition as it is opposed to the principles, in so far as the thing borrowed is a trust and is not taken without permission, beyond the fact that it is not taken from a place of safe custody. They said that in the tradition there are some omissions, for it says that she stole and then states the denial of borrowed property. This is evident from the words of the Prophet, "Those before you were destroyed (for the reason) that if one of their élite committed theft they let him go". They maintained that this tradition is related by al-Layth ibn Saʿd from al-Zuhrī, with its chain, in which he says that the Makhzūmiyya committed theft. They claimed that this indicates she committed both offences, denial of borrowed property as well as theft. They also agreed that there is no amputation for the usurper or the quarrelsome dominating person, unless he is a highway robber bearing arms against the Muslims and threatening the highways, for his *ḥukm* is then the same as that of the brigand (*muḥārib*), as will be coming up in the discussion of the *ḥadd* of the *muḥarib*.

In the case of the thief for whom the *ḥadd* of *ṣariqa* becomes obligatory, they agreed that one of the conditions is that the thief should have legal capacity (be a *mukallaf*), whether free man or a slave, male or female, Muslim or *dhimmī*, except the dispute that is related since the earlier period about the amputation of the hand of the runaway slave when he commits theft. This was related from Ibn ʿAbbās, ʿUthmān, Marwān and ʿUmar ibn ʿAbd al-ʿAzīz; it was not disputed in the following period. Those who held that consensus can occur in the later period after the existence of disagreement, considered the matter as definitive, but those who did not consider it as such favoured the general meaning in the command for purposes of amputation. The opinion of those, who did not rule for the amputation of the hand of the runaway slave, is not supported by any argument except the analogy that waiving of half the penalty from him causes the entire penalty to be waived, that is, in the case of those penalties that are halved for the slaves, which is a weak argument.

The conditions for stolen property are disputed. The best-known condition among these is the stipulation of the *niṣāb* (the minimum scale). The majority are inclined to stipulate it, except what is related from al-Ḥasan al-Baṣrī, who said that amputation is invoked for small as well as larger amounts due to the general implication of the words of the Exalted, "As to the thief, both male and female, cut off their hands. It is the reward of their own deeds, an exemplary punishment from Allāh. Allāh is Mighty, Wise".[231] Perhaps he also argued on the basis of the tradition of Abū Hurayra, recorded by al-Bukhārī and Muslim, related from the Prophet that he said, "The curse of Allāh is on the thief, he steals a shield (could be an egg) and his hand is cut, he steals a rope and his hand is cut". This was also the opinion of the Khārijites and a group of the *Mutakallimūn*.

Those who upheld the imposition of the *niṣāb* for invoking the liability for amputation and these are the majority, differed extensively over its amount, though the best-known opinions among them are based upon established evidence and these are two. First, the opinion of the jurists of Ḥijāz, Mālik, al-Shāfiʿī and others. Second, the opinion of the jurists of Iraq.

The jurists of Ḥijāz invoked amputation for (property worth) three silver *dirhams* or one-fourth of a gold *dīnār*. They disagreed about the currency with which stolen property is to be evaluated. Mālik, in his well-known opinion, said that such valuation is to be undertaken by means of *dirhams* and not with one-fourth of a gold *dīnār*. This is in case the value of three *dirhams* becomes different from one-quarter of a gold *dīnār*, as, for example, when a quarter of a gold *dīnār*s drops to two and one-half *dirhams*. Al-Shāfiʿī said that the basis for valuation is one-fourth of a gold *dīnār*, which is also the basis for *dirhams* according to him; thus, amputation is not invoked for three *dirhams*, unless they are equivalent to one-fourth *dīnār*. Both *dīnārs* and *dirhams* are considered as independent bases by Mālik. Some jurists of Baghdad have related from him that for purposes of goods he takes into account the prevalent currency of the concerned land; if the prevalent currency is the *dirham*, valuation is in *dirhams*, but if the prevalent currency is the *dīnār*, valuation is by means of one-fourth of a *dīnār*. I believe that there are also those within the school who fix the value of a quarter *dīnār* by means of three *dirhams*. Abū Thawr, al-Awzāʿī and Dāwūd

[231] Qurʾān 5:38

had the same opinion, for purposes of valuation, as that of al-Shāfiʿī, while Aḥmad adopted Mālik's well-known opinion, that is, valuation with *dirhams*.

According to the jurists of Iraq the value of the *niṣāb*, because of which amputation becomes obligatory is ten *dirhams* and it does not become obligatory in an amount less than this. One group and among them are Ibn Abī Laylā and Ibn Shubrama said that the hand is not to be amputated for less than five *dirhams*, while it is also said four *dirhams*. ʿUthmān al-Battī was of the view that it (the amount) is two *dirhams*.

The reliance of the jurists of Ḥijāz is on what has been related by Mālik from Nāfiʿ from Ibn ʿUmar "that the Prophet (God's peace and blessings be upon him) ordered amputation for the theft of a shield (*mijann*) valued at three *dirhams*" and on the tradition of ʿĀʾisha, related as *mawqūf* by Mālik and by al-Bukhārī and Muslim with chains reaching up to the Prophet (God's peace and blessings be upon him), that he said, "The hand is amputated for a quarter of a *dīnār* or more". The reliance of the jurists of Iraq is on the tradition of Ibn ʿUmar mentioned above, but they said that the value of the shield was ten *dirhams*, a fact reported in some versions of the tradition. In addition, a number of Companions, like Ibn ʿAbbās and others, those who were of the view that the hand was cut because of a shield, went against Ibn ʿUmar regarding the value of the shield. Muḥammad ibn Isḥāq has related from Ayyūb ibn Mūsā from ʿAṭāʾ from Ibn ʿAbbās, who said that the price of a shield, in the days of the Prophet (God's peace and blessings be upon him), was ten *dirhams*. They said that when a disagreement exists about the price of the shield, it is necessary that the hand should not be amputated except in cases of certainty. This opinion that they expressed would be the best, but for the tradition of ʿĀʾisha, which was relied upon by al-Shāfiʿī in this issue fixing the basis as one-quarter of a *dīnār*.

The tradition of Ibn ʿUmar found support with Mālik from the tradition of ʿUthmān that he related, which states that amputation was carried out because of a citron valued at three *dirhams*. Al-Shāfiʿī explains away the tradition of ʿUthmān on the basis that the exchange value in those days was twelve *dirhams* (to the gold *dīnār*). Amputation because of three *dirhams* seeks to preserve smaller amounts of wealth, while amputation for ten *dirhams* passes over and overlooks trivial amounts attaching importance to the integrity of the limb. A reconciliation between the tradition of Ibn ʿUmar, that of ʿĀʾisha and the act of ʿUthmān is possible through al-Shāfiʿī's opinion and is not possible through the opinions of others. If reconciliation is better than preference, then al-Shāfiʿī's opinion is the best.

This is one of the conditions stipulated for amputation. Within it they disagreed about the well-known case, which relates to that of a group of thieves and the amount giving rise to amputation, that is, the *niṣāb* without the share of each amounting to a *niṣāb*—this would happen when they bring out together from the place of safe custody an amount equal to the *niṣāb* at the same time. For example, when they carried out together an amount or a box that was equal to the *niṣāb*. Mālik said that each will be subjected to amputation, which was also the opinion of al-Shāfiʿī, Aḥmad and Abū Thawr. Abū Ḥanīfa said that they are not liable for amputation, unless each one of them took out an amount equal to the *niṣāb*. Those who upheld amputation for all were of the view that the penalty is related to the amount of stolen property, that is, the amount of stolen property giving rise to the liability for amputation because of preservation of property. Those who were of the view that amputation relates to this amount, no less, for the protection of the hand, said that a number of hands cannot be amputated for an amount that the law has determined as the basis of liability for cutting one hand.

They disagreed about the time of valuation of the stolen property. Mālik said that this is the day of theft, while Abū Ḥanīfa said that it is the day judgment is delivered against him for amputation.

The second condition for the obligation of this *ḥadd* is the place of safe custody (*ḥirz*). All the jurists, whose opinions are widely respected and their disciples are agreed upon the stipulation of *ḥirz* for the obligation of amputation, though they did differ about what constitutes *ḥirz* and what does not. It will be fairly accurate to say about the definition of *ḥirz* that it is a place or a condition in which wealth is preserved in a manner that its taking is made difficult, like a covering, or a fence, or what is similar. The act committed by the thief is described as taking of property from the *ḥirz*, as we shall be discussing.

Those who upheld its stipulation include Mālik, Abū Ḥanīfa, al-Shāfiʿī, al-Thawrī and their disciples. The Ẓāhirites said that amputation is invoked for the person who steals the *niṣāb* even if this is not from the *ḥirz*. The legal basis for the majority is the tradition of ʿAmr ibn Shuʿayb from his father from his grandfather from the Prophet (God's peace and blessings be upon him) that he said, "There is no amputation for fruit hanging from the tree nor for that in rope nets, but when gathered at the threshing floor or the place for drying, amputation will be applied for what reaches the price of a shield" and also the *mursal* tradition of Mālik from ʿAbd Allāh ibn ʿAbd al-Raḥmān ibn Abī Ḥusayn al-Makkī conveying the same meaning as the tradition of ʿAmr ibn Shuʿayb. The reliance of the Ẓāhirites is on the general meaning of the words of the Exalted, "As to the thief, both male and female, cut off their hands".[232] They maintained that it is necessary to interpret the verse for its general meaning unless restricted by an established *sunna* and the established

[232] Qurʾān 5:38

sunna restricts it only to the extent of the amount for which amputation is to be applied. They rejected the tradition of ʿAmr ibn Shuʿayb on the grounds of the dispute over the soundness of his traditions. Abū ʿUmar ibn ʿAbd al-Barr said that the traditions of ʿAmr ibn Shuʿayb must be acted upon when related by reliable narrators.

Those who deemed *ḥirz* an obligatory stipulation agreed upon certain things and disagreed about others, like the door of a room and the covering of a place of safe custody and their disagreement about utensils, or their agreement about not applying amputation to one stealing from a room not jointly owned for residence, unless he moves it out of the room, or their disagreement about a room with shared residence. Mālik and most of those who stipulated *ḥirz*, said that the thief's hand is cut if he moves the property out of the room, while Abū Yūsuf and Muḥammad said that amputation is not applied unless he moves it out of the house. They also disagreed about the grave, whether it is a *ḥirz*, so that amputation may be applied to the *nabbāsh* (shroud-snatcher). Mālik, al-Shāfiʿī, Aḥmad and a group of jurists said that it constitutes a *ḥirz* and the *nabbāsh* is liable to amputation. This was also the opinion of ʿUmar ibn ʿAbd al-ʿAzīz. Abū Ḥanīfa said that there is no amputation for him. The same was upheld by Sufyān al-Thawrī and is related from Zayd ibn Thābit.

Ḥirz generally, according to Mālik, is each place where the stolen property in question could customarily be placed for safe custody. Thus, the place where animals are tied is a *ḥirz* for him, as are utensils, or the clothes worn by humans. A human being is a *ḥirz* for each thing worn or carried by him. Anything used, by one sleeping, as a pillow is a *ḥirz*, on the basis of what is related in the tradition of Ṣafwān ibn Umayya, which will come up shortly. Whatever is taken in view of a vigilant person amounts to *ikhtilās* (misappropriation). According to Mālik, amputation is not applied to a person who pilfers jewellery worn by a minor, unless there is someone who is guarding him. There is no amputation for one who steals from the Kaʿba, according to Mālik; similarly, in the case of mosques. It is said in the Mālik's school, however, that if the thief steals from these places during the night, his hand is to be cut. The cases, in this topic, pertaining to the question as to what constitutes *ḥirz* and what does not are numerous.

Those who upheld the stipulation of *ḥirz* agreed that any person who can be designated as one removing something from a *ḥirz*, irrespective of his having entered it, becomes liable for amputation. There is disagreement when such designation vacillates, like the disagreement within the school in the case of two thieves, one inside a room and the other outside it, with the one inside moving the property close to a hole in the wall and the other taking it. It is said that the person outside the room, who takes the property, is liable for amputation, while it is said that there is no *ḥadd* for either. It is also maintained that *ḥadd* is applied to the person who moves the property close to the hole. The disagreement in all this refers to the application of the designation of a certain person as the remover from *ḥirz*.

This, then, is the discussion of *ḥirz* and its stipulation for the liability of amputation. The person who throws property out of the *ḥirz*, taking it later, is subjected to amputation. Mālik reserved his view about the person who is arrested after he has thrown the property out of the *ḥirz*, but before he could take it; Ibn al-Qāsim said his hand is to be cut.

56.8.1. **Chapter 1: The Categories of Stolen Property**

The jurists agreed about the categories of stolen property (that lead to amputation), saying that it is each thing (legally) owned, lacking speech (not human), whose sale and acquisition of compensation, in lieu thereof, is permitted. Amputation becomes obligatory for the theft of such a thing, except for fresh (moist) eatables and things that are essentially *mubāḥ* (free; *res nullius*)—about which they differed. The majority maintained that amputation is invoked for the theft of each thing of value that can be sold and for which compensation can be taken. Abū Ḥanīfa said that there is no amputation for (the theft of) food, nor for things that are essentially *mubāḥ* like game, firewood and grass.

The reliance of the majority is upon the general meaning of the verse imposing amputation and on the general meaning of the traditions laying down the condition of *niṣāb*. The reliance of Abū Ḥanīfa for the prevention of amputation in the case of fresh (moist) food is on the words of the Prophet (God's peace and blessings be upon him), "There is no amputation for (theft of) food or of *kathar* (edible tuber on top of the palm tree)". This tradition was related without qualifications or additions. He also relied on the argument that there exists for the thief a doubt of ownership in things *mubāḥ*. They disagreed about what constitutes *shubha* (doubt) for waiving the *ḥadd*, which is also a condition stipulated for stolen property and relates to three things: genus, quantity and conditions. This issue will be taken up in what follows.

They disagreed within this topic about categories of stolen property like the *muṣḥaf* (whether stealing them leads to amputation). Mālik and al-Shāfiʿī said that the thief's hand is cut off, while Abū Ḥanīfa said it is not; perhaps, this is based on Abū Ḥanīfa's view that its sale is not permitted, or that each person has a right in it in so far as it is not property. They also disagreed within this topic about the person who abducts a minor non-Arab slave, who cannot talk or comprehend speech. The majority said that his hand is to be cut. When the abducted non-Arab slave was old enough to understand, Mālik said that the abductor's hand is to be cut, while Abū Ḥanīfa said it is not. They disagreed about (the abduction of) a minor who is free. According to Mālik, his abductor's hand is to be cut off, but not so according to Abū Ḥanīfa, which is also the opinion of Ibn al-Mājishūn from among the disciples of Mālik.

They agreed, as we have said, that a substantial doubt with respect to ownership has the effect of waiving this *ḥadd*; however, they disagreed about what constitutes doubt sufficient to waive this *ḥadd*. Among the cases is that of the slave pilfering his master's property. The majority of the jurists maintain that his hand is not to be cut off, but Abū Thawr said that it is to be cut and he did not stipulate any conditions for it. The Ẓāhirites said that it is to be cut, unless the master had entrusted the property to him. Mālik stipulated for the servant, in whose case the *ḥadd* is to be waived, that he should be performing services directly for his master personally. Al-Shāfiʿī stipulated this condition in one opinion, but on another occasion he did not. ʿUmar, may Allāh be pleased with him, and Ibn Masʿūd upheld waiver of punishment in this case and none of the Companions opposed them.

Another case is that of one spouse stealing from another. Mālik said that if they reside in separate rooms where their property is stored, then amputation is obligatory for one who stole from the other spouse. Al-Shāfiʿī said that caution requires relief from amputation due to the doubt that their property is mixed up and also the doubt of joint-ownership, but an opinion similar to that of Mālik is related from him, which was adopted by al-Muzanī. Among the issues is also that of close relatives. Mālik's view in this is that only the father's hand is not to be cut for what he stole from his son, due to the words of the Prophet (God's peace and blessings be upon him), "You and your wealth belong to your father", but all other relatives are liable to amputation. Al-Shāfiʿī said that all ascendants and descendants—that is, fathers, grandfathers, sons, son's sons—are exempt form the liability of amputation. Abū Ḥanīfa said that all blood relations within the prohibited categories are exempt from liability. Abū Thawr held that each person is liable to amputation except those exempted through consensus. One of the issues is about the person who steals from the common booty or from the *bayt al-māl*. Mālik said his hand is to be cut, but ʿAbd al-Malik, one of his disciples, said that it is not.

This ends the discussion of the things (stolen, *al-masrūq*) that give rise to liability in this offence.

56.8.2. Chapter 2: Consequential Liability

When the offence is committed in accordance with the description we have given, that is, about the attributes of the thief, of the stolen property and of the act of theft, then, the jurists agree that the consequential liability for the offence is amputation, in so far as it amounts to an offence and when the liability is not for amputation, the obligation is to compensate (the loss caused). They disagreed whether compensation could be combined with amputation. One group said that the thief is liable for compensation as well as amputation, which is the opinion of al-Shāfiʿī, Aḥmad, al-Layth, Abū Thawr and a group of jurists. Another group said that he is not to compensate if the owner cannot find his property among the (recovered) goods. Among those who upheld this opinion are Abū Ḥanīfa, al-Thawrī, Ibn abī Laylā and a group of jurists. Mālik and his disciples made a distinction and said that if the thief is in financial ease he is to pay the value of the stolen property, but if he is in financial straits he is not to pay the price even when his situation improves. Mālik stipulated the continuance of financial ease up to the time of amputation, according to what is related from him by Ibn al-Qāsim.

The reliance of those who combined the two penalties is that there exist two kinds of rights in the offence of theft, the right of Allāh and the right of men, with each right requiring its own liability. Further, if they (the contenders) agreed upon the recovery of the property when it is found in the possession of the thief, then it follows that (in case of its loss) it should become a financial liability due from him on the analogy of all other financial obligations. The reliance of the Kūfīs is upon the tradition of ʿAbd al-Raḥmān ibn ʿAwf that the Messenger of Allāh said, "The thief is not liable for compensation once the *ḥadd* has been applied to him". This tradition is weak according to the traditionists; Abū ʿUmar said that it is *maqṭūʿ*, according to them, but some narrated it with a complete chain and it is recorded by al-Nasāʾī. The Kūfīs say that the operation of two claims through one right is against the principles and they add that amputation is a substitute for compensation. It is for this reason that they maintain that if the thief steals property and is awarded *ḥadd* for it, he is not to be awarded *ḥadd* again if he steals the same property a second time. The distinction drawn by Mālik is based on *istiḥsān*, as a breach from analogy.

The study of amputation relates to the object of amputation and to the case of the thief whose limb to be cut is missing. The object of amputation is the right hand, to be severed from the wrist, by agreement of the jurists. This is upheld by the majority. One group said that only the fingers are to be severed. If a thief, whose right hand has already been amputated for a previous theft, steals again, they disagree, with the jurists of Ḥijāz and Iraq saying that the left foot is to be severed after the right hand. Some of the Ẓāhirites and also some of the *Tābiʿūn*, said that the left hand is to be amputated after the right hand and nothing more is to be amputated after this.

Mālik, al-Shāfiʿī and Abū Ḥanīfa, after their agreement about amputation of the left foot following the right hand, disagreed about the suspension of sentence if he steals a third time. Sufyān and Abū Ḥanīfa said that amputation is suspended for the third theft and the thief is made to compensate the stolen property. Mālik and al-Shāfiʿī said that if he steals a third time, his left hand is to be severed followed by his right foot for the fourth theft. Both opinions are related from ʿUmar and Abū Bakr, that is, the opinions of Mālik and Abū Ḥanīfa.

The reliance of those who do not uphold multiple amputations, except for the hands, is upon the words of the Exalted, "As to the thief, both male and female, cut off their hands",[233] the feet being mentioned in the case of brigands only. The reliance of those who uphold the cutting of the foot after the hand is upon the report "that the Prophet (God's peace and blessings be upon him) was brought a slave who had committed theft and he ordered the amputation of his right hand. He was brought a second time and he ordered amputation of his left foot. When brought the third time, he ordered amputation of the left hand and the fourth time the (remaining) foot was amputated". This is related in the tradition of Jābir ibn ʿAbd Allāh, which states that "he was brought a fifth time and was ordered by the Prophet to be executed". This tradition, however, is of the category of *munkar* (rejected) according to the traditionists and is opposed by the words of the Prophet, "These are abominations for which penalties are prescribed", but he did not mention execution. Reliance is also placed on the tradition of Ibn ʿAbbās "that the Prophet (God's peace and blessings be upon him) ordered amputation of the foot after the hand". According to Mālik, the thief is subjected to correction the fifth time.

When the object of amputation is missing, due to a reason other than amputation for theft, for example, the hand is paralysed, the view of the school is that amputation is transferred to the other hand, while it is said that it is transferred to the foot.

They disagreed about the location of amputation, with respect to the foot. It is said that it is severed from the joint connecting the foot with the leg; it is also said that the ankles are to be included in amputation, while it is said that they are not; and it is further maintained that severance is from the joint that is in the middle of the foot.

They agreed that it is the right of the owner of stolen property to forgive the thief as long as the matter has not been brought to the notice of the *imām*, because of what has been related from ʿAmr ibn Shuʿayb from his father from his grandfather that the Messenger of Allāh (God's peace and blessings be upon him) said, "Pardon the *ḥudud* among yourselves, for when a *ḥadd* is reported to me it becomes obligatory" and his words, "Even if it was Fāṭima,

[233] Qurʾān 5:38

the daughter of Muḥammad, I would have applied the *ḥadd* to her" and also because of what he said to Ṣafwān, "Would that this had taken place before you brought him to me".

They disagreed when the thief had stolen something that gave rise to the liability of amputation, after having been reported to the *imām*, but the owner of the property had gifted it to him or did so after the complaint and before amputation. Mālik and al-Shāfiʿī said that he is liable for *ḥadd*, as the matter has been reported to the *imām*. Abū Ḥanīfa and a group of jurists said that there is no *ḥadd* for him. The reliance of the majority is upon the tradition of Mālik from Ibn Shihāb from Ṣafwān ibn ʿAbd Allāh ibn Ṣafwān ibn Umayya that it was said to him, "One who has not migrated is at a loss. Ṣafwān ibn Umayya, then, travelled to Madina and slept in a mosque. He had a cloak, which he placed under his head. A thief came and stole this cloak, but Ṣafwān caught him and brought him up to the Messenger of Allāh (God's peace and blessings be upon him). The Messenger of Allāh ordered the amputation of his hand, upon which Ṣafwān said, 'I did not intend this, O Messenger of Allāh and it is donated to him as charity'. The Messenger of Allāh said, 'Would that this had been before you brought him to me'".

56.8.3. **Chapter 3: The Proof of Theft**

They agreed that theft is proved through two *ʿadl* witnesses and that it is also proved through a confession by a free man. They disagreed about the confession of a slave. The majority of the jurists said that a confession by him against himself renders *ḥadd* obligatory, but does not make him liable for compensation. Zufar said that the confession of a slave against himself is not valid for matters leading to his execution or amputation of his hand, because of his being the property of his master. This was the opinion of Shurayḥ, al-Shāfiʿī, Qatāda and a group of jurists, when the slave retracts his confession due to a doubt pertaining to a period prior to his retraction. If he retracts without the existence of any doubt, there are two opinions about it from Mālik. This is what the jurists of Baghdad have related from the school, but the later jurists go into details that are not useful for the present purpose, but are suitable for the (detailed discussion of) cases within the school.

56.9. THE BOOK OF *ḤIRĀBA* (BRIGANDAGE)

The source for this book are the words of the Exalted, "The only reward of those who make war upon Allāh and His Messenger and strive after corruption in the land will be that they will be killed or crucified, or have their hands and feet on alternate sides cut off, or will be expelled from the land".[234] This is so, as the majority maintain that this verse was revealed in the case of brigands. Some said that it was revealed in the case of persons who became apostates in the period of the Prophet (God's peace and blessings be upon him) and drove the camels away.[235] The Messenger of Allāh (God's peace and blessings be upon him) issued the verdict and their hands and feet were cut (from alternate sides) and their eyes were gouged. The correct view is that it relates to the *muḥāribūn* (brigands), due to the words of the Exalted, "Save those who repent before ye overpower them. For know that Allāh is Forgiving, Merciful", as the inability to overpower is not stipulated for the repentance of the non-believers, which confirms that it pertains to the brigands.

56.9.1. Chapter 1: The Discussion of *Ḥirāba*

They agreed that *ḥirāba* is a show of armed force and the obstruction of the highways outside the city. They disagreed about the brigands inside the city. Mālik said that they are the same inside or outside the city. Al-Shāfiʿī stipulated power (*shawka*), though he did not stipulate numbers. The meaning of *shawka*, according to him, is the strength to overpower, because of which he stipulated remoteness from settlements, as overpowering is usually from outside the settlements. Likewise, al-Shāfiʿī maintained that if (the political) authority weakens and domination by another is found in the city, it amounts to *muḥaraba*. In cases other than this, according to him, it amounts to misappropriation. Abū Ḥanīfa said that *muḥaraba* does not take place within a city.

56.9.2. Chapter 2: The Discussion of the *Muḥārib*

A *muḥārib* is each person whose life is protected before the commission of *ḥirāba*, that is, a Muslim and a *dhimmī*.

[234] Qurʾān 5:33

[235] The reference is to a group of Bedouin who stayed with the Prophet and then complained of the climate of Medina. He advised them to go to the desert where his own camels were kept, tended by some shepherds. After staying on for some time, during which they ate the meat of camels and drank their milk, thus, becoming quite healthy, they killed the shepherds, drove away the camels and became apostates.

56.9.3. Chapter 3: The Consequential Liability of the *Muḥārib*

They agreed that he is liable for the right of Allāh and the right of human beings. The right of Allāh, they agreed, requires execution, crucifixion, the cutting off of hands and feet from alternate sides and exile as has been ordained by Allāh. They disagreed about these punishments whether there is a choice between them or they are to be applied through a gradation corresponding to the gravity of the offence by the *muḥārib*. Mālik said that if he commits murder, he must be put to death and the *imām* has no option between amputation and exile, but there is an option between his execution and crucifixion. If he has misappropriated property, but has not murdered, there is no discretion about his exile; however, there is discretion regarding execution, crucifixion and amputation from alternate sides. When he obstructs the highways only, the *imām* has the choice between his execution, crucifixion, amputation and exile. The meaning of discretion, according to him, is that the matter depends upon the *ijtihād* of the *imām*. Thus, if the *muḥārib* is one of those who have a doctrine and organization, *ijtihād* would require his execution or crucifixion, as amputation would not do away with his menace. In case he does not have a doctrine, but is strong and powerful, his limbs are to be amputated from alternate sides. If none of these two traits is found in him, the least punishment is adopted, which is lashing and exile.

Al-Shāfiʿī, Abū Ḥanīfa and a group of jurists maintained that these penalties are dependent upon the offences, which lead to the punishment as determined by the *sharʿ*, thus, none of the brigands is to be executed unless he has slain someone, none is to be subjected to amputation unless he has misappropriated property and only those are to be exiled who have neither killed nor misappropriated property. A group of jurists said that, on the other hand, the *imām* has absolute discretion in their affair, irrespective of their having killed or misappropriated property.

The reason for the disagreement is whether the word "or" (*aw*) indicates discretion or the details of gradation in proportion to the gravity of the offence. Mālik interpreted it to mean detailed gradation for some offenders and discretion in the case of others. They disagreed about the meaning of the words "or crucified", with some saying that he is to be crucified till he dies of starvation, while others said that it means he is to be executed and crucified at the same time. Among the latter were those who said that he is to be executed first and then crucified, which is the opinion of Ashhab, but it is said that he is to be crucified first and then put to death on the wooden prop, which is the opinion of Ibn al-Qāsim and Ibn al-Mājishūn. Those who said that he is to executed first and then crucified, maintain that funeral prayers be said for him before crucifixion. Some of those who said that he is to be executed upon the prop, maintained that funeral prayers are not to be said for him as a sign of his rejection, but it is said that they should assemble behind the prop and pray. Saḥnūn maintained that if he is executed upon the prop, he is to be taken down and then prayers are to be said. Is he to be returned to the wooden prop? There are two opinions about this. Abū Ḥanīfa and his disciples maintained that he is not to be left on the prop for more than three days.

The words of the Exalted, "[O]r have their hands and feet on alternate sides cut off", imply that his right hand and left foot should be cut off, but if he repeats the offence, his left hand and right foot are to be cut off. They disagreed when he does not have the right hand. Ibn al-Qāsim said that his left hand and right foot are to be cut off, while Ashhab maintained that his left hand and left foot are to be cut off.

They also disagreed about the words of the Exalted, "[O]r will be expelled from the land". Some said that exile here means imprisonment, while it is said that exile means that he be expelled from one area to another and imprisoned there till such time that his repentance is manifest. This is the opinion of Ibn al-Qāsim related from Mālik. The distance between the two areas, at a minimum, should be one in which prayers are to be shortened while travelling. Both views are related from Mālik, with Abū Ḥanīfa adopting the first one. Ibn al-Mājishūn said that exile is their fleeing from the land of the *imām* before the application of *ḥadd* to them. Exile after capture, however, is not allowed. Al-Shāfiʿī said that exile is not the objective, but if they flee we keep pursuing them in the land; it is said that it is an intended penalty, therefore, they have to be exiled and imprisoned forever. All this is from al-Shāfiʿī. It is also said that the meaning of "expelled from the land", is from the land of Islam to that of the land of war (enemy). The meaning that is manifest indicates that expulsion is their exile from their own area, because of the words of the Exalted, "And if We had decreed for them: Lay down your lives or go forth from your dwellings, but few of them would have done it"[236]—that equate execution and exile, which is a well known form of punishment customarily awarded like stripes and execution. All that has been said about this issue, besides this, is not known either through practise or custom.

56.9.4. **Chapter 4: Discharging the Obligation through Repentance**

The basis for the question, what are the factors that lead to the waiving of the punishment, is to be found in the words of the Exalted, "Save those who repent before you overpower them".[237] They differed about this on several

[236] Qurʾān 4:66
[237] Qurʾān 5:34

points. The first is whether *tawba* (repentance) is acceptable. Second, if it is accepted, then, what are the attributes of the *muḥārib* from whom it is accepted? The jurists have two opinions about this. One opinion, which is better known, states that repentance from each offender is acceptable, due to the words of the Exalted, "Save those who repent before you overpower them". The second opinion is that his repentance is not acceptable, which is upheld by those who maintain that the verse was not revealed because of the *muḥāribūn*.

They disagreed into three opinions about the description of repentance by virtue of which the *ḥukm* is discharged. First, that *tawba* takes place in two ways. One of these is that he relinquish his activities, even if he does not appear before the *imām*, while the second way is that he cast away his weapons and surrender to the *imām*, which is the opinion of Ibn al-Qāsim. The Second opinion is that he relinquish his activities and come to his place of residence and socialize with his neighbours. If he is brought to the *imām* before his repentance becomes manifest, he will apply the *ḥadd* to him. This is the opinion of Ibn al-Mājishūn. The third opinion maintains that repentance is attained through a recourse to the *imām*. If he relinquishes his activities it will not absolve him from the application of one of the different *aḥkām* to him when he is captured before surrendering to the *imām*. The gist of all this is that repentance is attained if he presents himself before the *imām* prior to his capture; it is said that it is sufficient if only his repentance becomes manifest prior to his arrest; and it is said that it is accomplished by both ways together.

They disagreed about the situation of the *muḥārib* whose repentance is accepted into three opinions also. First, that he must be one who crossed over to the enemy. Second, that he must have a following. Third, that (his repentance is accepted) whatever his situation, irrespective of his having a following or having crossed over to the *dār al-ḥarb*. They disagreed about the *muḥārib* who refuses to surrender and the *imām* offers him asylum on the condition that he crosses back and surrenders. It is said that the *amān* is valid and he is absolved from the *ḥadd* of *ḥirāba*. It is also said that there is no *amān* for him as *amān* may be granted only to the Polytheists. They disagreed into four opinions about the question what is discharged by virtue of the repentance. First, that repentance discharges the *ḥadd* of *ḥirāba* only, but he is liable for all other claims based on the right of Allāh and the rights of human beings. This is Mālik's opinion. The second opinion maintains that repentance discharges the *ḥadd* of *ḥirāba* as well all rights of Allāh, like unlawful intercourse, drinking *khamr* and the liability for amputation due to theft, but he is to settle the financial claims of the people and those arising from murder, unless the heirs of the victim forgive him. Third, that repentance removes all claims related to the right of Allāh and they are liable for killing and financial claims to the extent of whatever resources are found in their possession, but no delayed liability is imposed on them. The fourth opinion is that repentance absolves him from all claims based on the right of Allāh or on the rights of human beings pertaining to wealth or killing, except for the property still existing in their possession.

56.9.5. Chapter 5: The Mode of Proof for this *Ḥadd*

How is this *ḥadd* proved? It is proved through confession and testimony. Mālik accepts the testimony of those plundered against those who plundered them. Al-Shāfiʿī said that the testimony of the troops is admissible against them if they do not claim for themselves or their acquaintances wealth that was misappropriated. According to Mālik, *ḥirāba* is proved through hearsay testimony.

56.9.6. *Section on* Muḥāribūn *with a Cause based on Interpretation*

The antagonist of the *muḥāribūn* who are pursuing a cause based on interpretation is the *imām*. If he takes any one of them captive, he is not to execute him unless the warfare is still continuing. Mālik said that the *imām* has the right to execute him if he fears that not doing so would support his companions against the Muslims. If, however, he is taken captive after the cessation of hostilities, his *ḥukm* is the same as that of an innovator who does not invite others to follow his innovation. It is said that he is asked to repent; if he does so (he is released) otherwise he is executed, while it is said that he is asked to repent and if he refuses he is to be subjected to correction, but is not to be executed.

Most of the innovators are imputed with *kufr*, implicitly. Mālik's opinion differed about attributing *kufr* by implication of the categorical claims. Consequential *takfīr* (means) that the innovators do not make categorical utterances that amount to *kufr*, but make statements which imply disbelief, though they do not believe in such an implication. The *ḥukm* of what is to be done with such people when they are taken captive is that the *ḥadd* of *ḥirāba* is not applied to them if they repent and they are not liable for the wealth that they took, unless it exists in their possession (in the same form), in which case it is returned to the owners.

They disagreed whether they are to be subjected to *qiṣāṣ* for those whom they killed. It is said that they are, which is the opinion of ʿAṭāʾ and Aṣbagh. Muṭarrif and Ibn al-Mājishūn, relating from Mālik, said that they are not, which was also the opinion of the majority, as each person who fights for a cause based on some sort of interpretation is not a disbeliever, the legal basis being the wars of the companions; similarly, an actual disbeliever, for he is one who rejects (a part of the basic creed) without a basis for interpretation.

56.10. Chapter on the *Ḥukm* of the *Murtadd* (Apostate)

An apostate, if taken captive before he declares war, is to be executed by agreement in the case of a man, because of the words of the Prophet (God's peace and blessings be upon him), "Slay those who change their *dīn*". They disagreed about the execution of a woman and whether she is to be required to repent before execution. The majority said that a woman (apostate) is to be executed. Abū Ḥanīfa said that a woman is not to be executed and compared her to an originally non-believing woman. The majority relied upon the general meaning implied (in the tradition). One group held a deviant opinion saying that she is to be executed even if she reverts to Islam.

Asking the apostate to repent was stipulated by Mālik as a condition prior to his execution, on the basis of what is related from ʿUmar. One group of jurists said that his repentance is not acceptable. If the apostate becomes a *muḥārib* first and then an apostate, he is to be executed because of *ḥirāba* and is not required to repent, whether his *ḥirāba* occurs in the Muslim territory or later when he crosses over to the *dār al-ḥarb*, except when he becomes a Muslim again. When the apostate *muḥārib* converts to Islam after he is captured or before it, they differ about his *ḥukm*. If his *ḥirāba* has occurred in the *dār al-ḥarb*, then, according to Mālik, his situation is like that of any *ḥarbī* who converts to Islam, he is not held liable for what he did during his apostasy. If his *ḥirāba* has occurred in the *dār al-Islām*, then his conversion to Islam absolves him of the liability to the *ḥukm* of *ḥirāba* only and his *ḥukm* is like that of an apostate for the offences committed by him during his apostasy in the *dār al-Islām* prior to conversion to Islam. The disciples of Mālik, however, differed in this with some, who took into account the day of offence, saying that his *ḥukm* is the *ḥukm* of the apostate, while others, who took into account the time of the *ḥukm*, said that his *ḥukm* is like that of a Muslim.

They disagreed within this topic about the *ḥukm* of the magician, with Mālik saying that he is to be executed as a disbeliever, while others said that he is not to be executed. The principle is that he is not to be executed, unless he becomes an apostate.

LVII
THE BOOK OF *AQḌIYA* (JUDGMENTS)

The principles of this book are covered in six chapters. First, the identification of persons whose judgments are permitted. Second, the identification of matters in which judgment is valid. Third, identification of procedures on the basis of which judgment is rendered. Fourth, identification of persons for, or against, whom judgment is rendered. Fifth, the mode of judgment. Sixth, the time of judgment.

57.1. Chapter 1: On the Identification of Persons whose Judgments are Permitted

The study in this chapter relates to those persons whose judgments are permitted, and to the qualifications that enhance their merit. The conditions stipulated for permissibility are that the person be a free, Muslim, major, male, sane, and *ʿadl*. It is said in the school that *fisq* leads to removal, but his judgments remain valid. They disagreed about his (the *qāḍīʾ's*) being one of those qualified for *ijtihād*. Al-Shāfiʿī said that it is necessary that he be a *mujtahid*. An identical opinion is related, in the school, by ʿAbd al-Wahhāb. Abū Ḥanīfa said that the judgment of a layman is valid. The Qāḍī (Ibn Rushd) said that this is also apparent from what my grandfather related, may Allāh have mercy on him, in the *Muqaddimāt* about the school, for he deemed the existence of the qualification of *ijtihād* as recommended.

They differed about the condition of being a male. The majority said that it is a condition for the validity of the judgment. Abū Ḥanīfa said that it is permitted for a woman to be a *qāḍī* in cases involving financial claims. Al-Ṭabarī said that it is permitted to a woman to be a judge in all things without any restrictions. ʿAbd al-Wahhāb said, "I do not know of any dispute among them about the qualification of freedom".[238]

Those who denied the right of a woman to be a judge compared it (the office of the *qāḍī*) to the office of the head of state, and also compared a woman

[238] This appears to be a gloss that was incorporated into the text; it relates to material that follows two paragraphs later.

to the slave due the deficiency in her legal capacity. Those who permitted her judgment in cases of financial claims, did so comparing it to the permissibility of her testimony in such claims. Those who considered her judgment as executed in each thing said that the principle is that any person who is able to render judgment among people his decision is valid, except in matters restricted by consensus, like the office of head of state.

There is no dispute about the stipulation of freedom. There is no disagreement in Mālik's school that hearing, sight, and speech are stipulated for the continuance in office, but are not conditions for the permissibility of appointment. This is so, as there are qualifications of the judge that are stipulated as conditions of permissibility in the school—and if a person lacking them assumes office he is dismissed and all the judgments he rendered are abrogated—while there are others that are conditions for continuing in office, but are not conditions for permissibility—if such a person assumes office, he is removed, but the judgments he rendered are executed, unless these were unjust. In this category, then, they stipulate these three qualifications.

One of the conditions, according to Mālik, is that the judge should be single. Al-Shāfiʿī permits that there be two judges in a city, but he does not permit the stipulation that their judgments be identical. If complete independence is stipulated for each judge, it is viewed from two aspects: permissibility and prohibition. He (al-Shāfiʿī) said that if a dispute occurs between two litigants in the jurisdiction in the choice of the judge, they draw lots.

The merits of the judicial office are many and scholars have mentioned these in their books. They disagreed about an illiterate person, however, whether he can be a *qāḍī*. Its permissibility is more likely because of the Prophet (God's peace and blessings be upon him) being an *ummī*. One group of jurists said that it is not permitted, and from al-Shāfiʿī both views are related, as it is probable that the Prophet's case was specific to him and was related to the miraculous nature of his office. There is no disagreement about the head of state rendering judgments; his delegation of authority to the *qāḍī* is a condition for the validity of the judgments of the latter, and I know of no disagreement about this.

They disagreed about a person selected by the parties to the dispute, a person who has not been appointed to judicial office (an arbitrator). Mālik said that this is permitted, while al-Shāfiʿī said, in one of his opinions, that it is not permitted. Abū Ḥanīfa said that it is permitted if his verdict is in conformity with the rulings of the city judge.

57.2. Chapter 2: The Identification of Matters in which Judgment is Valid

Regarding matters in which he renders judgment, the jurists agreed that the *qāḍī* adjudicates each right, whether it pertains to the right of Allāh or to the right of human beings. He is the representative of the head of state for this purpose, registering marriages and appointing executors. About the question whether he appoints the *imāms* in the *jāmiʿa* (congregational) mosques there is disagreement. Does he appoint his successors in case of absence caused by illness or a journey? There is disagreement over this too, unless he has been authorized to do so. He does not oversee public life nor the other various offices, but he supervises interdiction of the prodigal, according to those who interdict them.

One of the issues in this topic is whether a judge can grant relief to a petitioner, on the strength of the evidence, when the thing (such relief) is not permissible in reality. They agreed that the judgment of the *ḥākim* based on the apparent evidence cannot make lawful a prohibited thing or prohibit something that is lawful, this applies particularly to financial matters, because of the words of the Prophet (God's peace and blessings be upon him), "I am a human being like you; when you bring your disputes to me it is possible that one of you may present a more persuasive proof than the other and I would decide for him on the basis of what I hear from him. If I have granted a right to a person that actually belongs to his brother, he should not take anything from it, for surely I have carved out for him a share in the Fire".

They disagreed about the dissolution of the contract of marriage or its valid conclusion on the basis of the *prima facie* evidence—which the judge considers correct but is not in fact so, for the prohibited does not become lawful, nor the lawful prohibited, on the basis of the judgment of the judge, without actually being so—whether it is to be considered lawful. The majority said that property and sex are the same for this purpose, the ruling of the judge does not make the lawful among these prohibited or the prohibited lawful. For example, if two perjuring witnesses were to testify about strangers, a man and a woman, that she is the man's wife, when she is actually not, the majority said that she does not become his lawful wife, even if the judgment of the judge has declared her to be so. Abū Ḥanīfa and the majority of his disciples said that she is his lawful wife.

The reliance of the majority is on the generality of the preceding tradition. The impression of the Ḥanafites is that (in a similar situation) the *ḥukm* of *liʿān* is established by the law, though it is known that one of the parties is lying, and *liʿān* results in separation prohibiting the wife for her accusing husband, making her lawful for someone else (who may marry her). If he (the husband) is lying, she has become prohibited for him only by the judgment of the *hākim*. Similar is the case when she is lying (that is, the prohibition is caused by the *hākim*), for her unlawful intercourse does not give rise (by itself) to dissolution according to the opinion of a majority of the jurists. The majority of the jurists, however, maintain that dissolution in this case occurs as a penalty for the knowledge that one of them is a liar.

57.3. Chapter 3: The Identification of the Basis for the Judgment

A judgment may be based on (one or more of) four things: testimony, oath, refusal to take an oath and confession. It may also be based on a combination of these things. In this chapter, therefore, there are four sections.

57.3.1. *Section 1: Testimony* (Shahāda)

The discussion of witnesses relates to three things: qualifications, gender and number. The number of qualifications considered for the acceptance of a witness are five: *ʿadāla*, puberty, Islam, freedom and the absence of an accusation. Some of these are agreed upon, while others are disputed. The Muslim jurists agreed about *ʿadāla* and its stipulation for the acceptance of testimony, because of the words of the Exalted, "[O]f such as ye approve as witnesses",[239] and His words, "[A]nd call to witness two just men among you".[240]

They disagreed as to what was meant by *ʿadāla*. The majority maintained that it was a qualification in addition to Islam, which requires that the witness abide by the prescribed obligations as well as recommendations, avoiding prohibited and disapproved acts. Abū Ḥanīfa said that apparent adherence to Islam is sufficient for *ʿadāla* as long as no vile act is known of the witness.

The reason for disagreement, as we have noted, is that there is vacillation about the meaning of the term *ʿadāla* as against *fisq*, as they agreed that the testimony of a *fāsiq* is not acceptable due to the words of the Exalted, "O ye who believe! If an evil-liver bring you tidings, verify it, lest ye smite some folk in ignorance and afterward repent of what ye did".[241] They did not disagree, however, that a *fāsiq*'s testimony is acceptable after he is known to have repented, except the person whose *fisq* arises from the offence of *qadhf*, as Abū Ḥanīfa says that his testimony is not acceptable even if he repents, while the majority say it is. The reason for the disagreement is whether the exception—in the words of the Exalted, "And those who accuse honourable women but

[239] Qurʾān 2 : 282
[240] Qurʾān 2 : 282
[241] Qurʾān 2 : 282

bring not four witnesses, scourge them (with) eighty stripes and never (afterward) accept their testimony—They indeed are the evildoers—Save those who afterward repent and make amends. (For such) lo! Allāh is Forgiving, Merciful"[242]—is effective for the nearest-mentioned category or for the whole (preceding) sentence, except what is restricted by consensus, that is, repentance does not discharge his liability for *ḥadd*. This discussion has preceded.

They agreed that puberty is stipulated on the basis of *ʿadāla*. They disagreed about the testimony of minors against each other in bodily injuries and homicide. The majority of the jurists of the regions rejected it on the basis of what we have said about the occurrence of consensus that a condition for testimony is *ʿadāla*, and the condition for *ʿadāla* is puberty. Therefore, according to Mālik, it (the testimony of minors) does not, in fact, amount to testimony, but is circumstantial evidence. It is for this reason that Mālik stipulates that they testify together so that they do not cower. The disciples of Mālik differed whether their testimony is admissible when there is a major among them.

They did not differ about the stipulation of the prescribed number of witnesses who render testimony, but they did differ whether the stipulation of being male is to be made. They also differed whether their testimony is permitted for purposes of a homicide committed among them. Mālik has no reliance in this except that it is related from Ibn al-Zubayr. Al-Shāfiʿī said that if the contender gives an argument based on this, it is to be said to him that Ibn ʿAbbās had rejected it and the Qurʾān indicates its invalidity. The same opinion as Mālik's was expressed by Ibn Abī Laylā and by a group of the *Tābiʿūn*. Mālik's acceptance of such testimony belongs to the category of permissions based on the analogy of *maṣlaḥa*.

They agreed about Islam that it is a condition for the acceptance of testimony, and that the testimony of a disbeliever is not permitted, except for their disagreement regarding its permissibility in bequests made on a journey, because of the words of the Exalted, "O ye who believe! Let there be witnesses between you when death draweth nigh unto one of you, at the time of bequest—two witnesses, just men from among you, or two who are not from among you".[243] Abū Ḥanīfa said that it is permitted upon the conditions mentioned by Allāh, while Mālik and al-Shāfiʿī said that it is not permitted, and considered the verse as abrogated.

The majority of the jurists of the regions inclined toward stipulating freedom for the acceptance of testimony, while the Ẓāhirites said that the

[242] Qurʾān 24 : 4,5

[243] Qurʾān 5 : 106. Pickthall's translation has been changed slightly where he uses the words "another tribe" for *min ghayrikum*.

testimony of a slave is valid as the fundamental condition is *ʿadāla*; and bondage is not effective in the rejection of testimony, unless this can be established from the Book of Allāh or from *sunna* or consensus. It was as if the majority maintained that bondage was a relic of the times of disbelief and, therefore, must be effective in the rejection of testimony.

About the impeachment of a witness on the basis of affection for the litigant, the jurists were unanimous that it was effective in the rejection of testimony. They disagreed about the rejection of the testimony of an *ʿadl* witness through impeachment on the basis of feelings of love or hate, which causes worldly enmity. The jurists of the regions upheld its rejection, but they agreed about the points of operation of impeachment and points where it is invalidated, and on other points they disagreed with some accepting its operation and others rejecting it. The case about which they agreed is the testimony of a father in favour of his son or of the son in favour of his father; similarly, in the case of a mother for her son and that of the son for his mother. The point where they disagreed about the effectiveness of impeachment is that of spouses rendering testimony one for the other, with Mālik and Abū Ḥanīfa rejecting it and al-Shāfiʿī, Abū Thawr and al-Ḥasan accepting it. Ibn Abī Laylā said that the testimony of a husband for his wife is acceptable, but not that of the wife for her husband, which was also the opinion of al-Nakhaʿī. The case in which they agreed about the ineffectiveness of impeachment is the testimony of a brother, unless he is casting suspicion away from himself, according to Mālik, and as long as he is not completely dependent on his brother. The exception is al-Awzāʿī for he said it is not permitted. Within this topic is their disagreement about the acceptance of the testimony of an enemy against his enemy. Mālik and al-Shāfiʿī said that it is not acceptable while Abū Ḥanīfa said that it is.

The reliance of the majority, in the rejection of testimony on the basis of impeachment, is upon what has been related from the Prophet (God's peace and blessings be upon him) that he said, "The testimony of a rival or of a suspect person is not acceptable", and also upon what has been recorded by Abū Dāwūd of the words of the Prophet (God's peace and blessings be upon him), "The testimony of a Bedouin is not acceptable against a town-dweller", because of the rare occasions that a Bedouin can witness what happens in a city. These are their proofs by way of transmission. A rational argument relates to impeachment itself, and the majority agreed about its effectiveness in the *aḥkām sharʿiyya*, for example, a murderer will not inherit from the victim and that the wife divorced thrice during his death-illness will inherit, though it is disputed. The other group, who are Shurayḥ, Abū Thawr, and Dāwūd, maintained that even the testimony of a father favouring his son is acceptable, when he is *ʿadl*, as is that of others beside him. Their reliance is upon the words of the Exalted, "O ye who believe! Be staunch in justice, witnesses for Allāh, even though it be against yourselves or (your) parents or (your) kindred".[244] A command for a thing, they say, implies its validity, except what has been restricted by consensus regarding the testimony of an individual on his own behalf. By way of a rational argument, they are likely to say that the rejection of testimony as a whole is on the point of suspicion of falsehood, which the law has made operative in the case of the *fāsiq* and has suspended in the case of an *ʿadl* witness, and *ʿadāla* cannot mingle with suspicion.

About the discussion of number and gender, the Muslims agreed that the offence of *zinā* cannot be proved with less that four male *ʿadl* witnesses. They agreed that all claims, with the exception of *zinā*, are proved by two male *ʿadl* witnesses. Al-Ḥasan al-Baṣrī disagreed saying that no right is to be acknowledged with less than four witnesses on the analogy of *rajm*, but this is weak because of the words of the Exalted, "And call to witness, from among your men, two witnesses".[245] All are agreed on the point that a judgment becomes obligatory with testimony of two witnesses without the oath of the plaintiff, except that Ibn Abī Laylā said he must take an oath (as well). They agreed that financial claims are established through one male *ʿadl* witness and two female witnesses, because of the words of the Exalted, "And if two men be not (at hand) then a man and two women, of such as ye approve as witnesses".

They disagreed about their testimony for purposes of *ḥudūd*. The opinion that is adopted by the majority is that the testimony of women is not admissible in *ḥudūd*, with men or independently. The Ẓāhirites said that it is admissible, when accompanied by the testimony of a man and if there is more than one woman, for all kinds of litigation on the basis of the apparent meaning of the verse. Abū Ḥanīfa said that their testimony is accepted in financial claims and in matters other than the *ḥudūd* related to the personal law, like divorce, retraction of divorce, marriage, and emancipation. It is not accepted, according to Mālik, for any issue affecting the person. The disciples of Mālik differed about the acceptance of their testimony in financial claims related to the law of persons, like agencies and bequests that are related to financial matters only. Mālik, Ibn al-Qāsim and Ibn Wahb said that in these matters a male and two female witnesses are acceptable, while Ashhab and Ibn al-Mājishūn said that only two men can testify in such matters.

The independent testimony of women, that is, women unaccompanied by male witnesses, is acceptable according to the majority in matters of personal

[244] Qurʾān 4 : 135
[245] Qurʾān 2 : 282

law that are usually not accessible to men, like birth, consummation, and the defects of women. There is no dispute about any of these, except in suckling, about which Abū Ḥanīfa said that the testimony of women alone is not acceptable unless accompanied by that of a man, for according to him it is a matter of non-financial human rights that is accessible to women as well as men. Those who permitted the independent testimony of women (in these matters) differed about the number of women stipulated. Mālik said that two women are sufficient; it is said that this is so after the matter has been made public, and it is said that it may be without making it public. Al-Shāfiʿī said that no less than four are sufficient for this purpose, as Allāh, the Mighty and Powerful, has declared two women as equivalent to one male witness; he (al-Shāfiʿī) also stipulated rendering of testimony in pairs. One group of jurists said that at least three women is a number considered sufficient, which is a meaningless opinion.

Abū Ḥanīfa permitted the testimony of women (about women) for the area that is between the navel and the knees, and I think that the Ẓāhirites, or at least some of them, do not permit the independent testimony of women in any thing just as they allow it with men in everything, which seems to be the case. They disagreed over the testimony of a single woman about suckling, because of the words of the Prophet (God's peace and blessings be upon him) regarding the single woman, who rendered testimony about suckling, "How is that when she has nursed both of you". The apparent meaning here indicates rejection, therefore, Mālik's opinion was firm about it that it is disapproved.

57.3.2. *Section 2: Oaths* (Aymān)

They agreed about oath that the claim against the defendant is dismissed because of it, when the plaintiff does not have evidence. They disagreed whether the claim of the plaintiff can be established through it. Mālik said that the right of the plaintiff in what was denied by the defendant is established, and the rights established against him are extinguished if claimed by a person against whom their cancellation stands proved, in a case where the plaintiff has a stronger cause of action a *prima facie* chance of success. Other jurists said that a claim by the plaintiff cannot succeed on the basis of an oath, whether it is for the denial of a right established against him or for the securing of a right that is denied to him by the defendant.

The reason for their disagreement is the vacillation about the meaning of the words of the Prophet (God's peace and blessings be upon him)—"Evidence (testimony) is to be produced by the plaintiff and the (defendant) one who denies is to take the oath"—whether they are common for all defendants and plaintiffs, or whether the plaintiff is always required to produce testimony and the defendant always to take the oath, as the plaintiff usually has a weaker *prima facie* case than the defendant. Those who said that this *ḥukm* is general for all defendants and plaintiffs, and that the general meaning is not restricted, said that a claim cannot be established with an oath, nor can an established claim be annulled through it. Those who said that the defendant alone has been given this *ḥukm* on the basis that he has a stronger *prima facie* case, said that if there appears a case in which the position of the plaintiff, on the face of it, is stronger, his statement would be accepted. These jurists argued on the basis of the cases over which the majority have expressed agreement that the acceptable statement is that of the plaintiff, along with his oath. For example, in the plaintiff's claim that a deposit entrusted to him was destroyed, and in other similar cases, his claim is accepted with an oath. These jurists may say that the principle is as we have stated it, except what is restricted by agreement.

All of them are in agreement that the oath refuting a claim or establishing it, is an oath upon the name of Allāh, and that there is no god but He. The opinions of the jurists of the regions are similar in its description. According to Mālik it is, "By Allāh, The One beside Whom there is no god", without further additions. Al-Shāfiʿī adds to this, "He Who knows what is hidden, just as He knows what is declared".

Whether it is to be enhanced in solemnity by undertaking it in a special place where it is sworn, they disagreed about this. Mālik held that it is enhanced, but it relates to a determined amount. Al-Shāfiʿī had the same view, but they differed about the amount. Mālik said that if he (the plaintiff) makes a claim against him for three *dirhams* or more, the swearing of the oath has to be in the congregational mosque. If it is the Prophet's Mosque (in Medina), it is necessary that he swear it after mounting the pulpit, but when it is another mosque there are two narrations from him about it: first, wherever it may take place; second, it is to be (sworn) by the pulpit. It is related from him by Ibn al-Qāsim that the defendant swears the oath about important claims in any congregational mosque, and he did not determine a spot for this. Al-Shāfiʿī said that he is to swear the oath in Medina by the pulpit, but in Mecca he swears it between the corner of the House and the station (*maqām*) of Abraham; similarly, he is to swear it by the pulpit, according to him, in other towns. The minimum scale (*niṣāb*) for this purpose, according to him, is twenty *dīnārs*. Dāwūd said that he swears by the pulpit for all small and large amounts. Abū Ḥanīfa said that the solemnity of an oath is not to be enhanced with the location.

The reason for disagreement is whether the solemnity of swearing an oath at the pulpit of the Prophet's Mosque (in the tradition) implies an obligation of swearing at the pulpit. Those who said that it does imply an obligation said that if this was not the case the enhancement of solemnity would have no meaning. Those who attributed to the enhancement of solemnity a meaning other than the obligation of taking the oath at the pulpit said that it is not obligatory to swear at the pulpit. The tradition laid down about such enhancement is that of Jābir ibn ʿAbd Allāh al-Anṣārī that the Messenger of Allāh said, "One who swears falsely at my pulpit prepares a place for himself in the Fire". They also argued on the basis of judicial precedent (*ʿamal*) saying that it was the practice of the Caliphs. Al-Shāfiʿī said that judicial practice, about it, did not cease in Medina and Mecca. They said that if enhancement had not implied the obligation of swearing the oath at the place of enhancement there would have been no use for it, except the avoidance of an oath at that spot. They (these jurists) said that if the ordainment of enhancement for the oath in the words of the Prophet (God's peace and blessings be upon him), "One who demolishes (or takes away) the right of a Muslim with his oath, Allāh will prohibit *janna* for him and make the Fire obligatory for him", makes it obligatory to render judgment on the basis of an oath, then the case of enhancement laid down in the case of location must be similar. The other group said that the enhancement of solemnity of the oath does not imply the obligation of rendering judgment on the basis of an oath. And if enhancement of the oath does not imply the rendering of the judgment on the basis of the oath, enhancement of location does not imply the undertaking of the oath in a special place. There is no consensus of the Companions supporting it. On the other hand, disagreement is implied in it through the case concerning Zayd ibn Thābit. The oath was enhanced for solemnity through location, by Mālik, in the case of *qasāma* and *liʿān*, so also by the prescription of time, for he said that the oath of *liʿān* is to be sworn after the afternoon prayer, on the basis of reports indicating enhancement when it is sworn after the afternoon prayer.

They disagreed about a judgment based upon oath along with a supporting witness. Mālik, al-Shāfiʿī , Aḥmad, Dāwūd, Abū Thawr, the seven jurists of Medina and a group said that a judgment may be rendered on the basis of an oath and a supporting witness in cases of financial claims. Abū Ḥanīfa, al-Thawri, al-Awzāʿī and the majority of the jurists of Iraq said that no judgment can be based upon an oath and a supporting witness. This was also the opinion of al-Layth from among the disciples of Mālik. The reason for disagreement in this issue is based upon the conflict of texts. Those who support it argue on the basis of a number of traditions, which include the tradition of Ibn ʿAbbās, the tradition of Abū Hurayra, the tradition of Zayd ibn Thābit and the tradition of Jābir. The tradition related from Ibn ʿAbbās which reads, "The Messenger of Allāh rendered verdicts on the basis of an oath and a witness", is recorded by Muslim, but has not been recorded by al-Bukhārī. Mālik relied for this purpose upon his *mursal* report from Jaʿfar ibn Muḥammad from his father "that the Messenger of Allāh rendered judgments based on an oath and a witness", as acting upon *mursal* traditions is obligatory according to him.

The text opposing these comprises the words of the Exalted, "And if two men be not (at hand) then a man and two women, of such as ye approve as witnesses".[246] They said that this imposes a limitation, thus, any addition to it would amount to abrogation, and the Qurʾān cannot be abrogated by a *sunna* that is not related by countless number of Companions (*mutawātir*). For the contenders, this does not amount to abrogation, but is an addition that does not alter the *ḥukm*. From the *sunna* they seek support from what has been recorded by al-Bukhārī and Muslim from Ashʿat ibn Qays, who said, "There was between me and a man a dispute over something. We took up the matter with the Prophet (God's peace and blessings be upon him), who said, 'Your two witnesses or his oath'. I said, 'Then let him swear, I do not mind'. The Prophet (God's peace and blessings be upon him) said, 'One who swears an oath devouring thereby the wealth of a Muslim is a perjurer, he will be meeting Allāh when He is angry with him' ". They said that this is the imposition of a limitation from the Prophet (God's peace and blessings be upon him) and is a rejection of the evidence adduced by each litigant, and the Prophet (God's peace and blessings be upon him) had to exhaust all legitimate forms of evidence. Those who uphold (a judgment based upon) an oath and a supporting witness abide by their principle that an oath is a form of evidence permitted to the litigant with a *prima facie* stronger case, and in this case the proof of the plaintiff is strengthened further through a witness as it is strengthened in the case of *qasāma*.

These jurists disagreed about the rendering of judgment on the basis of an oath and two witnesses who are women. Mālik said that it is permitted as two women have been made to stand in the place of one man. Al-Shāfiʿī said that it is not permitted as a woman can be a substitute with one male witness, not alone nor with another woman. Is judgment to be rendered on the basis of an oath in *ḥudūd* that are related to the rights of human beings, like *qadhf* and bodily injuries? There are two opinions about it in the school (of Mālik).

57.3.3. *Section 3: Defendant's Refusal to take the Oath* (Nukūl)

The jurists also disagreed about establishing a right against the defendant by his refusal to take the oath. Mālik, al-Shāfiʿī, the jurists of Ḥijāz and a group of the Iraqi jurists said that if the defendant refuses to take the oath no right is established for the plaintiff by the refusal itself, except when the plaintiff takes an oath or he has one witness. Abū Ḥanīfa, his disciples and the majority of the Kūfīs said that he is to render judgment for the plaintiff against the

[246] Qurʾān 2 : 282

defendant on the basis of the refusal itself, in cases of financial claims, after asking him thrice to take the oath.

The rebuttal of an oath with an oath (reversal), according to Mālik, may take place in cases in which the testimony of a male and two female witnesses is admissible, or in which testimony of a male witness accompanied by plaintiff's oath is admissible. According to al-Shāfiʿī, such rebuttal is permissible in all cases where an oath is acceptable. Ibn Abī Laylā said that the oath is to be offered to the plaintiff in cases of accusation, but not otherwise. There are two opinions from Mālik in the case of reversal due to accusation.

The reliance of those who upheld the reversal of an oath is what is related by Mālik "that the Messenger of Allāh (God's peace and blessings be upon him) offered the oath of rebuttal to the Jews in *qasāma* after commencing with the Anṣār". Among Mālik's proofs is the argument that rights are established in two ways, either through an oath with an accompanying witness, or through *nukūl* and a witness or plaintiff's oath. The principle, according to him, is to accept evidence in pairs. According to al-Shāfiʿī, the judge is not to render judgment on the basis of a witness and refusal.

The reliance of those who maintained the rendering of judgment on the basis of *nukūl* is on the argument that as testimony is for the establishment of the claim and oath is for its dismissal, it is necessary that the claim be established against him because of his refusal to take the oath. They said that its transference from the defendant to the plaintiff is against the texts, as the texts explicitly state that an oath is one of the means (available) for the defendant. These are the fundamentals of the different kinds of evidence on the basis of which the judge renders his judgment.

One of the things about which they agreed under this topic is the judgment of a *qāḍī* on the basis of an epistle received from of another *qāḍī*. According to the majority, this is possible with supporting testimony, I mean, when the *qāḍī*, before whom the case has been proved through two *ʿadl* witnesses, testifies that the case stands proved, that is, this should be recorded in the epistle that he sends to the other *qāḍī*, with two witnesses testifying to the fact that it is the epistle of the *qāḍī*, and that he records their testimony for its proof. It is also said that it is sufficient if it is recorded in the *qāḍī*'s own writing, and this was the earlier practice. Mālik, al-Shāfiʿī and Abū Ḥanīfa disagreed when he records their testimony about the epistle, but does not read it out to them. Mālik said that it is permitted, while al-Shāfiʿī and Abū Ḥanīfa said that it is not permitted, and the testimony is not valid.

They disagreed about the string and the bag in the case of found wealth, whether he renders judgment based on them without testimony, or whether testimony is necessary. Mālik said that he may render judgment based on them, while al-Shāfiʿī said that there must be two witnesses, which was also the opinion of Abū Ḥanīfa. Mālik's opinion in this depicts greater conformity with the traditions, while the opinion of the other jurists agrees more with the derived principles.

An issue about which they differed is the judgment of the judge based upon his own knowledge. The jurists agreed that the *qāḍī* may decide matters of *ʿadāla* and the discrediting of witnesses on the basis of his own knowledge, but if witnesses render testimony contrary to his own knowledge, he is to abstain from rendering judgment on the basis of his own knowledge. They also agreed that he may decide on the basis of his own knowledge about the confession or denial of the litigant, except for Mālik, who said that he must have two witnesses for the confessions and denials of litigants.

They agreed that he decides on the basis of his own knowledge to prefer one of the proofs on a point of law adduced by the parties when these are not conflicting. They disagreed when the proofs on the issue were in conflict. One group of jurists said that his judgment is not to be overturned if it does not violate a point of consensus (*ijmāʿ*). Another group of jurists said that if it is a deviant opinion (it is to be overturned). A third group of jurists said that his decision is overturned when it is based upon analogy and there is a text from the Book or *sunna* opposing analogy, which is more equitable, except when the analogy is supported by principles, while texts from the Book that are liable to interpretation and the (opposing) *sunna* is not *mutawātir*. This is the interpretation that must be assigned to the opinions of those jurists who prefer analogy in some cases over traditions, like what is attributed to Abū Ḥanīfa by agreement and to Mālik with dispute.

They disagreed whether he issues a decision based upon his own knowledge for someone without there being any testimony or confession, or that he is not to render judgment without evidence or a confession. Mālik and most of his disciples said that he does not decide except on the basis of testimony or confession, which was also the opinion of Aḥmad and Shurayh. Al-Sḥāfiʿī the Kūfī, Abū Thawr and a group of jurists said that the *qāḍī* has the right to decide on the basis of his own knowledge. For each group there are precedents among the verdicts of the Companions and the *Tābiʾūn*, and each relied on the texts and on rational arguments.

The reliance of the group of jurists who disallowed this includes the tradition of Maʿmar from al-Zuhrī from ʿUrwa from ʿĀʾisha "that the Prophet (God's peace and blessings be upon him) sent Abū Jahm for the collection of *ṣadaqa*, and there was a scuffle about the obligation with a man that led to injuries. They came to the Prophet (God's peace and blessings be upon him) and informed him about it, so he awarded them *arsh* (estimated compensation). The Prophet (God's peace and blessings be upon him) then said to them, 'I wish to address the people and inform them about this that you have agreed. Have you agreed?' They said, 'Yes'. The Messenger of Allāh (God's peace and blessings be upon him) mounted the pulpit and addressed the people mentioning the incident. He then said to them, 'Are you satisfied?' They said, 'No!' The *Muhājirūn* were distressed because of them and the Messenger of Allāh (God's peace and blessings be upon him) came down and granted them the compensation, mounted the pulpit and started addressing again. He said, 'Are you satisfied?' They said, 'Yes' ". This makes it evident that the Prophet did not decide on the basis of his own knowledge. As a rational argument they said that it gives rise to an accusation against the *qāḍī*, and they agreed that an accusation has a legal force in law. The example is that the murderer does not inherit from the person whom he killed, according to the majority. Another example is that the testimony of a father for his son is rejected. There are other examples too that are upheld by the majority.

The reliance of those who permitted it with respect to transmission is the tradition of ʿĀʾisha in the incident of Hind, daughter of ʿUtba ibn Rabīʿa, the wife of Abū Sufyān ibn Ḥarb, when the Prophet (God's peace and blessings be upon him) said to her, upon her complaint against Abū Sufyān, "Take what is customarily sufficient for you and your children", without even listening to the argument of the other party. They advance a rational argument saying that when he can render judgment on the basis of the testimony of a witness about whom there can be a doubt in his mind, it is appropriate that he render judgment on the basis of his conviction.

Abū Ḥanīfa and his disciples restricted what the *qāḍī* decides on the basis of his own knowledge, saying that he is not to render judgment on the basis of his own knowledge in the *ḥudūd*, but he can do so in matters other than these. Abū Ḥanīfa further restricted the knowledge on the basis of which he decides, saying that he is to decide on the basis of knowledge that is acquired during the judicial proceedings, but not on the basis of knowledge that was acquired prior to that. It is related from ʿUmar that he ruled on the basis of his own knowledge against Abū Sufyān for a man from Banū Makhzūm. Some of the disciples of Mālik said that he decides on the basis of knowledge acquired during a judicial session, that is, on the basis of what he heard during the judicial session even if it did not amount to testimony. This is the opinion of the majority as we have said. The opinion of al-Mughīra is in conformity with the principles, as the principle in this *sharīʿa* is that he is not to render judgment, except on the basis of evidence, even if the conviction attained through it (his own knowledge) is stronger than the conviction about the veracity of the witness.

57.3.4. *Section 4: Confession/Acknowledgement* (Iqrār)

When a confession is explicit, there is no disagreement about the obligation of judgment based upon it. The examination of this topic relates, however, to the person whose confession is valid. When the confession is ambivalent, there is no disagreement about it(s rejection). The discussion of the person whose confession is valid has preceded.

The discussion about the effective number of confessions has preceded in the section on *ḥudūd*. There is no disagreement among them that a single acknowledgement is operative in financial claims. In the issues related to it, about which they disagreed, the controversy centres around the interpretation of words, and if you like to focus on it then have recourse to the Book of Cases (*furūʿ*).

57.4. **Chapter 4: The Persons for Whom He Can Render Judgment**

Against whom does he render judgment, and for whom? The jurists agreed that he renders judgment for a person in whose case no suspicion can arise. They disagreed about the person whose case will give rise to suspicion. Mālik said that his judgment is not valid for a person in whose case his testimony would not be admissible. A group of jurists said that it is permitted as judgment is based on means that are evident, but testimony is not.

Against whom can he render render judgment? They agreed that he can render judgment against a Muslim who is present, but they differed about one who is absent and also about the People of the Book. About the person who is absent, Mālik and al-Shāfiʿī said that he can render judgment against a person who has been absent for a long time. Abū Ḥanīfa said that he does not render judgment against an absent person at all. This was also the opinion of Ibn al-Mājishūn. It is sometimes related from Mālik that he does not render judgment about property that involves third-party rights.

The reliance of those who uphold his judgment (in the case of absent parties) is upon the tradition about Hind that has preceded, but there is no persuasive force in it as he was not deciding a case of an absent party. The reliance of those who do not uphold his judgment in such a case is upon the words of the Prophet (God's peace and blessings be upon him), "I decide for him in accordance with what I hear", and also what has been related by Abū Dāwūd and others from ʿAlī that the Prophet (God's peace and blessings be upon him) said to him when he sent him to Yemen, "Do not decide in favour of one of the parties till you hear out the other".

There are three opinions about the judgment against *dhimmī*s. First, that he may judge between them if they bring up the matter to him seeking the same *ḥukm* as that for the Muslims. This is Abū Ḥanīfa's opinion. Second, that he has a choice, which is Mālik's opinion, with al-Shāfiʿī holding both opinions. Third that it is obligatory upon the judge to adjudicate their affair even if they do not take up the matter with him. The reliance of those who stipulate their recourse to the judge is upon the words of the Exalted, "If then they have recourse unto thee (Muḥammad) judge between them or disclaim jurisdiction".[247] Those who upheld an option, also sought support from this. Those who made it obligatory relied upon the words of the Exalted, "So judge between them by that which Allāh hath revealed",[248] and maintained that this verse has abrogated the verse ordaining an option. Those who upheld the obligation of the judgment even if they do not take up the matter with him relied upon their consensus that if a *dhimmī* commits theft his hand is to be amputated.

57.5. **Chapter 5: The Method of Rendering Judgment**

They agreed unanimously about how the *qāḍī* renders judgment, saying that it is obligatory upon him to maintain exact equality between the two parties during the judicial session, and that he should not hear one of them in the absence of the other. He should commence with the plaintiff and ask him to produce testimony if the defendant denies the claim. If he does not have any evidence (testimony) and the matter relates to a financial claim, an oath becomes obligatory upon the defendant by agreement. If the case relates to divorce, or marriage, or homicide, the oath becomes obligatory upon the defendant, according to al-Shāfiʿī, by the mere filing of the claim. Mālik said that it does not become obligatory unless it is accompanied by a male witness. If the matter relates to a financial claim, does the defendant take an oath about it by virtue of the claim itself or he delays the oath till the plaintiff proves the mingling of rights? They disagreed about this, with the majority of the jurists of the regions saying that an oath becomes binding on the defendant by the filing of the claim itself due to the general meaning in the words of the Prophet (God's peace and blessings be upon him) in the tradition of Ibn ʿAbbās, "The burden of evidence is upon the plaintiff and the taking of oath is upon the defendant". Mālik said that the oath does not become obligatory, except through the proof of rights (by the plaintiff). This was also the opinion of the seven jurists of Medina.

The reliance of those who upheld it is the consideration of *maṣlaḥa* so that people are not led, through the filing of suits, to torment others and waste

[247] Qurʾān 5 : 42
[248] Qurʾān 5 : 49

their energies. It was because of this that Mālik did not allow a wife to require her husband to take an oath when she claimed that he had divorced her, unless there was a witness to support her claim; similarly, when a slave requires his master to take the oath in a case of alleged manumission.

A claim can either be for corporeal property or for the performance of an obligation. If the claim is for an obligation and the defendant denies a liability for such an obligation, having supporting testimony, he must, by agreement, hear the testimony. Similarly, when the claim relates to a contract about property, like sale or something similar. If, however, the claim is about (restitution of) property, which is called *istiḍḥqāq*, they disagreed whether he should hear the testimony adduced by the defendant. Abū Ḥanīfa said that he is not to hear the testimony of the defendant, except in the case of marriage and those things that cannot recur. Other jurists said that he should not hear it for any issue. Mālik and al-Shāfiʿī said that he hears it, that is, if the testimony of the defendant demonstrates to the plaintiff that it is his wealth in his ownership (the defendant's).

The reliance of those who said that he should not hear it is that the law has assigned testimony to be in the domain of the plaintiff and the oath to be in the domain of the defendant; it is, therefore, necessary that the matter should not be reversed, and it was to them like a ritual. The reason for the disagreement is whether the testimony of the defendant exhibits a meaning beyond the fact that the disputed thing exists in the possession of the defendant. Those who said that it does not convey an additional meaning said that such testimony is futile, but those who said that it does convey additional information, took it into account.

If we uphold the admissibility of the defendant's testimony, and then a conflict occurs between the two testimonies when none of them is establishing an additional fact that is not likely to recur in the ownership of the owner, the *ḥukm*, according to Mālik, is that he is to render judgment on the basis of testimony that is more sound in terms of *ʿadāla*, but is not to take into account the larger number (of witnesses). Abū Ḥanīfa said the testimony of the plaintiff is considered preferable as a matter of principle, and is not to be preferred on the basis of *ʿadāla*—just as it is not preferred according to Mālik on the basis of number. Al-Awzāʿī said that it is to be preferred on the basis of number.

When the testimonies are equal in terms of *ʿadāla*, it is deemed to be a case of no evidence, and, according to Mālik, the defendant is asked to take the oath. If he refuses, the plaintiff swears the oath and the right is determined, as the possession of the defendant supports him. It was because of this strong position that he is required to produce the weakest type of evidence, that is, the oath.

When the defendant acknowledges the claim, and the thing disputed is property, it has to be delivered to the claimant, by agreement. If, on the other hand, it is an amount to be paid as dues, the person acknowledging is to be considered a debtor (and has to settle the debt). If he claims the non-existence of funds, the *qāḍī* is to imprison him, according to Mālik, till such non-existence is proven, either by the length of imprisonment or through evidence, if he is suspected. When his being destitute becomes manifest, he is to be released due to the words of the Exalted, "And if the debtor is in straitened circumstances, then (let there be) postponement to (the time of) ease".[249] One group of jurists said that he is to be employed for compensatory services, which was the opinion of Aḥmad and has been related from ʿUmar ibn ʿAbd al-ʿAzīz. It is related from Abū Ḥanīfa that his creditors have a right to follow him around wherever he goes.

There is no disagreement that if the defendant is able to discredit the testimony, the claim is dismissed, if this is done before the judgment is rendered. If it is done after the issuance of the verdict, the judgment is not to be set aside, according to Mālik, but al-Shāfiʿī said that it is. When the witnesses retract from their testimony, it depends on whether it happens before the judgment or after it. If it happens before the judgment, the majority maintain that the case is not established, while some jurists said that it is. If it takes place after the judgment, Mālik said that the *ḥukm* stands established, but others held that it is not.

According to Mālik, the witnesses indemnify what is destroyed through their testimony. If this is wealth, they compensate it in all circumstances. ʿAbd al-Malik said that they do not in the case of an error. Al-Shāfiʿī said that they do not compensate wealth. If it is life, and they claim to have made an error, they are liable for *diya*. If they confess (about premeditated intention) they are to be subjected to *qiṣāṣ*, according to the opinion of Ashhab, while they are not according to the opinion of Ibn al-Qāsim.

57.6. **Chapter 6: The Time of Rendering Judgment**

When does he issue the judgment? This invokes conditions, some of which refer to the (mental) state of the *qāḍī*, some refer to the time of execution of the judicial order and the time of decision, and some refer to the restraining of the disputed property and its recovery, in case it is corporeal property.

The time when the *qāḍī* renders his judgment is that when he is not emotionally disturbed, because of the words of the Prophet (God's peace and

[249] Qurʾān 2 : 280

blessings be upon him), "The *qāḍī* is not to render judgment, if at such time he is in anger". On similar grounds, Mālik held the opinion that the *qāḍī* is not to render judgment when he is thirsty, hungry, in fear, or in some such state that interferes with his understanding. If, however, he renders a correct judgment in any of these states, they agreed, as far as I know, that his judgment is to be executed. It is possible to say that no judgment is to be executed in the particular case that has been mentioned by the text, which is that of anger, as the prohibition depicts the invalidity of the thing prohibited.

The time of execution of his judgment is after the determination of a period and the granting of an opportunity for raising of objections. The meaning of execution here is that he confirms or rejects the proofs adduced by the plaintiff. Does he have the right to hear further arguments after the judgment? There is a disagreement within the opinions of Mālik. The best known is that he may hear arguments in things pertaining to the right of Allāh, like *waqf* (trust) and manumission, but not in other cases. It is said that he may not hear arguments after the execution of judgment, and this is called *taʿjīz* (inability). It is said that he does not hear arguments from any of them, while it is also said that a distinction has to be made between the plaintiff and the defendant, which is after he has expressed his inability to do so.

The time for restraining the property arises when the case is established, but before objections are raised. This takes place when the person, who is in possession of the claimed property, does not wish to litigate, and has recourse to the seller for the price he paid. If he should need to claim it from the seller, it is up to the seller to agree with him in this so that its purchase from him is established, in case the other person is denying it, or confirm it for him if he is acknowledging it. The person in possession, from whom the property is being claimed, may take the property from the person claiming it by paying him its value. Al-Shāfiʿī said that he should buy it from him (paying the price not the value). If the property perishes in the hands of the possessor, he is to compensate it, but if it perishes during the litigation, they disagreed as to who is to compensate it. It is said that if it perishes after the claim is established, the compensation is upon the claimant, and it is said that the claimant compensates after the judgment, but after proof of the claim and prior to the judgment, it is the person from whom it is claimed who compensates it.

The Qāḍī (Ibn Rushd), may Allāh be pleased with him, said: It is necessary to know that the *aḥkām* of the *sharīʿa* are divisible into two kinds. One of these kinds is adjudicated by the judges, and the majority of the *aḥkām* we have mentioned fall under this category. The second kind are those not adjudicated by the judges, and most of these are in the recommended (*mandūb*) category. This category of the *aḥkām* are like responding to the Muslim greeting (*salām*), blessing one who sneezes, and the like, which are mentioned by the jurists at the end of their books that are called *Jawāmiʿ*. We have also thought of mentioning the best known of this category, God willing.

It is necessary, before this, to know that the legal *sunan* (practices) pertaining to conduct have as their purpose the virtues of the believer. Some of them refer to respect, to whom it is due, and to the expression of gratitude, to whom that is due. The *ʿibādāt* are included in this category. These are the *sunan* relating to ethical values. Some of the *sunan* relate to the virtue called *ʿiffa* (chastity, abstinence from undignified habits), and are of two kinds: *sunan* laid down about food and beverages, and *sunan* laid down about marital affairs. Some *sunan* refer to the requirement of justice and abstention from tyranny. These are the categories of *sunan* that require the maintenance of a balance in financial dealings, and the maintenance of a balance in personal relations (physical contact). Related to this category are (the *aḥkām* of) *qiṣāṣ*, wars, and punishments, as the maintenance of justice is the aim of all of these. Among them are *sunan* laid down for individual integrity, and *sunan* laid down for all kinds of wealth and its valuation, through which is intended the attainment of the merit called generosity, and the avoidance of the meanness called *bukhl* (covetousness). *Zakāt* is included in this category from one aspect, and is included in the communal sharing of wealth from another; same is the case with charity (*ḍṣadaqāt*). There are *sunan* laid down for social life, which is the essential condition for human life, and the preservation of its benefits relating to conduct and knowledge, which are called statehood. It is for this reason that these *sunan* should be upheld by the leaders and the upholders of the *Dīn*. Among the important *sunan* for social life are those related to love and hate, and to co-operation for the maintenance of all these *sunan*, which is called *al-nahy ʿan al-munkar, waʾl-amr biʾl-maʿrūf* (prohibiting the blameworthy and requiring what is good), and which is love and hate, that is religious, which occurs either due to the evasion of these *sunan* or due to the evil intent of the believer in the *sharīʾa*. Most of what the jurists mention in the *Jawāmiʿ*, among their books, is that which deviates from the four categories that are the merit of chastity, the merit of justice, the merit of courage, and the merit of generosity, and all kinds of worship (*ʿibāda*) are like conditions for the fulfilment of these merits.

The Book of Judgments is now complete, and with its completion is completed the entire manual. Praise be to Allāh, as is His due, many times over.

Glossary

abkār: Plural of *bikr*, which means virgin.

ʿadāla: The attribute of justice; probity; moral uprightness. The qualification of being a legally acceptable witness in the court of a *qāḍī*.

ʿadhala: To blame; criticize.

adhān: Call for prayer.

adilla: The plural of *dalīl*, which means guide. In the technical sense, the term *dalīl* is applied to mean evidence leading to the discovery of a rule of law or *ḥukm*. The term *adilla tafṣīliyya* is used for specific evidence within the general evidence, like the individual verses of the Qurʾān, and is distinguished from the term *adilla ijmāliyya* in so far as the latter term applies to general evidence that contains the specific evidence; namely, the Qurʾān, *sunna*, *ijmāʿ*, and *qiyās*.

ʿadl: Justice. See *ʿadāla*.

āḥād: Derivative of *wāḥid* (single). *Ḥadīth al-āḥād* means a tradition that has not reached the level of a continuous narration. To be specific, it is an individual narration, that is, it was narrated by a single individual in the first generation after the Prophet, as compared to a continuous narration (*mutawātir*), which has multiple chains.

aḥkām: (Plural of *ḥukm*). See *ḥukm*.

ahl al-dhimma: Free non-Muslims who are citizens of a Muslim state or country.

ahl al-ḥadīth: The traditionists. The meaning also includes jurists who followed the apparent meaning of traditions as distinguished from the *ahl al-raʾy*, who followed the meanings in the traditions after ascertaining their compatibility with general principles emerging from the Qurʾān and the *sunna*.

ahl al-qibla: Those who turn towards a *qibla*; includes the Jews.

ahl al-ẓāhir: A title for the Ẓāhirī school, which is extinct. They followed the *ẓāhir* or apparent meaning of the texts and did not consider *qiyās* to be a valid method of interpretation. As a result of this, their method of interpretation was literalist in nature.

ajal: The period of credit in sale and *salam*.

ajīr khāṣṣ: A person hired for wages who is dedicated to the service of a single employer, as distinguished from the *ajīr mushtarak*, who is paid on the basis of work done by different people, like a tailor.

amāna: A trust; an item deposited on trust.

ama: Slave-girl.

ᶜamal: Act; practice. The term includes internal acts like intention. In the technical sense, it is means the juristic principle adopted by Mālik, and in that sense it is applied to mean the rules of law maintained by the jurists of Medina. It is also understood generally to mean the practice of the people of Medina, but there is a need to be careful in the use of this term, because usually Ibn Rushd uses this term to mean the jurists of Medina, though the wider application is not excluded.

amān: The assurance of safe custody given by a free Muslim to a foreigner, especially from an enemy state, planning to visit the grantor's country. A kind of a visa.

amāna: A trust; an item deposited on trust.

ᶜamd: Intention. In the technical sense, it means *mens rea* in murder or in culpable homicide not amounting to murder, that is, *shibh al-ᶜamd* or voluntary manslaughter.

ᶜāmil: Worker; official appointed for the collection of *zakāt*.

āmir: One in authority issuing a command to a subordinate for the commission of an act. In the criminal law, the term is used for explaining the cases of coercion or abetment.

ᶜāmm: A general word that includes all the categories to which it is applied. If an injunction is expressed in general terms, it is considered to apply to all its categories, that is, the *ḥukm* contained within the general word is applicable to each category without restriction or qualification. The implication of such a command is considered to be definitive (*qaṭᶜī*) by the Ḥanafīs, who maintain that such a command will apply to all its categories unless other equally strong and definitive evidence singles out one of its categories and assigns it a different *ḥukm*. The Shāfiᶜīs do not consider a general word to be definitive, thus they permit its restriction by probable evidence.

amr: A command that is the bearer of a *ḥukm*.

ʿaqd: Tie; knot. Technically, the term is used for a contract that is concluded through an offer and acceptance within the session of the contract.

ʿāqila: A group of persons responsible for paying the blood-money (*diya*) on behalf of an offender. Usually they are agnates or all the relations on the paternal side, but the term was also applied to the *dīvān* of a soldier.

ʿaql: Reason; intellect. Reason or *ʿaql* is the basis for the capacity for execution of an individual (*ahliyat al-adāʾ*). *ʿAql* is also the fourth purpose of the law; its preservation and protection is an acknowledged goal of the *sharīʿah*. The word *ʿaql* is also used to mean the liability of the *ʿāqila*.

ʿāriya: The lending of commodities and utensils; commodity loan.

ʿariyya: Plural *ʿarāyā*. The fruit left on the trees by the owner of an orchard for the consumption of the poor. The sale of *ʿariyya*, on the other hand, involves the exchange of dry dates with fresh dates still on the trees. The transaction is permitted as an exemption from the provisions of *ribā* and *salam*.

arkān: Plural of *rukn* (element). The essential ingredient of an act of worship, other act, or contract, the absence of which renders such act or transaction invalid.

arsh: A kind of penalty to be paid for injuries; estimated damages.

arṭāl: Plural of *raṭl* (pound); a unit of weight.

aṣhār: Relations through marriage.

aṣl: Origin; root; foundation. Source of law. The established case that forms the basis of the extension of the *ḥukm* in *qiyās* (analogy). A principle of law. The principal amount in a debt.

aṣnām: Plural of *ṣanam* (idol).

ʿaṭāʾ: Donation. The time of *ʿaṭāʾ* is the time of payment of *zakāt*.

athar: Plural *āthār*. Acts and sayings attributed to the Companions of the Prophet. The term is also applied to mean the legal effects of a contract or transaction.

ʿaṭiyya: Bestowal; an act of charity.

ʿawl: The doctrine of *ʿawl* in inheritance. It is a method of reduction through which fractional shares not amounting to a whole are allocated.

awliyāʾ: Plural of *walī* (guardian).

awsuq: It is the plural of *wasq*, which is a unit of measure that is equal to one camel-load.

ʿayn: Plural *aʿyān*. A thing present and ascertained by weighing or measuring in a contract of sale as compared to a counter-value that has not been ascertained or whole possession has not been taken, and which is called *dayn*.

ayyim: Widow.

ʿazl: Ejaculating outside the vagina.

bāḍiʿa: A wound that exposes the flesh.

bāligh: A person who has attained the age of marriage, that is, puberty.

baghy: Rebellion.

banāt labūn: A camel that has completed two years of age and has entered the third.

barāʾa: Absolution; removal of liability. *Barāʾa aṣlīya* is freedomfrom liability. It is the original rule of permissibility for an act that is asserted in the absence of a rule or *ḥukm*for such an act.

baraṣ: A skin disease.

bayān: Elaboration; explanation. In Islamic jurisprudence, the term is applied generally to mean interpretation. In a restricted sense it means the explanation or elaboration required for an obscure term in the texts called *mujmal*. The explanation in such a case is usually sought from the *sunna*.

bayʿ: Sale.

bayʿ al-ḥaṣāt: Sale by throwing or dropping stones. It is declared as a hazardous sale and consequently prohibited.

bayʿ al-ʿariyya: Sale of dry dates for fresh.

bayʿ al-khiyār: Sale with an option.

bayt al-māl: The treasury.

bidʿa: An innovation in matters of religion as distinguished from the established practice, the *sunna*.

bint labūn: See *banāt labūn*.

bint makhāḍ: A camel that has completed the first year of its age and has entered the second.

bulūgh: The literal meaning is "attaining" or "reaching". In the technical sense it means reaching the age of marriage. The apparent sign for such age is the attainment of puberty. In the absence of such signs the age is eighteen for a male and seventeen for a female in the opinion of Abū Ḥanīfa. The age for the presumption of puberty is fifteen for females according to the majority of the jurists.

bunūwwa: Sonship.

buyūʿ: Plural of sale.

buyūʿ al-ājāl: Sales with periods of delay, that is, credit sales.

buyūʿ al-gharar: Sales involving an element of risk or hazard usually because of uncertainty.

daʿ wa taʿajjal: A statement made by the creditor to encourage the debtor to pay. It means reduce the amount and hasten the payment. Thus, it is a discount offered by the creditor.

ḍaʿīf: Weak; used for a weak opinion or weak tradition.

dalīl: See *adilla*.

dalīl al-khiṭāb: The evidence gathered from the meaning of the text through an indirect implication.

ḍamān: Compensation; damages.

dāmiya: A wound that bleeds.

dār al-ḥarb: Enemy territory

dār al-Islām: The area within the jurisdiction of the Islamic state as distinguished from the *dār al-ḥarb*, which is enemy territory.

dār al-kufr: Area under the jurisdiction of the disbelievers.

ḍarar: Harm; injury.

dayn: Debt. It is distinguished from *ʿayn*, which is a commodity or property that is present, because a debt is not tangible and present, it is associated with the *dhimma* as a liability. See also *ʿayn*.

dharīʿa: Means; means to an end.

dhawū l-arhām: Distant relatives.

dhawū nasab: Blood relatives.

dhimma: Liability. The equivalent of legal personality in positive law. The receptacle for the capacity of acquisition.

dhimmī: A non-Muslim citizen of an Islamic state.

dīwān: The military unit to which a soldier belongs.

diya: Reparation; wergild. Fixed compensation for loss of life or limbs.

fāḥisha: Indecency. A general term that includes the indecency of unlawful sexual intercourse.

faḥwā al-khiṭāb: The various ways in which the meanings of a statement can be understood.

farāʾiḍ: The prescribed shares in the estate of the deceased, usually termed as inheritance.

farḍ: Obligatory; prescribed share.

farḍ ʿayn: Universal obligation.

farḍ kifāya: Communal obligation.

farʿ: Branch; issue; case.

fasād: Vitiation; irregularity.

fāsid: Vitiated; irregular; voidable.

fāsiq: Disobedient.

fayʾ: Booty acquired during war without fighting.

fidāʾ: Ransom.

fidya: Ransom.

fiqh: Knowledge; understanding. Knowledge of the law, which is the *sharīʿa*, that is, its jurisprudence. In its technical sense, it is the knowledge of the legal rules pertaining to conduct that has been derived from the detailed evidence in the general sources.

firāq: Separation.

firāsh: Bed. In law, it means legal access for sexual intercourse.

fisq: Disobedience; violation of religious injunctions.

fuḍūlī: Unauthorized agent.

fulūs: Plural of *fals*, a copper coin.

fuqahāʾ: Jurists; experts in *fiqh*. The term is distinguished from *mujtahid* in so far as the *mujtahid* is a jurist who is qualified to derive the law independently, while the *faqīh* may not be qualified to derive the law independently though he is trained in the law.

furūʿ: The branches of the law as distinguished from the *uṣūl*, which are its sources.

ghāṣib: Usurper.

ghīla: Treachery; ambush. It is used to refer to killing by concealed means, which is called *qatl al-ghīla*.

ghaṣb: Usurpation; kidnapping.

ghabn: Misrepresentation.

ghalla: Revenue; produce.

ghanam: Cattle.

gharar: Uncertainty; hazard; risk.

ghishsh: Fraud; deception.

ghurra: The white mark on the forehead of a horse. The compensation to be paid for the loss of the foetus or miscarriage.

ḥajb: Exclusion from inheritance of one heir due to the presence of the other.

ḥākim: Lawgiver. In Islamic law the term is applied to mean Allāh as the sole Lawgiver.

ḥārisa: A bruise that ruptures the skin.

ḥaḍāna: Custody of children.

ḥabl al-ḥabla: The sale of the foetus with the mother or the sale of the foetus before it is delivered.

ḥadd: A fixed penalty prescribed in the texts as a right of Allāh, like the penalties for unlawful sexual intercourse and theft. In general terms the word is used for all duties determined to be the rights of Allāh.

ḥadīth: Saying. In the technical sense, the term is used for the written record of the *sunna*, thus, a *ḥadīth* may contain more than one *sunan*.

ḥajj: Annual pilgrimage to Mecca.

ḥajr: Interdiction.

ḥalāl: Permitted. In a technical sense, the Lawgiver is indifferent to the performance of the act. In another sense, each permitted category may be obligatory or prohibited as a whole. Thus, the Lawgiver is indifferent how much a person eats, but total abstention from eating is prohibited in so far as it leads to the loss of life. In such a case it is obligatory for the person to eat for the preservation of his life, which is an acknowledged purpose of the *sharīʿah*.

ḥamāla: Surety. Another name for *kafāla*.

ḥamāla biʾl-māl: a guarantee provided for payment by a third party.

ḥamāla biʾl-nafs: The furnishing of a bail bond.

ḥarām: Prohibited.

ḥarbī: enemy.

ḥasan: A tradition that has within it all the conditions laid down for a *ṣaḥīḥ* (sound) tradition, but one of its narrators is considered weak, because he may not have a sound memory.

ḥashafa: Glans penis.

hāshima: An injury that fractures the bones without dislocating them.

ḥawāla: Endorsement; transfer of a debt.

ḥawl: One year. The period is relevant for purposes of *zakāt*.

hiba: Gift.

hirāba: Armed robbery; brigandage.

ḥijāb: Veil.

ḥikma: Wisdom. The underlying reason of a legal provision. It is different from the *ʿilla*, which is an outward attribute. Thus, the accompanying hardship is the *ḥikma* for the curtailment of prayer during travel, but the *ʿilla* is the journey itself.

ḥinṭa: Wheat.

ḥiqqa: A she-camel that has entered the fourth year of her life.

ḥirz: Place of safe custody. The removal of property from the *ḥirz* is an essential condition for the cutting of the hand in case of theft.

ḥudūd: Plural of *ḥadd*.

ḥujja: Demonstrative proof.

ḥukūma: Government. In criminal law, it is the estimation of the damage caused by an injury.

ḥukm: A rule of law; judgment; decision. The word is also used for the effects of a contract.

ḥulum: The attainment of the age of marriage or puberty.

ḥumalāʾ: Immigrants; gypsies.

iʿāra: Lending. See *ʿāriya*.

ibāḥa: Permissibility. It covers a category of acts that the Lawgiver is indifferent about, that is, He neither commands their commission nor their omission.

ibn labūn: A camel that has completed two years of age and has entered the third.

ibn makhāḍ: A camel that has completed the first year of its age and has entered the second.

ʿibādāt: Plural of *ʿibāda* (worship).

ʿibāda: Worship.

ʿidda: The period for which a woman has to wait after divorce or death of her husband before she can marry again.

ʿiffa: Chastity.

iflās: Insolvency.

ightiyāl: Devouring; converting another's property to one's own use.

iḥdād: Mourning. See also *ḥidād*.

iḥrām: Intention; the dress required for performing *ʿumra* and *ḥajj*.

iḥṣān: The state of being a *muḥṣan*, which usually means married. The term also means chaste as well as free.

ijāra: Hire. The contract of hire.

ijāza: Permission; authorization.

ijmāʿ: Consensus. In the technical sense it is the consensus of the jurists within a period of time after the death of the Prophet on a *ḥukm sharʿī* (point or rule of law).

ijtihād: Striving. In Islamic law it is the effort that the jurist exerts to discover the law from the sources. *Ijtihād* is not a source of law, as is assumed by some; it is merely the effort invested in interpretation according to a prescribed methodology.

ikhtilāṭ: Mixing. The mixing of capital contributed by persons entering into a partnership so that the capital of one becomes indistinguishable from that of the other.

ikhtilās: Misappropriation. It is the taking of property while the owner of the property is watching, as distinguished from theft (*sariqa*), which is the taking of property by way of stealth.

īlāʾ: Vow of continence. It is the swearing of an oath by a man that he will not have intercourse with his wife, either for a period in excess of four months, or for a period of four months, or for an unlimited period.

ʿilla: Underlying cause for a rule; *ratio decidendi.*

ʿilm al-nahw: Grammar.

iltiqāṭ: Taking found property into custody.

imām: The Muslim ruler or leader. The term is also applied to mean the person leading congregational prayers.

ʿīna: A dual contract used for evading the provisions of *ribā* (interest). The lender buys from the borrower some item for cash and then sells it back to him for a higher price on credit. The difference in the two prices is the interest charged.

iqāla: The rescission of a sale at a negotiated value.

ʿirq: Share.

ishtirāk: The case where a word has more than one meaning, that is, homonym.

iskān: The right of residence.

isnād: The chain of transmission of a tradition.

istiḥqāq: The right or claim of a third party.

istiḥsān: A principle used by the Ḥanafīs and Mālikīs in which the rule pointed to by strict analogy or syllogism is ignored and another rule based on other factors, like a general principle or necessity, is preferred. An example is the contract of hire. Strict syllogism (*qiyās*) maintains that a contract cannot be concluded for benefits that are not in actual existence. In the contract of hire for wages, for example, the services of the worker will emerge when he commences work, but they do not exist at the time of the contract. The Ḥanafīs would say that the contract is permissible on the basis of necessity, because there is no way that the benefits to be derived from the worker can be brought into existence before the contract. The same situation prevails in the hiring of property and many other cases. The juristic preference here is called *istiḥsān*.

istiṣḥāb: Maintenance of the original rule.

istiṣḥāb al-ḥāl: See *istiṣḥāb*.

istibrāʾ: Ascertaining the vacation of the womb.

istithnāʾ: Exception; exemption.

ʿitq: Emancipation of a slave; manumission.

iʿtiṣār: Retraction or taking back of gift.

iʿtikāf: Ritual seclusion in a mosque for worship.

jāʾifa: A wound affecting the body cavities, like the piercing of the ribs or penetration of the belly.

jāʾiz: Permitted; authorized.

jāʿil: The person making the offer in *juʿl* or *jiʿāla*.

jadhaʿ: A two-year-old goat.

jahl: Ignorance; uncertainty. Lack of knowledge about the essential details of a contract.

jald: Infliction of stripes; lapidation.

janīn: Foetus.

jarr al-walā: The name of a legal issue in which two slaves, male and female, who have children are manumitted separately and it is not settled to whom the custody of the children belongs. The issue is also relevant to inheritance.

jiʿāla: A contract in which the entitlement to wages depends upon the completion of the task, that is, the contractentered into by independent contractors.

jihād: War prescribed for Muslims for the defence of their faith and lands.

jizya: Poll-tax levied on the non-Muslim citizens of a Muslim state.

juʿl: See *jiʿāla*.

judhām: Leprosy.

jumhūr: Majority; majority of the jurists.

Jumuʿa: Friday congregational prayer.

jurḥ: Wound.

juzāf: Heaps; estimate; goods sold in heaps or by estimate.

kafāʾa: The doctrine of equal or proportionality of status in marriage.

kāfir: Disbeliever.

kafāla: Surety; guaranty; bail.

kaffāra: Expiation

khabar al-wāḥid: It is a report from the Prophet that does not reach the status of *mutawātir*, or *mashhūr* according to the Ḥanafīs, that is, there are one or two narrators in its chain in the first three generations: Companions, *Tābiʿūn*, and their followers. As compared to this, the *mashhūr* report has one or two narrators among the Companions, but it reaches the status of *mutawātir* in the second generation.

kalāla: The case of the deceased who at the time of death does not have four types of relations: parents, grandparents, children, and children's children. This definition is provided by Ibn Rushd.*khāṣṣ*: The specific word that applies to a single category.

khalṭ: See *ikhtilāṭ*.

khamr: Wine from grapes, as distinguished from other forms of liquor.

al-kharqāʾ: A well-known case of inheritance in Islamic law in which the deceased leaves behind a mother, a sister, and a grandfather. The jurists settled this case in five different ways.

khaṭaʾ: Mistake. The term is used alone to mean *qatl khaṭaʾ*, that is, involuntary manslaughter.

khayr: Good.

khiṭāb: Speech; address; communication.

khiṭba: Marriage proposal.

khilāf: The discipline recording juristic differences.

khilāfa: Caliphate.

khilsa: Pilferage.

khinzīr: Swine.

khiyār: Option.

khiyār al-majlis: Option during the session (*majlis*) of the contract.

khiyār al-ruʾya: Option of inspecting the goods.

khulʿ: Redemption in marriage.

kitāba: The contract between a master and a slave in which the slave buys his freedom, usually by making regular payments as he earns.

kufʾ: Equality of status. See *kafāʾa*.

kufr: Disbelief.

lāzim: Binding; the immediate contract.

laban al-faḥl: The milk of a male—a hypothetical case.

laqīṭ: Foundling.

lawth: Suspicion.

liʿān: Imprecation. The procedure followed when the husband accuses his wife of unlawful sexual intercourse for which he cannot produce four witnesses.

luqṭa: Found property.

mabīʿ: The sold commodity.

maḍāmīn: Sales involving the foetus of an animal.

maʾdhūn: A slave permitted by his master to trade on his behalf.

maḥall al-ʿaqd: The subject-matter of the contract.

maḥjūr: A person subject to interdiction.

maḥram: Husband or relative of the prohibited degree for marriage.

mahr: Dower.

mahr al-mithl: Reasonable dower, that is, dower that a woman would be entitled to because of her status.

majhūl: Something unknown.

majlis: Session.

makhṭūba: A woman proposed to.

makrūh: Disapproved; abominable; reprehensible.

māl: Wealth; property.

malāqīḥ: Sale of animal sperm.

malṭāʾ: A wound that *simḥāq*, reaches the thin (fibrous) membrane between the flesh and the bones (periosteum); it is also called *simḥāq*.

maʿlūl: Defective.

maʾmūma: An injury that reaches the cerebral membrane.

maʾmūr: One ordered to do something.

mandūb: Recommended.

manfaʿa: Benefit; utility.

maqdhūf: The victim of the offence of *qadhf*.

maqṭūʿ: Mutilated; cut up. A report with a cut-up chain.

maʿqūd ʿalayh: The subject-matter of the contract.

marfūʿ: A report that reaches the Prophet.

marhūn: The pledge; pawned property.

marhūn fīhi: Consideration for the pledge.

marīḍ: The sick person.

mashfūʿ ʿalayh: The buyer of the property subject to pre-emption (*shufʿa*).

mashfūʿ fīh: The property that is subject to pre-emption.

mashhūr: A report that reached the level of *tawātur* in the second generation. See also *khabar al-wāḥid*.

maṣāliḥ: Jurisprudential interests.

maṣlaḥa: An interest the preservation and protection of which is the acknowledged purpose of the *sharīʿa*.

maṣlaḥa mursala: An interest that is not tied down to the texts, that is, it has been subjected to *irsāl* (release).

mathmūn: Something having a price.

mawālī: Relations established through contract.

mawāt: Barren lands not owned by anyone.

mawhūb lahu: Donee.

mawlā: The master of a slave who has been emancipated.

mawqūf: Suspended.

mayta: Carrion.

mijann: Helmet.

milk: Ownership.

milk yamīn: Ownership of slaves.

mithl: Similar; fungible.

mithqāl: A measure of weight.

muʿār: Borrowed property.

muʿāwaḍa: A counter-value.

muʿāwama: Sale of fruit-bearing trees for several years.

muḍāraba: Commenda. A contract in which the owner of capital shares profits with a worker, but bears all the loss.

muʿīr: Lender.

muṣārafa: Transaction in currency or gold and silver.

muṣḥaf: A written copy of the Qurʾān.

muṣarrāt: The case where milk of an animal is allowed to remain in the udder for several days so as to give the impression of a more valuable animal.

muʿarrī: Donor.

muʿarra lahu: Donee.

mubāḥ: Permissible

mubāraʾa: Transaction in which money is paid by wife for obtaining divorce; same as *khulʿ*.

mubāshir: A person who commits an act directly.

mudabbar: Slave about whom his master has declared that he will be emancipated upon the master's death.

mudabbir: The master of a *mudabbar* slave.

mudd: A unit of measure.

muddaʿā ʿalayh: Defendant.

mūḍiḥa: A wound that uncovers or exposes the bones.

mufāwaḍa: A kind of partnership in which the partners contribute their entire belongings, that is, they have unlimited liability. This is the meaning according to the Ḥanafites. The *mufāwaḍa* partnership approved by the Malikites is more like the *ʿinān* form of partnership.

muflis: Insolvent, that is, a person reduced to *fulūs* (copper coins).

muftī: A jurist who issues *fatwas* (opinions; verdicts).

muḥāl: The creditor.

muḥāl ʿalayh: The person to whom a debt is endorsed or transferred.

muḥāqala: Renting out land on a third or fourth share of the produce.

muḥārib: A person who commits the offence of *hirāba*.

muḥīl: The person endorsing or transferring the debt to another.

muḥṣan: The term is usually applied to mean a person who is married for purposes of the offence of *zinā*; however, the term has other meanings too, namely, chaste and free.

muḥaṣṣa: Apportionment of shares.

muḥallil: A person who marries a woman with the intention of divorcing her so that she becomes lawful for her previous husband.

muḥrim: A person in the ritual state of *iḥrām*.

mujmal: A word whose meaning has not been elaborated; an obscure word.

mujtahid: A jurist who has the ability to undertake *ijtihād* independently.

mukātab: A slave who has entered into a contract with his master for emancipation through periodic payments.

mukallaf: A person who is legally liable for all kinds of obligations and duties; a person having legal capacity.

mukhāṭara: A sale involving risk.

mukhābara: Renting of land with part of its produce.

mulāʿana: A woman subjected to the proceedings of *liʿān*.

mulāmasa: A form of sale practised during the *jāhiliyya* in which the buyer could only feel a dress and not spread it out (for examination), or he would buy something on a dark night not knowing what was within.

multaqiṭ: The person who takes possession of found property.

munābadha: A sale in which each party to the sale used to fling a dress at the other, without determining the reciprocity of either, deferring the matter to their subsequent agreement.

munaqqila: An injury causing the fracture of the bones and their dislocation.

munkar: A category of tradition that is rejected by the traditionists.

munqatiʿ: A tradition with a defective chain of narration, that is, in which the names of some of the narrators are missing.

muqāraḍ: The worker in a *qirāḍ* or *muḍāraba*.

muqāriḍ: The owner of capital in a *qirāḍ* or *muḍāraba*.

muqāsama: See *qisma*.

muqayyad: Qualified; determined.

murāṭala: Exchange of the same species by weight.

murābaḥa: Sale at stated cost price.

mursal: A tradition in which the last part of the chain is missing (the name of the Companion according to the traditionists) and the report is attributed directly to the Prophet.

musāqā: Share-cropping.

musāwama: A term that is used for most sales other than *murābaḥa*.

mushtarak: A homonym; equivocal term.

muslam fīh: The subject-matter of the contract of *salam*.

muslam ilayh: The person to whom the advance payment is made in a contract of *salam*.

muslim: The person making the advance payment in a contract of *salam*.

mustaʿīr: Borrower.

mūṣā bih: Bequeathed property.

mūṣā lahu: Legatee.

mūṣī: Testator.

mutalāḥima: A flesh wound.

muthaqqal: A blunt weapon used for killing. There is a disagreement among jurists whether the use of such a weapon leads to the offence of murder or to that of voluntary manslaughter.

muwādaʿa: Place of stay of a slave mutually agreed to by the parties to a sale.

muwakkil: Principal in a contract of agency, that is, the person appointing an attorney.

muzābana: The sale of fresh (moist) dates for dry dates.

muzāriʿ: Land-tenancy.

muzāyada: Auction.

nājiz: Immediate; immediate contract.

nabbāsh: Shroud-snatcher.

najāsa: Filth; ritual impurity.

najis: Ritually impure.

najsh: The raising of bids without having an intention to buy.

nasāʾ: The delay in the exchange of two commodities. It is the same thing as *nasīʾa*.

nasīʾa: The delay in the exchange of two commodities. It is the same thing as *nasīʾa*.

naskh: Abrogation.

niṣāb: The minimum scale fixed for a number of things. For*zakāt* and *sariqa* it is a minimum amount of wealth. In evidence it is the ratio two women for one man.

nikāḥ: Marriage.

nikāḥ al-muḥallil: Marriage with a man who intends to divorce the woman he is marrying so that she can marry her previous husband who had divorced her.

nikāḥ al-shighār: It is a form of marriage in which one man gives his female ward in marriage to another on the condition that the other will give his ward in marriage to the first, without there being any dower except the body of one woman in exchange for that of the other. Such a contract is not permitted.

nukūl: Refusal to take oath.

al-Qāfa: A group of people who used to practice physiognomy.

qīma: The value of a thing as distinguished from its price.

qadhf: False accusation of unlawful sexual intercourse.

qarḍ: Loan. In Islamic law the term is used to mean an interest-free loan in which the lender is consciously gifting away the use of the sum borrowed by the loanee.

qarn: A disease of the sex organ that prevents intercourse—*qarn* or *ratq* is a birth defect in which the vulva is blocked, or the sides of the vulva are joined together.

qasāma: A procedure in which a group of people take an oath to establish the guilt of the accused. It is different from compurgation in so far as compurgation works to clear the name of the accused or to prove his innocence, while*qasāma* is a procedure through which the guilt of the accused is established.

qaṭʿī: Definitive.

qatl: Homicide.

qatl al-ghīla: Homicide by ambush or by deception.

qatl al-khaṭaʾ: Involuntary manslaughter.

qawad: Retaliation; same as *qiṣāṣ*.

qiṣāṣ: Retaliation; *lex talionis*.

qiṭāʿa: A contract similar to *kitāba* with the difference that emancipation is immediate in exchange for the wealth in the possession of the slave.

qirāḍ: Commenda; a contract in which the owner of capital shares the profits with the worker who uses the capital, but the loss is borne entirely by the owner of capital.

qisma: Partition.

qiyās: Analogy; syllogism. The extension of the *ḥukm* of a specific case established by the texts to a new case awaiting decision on the basis of a common underlying cause.

qiyās al-ʿilla: The regular form of analogy in which an underlying cause is employed for the extension of the *ḥukm*, as distinguished from *qiyās al-maʿanā* or even *qiyās al-shabah*.

qiyās al-maʿnā: The extension of the *ḥukm* from a lower-order meaning to a case falling under the higher-order meaning identified through the implication of the text. If the text of the Qurʾān says, for example, that one should not say even 'fie' to parents, then, taking this as the lower-order meaning we may extend the *ḥukm* to more grievous cases of abuse. This form is considered the strongest type of analogy. According to the Ḥanafīs, this is not analogy, but the implication of the text—*dalālat al-naṣṣ*.

qiyās al-shabah: Analogy on the basis of attributes that cannot qualify as underlying causes in the strict form of *qiyās al-ʿilla*. Thus, it is a form of analogy that is more flexible than *qiyās al-ʿilla*.

qiyās mursal: A kind of analogy in which the hold of individual texts is released and reasoning proceeds from a general principle based on the texts considered collectively.

rāhin: Mortgagor.

raʾs al-māl: Capital; business capital.

rabb al-māl: The owner of business capital.

radd: The doctrine of *radd* or return of the residue of the estate to the sharers.

rahn: Mortgage; pledge; pawned property.

rajm: Lapidation; stoning to death.

rashīd: A person who has attained discretion at the time of attaining puberty or after it.

ratq: See *qarn*.

ribā: Excess in the exchange of two counter-values in a transaction of sale; usury; interest.

rujūʿ: Recourse; retraction.

rukbān: Caravans.

rukhṣa: Plural *rukhaṣ*. Exemption.

rukn: The essential ingredient or element of an act without which the act is not complete.

rushd: Discretion. See also *rashīd*.

ṣāʿ: A unit of measure; a container used for measuring.

ṣabī: Minor.

sabr wa al-taqsīm: A method of discovering the underlying cause or *ʿilla* that uses the process of elimination.

ṣadāq: Dower.

ṣadāq al-mithl: Reasonable dower; dower for one of equivalent status.

ṣadaqa: Charity. The word is sometimes used to mean *zakāt*.

sadd al-dharīʿa: The prohibiting of lawful means to an unlawful end.

safīh: Prodigal; spendthrift, that is, one indulging in *safah*.

ṣaḥīḥ: Valid; sound. Used for a valid act or sound tradition.

salam: A contract permitting advance payment for goods to be supplied or produced.

sanad: The evidence on which reliance has been placed in the derivation of a rule of law.

sariqa: Theft for which the prescribed penalty is the cutting of the hand.

ṣaraf: Extravagance.

ṣarf: Exchange of currency or precious metals.

sāriq: A thief guilty of *sariqa*.

shabah: Resemblance. See also *qiyās al-shabah*.

shafīʿ: Pre-emptor. The plaintiff in a suit for pre-emption.

shahīd: Witness.

sharīʿa: The law of Islam as distinguished from *fiqh*, which is the knowledge or jurisprudence of this law.

sharika: Partnership.

sharikat al-ʿinān: A partnership in which the partners contribute capital and share profits and losses according to a determined ratio.

sharikat al-abdān: A partnership in which the partners contribute their labour in return for profits in a fixed ratio.

sharikat al-amwāl: Same as *sharikat al-ʿinān*.

sharikat al-mufāwaḍa: A partnership in which the partners contribute their entire belongings as capital along with their labour.

sharikat al-wujūh: A partnership that works on credit and the credit worthiness of the partners is their capital.

shawka: Power; political or military power.

shibh al-ʿamd: Quasi-wilful murder; voluntary manslaughter; culpable homicide not amounting to murder.

shibh al-khataʾ: Involuntary manslaughter.

shijāj: Plural of *shajja* (wound).

shubha: Doubt.

shubhat al-milk: Doubt as to the ownership of a thing in the mind of the offender.

shufʿa: Pre-emption.

shurakāʾ: Partners.

ṣīgha: Form; form of a contract, that is, the mode of offer and acceptance.

ṣighar: Minority.

ṣiḥḥa: Validity of an act.

sifā: Fornication.

simḥāq: A wound that reaches the thin (fibrous) membrane between the flesh and the bones (periosteum); it is also called *malṭāʾ*.

ṣulḥ: Settlement.

sult: Barley without shell.

taʿabbud: Ritual obedience as distinguished from something based upon a rational underlying cause.

taʿaddī: Tort; delict.

taʿḍiya: The attribute, in an underlying cause, of being extendible.

tafāḍul: Excess revealed through weight or measure for purposes of *ribā*.

tafwīḍ: Delegation. The term is used by the Ḥanafites for delegation of the right of divorce, but is used by the Author for a contract of marriage concluded without dower.

taghlīẓ: Enhancement; enhancement of blood-money (*diya*).

taghrīb: Exile.

ṭāhir: Pure; ritually clean.

taḥlīl: Marriage with the intention to divorce to facilitate the remarriage of a divorced couple.

taʿjīz: The inability of the judge to hear arguments after the execution of a judgment.

takhyīr: Choice; the choosing of opinions from various systems to arrive at a rule.

taklīf: Obligation; duty.

ṭalāq: Divorce.

taʿlīl: The discovery of an underlying cause for a *ḥukm*.

ṭalqa wāḥida: A single pronouncement of divorce.

taʿmīr: A term used by the Mālikites for the right of residence.

tamlīk: The passing of the right to divorce to the wife.

tanzīl: The doctrine of substitution in inheritance that places a person in the position of one through whom that person is related to the deceased.

taqlīd: Following the opinion of another without questioning thelegal basis for that opinion.

tarjīḥ: Preference of one evidence over another.

tawātur: Continuous narration of traditions; narration by such a large number that the possibility of falsehood is ruled out.

tawba: Repentance.

tawkīl: The act of appointing an agent.

tawliya: A friendly sale.

tazwīj: Marriage.

thaman: Price.

thawāb: Reward; spiritual reward.

thayyib: Virgin.

ṭuhr: Ritual purity.

ubūwwa: Paternity.

ʿuhda: The period of contractual obligation.

umm al-walad: A slave-girl who has borne a son for her master.

ummī: Illiterate.

umma: The Muslim nation.

ʿumrā: The visit to the Kaʿba for worship.

unmula: Phalange.

ʿurūḍ: Goods.

ʿurbān: Sale with earnest money.

uṣūl: Roots; principles; sources of law.

uṣūl al-fiqh: The principles with the help of which the jurists derive the rules of law from their detailed evidence.

wāhib: Donor.

wajh: Creditworthiness.

wājib: Obligatory.

wakāla: Agency.

walāʾ: Clientage.

walī: Guardian.

walī al-dam: The person inheriting the right to retaliation.

waqf: Trust.

waṣī: Executor.

waṣiyya: Bequest.

wilāya: Guardianship.

wujūb: Obligation.

yamīn: Oath.

yatīm: Orphan.

zaʿāma: Surety.

ẓāhir: A word whose meaning is apparent.

ẓannī: Probable; conjectural.

ẓihār: Injurious assimilation. A man prohibiting himself intercourse with his wife by equating her with the back of his mother.

zinā: Unlawful sexual intercourse.

Index for Volume Two